Business Analysis
WITH MICROSOFT EXCEL

Second Edition

Business Analysis
WITH MICROSOFT EXCEL

Second Edition

Conrad Carlberg

800 East 96th Street
Indianapolis, Indiana 46240

Business Analysis with Microsoft Excel, Second Edition

International Standard Book Number: 0-7897-2552-5

Library of Congress Catalog Card Number: 20-01092851

Printed in the United States of America

First Printing: September 2001

05   8   7   6

Trademarks

Warning and Disclaimer

ASSOCIATE PUBLISHER
Greg Wiegand

ACQUISITIONS EDITOR
Stephanie J. McComb

DEVELOPMENT EDITOR
Susan Hobbs

MANAGING EDITOR
Thomas Hayes

PROJECT EDITOR
Tricia S. Liebig

COPY EDITOR
Sossity Smith

INDEXER
Chris Barrick

PROOFREADER
Jessica McCarty

TECHNICAL EDITOR
Peter Kushar

TEAM COORDINATOR
Sharry Lee Gregory

INTERIOR DESIGNER
Anne Jones

COVER DESIGNERS
Alan Clements
Anne Jones

PAGE LAYOUT
Cheryl Lynch

Contents at a Glance

Table of Contents

II Financial Planning and Control

About the Author

Conrad Carlberg is president of Network Control Systems, Inc., a software development and consulting firm that specializes in statistical and database applications. He holds a Ph.D. in statistics and is a many-time recipient of Microsoft's Most Valuable Professional award. He lives near San Diego where he is trying, with only moderate success, to learn the difference between a spinnaker and a jib.

Dedication

For Buttonhook and Tigger: We still miss you. We always will.

Acknowledgments

I would like to thank and acknowledge the following Que staff and associates for their energy and good works, and especially for helping me deflate some pretentious language that marked this book's original edition: Stephanie McComb, Susan Hobbs, Sossity Smith, and Tricia Liebig.

Mark Randall, Jennifer Greenlee, and Diane Bartholomew, who provided contributions to several chapters.

And Peter Kushar for his technical edit. If there are any mistakes left, they're mine, all mine.

We Want to Hear from You!

As the reader of this book, *you* are our most important critic and commentator. We value your opinion and want to know what we're doing right, what we could do better, what areas you'd like to see us publish in, and any other words of wisdom you're willing to pass our way.

As an associate publisher I welcome your comments. You can email or write me directly to let me know what you did or didn't like about this book—as well as what we can do to make our books better.

Please note that I cannot help you with technical problems related to the topic of this book. We do have a User Services group, however, where I will forward specific technical questions related to the book.

When you write, please be sure to include this book's title and author as well as your name, email address, and phone number. I will carefully review your comments and share them with the author and editors who worked on the book.

Email: `feedback@quepublishing.com`

Mail: Greg Wiegand
         Associate Publisher
         Que Publishing
         800 East 96th Street
         Indianapolis, IN 46240 USA

For more information about this book or another Que title, visit our Web site at `www.quepublishing.com`. Type the ISBN (excluding hyphens) or the title of a book in the Search field to find the page you're looking for.

Introduction

The book you just opened is different from most others on Excel that you may have seen because it focuses on a topic that is deeply important to all of us: money.

Rex Stout once wrote, "The science of accounting has two main branches, one being addition, and the other being subtraction." I took these words to heart when I was casting about for the book's theme. I wanted to write a book that would show people how to maximize profit, the result of the two branches Stout cited.

Profit, of course, is not revenue. I can't teach you how to create revenue—that's more a matter for the heart, not the head—nor would I want to offer you MBA or CPA material. I did set out to write a book that any person engaged in any level of business could use as a refresher, from basic financial documents such as general ledgers and income statements, to operational methods such as statistical process control, to procedures that underlie investment decisions such as business case analysis.

I also wanted to structure the book around the most popular and sophisticated spreadsheet program available, Microsoft Excel. Therefore, each chapter in *Business Analysis with Microsoft Excel, Second Edition* provides information about a different business task or procedure, and discusses how best to apply Excel in that situation.

You will find reference to many Excel functions and capabilities that you may already use in your business activities on a daily basis. But you may also find discussions of tools that you have never used, or that you might never have considered using in the context of business analysis.

After all, no one can be completely familiar with every option in an application such as Excel. There are several Internet newsgroups frequented by Excel users where technical questions are posed and answered. Several years ago a question appeared about how to enter a number in a worksheet cell so that Excel would treat the number as text (this is quite a basic operation). Surprisingly, the question was posted by one of the most experienced, best known, and creative Excel consultants in the country. I thought that it was a put-on and responded in kind, but it turned out that the question was genuine.

So we all have gaps in our knowledge. The purpose here is to help fill in some of the gaps that may have appeared in your knowledge base since your last course in business, or since you first learned how to use a spreadsheet.

Business Analysis with Microsoft Excel, Second Edition makes liberal use of case studies: that is, situations that are typical of decisions or problems that you might face on any given workday. These case studies discuss, first, the problem itself: why it represents a problem and how a solution can contribute to a company's profitability. Then the case studies demonstrate at least one possible solution that uses Excel as a tool. The intent is for you to mentally put yourself in the situation described, work through it, and then apply the solution to an actual situation that you face.

How This Book Is Organized

You can look in the table of contents or the index of *Business Analysis with Microsoft Excel, Second Edition* whenever you encounter an unfamiliar or obscure situation, and read about how to solve it by means of the analysis tools in Excel. To make it easier to find related situations, the book is divided into four parts:

- **Part I, "Financial Statements and Statement Analysis."** This section discusses fundamental financial concepts and tools such as income statements, balance sheets, cash flow, and ratio analysis.
- **Part II, "Financial Planning and Control."** This section covers budgeting methods such as pro formas, forecasting trends, and quality control procedures including process measurement and defect analysis.

- **Part III, "Investment Decisions."** You will find business case analysis and profit planning in the chapters in this section. Strategies for structuring and testing business cases are covered here, as well as ways to quantify the degree of risk involved in entering a new line of business. You will also find in this section a chapter on fixed assets, which normally account for the greatest portion of a company's capital investment.

- **Part IV, "Sales and Marketing."** Sales and marketing analysis, costing and pricing, and margin analysis are covered here. Since the publication of the original edition of this book, many businesses have placed their financial and operational records in true relational databases. Therefore this edition includes a chapter that explains the most effective ways to import data into Excel directly from databases and from Web sites.

There is also a glossary that briefly defines important terms.

As mentioned previously, it's important that you be able to dip into this book to find particular topics, and to make use of the information without necessarily reviewing everything that came before. Therefore, certain tips and recommendations on using Excel are (briefly) repeated from time to time. And in each chapter you will find full, step-by-step descriptions of how to accomplish a given task using Excel.

Two Special Skills: Names and Array Formulas

Have you ever had to interpret someone else's worksheet? Or have you ever had to use a worksheet that you constructed, months or perhaps years ago, and then been completely unable to figure out what you had in mind when you constructed it? You probably have, and if so you know what a headache it can be.

The main difficulty with many otherwise useful worksheets is that their authors don't document them. Consider this worksheet formula:

```
=IF(AND(B12<3000,A12<5),C14*D14*.05,C14*D14*.075)
```

It could take you several minutes to figure out what that formula is up to, even if you know the worksheet's basic purpose. It would take you only a few seconds if the author had used this formula instead:

```
=IF(AND(YearToDateSales<3000,Tenure<5),Units*Price*LowCommission,Units*Price*
➥HighCommission)
```

It is not too difficult to infer that this formula says:

> "If this person's sales during this year are less than $3,000, and this person was hired fewer than 5 years ago, return the sales amount times the lower commission; otherwise return the sales amount times the higher commission."

So, to help make your work self-documenting, you should in many instances give names to Excel worksheet cells, ranges, and constants. Because you will find this approach taken throughout the book, it's reviewed here.

Assigning Names

To name a cell or range, begin by selecting it on the worksheet. Then, choose Insert, Name, Define and type the name you want to use in the Names in Workbook edit box. Or, use this quicker method: after you have highlighted the cell or range, click in the Name box (immediately above the column header for column A and left of the drop-down arrow), type the name, and press Enter.

To name a constant such as "LowCommission," choose Insert, Name, Define and type the name of the constant in the Names in Workbook edit box. Then, in the Refers to edit box, type the value that you want to assign to the constant. You cannot use the Name box to define a constant.

A side benefit of using names instead of cell or range addresses is that you can paste names into formulas as you are creating them. After you have started typing a formula, you can choose Insert, Name, Paste and select the name you want to use from the Paste Name list box. This approach saves you keystrokes and helps prevent misspellings. Most important, you don't have to remember existing names: they're right there in the list box.

When you choose a name for a range or a constant, consider using both uppercase and lower-case letters: for example, "TotalLiabilities." Mixing uppercase and lowercase makes the name easier to read (compare with "totalliabilities.") You should probably avoid using all uppercase letters. Excel's worksheet function names (for example, SUM and AVERAGE) use all upper-case letters, and you don't want to define a name that could be confused with a function.

Blank spaces aren't allowed in names. Some people like to use an underscore in place of a space, preferring to see "Total_Liabilities" instead of "TotalLiabilities."

Using Array Formulas

Many of the formulas described in this book are a special type of Excel formula termed an *array formula*. An array formula contains an array of values, or a reference to an array of worksheet cells, such as:

```
=SUM(IF(MOD(ROW(SheetRange),2)=0,SheetRange))
```

which sums the values in the worksheet range named "SheetRange" if and only if they are in an even-numbered row. The formula requires a special keyboard sequence to enter it correctly. On a computer running Windows, the sequence is Ctrl+Shift+Enter: that is, simultaneously hold down the Ctrl and Shift keys as you press Enter.

You can tell that Excel has interpreted your formula as an array formula if you see curly (sometimes termed French) braces around it in the formula bar. For example, the formula shown previously appears in the formula bar like this:

```
{=SUM(IF(MOD(ROW(SheetRange),2)=0,SheetRange))}
```

Do not type the braces yourself. If you do so, Excel interprets the formula as text.

These are termed array formulas because they have within them arrays that you don't usually see. For example, if expanded, the prior formula would show an array of the values in SheetRange. You can explore the inner workings of array formulas by using a tool that's new in Excel 2002, Evaluate Formula (begin by choosing Tools, Formula Auditing).

Conventions Used in This Book

Business Analysis with Microsoft Excel, Second Edition uses a few typeface, terminology, and formatting conventions to denote special information:

- A sequence like this:

  Ctrl+Enter

  means that you should hold down the Ctrl key as you press Enter.
- When you should select a sequence of options from an Excel menu, you will see this:

  Choose Tools, Goal Seek.

  This means that you should first click on the Tools option in Excel's main menu, and then click on Goal Seek in the Tools menu.
- Data or formulas that you enter in an Excel worksheet cell are shown like this:

  `=SUM(CumulativeNetIncome)/ProductLife`
- If you're asked to type something other than a formula it will be **boldfaced**.
- New terms, or information that needs special emphasis, are shown in *italic*.
- Information about performing a task more efficiently or alternative ways to go about a task appear in tips. Tips are set apart from the main text like this:

TIP To select a range of cells, even if it contains some blank cells, press Ctrl+*.

- Information that is related to the current topic, but that might not apply to it directly, is shown like this:

N O T E There is one distinct IRR for each change in sign in a series of cash flows. ■

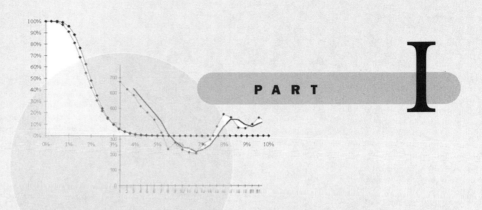

P A R T

I

Financial Statements and Statement Analysis

Working with Income Statements

In many ways, operating a business is like playing a game, and keeping track of your business is very similar to studying games such as baseball. Serious baseball fans know hundreds of statistics, such as batting averages and earned run averages. Similarly, if you are serious about your business, you need to be able to measure and understand the statistics that describe how your business operates. Accounting generally, and financial statements in particular, are the scorecards.

This chapter is not a treatise on accounting and finance, but it does describe tools that you can use to better understand certain financial aspects of operating your business. There are plenty of textbooks on the generally accepted practices of accounting and finance. This chapter highlights and demonstrates some practical techniques used in these disciplines.

Keeping Score

Accounting translates the actions that take place in the business world into a set of numbers that you can use to make informed decisions. It captures information on how well a company operates, the hundreds of obstacles that a company needs to overcome, and the company's prospects for the future.

Accounting rules enable you to compare your company with other companies and with other industries. These comparisons are important when you want to seek additional funds for expansion, such as by borrowing or by inviting capital investment. Following the rules can open opportunities to succeed and to receive equal treatment in a very rugged marketplace. But you don't need to be a CPA to use accounting for solid decision making. Often, it is as simple as subtracting your expenses from your revenues to determine your profits.

Accounting quantifies the everyday world of buying and selling. Would you buy something for more than you can sell it? Of course not—but many companies do exactly that every year. The demise of many of the dot-com startups can be traced to precisely that failing. Too often, businesses look at only the up-front costs, but ignore the related costs. The devil is in the details, and finance and accounting help keep the demons in their place.

Choosing the Right Perspective

We all tend to think of accounting as an exact science, one that is fully governed by the rules of arithmetic, but the numbers generated are actually only best estimates. While the rules, procedures, and methods make the numbers appear to be absolute facts, they are not.

But the numbers can and do represent how well the managers are running the business. Balance sheets and income statements are not commandments. They are guides, and different users have different purposes for them.

Defining the Categories

This book classifies accounting according to two kinds of decision makers:

- *Management* accounting provides information to decision makers who are inside the company. If you want to bring a new product to the marketplace, you would analyze data concerning cost, price, market demand and competition so as to assess the product's potential. You make judgments about the product—whether to introduce it, how to manage it, whether it has run its course—on the basis of the data you have available.

- *Financial* accounting provides information to decision makers outside the company, such as investors, creditors, and governments. Suppose that you wanted to raise funds by making your company a public corporation and issuing shares of stock to the investment community. Potential investors would demand detailed financial accounting information (and the law would require you to make it available). An investor wants to know that a set of rigid guidelines was used to create the information. Otherwise, there is no way to make an informed investment choice.

When you decide whether to introduce a new product, or make any other management decision, you use a more flexible analytic framework than when you are trying to raise capital in the investment community. You often need room to maneuver, and management accounting provides you with that room.

Both aspects of accounting are necessary tools, and this book discusses financial accounting from time to time. However, the principal focus is on making information as useful as possible for internal decision-making purposes.

To use accounting information for routine decision making, it is not necessary to explore in depth the nuances and technicalities of the accounting profession. But if you understand this information well enough to use it on a routine basis, you will be much better prepared to make good use of your accountant's time when a tricky decision *is* required.

Using the Income Statement

The income statement is a powerful tool for decision making. It portrays the flow of money and the relationship of revenues to expenses over a period of time. It tells us how much money was made in a year. The terms *profit*, *net income*, and *earnings* are commonly used to state the bottom line.

The income statement provides a starting point in the analysis of a business. The popular press frequently reports earnings and nothing more: *"Today, U.S. Widgets reported quarterly income of $240 million."* This is positive, but there is more to the story.

Businesses need to measure and report income. This sounds straightforward enough, but it gets complex in a hurry. Both measurement and reporting can, and are, complex enough to fill several texts. It is not the purpose here to go to that level of detail, but to provide highlights that simplify the process of measurement and reporting, and that enable you to make use of the results in day-to-day operational decisions.

Choosing a Reporting Method

The measurement of net income is an attempt to match the value generated by a business (its revenues) with the resources it consumes (its expenses). This sentence: "In fiscal year 2001, we sold $200 million of product and services, at a cost of $175 million, for a profit of $25 million," quantifies the operation of the business over a one-year period. The business now has a track record: a place to begin the analysis of its operations.

However, to measure and report income in a generally accepted fashion, more is needed. Accountants use a series of conventions that strengthen the validity of the income statement report. If you read an income statement that you believe to have been prepared using these conventions, you generally have greater faith that the information is valid and credible. Perhaps the company is worth investing in. This is the world of debits and credits, Generally Accepted Accounting Principles, tax rules, and so on. These are rules of the game that make the measurement of the operation of the business valid for the purposes of an income statement.

There is no one way to format an income statement. Your choice will depend on the use you intend to make of the statement, and the picture that you want to present. The key is for the information to be useful in support of decision making. Your audience could be potential investors, creditors, or internal (sometimes, external) managers.

Some examples of commonly used income statement formats are shown in Figures 1.1 through 1.4.

Case Study: Documentation for a Bank Loan

FiberOps, Inc., wants to obtain a bank loan for the purchase of some new equipment. As FiberOps's president, you oversee the day-to-day activities of the company. The bank has only a secondary interest in such matters as the amount of your variable costs relative to your earnings, or what your margins are on a product-by-product basis.

The bank is, however, keenly interested in your sales volume, your gross profit, and your operating profit. You could use a format such as the one shown in Figure 1.1 for the income statement that accompanies your loan application.

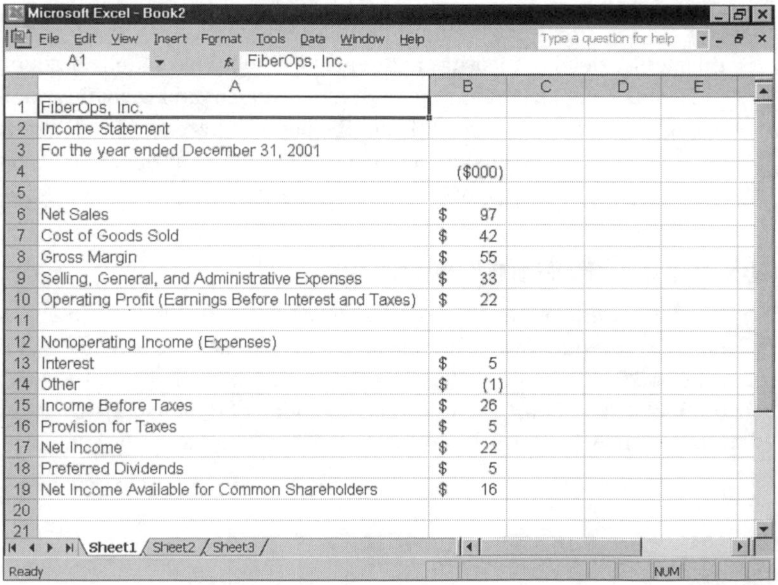

FIGURE 1.1

An income statement format suitable for external reporting usually omits details such as inventory levels, but includes all categories that affect net income.

	A	B	C	D	E
1	FiberOps, Inc.				
2	Income Statement				
3	For the year ended December 31, 2001				
4		($000)			
5					
6	Net Sales	$ 97			
7	Cost of Goods Sold	$ 42			
8	Gross Margin	$ 55			
9	Selling, General, and Administrative Expenses	$ 33			
10	Operating Profit (Earnings Before Interest and Taxes)	$ 22			
11					
12	Nonoperating Income (Expenses)				
13	Interest	$ 5			
14	Other	$ (1)			
15	Income Before Taxes	$ 26			
16	Provision for Taxes	$ 5			
17	Net Income	$ 22			
18	Preferred Dividends	$ 5			
19	Net Income Available for Common Shareholders	$ 16			
20					
21					

Figure 1.1 shows a typical format for an income statement used for external reporting purposes. It could also, for example, be used in an annual report. Notice that there are apparent math errors in the report, in rows 17 and 19. These are caused by the rounding that Excel applies when a currency format obscures significant digits. When, for purposes of space and simplicity, you divide actual figures by, say, 1000 and indicate by a column header that the entries are in $1000's, it's best to use Excel's ROUND() function. For example:

```
=ROUND(4690/1000,0)
```

Had this been used in cell B16 of Figure 1.1, instead of the actual entry of 4.69 (apparently rounded by means of the cell format to 05) then the result of the calculation in cell B17 would have been the correct value of $21 instead of $22. (You could also fill the Tools, Options, Calculation, Precision as Displayed check box on the Calculation tab, but this is a risky procedure. So doing would permanently change a value stored as 4.69 to a value stored as 5. Usually that's not a good thing.)

There are many types of income statement formats and uses. The same firm might modify and adjust its report of income and costs, based on the type of business that it conducts and, as a result, the income statement needs to reflect a different set of requirements.

Case Study: Inventory Control in a Merchandising Firm

Suppose that you are in charge of purchasing products for resale by a retail store. To hold down inventory carrying costs, and to avoid the use of cash until absolutely necessary, you have instituted JIT (Just In Time) inventory procedures. If these procedures are working as you designed, your inventory levels at the end of the year should be about the same as—or, ideally, lower than—the levels at the start of the year and match the turnover of the products of your business. For your management purposes, you might arrange to obtain an income statement similar to the one shown in Figure 1.2.

Another variation of an income statement format might be used by a manufacturing firm (see Figure 1.3). The major difference between the structure of the manufacturing firm's income statement and that of the merchandising firm is in the cost of goods sold. For the manufacturer, the cost of goods manufactured is added to the opening inventory. For the merchandiser, purchases from suppliers are added to the opening inventory. The manufacturer is likely to have various cost subcategories within the cost of goods manufactured, such as raw materials, factory overhead, and labor costs; these are often detailed in a supplement to the income statement. These subcategories do not appear in the merchandiser's income statement: the cost of purchases is seldom broken down further.

One type of income statement that deserves special mention targets the purpose of managing the business from the perspective of specific products and expenses. Figure 1.4 provides an example.

FIGURE 1.2

An income statement format suitable for certain management purposes in a merchandising firm might exclude dividend information but provide details on inventory levels.

	A	B	C	D	E	F
1	Davis Office Furniture					
2	Income Statement					
3	For the year ended December 31, 2001					
4						
5		($000)	($000)			
6						
7	Sales		$ 332			
8	Less Cost of Goods Sold					
9	Opening Inventory	$ 43				
10	Add Purchases	$ 52				
11	Goods Available for Sale	$ 95				
12	Ending Inventory	$ 27				
13	Cost of Goods Sold	$ 68				
14						
15	Gross Margin		$ 264			
16						
17	Less Operating Expenses					
18	Administrative Expenses	$ 82				
19	Selling Expenses	$ 51				
20	Operating Expenses		$ 133			
21						
22	Operating Income		$ 131			
23						

FIGURE 1.3

An income statement for a manufacturing firm, formatted for planning purposes, often includes information about the cost of goods manufactured in a supplement.

	A	B	C	D	E
1	Clark Manufacturing, Inc.				
2	Income Statement				
3	For the year ended December 31, 2001				
4					
5		($000)	($000)		
6					
7	Sales		$ 223		
8	Less Cost of Goods Sold				
9	Opening Finished Goods Inventory	$ 58			
10	Cost of Goods Manufactured (see Supplement)	$ 127			
11	Goods Available for Sale	$ 185			
12	Ending Finished Goods Inventory	$ 62			
13	Cost of Goods Sold	$ 123			
14					
15	Gross Margin		$ 100		
16					
17	Less Operating Expenses				
18	Administrative Expenses	$ 34			
19	Selling Expenses	$ 20			
20	Operating Expenses		$ 54		
21					
22	Operating Income		$ 46		
23					

This income statement excludes such items as interest and amortization, and can be used for everyday operations. It provides a detailed look at revenue and expense, and is an example of the type of income statement a manager needs to guide a department.

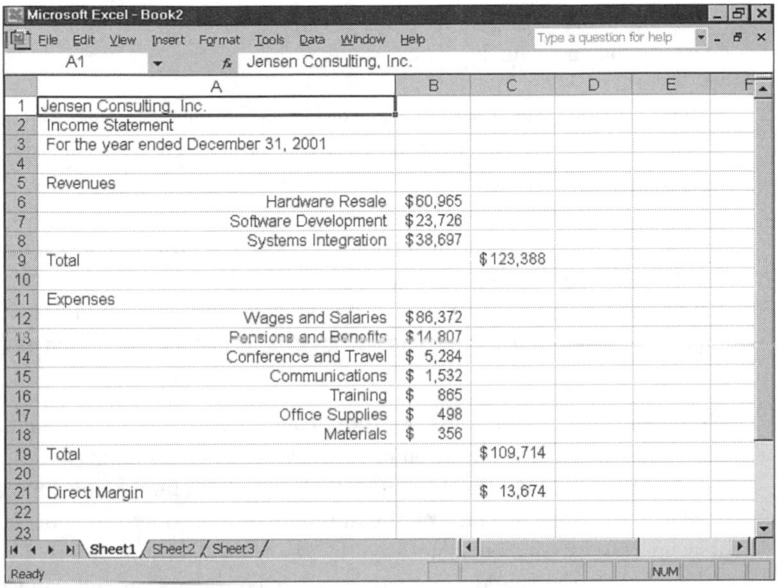

FIGURE 1.4
An income statement format that is used for revenue and expense management purposes details the sources and uses of funds.

	A	B	C	D	E	F
1	Jensen Consulting, Inc.					
2	Income Statement					
3	For the year ended December 31, 2001					
4						
5	Revenues					
6	Hardware Resale	$60,965				
7	Software Development	$23,726				
8	Systems Integration	$38,697				
9	Total		$123,388			
10						
11	Expenses					
12	Wages and Salaries	$86,372				
13	Pensions and Benefits	$14,807				
14	Conference and Travel	$ 5,284				
15	Communications	$ 1,532				
16	Training	$ 865				
17	Office Supplies	$ 498				
18	Materials	$ 356				
19	Total		$109,714			
20						
21	Direct Margin		$ 13,674			
22						
23						

Ideally, you should tailor the income statement to a format that you and your managers can use daily. You can expand the level of detail shown in Figures 1.1 through 1.4 to include the data that you need most often. It is here that judgment, as well as creativity, becomes critical. A simple reformat of data, or adding a detail line item, can enrich your insight into the way that your business operates.

For example, you could drive the behavior of your management team by means of a link between your bonus systems and a customized income statement. This link could take the form of the addition of a very specific measurement. Suppose that you want to push your sales force toward the creation of new accounts. Your income statement might show revenue figures both as sales to existing accounts and as new business, and might include cost figures for new business bonuses. This could help prod the sales force to concentrate on the more difficult process of new business sales.

As Figures 1.1 through 1.4 imply, there are many possible ways to structure an income statement. Each one reflects a different set of circumstances, defined by the business's specific situation. There are guidelines, but there is also flexibility within those guidelines to tailor a statement to your particular needs. Your business and the way that you want to use the data set the direction for the type of income statement you use.

Measuring the Operating and Non-Operating Segments

An income statement records the flow of resources over time. Operating income measures the extent to which revenues generated during the accounting period exceeded expenses incurred in producing the revenues. This measure tells whether the firm's core operating business made money or not.

NOTE   It's useful to distinguish operating income, the difference between revenues and expenses, from net income, which takes the additional effect of taxes, interest, and other charges into account. ▪

Income statements commonly divide this resource flow into operating and non-operating segments. The operating segment represents what occurred on a day-to-day basis. The non-operating segment represents the assets that the firm might have financed, the tax impacts of being in business, and extraordinary occurrences such as the one-time sale of a company asset.

When you analyze a business, it is important to keep the two segments separate. If you were considering the expansion of your own business, you might first ask yourself whether the firm made money, and whether you can fund an expansion by means of the profits. Your focus would be on the numbers produced by your normal, everyday business operations. You would not want to base your decision on the effect of a one-time, unique event. You would take that event into consideration, but you would not rely on its effect on future earnings.

An income statement's operating segment represents the results of the company's major, ongoing activities, while the non-operating segment represents all the company's secondary or ancillary activities. The company needs to understand both segments so as to grasp the total picture, as well as to know how best to prepare for its future.

Moving from the General Journal to the Income Statement

It is typical for a business to record its daily transactions in a General Journal. This record keeps track of every individual transaction in every account, whether cash investments, cash paid, accounts receivable, accounts payable, and so on.

Getting the General Journal into Excel

There are many different software programs available to help you record and store this information. Because some programs provide the user with such conveniences as a predefined chart of accounts, many people prefer to use software other than Excel to gather information on individual transactions. (A *chart of accounts* is simply a list that associates account names with numbers that identify the account: for example, you might decide to identify Accounts Payable with the number 20.) Excel is, of course, a sensible choice of platform for entering, storing, and retrieving information about individual transactions (although for these purposes Excel is much less powerful and flexible than a true database such as Oracle or, on a much smaller scale, Microsoft Access). If you choose Excel for this purpose, you will have to build many features from scratch, including your own categories for transactions, the double-entry nature of recording individual transactions, and so on.

Once you have imported the data into Excel, you can then manipulate the data to meet your requirements, including anything from category subtotals to statistical analysis. Few accounting packages allow for detailed manipulation of the accounting data but most provide an export feature that creates data files that Excel can open. Excel is a wonderful adjunct tool for accountants, regardless of the specific accounting software they prefer.

On the other hand, if you enter and store individual transactions using software other than Excel, you may on occasion have difficulty importing files into Excel. Although most such programs have an option that allows you to export data in ASCII (text) format, the arrangement of the exported data might not be ideal for import into Excel. For example, some programs export each part of a record onto a different line of the ASCII file: one line for the account number, another line for the account name, another line for the transaction amount, and so on.

N O T E   Attractive alternatives include the use of Structured Query Language (SQL, pronounced *sequel*) tools and Data Access Objects. If the software that handles your transactions conforms to certain standards, then you can arrange to import the data into Excel in a form that is ready for use in reports such as income statements and balance sheets. This book provides detailed information on SQL and Data Access Objects in Chapter 18, "Importing Business Data into Excel." ▪

Certainly, you can import ASCII files into an Excel worksheet quite easily by choosing File, Open. However, after you have imported the information, you might find it necessary to move the account name and the transaction amount onto the same line as the account number. If you have many transactions to import, this cutting and pasting can become tedious, and you should consider recording and then running an Excel macro to do the rearrangement for you.

Understanding Absolute, Relative, and Mixed References

Consider this formula:

```
=SUM($A$1:$B$2)
```

Entered into a cell in a worksheet, it returns the total of the values in cells A1, A2, B1, and B2. Suppose that you entered it in cell C3. If you then copied the formula and pasted it into cell Q15, or cell AA100, or cell IV65536, it would still refer to that same range of cells, $A$1:$B$2. It's an *absolute* reference. It's made absolute by the dollar signs that precede the column letters and row numbers.

In contrast, suppose you entered this formula in cell C3:

=SUM(A1:B2)

It has no dollar signs. It's a *relative* reference: relative to whatever cell was active when you created the reference. In this example, that's cell C3. If you now copy and paste the formula into cell D3 (same row, one column to the right) the formula adjusts accordingly, and becomes:

=SUM(B1:C2)

You pasted it one column to the right of where you originally entered it, and the relative reference responds by adjusting its columns: A becomes B, and B becomes C.

Similarly, if you copied it from cell C3 and pasted it into cell C4, it would become:

=SUM(A2:B3)

You've copied the formula down one row, so the row numbers in the relative reference adjust: 1 becomes 2, and 2 becomes 3.

A third type of reference is the *mixed* reference, where either the column or the row— but not both—is anchored by means of the dollar sign. For example:

=SUM($A1:$A2)

If you enter this formula in cell A3, you can copy and paste it to a cell in any other column and it will still depend on values in column A: the dollar signs anchor it there. But if you copy it from cell A3 into any other row, the rows in the reference will adjust accordingly. So, if you were to copy the formula from cell A3 into cell B4, the formula in B4 would be:

=SUM($A2:$A3)

It's the same with range names. By default, Excel makes absolute the cell or range of cells that a range name refers to. But you can edit that reference in the Insert Name dialog box, so as to make the reference mixed or relative.

Why should you care about all this? The next section shows you the reasons.

Getting the Journal Data to the Ledger

Whether you enter the General Journal data directly into Excel or import it from another software application, the next step is usually to collect the transactions in their proper accounts within the General Ledger. Figure 1.5 shows an example of entries in a General Journal, and Figure 1.6 shows how you could collect these entries in the General Ledger.

For ease in collecting the General Journal entries into the General Ledger, four range names are defined on the General Journal sheet: EntryDate ($A$5:$A$26), AccountNumber ($C$5:$C$26), JournalDebits ($D$5:$D$26), and JournalCredits

($E$5:$E$26). Each of these names, and their associated columns, refer to the General Journal worksheet in Figure 1.5.

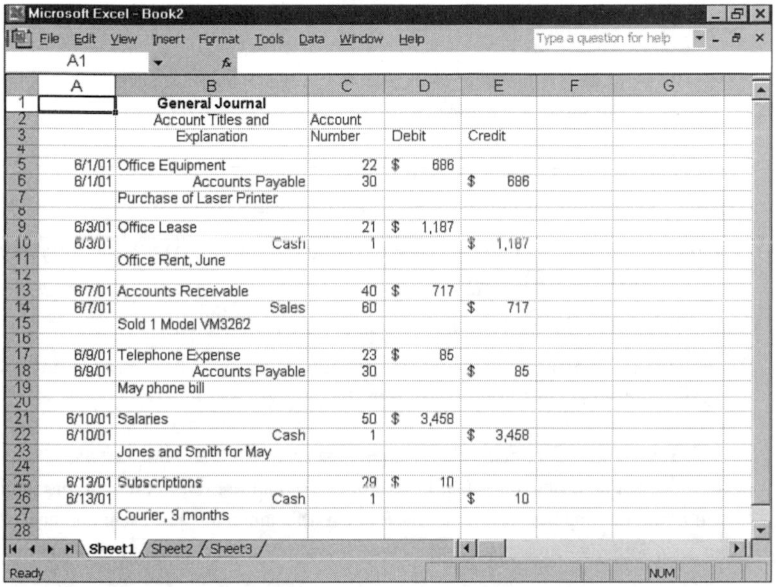

	Account Titles and Explanation	Account Number	Debit	Credit
	General Journal			
6/1/01	Office Equipment	22	$ 686	
6/1/01	Accounts Payable	30		$ 686
	Purchase of Laser Printer			
6/3/01	Office Lease	21	$ 1,187	
6/3/01	Cash	1		$ 1,187
	Office Rent, June			
6/7/01	Accounts Receivable	40	$ 717	
6/7/01	Sales	60		$ 717
	Sold 1 Model VM3282			
6/9/01	Telephone Expense	23	$ 85	
6/9/01	Accounts Payable	30		$ 85
	May phone bill			
6/10/01	Salaries	50	$ 3,458	
6/10/01	Cash	1		$ 3,458
	Jones and Smith for May			
6/13/01	Subscriptions	29	$ 10	
6/13/01	Cash	1		$ 10
	Courier, 3 months			

FIGURE 1.5
General Journal entries record individual transactions in chronological order as debits and credits.

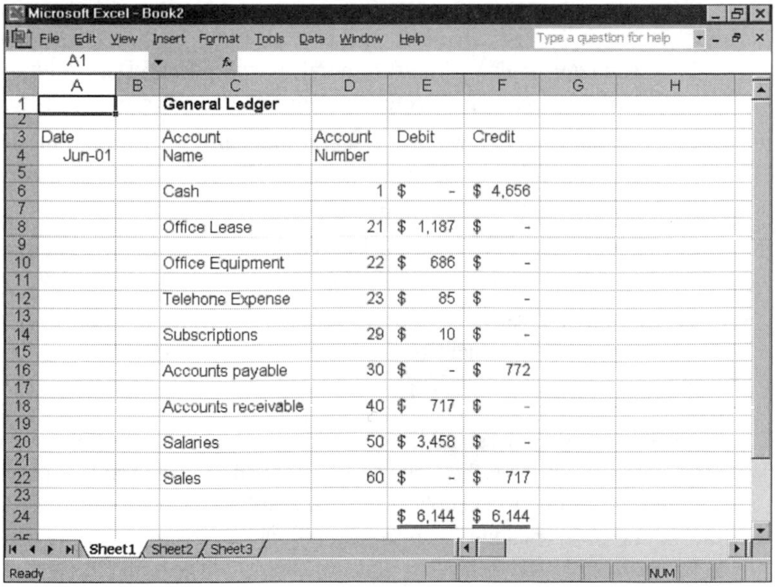

Date	Account Name	Account Number	Debit	Credit
	General Ledger			
Jun-01				
	Cash	1	$ -	$ 4,656
	Office Lease	21	$ 1,187	$ -
	Office Equipment	22	$ 686	$ -
	Telehone Expense	23	$ 85	$ -
	Subscriptions	29	$ 10	$ -
	Accounts payable	30	$ -	$ 772
	Accounts receivable	40	$ 717	$ -
	Salaries	50	$ 3,458	$ -
	Sales	60	$ -	$ 717
			$ 6,144	$ 6,144

FIGURE 1.6
General Ledger entries accumulate individual transactions from the General Journal into specific accounts.

Two additional names are defined in the General Ledger: Ledger Date refers to cell $A$4, and GLAccount (short for General Ledger Account) refers to cell $D6. Notice that LedgerDate refers to an absolute reference, and GL Account refers to a mixed reference. The effect of this referencing is explained in more detail later in this chapter.

N O T E If you're unfamiliar with the concept of names in Excel, refer to this book's Introduction for a brief discussion. ▪

On the General Ledger worksheet, the following formula in its Debit column accumulates the appropriate entries from the General Journal:

```
=SUM(IF(MONTH(EntryDate)=MONTH(LedgerDate),1,0)*IF(AccountNumber =
    GLAccount,1,0)*JournalDebits)
```

and this formula accumulates the appropriate credits:

```
=SUM(IF(MONTH(EntryDate)=MONTH(LedgerDate),1,0)*IF(AccountNumber =
    GLAccount,1,0)*JournalCredits)
```

N O T E The two formulas shown here must be entered as *array formulas*. After typing the formula, simultaneously hold down Ctrl+Shift and press Enter. In the Formula Bar, you will see a pair of curly braces around the formula. This indicates that Excel has accepted the formula as an array formula. Do not enter the braces yourself from the keyboard, or Excel will interpret the formula as text. ▪

The formulas instruct Excel to do the following:

1. Evaluate each entry in the General Journal's EntryDate column. If the month of that date equals the date for the General Ledger, return 1; otherwise, return 0.

2. Evaluate each entry in the General Journal's AccountNumber column. If the account number is the same as the account number for the current General Ledger account, return 1; otherwise, return 0.

3. Multiply the result of step 1 by step 2. Only when both conditions are true will this step return a 1; otherwise, it will return 0.

4. Multiply the result of step 3 by the General Journal's entries in the Journal Debits range (or its Journal Credits range, in the second of the previous two formulas).

5. Return the sum of step 4.

Be sure that you understand the following aspects of the names used in these formulas. First, they assume that the General Journal and the General Ledger worksheets both belong to the same workbook. If the General Journal belonged to a workbook named, say, "General Journal.xls" then the definitions of the names in the formulas would have to be qualified by references to that workbook. For example:

```
='C:\Financials\[General Journal.xls]JournalSheet'!$A$4:$A$27
```

Second, consider the definitions of the names LedgerDate and GLAccount. Ledger Date refers to cell $A$4: because this is an absolute reference (note the two dollar signs), LedgerDate returns the same value regardless of the location of the cell where it is entered.

GLAccount, on the other hand, refers to cell $D6. This is a mixed reference: only the column is fixed, and the row can change depending on where a reference to GLAccount is entered.

Therefore, this formula,

```
=SUM(IF(MONTH(EntryDate)=MONTH(LedgerDate),1,0)*IF(AccountNumber =
    GLAccount,1,0)*JournalCredits)
```

if entered in cell F6 shown in Figure 1.6, uses the value 1 (in cell D6) for GLAccount. But if the formula is entered in cell F8, it uses the value 21 (in cell D8). Because the name GLAccount refers to the mixed reference $D6, the name itself acts as a mixed reference.

The effect of the mixed reference in this case is to anchor the reference to column D, because of the dollar sign before the column letter, and to allow the row to adjust, because of the absence of a dollar sign before the row number.

By using these formulas, all the individual transactions from the General Journal are accumulated into the General Ledger, according to the account that they have been posted to and according to the correct date for the current General Ledger entry.

TIP If you're familiar with Excel's pivot tables, you may wonder why you would not use one to summarize data from the General Journal into a General Ledger. You can do so if you arrange the General Journal data as a three-column list: one column containing the name of the account, one column identifying the transaction as a debit or a credit, and the third column containing the amount. Now if you use that list as the source data for a pivot table, with the account name as the Row field, the type of entry as the Column field and the amount as the Data field, your pivot table will emulate a General Ledger.

Getting the Ledger Data to the Income Statement

You can use a similar approach to accumulate the information in the General Ledger in your income statement.

The procedure suggested here makes use of a convention that you might use in defining your chart of accounts. Perhaps you have decided to number all accounts that pertain to fixed administrative expenses by means of the numbers 20 through 29. If you name the range in the General Ledger that contains the account numbers as LedgerAccounts, the range containing the credits as LedgerCredits, and the range containing the debits as LedgerDebits, then this array formula,

```
=SUM(IF(TRUNC(LedgerAccounts/10)=2,LedgerCredits-LedgerDebits,0))
```

returns the required information to the Income Statement's appropriate cell. (Remember to enter it as an array formula: use Ctrl+Shift before pressing Enter.)

The array formula first evaluates the elements in the range named LedgerAccounts, and divides their values by 10. Then, if the integer portion of the result equals 2 (as it will if the account number is between 20 and 29 inclusive), it returns the sum of the difference between the accounts' debits and credits.

You could then use this formula to return the entry in your income statement that pertains to fixed administrative expenses. Similarly, if your chart of accounts assigned all accounts pertaining to fixed production expenses to two-digit numbers beginning with 3 (30, 31, ... , 39), you would use:

```
=SUM(IF(TRUNC(LedgerAccounts/10)=3,LedgerCredits-LedgerDebits,0))
```

NOTE The procedures suggested previously work most easily if you maintain your General Journal, General Ledger, and Income Statement all in the same workbook. However, Excel does not permit you to use the same name more than once in the same workbook unless you qualify it with a sheet name. Thus, you cannot create two instances of Debits, for example, once as a name that refers to the General Journal and once as a name that refers to the General Ledger in the same workbook. One option is to use names such as GeneralJournal!Debits, where GeneralJournal is the name of a sheet. Another option, used in the previous examples, is to use the name JournalDebits to distinguish that range from LedgerDebits. ■

You can accumulate most of the entries on an income statement in a similar fashion, working from the General Journal to the General Ledger to the Income Statement. Two types of entries in particular, entries such as accounts payable and accounts receivable that involve accrual, and assets that are subject to depreciation, usually require special attention. Both affect the timing of your company's earnings. Accrual accounting is discussed next, and depreciation is covered in the discussion of fixed assets in Chapter 16, "Fixed Assets."

Managing with Accrual Accounting

Accrual accounting involves two steps: identifying the revenues for a given period, and matching the associated costs to those revenues. This is called the *matching principle* and is a basic concept that is used throughout the accounting process.

The notion of matching revenues to costs might seem obvious, but it has some subtle implications. Suppose that you purchase license plates for a company vehicle. You pay $400 for the plates in January. You write off the full $400 in January (that is, you show it as a cost that you incurred fully during that month). You produce revenue or otherwise conduct business by using your vehicle both during January and during the next 11 months.

In this case, you have overstated your cost of doing business in January, understated it from February through December, and have failed to match the subsequent revenues with the initial expense. Accrual accounting allows you to spread the cost of the vehicle over (in this case) the full 12 months, and to match the revenues the vehicle produces to the expense you incurred for the license plates.

Revenue is not the same as cash received, and expense is not the same as cash spent. You normally recognize revenue when the effort required to generate the sale is substantially complete, and there is reasonable certainty that you will receive payment. The accountant views the timing of the actual cash receipts, or the actual cash outlay, as only a technicality.

(Another approach, termed the *cash method*, is sometimes used instead of the accrual method. Under the cash method, the business records revenue when the cash is received and costs or expenses when the cash is spent. Although the cash method is a less accurate means of associating revenues with costs and expenses, small businesses sometimes forego the extra accuracy of the accrual method for the extra simplicity of the cash method.)

For credit sales, the accrual principle means that you recognize the revenue at the time of the sale, not when the customer makes payment. Suppose that you use your credit card to buy a new set of golf clubs at your local sporting goods store. The store recognizes the revenue when you sign the credit slip, but it does not receive cash until your credit card company sends it payment. The lag between recognition of revenue and cash payment can be significant. The fact that a company is profitable is no assurance that its cash flow will be sufficient to keep it solvent.

Income statements are necessary for a company's management to understand the relationship between the company's revenues and its expenses—its profitability—over a given *period* of time. Balance sheets, covered in Chapter 2, "Balance Sheet: Current Assets," Chapter 3, "Valuing Inventories for the Balance Sheet," and Chapter 4, "Summarizing Transactions: From the Journals to the Balance Sheet," are necessary for management to understand the relationship between the company's assets and its liabilities—its worth—at a given *point* in time. Cash flow statements, covered in detail in Chapter 5, "Working Capital and Cash Flow Analysis," enable management to assess the company's solvency: whether or not sufficient working capital exists and will exist to continue business operations.

These three types of statements—income statements, balance sheets, and cash flow statements—are intimately related, even though they serve different purposes and provide different perspectives on a company's overall financial position. These relationships are determined in large measure by the principal of matching costs to revenues in the income statement via accrual.

For example, increases in revenues cause increases in the owner's equity on the credit side of the balance sheet, and increases in accrued expenses cause decreases in owner's equity on the debit side of the balance sheet.

Actual cash receipts and outlays, shown on cash flow statements, summarize the effects of increases and decreases in revenues and expenses on the amount of the company's working capital. The cash flow statements may or may not accurately reflect how the process of accrual apportions revenues and expenses during a given accounting period.

The fact that cash flows might or might not reflect the accrual of revenues and expenses highlights the need for *adjusting entries*. When your company acquires an asset, such as an insurance policy, you might or might not use that asset up in order to create revenue during a particular accounting period.

Case Study: Adjusting Entries

Martin Consulting is a small business that provides assistance to its customers in assessing the quality of ground water. Figure 1.7 shows several examples of how Martin Consulting uses adjusting entries to record transactions via accrual.

Martin begins by getting a trial balance. This process involves totaling the balances of accounts with debit balances and then doing the same for accounts with credit balances. When the two totals agree the ledger is in balance. See columns B and C in Figure 1.7.

	A	B	C	D	E	F	G
1	Martin Consulting worksheet, 7/31/2001	Trial Balance		Adjustments		Adjusted Trial Balance	
2		Debit	Credit	Debit	Credit	Debit	Credit
3	Cash	$ 32,650				$ 32,650	$ -
4	Accounts Receivable	$ 3,472				$ 3,472	$ -
5	Unexpired Insurance	$ 684			$ 57	$ 684	$ 57
6	Supplies	$ 592			$ 136	$ 592	$ 136
7	Office Equipment	$ 3,470				$ 3,470	$ -
8	Office Equipment: Accumulated Depreciation		$ 1,157		$ 96	$ -	$ 1,253
9	Accounts Payable		$ 4,223			$ -	$ 4,223
10	Unearned Consulting Fees		$ 1,280			$ -	$ 1,280
11	Chris Martin, Capital		$ 31,884	$ 160		$ 160	$ 31,884
12	Consulting Fees Earned		$ 6,250			$ -	$ 6,250
13	Advertising	$ 145				$ 145	$ -
14	Salaries	$ 3,600		$ 465		$ 4,065	$ -
15	Communications	$ 181				$ 181	$ -
16							
17	Insurance			$ 57		$ 57	$ -
18	Supplies			$ 136		$ 136	$ -
19	Consulting Fees Earned				$ 160	$ -	$ 160
20	Depreciation Expense: Office Equipment			$ 96		$ 96	$ -
21	Salaries Payable				$ 465	$ -	$ 465
22		$ 44,794	$ 44,794	$ 914	$ 914	$ 45,708	$ 45,708
23							
24							

FIGURE 1.7
Adjusting entries help to accrue revenues and expenses in the proper period.

At the end of July, Martin Consulting prepares this worksheet as the basis for its income statement and balance sheet. On July 1, an errors-and-omissions insurance policy was purchased in full to provide protection against faulty advice that might be given to the company's clients. The policy will remain in effect for 12 months. The cost of this policy is debited to an asset account in row 5, column B of the worksheet. When the worksheet is prepared at the end of the month, 1/12th of the value of the policy has expired: that value now becomes an expense incurred during the month of July. Row 5, column E contains $57 as an *adjusting credit entry*, reflecting that 1/12th of the policy's asset value has expired. Row 5, column F shows the remaining value of the asset, or $627. The *adjusting debit entry* appears in row 17, column D.

During the same period, Martin Consulting uses office supplies (stationery, photocopy toner, printing supplies, and so forth) in the amount of $136 to support the production of its revenues. Another adjusting entry of $136 appears in row 6, column E, reflecting the decrease in the value of the original office supplies asset of $592, and applied against that amount in row 6, column F to show its remaining value of $456 at the end of the month. The adjusting debit entry appears in row 18, column D.

It is fairly easy to see the rationale for these adjusting entries. On July 1, the company owned 12 months of insurance, and owns 11 months worth of insurance on July 31. Similarly, it owns $592 in office supplies on July 1 and $456 on July 31. These amounts are directly measurable and Martin Consulting can easily enter, as adjusting debits and credits, the portions that expire or are used as expenses during the month of July.

But office equipment is another matter. At the beginning of July, the company owned equipment originally valued at $3,470 (row 7, column B). How much of that $3,470 was used up in the production of the month's revenues? The equipment is still there: the computer is still creating worksheets, the photocopier is still making copies, the telephone is still ringing. And yet some value was taken from the equipment in order to generate revenue.

Depreciation is the means used to account for the fact that the equipment provided value to the process of revenue generation. In contrast to counting the precise number of months that expire on an insurance policy, or the number of mailing envelopes that are used up, Martin must estimate the value of the office equipment "used" during the month of July.

Martin can use one of several methods of calculating depreciation in order to arrive at this estimate. These are covered in detail in Chapter 16; for now, suppose that Martin uses the straight-line method of depreciation. The assumption is that the office equipment has a useful life of three years. Then, for each month that passes, it is assumed that the value of the equipment declines by 1/36th of its original value: that is, the equipment depreciates each month by 1/36th, or $96. The adjusting credit entry is in row 8, column E, and the adjusting debit entry is shown in row 20, column D.

TIP To avoid apparent errors in how your worksheet displays values when multiplication and division are involved, use the ROUND() function. For example:

```
=ROUND(3470/36,0)
```

By estimating the amount of monthly depreciation, Martin can assign an office equipment expense for the month. This makes it possible to associate the expense with the revenue, and to obtain a clearer picture of the month's income. Again, the matching principal holds that revenues should be matched with the expenses that helped to produce the revenues.

Adjusting entries are needed to accrue not only expenses but revenues. Suppose that toward the end of July, Martin has signed an agreement and accepted cash payment to perform eight hours of consulting at $160 per hour. The full amount of $1,280 is credited to an asset account called Unearned Consulting Fees. Before the end of the month Martin performs one of the eight contracted hours. Actually doing that work converts some of the unearned fees to an earned status. Adjusting entries, shown in row 10, column D and row 19, column E show how much—$160—of the unearned fee has been earned during July.

The four adjusting entries previously described pertain to activities that both begin and end during an accounting period: for example, the use of $136 in office supplies began on July 1 and ended on July 31. An adjusting entry can also be used to record an activity that *spans* accounting periods. Suppose that Martin prepares an assistant's salary check, in payment for the prior two weeks, one week before the end of the month. The assistant then accrues one week of salary from July 25 through July 31. In order to show that this accrued salary is an expense attributable to July, rather than to August, Martin makes adjusting entries in row 14, column D. To show that it is a liability that will be met subsequently (probably, in August) it is also entered as a credit in row 21, column E.

Excel makes it simple to accumulate the trial balance and the adjusting entries into an adjusted trial balance. The actual formulas used in columns F and G of Figure 1.7 (the adjusted debit and credit balances) are discussed in detail in Chapter 5. For now, be aware that:

- Each adjusted debit entry is the sum of the trial balance and adjusting debits, less the sum of the trial balance and adjusting credits.

- Each adjusted credit entry is the sum of the trial balance and adjusting credits, less the sum of the trial balance and adjusting debits.

The totals of the adjusting entries and of the adjusted entries appear in row 22, columns D through G. The equality of the debit and credit totals *prove* that the entries are in balance.

TIP Excel provides several underline formats, including Single Accounting and Double Accounting. These are often used for, respectively, subtotals and totals. To access these formats, use Format, Cells, and select the Font tab. Then, choose the Underline combo box.

Finally, it's time to move this information to a balance sheet and an income statement. See Figure 1.8.

FIGURE 1.8
Entries are copied from the adjusted trial balance columns to income statement and balance sheet columns.

Microsoft Excel - Book2

A1 | Martin Consulting worksheet, 7/31/2001

	A	H	I	J	K
1	Martin Consulting worksheet, 7/31/2001	Income Statement		Balance Sheet	
2		Debit	Credit	Debit	Credit
3	Cash			$ 32,650	$ -
4	Accounts Receivable			$ 3,472	$ -
5	Unexpired Insurance			$ 684	$ 57
6	Supplies			$ 592	$ 136
7	Office Equipment			$ 3,470	$ -
8	Office Equipment: Accumulated Depreciation			$ -	$ 1,253
9	Accounts Payable			$ -	$ 4,223
10	Unearned Consulting Fees			$ -	$ 1,280
11	Chris Martin, Capital			$ 160	$ 31,884
12	Consulting Fees Earned	$ -	$ 6,250		
13	Advertising	$ 145	$ -		
14	Salaries	$ 4,065	$ -		
15	Communications	$ 181	$ -		
16					
17	Insurance	$ 57	$ -		
18	Supplies	$ 136	$ -		
19	Consulting Fees Earned	$ -	$ 160		
20	Depreciation Expense: Office Equipment	$ 96	$ -		
21	Salaries Payable				$ 465
22		$ 4,680	$ 6,410	$ 41,028	$ 39,298
23	Operating Income	$ 1,730			$ 1,730
24		$ 6,410	$ 6,410	$ 41,028	$ 41,028
25					

Sheet1

Rows 3 through 11 and 21 represent asset and liability accounts. They are copied from the adjusted trial balance to the balance sheet columns. Rows 12 through 20 represent revenue and expense accounts, and are copied to the income statement columns. Then, in row 22 of columns H through K, the debits and credits are totaled. Notice that they are no longer in balance, nor should they be. The company's revenues for July exceeded its expenses, and the difference is its operating income. To arrive at this figure, subtract the total expenses of $4,680 in cell H22 from the total revenues in cell I22. The result, $1,730, appears in cell H23, and is the operating income for the month of July. Adding that to the total expenses of $4,680 results in $6,410, which equals the total revenues for the month.

A similar process is used to obtain the information for the balance sheet. Notice that this final step, copying information from the adjusted trial balance to the income statement and balance sheet, is merely a matter of segregating the revenue and expense data from the asset and liability data. The former go to the income statement; the latter to the balance sheet.

Organizing with Traditional Versus Contribution Approaches

The traditional approach organizes income statements around the functions a business performs, such as production, administration, and sales. This functional method of cost classification does not allow for the examination of cost behavior. Traditional income statements are not set up to describe the cost drivers of the business.

There are no subcategories to analyze, or to use in the management of the behavior of costs within each classification. All costs are grouped without respect to whether they are fixed, variable, inherent or some other characteristic of cost behavior. When an income statement lumps everything together in this fashion, it is difficult to analyze, to make decisions, and to offer recommendations.

The contribution format supplies answers to many additional questions. For example:

- What are the variable selling expenses for a given product?
- What percentage of total costs is represented by our fixed costs?
- New equipment will increase our fixed costs because it must be depreciated. Will it reduce our variable costs enough to result in lower *total* costs?

A manager needs more specific information than is available in the traditional income statement to answer questions like these.

This is not to say that there is no place for the traditional format: quite the contrary. Almost certainly, you would use a traditional format if you were applying for a business loan, considering the sale of your business, or preparing for an initial public stock offering.

In contrast, the contribution format is intended mainly for internal purposes, and is used by management for day-to-day, operational decisions. Consider the example shown in Figure 1.9:

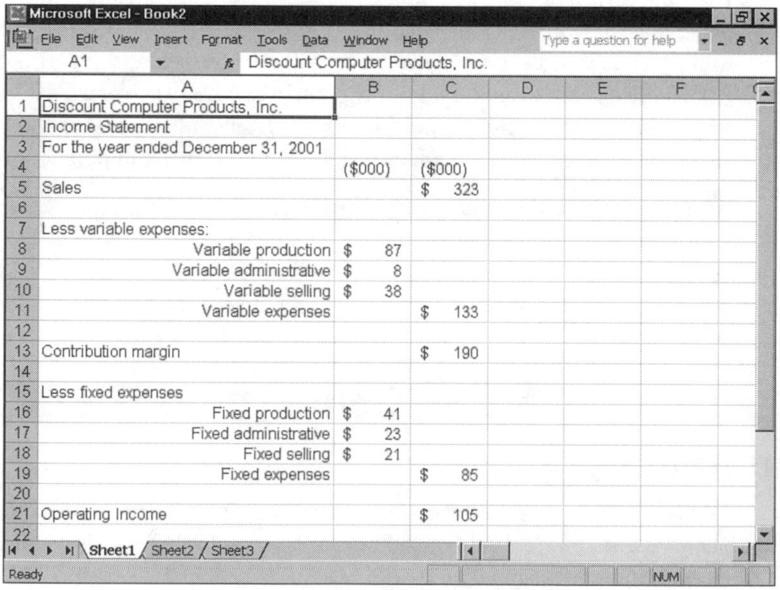

FIGURE 1.9

The contribution format of an income statement focuses on data helpful for operational decisions.

	A	B	C	D	E	F
1	Discount Computer Products, Inc.					
2	Income Statement					
3	For the year ended December 31, 2001					
4		($000)	($000)			
5	Sales		$ 323			
6						
7	Less variable expenses:					
8	Variable production	$ 87				
9	Variable administrative	$ 8				
10	Variable selling	$ 38				
11	Variable expenses		$ 133			
12						
13	Contribution margin		$ 190			
14						
15	Less fixed expenses					
16	Fixed production	$ 41				
17	Fixed administrative	$ 23				
18	Fixed selling	$ 21				
19	Fixed expenses		$ 85			
20						
21	Operating Income		$ 105			
22						

In Figure 1.9, variable expenses are deducted from sales to derive what is known as a contribution margin. See Chapter 20, "Pricing and Costing," for more information, but here we note that a contribution margin is the result of subtracting variable expenses from revenues. The contribution margin can then be used to meet fixed expenses, and to contribute toward a company's profit.

This information is critical for business decisions that pertain to products. For example, Figure 1.9 shows that Discount Computer's largest cost category is Variable Production expenses. A variable expense is one that changes depending on the number of units sold. The more computer products that this firm sells, the larger its variable production expense.

The contribution format of the income statement in Figure 1.9 directs a manager's attention to the costs involved in producing products. In the absence of this data, the manager who wants to cut costs might focus (perhaps inefficiently) on reducing *fixed* production costs.

The contribution approach is useful in making decisions about product profitability, product pricing, marketing channels, and many situational decisions. It enables you to understand the contribution that each product brings to the bottom line, and how much to variable costs. It helps you to better understand the cost drivers of your business.

American business focuses on cost reduction, on productivity, and (if it has the stamina) on quality management. To sharpen that focus, it is necessary to understand the structure of the costs that reduce your profitability. You will see more on this matter in future chapters.

Summary

In this chapter, you have learned about different formats and different purposes for income statements. They can be structured very differently depending on their audience and which management functions they support.

You have seen how absolute, relative, and mixed references are used to return results that are independent of, fully dependent, or partly dependent on their placement on the worksheet.

You have learned ways to use Excel to maintain a General Journal of transactions, and how to roll those transactions up into a General Ledger and an Income Statement.

You have also read about accrual accounting and the matching principal, under which costs are associated with the revenues that they help to produce.

The income statement is fundamental to an understanding of how your business operates. It has various uses and a virtually unlimited number of formats. The statement structure and format that you choose depends both on your audience and your purpose for a particular income statement.

There are guidelines for the construction of the statement, but you have broad latitude in selecting the data that you portray. You can measure and report income, but ultimately you have to make a business decision from the data. The key to making the best possible decision is to structure the statement so that it offers the most pertinent information available.

Balance Sheet:
Current Assets

The balance sheet complements the income statement, discussed in Chapter 1, "Working with Income Statements." You need both to keep track of your company's financial status. It is termed a *balance sheet* because its two primary sections—Assets and Liabilities—must be in *balance*; that is, the total of the company's assets must equal the total of its liabilities and its equity.

The balance sheet summarizes a company's financial position at the end of a given period. Whether that period is a month, a quarter, or a year, it tells you the value of the company's assets. It also describes the various classifications of liabilities, such as Accounts Payable, Debt, and Equity, that have claims against the company's assets.

For example, suppose that your company has $5,000 worth of inventory in stock. That's an asset: you can, and presumably intend to, convert it into cash by selling it to your customers. Now suppose that your company acquired that inventory partly with $2,500 in cash and partly on credit.

Those amounts are liabilities. The company has assumed $2,500 in Accounts Payable, which is the credit portion of the purchase. The remaining $2,500 worth of inventory is part of the Owner's Equity, which is the portion of the company's Total Assets owned by its investors. Owner's Equity is grouped with liabilities such as Accounts Payable because it represents whatever difference exists between the assets and liabilities.

By showing the $5,000 worth of inventory once in Assets and once in Liabilities, the balance sheet keeps the company's holdings and obligations in balance. If this were all there is to a balance sheet, it wouldn't be of much interest; however, as you will learn later in this book, the balance sheet is the starting point for a variety of analyses. Using Excel to analyze the balance sheet can give you insight into how a company is run, how well it manages its resources, and how it creates profit.

First, though, it's necessary to build the balance sheet. This chapter, along with Chapters 3, "Valuing Inventories for the Balance Sheet," and 4, "Summarizing Transactions: From the Journals to the Balance Sheet," describe that process.

Designing the Balance Sheet

In contrast to the income statement discussed in Chapter 1, the balance sheet usually follows a fairly rigid format. Figure 2.1 shows a typical example.

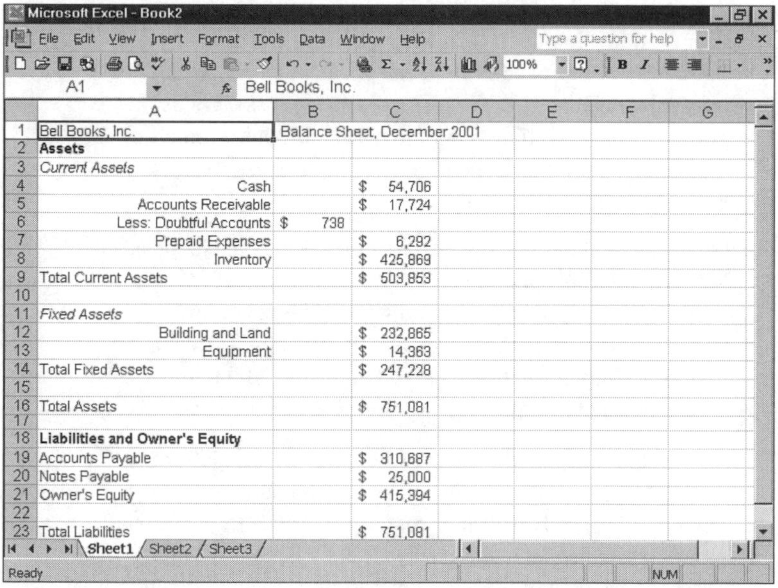

	A	B	C
1	Bell Books, Inc.	Balance Sheet, December 2001	
2	**Assets**		
3	*Current Assets*		
4	Cash		$ 54,706
5	Accounts Receivable		$ 17,724
6	Less: Doubtful Accounts	$ 738	
7	Prepaid Expenses		$ 6,292
8	Inventory		$ 425,869
9	Total Current Assets		$ 503,853
10			
11	*Fixed Assets*		
12	Building and Land		$ 232,865
13	Equipment		$ 14,363
14	Total Fixed Assets		$ 247,228
15			
16	Total Assets		$ 751,081
17			
18	**Liabilities and Owner's Equity**		
19	Accounts Payable		$ 310,687
20	Notes Payable		$ 25,000
21	Owner's Equity		$ 415,394
22			
23	Total Liabilities		$ 751,081

FIGURE 2.1
The balance sheet for Bell Books, Inc., December 2001, demonstrates the equality of its Assets with the total of its Liabilities and its Owner's Equity.

The first section of the balance sheet describes the company's Assets. The second section of the balance sheet summarizes the company's Liabilities and Owner's Equity.

Understanding Balance Sheet Accounts

The Current Assets classification is normally composed of Cash, Accounts Receivable, Prepaid Expenses, and Inventory. Because Inventory can require special techniques of management and analysis, this book discusses Inventory separately in Chapter 3. The remaining Current Asset classifications are discussed in this chapter.

Fixed Assets normally include items such as Land, Buildings, and Equipment. The conceptual difference between Current Assets and Fixed Assets is that Current Assets can be converted into cash fairly quickly—usually, within a year or less—without disrupting the business's normal operating procedures.

So, if your company conducts its business in a particular building that it owns, located on land that it owns, you would regard both the building and the land as Fixed Assets. Even if you could sell them in a week, to do so would interfere with your normal business operations. In contrast, if your company owns a building and land, but conducts no business there, it might be appropriate to regard them as Current Assets.

In the same way, liabilities are classified as current and long-term. A *current liability* is a debt that a business must pay within the same time period it uses to define its current assets: again, this is usually defined as a year or less. An example is a bank loan that must be repaid within 12 months. An example of a long-term liability is, say, a 10-year note used to acquire your place of business.

Understanding Debit and Credit Entries

Figure 2.1 showed a balance sheet for a book retailer, Bell Books, Inc. The cash worksheet that supports Bell Books' balance sheet is shown in Figure 2.2.

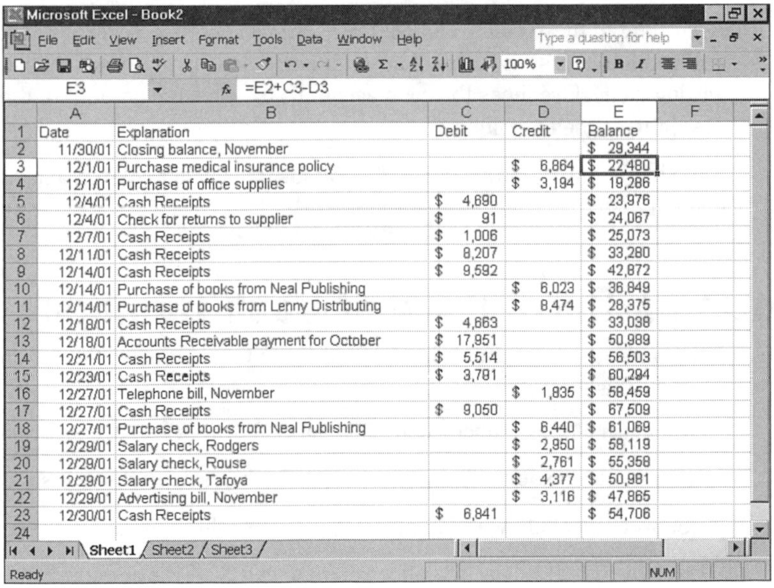

FIGURE 2.2
The cash worksheet for Bell Books records cash outlays as credits and cash receipts as debits.

	Date	Explanation	Debit	Credit	Balance	
1	Date	Explanation	Debit	Credit	Balance	
2	11/30/01	Closing balance, November			$ 29,344	
3	12/1/01	Purchase medical insurance policy		$ 6,864	$ 22,480	
4	12/1/01	Purchase of office supplies		$ 3,194	$ 19,286	
5	12/4/01	Cash Receipts	$ 4,690		$ 23,976	
6	12/4/01	Check for returns to supplier	$ 91		$ 24,067	
7	12/7/01	Cash Receipts	$ 1,006		$ 25,073	
8	12/11/01	Cash Receipts	$ 8,207		$ 33,280	
9	12/14/01	Cash Receipts	$ 9,592		$ 42,872	
10	12/14/01	Purchase of books from Neal Publishing		$ 6,023	$ 36,849	
11	12/14/01	Purchase of books from Lenny Distributing		$ 8,474	$ 28,375	
12	12/18/01	Cash Receipts	$ 4,663		$ 33,038	
13	12/18/01	Accounts Receivable payment for October	$ 17,951		$ 50,989	
14	12/21/01	Cash Receipts	$ 5,514		$ 56,503	
15	12/23/01	Cash Receipts	$ 3,791		$ 60,294	
16	12/27/01	Telephone bill, November		$ 1,835	$ 58,459	
17	12/27/01	Cash Receipts	$ 9,050		$ 67,509	
18	12/27/01	Purchase of books from Neal Publishing		$ 6,440	$ 61,069	
19	12/29/01	Salary check, Rodgers		$ 2,950	$ 58,119	
20	12/29/01	Salary check, Rouse		$ 2,761	$ 55,358	
21	12/29/01	Salary check, Tafoya		$ 4,377	$ 50,981	
22	12/29/01	Advertising bill, November		$ 3,116	$ 47,865	
23	12/30/01	Cash Receipts	$ 6,841		$ 54,706	
24						

Notice that deposits to Bell Books' cash account worksheet are labeled Debits, and withdrawals from the account are labeled Credits. If it's been a while since you looked closely at an accounting statement, you might wonder why deposits go under Debits and withdrawals go under Credits. It's mainly a matter of convention.

When you create an account in a worksheet, you normally have two columns: one to record increases in the account balance, and one to record decreases in the account balance. (This format is referred to as a *T-account*, because a horizontal line drawn beneath the column headers, and a vertical line drawn between the columns themselves, together resemble a "T.")

In the context of your business's accounts, the words debit and credit do not have the same implications that they have in everyday usage—that is, indebtedness versus reserves. Instead, these terms simply refer to the left (debit) and right (credit) columns of a T-account. Accountants have four fundamental rules for entering amounts in these columns:

- If the account is an asset account, record an increase in the amount of the asset in the left (debit) column.

- If the account is an asset account, record a decrease in the amount of the asset in the right (credit) column.

- If the account is a liability or Owner's Equity account, record an increase in the liability in the right (credit) column.

- If the account is a liability or Owner's Equity account, record a decrease in the liability in the left (debit) column.

According to these rules, deposits to a cash account are recorded in the account's left, or debit, column: cash is an asset account and a deposit increases its balance. Similarly, because writing a check reduces the cash account's balance, the amount of the check is recorded in the right, or credit, column.

Keep in mind that, in this context, debit just means left column and credit just means right column.

Getting a Current Asset Cash Balance

In the balance sheet shown in Figure 2.1, the Cash classification of Current Assets section contains this formula:

```
=NovemberEndCashBalance+SUM(DecemberCashDebits)-SUM(DecemberCashCredits)
```

The names in this formula refer to ranges in the cash worksheet shown in Figure 2.2.

In the worksheet shown in Figure 2.2, there are three named ranges:

- NovemberEndCashBalance refers to cell E2. This amount is the closing cash balance at the end of November, the prior month.

- DecemberCashDebits refers to cells C3:C24. This range contains all the deposits to Bell Books' corporate checking account that were made during December.

- DecemberCashCredits refers to cells D3:D24. This range contains all the withdrawals from Bell Books' corporate checking account that were made during December.

Cell E2, named NovemberEndCashBalance, contains the value $29,344. Cell E3 contains this formula:

```
=E2+C3-D3
```

Each entry in the cash worksheet is either a debit or a credit: there are no entries that contain both a debit and a credit. The formula in cell E4, therefore, either adds to the prior balance (cell E3) a debit figure from column C, or subtracts a credit figure from column D.

The formula is copied from cell E4 and is pasted into the range E5:E24. The process of copying and pasting the formula adjusts its relative cell references, so each balance depends on the prior balance as well as on the current debit or credit. Cell E24 contains the ending balance for the month of December, and this balance will be used as the beginning cash balance when it comes time to create the cash worksheet for January.

It would be possible, and perhaps preferable, to create the name DecemberEndCashBalance to represent cell E24 of Figure 2.2. Then, the Cash classification in Figure 2.1 could contain this formula:

```
=DecemberEndCashBalance
```

As the worksheets are constructed, the ending cash balance for December is calculated twice: once on the cash worksheet and once on the balance sheet. We have used this construction partly for illustration, and partly to make the calculations explicit.

Using Sheet Level Names

Before continuing with Bell Books' cash accounts, it's necessary to discuss an enhancement to the *workbook level* names that this book has used thus far.

The Introduction explained how to define a name that refers to a constant or to a range of cells. Unqualified by the name of a worksheet, these are workbook level names. They can be used by formulas anywhere in the workbook. If you defined the workbook level name *FICA* as referring to the constant 7.65%, you could enter this formula:

```
=FICA * C2
```

on any worksheet and it would return 7.65% times whatever value is in cell C2 of that worksheet. The *scope* of the workbook level name is the entire workbook.

The worksheets shown in Figures 2.3 and 2.4 make use of *sheet level* names. The worksheet in Figure 2.3 contains these sheet level names:

- The name FirstNational!Debits refers to the range FirstNational!$C$6:$C$12.
- The name FirstNational!Credits refers to the range FirstNational!$D$6:$D$12.
- The name FirstNational!BeginningBalance refers to the cell FirstNational!$E$5.

Notice two aspects of these range names:

- The name itself (for example, *Debits*) is qualified by the name of the worksheet (here, *FirstNational*), and the two are separated by an exclamation point.
- The range (for example, $C$6:$C$12) is also qualified by the name of the worksheet, and again the two are separated by an exclamation point.

Defining the names in this fashion makes them *sheet level* names: that is, the name refers specifically to the sheet where the range exists. Using sheet level names, instead of the workbook level names that this book has used so far, has some consequences:

- Unless it is qualified by the name of the sheet where it exists, the name is not accessible from any other sheet in the workbook. Suppose that you have defined the sheet level name JanuaryResults!Revenues. If a worksheet named, say, AnnualRollup is active, you cannot use this formula:

```
=SUM(Revenues)
```

to get the total of January's revenues. You would have to use this:

```
=SUM(JanuaryResults!Revenues)
```

- However, on the worksheet where the sheet level names are defined, you can use them without qualification. If the worksheet named JanuaryResults is active, you can use this formula:

```
=SUM(Revenues)
```

to return the sum of the values in the range that the sheet level name JanuaryResults!Revenues refers to.

Sheet level names are extremely useful. Suppose that you have a workbook with a different worksheet for each month of the year—JanuaryResults, FebruaryResults, MarchResults, and so on. If you define sheet level names such as JanuaryResults!Revenues and FebruaryResults!Revenues, you can use this formula:

```
=SUM(Revenues)
```

(or one like it) on each of those worksheets, and you will know that it returns the sum of the range that's named Revenues *for that worksheet only*. January's revenues are segregated from February's and from those on all other worksheets.

Getting a Cash Balance for Multiple Cash Accounts

It would be unusual for a company of any size to maintain only one bank account. More often, companies use several bank accounts, often for different purposes. In this case, a 3-D reference would be useful, because you generally want a different worksheet for each cash account. You would use the 3-D reference to sum the balance of the account in each worksheet.

Suppose that Bell Books uses an account at the First National Bank to handle all cash transactions *except* cash receipts and purchases from inventory suppliers. Figure 2.3 shows these transactions for the month of December.

FIGURE 2.3
The cash worksheet for First National account shows all operating expenses except those involving suppliers.

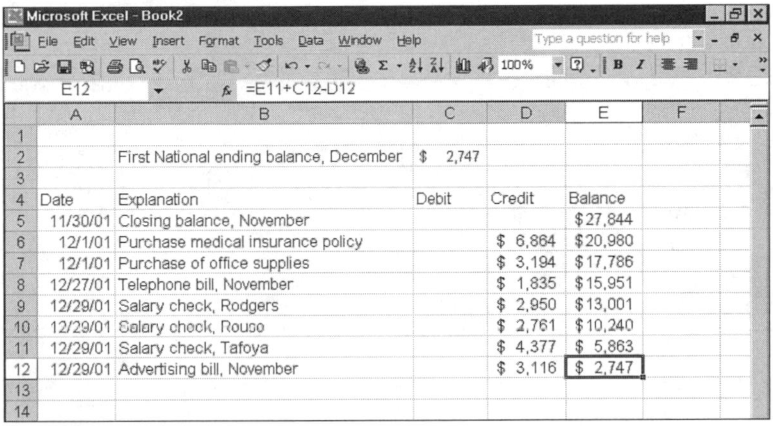

	A	B	C	D	E	F
1						
2		First National ending balance, December	$ 2,747			
3						
4	Date	Explanation	Debit	Credit	Balance	
5	11/30/01	Closing balance, November			$27,844	
6	12/1/01	Purchase medical insurance policy		$ 6,864	$20,980	
7	12/1/01	Purchase of office supplies		$ 3,194	$17,786	
8	12/27/01	Telephone bill, November		$ 1,835	$15,951	
9	12/29/01	Salary check, Rodgers		$ 2,950	$13,001	
10	12/29/01	Salary check, Rouse		$ 2,761	$10,240	
11	12/29/01	Salary check, Tafoya		$ 4,377	$ 5,863	
12	12/29/01	Advertising bill, November		$ 3,116	$ 2,747	
13						
14						

Cell C2 in Figure 2.3 contains this formula:

```
=BeginningBalance+SUM(Debits)-SUM(Credits)
```

which returns the ending balance in the First National account at the end of December. Why the First National account? Because the formula is entered on the worksheet where the sheet level names *Debits* and *Credits* are defined. Therefore, the references *must* be to ranges on the sheet where the formula is entered.

Suppose further that Bell Books uses an account at the Second National Bank to handle all cash receipts and purchases from inventory suppliers. Figure 2.4 shows those transactions for the month of December.

The worksheet in Figure 2.4 contains these sheet level names:

- The name SecondNational!Debits refers to the range SecondNational!$C$6:$C$19.
- The name SecondNational!Credits refers to the range SecondNational!$D$6:$D$19.
- The name SecondNational!BeginningBalance refers to the cell SecondNational!$E$5.

Cell C2 in Figure 2.4 contains the formula

```
=BeginningBalance+SUM(Debits)-SUM(Credits)
```

that is identical to the formula in cell C2 of Figure 2.3; however, because of the use of sheet level names, *Debits* in Figure 2.4 refers specifically to the name *Debits* on the worksheet named SecondNational. Similarly, *Debits* in Figure 2.3 refers specifically to the name *Debits* on the worksheet named FirstNational. The arguments to the SUM functions, therefore, represent different ranges and normally return different results.

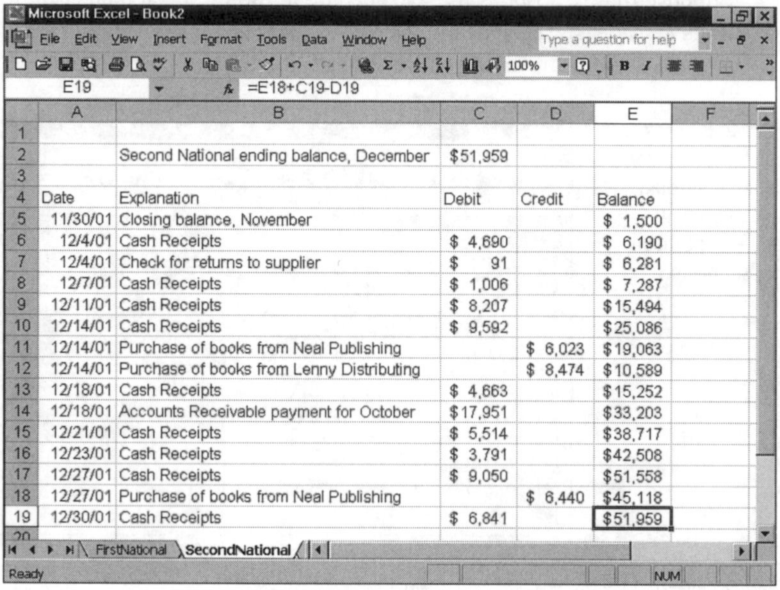

E19 =E18+C19-D19

	A	B	C	D	E
1					
2		Second National ending balance, December	$51,959		
3					
4	Date	Explanation	Debit	Credit	Balance
5	11/30/01	Closing balance, November			$ 1,500
6	12/4/01	Cash Receipts	$ 4,690		$ 6,190
7	12/4/01	Check for returns to supplier	$ 91		$ 6,281
8	12/7/01	Cash Receipts	$ 1,006		$ 7,287
9	12/11/01	Cash Receipts	$ 8,207		$15,494
10	12/14/01	Cash Receipts	$ 9,592		$25,086
11	12/14/01	Purchase of books from Neal Publishing		$ 6,023	$19,063
12	12/14/01	Purchase of books from Lenny Distributing		$ 8,474	$10,589
13	12/18/01	Cash Receipts	$ 4,663		$15,252
14	12/18/01	Accounts Receivable payment for October	$17,951		$33,203
15	12/21/01	Cash Receipts	$ 5,514		$38,717
16	12/23/01	Cash Receipts	$ 3,791		$42,508
17	12/27/01	Cash Receipts	$ 9,050		$51,558
18	12/27/01	Purchase of books from Neal Publishing		$ 6,440	$45,118
19	12/30/01	Cash Receipts	$ 6,841		$51,959

FIGURE 2.4
The cash worksheet for Second National account shows all cash receipts and those transactions that involve suppliers.

Sheet level names have some other effects. For example, suppose that you activate a worksheet other than FirstNational or SecondNational, and choose Insert, Name, Define. The sheet level names on the FirstNational and SecondNational worksheets would not appear in the dialog box: their scope is limited to their specific worksheets.

As another example, if you were to activate the FirstNational worksheet and then activate the Name Box in the Formula Bar, you would see the names *BeginningBalance, Credits,* and *Debits.* These range names would not be qualified by their sheet names because the sheet where they exist is active.

Although this preliminary work might seem onerous, it helps to make your workbook formulas more self-documenting, and it leads to easier name usage. For example, notice that the ending balance for each bank account in Figures 2.3 and 2.4 is in cell C2 of each sheet. This allows you to create a 3-D reference in the workbook, one that crosses multiple sheets. To do so, follow these steps:

1. Choose Insert, Name, Define.
2. In the Names in Workbook edit box, type **CashBalance**.
3. In the Refers To edit box, select whatever reference is presently there by dragging across it with the mouse pointer.

4. Click the sheet tab named FirstNational, hold down the Shift key, and then click the sheet tab named SecondNational. Both tabs are selected, and the Refers To edit box now contains =FirstNational:SecondNational!

5. The active sheet is the one whose tab you first clicked: in this example, that sheet is the one named FirstNational. Click cell C2, which contains the ending balance for December.

6. Choose OK.

You will now have a 3-D name: CashBalance refers to cell C2 in the worksheets named FirstNational and SecondNational. Finally, you are in a position to use all these sheet level and 3-D names. In the balance sheet worksheet, cell C4 of Figure 2.1, you can enter this formula:

=SUM(CashBalance)

which returns the sum of all the cells that compose the 3-D name CashBalance. In this case, the formula adds the value in cell C2 of the FirstNational worksheet ($2,747) to the value in cell C2 of the SecondNational worksheet ($51,959) to return the value $54,706. This is the total of Bell Books' current asset for its cash accounts.

TIP   3-D names do not appear in the Name box. The Name box displays only workbook level names and sheet level names that belong to the active sheet. Because a 3-D name belongs to at least two sheets, but is not a workbook level name, it does not conform to the rules for names that can appear in the Name box.

To review:

- The sheet level names *Debits*, *Credits,* and *BeginningBalance* are defined on each worksheet that contains a cash account.
- A cell that occupies the same position in each cash account worksheet contains the formula

  =BeginningBalance+SUM(Debits)-SUM(Credits)

  and returns the ending balance for the cash account contained in that worksheet.
- A 3-D name is created. It refers to the same cell in each worksheet that has a cash account ending balance. This is the balance created in step 2. The 3-D range is given a name such as *CashBalance*.
- On the balance sheet, the formula

  =SUM(CashBalance)

  returns the sum of the cells in the workbook that compose the CashBalance range.

Handling Restricted Cash Accounts

Because cash is the most liquid, and is therefore the most current of current assets, it's easy to think of all cash accounts as current assets. This is not necessarily true. Some of your cash accounts might be restricted, either as to their usage or as to the point in time that you can access them.

Suppose that your company builds houses. A new customer approaches you, asking you to build a custom house to particular specifications. You estimate that it will take about 18 months to complete the work, and you request that the customer pay you a substantial amount of the cost at the beginning of the project. This payment is to ensure that the customer will not simply walk away prior to making full payment.

You and the customer agree to put this preliminary payment in an escrow account. Neither party may access the account prior to the completion of construction. Although this account contains cash, it is not available to pay current liabilities, per the terms of your agreement with the customer. Therefore, you should not include it in a balance sheet as a current asset. Instead, you might include it as Unearned Revenue in an Other Assets classification on the balance sheet.

You might find that the interest rates on cash accounts that are denominated in a foreign currency are attractive, or you might anticipate that the value of the U.S. dollar will fall in relation to that currency. Having no other operational use for the funds, you invest $10,000 in a foreign savings account with a term of two years. Because you cannot withdraw these funds prior to completion of the term of the account, you cannot use them to pay current liabilities. Again, you would represent this investment as an asset on the balance sheet, but in a classification other than Current Assets.

Getting a Current Asset Accounts Receivable Balance

Credit sales are a fact of business life. If yours is a retail business with any appreciable degree of competition, you almost certainly must accept credit cards as a method of payment or risk losing business to your competitors. If your principal customers are themselves businesses, you must contend with the fact that they, like you, want to use their assets most efficiently. One way to do so is to use a good credit history to acquire more goods on credit.

The result is that you must temporarily show these credit sales as funds that you expect to receive at some point in the future. The matching principal, which was discussed in Chapter 1, applies here: it requires that you match revenues to the expenses required to produce the revenues in the same time period. Because you have not yet received payment for these credit sales in cash, it's necessary to record them as funds to be received: thus the term *accounts receivable*. Figure 2.5 shows an example of Accounts Receivable for Bell Books.

Notice that the ending balance for Accounts Receivable, shown in cell E23 of Figure 2.5, is identical to the Accounts Receivable balance shown in Bell Books' balance sheet (refer to Figure 2.1).

FIGURE 2.5
The Accounts
Receivable worksheet
for Bell Books details
the credit sales made
during December,
2001.

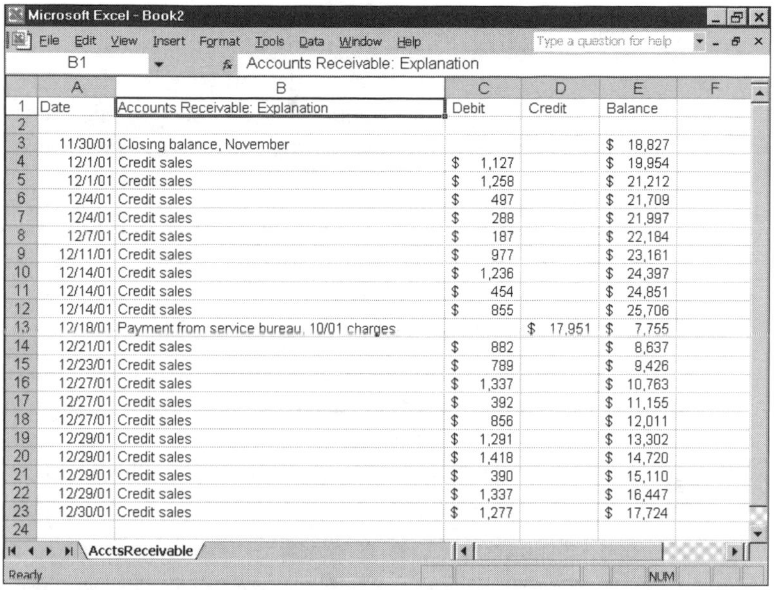

	A	B	C	D	E	F
		B1	▼	*fx* Accounts Receivable: Explanation		
1	Date	Accounts Receivable: Explanation	Debit	Credit	Balance	
2						
3	11/30/01	Closing balance, November			$ 18,827	
4	12/1/01	Credit sales	$ 1,127		$ 19,954	
5	12/1/01	Credit sales	$ 1,258		$ 21,212	
6	12/4/01	Credit sales	$ 497		$ 21,709	
7	12/4/01	Credit sales	$ 288		$ 21,997	
8	12/7/01	Credit sales	$ 187		$ 22,184	
9	12/11/01	Credit sales	$ 977		$ 23,161	
10	12/14/01	Credit sales	$ 1,236		$ 24,397	
11	12/14/01	Credit sales	$ 454		$ 24,851	
12	12/14/01	Credit sales	$ 855		$ 25,706	
13	12/18/01	Payment from service bureau, 10/01 charges		$ 17,951	$ 7,755	
14	12/21/01	Credit sales	$ 882		$ 8,637	
15	12/23/01	Credit sales	$ 789		$ 9,426	
16	12/27/01	Credit sales	$ 1,337		$ 10,763	
17	12/27/01	Credit sales	$ 392		$ 11,155	
18	12/27/01	Credit sales	$ 856		$ 12,011	
19	12/29/01	Credit sales	$ 1,291		$ 13,302	
20	12/29/01	Credit sales	$ 1,418		$ 14,720	
21	12/29/01	Credit sales	$ 390		$ 15,110	
22	12/29/01	Credit sales	$ 1,337		$ 16,447	
23	12/30/01	Credit sales	$ 1,277		$ 17,724	
24						

Roughly every third day during the month of December, Bell Books records new credit sales in the *debit* column of the Accounts Receivable account. This is according to the rule for recording increases to asset accounts: you record such increases in the asset account's debit column.

In Figure 2.5, a credit entry of $17,951 appears in cell D13. This represents a payment to Bell Books by the credit card firm that Bell Books uses. This is according to the rule for recording decreases to asset accounts: you record decreases in the asset account's credit column. The amount of $17,951 also appears in Figure 2.2, showing that Bell Books' cash account balance has increased per the deposit of the check in the bank.

That payment reduces the (debit) balance of Accounts Receivable for December, and increases the (debit) balance of Cash by an identical amount. Notice that this transaction has no net effect on Total Assets. It simply shifts the asset from Accounts Receivable to Cash, to reflect the fact that you have finally received payment for purchases that occurred in October.

Allowing for Doubtful Accounts

Unfortunately, not all credit purchases result in eventual, actual cash payment. The longer a customer's account goes unpaid, the more doubtful it is that the customer will ever make good on the debt. Some business customers go bankrupt subsequent to making a purchase on credit; others simply disappear. Recognized credit cards, such as MasterCard or American Express, help to minimize this risk. In most cases, if you accept one of these cards as payment for a product or service, you can count on receiving payment from the credit card company.

In return for accepting the risk of non-payment (and for associated services), the credit card company charges you some percentage of the credit purchases from your business. For every $100 worth of sales, you might receive $97 from the credit card company. Many firms view this avoidance of risk as an additional benefit of accepting credit cards as payment. (And, if they're smart, those firms get their paying customers to pick up the 3% tab for the dead-beats.)

Many businesses also extend credit terms directly to regular customers and clients, instead of (or in addition to) extending credit via an intermediary such as a credit card firm. In these cases, the business assumes the risk that it will never receive payment. Of course, the business avoids the payment of a service charge to a credit card firm in cases like these.

When you assume the risk of non-payment, you must anticipate that some customers will fail to pay you. Then, the matching principle requires that you estimate the amount of credit sales during a given period will eventually turn out to be uncollectible. In accordance with the principle, estimating uncollectible accounts reduces the revenue that is recorded for the period during which the sales occurred.

There are two basic approaches to estimating the amount of credit sales that will become uncollectible: the *aging approach* and the *percentage of sales approach*. Both depend on historic estimates of the percentage of credit sales that you will eventually have to write off.

Using the Aging Approach to Estimating Uncollectibles

The aging approach depends on an analysis of the aging of credit sales (see Figure 2.6).

FIGURE 2.6
The PastDue worksheet details individual accounts receivable for Bell Books that are past due as of December 31, 2001.

	A	B	C	D	E	F	G	H
	D2	▼	fx =MAX(0,$G$1-30-C2)					
1	Account number	Amount due	Date of sale	Days past due		Closing Date:	12/31/01	
2	2490 $	655.83	11/28/01	3				
3	1281 $	732.90	11/21/01	10				
4	5378 $	139.47	11/20/01	11				
5	1528 $	144.22	11/17/01	14				
6	7585 $	84.83	11/10/01	21				
7	5706 $	894.14	11/10/01	21				
8	1281 $	129.29	11/10/01	21				
9	7165 $	1,101.34	11/6/01	25				
10	1379 $	926.40	11/5/01	26				
11	6235 $	862.78	11/1/01	30				
12	5482 $	54.43	10/29/01	33				
13	3253 $	505.72	10/26/01	36				
14	2065 $	453.73	10/24/01	38				
15	3157 $	514.75	10/17/01	45				
16	8798 $	157.49	10/16/01	46				
17	6495 $	96.91	10/15/01	47				
18	8945 $	79.18	10/12/01	50				
19	4552 $	87.79	10/3/01	59				
20	6838 $	116.00	9/18/01	74				
21	8705 $	156.23	9/18/01	74				
22	1843 $	137.56	9/7/01	85				
23	8186 $	120.82	9/6/01	86				
24	2824 $	532.39	9/4/01	88				
25	461 $	532.00	8/25/01	98				

The worksheet shown in Figure 2.6 details the purchases made by individual accounts, the sales amount, the date of sale, and the number of days past due for each purchase. The following formula returns the number of days that an account is past due, in cell D2 of Figure 2.6:

```
=MAX(0,DATE(2001,12,31)-30-C2)
```

Bell Books extends a 30-day grace period to its customers, after which it considers the account past due. The formula uses the closing date for the balance sheet (12/31/01), subtracts the 30-day grace period, and then subtracts the date of the sale (the date value in cell C2). This results in the number of days past due for that sale. The formula is surrounded by the MAX function to prevent it from returning a negative value if the date of sale was within 30 days of the closing date.

The worksheet shown in Figure 2.7 summarizes this information.

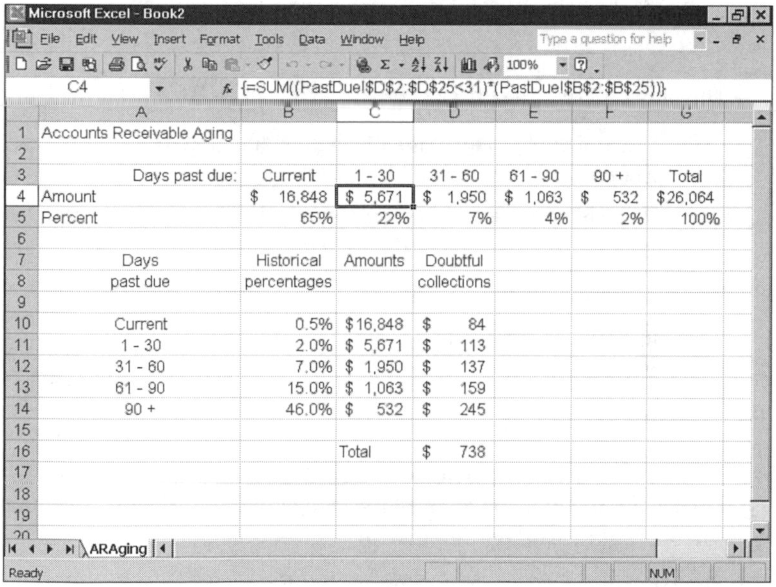

	A	B	C	D	E	F	G
1	Accounts Receivable Aging						
2							
3	Days past due:	Current	1 - 30	31 - 60	61 - 90	90 +	Total
4	Amount	$ 16,848	$ 5,671	$ 1,950	$ 1,063	$ 532	$26,064
5	Percent	65%	22%	7%	4%	2%	100%
6							
7	Days	Historical	Amounts	Doubtful			
8	past due	percentages		collections			
9							
10	Current	0.5%	$16,848	$ 84			
11	1 - 30	2.0%	$ 5,671	$ 113			
12	31 - 60	7.0%	$ 1,950	$ 137			
13	61 - 90	15.0%	$ 1,063	$ 159			
14	90 +	46.0%	$ 532	$ 245			
15							
16			Total	$ 738			
17							
18							
19							
20							

FIGURE 2.7
The aging approach to analysis of accounts receivable for Bell Books, December 31, 2001, summarizes the amount receivable according to the length of time the payment is past due.

NOTE Does it seem strange to subtract a number from a date? Excel keeps track of dates by means of a serial number system. By default, January 1, 1900 is serial number 1; January 2, 1900 is serial number 2; and so on. The DATE function accepts a year, month, and day as its arguments, and returns the serial number for that date. Even though a cell's format causes it to display, say, 12/31/2001, the actual value in the cell is the date's serial number. Therefore, the formula in cell D2 works out to

```
=35064-30-35031
```

The amount of $16,848 in cell B4 of Figure 2.7 is the total of all credit sales in Accounts Receivable that are current as of 12/31/01. The formula that sums the values in DecemberARDebits (cells C4:C23 in Figure 2.5) is

`=SUM(DecemberARDebits)`

The value in cell C4, $5,671, is returned by the array formula

`=SUM((PastDue!$D$2:$D$25<31)*(PastDue!$B$2:$B$25))`

(The worksheet named PastDue is shown in Figure 2.6.) This array formula examines the values in the range $D$2:$D$25, and returns an array of TRUE (if the value is less than 31) or FALSE (if the value is not less than 31). Excel converts these TRUE and FALSE values to 1s and 0s, and then multiplies the 1s and 0s by the corresponding dollar amounts in the range $B$2:$B$25. Finally, Excel sums the results of the multiplication, to return the value of $5,671.

Similarly, the value in cell D4, $1,950, is returned by this array formula:

`=SUM((PastDue!$D$2:$D$25>30)*(PastDue!$D$2:$D$25<61)*(PastDue!$B$2:$B$25))`

The only differences between the two array formulas are

- The first comparison restricts the SUM function to accounts where the number of days past due is greater than 30.

- There is now a second comparison, which restricts the SUM function to accounts where the number of days past due is less than 61.

The array formula interprets the account shown on line 12 in Figure 2.6 as follows:

- TRUE for the first condition, because 33 days past due is greater than 30.
- TRUE for the second condition, because 33 days past due is less than 61.
- $54.43 for the third term.

As Excel interprets the array formula, TRUE * TRUE * $54.43 is equivalent to 1 * 1 * $54.43. Finally, the SUM function adds all the values (either the actual sale amount or 0, depending on whether both conditions are true for a given sale).

The percentage values shown in row 5 of Figure 2.7 can be useful as a means of evaluating the store's credit policies. If they stray too far from percentages that management considers acceptable for a given aging period, it may be necessary to either tighten or relax the requirements for extending credit to a particular customer.

Cells B10:B14 contain historical information about the percentage of accounts that become uncollectible after a given period of time has elapsed. Bell Books' past experience has shown that half of 1% of all current credit sales go unpaid, 2% of credit sales from 1 to 30 days are past due, and so on. These percentages are multiplied by the dollar amounts in each aging category. The results of these calculations consist of the values shown in cells D10:D14.

Their sum, $738, appears both in cell D16 of Figure 2.7 and in cell B6 of Figure 2.1. This is the amount that Bell Books estimates as uncollectible accounts receivable as of 12/31/01, the date of the balance sheet.

Using the Percentage of Sales Approach to Estimating Uncollectibles

A much simpler method of estimating uncollectible accounts receivable depends on historical information about the ratio of dollars lost due to nonpayment to sales dollars. If you know that some percentage of sales eventually becomes uncollectible, you can simply multiply that percentage by your sales dollars for a given period.

If you decide to use this method, it's best to calculate the historic percentage of uncollectibles as a ratio of credit sales. This is because a cash sale never becomes uncollectible, so it does not help to include cash sales in the calculation. Furthermore, the relationship between the total credit sales and total cash sales in a given period might be substantially different than their relationship during the basis period. In that case, you are likely to seriously mis-estimate the amounts that you will never collect.

The aging approach is usually more accurate than the percentage of sales approach, because it forces you to focus on the actual length of time that individual accounts are past due. The sad fact is that the longer an account is past due, the less likely that you will ever receive payment.

Additionally, the process of focusing on specific aging periods enables you to evaluate your policies for granting credit. For these reasons, the aging approach is usually the recommended procedure for estimating an allowance for doubtful accounts.

Getting a Prepaid Expenses Balance

The entries to the balance sheet that this chapter has discussed so far—Cash and Accounts Receivable—are both driven by transactions that occur during the period covered by the balance sheet. Another category of Current Assets covers a subset of a business's resources that span accounting periods. Transactions that occur during the period in question might, or might not, change the value of these assets. But whether such a transaction changes the value of the asset, it usually requires that you make an *adjusting entry*.

Suppose, for example, that your business uses a postage meter. From time to time, you take the meter to the post office, write a check for a few hundred dollars, and a clerk increases the amount of postage shown in the meter by that amount.

In effect, what you have done is *prepay* a few months of expenses by decreasing the value of one current asset—Cash. If you were to prepare an income statement and a balance sheet at the end of each month, you would show the amount of metered postage that you actually used during that month as an operating expense on the income statement. However, postage remaining in the meter at the end of the month is an asset—one that you need to account for on the balance sheet.

In this way, you can associate the postage that you actually use during the month—the operating expense—with the revenues that the expense helped to generate. Doing so results in an accurate estimate of your profit for that period. Similarly, on the balance sheet, you can accurately estimate the (admittedly, small) contribution that the postage remaining in the meter makes to the worth of your company.

During the months that you are using the postage in the meter, no transaction occurs that triggers an entry in a postage journal, which would eventually show up in an income statement or balance sheet. (It would be very unusual to track each individual usage of the postage meter in a journal: that's overkill.) But the use of the postage has to be accounted for somewhere, and that's usually done by means of an adjusting entry at the end of each accounting period. The process of making adjusting entries is discussed in more detail in Chapter 5, "Working Capital and Cash Flow Analysis," which covers the topic of adjusted trial balances.

While there are many types of prepaid expenses that your business might incur, there are two that nearly every company must deal with at some point: supplies and insurance.

Although the acquisition of office supplies is, formally, a prepaid expense, most businesses do not bother with recording it as such in their financial statements. Their position is that it is too much trouble to perform a physical count of office supplies at the end of every accounting period in order to determine the value of supplies used during that period. A large corporation might treat supplies as a prepaid expense in its financial statements. However, it is likely to use an estimate of the supplies used during the period in question, rather than taking a formal inventory of all the pencils, stationery, and staples in its possession.

Insurance, however, is another matter. It is relatively easy to quantify the amount of insurance that expires during a period of time, and its value is usually considerably higher than that of office supplies. The brief example that follows will clarify the treatment of insurance as a current asset.

Dealing with Insurance As a Prepaid Expense

Bell Books purchases a medical insurance policy for its employees on December 1, 2001. The policy will remain in force for one year, during which the company enjoys the benefits provided by the insurance. Therefore, Bell Books can consider the cost of the policy a prepaid expense: an asset whose value declines over time and may require adjusting entries at the end of each accounting period. The purchase of the policy is recorded in the General Journal as shown in Figure 2.8.

FIGURE 2.8
Both the original purchase of an asset such as insurance, and its periodic expiration, are recorded as journal entries.

	A	B	C	D	E
1	Date	Explanation	Account	Debit	Credit
2					
3	12/1/01	To record purchase of medical insurance policy	Medical Insurance	$6,864	
4			Cash		$6,864
5	12/31/01	Expiration of one month of medical policy	Medical Insurance Expense	$ 572	
6			Medical Insurance		$ 572
7	12/1/01	To record purchase of office supplies	Office Supplies	$3,194	
8			Cash		$3,194
9	12/31/01	To record use of office supplies, December	Office Supplies Expense	$ 526	
10			Office Supplies		$ 526
11					
12					

Medical Insurance is an asset account. After purchasing the policy, the company has an additional asset in the form of insurance for its employees against the cost of medical treatment. According to the rules on debit entries and credit entries for asset accounts, an increase in the asset account's balance is recorded as a debit. Therefore, the amount of coverage provided by the policy shows up in both the General Journal and the Medical Insurance asset account (see Figure 2.9) as a debit.

FIGURE 2.9
The journal entries for the purchase and partial expiration of the Medical Insurance policy are also recorded as asset account ledger entries.

	A	B	C	D
1	Asset Account	Medical Insurance		
2				
3	Date	Explanation	Debit	Credit
4	12/1/01	Purchase of medical policy	$ 6,864	
5	12/31/01	Expiration of one month coverage		$ 572
6				
7	Balance		$ 6,292	
8				
9				

After one month of coverage, on December 31, one twelfth of the policy has expired, and the value of the asset therefore declines by one twelfth. Again, the rules for debits and credits in asset accounts state that a decline in the value of an asset is recorded as a credit. Therefore, on December 31, Bell Books makes credit entries in its General Journal and its General Ledger Medical Insurance accounts. These entries reflect the expiration of one twelfth of the value of the policy (refer to Figures 2.8 and 2.9).

Because this is a prepaid expense, the expiration of the one month of coverage should also be recorded in an expense account. An expense results in a decrease in Owner's Equity, and according to the debit and credit rules a decrease in a liability or Owner's Equity account is recorded as a debit. Therefore, the expense incurred as a result of the expiration of one month of insurance coverage is recorded as a debit to the Medical Insurance account, as shown in Figure 2.10.

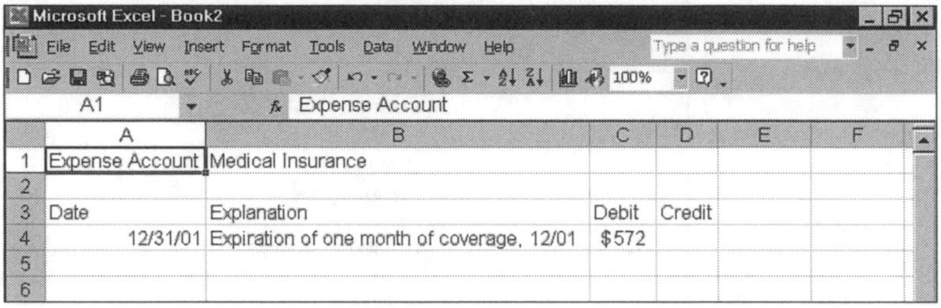

FIGURE 2.10
Debiting the Medical Insurance expense account ledger entry offsets the credit to the Medical Insurance asset account.

	A	B	C	D	E	F
1	Expense Account	Medical Insurance				
2						
3	Date	Explanation	Debit	Credit		
4	12/31/01	Expiration of one month of coverage, 12/01	$572			
5						
6						

There is one more place that the prepaid expense must have an effect: the Prepaid Expenses asset category on the balance sheet. At the end of the first month of coverage, the value of the policy has dropped by $572. During the remaining 11 months of coverage provided by the policy, this prepaid expense balance will continue to decline. If Bell Books prepares a balance sheet at the end of each of those 11 months, the Medical Insurance portion of the Prepaid Expenses asset will continue to decline until it has no value left.

Getting a Current Asset Balance

Chapter 3 goes into considerable detail on the topic of valuing inventories. However, because a company's inventory is also a current asset, some of the mechanics of moving inventory asset amounts among various accounts as the balance sheet is being prepared are discussed here.

At the end of an accounting period, when you are preparing an income statement and a balance sheet, it is usual to bring the balances of the various revenue and expense accounts to zero. The reason for this is that the next time you prepare these statements, you want them to reflect the activity that takes place during the *next* period.

A starting value of zero in the revenue and expense accounts allows you to accurately determine the profit that you earn during that period. If there are dollar amounts from a prior period remaining in those accounts, you will be unable to subtract the correct amount of expenses from the correct amount of revenues to arrive at an accurate earnings estimate.

The following three steps define the process of bringing the revenue and expense accounts to zero (also called *closing the accounts*):

1. For revenue accounts, which normally carry credit balances, make an offsetting debit entry to bring its balance to zero. For expense accounts, which normally carry debit balances, make an offsetting credit entry to close them.

2. Make these closing entries in a special, temporary account in the General Journal, termed an Income Summary. The revenue account's debit entry is offset by a credit to the Income Summary. The expense account's credit entry is offset by a debit to the Income Summary. The difference between the sum of the revenue entries and the sum of the expense entries represents the earnings for the period that are attributable to operations.

3. Close the temporary Income Summary account by means of a debit entry in the amount of its balance, and place the same entry as a credit to Retained Earnings.

The result of this process is that the next period can begin afresh with zero amounts in the revenue and expense accounts. It also places the earnings from the current period (whether positive or negative) in the appropriate balance sheet account.

The procedure that you use for asset and liability accounts is different from the procedure for revenue and expense accounts. The dollar amounts in asset and liability accounts fluctuate over time, as resources grow and debts are paid. To arrange for an asset account to have a zero balance at the beginning of an accounting period would be to say that the company's assets somehow vanished at the end of the prior period.

One such asset account is Inventory. If your business produces products or resells them to retailers or consumers, you have inventory to account for. (If your business provides only services for its customers, you might well carry no inventory at all.)

Understanding the Inventory Flow

At the beginning of a period, you normally have some amount of goods in your inventory. During the period, you might purchase additional goods from your suppliers—these purchases have the effect of increasing the inventory. At the same time, you sell as many items from the inventory to your customers—these sales decrease your inventory. The result of these activities is your ending inventory: beginning inventory, plus purchases, minus the goods used in the sales that you make to your customers.

N O T E   By rearranging this equation, you can arrive at the Cost of Goods Sold (COGS). This is an important element in determining your company's gross profit, which is defined as Sales minus COGS. COGS is calculated by the equation

`COGS = Beginning Inventory + Purchases - Ending Inventory`

In words, the cost of goods available for sale is the sum of the beginning inventory and any purchases that were made. The difference between the cost of goods available for sale and the ending inventory is the cost of the goods that you actually sold to your customers. ▪

Of course, many events can occur that complicate these basic relationships. You might have an arrangement with your suppliers that allows you to return to them, for any reason and for credit, some portion of the goods you purchase from them. It might be that some goods are damaged or otherwise unacceptable.

Your purchase terms might call for discounts if you make payment within a specified period. Adjusting entries or special accounts are sometimes necessary to quantify the effects of these occurrences. Nevertheless, they do not materially change the basic flow of starting inventory, through purchases and sales, to ending inventory—which becomes the starting inventory for the next accounting period.

Closing the Inventory Account

At the end of the period, a company often performs a physical count of the ending inventory. When it subsequently applies one of the valuation methods described in the next chapter, the result is the value of the inventory. This is the value that is used in the Current Assets section of the balance sheet.

This probably seems a little anticlimactic after all the discussion previously about closing accounts, inventory flow, and Income Summaries. In practice the process is more complex than simply performing an inventory count and entering the result on the balance sheet, as shown in Figure 2.11.

FIGURE 2.11
Closing accounts at the end of a period takes revenue and expense accounts to a zero value, but normally leaves a value in asset and liability accounts.

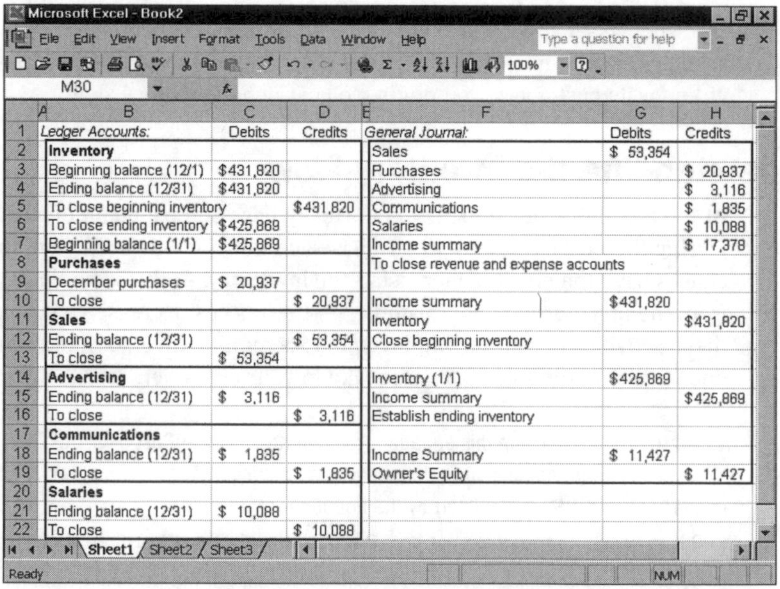

	B	C	D	F	G	H
1	Ledger Accounts:	Debits	Credits	General Journal:	Debits	Credits
2	**Inventory**			Sales	$ 53,354	
3	Beginning balance (12/1)	$431,820		Purchases		$ 20,937
4	Ending balance (12/31)	$431,820		Advertising		$ 3,116
5	To close beginning inventory		$431,820	Communications		$ 1,835
6	To close ending inventory	$425,869		Salaries		$ 10,088
7	Beginning balance (1/1)	$425,869		Income summary		$ 17,378
8	**Purchases**			To close revenue and expense accounts		
9	December purchases	$ 20,937				
10	To close		$ 20,937	Income summary	$431,820	
11	**Sales**			Inventory		$431,820
12	Ending balance (12/31)		$ 53,354	Close beginning inventory		
13	To close	$ 53,354				
14	**Advertising**			Inventory (1/1)	$425,869	
15	Ending balance (12/31)	$ 3,116		Income summary		$425,869
16	To close		$ 3,116	Establish ending inventory		
17	**Communications**					
18	Ending balance (12/31)	$ 1,835		Income Summary	$ 11,427	
19	To close		$ 1,835	Owner's Equity		$ 11,427
20	**Salaries**					
21	Ending balance (12/31)	$ 10,088				
22	To close		$ 10,088			

Figure 2.11 contains seven sections, indicated by their bold borders. These sections could be maintained in separate Excel worksheets, but to conserve space, they are shown here on one sheet.

The first section, labeled Inventory, shows the amount of inventory at the beginning of the period ($431,820), and the ending balance (also $431,820). Under a periodic inventory system (see Chapter 3 for details), no changes are made to the Inventory account during the period: purchases are recorded in their own account. A closing entry, equal to the ending balance, is made in the account's credit column. This amount is also entered in the General Journal's Income Summary (cell G10). A physical inventory count is taken, and entered as a debit ($425,869 in cell C6), and also to establish the beginning inventory for the next period (cell C7).

Purchases made to inventory during the period are also closed out by a debit entry in the ledger (cell D10) and transferred to the Income Summary with a credit entry (cell H3).

Closing the Revenue and Expense Accounts

As mentioned earlier in this chapter, at the end of the accounting period the revenue and expense accounts are left with a zero balance, but asset and liability accounts such as Inventory are not. For example, the Sales account is given a zero balance at the end of one period and, thus, at the beginning of the next. Its ending balance, $53,354, is entered twice at closing: once as a debit to the ledger account, to close it, and once as a debit in the Income Summary. The latter entry begins the process of moving revenue out of its ledger account and into the balance sheet.

The formula used in cell D12 to calculate Sales is an array formula:

```
=SUM(IF(SecondNational!B5:B19="Cash Receipts",SecondNational!C5:C19,0))+
    SUM(IF(AcctsReceivable!B3:B23="Credit Sales", AcctsReceivable!C3:C23,0))
```

This array formula looks to a different worksheet, here named "SecondNational", to find any values in cells B5:B19 that match the value "Cash Receipts." For any matching values, the formula sums the corresponding dollar amounts in cells C5:C19 (refer to Figure 2.4).

The same process is completed for the credit sales recorded in the Accounts Receivable worksheet, and the results of the two SUM functions are totaled to give the full amount of sales for the month. In practice, just as here, you keep these two accounts separate, and add their closing balances together for the purpose of the Income Summary.

The next three sections in Figure 2.11, labeled Advertising, Telephone, and Salaries, each represent expenses incurred during the current period. The details of the activity in each account during the period have been omitted, and only the ending balance and the closing entry are shown.

The closing entries in the ledger accounts also appear in the General Journal's temporary Income Summary account. Note that the values in cells D16, D19, and D22 are identical to the values in cells H4:H6 in the figure.

Notice also the value of $17,378 in cell H7 of Figure 2.11. It is the result of subtracting the period's expenses (Purchasing, Advertising, Telephone, and Salaries) from the period's sales revenue ($53,354).

Cell G18 contains the formula

```
=H7+(H15-G10)
```

which adds the difference between the ending inventory and the beginning inventory to the Income Summary. This amount, $11,427, represents the change in equity for the period: sales, less operating expenses, plus the change in the inventory valuation. Because the value of inventory dropped during the period, its effect is to reduce the amount that is added to Owner's Equity. Had the inventory grown, its effect would have been to increase the amount added to Owner's Equity.

Summary

In this chapter, you have learned about some of the preliminary aspects of balance sheets: their uses, their construction, their current asset components, and their relationships to underlying accounts. Changes over time in these accounts cause changes in your company's worth, and thus in its balance sheet. However, revenue and expense accounts are treated differently at the end of an accounting period than are asset and liability accounts.

While it is not this book's purpose to teach accountancy, the use of some accounting terminology is necessary in a discussion of the measurement of profit. As well, some discussion of certain rules used in double-entry accounting—such as recording an increase in an expense account as a debit entry—is necessary if you are to measure your profits in a way that others can understand.

The reason is that potential investors and creditors, as well as the accountants who will inevitably insist on examining your books, will insist that you follow accepted principles and practices in the creation of your financial statements. This chapter has introduced some of these concepts; more will be covered in subsequent chapters, but only to the extent necessary to help you create your financial statements.

Because the valuation of inventory is a somewhat complicated topic, Chapter 3 covers it in detail. Choosing the appropriate method for valuing the items in your business's inventory is essential if you are to estimate the worth of your business properly. The measurement of your profits also depends on your choice of valuation method. After this excursion into the topic of inventory valuation, this book returns to the balance sheet with a consideration of Liabilities and Owner's Equity.

Valuing Inventories for the Balance Sheet

Particularly for a line of business that manufactures or sells tangible goods, the size of the company's inventory exerts a powerful influence on its profitability. The inventory of goods is often the company's major current asset, and therefore contributes heavily to the calculation of the company's worth. Because the cost of goods sold is dependent on the valuation of the inventory, it also largely determines the company's gross profit (and, thus, its net income).

How you calculate the value of your company's inventory has a profound effect on the balance sheet: inventory is an asset and has an equally profound effect on the income statement (you combine the cost of goods sold with revenue to determine the gross profit).

Because of the importance of inventory analysis to a company's worth and profitability, you have at your disposal a variety of methods to value an inventory and techniques to categorize it. Because you are expected to be consistent from year to year as to your inventory valuation and accounting methods, it's important to make sound choices early on. Using Excel's tools and capabilities properly helps you with these choices.

This chapter describes the different methods you can use to assign a value to your inventory, and the different ways available to account for it. You will learn how your choice of a technique to assign a value to your inventory affects both your profitability and your business's calculated worth.

Valuing Inventories

The basic principle of inventory valuation is that the value of a unit of inventory is its cost. For example, if your company purchases products at a wholesale cost and resells them to consumers at a retail price, then the value of your inventory of goods is determined by the amount you pay to acquire them. The inventory itself consists of whatever you have purchased for the purpose of resale, in your normal business operations. So inventory would not include the building that you purchased for office space: although you might resell it, you wouldn't expect to do so as part of normal business operations.

On the other hand, if your company manufactures or otherwise produces goods, the situation is more complicated. In that case, there are typically three categories of inventory: raw materials, work in process, and finished goods. You would value each category differently. The value of the raw materials is simply their acquisition cost. The value of work in process is the cost of the raw materials plus any labor costs incurred to date. And the value of finished goods consists of the material cost plus all the labor costs involved in bringing the product to completion—including factory overhead.

There are three basic methods you can use to assign a value to your inventory:

- *Specific identification*. This method assigns the actual cost of acquiring each inventory unit to that unit. Historically, it has been companies that resell relatively few but relatively costly products that use specific identification. If your business sells expensive jewelry, you find it fairly easy to attach a specific acquisition cost to each unit. But if your company sells art supplies, you find it difficult to do so. It is much harder to keep track of the amount you paid for each of 100 paintbrushes.

- *Average cost*. This method is relatively simple to apply. The average cost per unit of inventory is just the total of your payments to suppliers, divided by the number of units in stock. Because the actual unit cost usually varies, due to changes in your supplier's pricing over time and to changing suppliers, this method can be less accurate than specific identification. But average cost is often a feasible method when specific identification is not.

- *FIFO* and *LIFO*. FIFO stands for first-in, first-out, and LIFO stands for last-in, first-out. These methods involve assumptions about when you acquired a unit of inventory and about when you sell it. Because your acquisition costs normally change over time, your cost of goods sold changes accordingly. Both your profitability and your total assets depend on whether you bought a unit for $50 and sell it for $75, or whether you bought an identical unit for $60 and sell it for $75.

The following sections in this chapter discuss each of these methods in detail.

Using Specific Identification

As mentioned previously, it is relatively easy to use specific identification as a means of valuing inventory if you have relatively few units to value. And as a practical matter, this has usually meant that those items are quite costly: a business that has just a few items to sell must either sell them at a substantial profit or cease operations for lack of cash.

In recent years, however, the proliferation of such technology as point-of-sale terminals at retail stores, the imprinting of serial numbers on many different kinds of electronic equipment, and the widespread use of computer-based support systems, has changed that situation—in the retail industry, at least. It is now much less onerous to track each and every unit from its acceptance into inventory through its eventual sale.

Although specific identification is probably the most intuitively satisfying of the valuation methods, it will become apparent that it is not always preferable to its alternatives— particularly from the profitability standpoint. Consider the case of a retail store that sells electronic equipment.

Case Study: Evans Electronics

Evans Electronics, a retail store newly located in a shopping mall, sells personal computers, data communications equipment, and ancillary products such as printers and disk drives. The store has put in place a small database, using Microsoft Access as the database management system. This database enables the sales staff to record the serial number and product code of every item that the store sells.

The system also maintains information about inventories. It records the date that a unit of stock was purchased, its cost, and its product code. This information is recorded in a table whose structure is shown in Figure 3.1.

The database also contains several predefined *queries*. Although queries perform several different kinds of tasks, one of their primary functions is to return data from tables to files, to workstation monitors, and to other applications. The data returned by queries might be record-by-record or it might be summarized.

Chapter 18, "Importing Business Data into Excel," goes into these matters in considerably more detail than is covered here. For now, take the following information as background to the matter at hand, inventory valuation:

- You can arrange to have the most current data from a database moved into an Excel workbook whenever you open the workbook. The source database is not necessarily one designed using Microsoft Access.
- The information that is retrieved into Excel can come directly from tables in the database, or indirectly via queries that extract data from the tables.

■ If the information is returned by queries, you can also arrange for runtime criteria. Don't be intimidated by that terminology—those are just words. Put differently, you can specify criteria such as beginning and ending dates that take effect at runtime, when the query extracts the data from the tables.

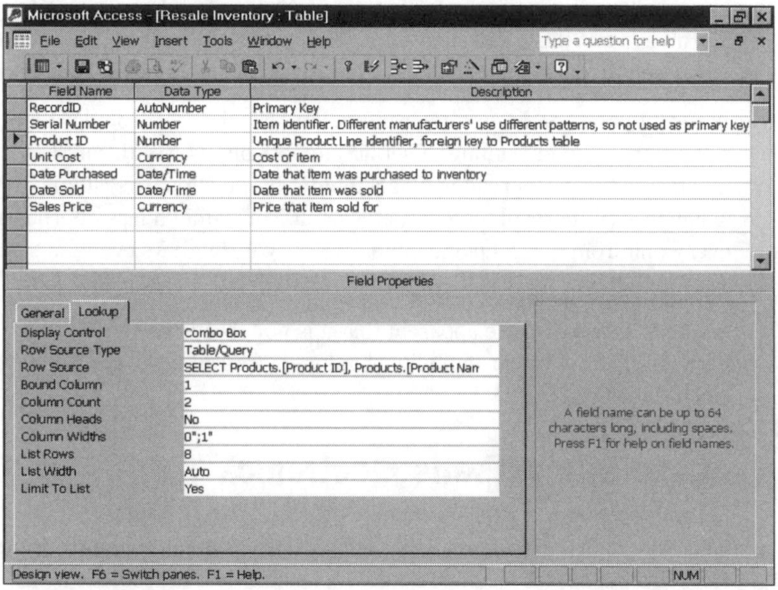

FIGURE 3.1

By specifying a table lookup and a row source, you can display (for example) descriptive text instead of nondescriptive identification numbers.

Using a predefined query, Evans Electronics extracts data from its database into the Excel worksheet. Summary information on the starting inventory as of 4/1/2001 and quantities purchased during the month are both displayed in Figure 3.2.

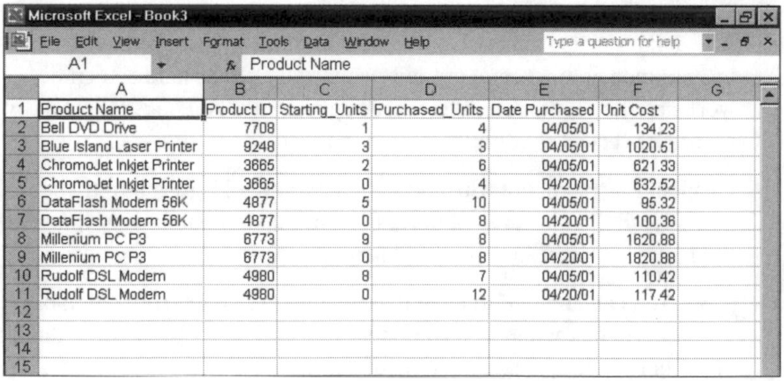

FIGURE 3.2

Evans Electronics' starting inventory and quantities purchased during April 2001 form the basis for valuation at the end of the period.

	A	B	C	D	E	F	G
1	Product Name	Product ID	Starting_Units	Purchased_Units	Date Purchased	Unit Cost	
2	Bell DVD Drive	7708	1	4	04/05/01	134.23	
3	Blue Island Laser Printer	9248	3	3	04/05/01	1020.51	
4	ChromoJet Inkjet Printer	3665	2	6	04/05/01	621.33	
5	ChromoJet Inkjet Printer	3665	0	4	04/20/01	832.52	
6	DataFlash Modem 56K	4877	5	10	04/05/01	95.32	
7	DataFlash Modem 56K	4877	0	8	04/20/01	100.36	
8	Millenium PC P3	6773	9	8	04/05/01	1620.88	
9	Millenium PC P3	6773	0	8	04/20/01	1820.88	
10	Rudolf DSL Modem	4980	8	7	04/05/01	110.42	
11	Rudolf DSL Modem	4980	0	12	04/20/01	117.42	
12							
13							
14							
15							

Evans' supplier raised its prices during April 2001: notice that identical products have entered the inventory at different times and at different costs. For example, Evans acquired seven DSL modems on 4/5/2001 at a unit cost of $110.42, and another 12 units of the same modem on 4/20/2001 at a unit cost of $117.42.

The worksheet shown in Figure 3.2 contains four named ranges that will become important later in this chapter:

- Inventory_Product_Code refers to the range B2:B11. It contains the identifier that distinguishes, say, a fax modem from a laser printer. Although this range uniquely identifies a product, it does not uniquely identify a product at a particular cost.

- Start_Units refers to the range C2:C11. It contains data on the number of units of each product code *at a particular unit cost* that are in the inventory at the beginning of the period.

- Purchase_Units refers to the range D2:D11. It shows how many units were purchased to the inventory during the period—again, at a particular unit cost.

- Inventory_Unit_Cost refers to the range F2:F11. This is the cost of each product that was acquired from the supplier *at a particular time*.

When it is time to close the books at the end of each month, the information on products sold is copied from the database, maintained in Microsoft Access, to an Excel worksheet.

You usually set up queries for Microsoft Access by means of a graphical user interface. By dragging tables and fields around on the screen you indicate which fields you want the query to return. You establish criteria that specify the records to return in the same way. The user interface hides the Torquemada-like machinations that go on behind the scenes and that result in the Structured Query Language code that actually extracts the data from the database. For example, here's the code that returns Evans' sales for April:

```
SELECT Products.[Product Name], Products.[Product ID],
[Resale Inventory].[Serial Number], [Resale Inventory].[Unit Cost],
[Resale Inventory].[Sales Price]

FROM [Resale Inventory] LEFT JOIN Products ON
[Resale Inventory].[Product ID] = Products.[Product ID]

WHERE (((([Resale Inventory].[Date Sold])
Between #4/1/2001# And #4/30/2001#))

ORDER BY [Resale Inventory].[Serial Number];
```

This code is actually fairly easy to understand—that's one of the more pleasant aspects of Structured Query Language. Here's a brief walkthrough:

- The SELECT statement identifies the tables and fields that are involved in the query. Here, the tables are Products and Resale Inventory. The fields from each table follow the table name. So, for example, the code says to select the Product Name field from the Products table.

■ In the FROM statement, the relationship (or *join*) between the two tables is specified. A record from Products is related to a record in Resale Inventory when they share the same Product ID.

■ The WHERE statement specifies any criteria that the query is to apply. In this example, the criterion is that only records with a Date Sold value between 4/1/2001 and 4/30/2001 are to be returned.

■ The ORDER BY statement calls for the records to be returned in ascending (that's the default) Serial Number order.

Once the queries have been set up (Chapter 18 provides more information on the process), getting the data out of the database and into the worksheet is no more difficult than choosing Refresh Data from Excel's Data menu.

The worksheet for sales during April is shown in Figure 3.3. Because the specific identification method is being used, each row contains information on the Product ID and Serial Number of each unit sold. Because this information uniquely identifies a particular unit, the sales database also contains, and passes to Excel, Evans Electronics' cost for that specific unit.

FIGURE 3.3

The record of Evans Electronics' product sales for April 2001 shows that some units that were sold had different acquisition costs.

	Product Name	Product ID	Serial Number	Unit Cost	Sales Price
1	Product Name	Product ID	Serial Number	Unit Cost	Sales Price
2	DataFlash Modem 56K	4877	196482	95.32	127.02
3	DataFlash Modem 56K	4877	861710	100.36	127.02
4	DataFlash Modem 56K	4877	66202	100.36	127.02
5	Rudolf DSL Modem	4980	508461	110.42	138.54
6	Rudolf DSL Modem	4980	810263	110.42	138.54
7	Rudolf DSL Modem	4980	923172	117.42	138.54
8	Rudolf DSL Modem	4980	692294	117.42	138.54
9	Millennium PC P3	6773	160082	1820.88	2130.42
10	Millennium PC P3	6773	383226	1820.88	2130.42
11	Millennium PC P3	6773	876481	1820.88	2130.42
12	Millennium PC P3	6773	139456	1820.88	2130.42
13	Millennium PC P3	6773	816001	1820.88	2130.42
14	Blue Island Laser Printer	9248	235806	1020.51	1298.31
15	Bell DVD Drive	7708	7853	134.23	167.39
16	Bell DVD Drive	7708	344181	134.23	167.39
17	ChromoJet Inkjet Printer	3665	336457	621.33	774.95
18	ChromoJet Inkjet Printer	3665	563523	621.33	774.95
19	ChromoJet Inkjet Printer	3665	574032	621.33	774.95
20	ChromoJet Inkjet Printer	3665	823942	632.52	774.95
21	ChromoJet Inkjet Printer	3665	146566	632.52	774.95
22					
23	Totals			13874.12	17095.16
24					

Although the unit costs for some products are different, Evans sold each product at the same price. As a new business, Evans made a tactical decision not to increase the sales price during the first month of operation. Clearly, Evans' decision to absorb the supplier's price increase, rather than to pass it on to its own customers, reduces its profitability. This is not an unusual decision, but the fact that the inventory contains identical units acquired at different costs has consequences both for the store's gross profit and for the balance sheet's asset evaluation.

Using the specific identification method of valuation, Evans can analyze its inventory for the month of April as shown in Figure 3.4.

FIGURE 3.4
By matching product codes and costs to the sales database, Evans Electronics can tell how many units of each product were sold.

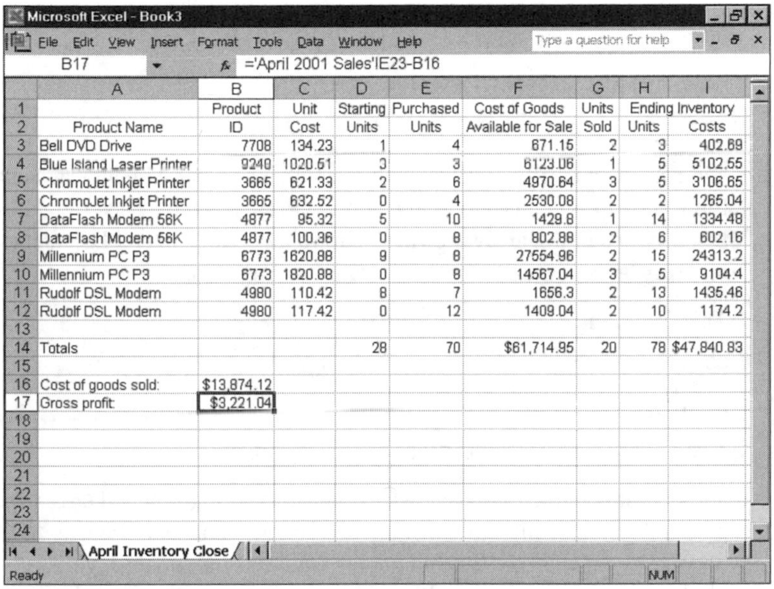
Microsoft Excel - Book3

B17 ='April 2001 Sales'!E23-B16

	A	B	C	D	E	F	G	H	I
1		Product	Unit	Starting	Purchased	Cost of Goods	Units	Ending Inventory	
2	Product Name	ID	Cost	Units	Units	Available for Sale	Sold	Units	Costs
3	Bell DVD Drive	7708	134.23	1	4	671.15	2	3	402.69
4	Blue Island Laser Printer	9240	1020.61	3	3	6123.06	1	5	5102.55
5	ChromoJet Inkjet Printer	3665	621.33	2	6	4970.64	3	5	3106.65
6	ChromoJet Inkjet Printer	3665	632.52	0	4	2530.08	2	2	1265.04
7	DataFlash Modem 56K	4877	95.32	5	10	1429.8	1	14	1334.48
8	DataFlash Modem 56K	4877	100.36	0	8	802.88	2	6	602.16
9	Millennium PC P3	6773	1620.88	9	8	27554.96	2	15	24313.2
10	Millennium PC P3	6773	1820.88	0	8	14567.04	3	5	9104.4
11	Rudolf DSL Modem	4980	110.42	8	7	1656.3	2	13	1435.46
12	Rudolf DSL Modem	4980	117.42	0	12	1409.04	2	10	1174.2
13									
14	Totals			28	70	$61,714.95	20	78	$47,840.83
15									
16	Cost of goods sold:	$13,874.12							
17	Gross profit:	$3,221.04							

April Inventory Close

In Figure 3.4, the columns for Product Name, Product ID, and Unit Cost contain the unique combinations of the variables from the worksheet in Figure 3.3: for example, there are only two possible combinations of product code and unit cost for the DataFlash 56K modem. The number of units in the starting inventory is obtained from the ending units in the March inventory summary. (When it's feasible, it's wise to perform a physical count on a periodic basis and reconcile the actual number of units counted with the number of units recorded in the database. The system described here can be either a perpetual or periodic system. See "Using Perpetual and Periodic Inventory Systems" later in this chapter for more information.) The cost of each item available for sale is the product of the unit cost and the number of units.

NOTE In the remainder of this section, Excel formulas are used to calculate results such as the number of units sold. These calculations are based on data returned from the database. It is also possible—and sometimes preferable—to carry out those calculations in the database itself and return the results to Excel as part of a query.

The critical portion of Figure 3.4 is in column G, Units Sold. Cell G8 contains this array formula:

```
=SUM((B8=Sales_Product_Code)*(C8=Sales_Unit_Cost))
```

which returns 2 as its value. Two DataFlash 56K modems that were purchased for $100.36 each were sold during April. To understand how this formula works, examine its components.

There is a range named `Sales_Product_Code`, which occupies cells B2:B21 in Figure 3.3. This fragment:

```
B8=Sales_Product_Code
```

evaluates to

```
{TRUE;TRUE;TRUE;FALSE;FALSE; . . . ;FALSE}
```

and returns an array of values that are `TRUE` or `FALSE`. The logical value depends on whether the value in B8 equals any values in the `Sales_Product_Code` range. In this case, the first three values in the array are `TRUE`. The value of 4877 in cell B8 equals the first three elements in `Sales_Product_Code` (see cells B2:B4 in Figure 3.3).

This fragment:

```
C8=Sales_Unit_Cost
```

evaluates to

```
{FALSE;TRUE;TRUE;FALSE;FALSE; . . . ;FALSE}
```

and operates in much the same way. There is a range named `Sales_Unit_Cost`, which occupies cells D2:D21 in Figure 3.3. It also returns an array of logical, `TRUE` or `FALSE` values, depending on whether the unit cost in C8, $100.36, equals any unit costs in the `Sales_Unit_Cost` range. In this case, only the second and third values are TRUE (see cells D3:D4 in Figure 3.3).

TIP

You can see the arrays of TRUE or FALSE values—indeed, the results of any portion of an Excel formula—by highlighting a fragment in the Formula bar and pressing the F9 key. When you have finished, be sure to press Esc. Otherwise, the results replace the original fragment.

Excel 2002 offers a new tool that accomplishes much the same end as the F9 key: Formula Evaluation. Select a cell that contains a formula and choose Tools, Formula Auditing, Evaluate Formula. In the Evaluate Formula window, press the Evaluate button repeatedly to watch expressions resolve into intermediate values and finally to the result you see on the worksheet. This new tool is a little less flexible but much more convenient than using the F9 key.

Excel can perform arithmetic operations on logical values. The rules are that TRUE*TRUE = 1, TRUE*FALSE = 0, and FALSE*FALSE = 0. So this fragment, which multiplies the first array of logical values times the second:

```
(B8=Sales_Product_Code)*(C8=Sales_Unit_Cost)
```

evaluates to

```
{0;1;1;0;0;0;0;0;0;0;0;0;0;0;0;0;0;0;0;0}
```

and returns an array of 1s and 0s. The first array contains TRUE in its first three elements, and the second array contains TRUE in its second and third elements; the remaining elements in each array are FALSE. So, the result of this multiplication is an array whose second and third elements are 1s and the remaining elements are 0s.

Finally, the full formula:

```
=SUM((B8=Sales_Product_Code)*(C8=Sales_Unit_Cost))
```

returns the sum of the array of 1s and 0s. In this case, that sum equals 2: the number of sales of products whose product code is 4877 and whose unit cost is $100.36.

The array formula just discussed is copied and pasted into each of the cells in the range G3:G12 in Figure 3.4. The references to the product code and unit cost adjust accordingly, but the range names, which represent absolute references, do not adjust. This results in a count of each unit that was sold during April at a given unit cost.

The units in the ending inventory for April (column H in Figure 3.4) are simply the result of subtracting the units sold from the starting inventory plus the units that were purchased. And the cost for each product at a given unit cost (column I in Figure 3.4) is the result of multiplying the number of units in the ending inventory by the associated unit cost.

By obtaining the total cost of the goods available for sale ($61,714.95), and subtracting from that figure the total cost of the ending inventory ($47,840.83), Evans can arrive at a cost of goods sold for the month of April of $13,874.12.

Therefore, Evans Electronics' income statement for April would show a gross profit of $3,221.04, the result of subtracting the cost of goods sold from its total sales revenue of $17,095.16 (refer to Figure 3.3). Its balance sheet for April would show ending inventory assets of $47,840.83.

Using Average Cost

Suppose that, as in the prior section, Evans Electronics has in its starting inventory items that carry different costs of acquisition but are otherwise identical. What if the store had no means of knowing which specific item it sold? That is, suppose that when it sells a Millennium PC P3 computer, Evans does not know whether it is a unit that was purchased from the supplier for $1,620.88 or for $1,820.88. Quite possibly, as will become apparent in this section, Evans doesn't *care* to know.

In cases such as these, you would typically choose to use the *average cost* method of valuing your inventory. There can be other reasons to use this method. For example, if you had some means of recognizing whether a computer cost you $1,620.88 or $1,820.88, it would be possible for you to use the specific identification method—possible, although perhaps not feasible.

But if you use specific identification, your gross profit on a sale would depend in part on which of several functionally identical computers your customer happened to take off the shelf. In this sort of situation, your gross profit should surely be irrelevant to the customer's purchasing choice. The average cost method recognizes this: it assigns a cost to each unit of inventory that is a weighted average of all the unit costs for a particular product. Figure 3.5 illustrates the average cost method as it might be used by Evans Electronics.

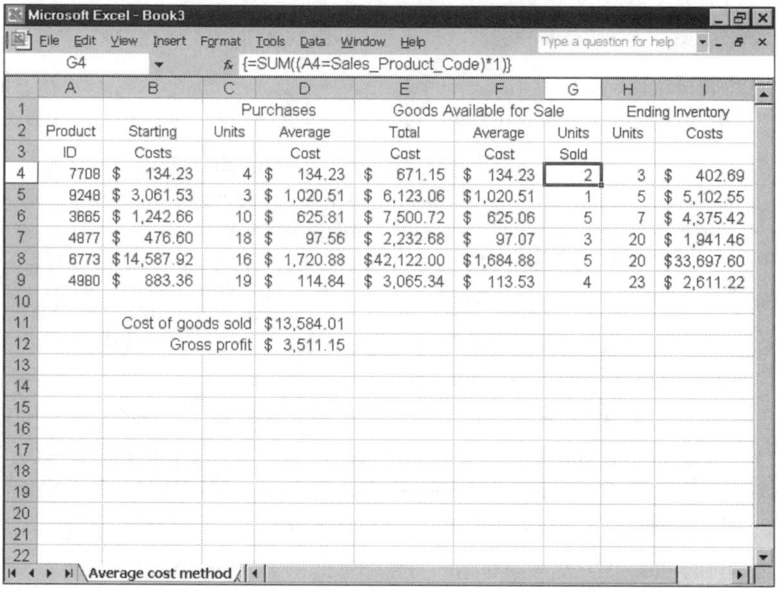

	A	B	C	D	E	F	G	H	I
1			Purchases		Goods Available for Sale			Ending Inventory	
2	Product	Starting	Units	Average	Total	Average	Units	Units	Costs
3	ID	Costs		Cost	Cost	Cost	Sold		
4	7708	$ 134.23	4	$ 134.23	$ 671.15	$ 134.23	2	3	$ 402.69
5	9248	$ 3,061.53	3	$ 1,020.51	$ 6,123.06	$1,020.51	1	5	$ 5,102.55
6	3665	$ 1,242.66	10	$ 625.81	$ 7,500.72	$ 625.06	5	7	$ 4,375.42
7	4877	$ 476.60	18	$ 97.56	$ 2,232.68	$ 97.07	3	20	$ 1,941.46
8	6773	$14,587.92	16	$ 1,720.88	$42,122.00	$1,684.88	5	20	$33,697.60
9	4980	$ 883.36	19	$ 114.84	$ 3,065.34	$ 113.53	4	23	$ 2,611.22
10									
11		Cost of goods sold		$13,584.01					
12		Gross profit		$ 3,511.15					

FIGURE 3.5
Evans Electronics' starting and ending inventory for April 2001 with the average cost method returns different results than with specific identification.

In contrast to Figure 3.4, which shows ten combinations of product code by unit cost, Figure 3.5 shows six product codes, each with just one unit cost. The average cost method derives a single unit cost for each product code, and therefore there is no need to represent the different actual costs for each product code on the inventory summary.

Column B of Figure 3.5 displays the result of multiplying the starting inventory for each product by its unit cost. This represents the cost of Evans' inventory at the beginning of April.

Column C of Figure 3.5 shows the count of each product code purchased to inventory. Cell C4 calculates this with the array formula:

```
=SUM(IF(A4=Inventory_Products_Code,Purchase_Units,0))
```

Notice that there is only one array of logical values in this formula, so no multiplication of logical values is involved. The fragment

```
A4=Inventory_Products_Code
```

returns this array of `TRUE/FALSE` values:

```
{TRUE;FALSE;FALSE;FALSE;FALSE;FALSE;FALSE;FALSE;FALSE;FALSE}
```

In words, the value 7708 in cell A4 equals the first, and only the first, value in the range named `Inventory_Products_Code`.

Surrounding this fragment with the `IF` function and the reference to `Purchase_Units` causes Excel to return the number of units purchased if the product code equals 7708:

```
IF({TRUE;FALSE;FALSE;FALSE;FALSE;FALSE;FALSE;FALSE;FALSE;FALSE},Purchase_Units,0)
```

which returns this numeric array:

```
{4;0;0;0;0;0;0;0;0}
```

Using this array as the argument to the `SUM` function returns 4, the total of the values in the array. The formula is copied from cell C4 and pasted into cells C5:C9 to complete the count of the units purchased.

Column D in Figure 3.5 shows the average cost for each product code. It begins with cell D4, which contains this array formula:

```
=SUM(IF(A4=Inventory_Products_Code,Inventory_Unit_Cost*Purchase_Units))/C4
```

Again, this fragment

```
A4-Inventory_Products_Code
```

returns this array of logical values:

```
{TRUE;FALSE;FALSE;FALSE;FALSE;FALSE;FALSE;FALSE;FALSE;FALSE}
```

which act as the criteria for the `IF` function. When the criterion is `TRUE`, Excel returns the product of the unit cost and the number of units; else, Excel returns `FALSE`. That is, this fragment

```
IF(A4=Inventory_Products_Code,Inventory_Unit_Cost*Purchase_Units)
```

returns

```
{536.92;FALSE;FALSE;FALSE;FALSE;FALSE;FALSE;FALSE;FALSE}
```

The first value in the array, 536.92, is the result of multiplying the unit cost of the product by the number of units purchased: 134.23 * 4. The total of the array is returned by the `SUM` function. The `FALSE` values are treated as zeros, so the total is 536.92. Dividing that sum by the value in A4, or 4, results in 134.23, the value shown in cell D4 of Figure 3.5.

All that tells you is that the average cost of units that were bought for $134.23 is $134.23: in this particular case, a trivial outcome. It was discussed simply to illustrate the mechanics of the array formula. From the standpoint of understanding how average cost works, consider the formula in cell D6 of Figure. 3.5:

```
=SUM(IF(A6=Inventory_Products_Code,Inventory_Unit_Cost*Purchase_Units))/C6
```

The formula is identical to the formula in D4, except that it refers to the product code in cell A6 and the number of units purchased in cell C6. In this case, the `TRUE`/`FALSE` array returns these values:

```
{FALSE;FALSE;TRUE;TRUE;FALSE;FALSE;FALSE;FALSE;FALSE;FALSE}
```

So the product code found in cell A6, 3665, is found in the third and fourth positions (corresponding to the TRUE values in the array) of the range named Inventory_Products_Code. When those array values are TRUE, the IF function says to return the product of the unit cost times the number of units purchased. The result of that is

`{FALSE;FALSE;3727.98;2530.08;FALSE;FALSE;FALSE;FALSE;FALSE}`

The third value, 3727.98, is the result of multiplying the cost 621.33 by 6, the number of units purchased at that cost: see cells C5 and E5 in Figure 3.4. These are the six units of product 3665 that were purchased for the earlier, lower price of $621.33 each.

The fourth value in the array, 2530.08, comes about by multiplying the cost 632.52 by 4, the number of units purchased: see cells C6 and E6 in Figure 3.4. These are the four units of product 3665 that were purchased for the later, higher price of $632.52.

The SUM function adds 3727.98 and 2530.08, treating the FALSE values in the array as zeros. Finally, this sum is divided by 10, the total number of units purchased for that product code, which is the value in cell C6.

Notice that this is a *weighted* average: each of the two unit costs ($621.33 and $632.52) is weighted by multiplying it by the number of units purchased at that cost. So, six units at $621.33 cost $3727.98, the third value in the array shown previously. Four units at $632.52 cost $2530.08, the second value in the array. $3727.98 plus $2530.08, or $6258.06, is the total cost of the purchases of this product. Dividing by the total number of purchased units, 10, yields an average cost of $625.81 for this product, as shown in cell D6 of Figure 3.5.

Then, the product code's total cost is placed into E4:E9 by adding the total starting cost to the total cost of the purchased products. The result is the total cost of the goods available for sale: starting costs plus purchase costs.

Column F contains the average cost of the goods available for sale, on a unit basis. It is simply the result of dividing the amount in column E by the number of units in the starting inventory plus the number of units purchased. Notice, for example, the value $113.53 in cell F9 for Figure 3.5. Referring to Figure 3.4, consider this formula:

`=((D11+E11)*C11+(D12+E12)*C12)/SUM(D11:E12)`

That formula totals the number of units in stock and the number of units purchased at each of two costs. It multiplies each total by the appropriate cost and adds the results, to get the total paid for all units of that product. It then divides by the total number of units for that product. The result is its average cost. If entered in the worksheet shown in Figure 3.4, the formula just given would return 133.53, the same as the value found in cell F9 in Figure 3.5.

Column G contains the number of units sold for each product code. It is considerably simpler than the corresponding calculation for the specific identification method. In this case, there is a single average unit cost associated with each product code, and the number of units sold can be retrieved by this formula, used in cell G6 of Figure 3.5:

```
=SUM((A6=Sales_Product_Code)*1)
```

The range named Sales_Product_Code is as shown in Figure 3.3, cells B2:B21. This fragment:

```
A6=Sales_Product_Code
```

returns an array of TRUE/FALSE values. To convert the TRUEs and FALSEs to 1s and 0s, it's necessary to multiply them by 1. Then, the 1s and 0s are summed to determine the number of units sold.

Column H, the ending inventory in units, is obtained by subtracting the units sold from the units in the starting inventory plus the units purchased. Column I, the total cost of each product line in the ending inventory, is the product of the number of units in the ending inventory times their average unit cost.

The cost of goods sold is the total cost of the starting inventory, plus the cost of purchases, less that of the ending inventory, just as it is using specific identification. However, the value of the cost of goods sold is different. Under specific identification, the cost of goods sold is $13,874.12, whereas under average cost it is $13,584,01, about $300 less.

This is because the average cost method results in a different unit cost than does specific identification. The two methods result in a different cost of each unit sold. Under average cost, the actual amount paid for each unit sold is unknown, and the average cost is used in place of the actual amount paid.

The difference of $300 in cost of goods sold (between the average cost method and the specific identification method) is small in this illustration, because there are roughly the same numbers of units carrying different average costs in the starting inventory. The difference would be larger if the starting inventory had one Millennium PC P3 computer at a cost of $1,620.88, and 15 at a cost of $1,820.88.

Under the average cost method, Evans Electronics' income statement for April would show a gross profit of $3,511.15, the result of subtracting the cost of goods sold (the total cost of the goods available for sale less the total cost of the ending inventory) from its total sales revenue of $17,095.16. Its balance sheet for April would show inventory assets of $48,130.94. Thus, its gross profit is about $300 more, and its inventory assets about $300 less, than with specific identification.

NOTE Note that this result is not a general rule about the relationship between the two valuation methods. The use of average cost could cause a gross profit either greater or less than specific identification, and the same is true of asset valuation. Both the direction and the size of the difference between the two methods depend on the difference in the number of units in the inventory that carry different actual unit costs. In fact, if the numbers of units are equal, the two methods return the same result. ▪

Part

I

Ch

3

Using FIFO

FIFO, or *first-in, first-out,* is a method of valuing inventory that, like specific identification, uses the actual cost of a unit of inventory. Unlike specific identification (but like average cost) FIFO makes an assumption about the cost of the unit that is actually sold.

The average cost method assumes that the cost of a unit is the weighted average of the costs of all such units in the starting inventory. In contrast, FIFO assumes that the first unit sold during the month has a cost equal to that of the first unit purchased to the starting inventory. Thus, first-in to inventory, first-out of inventory.

When, for the first time during April, a customer purchases a DataFlash modem from Evans Electronics, it is not known whether the supplier charged Evans $95.32 or $100.36 for that specific modem. It is assumed, though, that the modem's cost is the same as that of the first modem purchased to the starting inventory: $95.32.

Figure 3.6 illustrates the FIFO valuation method.

FIGURE 3.6
Using FIFO, Evans Electronics assumes that the cost of a unit sold is the cost of the unit that entered its inventory the earliest.

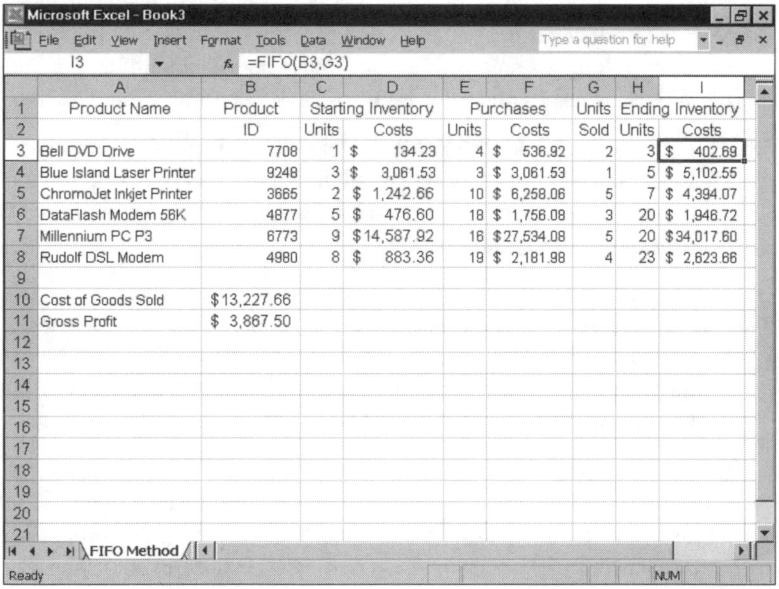

	A	B	C	D	E	F	G	H	I
1	Product Name	Product	Starting Inventory		Purchases		Units	Ending Inventory	
2		ID	Units	Costs	Units	Costs	Sold	Units	Costs
3	Bell DVD Drive	7708	1	$ 134.23	4	$ 536.92	2	3	$ 402.69
4	Blue Island Laser Printer	9248	3	$ 3,061.53	3	$ 3,061.53	1	5	$ 5,102.55
5	ChromoJet Inkjet Printer	3665	2	$ 1,242.66	10	$ 6,258.06	5	7	$ 4,394.07
6	DataFlash Modem 56K	4877	5	$ 476.60	18	$ 1,756.08	3	20	$ 1,946.72
7	Millennium PC P3	6773	9	$ 14,587.92	16	$ 27,534.08	5	20	$ 34,017.60
8	Rudolf DSL Modem	4980	8	$ 883.36	19	$ 2,181.98	4	23	$ 2,623.66
9									
10	Cost of Goods Sold	$ 13,227.66							
11	Gross Profit	$ 3,867.50							

The value of the ending inventory, shown in column I in Figure 3.6, is determined by means of a user-defined function (UDF) named FIFO. This function is called in cell I5 of Figure 3.6 with this entry:

```
=FIFO(B5,G5)
```

Its arguments, cells B5 and G5, contain the particular product code being analyzed and the number of units of that product that were sold during April. The FIFO function is written in Visual Basic for Applications (VBA) code, and is shown in Figure 3.7.

FIGURE 3.7
This VBA code calculates the value of ending inventory using the FIFO method.

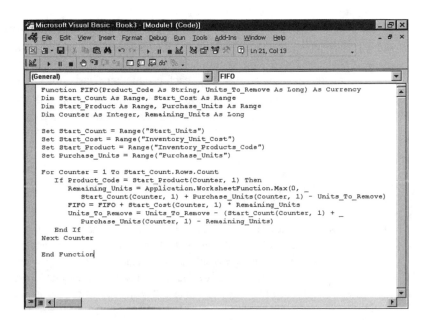

The function works as described next. The first line of code:

```
Function FIFO(Product_Code As String, Units_To_Remove As Long) As Currency
```

declares the function by giving it the name FIFO, specifies that its arguments are a text (String) value and a long integer (Long) value, and that it is to return a Currency data type. Used in cell I5 of Figure 3.6, the argument Product_Code represents the value in cell B5, and the argument Units_To_Remove represents the value in cell G5.

The function's next three statements:

```
Dim Start_Count As Range, Start_Cost As Range
Dim Start_Product As Range, Purchase_Units As Range
Dim Counter As Integer, Remaining_Units As Long
```

declare several variables, four of which are *object* variables. Object variables are used to represent Excel objects, such as cells, ranges of cells, worksheets, toolbars, and so on. The four object variables used here are declared as the Range type, so they can represent ranges of cells on the worksheet (they can also represent single cells, which are a special case of Range objects).

- ▓ *Start_Count* is an object variable that will represent a range of worksheet cells. The FIFO function will use Start_Count to represent the worksheet range that contains the number of units of each product that are in the starting inventory.

- ▓ *Start_Cost* is an object variable. It will represent the workbook range that contains the unit cost of each product.

- *Start_Product* is an object variable. It is used to represent the workbook range that contains the product codes in the starting inventory.

- *Purchase_Units* is an object variable. It is used to represent the workbook range that contains the number of units of each product purchased during the month.

- *Counter* is an Integer variable. It is used to control a loop in the FIFO function that examines each product in the starting inventory to see whether it should contribute to the product's valuation in the ending inventory.

- *Remaining_Units*, a Long variable, is used to determine how many inventory units are left in inventory after the units sold have been subtracted. A variable with a Long data type can take on integer values with greater maximums and minimums than can a variable with an Integer data type.

N O T E A Long variable is an Integer variable that can accommodate values as large as plus or minus 2,147,483,647. It requires slightly more memory than an Integer variable. The small premium in additional memory is often worth the variable's extra capacity. Integer variables cannot take on values greater than 32,767. Therefore, it's sometimes best to declare variables that index a worksheet's rows as Long instead of Integer. A worksheet can contain up to 65,536 rows. ■

The next four statements:

```
Set Start_Count = Range("Start_Units")
Set Start_Cost = Range("Inventory_Unit_Cost")
Set Start_Product = Range("Inventory_Products_Code")
Set Purchase_Units = Range("Purchase_Units")
```

associate each object variable with the proper range in the workbook. The first of the four, for example, specifies that Start_Count represents the range named Start_Units.

The Long variable Units_To_Remove is the second argument to the FIFO function: in this example, it is the value in cell G5 in Figure 3.6. Because G5 contains the value 5, Units_To_Remove starts life with the value of 5.

FIFO's For loop contains the meat of the function:

```
For Counter = 1 To Start_Count.Rows.Count
   If Product_Code = Start_Product(Counter, 1) Then
      Remaining_Units = Application.WorksheetFunction.Max(0, _
         Start_Count(Counter, 1) + Purchase_Units(Counter, 1) - Units_To_Remove)
      FIFO = FIFO + Start_Cost(Counter, 1) * Remaining_Units
      Units_To_Remove = Units_To_Remove - (Start_Count(Counter, 1) + _
         Purchase_Units(Counter, 1) - Remaining_Units)
   End If
Next Counter
```

The For and the Next statements cycle the loop through all the rows of the Start_Count range: that is, the loop executes once for each row in the range that is represented in the function by the Start_Count variable. Start_Count represents the range named Start_Units, which is contained in cells C2:C11 of Figure 3.2. That range has 10 rows, so the loop will execute 10 times as its control variable, Counter, progresses from 1 to 10.

Within the loop, the `If . . . End If` block tests whether the value of `Product_Code` passed to the function equals the current value of the `Start_Product` range. If it does, then the statements within the `If` block are executed; else, the `For` loop continues to the next value of `Counter` and thus to the next value in the `Start_Product` range.

For example, suppose that `Product_Code` is equal to 3665, as it is when the value in cell B5 of Figure 3.6 is passed to FIFO's first argument. The third time that the loop executes, `Counter` equals 3. Then, the expression

```
Start_Product(Counter, 1)
```

represents the third row of the first (and only) column of the `Start_Product` range. That range is cells B2:B11 in Figure 3.2. The third row in that range contains 3665. Therefore, `Product_Code` equals `Start_Product(Counter,1)`, and the statements within the `If . . . End If` block are executed.

In contrast, `Counter` equals 5 during the fifth time that the loop executes. `Product_Code` still equals 3665: nothing that occurs in the loop changes that value. But now, the expression

```
Start_Product(Counter, 1)
```

refers to the *fifth* row of the range B2:B11 in Figure 3.2. That cell contains the value 4877. Now, `Product_Code` no longer equals `Start_Product(Counter, 1)`. The statements within the `If . . . End If` block are skipped, the `Next` statement increments the `Counter` variable to 6, and the loop continues.

So, given that we pass the value 3665 to the `FIFO` function, the statements in the `If . . . End If` block are executed when `Counter` equals 3 and when `Counter` equals 4. Follow the logical flow of those statements:

```
Remaining_Units = Application.WorksheetFunction.Max(0, _
    Start_Count(Counter, 1) + Purchase_Units(Counter, 1) - Units_To_Remove)
```

`Application.WorksheetFunction.Max` invokes Excel's worksheet function `MAX()`. Therefore, this statement returns the larger of 0, or the result of adding the number of units in the starting inventory, plus the number of units purchased, less the current number of `Units_To_Remove`. This usage of the `Max` worksheet function prevents `Remaining_Units` from taking on a negative value if the number of units sold is greater than the number of units in the available inventory at a given unit cost.

When `Counter` equals 3, the number of starting units equals 2, and the number of purchased units equals 6 (see Figure 3.2 cells C4 and D4). `Units_To_Remove` was passed to the `FIFO` function with the value 5 (that is, the number of units sold) before the loop began. So `Remaining_Units` equals 2+6–5, or 3. This is the number of units remaining in inventory at a given cost after accounting for the number that was sold.

```
FIFO = FIFO + Start_Cost(Counter, 1) * Remaining_Units
```

Part
I

Ch
3

FIFO starts life with a value of zero, and nothing happens during the first two times through the loop because the `Product_Code` test fails. So when `Counter` equals 3, FIFO's value is still zero. The prior assignment statement increments `FIFO` by the product of the unit cost times the number of units remaining in inventory. `Start_Cost(Counter, 1)` equals 621.33 when `Counter` equals 3 (see cell F4 of Figure 3.2). `Remaining_Units` equals 3, so `FIFO` is set equal to 621.33 * 3, or 1863.99.

```
Units_To_Remove = Units_To_Remove - (Start_Count(Counter, 1) + _
    Purchase_Units(Counter, 1) - Remaining_Units)
```

Before this statement executes, `Units_To_Remove` equals 5 (that is the value passed to the function). `Start_Count(Counter, 1)` equals 2, `Purchase_Units(Counter, 1)` equals 6, and `RemainingUnits` equals 3. The statement resolves to:

```
Units_To_Remove = 5-(2+6-3) = 5-5 = 0
```

The `If . . . End If` block is now complete. The `Next` statement increments the value of `Counter` to 4. The `If` statement is tested again, and it passes the test because the fourth value in `Start_Product` is still 3665. Execute the statements in the `If . . . End If` block once again, with `Counter` equal to 4:

```
Remaining_Units = Application.WorksheetFunction.Max(0, _
    Start_Count(Counter, 1) + Purchase_Units(Counter, 1) - Units_To_Remove)
```

At present, the value of `Units_To_Remove` is zero, so `Remaining_Units` is set equal to the value of the fourth row of `Start_Count` plus the fourth row of `Purchase_Units`. Those values are 0 and 4 (see cells C5 and D5 of Figure 3.2).

```
FIFO = FIFO + Start_Cost(Counter, 1) * Remaining_Units
```

At present, `FIFO` equals 1863.99. To that value is added the product of the fourth row of `Start_Cost` and `Remaining_Units`. `Start_Cost(4,1)` equals 632.52 (see Figure 3.2 cell F5). `Remaining_Units` equals 4, so `FIFO` is set equal to 1863.99 + 632.52 * 4, or 4394.07.

Because there are only two instances of 3665 in `Start_Product`, the `If . . . End If` block will not execute again, and the final value of `FIFO` is 4394.07. This is the value returned to cell I5 in Figure 3.6.

Conceptually, the `FIFO` function has looked for every instance of 3665 in the starting inventory. It subtracts the number of units sold from the first instance of 3665, and adds to the value of `FIFO` the number of units remaining times their unit cost. In accordance with FIFO's basic assumption, the units sold are considered to be the first units to enter the inventory. The number of units sold is subtracted from the first units that `FIFO` encounters in its loop through the starting inventory.

You may find it a useful exercise to go through this same step-by-step progression by setting the number of units sold to a value greater than the first row of `Start_Count` plus the first row of `Purchase_Units` for a given product. For example, try setting the value in cell G6 of

Figure 3.6 to 17. Doing so would cause FIFO to account for all the units of the DataFlash modem, Product ID 4877, in the inventory that cost $95.32, plus two of the units that cost $100.36, resulting in an ending inventory value for Product ID 4877 of $602.16. In particular, watch what happens to Remaining_Units and Units_To_Remove as Counter changes from 5 to 6.

The cost of goods sold shown in Figure 3.6 is the difference between the total cost of the starting inventory and that of the ending inventory, just as it is using specific identification and average cost. Under the average cost method, the cost of goods sold is $13,584.01, about $350 more than under the FIFO method ($13,227.66). This is because the average cost method uses the weighted average of all units in the starting inventory to calculate the cost of goods sold. In contrast, FIFO uses the costs of, say, the three units that entered the starting inventory first to calculate the cost of goods sold. Keep in mind that the earliest costs are used, even though the actual, physical units that were sold might be the ones that entered the starting inventory last.

Under FIFO, Evans Electronics' income statement for April would show a gross profit of $3,867.50, the result of subtracting the cost of goods sold from its total sales revenue of $17,095.16. Its balance sheet for April would show inventory assets of $48,487.29. Thus, its gross profit is about $350 more, and its inventory assets about $350 less, than with the average cost method.

Again, this is not a general rule about the relationship between the two valuation methods. FIFO's effect is different according to whether supplier prices are rising or falling over time. If supplier prices are rising, FIFO returns a lower cost of goods sold on the income statement, and a greater valuation of ending inventory on the balance sheet. This is because, when prices rise, units acquired earlier cost less than units acquired later, and FIFO assumes that the cost of goods sold are a function of the cost of goods acquired earlier.

In contrast, neither the specific identification nor the average cost method is sensitive to the timing of a purchase to starting inventory.

N O T E   If you have a practical application for the FIFO function provided here, bear in mind that you will need four worksheet ranges with the names specified in the function (of course, you can change those names in the function and in the workbook if you want). And the records in those ranges must begin with the earliest acquired and end with the most recent acquired.

Using LIFO

LIFO, or last-in, first-out, works in much the same way as FIFO. The difference is that the cost of a unit sold is assumed to be the cost of units that entered the inventory most recently, instead of the cost of the units that entered the starting inventory earliest.

Part

I

Ch

3

Just as with FIFO, the effect of LIFO is dependent on whether your supplier costs are rising or falling—although LIFO's effect is the reverse of FIFO's. Under LIFO, if your unit costs are rising, then your cost of goods sold will rise, your gross profit will be smaller, and your balance sheet assets will be smaller (because the cost of the units in ending inventory will be assigned the lower, earlier values). If your unit costs are falling, however, your cost of goods sold will be lower, your gross profit will be larger, as will your balance sheet assets. Therefore, your choice of a valuation method impacts your company's reported income (and, indirectly, its income taxes) as well as its worth as reported on the balance sheet.

Figure 3.8 illustrates the use of LIFO for Evans Electronics.

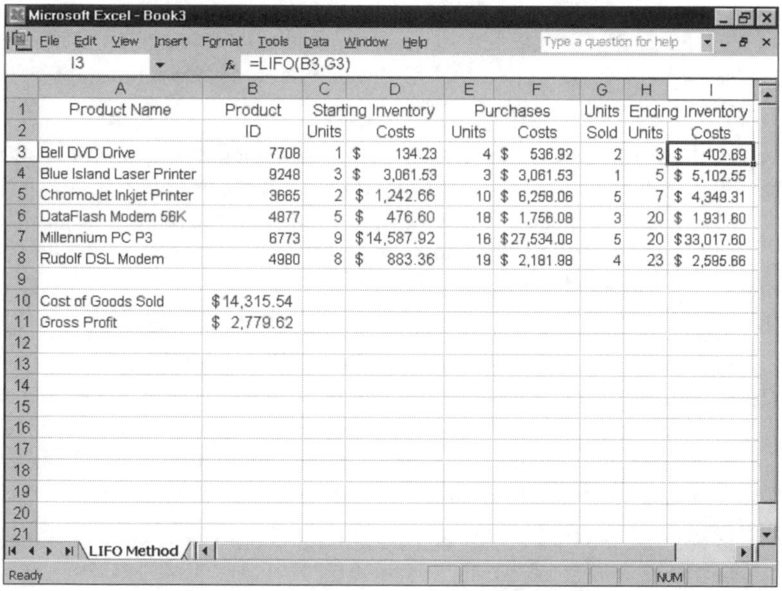

	A	B	C	D	E	F	G	H	I
1	Product Name	Product	Starting Inventory		Purchases		Units	Ending Inventory	
2		ID	Units	Costs	Units	Costs	Sold	Units	Costs
3	Bell DVD Drive	7708	1	$ 134.23	4	$ 536.92	2	3	$ 402.69
4	Blue Island Laser Printer	9248	3	$ 3,061.53	3	$ 3,061.53	1	5	$ 5,102.55
5	ChromoJet Inkjet Printer	3665	2	$ 1,242.66	10	$ 6,258.06	5	7	$ 4,349.31
6	DataFlash Modem 56K	4877	5	$ 476.60	18	$ 1,756.08	3	20	$ 1,931.60
7	Millennium PC P3	6773	9	$14,587.92	16	$27,534.08	5	20	$33,017.60
8	Rudolf DSL Modem	4980	8	$ 883.36	19	$ 2,181.98	4	23	$ 2,595.66
9									
10	Cost of Goods Sold	$14,315.54							
11	Gross Profit	$ 2,779.62							
12									
13									
14									
15									
16									
17									
18									
19									
20									
21									

FIGURE 3.8
The `LIFO` method values inventory under the assumption that the most recently acquired goods are sold first; equivalently, the goods acquired earliest remain in inventory at the end of the period.

All the information in Figure 3.8 is the same as in Figure 3.6, except for the value of the ending inventory and the total cost of goods sold. The value of the ending inventory is determined by means of a UDF named LIFO. This function is called in cells I3 of Figure 3.8 with this entry:

```
=LIFO(B3,G3)
```

and is copied from I3 into I4:I8. The only difference between the entries in column I of Figure 3.8 and those in column I of Figure 3.6 is the call to LIFO instead of to FIFO. The VBA code for the user-defined LIFO function is shown in Figure 3.9.

There are three small differences between the FIFO and LIFO UDFs. First, the line that names the function and its arguments refers to LIFO rather than FIFO.

FIGURE 3.9
This VBA code calcu-
lates the value of end-
ing inventory using the
LIFO method.

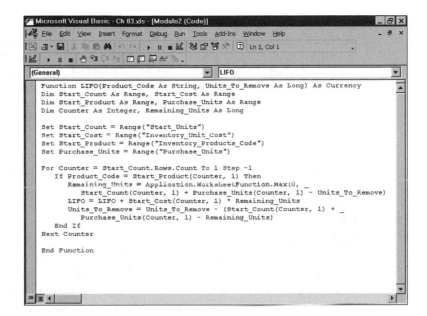

```
Function LIFO(Product_Code As String, Units_To_Remove As Long) As Currency
Dim Start_Count As Range, Start_Cost As Range
Dim Start_Product As Range, Purchase_Units As Range
Dim Counter As Integer, Remaining_Units As Long

Set Start_Count = Range("Start_Units")
Set Start_Cost = Range("Inventory_Unit_Cost")
Set Start_Product = Range("Inventory_Products_Code")
Set Purchase_Units = Range("Purchase_Units")

For Counter = Start_Count.Rows.Count To 1 Step -1
    If Product_Code = Start_Product(Counter, 1) Then
        Remaining_Units = Application.WorksheetFunction.Max(0, _
            Start_Count(Counter, 1) + Purchase_Units(Counter, 1) - Units_To_Remove)
        LIFO = LIFO + Start_Cost(Counter, 1) * Remaining_Units
        Units_To_Remove = Units_To_Remove - (Start_Count(Counter, 1) + _
            Purchase_Units(Counter, 1) - Remaining_Units)
    End If
Next Counter

End Function
```

Second, in LIFO, the loop that controls the progression through the starting inventory starts
at the bottom of those ranges rather than at the top:

```
For Counter = StartCount.Rows.Count To 1 Step -1
```

So, instead of progressing from 1 to 10, Counter might progress from 10 to 1 in increments of
–1. Because the ranges that describe the starting inventory are sorted, top to bottom, in earlier to later order, this means that the more recent entries are examined first, and the units
that have been sold are removed from the most recent additions to the starting inventory.

Therefore, items remaining in inventory at the end of the period are assigned the cost of
those that entered the inventory first. This is in accordance with the last-in, first-out approach.

And third, the statement that assigns a value to the name of the function refers to LIFO rather
than to FIFO:

```
LIFO = LIFO + Start_Cost(Counter, 1) * Remaining_Units
```

Notice, in Figure 3.8, that the cost of goods sold is $14,315.54. Using the FIFO method, the
cost of goods sold is $13,227.66 (see Figure 3.6). Therefore, choosing to use LIFO instead of
FIFO increases the cost of goods sold by $1,087.88. That is because in this case, the costs of
goods were increasing over time.

Comparing the Four Valuation Methods

As you might expect, each valuation method discussed in this chapter has both advantages
and drawbacks:

Part
I

Ch
3

■ *Specific identification* is the most intuitively satisfying method, because it adjusts the ending inventory valuation according to the actual cost of the specific items that were sold during the period. It avoids the average cost method's assumption that all otherwise identical units bear the same acquisition cost, and it avoids the assumptions made by FIFO and LIFO that a unit was purchased at a particular time. However, specific identification enables the (probably undesirable) manipulation of cost of goods sold, gross profit, and asset valuation. The person who chooses the actual unit that is provided to the customer controls the value of the unit that is leaving the inventory. Your company may not want its financial results to be under the direct control of a person who removes an item from stock. This would probably not constitute a problem if your business were, for example, the retail sale of custom jewelry. In this case, each item in your inventory might be unique, and the removal of a unit from inventory is left to the marketplace, not to a member of your staff.

Furthermore, if a company has thousands of units in its inventory, specific identification makes recordkeeping virtually unmanageable.

■ The *average cost* method treats each otherwise identical item in the inventory as though it had the same cost, regardless of how much it cost to bring it into inventory. This method makes no assumption as to when an item was acquired, as do LIFO and FIFO. Furthermore, the item's assigned cost is not affected by the choice of which physical unit to deliver to the customer, as is the case with specific identification.

But consider the effect of rising or falling supplier prices. If your costs of acquisition are changing substantially or swiftly, the current replacement cost of your inventory is changing to the same degree. Average cost combines the cost of older but functionally identical units with the cost of newer units. This can cause you to under- or over-value your inventory. And it can cause inaccurate pricing decisions if you base your selling price as a fixed percentage of your cost.

On the other hand, if you manage your inventories according to Just-in-Time principles (see "Calculating Turns Ratios" later in this chapter), their levels will tend to be small relative to the amounts that you buy into stock and sell from stock. In that case, the current costs of acquisition will enter the average cost equation with a greater weight, and provide quite an accurate valuation.

■ The *FIFO* method values the ending inventory according to the cost of the units that were most recently acquired. Therefore, the valuation of the inventory assets on the balance sheet tends to be more closely in accord with their current replacement cost. And, as a result, the value of the business on its balance sheet tends to be more accurate.

On the other hand, the time lag between the acquisition of older units and the sale of the merchandise is greater than the lag between the acquisition of the newer units and the sale of the merchandise. Therefore, from the standpoint of the income statement, FIFO is less accurate than LIFO. This is because the measurement of the gross profit is based on the revenues that derive from current market conditions and the costs that derive from earlier market conditions.

■ The *LIFO* method values the units sold during the period at the cost of the units that were most recently acquired. Therefore, the calculation of the gross profit is in closer accord with current market conditions, resulting in a more accurate income statement.

However, LIFO values the inventory at the end of the period according to the costs of the units that were acquired earliest. This can cause a mis-estimate of the current value of the inventory assets for the purpose of reporting the worth of the business on its balance sheet.

Because of changes in income tax laws, changes in market conditions such as rising and falling costs, and occasional changes in accounting standards, no one can offer broad-brush advice about which method of inventory valuation is best, even for a given company. Use the knowledge you have gained about inventory valuation to select the appropriate method in consultation with your accountant or tax lawyer, and implement that method in your daily operations.

Part
I
Ch
3

Handling Purchase Discounts

It often happens that a supplier will offer a discount from cost in return for quick payment for goods. This purchase discount is not applied to the valuation of the inventory, but is recorded in a Purchase Discounts account. In turn, the entries in the Purchase Discounts account are used to adjust the income statement's Purchases account.

N O T E Some companies handle purchase discounts as adjustments to their inventory accounts. However, because this complicates the process of valuing the inventory, most companies use the approach outlined here. ■

Is it to your advantage to pay a supplier promptly and thus obtain a purchase discount? As you might expect, that depends on the amount of the discount as well as the payment deadline.

Suppose that Evans Electronics orders two PCs from its supplier. The supplier offers Evans a $30 discount if payment is made within 30 days. Payment must be made within 60 days (see Figure 3.10).

The extended cost (that is, the number of units times the unit cost) for the two PCs is $3,641.76. Evans' choices are to pay $3,611.76 (the extended cost less the purchase discount) within 30 days, or to pay the full extended cost within 60 days. Choosing the discount is, in concept at least, equivalent to borrowing $3,611.76 for the 30 days between the discount deadline and the payment deadline. The interest to be paid on this putative loan can be compared to the $30 discount that the supplier offers. Evans knows it is possible to obtain a bank loan at 9% annual interest. By entering the following formula in an Excel worksheet:

```
=IPMT(0.09/12,1,12,(D4-E4))
```

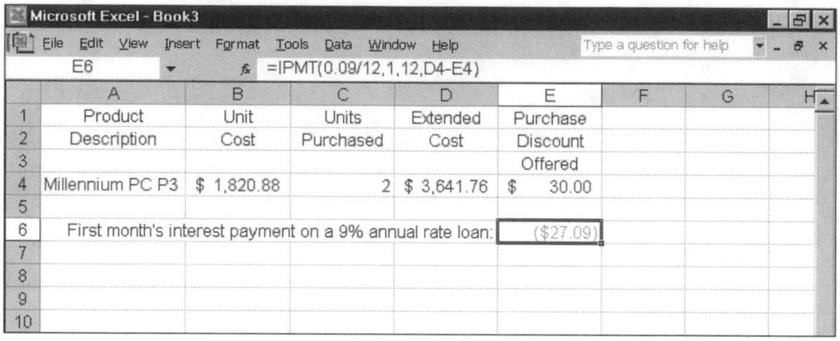

	A	B	C	D	E
1	Product	Unit	Units	Extended	Purchase
2	Description	Cost	Purchased	Cost	Discount
3					Offered
4	Millennium PC P3	$ 1,820.88	2	$ 3,641.76	$ 30.00
5					
6	First month's interest payment on a 9% annual rate loan:				($27.09)
7					
8					
9					
10					

FIGURE 3.10
Analyzing a purchase discount as though it were interest on a loan can help you decide whether to take the discount.

Evans can compare the purchase discount to the cost of the money. The first month's interest on a bank loan would be $27.09, as shown (as a negative value) in cell E6 of Figure 3.10. Therefore, it is to Evans' advantage to make payment before (but not long before) the discount deadline, because the discount obtained exceeds the cost of money for the same period.

This worksheet function, `IPMT` (*i*nterest *p*ay*m*en*t*), takes four required arguments:

- **The interest rate per period.** In the example, the annual interest rate is 9% or .09. Because the payment period is monthly, the interest rate is .09/12, or 0.75%.
- **The period for which the payment amount is desired.** In the example, 1 is used to return the first month's interest payment for a 12-month loan.
- **The number of payment periods in the loan.** For monthly payments on a one-year loan, the example uses 12.
- **The principal amount of the loan.** The example uses the result of (D4–E4), or $3,611.76, as this argument.

NOTE In Excel's annuity functions, including `IPMT`, the result of the function itself and any argument to the function are positive if they indicate a credit and negative if they indicate a debit. Because this example analyzes a loan, the function's fourth argument is entered as a positive value. Because Evans would pay out $27.31 in interest for the first month, the function returns a negative value.

Using Perpetual and Periodic Inventory Systems

As mentioned at the beginning of this chapter, businesses that deal in goods that carry a high value usually have an easier time tracking their inventories. A boat dealer, for example, tends to have fewer units in stock than does an office supply store. Other things being equal, it is easier for the boat dealer to do a physical count of the number of boats in the inventory than for the office supplier to count the number of reams of photocopy paper in stock.

The boat dealer can determine the cost of goods sold and the value of the ending inventory on a daily basis. It is simply a matter of counting the number of boats sold, shown on the sales receipts, and multiplying that number by the cost of each unit. The boat dealer might use any one of the four valuation methods discussed previously to calculate the cost of goods sold.

Similarly, the boat dealer can value the ending inventory by performing a physical count of the boats in stock at the end of the day, and multiplying by their unit costs. Again, any method of valuation could be used.

This approach is termed a *perpetual inventory* system, so named because it is both possible and feasible to directly determine the inventory on any given day.

On the other hand, using traditional methods of tracking inventory, the office supply dealer would have great difficulty maintaining a perpetual inventory. There would be thousands of units to count, both in the sales records and on the shelves and storerooms at the end of the business day. Furthermore, the office supply dealer typically has many different categories of merchandise and several different brands within each category. This is far too much information to track by hand in a perpetual inventory system.

Part
I
Ch
3

Of course, in recent years, point-of-sale terminals and electronic recordkeeping have put a perpetual inventory system within the reach of many businesses. Still, these systems are not pervasive as yet, and the alternative to a perpetual system, the *periodic inventory* system, remains in widespread use.

Under the periodic inventory system, a business conducts a physical count of the items in inventory at the end of an accounting period—typically, at the end of the month or the year. The count of each product is multiplied by that product's value, as determined by any one of the four valuation methods. (As a practical matter, it is unlikely that specific identification would be used. The same considerations that would lead a business to use a periodic inventory would normally preclude the use of specific identification.)

The total value of all products in stock at the end of the period has two uses: it becomes the value of the starting inventory for the next period, and it is used to determine the cost of goods sold during the period.

At the start of an accounting period, a business normally has units in stock: its starting inventory. During the period, the business normally acquires more units. The sum of the starting inventory and purchases made during the period is the *cost of goods available for sale*:

Cost of Goods Available for Sale = Starting Inventory + Purchases

With this information, and with knowledge of the value of the ending inventory, the company can calculate its cost of goods sold:

Cost of Goods Sold = Cost of Goods Available for Sale – Ending Inventory

For example, suppose that Evans Electronics could not record its sales on a daily basis. In that case, its inventory analysis and its figures for cost of goods sold and gross profit would be the same as shown in Figures 3.4 through 3.8, depending on the method of valuation that Evans selected. However, the number of units sold would be determined not by the sales records but by subtracting the ending inventory (physical count) from the starting inventory plus any purchases made during the period.

Calculating Turns Ratios

A *turns ratio* is a measure of how often inventory is depleted: that is, how frequently it turns over. Calculating turns ratios helps you understand how well you are managing your inventory.

The longer that units are in inventory, the longer your assets are tied up in stock, and thus unavailable for other uses. Holding units in stock often involves carrying costs: the costs involved in storing the goods and, possibly, the costs involved in financing their purchase. And during the time that units are in stock, you are not earning a profit on them unless you are holding them in the expectation that their replacement value will increase. (The latter effect, termed *inventory profits*, is something you should discuss with an accountant.)

Therefore, the concept of Just-in-Time (JIT) inventory is one to which many companies subscribe. The notion is that you do not want to tie up assets in inventory until the goods are actually needed for operational or resale purposes. The turns ratio is one measure of your ability to keep your inventory as low as possible, given operational and sales demands.

The turns ratio is expressed in terms of a time period: usually, a year. For example, an annual turns ratio of 4.5 means that the inventory turns over 4.5 times per year. This means that sales have been brisk enough, and inventories low enough, that it is necessary to replenish the stock 4.5 times in a 12-month period.

You can calculate a turns ratio in terms either of units or of costs (see Figure 3.11).

Rows 4 through 9 in Figure 3.11 show a snapshot calculation of the turns ratios achieved by each product during the month. No purchases to inventory were made between 3/31/2001 and 4/30/2001.

The turns ratio for product code 4877 is shown as 6.0 in cell G7. The formula in G7 is

`=E5/C5*12`

This is the number of units sold during the month divided by the number on hand at the beginning of the month, multiplied by 12 so as to annualize the ratio. A ratio of 6.0 means that the inventory would have to be replenished six times during the year. Notice that five units were sold during the month. At this rate, the stock for this product would have to be replenished every two months, or six times (that is, its turns ratio) during the year.

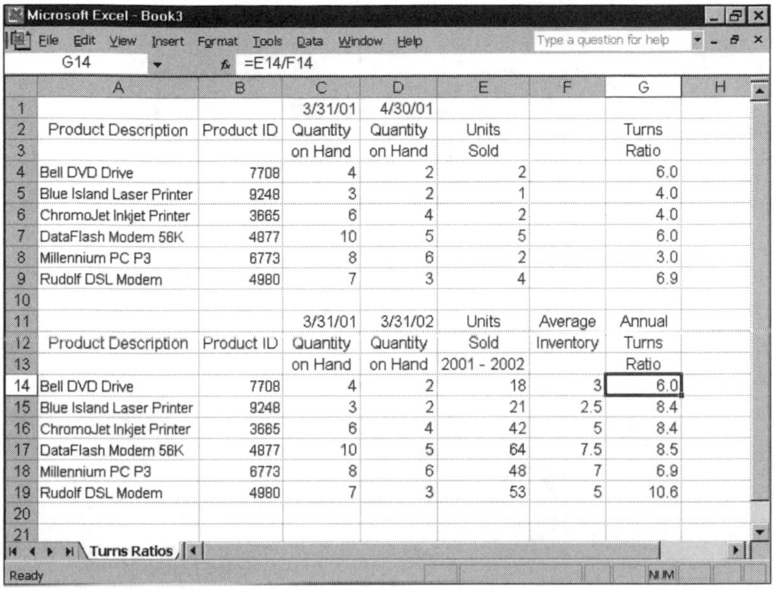

FIGURE 3.11
You can use actual units sold to calculate turns ratios, or use average inventory levels to estimate turns ratios.

	A	B	C	D	E	F	G	H
1			3/31/01	4/30/01				
2	Product Description	Product ID	Quantity	Quantity	Units		Turns	
3			on Hand	on Hand	Sold		Ratio	
4	Bell DVD Drive	7708	4	2	2		6.0	
5	Blue Island Laser Printer	9248	3	2	1		4.0	
6	ChromoJet Inkjet Printer	3665	6	4	2		4.0	
7	DataFlash Modem 56K	4877	10	5	5		6.0	
8	Millennium PC P3	6773	8	6	2		3.0	
9	Rudolf DSL Modem	4980	7	3	4		6.9	
10								
11			3/31/01	3/31/02	Units	Average	Annual	
12	Product Description	Product ID	Quantity	Quantity	Sold	Inventory	Turns	
13			on Hand	on Hand	2001 - 2002		Ratio	
14	Bell DVD Drive	7708	4	2	18	3	6.0	
15	Blue Island Laser Printer	9248	3	2	21	2.5	8.4	
16	ChromoJet Inkjet Printer	3665	6	4	42	5	8.4	
17	DataFlash Modem 56K	4877	10	5	64	7.5	8.5	
18	Millennium PC P3	6773	8	6	48	7	6.9	
19	Rudolf DSL Modem	4980	7	3	53	5	10.6	
20								
21								

Rows 14 through 19 illustrate a convenient way to examine the turns ratios for a full year. This represents a look back as of 3/31/02, rather than a look forward as of 4/30/01. The quantities on hand at the beginning and end of the year are shown in C14:D19. The units sold, E14:E19, are obtained from the sales records for the year. The average inventory, F14:F19, is estimated by means of averaging the quantity on hand at the beginning of the year and the quantity on hand at the end of the year. Finally, the annual turns ratio is the number of units sold divided by the average inventory.

TIP Turns ratios in the range of 4 to 6 are normally regarded as quite good: the inventory is being managed well. A turns ratio of less than 1, indicating that it takes more than a year to turn the stock over, is terrible.

On a broader scale, it is also possible to calculate a turns ratio for an entire stock, rather than on a product-by-product basis (see Figure 3.12).

Figure 3.12 shows the cost of goods sold, the starting inventory, and the ending inventory for the 12-month period. The average inventory is again the average of the starting and ending values. The turns ratio is the cost of goods sold, divided by the average inventory.

Note that a company's choice of method to value its inventory (specific identification, average cost, FIFO, or LIFO) impacts its turns ratios when they are based on cost data rather than units. Particularly using LIFO or FIFO, the total inventory valuation can be based on different costs at the beginning of the year than it is at the end of the year.

Part
I

Ch
3

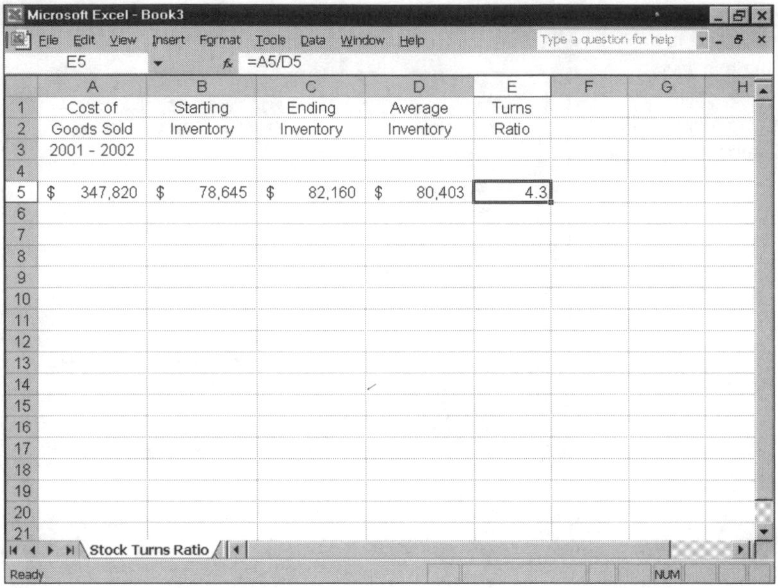

FIGURE 3.12

A turns ratio can be calculated for an entire inventory, irrespective of product-by-product differences.

Normally, a purchasing manager will be interested in the turns ratios on a product-by-product basis. These can help guide purchasing decisions, as well as the minimum and maximum units that should be on hand at any given time.

An overall look at a company's turns ratio, such as is shown in Figure 3.12, would normally be of greater interest to a principal in the company, or to an outside investor or creditor. Product-by-product turns ratios tend to be of little interest to those requiring an overall view of how a business manages its inventories, but are of great interest to those responsible for managing them.

Summary

In this chapter, you have learned about four methods of valuing inventory and how to implement them using Excel. Their effects on both the income statement (via the gross profit calculation) and on the balance sheet (via the amount of company assets in ending inventory) were discussed. You have seen how user-defined functions, such as LIFO and FIFO, can automate worksheet tasks in general. And you have learned how to use different sorts of turns ratios to evaluate how well a company manages its assets.

The next chapter turns from a focus on a company's assets to a focus on its liabilities.

CHAPTER 4

Summarizing Transactions: From the Journals to the Balance Sheet

Chapter 3, "Valuing Inventories for the Balance Sheet," covered the topic of inventory valuation in detail. The various methods discussed there are needed to properly complete the current assets section of the Balance Sheet. This chapter focuses on recording transactions in journals, cataloging transactions in ledgers, and summarizing the information in the Balance Sheet.

To review the basic structure of the Balance Sheet:

- The Assets section consists of the company's current assets (typically including Cash, Accounts Receivable, Inventory, and Prepaid Expenses), and its fixed assets. This section also contains any other assets that do not fit within the current and fixed classifications.

- The Liabilities and Owner's Equity section consists of the company's current and long-term liabilities. Typically, these include Accounts Payable, Short- and Long-term Notes Payable, and a few other types of liabilities that will vary according to a company's line of business.

■ The difference between the company's assets and its liabilities represents its equity—that portion of the company's worth that belongs to its owner or owners.

The first three chapters of this book have introduced some fundamental concepts, such as accounts, revenues, assets, debits, and credits. They have also discussed some of the functional relationships among these concepts.

This chapter introduces ways that you can use Excel to establish the *structural* relationships among such tools as accounts, journals, and ledgers. It describes how to manage the flow of information about revenue, expenses, and profit by using Excel workbooks, worksheets, and Visual Basic for Applications (VBA) code. This chapter illustrates these techniques with concepts that were introduced in Chapters 1 through 3.

Understanding Journals

The basic flow of information about business transactions follows this sequence of events:

1. A business transaction occurs—for example, a sale, a purchase, a receipt of funds, or an expenditure of funds.

2. Information about the transaction is recorded in a *journal*. The journal usually retains the information about the transactions in chronological order: so, one record might contain data on a sale that took place on March 1, the next record might describe a purchase that was made on March 2, the next record might have data on a payment due on March 3, and so on.

3. Information about the transactions is copied (or *posted*) from the journal to a *ledger*. This ledger has different sections: one for each type of account, such as Accounts Receivable or Notes Payable. Within each of these sections, information is usually recorded chronologically. The main difference between the journal and the ledger is that the ledger categorizes the information from the journal into specific accounts.

4. Information in the ledger is summarized, to obtain a total for each account at the end of an accounting period. These totals are used to prepare financial statements such as the Income Statement and the Balance Sheet.

See Figure 4.1 for an example of a General Journal.

Why qualify the term "journal" with the word "general?" Because keeping just one journal and just one ledger tends to become cumbersome. If you had only one journal, the task of posting information from the journal to the ledger could become too time-consuming. Furthermore, to use one journal only makes finding information about a specific sale or a specific payment more difficult—even if you use Excel's lookup functions.

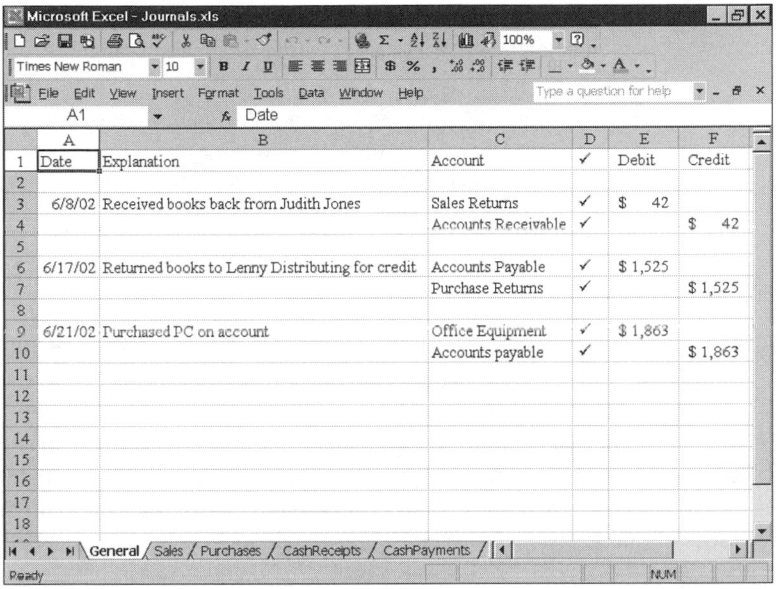

	A	B	C	D	E	F
1	Date	Explanation	Account	✓	Debit	Credit
2						
3	6/8/02	Received books back from Judith Jones	Sales Returns	✓	$ 42	
4			Accounts Receivable	✓		$ 42
5						
6	6/17/02	Returned books to Lenny Distributing for credit	Accounts Payable	✓	$ 1,525	
7			Purchase Returns	✓		$ 1,525
8						
9	6/21/02	Purchased PC on account	Office Equipment	✓	$ 1,863	
10			Accounts payable	✓		$ 1,863
11						
12						
13						
14						
15						
16						
17						
18						

FIGURE 4.1
The General Journal can be used as a catchall for transactions that don't belong in special journals.

Notice, in Figure 4.1, that there are only three transactions shown in the General Journal. These transactions pertain to three relatively infrequent events: the return of some merchandise from a customer, the return of some inventory to a supplier, and the purchase of office equipment. All the remaining transactions during June are kept together in special journals.

Understanding Special Journals

Companies often use *special journals*, which are places to record information about particular types of transactions. The most frequently occurring transactions tend to be sales to customers and payments to creditors. Also, many companies do business with their customers and suppliers on both a cash basis and a credit basis. This implies the use of four special journals:

- A *Cash Receipts* journal contains information about payments that you receive from customers. These payments could take the form of currency, as when a customer hands you $20 to purchase an item, or a check, as when you receive payment for a credit purchase. It also contains other information about cash that the company receives, such as capital investments that you make in the company or any funds that you borrow.
- A *Cash Payments* journal contains information about payments that you make to creditors and suppliers. Normally, these payments are checks that you write, but of course they could also be payments made in currency. It also contains information about operating expenses that you pay in cash, such as salaries or a building lease.

■ A *Sales* journal contains information about credit sales that you make. Together with sales information in the Cash Receipts journal, this accounts for all sales that your business makes.

■ A *Purchases* journal contains information about credit purchases that you make from your suppliers. Together with cash purchase information in the Cash Payments journal, this accounts for all purchases that your business makes from suppliers.

There are, of course, many types of transactions other than those that go in these special journals. These remaining transactions are recorded in the General Journal, which then becomes a sort of catchall for miscellaneous transactions.

Your own business might have a category of transactions that are both frequent and that do not fit into the structure outlined previously. There is no special reason to adopt this structure for journals: any structure that has special journals for the most frequently occurring types of transactions will do. For example, suppose that you run a car rental agency. It is likely that the purchase of cars from suppliers is a relatively rare event, but that the maintenance of your cars by garages and body shops occurs frequently. In that case, you might dispense with a special Purchases journal, and use a special Repairs and Maintenance journal instead.

Structuring the Special Sales Journal

The structure of your special journals differs according to the the journal's purpose and the nature of the information you intend to keep in it. Figure 4.2 shows an example of a special Sales journal.

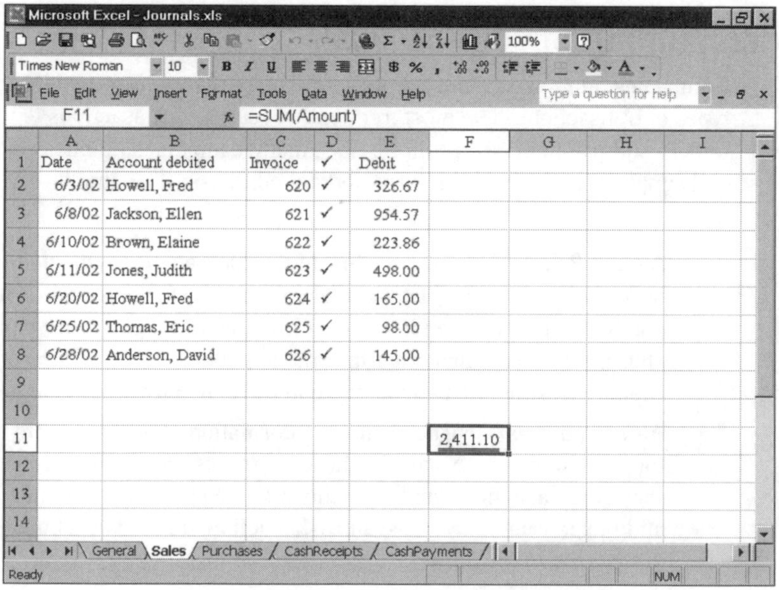

FIGURE 4.2
The special Sales journal for Bell Books records credit purchases by its customers.

There are several items to notice about this special Sales journal:

- Each account has a different customer name (for example, Fred Howell, Ellen Jackson, and so on). These accounts are also found in the Accounts Receivable ledger account, so that Bell Books can keep track of whether a customer owes money on an account (and if so, how much) or whether the account is paid up.

- A journal, whether the General Journal or a special journal such as Sales, contains transactions in chronological order. Therefore there can be—and often will be—several transactions that involve a particular account. For example, Figure 4.2 shows that Fred Howell has made two purchases during June. This account is summarized, to obtain a current balance, in an Accounts Receivable account found in the ledger. The accounts are not summarized in the journal.

- There is no column headed "Credit" as there is in the General Journal shown in Figure 4.1. This is because the only activities recorded in the Sales journal are non-cash sales, and the offsetting credit amounts are accumulated in the General Ledger's Sales account (see the following).

- There is a column headed with a checkmark (√). This checkmark indicates that a particular transaction has been posted from the Sales journal to the Sales account in the General Ledger.

> **TIP**
>
> You can show a variety of special characters in Excel by choosing a particular font. These characters can represent the entire cell entry, or only a portion of the entry. For example, to show the checkmark in Figure 4.2, the cells were formatted using the Wingdings TrueType font. When formatted with this font, putting the formula =CHAR(252) in the cell causes Excel to display a checkmark.
>
> To find a particular symbol, you can use Edit, Fill, Series to enter a numeric series from 0 to 255 in, say, cells A1 to A256 of a worksheet. In cell B1, enter this formula:
>
> =CHAR(A1)
>
> and copy and paste this formula into the range B2:B256. Then, select B1:B256 and choose Format, Cells. Using the Font tab, assign the range a font such as Symbol. After choosing OK, you can examine the B1:B256 range to see whether it contains the symbol you want. After you have found it, you can use the combination of the value, the CHAR function, and the font to display the symbol. Note that you can assign different fonts to different characters in a text entry by highlighting the character and continuing exactly as you would to format a full cell.

Structuring the Special Purchases Journal

The purpose of the special Purchases journal differs from that of the special Sales journal, and therefore it's structured differently. Bell Books' special Purchases journal is shown in Figure 4.3.

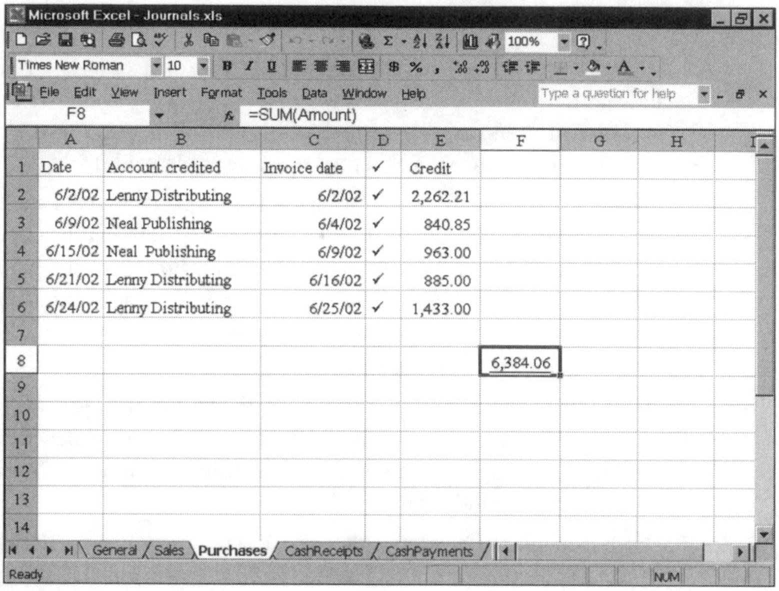

FIGURE 4.3
The special Purchases journal for Bell Books records credit purchases from its suppliers.

For tracking purposes, the Sales journal uses the invoice *number* in column C. In contrast, the Purchases journal uses the *date* of the supplier's invoice: this enables Bell Books to keep track of the length of time a payable invoice has been outstanding. Should the user want, of course, the supplier's invoice number can also be shown in the Purchases journal.

Another difference between the Sales and Purchases journals is that the amount of the purchase is shown as a credit, whereas the amount of a sale is shown as a debit. When a purchase is posted from the Purchases journal, it is posted as a credit to the ledger account Accounts Payable.

Again, there is no debit column because all entries in this journal are non-cash purchases. The offsetting debit entry is found in the ledger account Purchases.

Using Dynamic Range Names in the Journals

Each of the first three chapters of this book has discussed range names. You have seen how to identify a particular range of cells by means of a name, such as Inventory_Product_Code. Those range names were static: that is, the name always refers to the same set of cells, until and unless the user changes the address of the name's range.

Although there are advantages to using static range names, there are also drawbacks. Suppose that you have five values in the range A1:A5. These values represent your company's revenues for the first five months of the year, and you have given the range A1:A5 the name Revenues. Elsewhere on the worksheet, you use the formula =SUM(Revenues) to display your total year-to-date revenues.

Come the end of June, you enter June's revenue figure in cell A6. Now, to get the correct result for =SUM(Revenues) you have to use Insert, Name, Define and include A6 in the Revenues range. And that's a hassle you don't need every month.

What's needed is a way to make the name Revenues respond to the presence of new values. In other words, you need a *dynamic* range name. You can arrange that by using Excel's OFFSET function. When you use Insert, Name, Define, you're not required to enter a specific worksheet address in the Refers To box. You can enter a value, or a formula. In particular, you could use this formula:

```
=OFFSET($A$1,0,0,COUNT($A:$A),1)
```

Meet the OFFSET function. It returns a reference to a range of cells. It takes these arguments:

- An anchor cell (or range of cells). In the prior example, it's one cell, $A$1. The anchor cell informs OFFSET what cell to use as a basis.

- A Rows argument, which is the first zero in the example. The reference that OFFSET returns is shifted (or *offset*) that many rows from the anchor cell. In this case, the reference will be shifted from $A$1 by zero rows.

- A Columns argument, the second zero in the example. OFFSET shifts the reference by that many columns from $A$1. Again, this example shifts the reference by zero columns.

- A Height argument, which in the example is COUNT($A:$A). Using the COUNT function informs OFFSET how many numeric values there are in (here) column A. This is the heart of the dynamic range definition. When the number of numeric values in column A changes, that event causes COUNT to recalculate. In turn, the OFFSET function recalculates and returns a reference with a different number of rows.

- A Width argument, the number 1 in the example. It defines the number of columns in the range that OFFSET returns.

So, this formula:

```
=OFFSET($A$1,0,0,COUNT($A:$A),1)
```

returns a reference that depends on the number of numeric values in column A. Suppose that there are six numbers in column A. The formula returns a reference that is offset from A1 by zero rows and by zero columns. The reference is six rows high and one column wide. So it returns the reference A1:A6.

As soon as a seventh number is entered in column A, the COUNT and OFFSET functions combine to make the reference one row larger. The reference would then be A1:A7. The name Revenues, defined in this fashion, is a dynamic range name.

The dynamic range name removes the drawback to static range names mentioned at the beginning of this section. You no longer need to manually redefine the name Revenues when a new revenue figure is put with the existing values. Your formula =SUM(Revenues) will automatically recalculate and return the sum of all the values in the Revenues range.

Unfortunately, the dynamic range name comes with a drawback of its own. A spurious value in the range causes the range to become spuriously larger. Continuing the Revenues example, suppose that you inadvertently entered a date value (a date is a numeric data type) in column A. The COUNT function, and thus the OFFSET function, would respond to the date's presence, even if it were all the way down in cell A65536. The Revenues range would contain one more row than there are revenue values.

In this particular example that probably wouldn't make any difference. But there are plenty of other situations in which you'd wind up with a serious error.

One further point: you must keep formulas that refer to the dynamic range outside of that range. Suppose you put your =SUM(Revenues) formula in column A. The formula gets counted as one of the values that define the extent of the range, and that means that the Revenues range in the SUM function is helping to define itself. That's a circular reference error and Excel won't let you get away with it.

The Sales and the Purchases journals make use of several dynamic range names. The range names are qualified by the name of the worksheet to make them sheet-level: for example, Purchases!Amount and Sales!Amount. Each journal has these names and definitions:

- **TransactionDate.** In the case of the Sales journal, this range is defined as
  ```
  =OFFSET(Sales!$A$1,1,0,COUNT(Sales!$A:$A),1)
  ```

- **Account.** It's useful to make this name, as well as the names Posted and Amount, depend on the TransactionDate range. Account is defined as
  ```
  =OFFSET(Sales!TransactionDate,0,1)
  ```
  and so the reference it returns is offset from TransactionDate by zero rows and one column. When, as here, you do not supply a Height or a Width argument, they default to the Height and Width of the anchor argument. That's the TransactionDate range, so the Account reference has as many rows and columns as does TransactionDate.

- **Posted.** This name is defined as
  ```
  =OFFSET(Sales!TransactionDate,0,3)
  ```
  It is offset from TransactionDate by zero rows and three columns.

- **Amount.** The definition is
  ```
  =OFFSET(Sales!TransactionDate,0,4)
  ```

The corresponding names on the Purchases journal use the sheet name Purchases instead of Sales before the exclamation point, but are defined identically otherwise.

Structuring the Cash Receipts Journal

The two special journals, Sales and Purchases, together account for all of Bell Books' non-cash transactions. It's still necessary to account for the cash receipt and cash payment transactions. Figure 4.4 shows the special Cash Receipts journal.

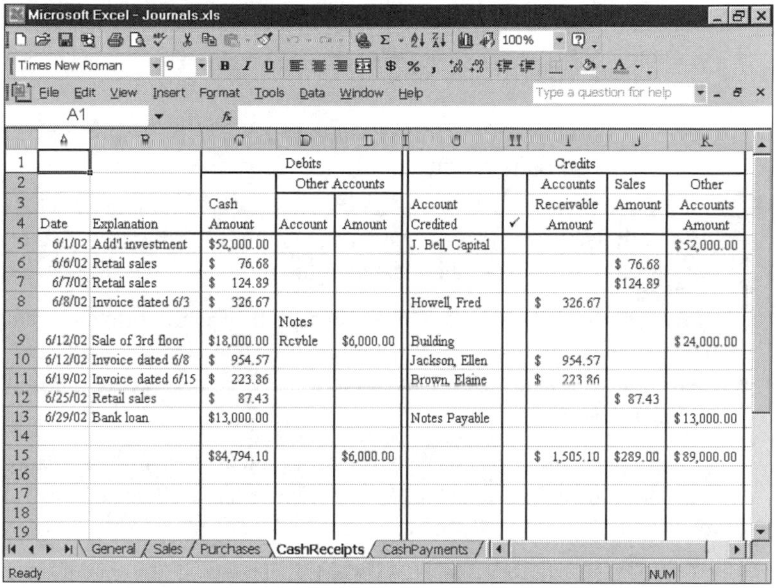

FIGURE 4.4
Normally, the Cash account should be debited for the receipt of cash.

The structure of the Cash Receipts journal is quite different from the structure of the Sales and Purchases journals. As explained previously, *all* transactions entered in the Sales journal are destined for one ledger account: the Sales account. Similarly, all transactions in the Purchases journal are placed in the Purchases ledger account. However, cash transactions, whether receipts or payments, can be posted to a variety of accounts.

Usually, a transaction in the Cash Receipts journal is posted to the ledger account named Cash. The total ($84,794.10) of all the transactions whose amounts appear in column C of Figure 4.4 will be posted to the Cash account in the General Ledger. For example, the owner of Bell Books invests an additional $52,000 in the company on June 1 (see cell C5 of Figure 4.4). This investment comes in the form of cash, and consequently will be posted—as part of the total cash receipts in column C—as a debit to the General Ledger's Cash account.

Notice, however, that on June 12 Bell Books sells the third floor of its building to another company for $24,000. Bell Books receives $18,000 of the $24,000 in cash, and accepts a Note Payable from the buyer for the $6,000 remainder of the amount due. (See cells C9 and E9 of

Part

I

Ch

4

Figure 4.4.) The $6,000 *could* have been entered in the General Journal instead of in the Cash Receipts journal; however, it's convenient to keep the two portions of the transaction together, so that the entire transaction can be seen in one place.

This is the purpose of the columns headed "Other Accounts," columns D and E of the worksheet. Column D contains the name of the ledger account where the transaction will be posted, and column E contains the debit amount that will be posted there.

So, the amounts in the debits section of the Cash Receipts journal are posted to the General Ledger as follows:

- The *total* of the receipts in column C, $84,794.10, is posted as one value to the General Ledger's Cash account.

- The *individual amounts* of any receipts in column E are posted in the General Ledger to the accounts that are named in column D. In Figure 4.4, that's just one account: Notes Receivable (abbreviated in the figure to *Notes Rcvble*).

Figure 4.4 also shows the credits section of the Cash Receipts journal, which is similar in structure to the debits section. There are two main ledger accounts that are to be credited when transactions are posted from the Cash Receipts journal: Accounts Receivable (column I) and Sales (column J).

For example, Bell Books receives a check on 6/8/02 from Fred Howell. This check is payment for an invoice dated 6/3/02. The transaction is shown in row 8 of the Cash Receipts worksheet in Figure 4.4, and results in the following actions:

1. An entry showing the amount of the check is made in cell C8, indicating that the General Ledger account Cash is to be debited by $326.67.

2. An entry showing the account that is to be credited is made in cell G8: Fred Howell's account will be credited by $326.67.

3. An entry showing the amount of the check is made in cell I8, indicating that the ledger account named Accounts Receivable is to be credited by $326.67.

4. When the amount of $326.67 is actually posted to Accounts Receivable, a checkmark is entered in cell H8, to indicate that the posting has been made.

The posting of $326.67 as a debit to Cash and as a credit to Accounts Receivable ensures that the amount is moved *into* Cash (an asset in hand) and *from* Accounts Receivable (an asset not yet in hand) at the point that the payment is received.

As another example, when a customer makes payment with $76.68 in currency on June 6 (see row 6 in Figure 4.4), this amount is entered in cell C6, to show that the General Ledger account named Cash is to be debited by that amount, and the same figure is entered in cell J6 to show that the ledger account named Sales is to be credited by $76.68.

The reason for entering the sale amount of $76.68 in both the Cash and the Sales ledger accounts is due to a concept that this book has, so far, assumed but not yet made explicit:

double-entry accounting. Every business transaction must be entered as both a debit and a credit, and these entries must be made in different accounts. Among other benefits of the double-entry method is the result that the sum of all debit entries in the ledger must equal the sum of all credit entries, which helps prove that the business's accounts are in balance.

For example, consider the transaction shown in row 13 of Figure 4.4. On June 29, Bell Books assumes a bank loan in the amount of $13,000. In return for signing the note, the bank writes a check to Bell Books for $13,000, and the company deposits it in a checking account. Therefore, Bell Books' cash assets have increased by $13,000. But the company has not suddenly become $13,000 richer by virtue of depositing a check: eventually, it will have to repay the loan. Therefore, the company's liabilities have increased by $13,000, and to document this fact the account named Notes Payable is increased by the same amount.

The net effect, of course, is that the company's worth remains unchanged, because loans themselves do not contribute directly to profit. But when Bell Books sells a book to a customer for cash, four events occur:

1. Its Cash account (an asset account) is debited.
2. Its Sales account (a revenue account) is credited.
3. Its Inventory (an asset account) is eventually credited.
4. Its Cost of Goods Sold (a revenue account) is eventually debited.

If the amount involved in 1 and 2 is greater than the amount involved in 3 and 4, the company obtains a profit. Buy low and sell high.

Finally, notice that column H, in the credits section of the Cash Receipts journal, indicates with a checkmark whether a receipt of funds has been posted. The only entries in this journal that are ever marked as posted are payments to Accounts Receivable. The reason is that the ledger account maintains detailed information about specific accounts (for example, Fred Howell's account, Ellen Jackson's account, and so on). Therefore, when funds are received in payment for a specific account, Bell Books posts the amount to a specific customer account.

In contrast, the company can post a *total* amount for cash sales to the General Ledger's Sales account. In that account, there's no reason to maintain information about who bought an item from Bell Books for cash.

Structuring the Cash Payments Journal

The Sales journal and the Purchases journal collect information about non-cash transactions, and the Cash Receipts journal collects information about cash paid to the company. Unfortunately, the company must also pay cash out, and recording that information is the purpose of the final special journal discussed here is the Cash Payments journal. It is shown in Figure 4.5.

FIGURE 4.5
Normally, the Cash
account is credited for
cash payments.

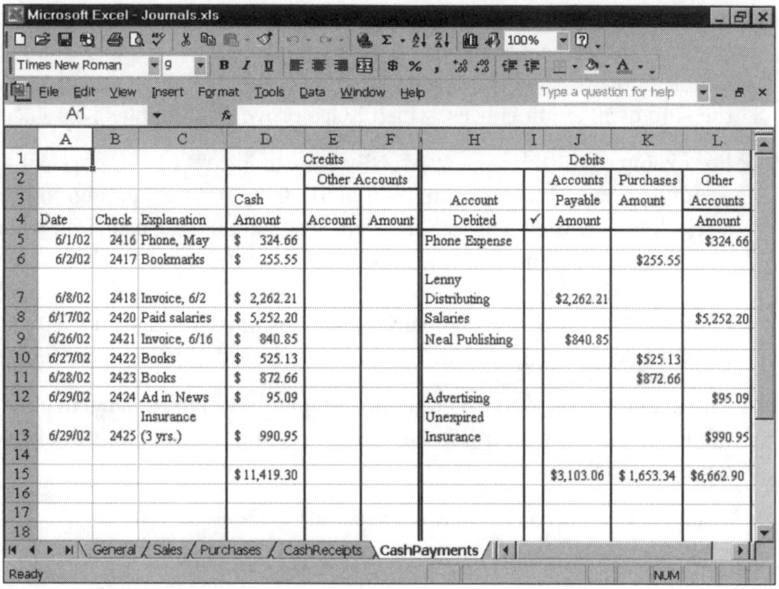

	A	B	C	D	E	F	H	I	J	K	L
1					Credits				Debits		
2					Other Accounts				Accounts	Purchases	Other
3				Cash			Account		Payable	Amount	Accounts
4	Date	Check	Explanation	Amount	Account	Amount	Debited	✓	Amount		Amount
5	6/1/02	2416	Phone, May	$ 324.66			Phone Expense				$324.66
6	6/2/02	2417	Bookmarks	$ 255.55						$255.55	
7	6/8/02	2418	Invoice, 6/2	$ 2,262.21			Lenny Distributing		$2,262.21		
8	6/17/02	2420	Paid salaries	$ 5,252.20			Salaries				$5,252.20
9	6/26/02	2421	Invoice, 6/16	$ 840.85			Neal Publishing		$840.85		
10	6/27/02	2422	Books	$ 525.13						$525.13	
11	6/28/02	2423	Books	$ 872.66						$872.66	
12	6/29/02	2424	Ad in News	$ 95.09			Advertising				$95.09
13	6/29/02	2425	Insurance (3 yrs.)	$ 990.95			Unexpired Insurance				$990.95
14											
15				$11,419.30					$3,103.06	$ 1,653.34	$6,662.90
16											
17											
18											

The overall structure of this journal is the same as that of the Cash Receipts journal, with one major difference: the credits section is shown on the left, instead of on the right of the debits section. Normally, debits are shown to the left of credits, but in a special journal it's normal practice to allow the columns to be in any sequence.

It's more convenient to show the credits section to the left of the debits section in the Cash Payments journal because doing so places the Cash column on the left side of the worksheet, where it is easily accessible. The accessibility is important because in Cash transaction journals every transaction will contain a Cash entry.

Notice in Figure 4.5 that the specific ledger accounts referenced in columns J and K are Accounts Payable and Purchases, respectively. This is because these accounts are the accounts most frequently debited when a cash payment is made. Other accounts, such as salaries and telephone expenses, are typically debited only once a month, when checks are written to employees and to the phone company. Again, the way that your company does business should dictate which accounts you show as columns in the Cash Payments journal, and which ones you show as line items in the Other Accounts column (Figure 4.5, column L).

Understanding Ledgers

Your decision about what sorts of ledgers to maintain follows reasoning similar to the decision to maintain special journals. If you kept only one ledger, with detailed information about all accounts, it would lose much of its value as a summary document.

Therefore, it's normal to establish *subsidiary ledgers* that contain detailed information from the journals. You can then keep the detailed information about specific sales and specific purchases in the subsidiary ledgers, and transfer totals from them to a general ledger. Because of the frequency of transactions involving sales and purchases, many businesses maintain an Accounts Receivable subsidiary ledger and an Accounts Payable subsidiary ledger.

Creating the General Ledger

By keeping detailed information from the journals in these subsidiary ledgers, it's easier to keep up with the status of your individual accounts with both creditors and customers. At the same time you can keep the General Ledger from becoming cluttered with detailed Information about customers who owe you money, and about creditors who expect to be paid (see Figure 4.6, which displays the General Ledger's asset and liability accounts).

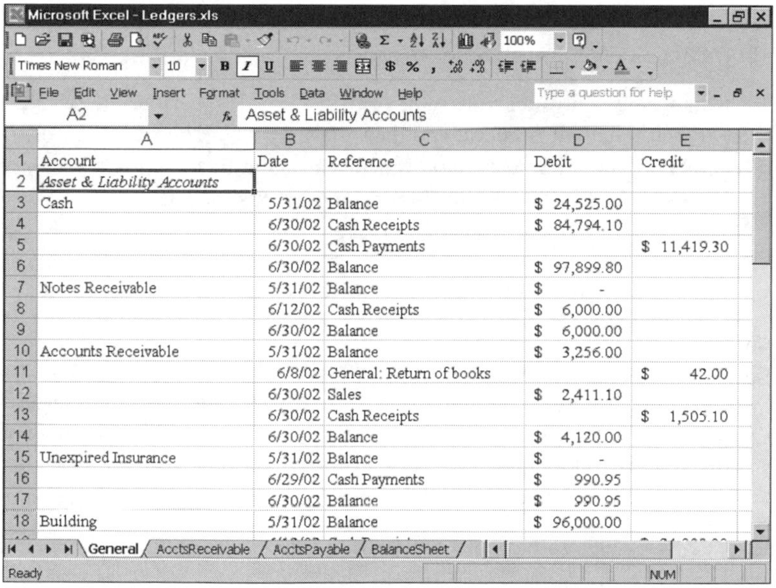

FIGURE 4.6
The General Ledger should show the account, date, and journal reference for each debit and credit.

Part

I

Ch

4

Every dollar entry in this ledger either refers directly to an entry in a journal, or to a total of transactions in a journal. For example, the formula in cell D8 is

```
=[Journals.xls]CashReceipts!$E$9
```

Figure 4.4 shows the Cash Receipts journal. Notice that the value of $6,000 in cell D8 of the General Ledger is the single entry in the Cash Receipts journal that represents the note accepted by Bell Books in partial payment for the third floor of its building. In contrast, the formula in cell D4 of Figure 4.6 is

```
=[Journals.xls]CashReceipts!$C$15
```

Cell C15 of the Cash Receipts journal also appears in Figure 4.4. Notice that the value of $84,794.10 is the total of all cash receipts during June. This illustrates how a ledger entry summarizes all the transactions in a given category that appear individually in a journal.

So, debits to the General Ledger's Cash account are based on the Cash Receipts journal. In contrast, credits to the General Ledger's Cash account are based on the Cash Payments journal. The formula in cell E5 of Figure 4.6 is

```
=[Journals.xls]CashPayments!$D$15
```

Figure 4.5 shows the Cash Payments journal, and cell D15 is the sum ($11,419.30) of the cash payments made during the month. The outflow of cash is represented in the General Ledger by credits to its Cash account.

Consider the Accounts Receivable classification in Figure 4.6. There are three amounts: $42.00, $2,411.10, and $1,505.10. The $42.00 value represents the return of merchandise from a customer, and is taken from the General Journal. This formula returns the $2,411.10 value

```
=SUM([Journals.xls]Sales!Amount)
```

which totals the values of credit sales in the Sales journal. There is a range in the Sales journal that is named Amount, and that refers to cells E2:E8 of that worksheet, shown in Figure 4.2. (The range name *Amount* was discussed in this chapter's section on dynamic range names.) The $1,505.10 value is returned by this formula:

```
=[Journals.xls]CashReceipts!$I$15
```

which refers to the total of the credits to Accounts Receivable, from the credits section of the Cash Receipts journal (see Figure 4.4).

In this way, the activity in the Accounts Receivable account is summarized for the month. New purchases on credit are totaled in cell D12, and payments for purchases on credit are totaled in cell E13, both in the General Ledger. You will find it useful to open the Ledgers.xls file and inspect each of its entries to determine their source in the journals. (If you do so, you will find that every value for June in the General Ledger refers to an entry in a journal.)

The Revenue and Expense section of the General Ledger is shown in Figure 4.7.

The entries in this section follow the pattern established in the assets and liabilities section: that is, each entry comes from a journal, and is either a specific journal entry or the total of several journal entries that belong to the same account.

The values in cells D60 and E60 of Figure 4.7, $210,698.10, help to demonstrate that the accounts are in balance. As noted previously, the double-entry method is intended to ensure that the total of the debits for a given period equals the total of the credits for the same period. Each transaction that occurs exists as a debit to one account, and as a credit to another account.

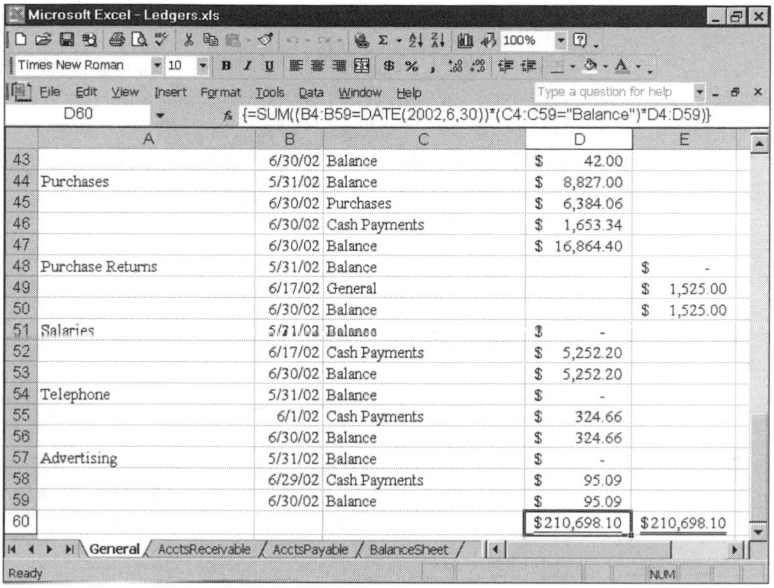

FIGURE 4.7
General Ledger entries should all be linked to General Journal or special journal transactions.

	A	B	C	D	E
43		6/30/02	Balance	$ 42.00	
44	Purchases	5/31/02	Balance	$ 8,827.00	
45		6/30/02	Purchases	$ 6,384.06	
46		6/30/02	Cash Payments	$ 1,653.34	
47		6/30/02	Balance	$ 16,864.40	
48	Purchase Returns	5/31/02	Balance		$ -
49		6/17/02	General		$ 1,525.00
50		6/30/02	Balance		$ 1,525.00
51	Salaries	5/31/02	Balance	$ -	
52		6/17/02	Cash Payments	$ 5,252.20	
53		6/30/02	Balance	$ 5,252.20	
54	Telephone	5/31/02	Balance	$ -	
55		6/1/02	Cash Payments	$ 324.66	
56		6/30/02	Balance	$ 324.66	
57	Advertising	5/31/02	Balance	$ -	
58		6/29/02	Cash Payments	$ 95.09	
59		6/30/02	Balance	$ 95.09	
60				$210,698.10	$210,698.10

D60 = {=SUM((B4:B59=DATE(2002,6,30))*(C4:C59="Balance")*D4:D59)}

Cells D60 and E60 total the debit and credit account balances in the General Ledger, and are equal: this is evidence that accounts are in balance. The two cells' equality does not *prove* that all entries are accurate, because the possibility of, for example, compensating errors exists. But if the two amounts were unequal, that would demonstrate that at least one error existed somewhere.

Creating Subsidiary Ledgers

Bell Books uses two subsidiary ledgers: Accounts Receivable and Accounts Payable. The purpose of these ledgers is to help to keep tabs on accounts that customers have with Bell Books, and that Bell Books has with its suppliers. Figure 4.8 shows the Accounts Receivable ledger.

Neither the Accounts Receivable ledger nor the Accounts Payable ledger links to the General Ledger. Each simply replicates some of the information in the General Ledger: specifically, the Accounts Receivable ledger provides details about the individual accounts maintained by Bell Books' credit customers.

There are two worksheet buttons on the Accounts Receivable ledger. One is labeled *Post from Sales Journal*. That button has assigned to it VBA code that posts information about non-cash sales from the Sales journal to the Accounts Receivable ledger. Clicking the button causes that VBA code to run. The button labeled *Post from Cash Receipts Journal* also has VBA code assigned to it. That code posts information from the Cash Receipts journal to the Accounts Receivable ledger. The cash receipts represent payments for credit sales that were recorded in the Sales journal.

Part
I
Ch
4

FIGURE 4.8
The Accounts Receivable ledger helps to track the status of individual accounts.

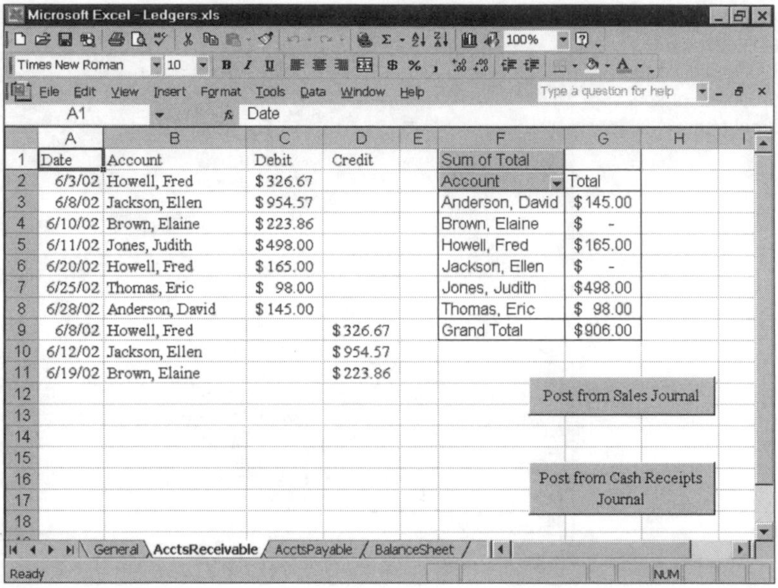

Date	Account	Debit	Credit
6/3/02	Howell, Fred	$326.67	
6/8/02	Jackson, Ellen	$954.57	
6/10/02	Brown, Elaine	$223.86	
6/11/02	Jones, Judith	$498.00	
6/20/02	Howell, Fred	$165.00	
6/25/02	Thomas, Eric	$ 98.00	
6/28/02	Anderson, David	$145.00	
6/8/02	Howell, Fred		$326.67
6/12/02	Jackson, Ellen		$954.57
6/19/02	Brown, Elaine		$223.86

Sum of Total	
Account	Total
Anderson, David	$145.00
Brown, Elaine	$ -
Howell, Fred	$165.00
Jackson, Ellen	$ -
Jones, Judith	$498.00
Thomas, Eric	$ 98.00
Grand Total	$906.00

The Accounts Receivable ledger also contains a pivot table. This pivot table provides the current balance for each of the accounts receivable.

Notice in Figure 4.8 that cell D9 contains the value $326.67. This value represents the payment that was received from Fred Howell on June 8, and that was entered into the Cash Receipts journal (refer to cell I8 of Figure 4.4). The value $326.67 is also entered in the General Ledger in cell E13, as part of the total of the credits to Accounts Receivable.

This illustrates that amounts that are posted to subsidiary ledgers must be posted twice: once to the General Ledger, and once to the subsidiary ledger. Doing so ensures that the account as shown in the General Ledger equals the amount shown in the subsidiary ledger.

Automating the Posting Process

There are various types of buttons that you can use in Excel: buttons on worksheets, buttons on dialog boxes, and buttons on toolbars are examples. You can arrange for a custom toolbar by using View, Toolbars, choosing Customize, and clicking New. However, if you do so, that toolbar—and any button that you put on the toolbar—will appear regardless of which sheet in the workbook is active.

To place a button on a worksheet so that it appears on that sheet only, use the Control Toolbox:

1. Choose View, Toolbars, and click the Control Toolbox item in the cascading menu.
2. The Control Toolbox toolbar appears on the active worksheet. Click the Command button on the toolbar. When you move the mouse pointer away from the Control Toolbox the pointer changes from an arrow to crosshairs.

3. Holding down the left mouse button, drag across and down on the worksheet to indicate where you want the button to appear. Then, release the mouse button.

4. The Command button is established on the worksheet. Right-click the Command button to invoke a shortcut menu. One of its items is View Code. When you are ready to provide the VBA code that is to run when the button is clicked, choose the View Code item.

5. The button has a default label, *CommandButton1* if it's the first Command button on the worksheet. There are various ways to change the label. One is as follows: right-click the button and choose CommandButton Object, Edit from the shortcut menu. When you move your mouse pointer over the button's label, the pointer changes to an I-bar. Hold down the left mouse button and drag across the label to highlight it. Then type whatever text you want to appear on the button.

6. Deselect the button by clicking any worksheet cell.

The Post from Sales Journal button shown in Figure 4.8 is linked to the VBA procedure named PostFromSalesToAR, shown next, which actually performs the posting.

```
Option Explicit
Option Base 1

Sub PostFromSalesToAR()
Dim SalesDate As Range, Acct As Range, Posted As Range, SalesAmount As Range
Dim ThisTransaction As Integer, NextEntryRow As Long

Workbooks("Journals.xls").Activate
Sheets("Sales").Select
Set SalesDate = Range("TransactionDate")
Set Acct = Range("Account")
Set Posted = Range("Posted")
Set SalesAmount = Range("Amount")
NextEntryRow = ThisWorkbook.Sheets("AcctsReceivable") _
    .Range("TransactionDate").Rows.Count
For ThisTransaction = 1 To Acct.Rows.Count
    If Posted(ThisTransaction) <> Chr(252) Then
        With ThisWorkbook.Sheets("AcctsReceivable")
            .Range("TransactionDate").Offset(NextEntryRow, 0).Resize(1, 1) = _
                SalesDate(ThisTransaction)
            .Range("AccountNames").Offset(NextEntryRow, 0).Resize(1, 1) = _
                Acct(ThisTransaction)
            .Range("Purchases").Offset(NextEntryRow, 0).Resize(1, 1) = _
                SalesAmount(ThisTransaction)
        End With
        Posted(ThisTransaction).FormulaR1C1 = "=CHAR(252)"
```

```
        NextEntryRow = NextEntryRow + 1
    End If
Next ThisTransaction

ThisWorkbook.Activate
ThisWorkbook.Sheets("AcctsReceivable").PivotTables("ARSummary").PivotCache.Refresh
End Sub
```

The first two lines of code set two general options. *Option Explicit* requires that all variables used in the code be explicitly declared. If this option were not set, new variables could be created on the fly—simply typing a variable name would create it. Because this approach makes the code much more difficult to trace and debug, it's wise to use Option Explicit and to specifically declare each variable (see the discussion of the Dim statements later in this section).

The second option, *Option Base 1*, requires that the first element of all VBA arrays be element number one. Omitting this option causes Excel to treat the first element of an array as element number zero. Suppose that the first element of MyArray were "Fred Howell." Using Option Base 1, you would refer to this value as MyArray(1). Without Option Base 1, you would refer to it as MyArray(0). If you prefer to start counting at one, rather than at zero, use Option Base 1 in your VBA code.

The next statement, *Sub PostFromSalesToAR()*, classifies the procedure and gives it a name. VBA has two types of procedures: functions and subroutines. The keyword *Sub* identifies the procedure as a subroutine. VBA procedures always have a set of parentheses following the name itself. If the parentheses enclose a variable name or names, it means that those variables are being passed as arguments to the subroutine. In this case, no variables are being passed to the subroutine.

The next two statements are *Dim* (short for *dimension*) statements. Using Option Explicit requires that the code explicitly declare all variables. The Dim statements declare the existence of several variables and their types. The variable ThisTransaction, for example, is declared as type Integer. This means that the variable cannot take on a numeric value that has a fractional component, such as 3.1416.

The four variables that are declared as type Range will later refer specifically to worksheet ranges. After the variables are declared with in the Dim statement, they are subsequently assigned to the ranges by means of the Set statements. In this case, the variables are simply conveniences: the code can refer to the variable instead of having to make reference to the name of the range in the worksheet where it exists, and in the workbook that contains the worksheet.

The next statements:

```
Workbooks("Journals.xls").Activate
Sheets("Sales").Select
```

cause Excel to make Journals.xls the active workbook, and to make the sheet named Sales in that workbook the active worksheet. The Sales worksheet, of course, contains the Sales journal. These two statements require that the Journals.xls workbook be open at the time that the statements are executed. This is managed elsewhere in the code, in a different procedure that runs when the Ledgers workbook is opened. See the "Opening the Workbooks" section later in this chapter for more information.

After the Sales journal worksheet is selected, the four Range variables are assigned to named ranges; for example

```
Set SalesDate = Range("TransactionDate")
```

This causes the variable *SalesDate* to stand in for the range that is named *TransactionDate* in the Sales journal.

After these range variables are set, the code determines the next available row in the AcctsReceivable sheet where a transaction can be posted. It does so by counting the number of rows that are presently in the AcctsReceivable range:

```
NextEntryRow = ThisWorkbook.Sheets("AcctsReceivable") _
  .Range("TransactionDate").Rows.Count
```

The statement names four objects that are separated by dots. In VBA, this is termed *dot notation* and it denotes a hierarchy: an object that follows the dot belongs to an object that precedes the dot.

This statement refers to a range named TransactionDate. That range belongs to a sheet named AcctsReceivable. In turn, that sheet belongs to the ThisWorkbook object—that is, the workbook that contains the VBA code that's executing.

The TransactionDate range has a Rows property, which returns a collection of the rows that belong to the TransactionDate range. That collection of rows itself has properties, and one of them is the Count property. The Count property returns the number of objects in a collection. As used here, it returns the number of rows in the TransactionDate range found on the AcctsReceivable sheet that is in the workbook that contains the VBA code.

The number of rows in the range is assigned to the variable NextEntryRow. That variable is used later in the code as an argument to the Offset function. At present, the TransactionDate range has one row only, and the statement therefore assigns NextEntryRow a value of 1.

Now the meat of the procedure begins. This statement:

```
For ThisTransaction = 1 To Acct.Rows.Count
```

starts a loop that executes once for each row in the range represented by the Acct variable. The approach is similar to that used to find the next entry row: *Acct.Rows.Count* returns the number of rows in the range represented by the Acct variable. The loop steps through the Sales journal row by row, looking for transactions that should be posted to the Accounts Receivable ledger.

The For loop starts at *1* and ends at *Acct.Rows.Count,* and therefore it will execute as many times as there are rows in that range. The Acct variable represents the range named Account on the Sales journal worksheet. So the loop executes once for each instance of an account name in that range.

The first statement inside the loop is

```
If Posted(ThisTransaction) <> Chr(252) Then
```

This statement causes the statements that follow it to execute if its condition is satisfied, and to be skipped if its condition isn't satisfied. The condition is that a particular value does not equal the ANSI character associated with the number 252 (that's a checkmark in the Wingdings font). The particular value that's tested is the element in the Posted range that corresponds to the current value of ThisTransaction. The Posted variable refers to the range named Posted in the Sales journal: notice how it's declared in the second line of the procedure.

In brief, the first time that the loop executes, ThisTransaction has a value of 1. Excel examines the first value in Posted, to see if it equals Chr(252)—that is, to see if it is a checkmark. If that value is not a checkmark, subsequent statements are executed because the transaction remains to be posted; otherwise, the statements are skipped.

Why look for the value returned by Chr(252) in Posted? Recall that the checkmarks in the Sales journal are created by putting the formula =CHAR(252) in their range, and formatting the range with the Wingdings font. A checkmark means that the transaction has been posted from the Sales journal to the Accounts Receivable ledger. Therefore, if the current formula in Posted is =CHAR(252), that transaction has already been posted, and you do not want to post it again.

N O T E   The VBA code discussed here uses the Chr function, whereas the CHAR function is used on the worksheet. VBA has its own set of functions, as does Excel. VBA's Chr function is equivalent to Excel's CHAR function. ▪

If, on the other hand, the current transaction has *not* yet been posted—if the result of Chr(252) is not found in the current element of the Posted range—the statements that follow the If should be executed. Executing those statements results in the posting of the transaction to Accounts Receivable.

Next, a With block is initiated:

```
With ThisWorkbook.Sheets("AcctsReceivable")
```

Inside With blocks are references to objects (such as a worksheet), methods (such as a worksheet's Activate method), and properties (such as a cell's Font property). Some are preceded by a dot (for example, .Rows) with nothing immediately preceding that dot. Anything with nothing but a dot preceding it is taken to belong to whatever object is named in the With statement. In this case, all objects, methods, and properties referred to inside the With block are deemed to belong to the sheet named AcctsReceivable, which in turn belongs to ThisWorkbook.

The With block is useful shorthand. Inside the block there are several statements that make use of ranges belonging to the AcctsReceivable sheet. If the With block wasn't used, the code would have to repeatedly qualify those ranges by referring to the sheet where it's found. But because the With block is in use, the code needs to refer to that sheet once only: in the With statement itself.

Each statement inside the With block accomplishes some task in the posting of a transaction from the Sales journal to the Accounts Receivable ledger. For example, this is the first statement inside the With block:

```
.Range("TransactionDate").Offset(NextEntryRow, 0).Resize(1, 1) = _
    SalesDate(ThisTransaction)
```

Notice the following aspects of the statement:

- The fragment *.Range("TransactionDate")*, because of the With statement, is taken to refer to the sheet named AcctsReceivable in ThisWorkbook.

- The Offset fragment defines a range that is offset from the TransactionDate range. It is offset from the TransactionDate range by *NextEntryRow* rows and by zero columns. The first time through the loop, NextEntryRow equals 1 (refer to the assignment statement that precedes the For loop). So the (1,0) offset to the TransactionDate range refers to one row below it and in the same column.

- The Resize fragment defines, temporarily, the size of the range as containing one row and one column: thus, one cell.

- This cell is set equal to the value in the Sales journal range, referred to by the variable SalesDate, for the current value of ThisTransaction—which is the transaction being posted. That is, the date of the current transaction is placed in the TransactionDate range in the AcctsReceivable ledger.

This process is repeated in the remainder of the With block, so that the values of AccountName and Purchases are also posted.

The With block is then terminated, and a checkmark is placed in the Posted range of the Sales journal by means of this statement:

```
Posted(ThisTransaction).FormulaR1C1 = "=CHAR(252)"
```

The variable that controls the offset to the ranges on the AcctsReceivable ledger is incremented. Therefore, the next time the loop executes the sales date, account and amount will be placed one row farther down:

```
NextEntryRow = NextEntryRow + 1
```

Part

I

Ch

4

Then, the If block is terminated with an End If (this marks the end of the statements that are executed if a transaction in the Sales journal has not yet been posted). The loop is terminated with

```
Next ThisTransaction
```

Control returns to the beginning of the loop if the value of ThisTransaction does not yet exceed Accts.Rows.Count. When the loop has executed once for each row in the range named Account in the Sales Journal, the loop ends.

After final instance of the loop has completed, the Ledgers workbook is activated and the pivot table on the AcctsReceivable sheet is refreshed. The purpose of refreshing the data in the pivot table is to cause the table to incorporate the transactions that have just been posted to the ledger:

```
ThisWorkbook.Activate
ThisWorkbook.Sheets("AcctsReceivable").PivotTables("ARSummary").PivotCache.Refresh
```

The purpose of the pivot table is to summarize the current status of all the accounts. Figure 4.8 shows the data posted from the Sales journal and from the Cash Receipts journal. Notice, for example, that Fred Howell has made two purchases, one for $326.67 and one for $165.00, and Accounts Receivable has been debited for those two transactions. Howell has made payment for the first transaction but not as yet for the second. And the pivot table shows that Howell still owes $165.00 for the second transaction.

This is managed by creating a calculated field named Total inside the pivot table, using that field as the pivot table's data field, and using Account as the row field. More specifically, the following steps are taken (and they need be taken only once, when the pivot table is first put on the worksheet):

1. With the AcctsReceivable sheet active, choose Insert, Name, Define. In the Names in workbook box type **DataRange**.

2. In the Refers to box type =OFFSET(TransactionDate,0,0,ROWS(TransactionDate),4), and click OK. This causes the name DataRange to refer to a range that is offset by zero rows and zero columns from the TransactionDate range, that has as many rows as does the TransactionDate range, and that has four columns. As things stand in Figure 4.8, DataRange refers to the range A1:D11. But notice that DataRange will redefine itself whenever the TransactionDate range gets new rows.

3. Select cell F1 and choose Data, PivotTable and PivotChart Report. This displays Step 1 of the PivotTable Wizard. Click Next and in Step 2 type **DataRange** in the Range box. Click Layout.

4. Drag the Account field into the Row area and the Debit field into the Data area. Choose OK and then click Finish. A new pivot table appears on the worksheet.

5. Right-click in any cell of the pivot table and choose Show PivotTable Toolbar. On the PivotTable toolbar, click the PivotTable dropdown and choose Formulas, Calculated Field from the shortcut menu.

6. In the Name box, type **Total**.

7. In the Formula box, type **= Debit – Credit** and click OK.

8. Right click any Debit field cell in the pivot table and choose Hide from the shortcut menu.

The result of this maneuvering is a pivot table with one row for each account. Associated with each account in the table is a calculated field, named Total in this example. That field expresses the difference between an account's debits and its credits, thus summarizing the information in the Purchases and the Payments ranges on the AcctsReceivable worksheet.

TIP Each sheet in Ledgers.xls contains a sheet-level range named TransactionDate. In some circumstances it can be necessary to qualify a reference to TransactionDate with the name of the sheet. But if you have, say, the AcctsReceivable sheet active when in Step 2 previously you chose Insert, Name, Define, it's not necessary to qualify the range name with the name of the sheet. Excel assumes that you mean the instance of the range that belongs to the active sheet.

Pivot tables do not respond immediately to changes in their underlying data sources, whether those sources be a worksheet range, and external data source or another pivot table. In this respect, pivot tables are different from worksheet formulas, defined names, and charted data series, which *do* recalculate immediately when their source changes.

If a change occurs to a pivot table's data source, it's necessary to *refresh* the pivot table, and that's the purpose of this VBA statement:

```
ThisWorkbook.Sheets("AcctsReceivable").PivotTables("ARSummary").PivotCache.Refresh
```

Once the pivot table has been refreshed, the subroutine ends with the End Sub statement.

There are slightly more efficient ways to write this VBA code. For example, you could create more variables that, via Set statements, refer to worksheet ranges in the AcctsReceivable worksheet as well as in the Sales worksheet. However, the structure was chosen in order to illustrate a variety of VBA capabilities, including the With statement, the Offset and Resize methods, and the automated redefinition of range addresses.

These VBA subroutines, and their associated buttons, are replicated for the Accounts Payable ledger (see Figure 4.9).

The main functional difference in the VBA code that posts to the Accounts Payable ledger is that the code accesses the Accounts Payable journal instead of Accounts Receivable.

Part

I

Ch

4

FIGURE 4.9
The Accounts Payable ledger details information about open accounts with the company's suppliers.

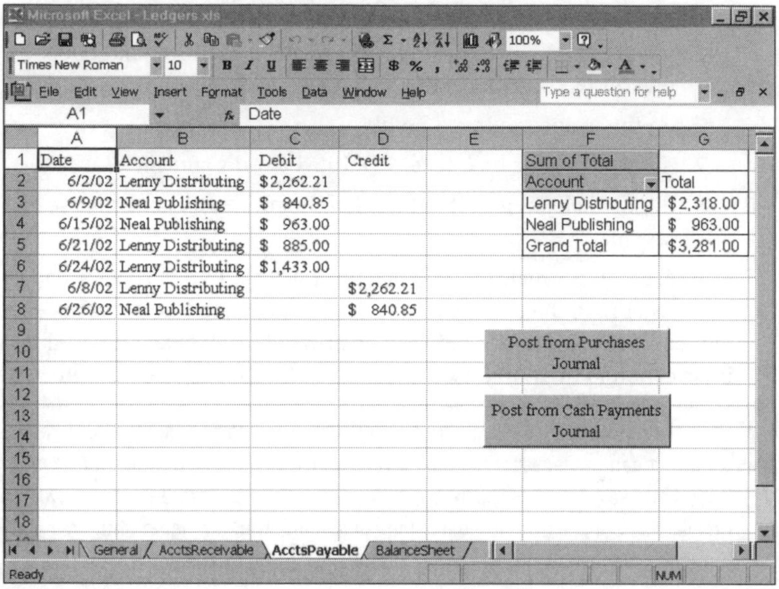

Opening the Workbooks

The previous section mentioned that the two workbooks, Journals.xls and Ledgers.xls, must both be open for them to work together properly. The reason is that the Ledgers workbook has automatic links to the dynamic range names in the Journals workbook. Excel cannot evaluate links from Ledgers.xls to dynamic range names in Journals.xls when the Journals workbook is closed. The result is that if you were to open Ledgers.xls without opening Journals.xls, the cells that contain the links to Journals would show the #REF! error value.

So Ledgers.xls has a procedure that runs automatically when the workbook is opened. Here is its code:

```
Private Sub Workbook_Open()
Dim LinkArray As Variant
Dim LinkIndex As Integer
LinkArray = ActiveWorkbook.LinkSources(xlExcelLinks)

For LinkIndex = LBound(LinkArray) To UBound(LinkArray)
   ActiveWorkbook.OpenLinks LinkArray(LinkIndex)
Next LinkIndex

ThisWorkbook.Activate
End Sub
```

A variable named LinkArray is declared as a Variant in the first Dim statement. A Variant variable can take on nearly any type of value—an integer, a text value, Boolean values, and so on. It's used here because a Variant can also be assigned an array of values in one statement. An integer variable, LinkIndex, is also declared. It will be used to loop through the array.

This statement:

```
LinkArray = ActiveWorkbook.LinkSources(xlExcelLinks)
```

uses the LinkSources method to put an array of links into LinkArray. The xlExcelLinks argument specifies links to Excel workbooks, so OLE and DDE links will not be put in the array.

Then a For loop is run. For each of the links in LinkArray, the OpenLinks method is invoked and the workbook that contains the link is opened. In this example, the only links that are in Ledgers.xls are to Journals.xls, so only that workbook is opened by the process.

The keywords Lbound and Ubound in the For statement specify where the loop is to begin and where it is to end. In words, the statement says to let LinkIndex begin with the lower bound (Lbound: the first element in the array) and end with the upper bound (Ubound: the final element in the array).

Once the loop terminates, Ledgers.xls is activated and the procedure terminates.

Notice the name of the procedure, Workbook_Open. It is termed an *event handler*, in this case one that responds to the event of the workbook opening, and it requires special treatment. In some earlier versions of Microsoft Excel, a subroutine named Auto_Open was used to carry out code when a workbook was opened. While you can still take that approach, there are good reasons for using the event handler approach instead (among them is consistency with responding to other events such as Worksheet.Activate).

To establish an event handler for opening a workbook, take these steps:

1. With the workbook in question active, choose Tools, Macro, Visual Basic Editor. The Visual Basic window appears.

2. If you do not see the Project Explorer window, choose View, Project Explorer. In that window, locate the ThisWorkbook object. It follows the final worksheet name in the Objects folder.

3. Right-click ThisWorkbook and choose View Code from the shortcut menu.

4. Type **Private Sub Workbook_Open()**. Then enter VBA code to carry out whatever actions you want to take place when the workbook opens.

5. To leave the Visual Basic Editor, choose File, Close and Return to Microsoft Excel.

Part

I

Ch

4

TIP

Unless someone has suppressed this capability, you can bypass an event handler for the Workbook.Open event. Hold down the Shift key as you open the workbook. (This tip also applies to opening Microsoft Access database files and Microsoft Word documents.)

Getting a Current Liabilities Balance

Now that a structure for journals and ledgers has been defined, it is straightforward to move amounts for liabilities into the Balance Sheet (see Figure 4.10).

FIGURE 4.10

The Balance Sheet for Bell Books, June 2002 (liabilities and owner's equity), links directly to the General Ledger's asset and liability accounts.

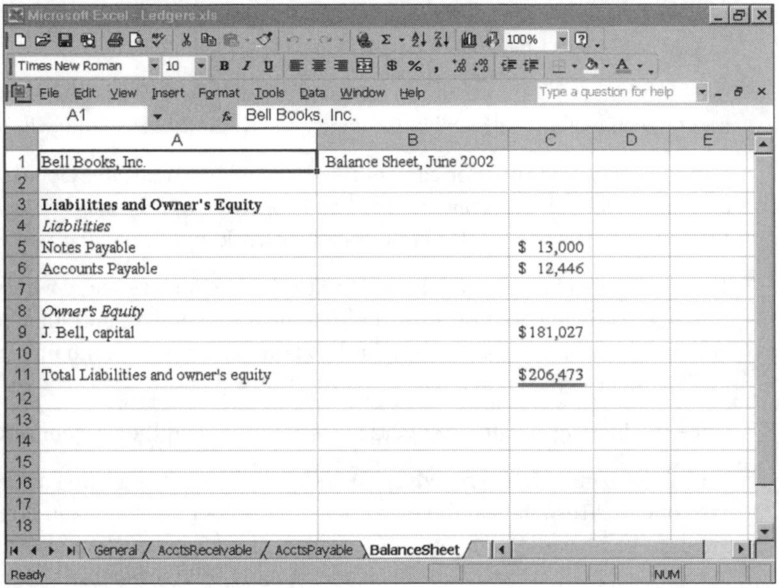

Both Notes Payable and Accounts Payable are copied from their General Ledger balances to the Balance Sheet.

Although this example illustrates only two types of liability, Accounts Payable and Notes Payable, there are other types of liability that you might need to account for in your ledger accounts. These include:

- **Taxes payable.** You will often need to estimate the taxes that will be due on both income and salaries. You should consult an accountant or tax lawyer to determine the percentage rates to apply against your estimated income and estimated salaries. With these amounts, you can establish journal and ledger accounts that contain the proper estimates.

- **Salaries payable.** It often happens that you pay employees' salaries on a date prior to closing your books. In that case, the days that elapse after payment is made and before the books are closed usually result in the accrual of salary amounts. Those accruals will have to be paid after closing the books. Journal and ledger accounts that accumulate these salaries help you keep track of these liabilities.

- **Interest payable.** Depending on whether a note is discounted, you might want to account for interest on the note on a periodic basis, rather than as of the date that the note is actually paid. An Interest Payable account will allow you to accrue this liability over time.

- **Unearned revenue.** Sometimes, a customer might pay you for a product or service that will not be delivered until after the books are closed. In that case, the revenue represents both an asset in the Cash account and a liability (until delivery has occurred), which you can account for with an Unearned Revenue account.

- **Long term debt.** If you have acquired a loan whose payable date is longer than a year from the date that the books are closed, you should keep this amount separate from the Current Liabilities section of the Balance Sheet. Its amount would be listed in a separate account, perhaps named Long Term Debt, and listed in a long-term liabilities section of the Balance Sheet.

Summary

This chapter has demonstrated how you can use Excel to create an account structure in a workbook that contains both a General Journal and special journals, and in a workbook that contains both a General Ledger and subsidiary ledgers. As they occur, transactions are entered in the journals in chronological order. The transactions are then posted to the appropriate accounts in the ledger workbook. This accounts for the bulk of the work involved in creating both the Assets and the Liabilities sections of a Balance Sheet.

You have also learned some VBA techniques for automating the process of posting from journals to their associated ledger accounts, and how to use Excel's pivot table facility to determine the current outstanding balance of an account, whether receivable or payable.

Chapter 5, "Working Capital and Cash Flow Analysis," discusses an important technique for determining your company's financial position. While the accrual method of accounting is, for most companies, the most accurate way to match revenue and expenses so as to determine profit, it tends to obscure how the company handles its most liquid asset, cash. You will learn techniques for tracking the flow of cash and working capital in Chapter 5.

Part
I

Ch
4

Working Capital and Cash Flow Analysis

Cash is the most liquid of all assets—so many managers are keenly interested in how much cash is available to a business at any given time. Because the flow of cash into and out of a business is mainly a matter of investing (purchasing assets) and disinvesting (disposing of assets), an analysis of cash flows can be a good measure of how well managers are performing their investing functions.

This chapter describes the process of accounting for and analyzing these cash flows. Although it doesn't replace them, the cash flow statement is a useful adjunct to income statements and balance sheets. Using tools that are available to you in the form of different functions and links, you will learn how to use Excel to convert the information in a balance sheet and income statement to a cash flow statement.

To set the stage, consider the issue of how costs are timed, discussed in the next section.

Matching Costs and Revenues

Several other chapters of this book discuss the *matching principle*—the notion that revenue should be matched with whatever expenses or assets produce that revenue.

This notion leads inevitably to the *accrual method* of accounting. If you obtain the annual registration for a truck in January, and use that truck to deliver products to your customers for 12 months, you have paid for an item in January that helped you produce revenue all year long.

To record the entire amount of the expense in January causes you to overstate your costs, and understate your profitability, for that month. It also causes you to understate your costs, and overstate your profitability, for the remaining 11 months.

It is largely for this reason that the accrual method evolved. Using the accrual method, you would accrue 1/12th of the expense of the truck registration during each month of the year. Doing so enables you to measure your expenses against your revenues more accurately, and so to measure your profitability more accurately throughout the year.

Similarly, suppose that you sell a product to a customer on a credit basis: you might receive the payment for the product over a period of several months, or you might receive payment in a lump sum several months after the sale. Again, if you wait to record that income until you have received full payment, you will mis-estimate your profit until the customer finishes paying you.

Some very small businesses—primarily sole proprietorships—use an alternative to accrual, called the *cash method* of accounting. They find it more convenient to record expenses and revenues during the period in which they were paid or received. An accrual basis is more complicated than a cash basis, and requires more effort to maintain. But it is often a more accurate method for reporting purposes.

The main distinction between the two methods is that if you record revenue and expenses during the time period that you incurred them, you are using the accrual method. If you record them during the time period that you received or made payment, you are using the cash method. As an example of the cash method of accounting, consider Figure 5.1.

Jean Marble starts a new firm, Marble Designs, in January. At the end of the first month of operations, she has made $8,000 in sales and paid various operating expenses: her salary, the office lease, phone costs, office supplies, and a computer. She was able to save 20% of the cost of office supplies by making a bulk purchase that she estimates will last the entire year. Recording all of these as expenses during the current period results in net income for the month of $1,554.

Contrast this result with Figure 5.2.

FIGURE 5.1
The cash basis understates income when costs are not associated with revenue that they help generate.

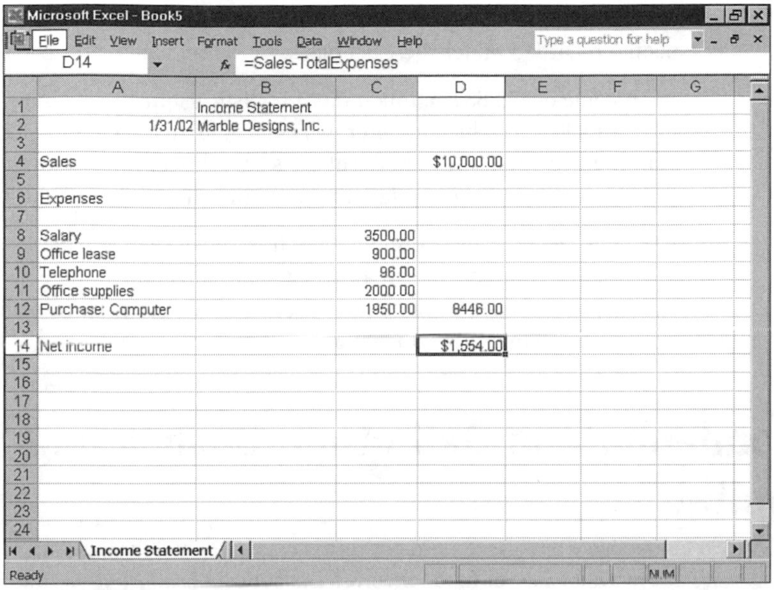

	A	B	C	D	E	F	G
1		Income Statement					
2		1/31/02 Marble Designs, Inc.					
3							
4	Sales			$10,000.00			
5							
6	Expenses						
7							
8	Salary		3500.00				
9	Office lease		900.00				
10	Telephone		96.00				
11	Office supplies		2000.00				
12	Purchase: Computer		1950.00	8446.00			
13							
14	Net income			$1,554.00			

Cell D14 = Sales-TotalExpenses

FIGURE 5.2
Marble Designs Income Statement: the accrual basis more accurately estimates income.

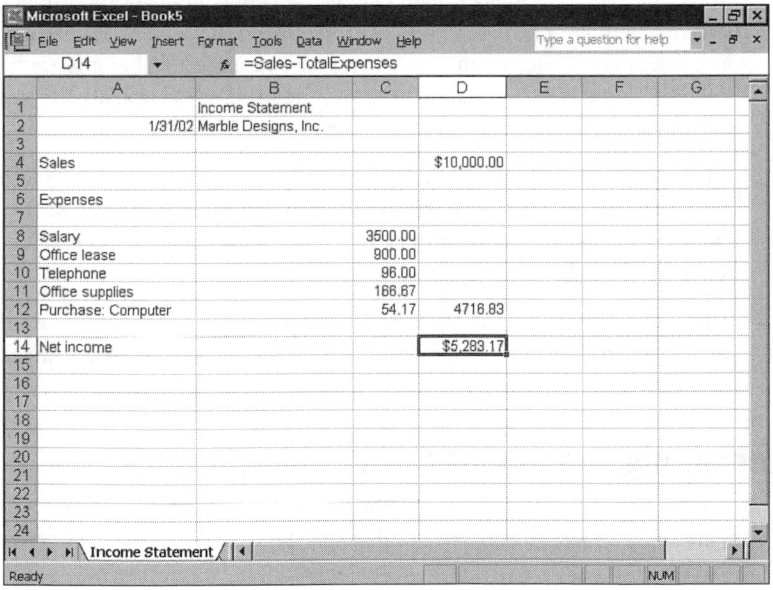

	A	B	C	D	E	F	G
1		Income Statement					
2		1/31/02 Marble Designs, Inc.					
3							
4	Sales			$10,000.00			
5							
6	Expenses						
7							
8	Salary		3500.00				
9	Office lease		900.00				
10	Telephone		96.00				
11	Office supplies		166.67				
12	Purchase: Computer		54.17	4716.83			
13							
14	Net income			$5,283.17			

Cell D14 = Sales-TotalExpenses

Using the accrual method, Marble Designs records 1/12th of the cost of the office supplies during January. This is a reasonable decision because they are expected to last a full year. It also records 1/36th of the cost of the computer as depreciation. The assumption is that the computer's useful life is three years. The net income for January is now $5,283; 3.4 times the net income recorded under the cash basis.

The net income of $5,283 is a much more realistic estimate for January than is $1,554. Both the office supplies and the computer will contribute to the creation of revenue far longer than one month. In contrast, the benefits of the salary, lease, and phone expenses pertain to that month only, and so it is appropriate to record the entire expense during January.

However, this analysis says nothing about how much cash Marble Designs has in the bank. Suppose that the company must pay off a major obligation in the near future. Under the accrual method, the income statement does not necessarily show whether Marble Designs is likely to be able to meet that obligation.

Broadening the Definition: Cash Versus Working Capital

So far, we have discussed funds in terms of cash only. A broader and more useful way of looking at the availability of funds involves the concept of *working capital*.

How does your company create income? If you manufacture a product, you use funds to purchase inventory, produce goods with that inventory, convert those goods into accounts receivable by selling them, and convert accounts receivable into cash when you receive payment. If yours is a merchandising firm, the process is basically the same, although you probably purchase finished goods rather than producing them.

Each of the components in this process is a current asset, such as an asset that you can convert into cash in a relatively short period (usually, but not always, one year) as a result of your normal business operations. Inventory and accounts receivable, for example, are not as liquid as cash, but your business expects eventually to convert both to cash.

Current liabilities, on the other hand, are obligations that you must meet during the same relatively short time period that defines your current assets. Notes payable, accounts payable, and salaries are examples of current liabilities.

Determining the Amount of Working Capital

Working capital is the result of subtracting current liabilities from current assets. It is a measure of a company's solvency, of its capacity to make large purchases and realize bulk discounts, and of its capability to attract customers by offering advantageous credit terms.

Case Study: Marble Designs' Working Capital

To complicate the activities of Marble Designs in January 2002 with one additional transaction, assume that the company purchases $2,000 worth of inventory on January 1. The inventory is purchased on credit, and Marble Designs uses $500 of the inventory during January to deliver products to customers.

The cash transactions that occur during January are shown in Figure 5.3.

FIGURE 5.3
The cash transactions undertaken by Marble Designs during January 2002 affect, but do not define, its working capital.

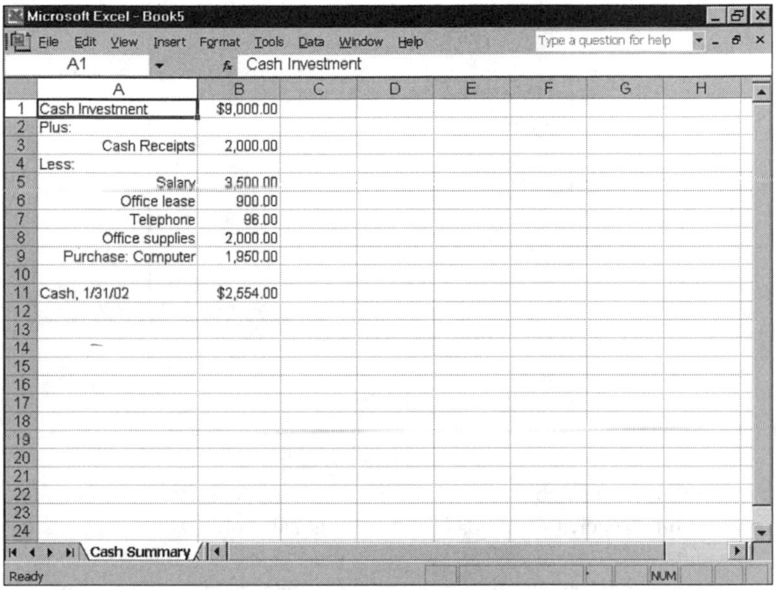

	A	B
1	Cash Investment	$9,000.00
2	Plus:	
3	Cash Receipts	2,000.00
4	Less:	
5	Salary	3,500.00
6	Office lease	900.00
7	Telephone	96.00
8	Office supplies	2,000.00
9	Purchase: Computer	1,950.00
10		
11	Cash, 1/31/02	$2,554.00

Jean Marble establishes capital for her new firm by investing $9,000 at the outset. Of the $10,000 in sales that she makes during the first month, she receives cash payment of $2,000: her cash account is now $11,000. Out of that $11,000, she makes cash payment for:

- $3,500 for her salary
- $900 for the monthly office lease
- $96 for the telephone line
- $2,000 in office supplies
- $1,950 for a computer

These transactions are shown in a format that helps you move to a Trial Balance, then to an Adjusted Trial Balance (see Figure 5.4), and subsequently to an income statement and balance sheet.

TIP

Figure 5.4 shows its six totals with double-underlines. Excel provides a special format for double-underlined totals and for single-underlined subtotals as well. Select the cell or cells whose values you want to underline, and choose Format, Cells. Click the Font tab, and select Single Accounting or Double Accounting from the Underline combo box. Choose OK to return to the worksheet.

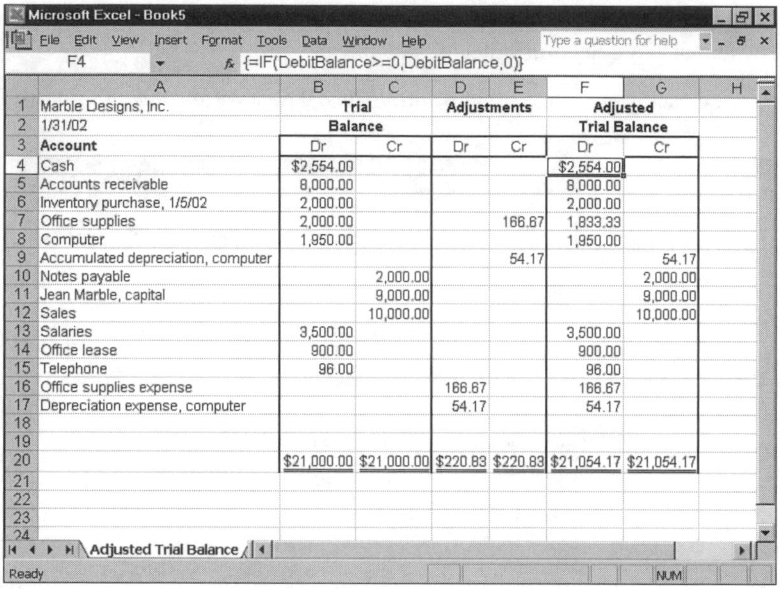

FIGURE 5.4

Marble Designs' Trial Balance, Adjustments, and Adjusted Trial Balance begin to focus on the company's working capital.

	A	B	C	D	E	F	G
		Trial		Adjustments		Adjusted	
1	Marble Designs, Inc.	Balance				Trial Balance	
2	1/31/02						
3	Account	Dr	Cr	Dr	Cr	Dr	Cr
4	Cash	$2,554.00				$2,554.00	
5	Accounts receivable	8,000.00				8,000.00	
6	Inventory purchase, 1/5/02	2,000.00				2,000.00	
7	Office supplies	2,000.00			166.67	1,833.33	
8	Computer	1,950.00				1,950.00	
9	Accumulated depreciation, computer				54.17		54.17
10	Notes payable		2,000.00				2,000.00
11	Jean Marble, capital		9,000.00				9,000.00
12	Sales		10,000.00				10,000.00
13	Salaries	3,500.00				3,500.00	
14	Office lease	900.00				900.00	
15	Telephone	96.00				96.00	
16	Office supplies expense			166.67		166.67	
17	Depreciation expense, computer			54.17		54.17	
18							
19							
20		$21,000.00	$21,000.00	$220.83	$220.83	$21,054.17	$21,054.17
21							
22							
23							
24							

F4 cell formula: `{=IF(DebitBalance>=0,DebitBalance,0)}`

On the left (or debit) side of the Trial Balance, are the ending cash balance of $2,554, the accounts receivable of $8,000 (recall that sales of $10,000 were made, and $2,000 in cash payments were received), the inventory purchased with the $2,000 loan, and the office supplies, computer, salary, lease, and telephone service paid for with cash.

On the right, or credit, side of the Trial Balance are Marble's initial capital investments into Cash, the $10,000 in sales, and the $2,000 borrowed to purchase the inventory.

The Adjustments to the Trial Balance include $54.17 in depreciation on the computer during the first of 36 months of its useful life, and the $166.67 worth of supplies consumed during the first month. The $54.17 in depreciation is found with this formula:

`=SLN(B8,0,36)`

This is the Excel function that returns straight-line depreciation. You will learn more about Excel's depreciation functions in Chapter 16, "Fixed Assets," but this particular entry computes the monthly depreciation on the value in cell B8 ($1,950), assuming that its eventual salvage value is $0 and that its useful life is 36 months.

NOTE Couldn't you just divide $1,950 by 36 to get the $54.17 straight-line monthly depreciation? Sure. But by using the SLN function, you make it explicit both that you are calculating depreciation, and that you assume 36 months useful life and a zero salvage value. A year from now, reviewing your income statement, you might appreciate that your calculation was unambiguous. ■

The value of the Office Supplies consumed during the month is $166.67: the value of $2,000 in cell B7 divided by 12.

These adjustments are combined with the Trial Balance to arrive at the debit amounts in the Adjusted Trial Balance. The worksheet accomplishes this by means of this array formula in cells F4:F18:

```
=IF(DebitBalance>=0,DebitBalance,0)
```

In the formula, *DebitBalance* is the name of another formula. That other formula is defined as:

```
=(TrialDebits-TrialCredits)+(AdjustDebits-AdjustCredits)
```

The formula for DebitBalance makes use of four named ranges (the cell references are to the worksheet shown in Figure 5.4):

- TrialDebits refers to B4:B18, the debit amounts in the Trial Balance.
- TrialCredits refers to C4:C18, the credit amounts in the Trial Balance.
- AdjustDebits refers to D4:D18, the debit amounts in the Adjustments.
- AdjustCredits refers to E4:E18, the credit amounts in the Adjustments.

The steps involved in defining the name DebitBalance are

1. Choose Insert, Name, Define.
2. In the Names in Workbook box, type **DebitBalance**.
3. In the Refers to box, type this formula:

   ```
   =(TrialDebits-TrialCredits)+(AdjustDebits-AdjustCredits)
   ```
4. Choose OK (or, if you're ready to continue defining more names, choose Add).

The formula subtracts any amounts in the Credit column of the Trial Balance from any amounts in its Debit column. It then adds any adjusting debits, and subtracts any adjusting credits. The result is the debit balance—thus the name of the formula.

As noted earlier in this section, DebitBalance is used in this array formula, which occupies cells F4:F18 in Figure 5.4:

```
=IF(DebitBalance>=0,DebitBalance,0)
```

To illustrate its effect, consider cell F7, the adjusted trial balance for the Office Supplies account. The Trial Balance provides a debit amount of $2,000, and no credit amount. The adjustments include no debit amount, but a credit amount of 166.67. So the named formula DebitBalance returns (2000 − 0) + (0 − 166.67), or 1833.33. Because that value is greater than zero, the condition in the array formula in cell F7 is satisfied, and returns the value 1833.33.

Before you continue, you might want to be sure that you understand why no non-zero value appears in cells F9:F12.

Cells G4:G18 contain this array formula:

```
=IF(CreditBalance>=0,CreditBalance,0)
```

It's similar to the array formula in cells F4:F18. The sole difference is that it relies on a different named formula, *CreditBalance*. Using Insert, Name, Define, CreditBalance is defined as:

```
=(TrialCredits-TrialDebits)+(AdjustCredits-AdjustDebits)
```

Notice that the formula reverses the relationship between debits and credits used in DebitBalance. Its purpose is to combine trial and adjusting credits and debits so that if credits exceed debits, the formula returns a positive value. Then the array formula in G4:G18 returns values greater than or equal to zero only.

You might have noticed that these various formulas call for Excel to return a zero amount if a condition is not met. For example, the array formulas in F4:F18 and G4:G18 return a DebitBalance or CreditBalance amount when the balances equal or exceed zero, but a zero when they do not. The figure does not show these zero amounts, primarily to avoid visual clutter.

TIP
You can suppress the display of any zero amounts in a worksheet by selecting Options from the Tools menu, choosing the View tab, and clearing the Zero Values checkbox.

With the cells in the Adjusted Trial Balance section completed, their revenue and expense information is carried over from the Adjusted Trial Balance to the Income Statement and Balance Sheet. See Figure 5.5.

FIGURE 5.5
Marble Designs Income Statement and Balance Sheet enables you to determine working capital.

	Account Type	Account	Income Statement Dr	Income Statement Cr	Balance Sheet Dr	Balance Sheet Cr
1		Marble Designs, Inc.				
2		1/31/02				
3	Account Type	Account	Dr	Cr	Dr	Cr
4	Assets	Cash			$2,554.00	
5	Assets	Accounts receivable			8,000.00	
6	Expenses	Inventory purchase, 1/5/02	2,000.00			
7	Assets	Office supplies			1,833.33	
8	Assets	Computer			1,950.00	
9	Liabilities	Accumulated depreciation, computer				54.17
10	Liabilities	Notes payable				2,000.00
11	Liabilities	Jean Marble, capital				9,000.00
12	Revenues	Sales		10,000.00		
13	Expenses	Salaries	3,500.00			
14	Expenses	Office lease	900.00			
15	Expenses	Telephone	96.00			
16	Expenses	Office supplies expense	166.67			
17	Expenses	Depreciation expense, computer	54.17			
18	Assets	Inventory, 1/31/02		1,500.00	1,500.00	
19			6,716.83	11,500.00	15,837.33	11,054.17
20		Net Income	4,783.17			4,783.17
21						
22			$11,500.00	$11,500.00	$15,837.33	15,837.33
23						

For the Income Statement, information on revenues and expenses are needed. The debit amounts are obtained by means of this formula:

`=IF(OR(AccountType="Revenues",AccountType="Expenses"),AdjustedDebits,0)`

The AdjustedDebits range occupies cells F4:F18 in Figure 5.4. The range named AccountType occupies cells A4:A18 in Figure 5.5, and contains values that identify the type of account: revenue, expense, asset, or liability. The values in AccountType enable the formula to bring only the needed accounts into the Income Statement. Similarly, the credit amounts in the Income Statement are obtained by means of this formula in cells D4:D18:

`=IF(OR(AccountType="Revenues",AccountType="Expenses"),AdjustedCredits,0)`

The AdjustedCredits range occupies cells G4:G18 in Figure 5.4.

There are two additional amounts required to bring the Income Statement into balance: Ending Inventory and Net Income. Both these amounts are as of the statement date, 1/31/02.

Ending Inventory is included as a credit amount, accounting for the remainder of the initial $2,000 purchase.

Net Income is included in the Debit Column, as the difference between the Income Statement's total Credits and its total Debits. The figure returned is $4,783. As a check, notice that this is the result of:

```
$10,000 (Gross Sales) - $500 (Cost of Goods Sold) - $4,717 (Total Operating
➥Expenses) = $4,783
```

and the inclusion of the Ending Inventory and Net Income brings the Income Statement into balance.

N O T E   Recall that Cost of Goods Sold equals Beginning Inventory (here, $0) plus Purchases ($2,000) less Ending Inventory ($1,500). ■

Finally, the debit and credit columns of the Balance Sheet are obtained by formulas that are similar to those used for the Income Statement. The debit amounts are returned by this formula:

`=IF(OR(AccountType="Assets",AccountType="Liabilities"),AdjustedDebits,0)`

and the credit amounts are returned by:

`=IF(OR(AccountType="Assets",AccountType="Liabilities"),AdjustedCredits,0)`

At last, Marble is in a position to calculate her working capital. Recall that this is defined as the difference between Current Assets and Current Liabilities. As of 1/31/02, Marble's Current Assets are

$2,554 (Cash)

$8,000 (Accounts Receivable)

Part

I

Ch

5

$1,833 (Office Supplies, a pre-paid expense)

$1,500 (Ending Inventory)

for a total of $13,887. Her Current Liabilities include only the $2,000 note payable. Her working capital is therefore $11,887, or $13,887 – $2,000.

NOTE Notice that the computer asset is not involved in determining working capital. This is because the computer is not a current asset: one that can quickly be converted to cash in the normal course of business operations.

Determining Changes in Working Capital

From a management perspective, it is important to understand how the amount of working capital changes over time. A comparative balance sheet is useful for this purpose. Figure 5.6 shows a balance sheet for Marble Designs, in a more condensed format than the one used in Figure 5.5.

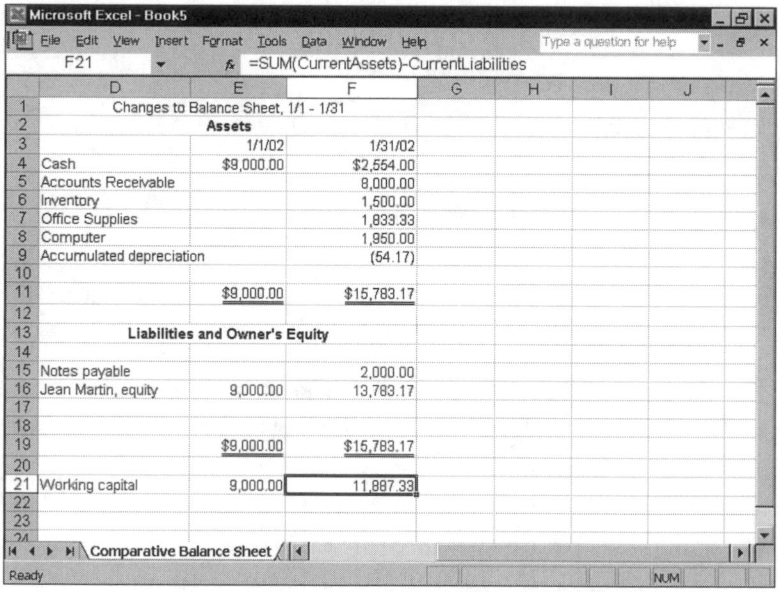

	D	E	F
1	Changes to Balance Sheet, 1/1 - 1/31		
2		**Assets**	
3		1/1/02	1/31/02
4	Cash	$9,000.00	$2,554.00
5	Accounts Receivable		8,000.00
6	Inventory		1,500.00
7	Office Supplies		1,833.33
8	Computer		1,950.00
9	Accumulated depreciation		(54.17)
10			
11		$9,000.00	$15,783.17
12			
13	**Liabilities and Owner's Equity**		
14			
15	Notes payable		2,000.00
16	Jean Martin, equity	9,000.00	13,783.17
17			
18			
19		$9,000.00	$15,783.17
20			
21	Working capital	9,000.00	11,887.33

FIGURE 5.6
A comparative balance sheet can clarify how your financial position changes over time.

The balance sheet section of Figure 5.6 lists Marble Designs' assets and liabilities. On 1/1/02, when the firm began operation, it had no liabilities and $9,000 in assets, consisting entirely of cash. Its working capital was therefore $9,000. By the end of the month, the sum of the firm's assets was $15,783 (as, of course, was the sum of its liabilities and owner's equity).

Not all these assets and liabilities are *current*, however. The current assets include cash, accounts receivable, inventory, and office supplies, which total $13,887. The sole current liability is the note for the purchase of the beginning inventory, for $2,000. The difference between the total of the current assets and the current liability is $11,887, which agrees with the amount arrived at via the information in Figure 5.5.

So, the change in working capital from the beginning to the end of the month is $11,887 – $9,000, or $2,887.

There are several different ways to calculate changes in working capital. It's useful to look at them, both to understand working capital from different perspectives, and because you might want to calculate working capital in the context of different worksheet layouts. One way to do so is shown in Figure 5.7.

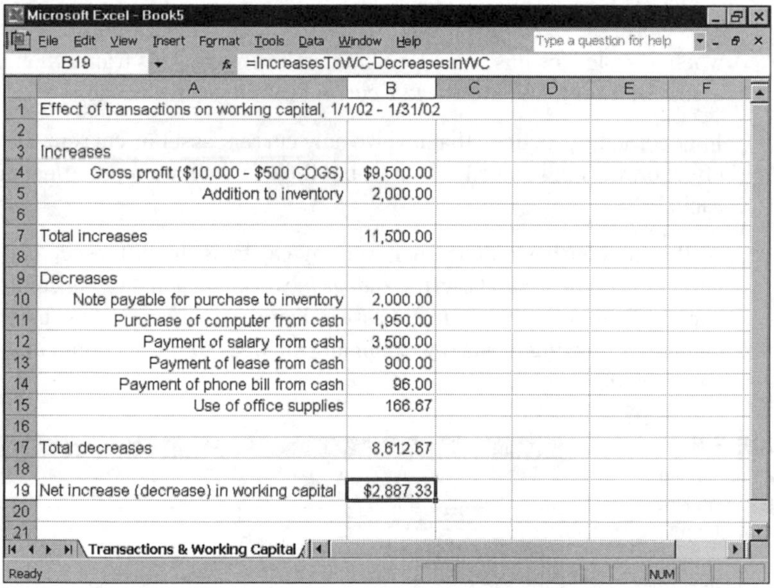

	A	B
1	Effect of transactions on working capital, 1/1/02 - 1/31/02	
2		
3	Increases	
4	Gross profit ($10,000 - $500 COGS)	$9,500.00
5	Addition to inventory	2,000.00
6		
7	Total increases	11,500.00
8		
9	Decreases	
10	Note payable for purchase to inventory	2,000.00
11	Purchase of computer from cash	1,950.00
12	Payment of salary from cash	3,500.00
13	Payment of lease from cash	900.00
14	Payment of phone bill from cash	96.00
15	Use of office supplies	166.67
16		
17	Total decreases	8,612.67
18		
19	Net increase (decrease) in working capital	$2,887.33
20		
21		

FIGURE 5.7
A laborious way to determine changes in working capital is by examining individual transactions.

During January, selling products for more than their cost increased working capital: the gross profit of $9,500. Placing $2,000 worth of materials in inventory also increased working capital. These are both current assets, totaling $11,500.

Acquiring an obligation of $2,000, the note payable that was used to purchase the inventory, decreased working capital. Working capital was also decreased by the payment of cash for the computer, for various operating expenses, and the use of office supplies. These are all current liabilities, totaling $8,613.

The net effect of the increase of $11,500 in working capital and the decrease of $8,613 in working capital is $2,887. During the month of January, Marble Designs was able to increase its working capital by this amount. Note that this is the same figure as was determined by the analysis in Figure 5.6 ($11,887 – $9,000).

Normally, you would not determine changes in working capital by examining each transaction that occurred in a given period: there are quicker ways. Also, many transactions occur that affect current assets and current liabilities to the same degree, and therefore have no net effect on working capital.

For example, when you collect payment for a product or service, this transaction has no effect on working capital. So doing merely increases one current asset (cash) and decreases another current asset (accounts receivable) by identical amounts. When you write a check for an account payable, you decrease both a current asset account (cash) and a current liability account (accounts payable) by equal amounts. There is no net effect on the amount of working capital.

Therefore, the example shown in Figure 5.7 could have ignored the transactions involved when Marble Designs acquired $2,000 in inventory. This transaction increased a current asset, inventory, and increased a current liability, notes payable, by identical amounts.

In general, transactions that involve only current asset or current liability accounts *do* have an effect on working capital accounts, but they *do not* have a net effect on the amount of working capital.

As this chapter has emphasized, working capital is the difference between current assets and current liabilities. Similarly, the *change* in working capital is the combined effect of *changes* in current liabilities and in current assets. Figure 5.8 shows how you can quickly determine the change in working capital by examining changes to the accounts that comprise current assets and liabilities:

FIGURE 5.8
You can determine changes in working capital by comparing changes in current assets and in current liabilities.

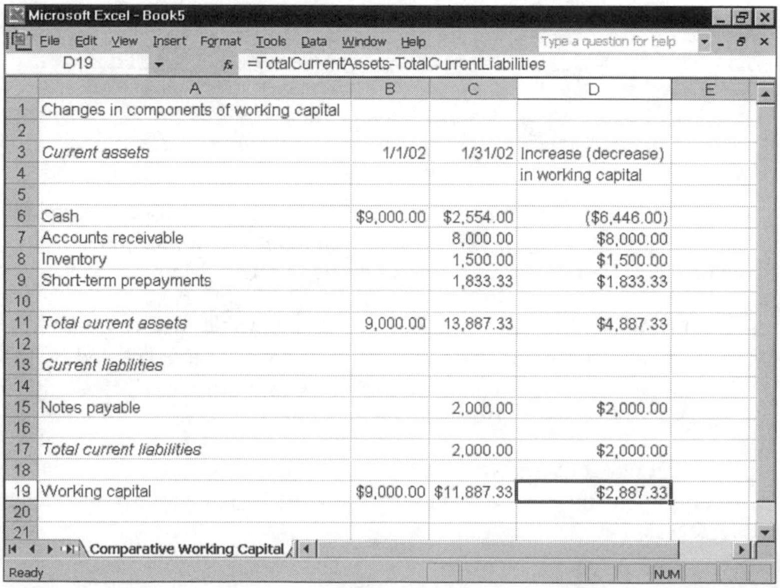

	A	B	C	D	E
1	Changes in components of working capital				
2					
3	Current assets	1/1/02	1/31/02	Increase (decrease)	
4				in working capital	
5					
6	Cash	$9,000.00	$2,554.00	($6,446.00)	
7	Accounts receivable		8,000.00	$8,000.00	
8	Inventory		1,500.00	$1,500.00	
9	Short-term prepayments		1,833.33	$1,833.33	
10					
11	Total current assets	9,000.00	13,887.33	$4,887.33	
12					
13	Current liabilities				
14					
15	Notes payable		2,000.00	$2,000.00	
16					
17	Total current liabilities		2,000.00	$2,000.00	
18					
19	Working capital	$9,000.00	$11,887.33	$2,887.33	
20					
21					

D19   fx =TotalCurrentAssets-TotalCurrentLiabilities

As it happens, the only current asset that declines during January is the Cash account. All other current asset accounts increase in value. One current liability account, Notes Payable, increases. The change in working capital can then be determined by subtracting the net increase in current liabilities from the net increase in current assets: $4,887 – $2,000 = $2,887.

One further means of determining changes in working capital is to compare its sources with its uses. Recall that transactions involving only current asset and current liability accounts have no net effect on working capital. The same is true of transactions that involve only non-current accounts. For example, when Marble records $54 as the month's depreciation on the computer, she adds $54 to a non-current account, with no net effect on working capital.

However, a transaction that involves a current account and a non-current account does affect the amount of working capital. For example, suppose that Marble were to invest an additional $1,000 in her business, recording it in both the capital account (non-current) and the cash account (a current asset). This transaction would have the effect of increasing working capital by $1,000.

Therefore, when determining changes to working capital, it is often convenient to limit the analysis to transactions affecting only current accounts and non-current accounts. Figure 5.9 gives an example.

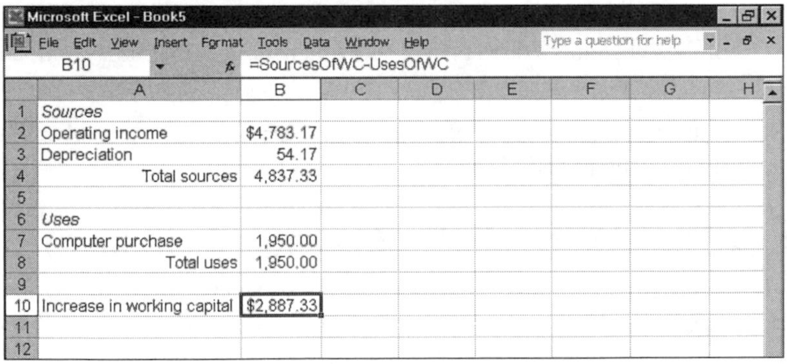

	A	B
1	Sources	
2	Operating income	$4,783.17
3	Depreciation	54.17
4	Total sources	4,837.33
5		
6	Uses	
7	Computer purchase	1,950.00
8	Total uses	1,950.00
9		
10	Increase in working capital	$2,887.33

FIGURE 5.9
Another way to determine changes in working capital is to examine current and non-current accounts.

The sources of working capital, in this case, consist solely of net income. What is depreciation doing there? Recall that depreciation is a non-cash expense that, for the purposes of the income statement, acts as an offset to gross profit in the calculation of net income. But no funds change hands as a result of recording depreciation. Therefore, when you use net income to calculate your sources of working capital, it is necessary to add depreciation back in: in other words, to reverse the effect of subtracting it in the calculation of net income.

The cash portion of net income, a non-current account, is deposited in the cash account, a current asset. Therefore, in combination with the act of adding depreciation back in, it can be used to calculate the change in working capital.

The sole use of working capital shown in Figure 5.9, the purchase of the computer, is also used to determine the change in working capital. Funds from the cash account, a current asset, were used to purchase Equipment, a non-current asset.

The difference between the total sources of working capital and the total uses of working capital is, once again, $2,887, just as was found by means of the analyses in Figures 5.6 through 5.8.

Analyzing Cash Flow

As noted previously, there are various reasons that you would want to determine how a company uses its cash assets. The choice to use cash to acquire an asset, meet a liability, or retire a debt is a process of investment and disinvestment, and there are always choices, some smart and some maladroit, that a manager can make. It's important to keep track of how well a company's management is making these choices.

Furthermore, the accrual method of accounting, for all its usefulness in matching revenues with expenses, tends to obscure how cash flows through a firm. One of the purposes of cash flow analysis is to highlight differences between, say, net income and the actual acquisition of cash. For example, accounts receivable is one component of net income, but it will not show up as cash until the check makes it to the bank. A company may have a healthy net income, but if its customers do not pay it on a timely basis it might have difficulty meeting its obligations. Cash flow analysis can illuminate problems, even impending problems, such as this.

To illustrate this process, consider what might transpire in Marble Designs' financial structure over the period of a year.

Case Study: Marble Designs (Continued)

During the 12 months following the analyses shown in Figures 5.1 through 5.9, Marble Designs enjoys successful operations, and engages in the following transactions:

- Makes $90,000 in sales to customers, using $24,500 in inventory to deliver on those sales. As of January 31, 2003, $5,500 remains in accounts receivable, so $84,500 has been received in payment.
- Uses cash to purchase $25,000 in materials to replenish its inventory.
- Collects the $8,000 that remained in accounts receivable at the end of January, 2002.
- Pays $53,951 in cash to cover operating expenses.
- Purchases a new computer in July for $2,320 in cash.
- Buys $2,000 in additional office supplies.
- Purchases office space in a new building for $30,000. Decides against occupying the space before construction of the building is complete, and sells the space for $35,000, making a $5,000 nonoperating profit.

- Retires the $2,000 note acquired during January 2002, and obtains a new note for $3,000.
- Depreciates the two computers, for a total of $1,037 from 1/31/02 through 1/31/03.

Some of these transactions are cash, some are transactions that pertain to normal operations, and some affect current assets and liabilities. Others are non-cash, non-operating, and long-term. To determine their effect on Marble Designs' cash flow, it's necessary to disaggregate them.

NOTE This is a relatively simple situation to analyze, and because it is illustrative it omits many of the transactions that you would normally take into account. For example, it assumes that Marble Designs is an S-corporation, and therefore the treatment of its income taxes is deferred. ▪

As a benchmark, against which the following analysis will be compared, Figure 5.10 shows the actual cash transactions that occur as a result of Marble Designs' activities during the 12-month period.

FIGURE 5.10
Marble Designs' cash positions can be tracked by examining individual cash transactions.

	A	B	C	D
	Cash transaction summary, 1/31/02 - 1/31/03	Deposits	Withdrawals	Balance
1				
2	Beginning cash balance			$2,554.00
3	Plus cash deposits from revenues	84,500.00		
4	Less purchases to inventory		25,000.00	
5	Plus payment of 1/31/02 accounts receivable	8,000.00		
6				
7	Less cash expenses		53,951.00	
8	Less purchase of new computer		2,320.00	
9	Less purchase of new supplies		2,000.00	
10	Plus gain on sale of office	5,000.00		
11	Less retirement of old note		2,000.00	
12	Plus acquisition of new note	3,000.00		
13	Ending cash balance			$17,783.00
14				
15	Increase in cash balance			$15,229.00

Cell D15 formula: =CurrentBalance-PriorBalance

Again, though, the information in Figure 5.10 is simply a benchmark used as a check on the cash flow analysis. You would almost never attempt to do a cash flow analysis using actual cash receipts and payments over any lengthy period of time: it's too time consuming and it's a less informative way of going about the analysis.

Developing the Basic Information

Instead of beginning with a checkbook register, start with the standard financial reports: the Income Statement and Balance Sheet. Figure 5.11 shows the Income Statement for the period 1/31/02–1/31/03 for Marble Designs, as well as a comparative Balance Sheet showing assets, liabilities, and equity at the beginning and end of that period.

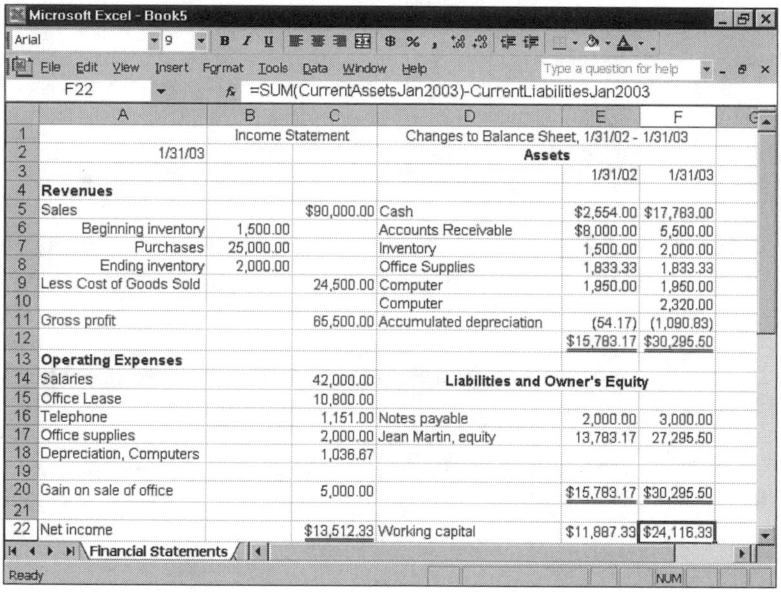

	A	B	C	D	E	F
1		Income Statement		Changes to Balance Sheet, 1/31/02 - 1/31/03		
2	1/31/03				**Assets**	
3					1/31/02	1/31/03
4	**Revenues**					
5	Sales		$90,000.00	Cash	$2,554.00	$17,783.00
6	Beginning inventory	1,500.00		Accounts Receivable	$8,000.00	5,500.00
7	Purchases	25,000.00		Inventory	1,500.00	2,000.00
8	Ending inventory	2,000.00		Office Supplies	1,833.33	1,833.33
9	Less Cost of Goods Sold		24,500.00	Computer	1,950.00	1,950.00
10				Computer		2,320.00
11	Gross profit		65,500.00	Accumulated depreciation	(54.17)	(1,090.83)
12					$15,783.17	$30,295.50
13	**Operating Expenses**					
14	Salaries		42,000.00	**Liabilities and Owner's Equity**		
15	Office Lease		10,800.00			
16	Telephone		1,151.00	Notes payable	2,000.00	3,000.00
17	Office supplies		2,000.00	Jean Martin, equity	13,783.17	27,295.50
18	Depreciation, Computers		1,036.67			
19						
20	Gain on sale of office		5,000.00		$15,783.17	$30,295.50
21						
22	Net income		$13,512.33	Working capital	$11,887.33	$24,116.33

FIGURE 5.11
The Income Statement and Balance Sheet provide starting points for a cash flow analysis.

The Income Statement shows that there was $1,500 worth of materials in inventory at the beginning of the period, an additional $25,000 worth was purchased during the period, and $2,000 was remaining at the end. Therefore, $24,500 in materials was used in the completion of $90,000 in sales for the period, resulting in a gross profit of $65,500.

Against that gross profit, various operating expenses were incurred: salaries, the cost of the office lease, and the telephone expense. The $1,833 in office supplies that remained at the end of 1/31/02 were consumed: this was a prepaid expense, because Marble purchased the entire stock of supplies at the beginning of January 2002. Another $2,000 were purchased during the period covered by the Income Statement.

The depreciation on the computers also appears in the Income Statement. This is, however, a non-cash expense. The formula used in cell C18 of Figure 5.11 is

```
=SLN(1950,0,3)+SLN(2320,0,3)*0.5
```

It makes use of Excel's straight-line depreciation function, whose arguments are *cost, salvage value,* and *life*. The cost is simply the item's initial cost; its salvage value is the item's value at the end of its useful life—here, Marble estimates that value will be zero; its life is the number of periods that will expire before the item reaches its salvage value. The function returns the amount of depreciation that occurs during one period of the item's useful life. So, this fragment:

```
SLN(1950,0,3)
```

returns $650, the amount of depreciation in the value of the first computer purchased, during one year of its assumed three-year life.

The second computer cost $2,320, and was purchased in July of 2002, halfway through the period covered by the Income Statement. Therefore, the depreciation on that computer during the second half of the year, $387, is returned by this fragment:

```
SLN(2320,0,3)*0.5
```

Together, the $650 in depreciation over 12 months for the first computer, and the $387 in depreciation over six months for the second computer, result in a total equipment depreciation of $1,037.

NOTE Expenditures, such as the purchase of the computer, that add to business assets are *capital expenditures*. They are recorded in asset accounts, which is why the cost of the computers does not appear in the income statement. Expenditures for repairs, maintenance, fuel, and so on are *revenue expenditures*, and do appear in the income statement. ■

It's important to keep in mind that this depreciation does not constitute a cash expense such as a salary check or the payment of a monthly telephone bill. As noted previously, no funds change hands when you record depreciation: It is merely a means of apportioning, or accruing, an earlier use of capital to a period in which the item contributes to the creation of revenue.

Lastly, the $5,000 profit from the acquisition (for $30,000) and subsequent sale (for $35,000) of the office space is recorded and added to obtain a total net income. Note that this $5,000 is nonoperating income: that is, it is profit created from an activity, the purchase and sale of property, that is not a part of Marble Designs' normal operations.

The Balance Sheet repeats from Figure 5.6, in column E, Marble Designs' assets, liabilities, and equity at the end of 1/31/02. Column F also shows these figures as of 1/31/03. As noted previously, the transactions that occurred during the 12-month period resulted in a healthy increase in cash, and minor changes to the remaining asset and liability categories. These entries are taken from ledger accounts; the exception is the owner's equity figure of $27,295.50. Just as explained in the discussion of the balance sheet shown in Figure 5.6, the owner's equity in cell F17 of Figure 5.11 is calculated as:

```
=E17+C22
```

That is, the prior equity figure of $13,783.17 in cell E17, plus the net income of $13,512.33 for the period in cell C22.

Summarizing the Sources and Uses of Working Capital

Figure 5.12 shows the changes in working capital that occurred during the year, determined by analyzing the effect of non-current accounts. Sources of working capital include operations, the non-operating profit realized from the purchase and sale of the office space, and borrowing on a new short-term note.

NOTE It can be easy to confuse the concept of working capital itself, the result of subtracting current liabilities from current assets, with an analysis of how working capital is created and used—the subject of the present section. As you work through this analysis, bear in mind that sources and uses of working capital involve non-current assets and liabilities.

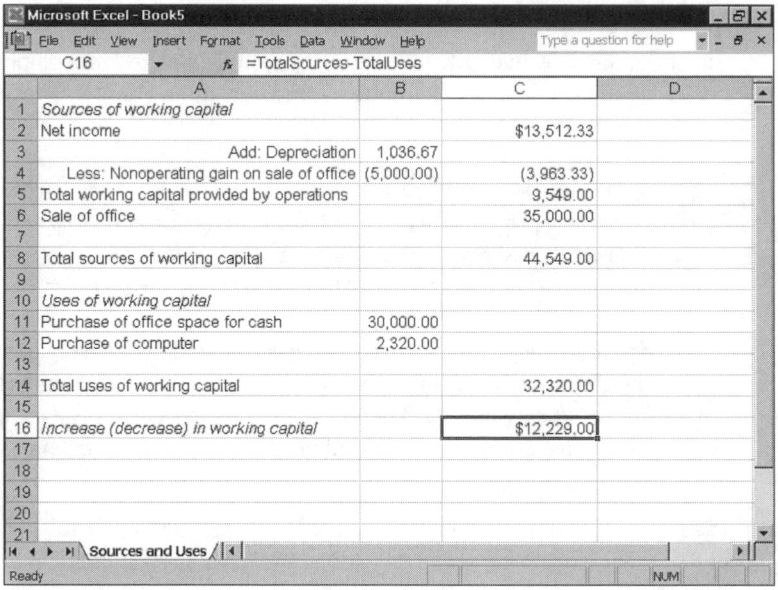

	A	B	C	D
1	*Sources of working capital*			
2	Net income		$13,512.33	
3	Add: Depreciation	1,036.67		
4	Less: Nonoperating gain on sale of office	(5,000.00)	(3,963.33)	
5	Total working capital provided by operations		9,549.00	
6	Sale of office		35,000.00	
7				
8	Total sources of working capital		44,549.00	
9				
10	*Uses of working capital*			
11	Purchase of office space for cash	30,000.00		
12	Purchase of computer	2,320.00		
13				
14	Total uses of working capital		32,320.00	
15				
16	*Increase (decrease) in working capital*		$12,229.00	
17				
18				
19				
20				
21				

FIGURE 5.12
Analyzing the sources and uses of working capital is often a useful indicator of how well a business is managing its resources.

There are three points to note about this analysis of sources and uses of working capital:

- You can *calculate* overall cash flow by determining the net change in the Cash account, but to *analyze* cash flow you need to examine all the changes in the balance sheet accounts—including working capital. The details and the overall effect of changes in working capital usually differ from those of cash transactions. Both the working capital and the cash impacts are important to an understanding of a company's financial position.
- Changes in working capital are not the same as changes in cash. In this case, cash increases during the accounting period by $15,229, whereas working capital increases by $12,229.

- Notice that the profit on the purchase and sale of the office space apparently has no effect on the increase in working capital. In fact, however, it does: the profit of $5,000 has already been included in net income. Figure 5.12 subtracts that profit from net income in order to provide a more accurate picture of operations as a source of working capital. Further, the transaction is shown both under sources and uses in order to show how capital has been generated and used, not simply to calculate the increase or the decrease over time.

Identifying Cash Flows Due to Operating Activities

The next step in analyzing cash flows is to focus on cash generated by and used in operations. Figure 5.13 shows this step.

FIGURE 5.13
Determining cash flows from operating activities.

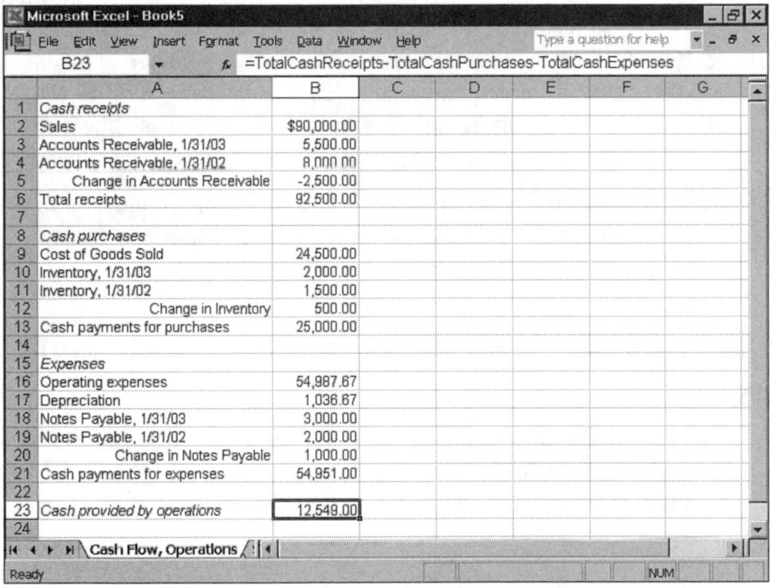

	A	B
1	*Cash receipts*	
2	Sales	$90,000.00
3	Accounts Receivable, 1/31/03	5,500.00
4	Accounts Receivable, 1/31/02	8,000.00
5	Change in Accounts Receivable	-2,500.00
6	Total receipts	92,500.00
7		
8	*Cash purchases*	
9	Cost of Goods Sold	24,500.00
10	Inventory, 1/31/03	2,000.00
11	Inventory, 1/31/02	1,500.00
12	Change in Inventory	500.00
13	Cash payments for purchases	25,000.00
14		
15	*Expenses*	
16	Operating expenses	54,987.67
17	Depreciation	1,036.67
18	Notes Payable, 1/31/03	3,000.00
19	Notes Payable, 1/31/02	2,000.00
20	Change in Notes Payable	1,000.00
21	Cash payments for expenses	54,951.00
22		
23	*Cash provided by operations*	12,549.00
24		

Generally, there are three sources or uses of cash that arise from operating activities:

- *Cash receipts from customers.* You can easily determine this amount by combining the value for sales (net of any discounts that may have been provided to customers) with changes in accounts receivable. That is, add accounts receivable at the end of the period to the sales figure, and then subtract accounts receivable at the end of the period. The logic is that if accounts receivable has declined during the period, you have collected more in cash than you have accrued into accounts receivable; if it has increased, you have accrued more than you have collected in cash.
- *Cash outlays for purchases.* From the standpoint of operating activities, there is one use of cash for purchases: inventory. Therefore, to summarize cash flow for operating

purchases, add to the cost of goods sold during the period of the ending inventory level, and subtract the beginning inventory level.

Additionally, you might have purchased inventory via a note or account payable to the suppliers of your inventory materials. In that case, you would add any decrease in these payables (because you would have used cash to decrease them) or subtract any increase in these payables (because you used credit, not cash, to acquire the materials).

■ *Cash outlays for expenses.* These are easily determined from the operating expenses portion of the income statement. Combine the total operating expenses with any changes in prepayments and accrued liabilities, such as employee salaries earned, but as yet unpaid, at the end of the period.

In the case of Marble Designs, applying these calculations as shown in Figure 5.13 indicates that sales, increased by a reduction of $500 in accounts receivable, results in cash receipts of $92,500. Cost of goods sold, increased by the $500 change in inventory level, results in $25,000 cash purchases. And total operating expenses were (a) reduced by $1,037 in depreciation, a non-cash, long-term prepayment, and (b) increased by a change in the amount of notes payable, converted to cash and used to acquire office supplies.

This completes the process of converting information contained in the income statement, receipts, and outlays represented as accruals, into a cash basis, represented as actual cash receipts and outlays occurring during the period in question.

Combining Cash from Operations with Cash from Non-Operating Transactions

The final step in developing the cash flow analysis is to combine the cash amounts used for normal operations with the cash transactions that apply to non-operating activities. Figure 5.14 provides this summary.

FIGURE 5.14
Marble Designs' cash flow statement, 1/31/02–1/31/03.

	A	B	C	D	E	F	G
1	Cash receipts						
2	Cash from operations	$12,549.00					
3	Sale of office	35,000.00					
4	Cash payments						
5	Purchase of equipment	2,320.00					
6	Purchase of office	30,000.00					
7							
8	Increase in cash	15,229.00					
9							
10	Change in cash balance						
11	(from Cash Transaction Summary)	$15,229.00					
12							

B8 — fx =SUM(CashReceipts)-SUM(CashPayments)

Cash receipts, in this case, are comprised of cash from operations and cash received from selling the office space. Cash outlays are comprised of the purchase of the new computer and the office space. The difference between the two, $15,229, represents the amount of cash generated by Marble Designs during the 12-month period, and should agree with the difference in the cash account between 1/31/02 and 1/31/03. Refer back to Figure 5.10: the difference between the ending balance of $17,783 and the beginning balance of $2,554 is $15,229, which agrees with the results of the cash flow analysis.

In reality, cash flow analysis is a much more complicated task than the relatively simple example provided here. There are many more transactions than were included in this example: the effect of taxes must be taken into account, accrued liabilities complicate the process, and such transactions as the issuance of stock, dividends, and long-term bonds affect the identification and calculation of cash flows. However, the example serves to illustrate the basic principles and the overall process of converting balance sheets and income statements into information about how a company creates and uses its cash resources.

Summary

In this chapter, you learned how to analyze working capital, its sources and uses, to move beyond the information in the balance sheet and income statement. Working capital is an important gauge of a company's financial health, and it can be hidden by the accrual basis used by other analyses.

This chapter also described how to analyze the flow of cash into, through, and out of a company as a result of its transactions. Because cash is the most liquid form of working capital, it is an important component of many financial ratios used by investors and potential creditors; you will learn more about these in Chapter 7, "Ratio Analysis." Cash flow analysis is also an important means of understanding the difference between such items as net income and actual receipts.

Further, the ways that a company uses its working capital, and in particular its cash, are good indicators of how well it manages its assets. They serve to highlight the choices of investments and dis-investments made every day by the company's management. Highlighted, those choices can give you insight into the way that management handles its responsibilities.

Part
I

Ch
5

Statement Analysis

Chapters 1 through 4 discussed the creation of income statements and balance sheets, and how to use them for reporting purposes. This chapter, as well as Chapter 7, "Ratio Analysis," describes how you can use the information in income statements and balance sheets to improve your insight into business operations.

Neither a particular dollar amount in a financial report, nor the report itself, stands on its own. The knowledge that a company's total operating expenses during 2001 were $250 million is not, by itself, very informative. To understand the meaning of that number, you have to know other figures such as gross profit and operating income. Similarly, although a balance sheet is fundamental to evaluating the financial condition of a company, it does not speak to questions such as these:

- Is the company's value increasing or decreasing over time?
- How do the company's current assets relate to its current liabilities?
- How well does the company's management use its resources to create economic value?
- How do the components of the company's assets, liabilities, and equity change over time?

The processes of statement analysis and ratio analysis provide you the contexts to make judgments like these. There are close relationships between the two. *Statement analysis* helps complete the picture of a company's operations, strategies and policies. *Ratio analysis* helps fill in the details of why a company's value is increasing or declining.

Fundamentally, statement analysis examines the relationships among items on an income statement or a balance sheet, and how they change over time. Ratio analysis focuses on certain relationships between individual numbers on a financial report.

At its heart, statement analysis depends on *common-sizing*, which converts the raw numbers to a common level of measurement.

Understanding a Report by Means of Common-Sizing

A common-sized report typically expresses every dollar category as a percentage of some other dollar category. Doing so enables you to more easily compare, for example, a company's present year with a prior year, or one company with another, or a company with an industry composite.

It's conventional, for example, to common size an income statement by dividing each entry by the total sales for the period covered by the statement. Doing so converts each dollar figure, from cost of goods sold to operating income to income taxes to operating expenses, to its percentage in terms of total sales.

The rationale for common-sizing in terms of total sales is that most of a company's activities depend on its revenues. The more the company sells, the greater its cost of goods sold. In a well-managed firm, greater revenues result in greater profits. And, although there are exceptional cases, a higher level of sales tends to cause a higher level of salaries. Because total sales exerts an effect on so many of the items in an income statement, a common-sized statement is usually based on total sales.

Using Common-Sized Income Statements

Figures 6.1 and 6.2 provide an example.

To convert the income statement shown in Figure 6.1 to a common-sized income statement based on total sales, follow these steps:

1. Highlight the worksheet range containing the entire statement: in Figure 6.1, this range is A1:C24.
2. Choose Edit, Copy.
3. Activate a new worksheet.
4. Choose Edit, Paste Special.

FIGURE 6.1
This Income Statement uses the regular dollar metric: it is not common sized.

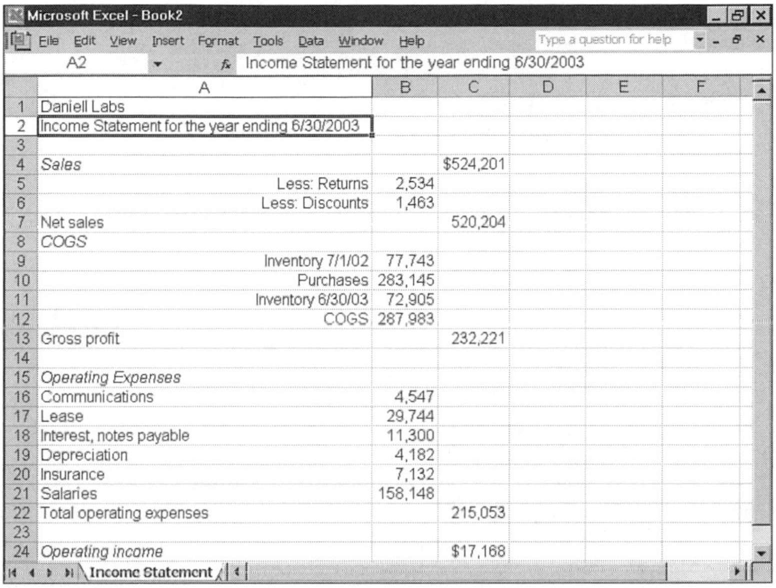

5. In the Paste Special dialog box, click Values in the Paste group box, and choose OK. This converts any formulas in the original income statement to values in the new worksheet.

6. Switch back to the original income statement. Highlight the cell that contains the value of total sales. In Figure 6.1, this is cell C4.

7. Choose Edit, Copy and switch back to the new worksheet.

8. Highlight the worksheet range containing the numbers in the entire statement; in Figure 6.2, this range is B4:C24.

9. Choose Edit, Paste Special.

10. In the Paste Special dialog box, click Divide in the Operation area, and choose OK. This divides all the values in the selected range by the value of the copied cell, Total Sales.

11. While the full range is still selected, choose Cells from the Format menu. In the Format Cells dialog box, click the Number tab. Select Percentage in the Category list box, adjust the number of Decimal Places, and choose OK.

TIP You might want to clear any cells in the range B1:C24 that now contain zero values. (The Skip Blanks option in the Paste Special dialog box refers to blanks in the range you are copying from, not in the range that you copy to.) Or, and perhaps better, you can select Tools, Options, choose the View tab, and clear the Zero Values checkbox. Clearing the cells removes the zero values from the worksheet; clearing the Zero Values checkbox just prevents them from showing.

Part

I

Ch

6

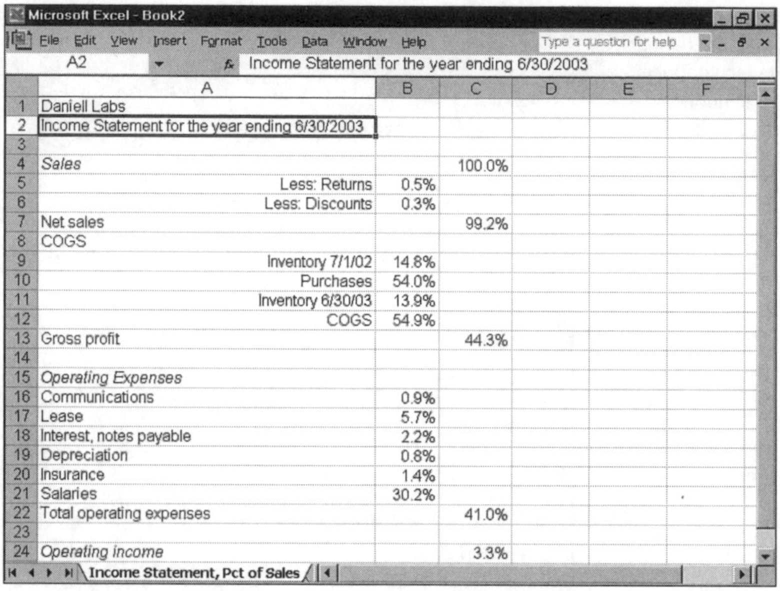

FIGURE 6.2
This Income Statement has been common sized on the basis of Total Sales.

	A	B	C	D	E	F
1	Daniell Labs					
2	Income Statement for the year ending 6/30/2003					
3						
4	*Sales*		100.0%			
5	Less: Returns	0.5%				
6	Less: Discounts	0.3%				
7	Net sales		99.2%			
8	COGS					
9	Inventory 7/1/02	14.8%				
10	Purchases	54.0%				
11	Inventory 6/30/03	13.9%				
12	COGS	54.9%				
13	Gross profit		44.3%			
14						
15	*Operating Expenses*					
16	Communications	0.9%				
17	Lease	5.7%				
18	Interest, notes payable	2.2%				
19	Depreciation	0.8%				
20	Insurance	1.4%				
21	Salaries	30.2%				
22	Total operating expenses		41.0%			
23						
24	*Operating income*		3.3%			

NOTE The reason that step 5, previously, recommends that you convert formulas on the income statement to values is that the subsequent Divide operation in step 10 does not work as intended (here) on a formula. For example, cell C7 in Figure 6.1 contains this formula:

=C4-B5-B6

If you copied this formula, and subsequently divided it by Total Sales, this formula would result:

=(C4-B5-B6)/544201

Because cells C4, B5, and B6 now contain percentages, this formula would return 0.00%, instead of the desired value of 99.27%.

Notice that, while the common-sized income statement in Figure 6.2 does not add any information to the raw dollar income statement, it makes it a little easier to answer some questions. For example, it's easy to see that the greatest cost incurred by Daniell Labs is its cost of goods sold (COGS). Although it's by no means unusual to find COGS around 50% of total sales, this alerts you that COGS is a good candidate for management attention in the search for greater profits.

Furthermore, if you have developed a feel for what a percentage of total sales *should* be in your business, the common-sized income statement makes it very easy to identify categories of income and expenses that are out of line.

Using Common-Sized Balance Sheets

You can do the same sort of analysis using a balance sheet. Figure 6.3 shows Daniell Labs' balance sheet, in both raw dollar format and common sized by Total Assets.

FIGURE 6.3
Balance sheets, as well as income statements, can be more informative when they have been common sized.

Microsoft Excel - Book2

A2 | Balance Sheet for the year ending 6/30/2003

	A	B	C	D	E	F
1	Daniell Labs					
2	Balance Sheet for the year ending 6/30/2003					
3						
4		Dollars			Percentage of Total Assets	
5	Cash		$9,544			8.94%
6	Accounts receivable		6,432			6.03%
7	Inventory		72,905			68.30%
8	Remaining insurance coverage		5,500			5.15%
9	Equipment		16,543			15.50%
10	Less: accumulated depreciation	4,182			3.92%	
11	Total assets		106,742			100.00%
12						
13	Liabilities					
14	Notes payable	12,409			11.63%	
15	Accounts payable	51,243			48.01%	
16	Total liabilities		63,652			59.63%
17						
18	Owner's equity					
19	Capital		43,090			40.37%
20	Total liabilities and owner's equity		$106,742			100.00%
21						
22						
23						
24						

Balance Sheet

Again, the use of component percentages in the common-sized balance sheet begins to answer some questions about how the company does business. You can immediately determine the relative importance of various assets and liabilities.

For example, Figure 6.3 immediately makes it clear that a very large percentage, over 68%, of the company's assets is in its inventory. This knowledge would probably cause you to focus on the firm's inventory management procedures. In a case like this, when you begin to analyze specific ratios (see Chapter 7), you might well begin with a careful look at the firm's inventory turns ratios.

The situation would, of course, be very different if Daniell Labs' inventory represented only 40% of its total assets. The point is that by looking at the component percentages in a common-sized financial report you can direct your attention immediately to sources of existing and impending problems.

Examining a common-sized balance sheet often gives you insight into a company's procedures for raising capital. By comparing the component percentages for short-term liabilities such as Accounts Payable, long-term liabilities such as Notes Payable, and Retained Earnings, you can determine how the company focuses its efforts to obtain resources. A relatively large component percentage for long-term Notes Payable, for example, would indicate a reliance on debt financing. On the other hand, a relatively large component percentage for Retained Earnings would suggest that a company relies on operating income to provide its resources.

Using Comparative Financial Statements

The advantages of using common-sizing become more apparent in comparative financial statements. Such statements display results side by side over time or across companies. Figure 6.4 shows a comparative income statement for Daniell Labs.

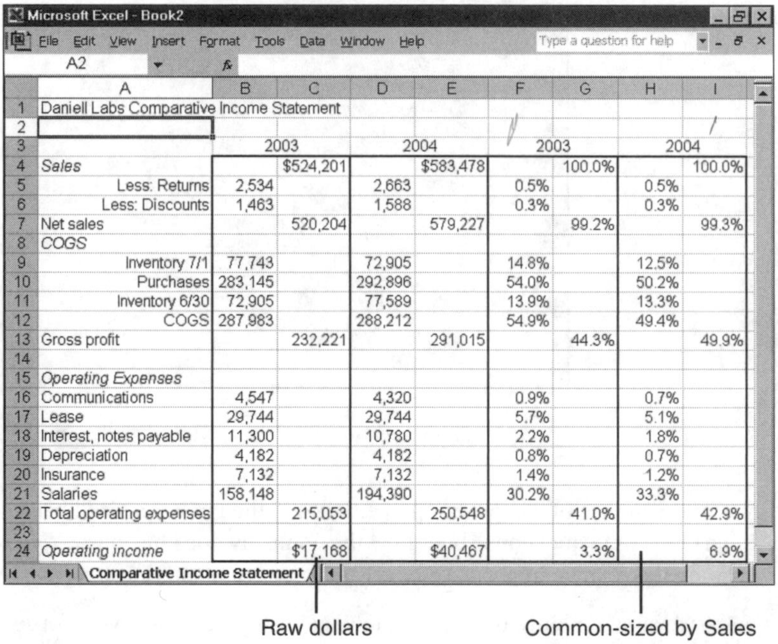

FIGURE 6.4
Comparative income statements, especially when common-sized, make it easier to assess year-to-year performance.

Raw dollars   Common-sized by Sales

	2003		2004		2003		2004	
Sales		$524,201		$583,478		100.0%		100.0%
Less: Returns	2,534		2,663		0.5%		0.5%	
Less: Discounts	1,463		1,588		0.3%		0.3%	
Net sales		520,204		579,227		99.2%		99.3%
COGS								
Inventory 7/1	77,743		72,905		14.8%		12.5%	
Purchases	283,145		292,896		54.0%		50.2%	
Inventory 6/30	72,905		77,589		13.9%		13.3%	
COGS	287,983		288,212		54.9%		49.4%	
Gross profit		232,221		291,015		44.3%		49.9%
Operating Expenses								
Communications	4,547		4,320		0.9%		0.7%	
Lease	29,744		29,744		5.7%		5.1%	
Interest, notes payable	11,300		10,780		2.2%		1.8%	
Depreciation	4,182		4,182		0.8%		0.7%	
Insurance	7,132		7,132		1.4%		1.2%	
Salaries	158,148		194,390		30.2%		33.3%	
Total operating expenses		215,053		250,548		41.0%		42.9%
Operating income		$17,168		$40,467		3.3%		6.9%

In Figure 6.4, the annual income statement for 2003 appears in columns B and C, and for 2004 in columns D and E. Focusing only on the firm's ending inventory dollar amounts (cells B11 and D11), you can tell that the amount of inventory has increased from the end of 2003 to the end of 2004. Initially, this tends to confirm your suspicion (from viewing the common-sized balance sheet) that Daniell Labs needs to tighten its inventory management procedures.

However, the common-sized income statements in columns F through I present a different picture. At the end of 2003, inventory amounted to 13.9% of total sales, whereas at the end of 2004 it amounts to 13.3% of total sales. Although you might not regard 0.6% as a sizable difference, at least the ending inventory levels are moving in the right direction, *when viewed in terms of total sales.* As sales increase (as they do from 2003 to 2004), you normally expect that inventory levels will increase, because management must allow for more contingencies in customers' requirements. Figure 6.4, however, shows that—relative to total sales—inventory levels decreased from 2003 to 2004. Inventory might still require further management attention, but there is some evidence that management has been taking steps to bring it under control.

Figure 6.4 also makes it apparent that Daniell Labs has been managing its profit levels more efficiently in 2004 than in 2003. Notice (cells F12 and H12) that as component percentages the cost of goods sold decreased during the two-year period, even though the raw dollar amounts increased slightly (compare cell B12 with cell D12). The decrease in the COGS percentage occurs because, although the dollars spent were virtually identical, the amount of total sales increased. This finding points to one of two conclusions: either Daniell Labs has increased its unit sales price while holding its unit COGS constant, or its production costs have fallen. Perhaps the company has obtained more favorable pricing from its suppliers, or reduced its labor costs, or has encountered some other favorable condition. Any of these could enable Daniell Labs to hold its unit sales price constant while its unit COGS decreases.

This effect also shows up in the company's gross profit margins (cells G13 and I13), which increase by 5.6% of sales from 2003 to 2004. Nearly the entire increase can be attributed to the change in the COGS percentage. And the greater gross profit margin flows down to the company's operating income, which increases by roughly 3.6% from 2003 to 2004.

The difference between the growth in the gross profit margin and the growth in operating income is due to the fact that, as component percentages, operating expenses did not rise as fast as did total sales. This effect emphasizes the importance of examining both the raw dollar statements and the common-sized statements.

This would not be clear if you looked only at the common-sized statements. By examining the raw dollar statements as well, you can tell what happened to the basis (total sales) of the component percentages. Doing so helps you better understand the context in which changes over time occur.

On the basis of the comparative income statements, you might conclude that business is proceeding satisfactorily for Daniell Labs. Figure 6.5, however, presents yet a different picture.

From 2003 to 2004, Total Assets (in dollars) are declining, as is Owner's Equity (in dollars and as a percent of Total Assets). At the same time, Accounts Payable is increasing. Two assets, Equipment and Remaining Insurance, are declining due to depreciation and the expiration of one year of prepaid insurance. These effects show up in both the raw dollar figures and in the common-sized balance sheet.

Particularly in view of the fact that operating income increased during the same period (refer to Figure 6.4), you should conclude that a working capital and cash flow analysis of the sort described in Chapter 5, "Working Capital and Cash Flow Analysis," is in order, so as to determine the uses that Daniell Labs made of its assets during 2004.

Part
I
Ch
6

FIGURE 6.5
Daniell Labs
Comparative Balance
Sheets for 2003 and
2004 show some ero-
sion in the company's
worth.

	A	B	C	D	E	F	G	H	I
1	Daniell Labs Comparative Balance Sheet								
2			Raw Dollars				Common Size (Total Assets)		
3			2003		2004		2003		2004
4			6/30/03		6/30/04		6/30/03		6/30/04
5	Cash		$9,544		$17,460		9%		16%
6	Accounts receivable		6,432		711		6%		1%
7	Inventory		72,905		77,589		68%		73%
8	Remaining insurance coverage		5,500		2,750		5%		3%
9	Equipment		16,543		16,543		15%		16%
10	Less: accumulated depreciation	4,182		8,364		4%		8%	
11	Total assets		106,742		106,689		100%		100%
12									
13	Liabilities								
14	Notes payable	12,409		6,733		12%		6%	
15	Accounts payable	51,243		68,946		48%		65%	
16	Total liabilities		63,652		75,679		60%		71%
17									
18	Owner's equity								
19	Capital		43,090		31,010		40%		29%
20	Total liabilities and owner's equity		$106,742		$106,689		100%		100%
21									
22									
23									
24									

Using Dollar and Percent Changes in Statement Analysis

Another way of viewing changes over time in income statements and balance sheets is by means of dollar changes and percentage changes (see Figure 6.6). To express changes over time in terms of dollars, you consolidate two reports into one by showing—for each category—the difference in dollars between the two. Or you might decide to consolidate the information by dividing each category in one report by the same category in the other. This expresses changes over time as percentages.

Assessing the Financial Statements

It's nearly always satisfying for an owner to view changes in dollar amounts such as those shown in Cash and Accounts Receivable from 2002 to 2003. Column H, which contains the difference in each classification from the end of the first year to the end of the second, shows that the company's assets increased dramatically during that period.

It is true that a major portion of the increase in assets was paid for by means of the acquisition of debt (Notes Payable and Accounts Payable), but it is also true that the amount of the increase in Total Assets is larger than the increase in debt.

Furthermore, including information about 2002 helps to put the changes from 2003 to 2004 (refer to Figure 6.5) in a slightly longer perspective. Viewed in the context of the large increases in assets and equity that occurred in 2003, the decreases in assets and increases in liabilities that occurred in 2004 (see column I of Figure 6.6) do not appear as threatening.

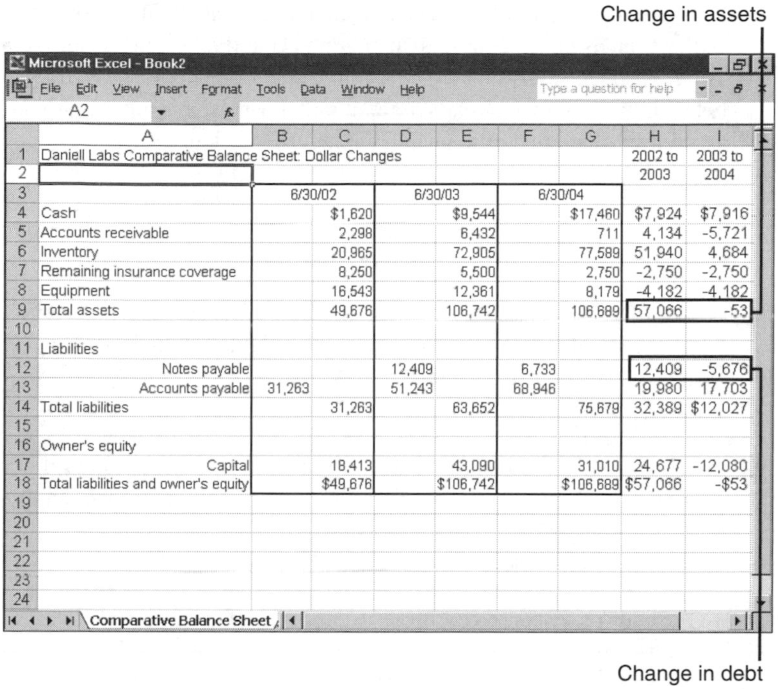

Change in assets

FIGURE 6.6
With comparative balance sheets and income statements, you can better focus on changes over time by calculating year-to-year differences.

But a better understanding yet of Daniell Labs' business operations is available from an examination of percentage changes (see Figure 6.7).

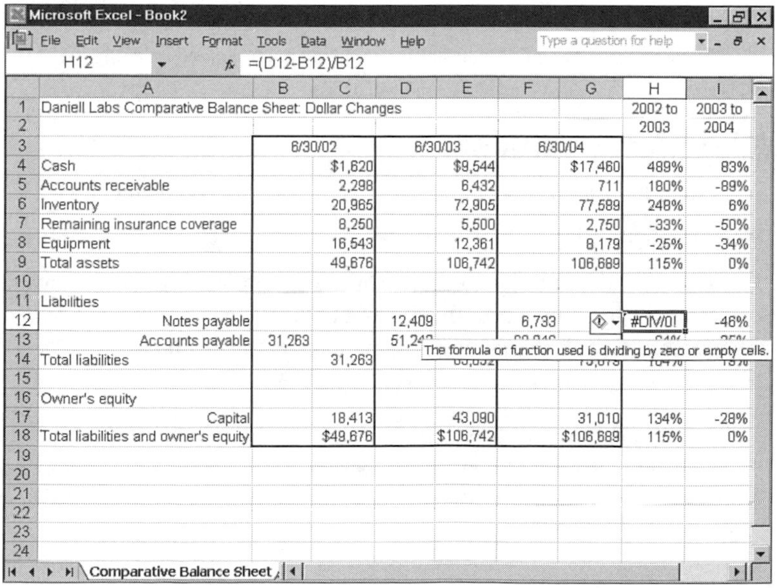

Change in debt

FIGURE 6.7
You can obtain further perspective on changes in financial position by means of ratios that represent percentage of change.

Part
I

Ch
6

In Figure 6.7, the year-to-year changes in each statement classification are shown as percents, rather than as dollar amounts, in columns H and I. The percents are *not* simple ratios, such as Total Assets for 2003 divided by Total Assets for 2002. Instead, they are the difference between a comparison year's amount and a base year's amount, divided by the base year's amount. For example, the formula in cell H5 of Figure 6.7 is

```
=(E5-C5)/C5
```

This represents the difference between 2003's Accounts Receivable and 2002's Accounts Receivable, expressed as a percentage of 2002's Accounts Receivable.

Notice that each year's balance sheet information occupies two columns, while the information on percentage changes occupies one column for each pair of years. This means that once you have entered this formula:

```
=(E5-C5)/C5
```

in cell H5, you cannot simply copy and paste it into cell I5 to get the analogous percentage change from 2003 to 2004. If you did so, the relative references in the formula would show up in I5 as

```
=(F5-D5)/D5
```

and would return the Excel error value #DIV/0!, because cell D5 is empty.

TIP

To overcome this relative referencing problem, copy the formula to the cell that will adjust the references properly. In this case, you could copy cell H5 to cell J5, so that the references would adjust to

```
=(G5-E5)/E5
```

Then, use either Edit, Cut and Edit, Paste, or use your mouse pointer to drag and drop the formula in J5 back into I5. Neither of these two operations is sensitive to relative references in the way that either Edit, Copy and Edit, Paste, or AutoFill is. This is just a matter of first using Copy to adjust the references properly, and then using Cut to adjust the formula's location.

Handling Error Values

Also in Figure 6.7, notice the Excel error value #DIV/0! in cell H12. Its formula is

```
=(D12-B12)/B12
```

Because cell B12 is a zero value (there is no amount for Notes Payable in 2002), the formula results in an error due to the attempt to divide by zero. You can avoid this type of error by means of Excel's IF statement. For example, the formula you enter in H12 might be:

```
=IF(B12<>0,(D12-B12)/B12,"")
```

This formula would cause Excel to examine the value in cell B12. If it does not equal zero, the cell would display the appropriate percentage change. If B12 does equal zero, the cell would display nothing, as indicated by the null string defined by the pair of empty quotation marks.

If you're an experienced user of Excel, comfortable with versions prior to Excel 2002, the additional error information shown in Figure 6.7 probably looks unfamiliar to you. In Excel 2002, when you induce an error value such as #DIV/0! or #NUM!, Excel inserts a triangle in the cell's upper-left corner, much like a comment indicator in a cell's upper-right corner.

If you then select that cell, Excel displays a control next to the error value. The control has an icon of an exclamation point on a traffic caution sign. If you move your screen pointer over the icon a drop-down arrow appears. If you leave the screen pointer there for a couple of seconds, you will also see a screen tip that explains the error. In Figure 6.7, that tip says, "The formula or function used is dividing by zero or empty cells."

If you click the drop-down arrow, you see a menu of actions that you can take. The list of menu items varies with the type of error value that has occurred. In the case of division by zero, the menu items include:

- *Help on This Error.* Click this item to see Help documentation that explains the error value and how to correct it.
- *Show Calculation Steps.* Clicking this item invokes the Audit Formula dialog box, also available from the main worksheet menu by choosing Tools, Formula Auditing, Evaluate Formula.
- *Ignore Error.* This item removes the error indicator from the cell and the warning icon next to it. You can change your mind later by choosing Tools, Options, clicking the Error Checking tab, and clicking the Reset Ignored Errors button.
- *Edit in Formula Bar.* This item just activates the Formula Bar so that you can change the formula, presumably to avoid an error value.
- *Error Checking Options.* Use this item to display the dialog box that you usually display by choosing Tools, Options, and clicking the Error Checking tab.
- *Show Formula Auditing Toolbar.* This toolbar, also available by choosing View, Toolbars, has buttons that help you determine what's going on with a formula. Suppose that C5 is the active cell. If you click the Auditing Toolbar's Trace Dependents button, it will display arrows that point from cell C5 to any cells containing formulas that refer to cell C5.

Evaluating Percentage Changes

Back to the discussion of the perspective that percentage changes can provide. Notice that in cells H8 and I8 of Figure 6.6, the raw dollar changes from year to year are constant. This is because Daniell Labs is using straight-line depreciation on its equipment, and this method results in a constant depreciation figure from period to period. Therefore, the book value of the firm's equipment declines by a constant $4,182 during each year. (See Chapter 16, "Fixed Assets," for a full discussion of depreciation methods in Excel.)

However, cells H8 and I8 of Figure 6.7 show that the decrease in the value of the equipment is accelerating from year to year, from a loss of 25% during 2002–2003 to a loss of 34% during 2003–2004. The reason for this, of course, is that each percentage difference uses a different base. As the size of that base decreases from 2002 (cell C8) to 2003 (cell E8), the formula's denominator decreases, and the size of the ratio increases.

In this case, the difference between a loss in value of –25% to –34% is not drastic, especially considering the associated, and rather small, raw dollar differences. If you were to observe a very large decrease in equipment valuation, you might want to check into the depreciation methods being used. The company might employ a very aggressive, accelerated depreciation method, which would tend to reduce its taxable income markedly while the equipment was still fairly new.

Alternatively, such a decrease in equipment valuation might suggest that the company has sold or written off a significant portion of its equipment. Did it do so in the normal course of operations, because the equipment had become obsolete? In that case, was the equipment replaced? At a lower cost? Or did the company sell the equipment to raise needed cash?

Examining period-to-period changes in balance sheets and income statements, measured both in dollar amounts and as percentage changes, can provide you with useful information about how a company is going about the management of its operations and financial position.

Common-Sizing for Variance Analysis

The term *variance analysis*, in the context of finance and accounting, means the examination of differences between one set of numbers and another. For example, if your company's actual total salaries during the first quarter differ from its budgeted first quarter salaries, there is a variance between the budget and the actual results.

Common-sizing can help you do variance analysis more quickly and easily. Speed and facility in variance analysis are particularly important, because companies spend an enormous amount of time and effort examining the differences between their plans and their actual results and between prior and current results. Consider the following case study on New Way Tours, a travel agency.

Case Study: New Way Tours

New Way Tours is a small business with five employees, two of whom work part-time. It specializes in planning and arranging for ski vacations; therefore, its business is highly seasonal, with the majority of its revenues occurring during the winter months.

New Way's owner, Gena Anderson, has prepared an operating budget for 2004, based on past information about revenues and operating expenses during the most recent five-year period (see Figure 6.8).

FIGURE 6.8
New Way Tours' operating budget for 2004.

	A	B	C	D	E	F	G	H	I	J	K	L	M
1		Jan	Feb	Mar	Apr	May	Jun	Jul	Aug	Sep	Oct	Nov	Dec
2	Gross profit	42589	53765	38846	15214	20512	21213	20674	12698	11854	12779	55155	52702
3	Salaries	20000	20000	20000	17500	17500	17500	17500	17500	17500	17500	20000	20000
4	Payroll taxes	5040	5040	5040	4410	4410	4410	4410	4410	4410	4410	5040	5040
5	Lease	1000	1000	1000	1000	1000	1000	1000	1000	1000	1000	1000	1000
6	Phone	500	500	500	500	500	500	500	500	500	500	500	500
7	Supplies	300	300	300	300	300	300	300	300	300	300	300	200
8	Insurance	500	500	500	500	500	500	500	500	500	500	500	500
9	Total OpEx	27340	27340	27340	24210	24210	24210	24210	24210	24210	24210	27340	27240
10	EBITDA	15249	26425	11506	-8996	-3698	-2997	-3536	-11512	-12356	-11431	27815	25462
11													
12	Gross profit	100%	100%	100%	100%	100%	100%	100%	100%	100%	100%	100%	100%
13	Salaries	47%	37%	51%	115%	85%	82%	85%	138%	148%	137%	36%	38%
14	Payroll taxes	12%	9%	13%	29%	21%	21%	21%	35%	37%	35%	9%	10%
15	Lease	2%	2%	3%	7%	5%	5%	5%	8%	8%	8%	2%	2%
16	Phone	1%	1%	1%	3%	2%	2%	2%	4%	4%	4%	1%	1%
17	Supplies	1%	1%	1%	2%	1%	1%	1%	2%	3%	2%	1%	0%
18	Insurance	1%	1%	1%	3%	2%	2%	2%	4%	4%	4%	1%	1%
19	Total OpEx	64%	51%	70%	159%	118%	114%	117%	191%	204%	189%	50%	52%
20	EBITDA	36%	49%	30%	-59%	-18%	-14%	-17%	-91%	-104%	-89%	50%	48%

Figure 6.8 shows, for each month in 2004, New Way's anticipated gross profit (its revenues less its sales discounts and any purchases subsequently canceled by its customers) based on average monthly results from 1999 through 2003.

TIP

Notice cells B1:M1 in Figure 6.8, which show the names of the months of the year in abbreviated form. Excel provides these names as a custom list; other predefined custom lists include months of the year (spelled out in full) and days of the week (abbreviated and spelled out). You can fill a range of cells with these values by typing, say, **Jan** in one cell, and then using AutoFill by dragging the cell's fill handle right or left, up or down. You can define your own custom lists by choosing Tools, Options and clicking the Custom Lists tab.

Figure 6.8 also shows the operating expenses (abbreviated "OpEx" in cells A9 and A19) for each month. The major operating expense is Salaries, which is higher during the winter than during the summer and varies with the number of hours worked by Anderson's two part-time employees. Payroll tax dollars vary with the monthly salaries. The cost of New Way's lease and insurance are expected to be constant throughout the year. Telephone expenses and office supplies are difficult to estimate on a monthly basis, and in any event are small enough in relation to gross profit that making a constant monthly estimate is a reasonable approach.

Row 9 shows the total of the monthly operating expenses, and row 10 shows the anticipated Earnings Before Interest, Taxes, Depreciation, and Amortization (EBITDA).

Rows 12 through 20 show the budget, common sized by Gross Profit: each entry in B12:M20 is the classification's percentage of that month's Gross Profit. Anderson can make some use

Part

I

Ch

6

of this common-sized information in isolation. For example, as noted previously, most of New Way's business occurs during the winter, and Anderson expects to lose money during the warmer months. This expectation is reflected in the fact that, from April through October, the total budgeted operating expenses are greater than 100% of gross profit. Anderson has made the business decision that it is more important to keep three experienced employees year around than to reduce the staff further during her business's slow months.

But it is the process of comparing the budgeted information with the actual results that helps to bring matters into focus (see Figure 6.9).

FIGURE 6.9
New Way Tours' actual financial results for 2004 are much worse than its budget antici-pated.

	A	B	C	D	E	F	G	H	I
1		Jan	Feb	Mar	Apr	May	Jun		
2	Gross profit	32,845	46,208	21,710	12,607	18,938	18,268		
3	Salaries	27,520	22,701	25,984	22,618	16,761	16,783		
4	Payroll taxes	6,935	5,721	6,548	5,700	4,224	4,229		
5	Lease	1,000	1,000	1,000	1,000	1,000	1,000		
6	Phone	562	737	608	678	486	259		
7	Supplies	142	263	132	299	106	158		
8	Insurance	500	500	500	500	500	500		
9	Total OpEx	36,659	30,922	34,772	30,795	23,077	22,929		
10	EBITDA: Actual	-3,814	15,286	-13,062	-18,188	-4,139	-4,661		
11	EBITDA: Plan	15,249	26,425	11,506	-8,996	-3,698	-2,997		
12									
13	Gross profit	100%	100%	100%	100%	100%	100%		
14	Salaries	84%	49%	120%	179%	89%	92%		
15	Payroll taxes	21%	12%	30%	45%	22%	23%		
16	Lease	3%	2%	5%	8%	5%	5%		
17	Phone	2%	2%	3%	5%	3%	1%		
18	Supplies	0%	1%	1%	2%	1%	1%		
19	Insurance	2%	1%	2%	4%	3%	3%		
20	Total OpEx	112%	67%	160%	244%	122%	126%		
21	EBITDA: Actual	-12%	33%	-60%	-144%	-22%	-26%		
22	EBITDA: Plan	46%	57%	53%	-71%	-20%	-16%		
23									

Figure 6.9 shows New Way Tours' actual financial results for the first two quarters of 2004. The planned, monthly EBITDA from Figure 6.8 is shown as well. January has been a disas-trous month. Besides a gross profit that is nearly $10,000 less than projected in the budget, Anderson has paid over $7,500 more in salaries than budgeted, in a failed attempt to increase revenues for the month. February is better, but the subsequent four months continue the pat-tern that began in January.

Anderson can easily perform this variance analysis by checking the common-sized EBITDA values in rows 21 and 22 of Figure 6.9. For January through June, EBITDA as a percentage of gross profit is less than budgeted, and if business does not turn around during the second half of the year New Way Tours will lose money for the year. Anderson will either have to find a way to increase gross profits or to decrease her operating expenses. Another way to view the actuals for the first six months of 2004, in the context of the 2004 budget, is to subtract the budgeted gross profit dollars from the actual gross profit dollars; the same can be done for budgeted and actual operating expenses. Anderson can also calculate the ratio of the actual-to-budgeted figures (see Figure 6.10).

FIGURE 6.10
Variances between budgets and actual results, expressed in both dollar amounts and as ratios, often help point to problems in a company's operations.

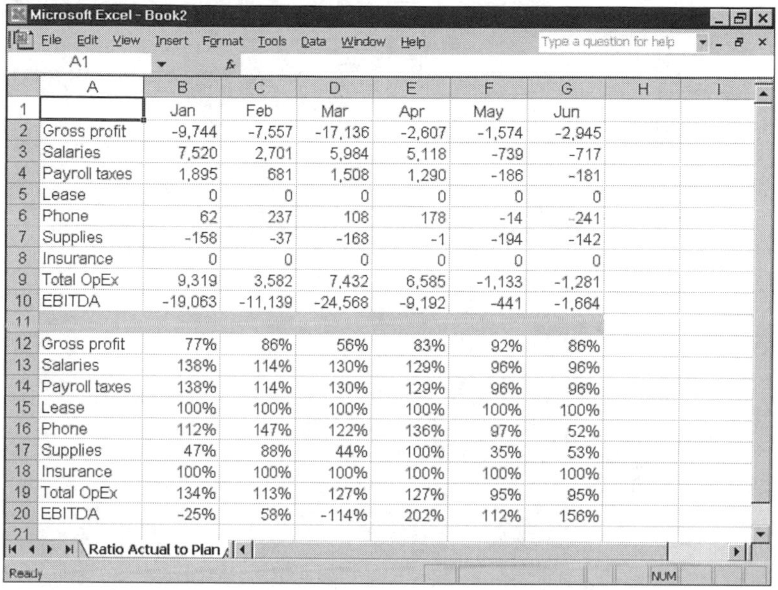

	A	B	C	D	E	F	G	H	I
1		Jan	Feb	Mar	Apr	May	Jun		
2	Gross profit	-9,744	-7,557	-17,136	-2,607	-1,574	-2,945		
3	Salaries	7,520	2,701	5,984	5,118	-739	-717		
4	Payroll taxes	1,895	681	1,508	1,290	-186	-181		
5	Lease	0	0	0	0	0	0		
6	Phone	62	237	108	178	-14	-241		
7	Supplies	-158	-37	-168	-1	-194	-142		
8	Insurance	0	0	0	0	0	0		
9	Total OpEx	9,319	3,582	7,432	6,585	-1,133	-1,281		
10	EBITDA	-19,063	-11,139	-24,568	-9,192	-441	-1,664		
11									
12	Gross profit	77%	86%	56%	83%	92%	86%		
13	Salaries	138%	114%	130%	129%	96%	96%		
14	Payroll taxes	138%	114%	130%	129%	96%	96%		
15	Lease	100%	100%	100%	100%	100%	100%		
16	Phone	112%	147%	122%	136%	97%	52%		
17	Supplies	47%	88%	44%	100%	35%	53%		
18	Insurance	100%	100%	100%	100%	100%	100%		
19	Total OpEx	134%	113%	127%	127%	95%	95%		
20	EBITDA	-25%	58%	-114%	202%	112%	156%		

Notice that for each month, the dollar differences for Gross Profit are negative, and for operating expenses they are positive (the formulas subtract the budgeted figures from the actual figures). These dollar differences help Anderson understand how much money is being lost. The ratios (actuals divided by budgeted figures) put the losses into a percentage context. For example, the actual gross profit during January is 77% of the budgeted figure, and the actual salaries paid for January are 138% of the budgeted amount.

These variance analyses, useful as they are, do not present the full picture. For example, because the gross profit varies from month to month, Anderson cannot directly compare the actual-to-budget ratios for January with the actual-to-budget ratios for February: the basis differs across months. One way to make direct comparisons is to take ratios of the ratios (see Figure 6.11).

The formula for the figure of 178% in cell B4 of Figure 6.11 is

```
='Variance, Actual vs. Plan'!B14/'Operating Budget'!B13
```

N O T E   Notice in the preceding formula that the cell references B14 and B13 are preceded by the names of the sheets that contain those cells.

Under some conditions, Excel encloses the sheet name in single quotes when it is used in a reference or in a defined name. These conditions include at least one space in the sheet name, one of the special characters (such as %) that is allowed in the sheet names, and when the sheet names begin with a numeral.

In the preceding formula, both sheet names contain spaces, so Excel inserts the single quote marks around them.

Part

I

Ch

6

FIGURE 6.11

New Way Tours' variance ratios for the first half of 2004 put the percentages on a common basis.

	A	B	C	D	E	F	G	H	I	J
		Jan	Feb	Mar	Apr	May	Jun			
1										
2	Gross profit	100%	100%	100%	100%	100%	100%			
3										
4	Salaries	178%	132%	232%	156%	104%	111%			
5	Payroll taxes	178%	132%	232%	156%	104%	111%			
6	Lease	130%	116%	179%	121%	108%	116%			
7	Phone	146%	172%	218%	164%	105%	60%			
8	Supplies	61%	102%	79%	120%	38%	61%			
9	Insurance	130%	116%	179%	121%	108%	116%			
10										
11	Total OpEx	174%	132%	228%	154%	103%	110%			
12										
13	EBITDA	130%	116%	179%	121%	108%	116%			

Ratio (Actual) to Ratio (Plan)

The numerator of this ratio is the percentage of January's actual gross profit accounted for by January's actual salaries paid. The denominator is the percentage of January's budgeted gross profit accounted for by January's budgeted salaries. Therefore, for the month of January, the actual salary expense ratio was nearly twice the budgeted salary expense ratio.

This analysis places the variance for expenses into the context of the shifting gross profit figures, which are equalized by taking the ratio of the ratios. Notice that the ratio of the actual gross profit percentage to the budgeted gross profit percentage is, in each month, 100%. Thus, Anderson can tell that, regardless of the actual monthly gross profit, her firm's actual expense levels are running well ahead of its budgeted expense levels.

The case study on New Way Tours discussed one basic kind of variance analysis: actuals to budget. This sort of analysis is the one done most frequently, but there are other types of variance analysis that you can perform.

For example, you might analyze the differences between your year-to-date actuals and your current estimate. A *current estimate* is a type of budget. During the year, you revise and update your budget for the current year to take account of changes in the assumptions that you used to build your initial budget. It's useful, then, to do variance analysis on the year-to-date actuals with the current estimate.

It's also helpful to do variance analysis on year-to-date actuals with the actuals from the prior year. Yet another form of variance analysis involves a different sort of common-sizing: expressing a statement's data in terms of headcount.

Common-Sizing by Headcount

Headcount, of course, refers to the number of people who are on the payroll at any given time. Particularly if you are in the midst of a downsizing (or, euphemistically, "rightsizing") situation, it is useful to common size on the basis of headcount. Doing so does not result in the type of information shown by earlier figures in this chapter, where the basis was revenue or assets and the result was a percentage of revenue or assets. In contrast, common-sizing on the basis of headcount usually results in some number of dollars per employee (see Figure 6.12).

FIGURE 6.12

New Way Tours' actual results for 2004, common sized by headcount, express operating expenses as dollars spent per employee.

	A	B	C	D	E	F	G	H	I
		Jan	Feb	Mar	Apr	May	Jun		
1									
2	Headcount	5	5	5	5	3	3		
3	Gross profit	32,845	46,208	21,710	12,607	18,938	18,268		
4	Salaries	27,520	22,701	25,984	22,618	16,761	16,783		
5	Payroll taxes	6,935	5,721	6,548	5,700	4,224	4,229		
6	Lease	1,000	1,000	1,000	1,000	1,000	1,000		
7	Phone	562	737	608	678	486	259		
8	Supplies	142	263	132	299	106	158		
9	Insurance	500	500	500	500	500	500		
10	Total OpEx	36,659	30,922	34,772	30,795	23,077	22,929		
11	EBITDA: Actual	-3,814	15,286	-13,062	-18,188	-4,139	-4,661		
12	EBITDA: Plan	15,249	26,425	11,506	-8,996	-3,698	-2,997		
13									
14	Gross profit	6,569	9,242	4,342	2,521	6,313	6,089		
15	Salaries	5,504	4,540	5,197	4,524	5,587	5,594		
16	Payroll taxes	1,387	1,144	1,310	1,140	1,408	1,410		
17	Lease	200	200	200	200	333	333		
18	Phone	112	147	122	136	162	86		
19	Supplies	28	53	26	60	35	53		
20	Insurance	100	100	100	100	167	167		
21	Total OpEx	7,332	6,184	6,954	6,159	7,692	7,643		
22	EBITDA: Actual	-763	3,057	-2,612	-3,638	-1,380	-1,554		
23	EBITDA: Plan	3,050	5,285	2,301	-1,799	-1,233	-999		

Cell reference: B14 =B3/B$2

Rows 14 through 23 of Figure 6.12 show the actuals for January through June (found in rows 1 through 12), divided by the number of employees on payroll for each month (headcount, shown in row 2). This range makes it clear that the fixed expenses, such as those for the office lease and insurance, vary on a per-employee basis as the headcount changes. Other expenses, particularly salaries and payroll taxes, vary almost directly with headcount.

If gross profit and an operating income figure such as EBITDA are *not* sensitive to headcount, while such major expense classifications as salaries *are* sensitive, then there can be a compelling business reason to reduce the number of employees. For example, if New Way Tours can expect roughly the same level of revenue regardless of its headcount, Gena Anderson should give serious thought to reducing the number of employees.

Of course, doing so can have unanticipated consequences. It might be that, while increasing headcount does not increase gross profit, decreasing headcount below some minimum level results in poor customer service—which is guaranteed, sooner or later, to reduce gross profit.

Part

I

Ch

6

On the other hand, if headcount is directly related to gross profit, there might well be an argument for increasing headcount, particularly if the business uses some method of direct sales. The trick is to increase the number of productive salespeople, and hold steady the number of staff who contribute only to expenses, not to gross profit. This process is tricky because, in most cases, the greater the gross profit the larger the number of staff required to support after-sale processes.

Suppose, however, that Anderson believes that she can convert the responsibilities of three of her current full-time staff from both sales and staff functions to sales only. She also considers hiring one additional salesperson. She believes that if these employees are free to perform a sales role only, instead of both revenue-producing activities and support activities, each salesperson can generate an average of $13,138 in gross profit per month instead of January's figure of $6,569. The remaining employees will devote 100% of their time to performing support activities. This projection is shown in Figure 6.13.

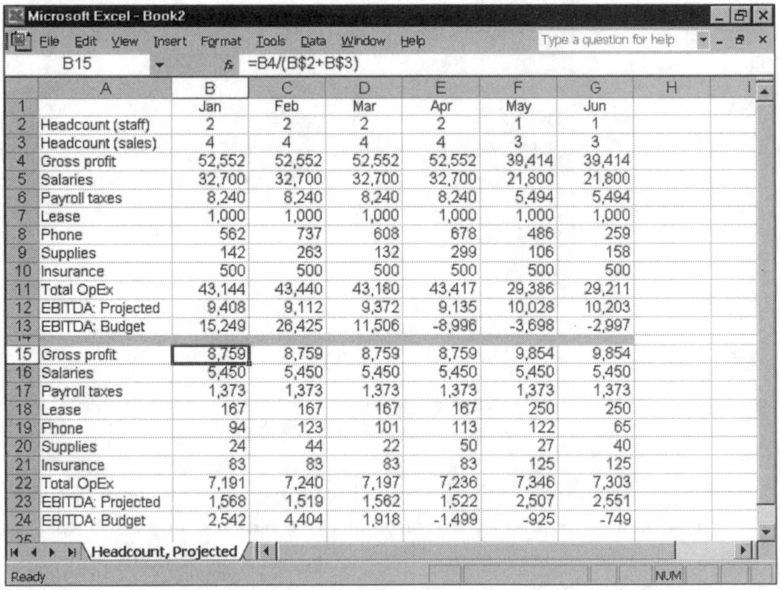

	A	B	C	D	E	F	G
1		Jan	Feb	Mar	Apr	May	Jun
2	Headcount (staff)	2	2	2	2	1	1
3	Headcount (sales)	4	4	4	4	3	3
4	Gross profit	52,552	52,552	52,552	52,552	39,414	39,414
5	Salaries	32,700	32,700	32,700	32,700	21,800	21,800
6	Payroll taxes	8,240	8,240	8,240	8,240	5,494	5,494
7	Lease	1,000	1,000	1,000	1,000	1,000	1,000
8	Phone	562	737	608	678	486	259
9	Supplies	142	263	132	299	106	158
10	Insurance	500	500	500	500	500	500
11	Total OpEx	43,144	43,440	43,180	43,417	29,386	29,211
12	EBITDA: Projected	9,408	9,112	9,372	9,135	10,028	10,203
13	EBITDA: Budget	15,249	26,425	11,506	-8,996	-3,698	-2,997
15	Gross profit	8,759	8,759	8,759	8,759	9,854	9,854
16	Salaries	5,450	5,450	5,450	5,450	5,450	5,450
17	Payroll taxes	1,373	1,373	1,373	1,373	1,373	1,373
18	Lease	167	167	167	167	250	250
19	Phone	94	123	101	113	122	65
20	Supplies	24	44	22	50	27	40
21	Insurance	83	83	83	83	125	125
22	Total OpEx	7,191	7,240	7,197	7,236	7,346	7,303
23	EBITDA: Projected	1,568	1,519	1,562	1,522	2,507	2,551
24	EBITDA: Budget	2,542	4,404	1,918	-1,499	-925	-749

FIGURE 6.13
New Way Tours' 2004 projections common sized by new headcount.

Anderson obtains the dollar figures for Gross Profit, in row 4 of Figure 6.13, by multiplying the Sales headcount in row 3 by her assumed gross profit level of $13,138 per salesperson. She also assumes that her average salary per employee will be $5,450. Restated, these assumptions are:

- Both total gross profit and average gross profit are sensitive to the number of sales employees.

■ Total salary expense is sensitive to the total number of employees, but average salary expense is constant.

The result, if Anderson's assumptions pay off, is that she can actually *increase* total headcount and cause New Way Tours' EBITDA to turn positive, even during its traditionally money-losing summer months. The assumptions involved are optimistic—particularly the notion that making some employees full-time salespeople will double the per-employee gross profit. But even if the per-employee increase in gross profit is only 50%, the results would increase the profit in good months, and reduce the loss in bad months.

N O T E This sort of headcount analysis is closely related to the concept of *leverage*, which is discussed in greater detail in Chapter 14, "Planning Profits." The common ground between leverage and common-sizing on the basis of headcount is that you seek to keep certain costs constant as variable revenues increase. ■

In large corporations, common-size analysis on the basis of headcount is done frequently and is especially tricky. It often happens that one division reduces its headcount so as to decrease its expenses, hoping that as it does so its revenues will not suffer. It can also happen that the employees who leave that division find employment in another division of the same large corporation: usually, one that is not currently under pressure to reduce its expenses.

The net result is that, although one division might improve its profitability through a reduction in expenses, another division's profitability suffers because of an increase in expenses. Then, the corporation, considered as a whole, has probably not improved its profitability. However, it has managed to disrupt people's lives, and probably to increase costs, such as those for training, that do not directly produce revenue.

Therefore, when divisions report that they have reduced headcount and consequently increased their profitability, it is incumbent on them to estimate the effect of doing so on the corporation as a whole. Although this estimate is often a difficult task, it is a necessary ingredient of an accurate estimate of the effects of their analysis and consequent actions.

Summary

In this chapter, you have learned some of the basic techniques of statement analysis, including variance analysis and common-sizing according to bases such as revenues, total assets, and headcount.

These are global techniques: that is, the results can serve to direct your attention to obstacles to your company's profitability, but they do not provide you as much specific information about problems as you might want. Chapter 7 discusses the particular ratios that you often want to calculate to obtain highly targeted information about your company's profitability and overall financial condition.

Part
I

Ch
6

Ratio Analysis

In earlier chapters of this book, you learned about various indicators of a company's financial condition. Quantities and values such as current assets, inventory levels, sales, and accounts receivable all help you understand how much money a company has, how much it owes, and its profitability.

These numbers can be informative if you happen to have intimate knowledge of the company itself. Suppose, for example, that you work for a company that today has $2 million worth of materials in its finished goods inventory. In that case, you probably know whether that's an acceptable figure, whether it's so low that the company will have difficulty delivering the products that it sells, or whether it's so high that the company might need to slow down its production rate. Because you are familiar with the company and its operations, you have a context to help interpret that $2 million figure.

But if you aren't familiar with the company, $2 million is just a number: it has no context to help you interpret it. Knowing that the company has $2 million worth of finished goods in stock tells you nothing about whether the company is doing well, poorly, or whether business is as usual.

However, if you also happened to know the amount of the company's current assets and current liabilities, you could quickly create a useful insight into the company's current financial situation. This formula

```
(Current Assets - Inventory)/(Current Liabilities)
```

would tell you how liquid the company is in the short term. This formula returns the *quick ratio*. If the company's current assets are $4 million and its current liabilities are $1 million, the formula would return

```
($4 million - $2 million)/($1 million) = 2
```

and the company's quick ratio is 2. The company's quickly accessible assets are twice its short-term liabilities: it is liquid.

N O T E Although inventory is part of current assets, it can take longer to convert inventory to cash than other current assets. So this formula removes the value of inventory to quantify quickly accessible assets. See this chapter's section on the quick ratio for more information. ◼

But if the company's current assets are $2.5 million, the formula would return:

```
($2.5 million - $2 million)/($1 million) = 0.5
```

The company's quickly accessible assets are only half its short-term liabilities.

A prospective employee would probably have a different attitude toward the company depending on whether the result of that formula is 2.0 or 0.5. If the value is 2.0, you would be more confident that your paycheck wouldn't bounce. As a prospective stockholder, you would be more confident of receiving a dividend check if the value is 2. As the company's CEO, you would have a meeting with the production and sales managers if the value is 0.5, and the meeting would probably be a testy one.

Of course, the value of the quick ratio does not depend solely on how well the company is managing its assets and liabilities. The ratio's value also depends on other considerations such as what business sector the company belongs to and how well that business sector is doing in the present economy. And companies in growth industries are expected to have smaller quick ratios than companies in mature industries. Too much cash on hand can mean that the company isn't using its assets to effectively take advantage of growth conditions.

Your evaluation of the quick ratio's value would take these considerations into account. You would also want to know how that ratio has behaved in the past: if the ratio has been consistently increasing, your confidence in the company's management and its financial structure would be greater than if it has been sliding for some time.

Ratios such as the quick ratio can tell you a great deal about a company's health, and relationships among ratios can help you locate sources of concern in the way a company is run. This chapter describes some of the most important ratios—those that are frequently published in financial reports and in commercially available data sources—as well as how to interpret them to determine a company's profit outlook.

Interpreting Industry Averages and Trends

Evaluating a ratio that describes a particular company in terms of the industry average for that ratio can be informative, but it can also be misleading. Consider one commonly reported indicator, the Price/Earnings (P/E) ratio.

Suppose that you know, from examining stock exchange tables in the newspaper or online or from some other source, that the P/E is 10 for a communications firm that you have some interest in. This means that stock in the company presently sells for 10 times its earnings. Perhaps you also know, by information obtained from a commercial service that the average P/E for the telecommunications industry is 15. At first glance, 10 looks like a good P/E, compared to the industry average: in terms of earnings, it is only two-thirds as expensive as other such stocks.

And 10 might be a good P/E ratio. However, there are various ways that this comparison can mislead you, as the next section illustrates.

Comparing Ratios Within Industries

For example, during the 1980s and 1990s, the telecommunications industry changed quickly and dramatically. Companies that once provided little more than basic telephone service aggressively entered new fields such as data communications, wireless communications, cable TV, financial and other business services, and electronic advertising.

These firms also entered into partnerships with companies such as software developers and firms that provide the programming that you see on television and in theaters. For a time, e-business in general and dot-coms in particular spread faster than bad news.

Some of these efforts bore fruit in the form of higher earnings and some resulted in drastic losses for the firms involved. It might be that the communications firm with a P/E of 10 has refrained from investing in newer opportunities. Therefore, a larger portion of its revenues is available in the form of earnings than is the case with a telephone company that has aggressively invested in alternatives to its basic, historic revenue base. Greater earnings will tend to lower the P/E ratio.

The fact that a firm has a P/E that is lower than its industry average is not clear evidence that it is better managed than the other companies in that industry group. In fact, to continue the present example, you might find that this company is rather poorly managed if it turns out that other communications firms do very well with their investment and partnering strategies. It's also possible that other investors have more and better information than you do, and this information has caused them to push the price down.

The point is that industry groups are gross classifications. Just because a company is categorized in the "Telecommunications Industry" does not mean that its business strategies, product mix, and investments are directly commensurate with other companies in its category. Before you put much credence in the comparison of a financial ratio such as P/E with its industry average, you should be sure that the company is really managed and operated as are other firms in its classification.

Part

I

Ch

7

But even if you are confident that you are comparing a ratio with an average that is derived from firms that are truly comparable, the question of accounting procedures comes into play. As was discussed in Chapter 1, "Working with Income Statements," there are ground rules that all companies must follow in computing their revenues, costs, expenses, earnings, and so on. Sometimes companies play fast and loose with those rules. Even in the vast majority of cases where companies act scrupulously, the rules leave room for choice, and the rules oper-ate differently in different situations.

For example, Chapter 5, "Working Capital and Cash Flow Analysis," briefly discussed the effect that depreciation has on net income: you subtract depreciation, along with other expenses, from your gross profit to arrive at a net income figure. As you will see in Chapter 16, "Fixed Assets," there are a variety of methods that you can use to compute depreciation, and these different methods usually return different figures. Different ways of figuring depre-ciation expense therefore result in different estimates of earnings. (Companies in a particular industry group tend to use the same procedures even when variation is permitted.)

You also saw in Chapter 3, "Valuing Inventories for the Balance Sheet," that there are differ-ent methods you can use to value inventories. The cost of goods sold is subtracted from sales to arrive at a figure for gross profit, and the cost of goods sold is often determined by this for-mula:

```
Cost of goods sold = Beginning Inventory + Inventory Purchases - Ending Inventory
```

So, the method a firm uses to value its inventory has an effect on its gross profit, and there-fore on the determination of its earnings.

In short, a financial ratio may not be commensurate among companies that are in the same line of business, because differences in accounting methods can bring about different results from computing the same ratio.

Analyzing Ratios Vertically and Horizontally

This sort of comparison of one company's ratio with that of an entire business sector is often termed *vertical* analysis. Another approach (termed, as you might expect, *horizontal* analysis) tracks financial ratios over time. Access to several years' worth of information on, say, the P/E reported by a given company enables you to determine whether its P/E has been increasing, decreasing, or remaining stable.

Horizontal analysis minimizes many of the problems associated with vertical analysis. When you focus on the changes to a ratio reported by one company over time, there is less reason to be concerned about the effect of different accounting methods on the comparisons. Although a company may alter some of its methods from time to time, it is required to report any material changes in those methods. You are therefore better able to tell whether a sub-stantial change in a financial ratio from one year to the next has been caused by a modifica-tion in accounting methods or by a change in the ways a company does business.

The major weakness of a strictly horizontal analysis is that it provides you no information about a *standard* for a given ratio. Suppose you know that a retailer's inventory turns ratio has increased steadily from 8 turns per year to 10 per year over a five-year period. On the face of it, this is a cheery finding: the company has been moving goods through its retail outlets faster and faster over time. But if other, similar retailers average 15 turns per year, then although this company is improving it might not yet be managing its inventory as well as it should. A strictly horizontal analysis would not give you this information.

Neither a vertical nor a horizontal analysis of financial ratios is completely informative. Doing both types of analysis can be better than doing just one, and is certainly better than doing neither, but there are still ways that you can be misled by doing both. It is best if you do not regard financial ratios as absolute, objective measures of a company's performance, but rather as clues: pointers to questions that you would want to ask about a company's financial structure and business strategies.

To return to an earlier example, if a company reports a quick ratio of .8, it matters little whether the ratio has been steadily improving from .1 over a period of time. It also makes little difference that other, directly comparable companies report quick ratios that average .5. What does matter is that the company has greater current liabilities than it does current assets less inventory. Knowing this puts you in a position to ask *why* that situation exists. The answers to that question might position you to take corrective action as a manager, or to make a more informed decision as a creditor or investor.

The remainder of this chapter discusses specific financial ratios, both their calculations, as well as what questions a ratio's value might prompt you to ask. By way of example, an income statement for a book publisher, Orinoco Books, is shown in Figures 7.1 and 7.2. The company's balance sheet is shown in Figures 7.3 and 7.4.

FIGURE 7.1
This Income Statement for Orinoco Books contains defined names, such as Sales and Net_Income, used to compute financial ratios.

			Q1	Q2	Q3	Q4	Total 2002
Sales							
	Sales		$2,652,077	$1,860,290	$1,498,534	$3,134,388	$9,145,289
	Cost of sales		$1,432,744	$978,673	$1,107,254	$3,103,300	$6,621,971
		Gross profit	$1,219,333	$881,617	$391,280	$31,088	$2,523,318
Expenses							
	Operating expenses		$756,796	$533,991	$496,472	$432,676	$2,219,935
	Interest		$18,232	$17,112	$19,227	$19,211	$73,781
	Depreciation		$32,500	$33,958	$33,958	$33,958	$134,374
	Amortization		$1,500	$1,500	$1,500	$1,500	$6,000
		Total expenses	$809,028	$586,561	$551,157	$487,345	$2,434,090
		Operating income	$410,305	$295,056	($159,877)	($456,257)	$89,228
Other income and expenses							
	Sale of assets		$87,500	$15,000	$2,000	$398,600	$503,100
	Other		$15,000	$65,000	$98,000	$202,000	$380,000
		Subtotal	$102,500	$80,000	$100,000	$600,600	$883,100
		Income before tax	$512,805	$375,056	($59,877)	$144,343	$972,328
	Taxes @ 30%		$153,842	$112,517	($17,963)	$43,303	$291,698
		Net income	$358,964	$262,539	($41,914)	$101,040	$680,630

Part

I

Ch

7

FIGURE 7.2
The continuation of the
Income Statement data
for Orinoco Books
breaks out categories
such as Interest, which
is used to calculate the
times interest earned
ratio.

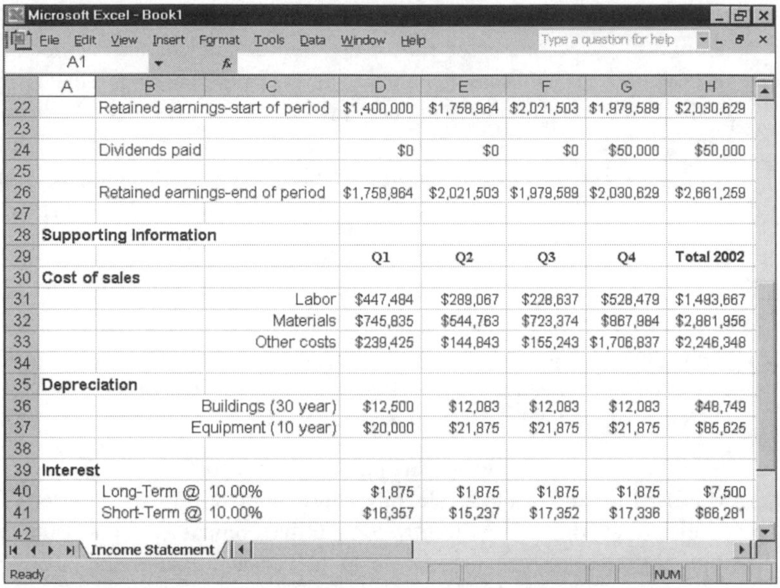

	A	B	C	D	E	F	G	H
22		Retained earnings-start of period		$1,400,000	$1,758,984	$2,021,503	$1,979,589	$2,030,629
23								
24		Dividends paid		$0	$0	$0	$50,000	$50,000
25								
26		Retained earnings-end of period		$1,758,984	$2,021,503	$1,979,589	$2,030,629	$2,661,259
27								
28	**Supporting Information**							
29				Q1	Q2	Q3	Q4	**Total 2002**
30	**Cost of sales**							
31			Labor	$447,484	$289,067	$228,637	$528,479	$1,493,667
32			Materials	$745,835	$544,763	$723,374	$867,984	$2,881,956
33			Other costs	$239,425	$144,843	$155,243	$1,706,837	$2,246,348
34								
35	**Depreciation**							
36			Buildings (30 year)	$12,500	$12,083	$12,083	$12,083	$48,749
37			Equipment (10 year)	$20,000	$21,875	$21,875	$21,875	$85,625
38								
39	**Interest**							
40		Long-Term @	10.00%	$1,875	$1,875	$1,875	$1,875	$7,500
41		Short-Term @	10.00%	$16,357	$15,237	$17,352	$17,336	$66,281
42								

FIGURE 7.3
The figures in the
Assets section of the
Balance Sheet are
important for determin-
ing profitability ratios.

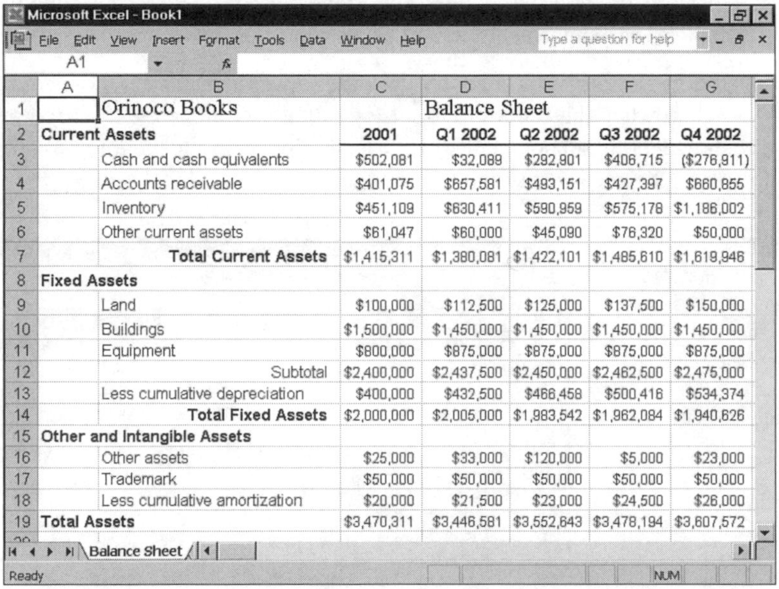

	A	B	C	D	E	F	G
1		Orinoco Books			Balance Sheet		
2	**Current Assets**		2001	Q1 2002	Q2 2002	Q3 2002	Q4 2002
3		Cash and cash equivalents	$502,081	$32,089	$292,901	$406,715	($276,911)
4		Accounts receivable	$401,075	$657,581	$493,151	$427,397	$660,855
5		Inventory	$451,109	$630,411	$590,959	$575,178	$1,186,002
6		Other current assets	$61,047	$60,000	$45,090	$76,320	$50,000
7		Total Current Assets	$1,415,311	$1,380,081	$1,422,101	$1,485,610	$1,619,946
8	**Fixed Assets**						
9		Land	$100,000	$112,500	$125,000	$137,500	$150,000
10		Buildings	$1,500,000	$1,450,000	$1,450,000	$1,450,000	$1,450,000
11		Equipment	$800,000	$875,000	$875,000	$875,000	$875,000
12		Subtotal	$2,400,000	$2,437,500	$2,450,000	$2,462,500	$2,475,000
13		Less cumulative depreciation	$400,000	$432,500	$466,458	$500,416	$534,374
14		Total Fixed Assets	$2,000,000	$2,005,000	$1,983,542	$1,962,084	$1,940,626
15	**Other and Intangible Assets**						
16		Other assets	$25,000	$33,000	$120,000	$5,000	$23,000
17		Trademark	$50,000	$50,000	$50,000	$50,000	$50,000
18		Less cumulative amortization	$20,000	$21,500	$23,000	$24,500	$26,000
19	**Total Assets**		$3,470,311	$3,446,581	$3,552,643	$3,478,194	$3,607,572

FIGURE 7.4
The figures in the Liabilities and Equity section of the Balance Sheet are used to compute liquidity ratios.

Microsoft Excel - Book1

	A	B	C	D	E	F	G
22	**LIABILITIES AND STOCKHOLDERS' EQUITY**						
23	**Current Liabilities**		**2001**	**Q1 2002**	**Q2 2002**	**Q3 2002**	**Q4 2002**
24		Accounts payable	$575,000	$300,345	$310,294	$326,551	$315,626
25		Notes payable	$125,000	$75,000	$75,000	$75,000	$75,000
26		Current portion of long-term debt	$100,000	$100,000	$100,000	$100,000	$100,000
27		Income taxes	$26,495	$116,178	$82,030	($53,183)	$11,860
28		Accrued expenses	$86,880	$88,474	$103,964	$91,991	$114,382
29		Other current liabilities	$16,772	$13,852	$11,457	$12,896	$13,128
30		**Total Current Liabilities**	$930,147	$693,849	$682,745	$553,255	$629,996
31	**Non-Current Liabilities**						
32		Long-term debt	$747,296	$554,267	$509,473	$594,062	$593,443
33		Deferred income	$132,704	$134,612	$117,076	$111,867	$117,690
34		Deferred income taxes	$37,101	$37,664	$30,487	$35,220	$31,443
35		Other long-term liabilities	$73,063	$117,225	$41,359	$54,201	$54,371
36		**Total Liabilities**	$1,920,311	$1,537,617	$1,381,140	$1,348,605	$1,426,943
37	**Stockholders' Equity**						
38		Capital stock issued	$100,000	$100,000	$100,000	$100,000	$100,000
39		Additional paid in capital	$50,000	$50,000	$50,000	$50,000	$50,000
40		Retained earnings	$1,400,000	$1,758,964	$2,021,503	$1,979,589	$2,030,629
41		**Total Equity**	$1,550,000	$1,908,964	$2,171,503	$2,129,589	$2,180,629
42		**Total Liabilities and Equity**	$3,470,311	$3,446,581	$3,552,643	$3,478,194	$3,607,572

Balance Sheet

The data shown in Figures 7.1 through 7.4 are used to compute each of the ratios discussed in the next several sections.

This chapter discusses the 12 important financial ratios listed in Table 7.1. The ratios are usually thought of as belonging to four basic categories: profitability ratios, liquidity ratios, activity ratios, and leverage ratios:

Table 7.1 Ratios That Provide Insights into a Company's Finances and Management Practices

Category	Ratio
Profitability ratios	Earnings Per Share
	Gross Profit Margin
	Net Profit Margin
	Return on Assets
	Return on Equity
Liquidity ratios	Current Ratio
	Quick Ratio
Activity ratios	Average Collection Period
	Inventory Turnover
Leverage ratios	Debt Ratio
	Equity Ratio
	Times Interest Earned

Analyzing Profitability Ratios

If you are considering investing money in a company, its profitability is a major concern. If the company intends to pay dividends to its stockholders, those dividends must come out of its profits. If the company hopes to increase its worth in the marketplace by enhancing or expanding its product line, then an important source of capital to make improvements is its profit margin. There are several different, but related, means of evaluating a company's profitability.

Finding and Evaluating Earnings Per Share

Depending on your financial objectives, you might consider investing in a company to obtain a steady return on your investment in the form of regular dividend payments, or to obtain a profit by owning the stock as the market value of its shares increases. These two objectives might both be met, but in practice they often are not. Companies frequently face a choice between distributing income in the form of dividends, or retaining that income to invest in research, new products, and expanded operations. The hope, of course, is that the retention of income to invest in the company will subsequently increase its income, thus making the company more profitable and increasing the market value of its stock.

In either case, Earnings Per Share (EPS) is an important measure of the company's income. Its basic formula is

```
EPS=Income available for common stock / Shares of common stock outstanding
```

EPS is usually a poor candidate for vertical analysis because different companies always have different numbers of shares of stock outstanding. It *may* be a good candidate for horizontal analysis, if you have access both to information about the company's income and shares outstanding. With both these items, you can control for major fluctuations over time in shares outstanding. This sort of control is important: it is not unusual for a company to purchase its own stock on the open market to reduce the number of outstanding shares. So doing increases the value of the EPS ratio, perhaps making the stock appear a more attractive investment.

Suppose for the purpose of this example that Orinoco Books has 1,000 shares outstanding.

The EPS for this company at the end of each quarter in 2002 is shown in Figure 7.5:

FIGURE 7.5

EPS ratios during 2002 vary as net income drops.

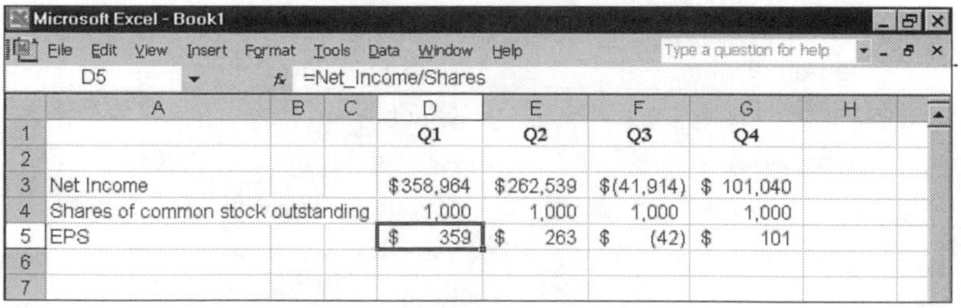

	A	B	C	D	E	F	G	H
1				Q1	Q2	Q3	Q4	
2								
3	Net Income			$358,964	$262,539	$(41,914)	$ 101,040	
4	Shares of common stock outstanding			1,000	1,000	1,000	1,000	
5	EPS			$ 359	$ 263	$ (42)	$ 101	
6								
7								

D5 = =Net_Income/Shares

Note that the EPS declines steadily throughout the year. Because, in this example, the number of shares outstanding is constant throughout the year, the EPS changes are due solely to changes in net income. The major impact to net income is the very small value of gross profit during the fourth quarter (see Figure 7.1, cell G6). In turn, that gross profit is due to the relatively large cost of sales during that quarter. The cost of sales is the sum of cells G31:G33 (shown in Figure 7.2).

Note also in Figure 7.2 that there is one very large "Other cost" of $1,706,837 during the fourth quarter. As a prospective shareholder, you would want to know the reason for this cost, whether it will be recouped in the future, or whether it will repeat. Any extraordinarily large cost such as this will certainly impact the market value of the company's stock, and might well impact the company's ability to pay any dividends that you expect to receive.

Many companies issue at least two different kinds of stock: ***common*** and ***preferred***. Preferred stock is issued under different conditions than common stock and is often callable at the company's discretion. It pays dividends at a different (usually, a higher) rate per share, it might not carry voting privileges, and often has a higher priority than common stock as to the distribution of liquidated assets if the company goes out of business.

Calculating EPS for a company that has issued preferred stock introduces a slight complication. Because the company pays dividends on preferred stock before any distribution to shareholders of common stock, it is necessary to subtract these dividends from net income:

```
EPS= (Net Income - Preferred dividends) / Shares of common stock outstanding
```

Determining Gross Profit Margin

The gross profit margin is a basic ratio that measures, for a manufacturing firm, the value that the market places on the company's non-manufacturing activities. For a firm that resells products, the ratio measures the value placed by the market on the activities that enhance those products.

Its formula is

```
Gross profit margin = (Sales - Cost of goods sold)/Sales
```

Orinoco Books' gross profit margin is shown in Figure 7.6:

FIGURE 7.6
The fourth quarter's gross profit margin is low due to its large cost of sales.

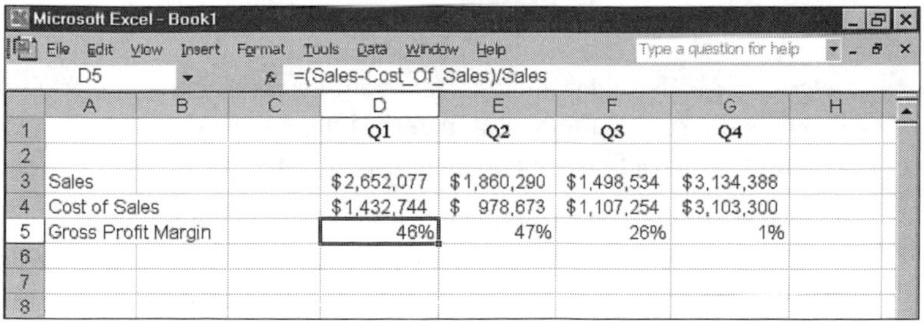

	A	B	C	D	E	F	G	H
1				Q1	Q2	Q3	Q4	
2								
3	Sales			$2,652,077	$1,860,290	$1,498,534	$3,134,388	
4	Cost of Sales			$1,432,744	$ 978,673	$1,107,254	$3,103,300	
5	Gross Profit Margin			46%	47%	26%	1%	
6								
7								
8								

Orinoco Books' Income Statement and Balance Sheet, in Figures 7.1 through 7.4, have several defined names. The name *Sales* is defined as referring to the range D3:H3 on the Income Statement, Figure 7.1. The name *Cost_Of_Sales* is defined as referring to the range D4:H4, also on the Income Statement, Figure 7.1. In turn, *Cost_Of_Sales* is the sum of rows 31 through 33 in Figure 7.2. These rows, in columns D through H, contain the cost of labor, materials, and other costs (usually taken to mean factory overhead) involved in the production of goods for sale. In other words, *Cost_Of_Sales* here is the Cost of Goods Sold, or COGS. The formulas used to calculate the gross profit margins in Figure 7.6 are as follows. The sales values for the four quarters, in cells D3:G3, are obtained by selecting that range, typing this formula:

```
=Sales
```

in the Formula Bar, and finishing with Ctrl+Enter. There are two points to note:

- When you select a range of cells and enter a formula (or even a static value) using Ctrl+Enter instead of just Enter, that formula is entered into each of the cells in the selected range.

- The name Sales refers to D3:H3 in Figure 7.1. In Figure 7.6, the range that returns the sales figures occupies columns D through G (column H on the Income Statement, containing annual totals, is omitted because the focus here is on the quarterly results). This means that the formula is able to take advantage of the implicit intersection: whatever is in column D in the named range is returned to column D in the formula's range—and similarly for columns E through G. If you entered the formula in a column that's not used by the defined name (here, anything left of column D or right of column H) you would get the #VALUE! error.

The same approach is used to get the Cost of Sales in cells D4:G4. That is, D4:G4 is selected, this formula:

```
=Cost_Of_Sales
```

is typed in the Formula Bar, and then entered with Ctrl+Enter.

Lastly, the gross profit margin in cells D5:G5 is obtained by selecting that range, typing this formula:

```
=(Sales-Cost_Of_Sales)/Sales
```

in the Formula Bar, and pressing Ctrl+Enter.

The cost of goods sold is an important component of the gross profit margin. It is usually calculated as the sum of the cost of materials the company purchases plus any labor involved in the manufacture of finished goods, plus associated overhead.

The gross profit margin depends heavily on the type of business in which a company is engaged. A service business, such as a financial services institution or a laundry, typically has little or no cost of goods sold. A manufacturing, wholesaling, or retailing company typically has a large cost of goods sold, with a gross profit margin that varies from 20% to 40%.

The gross profit margin measures the amount that customers are willing to pay for a company's product, over and above the company's cost for that product. As mentioned previously, this is the value that the company adds to that of the products it obtains from its suppliers. This margin can depend on the attractiveness of additional services, such as warranties, that the company provides. The gross profit margin also depends heavily on the ability of the sales force to persuade its customers of the value added by the company.

This added value is, of course, created by activities that cost money to undertake. In turn, these activities must be paid for largely by the gross profit on sales. If customers do not place sufficient value on whatever the company adds to its products, there will not be enough gross profit to pay for the associated costs. Therefore, the calculation of the gross profit margin helps to highlight the effectiveness of the company's sales strategies and sales management.

Determining Net Profit Margin

The net profit margin narrows the focus on profitability, and highlights not just the company's sales efforts, but also its ability to keep operating costs down, relative to sales. The formula generally used to determine the net profit margin is

```
Net profit margin = Earnings after taxes / Sales
```

The calculation of Orinoco Books' net profit margin is shown in Figure 7.7.

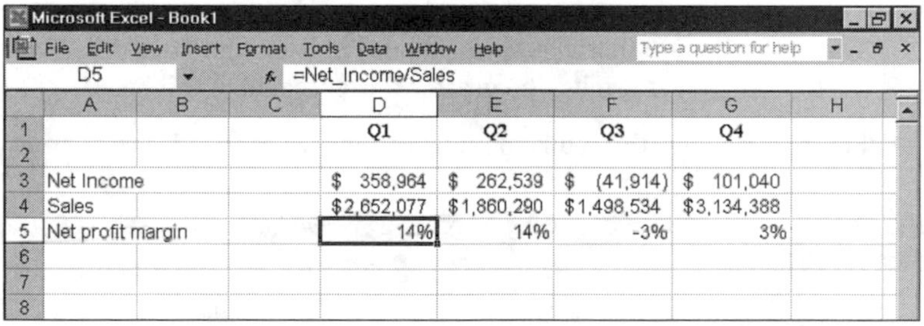

	A	B	C	D	E	F	G	H
1				Q1	Q2	Q3	Q4	
2								
3	Net Income			$ 358,964	$ 262,539	$ (41,914)	$ 101,040	
4	Sales			$2,652,077	$1,860,290	$1,498,534	$3,134,388	
5	Net profit margin			14%	14%	-3%	3%	
6								
7								
8								

FIGURE 7.7
The net profit margin, in contrast to the gross profit margin, takes expenses into account.

The quarterly earnings after taxes, in the range D3:G3, is returned by this formula, again entered with Ctrl+Enter:

```
=Net_Income
```

The name Net_Income is defined as the range D20:H20 on Orinoco Books' Income Statement (refer to Figure 7.1). As in the gross profit margin calculation, sales figures are returned in the range D4:G4 by:

```
=Sales
```

And the net profit margin for each quarter is returned in the range D5:G5 by:

```
=Net_Income/Sales
```

Why does the net profit margin fall so far from the first to the fourth quarters? One principal culprit is, again, the cost of sales. Notice in Figure 7.2 that the materials expense is $745,835 in the first quarter (cell D32). Even though sales fall by 30% from the first to the second quarter, and by 20% from the second to the third quarter, the company's production operations consumed a relatively large amount of materials during the fourth quarter.

Chapter 6, "Statement Analysis," described the use of common-sized statements to make more informed comparisons. In the present example, common-sized quarterly statements would help identify Orinoco's problem areas.

Another place to look when you see a discrepancy between gross profit margin and net profit margin is operating expenses. When the two margins co-vary closely, it suggests that management is doing a good job of reducing expenses when sales fall, and increasing expenses when necessary to support production and sales in better times.

Determining the Return on Assets

One of management's most important responsibilities is to bring about a profit by effective use of the resources it has at hand. The Return on Assets, or ROA, ratio measures the effectiveness of resource usage. There are several ways to measure this return; one useful method is

```
Return on assets = (Gross Profit - Operating Expense) / Total assets
```

This formula will return the percentage earnings for a company in terms of its total assets. The better the job that management does in managing its assets—the resources available to it—to bring about profits, the greater this percentage will be.

Figure 7.8 shows the return on total assets for Orinoco Books:

FIGURE 7.8
The return on total assets is usually computed on an annualized basis.

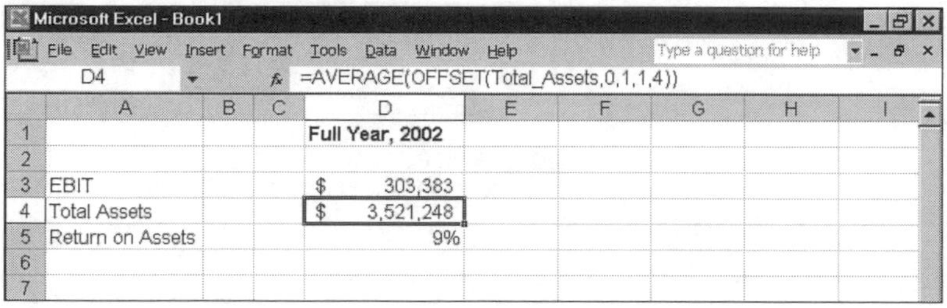

Earnings Before Interest and Taxes (EBIT) is shown in cell D3 of Figure 7.8. The formula used to obtain the figure is

```
=Income_2002 Gross_Profit - Income_2002 Operating_Expenses
```

This formula makes use of three range names: *Income_2002, Gross_Profit,* and *Operating_Expenses. Income_2002* refers to the annual total column in the Income Statement: specifically, the range H3:H26. *Gross_Profit* refers to D6:H6 on the Income Statement, and *Operating_Expenses* refers to D8:H8 in the Income Statement. Refer to Figure 7.1 to view all three of these ranges.

The formula uses the intersection operator, a blank space, between Income_2002 and Gross_Profit to specify the cell where these two ranges intersect; in Figure 7.1, that's cell H6. Similarly, it uses the same operator to specify the cell where Income_2002 intersects Operating_Expenses (Figure 7.1 cell H8). The formula for EBIT then subtracts the annualized operating expenses from the annualized gross profit to return the value of $303,383 shown in Figure 7.8.

It's normal to calculate the return on total assets on an annual basis, rather than on a quarterly basis: therefore, the range named Income_2002 is used to show the EBIT for the full year. The total assets portion of the formula—its denominator—is usually computed by taking an average of the company's total assets for the period in question.

The formula for total assets, cell D4 in Figure 7.8, is:

```
=AVERAGE(OFFSET(Total_Assets,0,1,1,4))
```

Orinoco Books' Balance Sheet defines the range Total_Assets as referring to cells C19:G19 (refer to Figure 7.3). The first cell in this range, C19, contains the value of total assets for the prior year, 2001. Because this cell must be ignored when calculating the company's average quarterly total assets for the current year, 2002, Excel's OFFSET function is used.

This OFFSET specifies a range *within* Total_Assets (first argument) that is offset by 0 rows (second argument) and 1 column (third argument): that is, the offset range is right-shifted from Total_Assets by one column, so as to ignore its first cell (C19). It also specifies that the offset range is one row high (fourth argument) and four columns wide (fifth argument). Therefore, the OFFSET function as used here returns the range D19:G19.

Enclosing the OFFSET function and its arguments within the AVERAGE function returns the average of the values within the offset range, D19:G19.

Lastly, the return on total assets in Figure 7.8 is calculated by this formula:

```
=D3/D4
```

Determining the Return on Equity

Another profitability measure, related to Return on Assets, is the Return on Equity, or ROE. ROE measures management's effectiveness in maximizing the return to holders of common stock. The formula for ROE is

```
Return on equity = (Net Income-Preferred Dividends)/Average common stockholders'
equity
```

Part

I

Ch

7

where the Average common stockholders' equity is the average of the equity at the beginning and at the end of the accounting period.

Figure 7.9 displays Orinoco Books' Return on Equity.

FIGURE 7.9
You can compare Return on Equity with Return on Assets to infer how a company obtains the funds used to acquire assets.

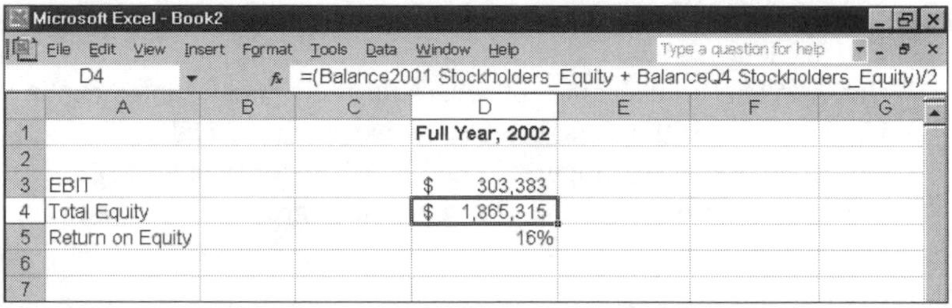

The principal difference between the formula for Return on Assets and for Return on Equity is the use of equity rather than total assets in the denominator. The stockholders' equity figures are obtained by this formula:

```
=(Balance2001 Stockholders_Equity + BalanceQ4 Stockholders_Equity)/2
```

which uses implicit intersections to return the values at the beginning and end of the period (cells C41 and G41 of the Balance Sheet shown in Figure 7.4).

Here, the technique of comparing ratios comes into play. By examining the difference between Return on Assets and Return on Equity, you can gain insight into how the company is funding its operations.

Assets are acquired through two major sources: creditors (through borrowing) and stockholders (through retained earnings and capital contributions). Collectively, the retained earnings and capital contributions constitute the company's equity. When the value of the company's assets exceeds the value of its equity, you can expect that the difference is made up by some form of financial leverage, such as debt financing.

In this chapter's example, Orinoco Books' Return on Assets is 9% while its Return on Equity is 16%. That the larger of the two ratios is Return on Equity points to the use of debt financing. And, as the Balance Sheet in Figure 7.4 shows, at the end of 2002 Orinoco Books has $75,000 in Notes Payable and $693,443 in Long-Term Debt ($100,000 of which is current).

Analyzing Leverage Ratios

The term *leverage* means the purchase of assets with borrowed money. Chapter 14, "Planning Profits," goes into this subject in detail. For now, consider this example: suppose that your company retails office supplies. When you receive an order for business cards, you pay one of your suppliers 50% of the revenue to print them for you. This is a variable cost: the more you sell, the greater your cost.

But if you purchase the necessary printing equipment, you could make the business cards yourself. So doing would turn a variable cost into a largely fixed cost: no matter how many cards you sell, the cost of printing them is fixed at however much you paid for the printing equipment (apart from consumables such as paper stock). The more cards you sell, the greater your profit margin. This effect is termed *operating leverage*.

If you borrow money to acquire the printing equipment, you are using another type of leverage, termed *financial leverage*. The cost is still fixed at however much money you must pay, at regular intervals, to retire the loan. Again, the more cards you sell, the greater your profit margin. But if you do not sell enough cards to cover the loan payment, your firm will have less revenue to cover other costs of doing business. In that case, it might be difficult to find funds either to make the loan payments or to cover your other expenses. In addition, your credit rating might fall, making it more costly for you to borrow other money.

Leverage is a financial tool that accelerates changes in income, both positive and negative. A company's creditors and investors are interested in how much leverage has been used to acquire assets. From the standpoint of creditors, a high degree of leverage represents risk because the company might not be able to repay a loan. From the investors' standpoint, if the Return on Assets (see earlier in the chapter) is less than the cost of borrowing money to acquire assets, then the investment is unattractive. The investor could obtain a better return in different ways—one way would be to loan funds rather than to invest them in the company.

Two ratios that help you to measure leverage are the debt ratio and the equity ratio.

Determining the Debt Ratio

The debt ratio shows what percentage of assets have been acquired through borrowing. It is defined by this formula:

```
Debt ratio = Total debt / Total assets
```

Figure 7.10 shows the debt ratio calculated for Orinoco Books.

FIGURE 7.10
The debt ratio indicates the company's use of financial leverage.

	A	B	C	D	E	F	G	H
				Q1	Q2	Q3	Q4	
1								
2								
3	Total Liabilities			$1,537,617	$1,381,140	$1,348,605	$1,426,943	
4	Total Assets			$3,446,581	$3,552,643	$3,478,194	$3,607,572	
5	Debt Ratio			45%	39%	39%	40%	
6								
7								

D5 — fx =Total_Liabilities/Total_Assets

The term *total debt* is, in this context, synonymous with the term *total liabilities*. The formula used in the range D3:G3 of Figure 7.10 to return the total debt is

```
=Total_Liabilities
```

Part
I

Ch
7

The range D4:G4 in Figure 7.10 returns the company's total assets for each quarter in similar fashion, and cell D5:G5 simply divides the total debt by the total assets as shown in the Formula Bar.

The comparison of the Return on Assets to the Return on Equity suggested some reliance by Orinoco Books on debt financing. It may be a healthy sign, then, that the company's debt ratio has fallen during 2002. A multi-year analysis of return ratios might be informative. As the return on assets falls, the net income available to make payments on debt also falls. If this has been happening, Orinoco Books should probably take action to retire some of its short-term debt, and the current portion of its long-term debt, as soon as possible.

Determining the Equity Ratio

The *equity ratio* is the opposite of the debt ratio. It is that portion of the company's assets financed by stockholders:

```
Equity ratio = Total equity / Total assets
```

In Figures 7.10 and 7.11 the equity ratio and debt ratio in each quarter total to 100%. This is generally true of any enterprise: assets are acquired either through debt or through equity (investment plus retained earnings).

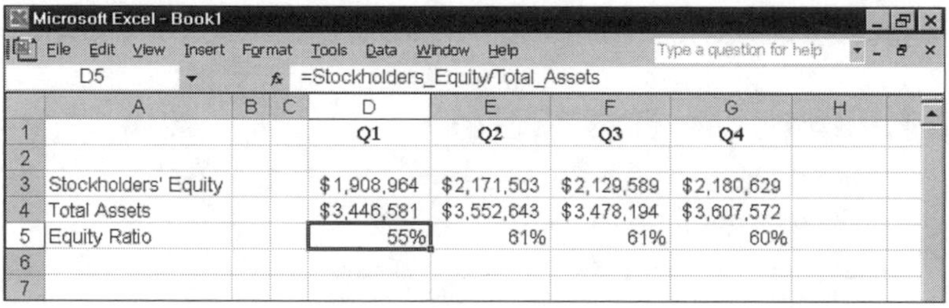

	A	B	C	D	E	F	G	H
1				Q1	Q2	Q3	Q4	
2								
3	Stockholders' Equity			$1,908,964	$2,171,503	$2,129,589	$2,180,629	
4	Total Assets			$3,446,581	$3,552,643	$3,478,194	$3,607,572	
5	Equity Ratio			55%	61%	61%	60%	
6								
7								

FIGURE 7.11
The equity ratio indicates the degree to which assets are acquired via capital contributions and retained earnings.

It is usually easier to acquire assets through debt than to acquire them through equity. There are certain obvious considerations. For example, you might need to acquire investment capital from many investors, whereas you might be able to borrow the required funds from just one creditor. Less obvious is the question of priority.

By law, if a firm ceases operations, its creditors have the first claim on its assets to help repay the borrowed funds. Therefore, an investor's risk is somewhat higher than that of a creditor, and the effect is that stockholders tend to demand a greater return on their investment than a creditor does on its loan. The stockholder's demand for a return can take the form of dividend requirements or return on assets, each of which tend to increase the market value of their stock.

But there is no "always" in financial planning. Because investors usually require a higher return on their investment than do creditors, it might seem that debt is the preferred method of raising funds to acquire assets. Potential creditors, though, look at ratios such as the return on assets and the debt ratio. A high debt ratio (or, conversely, a low equity ratio) means that existing creditors have supplied a large portion of the company's assets, and that there is relatively little stockholder's equity to help absorb the risk.

Determining the Times Interest Earned Ratio

One measure frequently used by creditors to evaluate the risk involved in loaning money to a firm is the Times Interest Earned ratio. This is the number of times in a given period that a company earns enough income to cover its interest payments. A ratio of 5, for example, would mean that the amount of interest payments is earned five times over during that period.

The usual formula is

```
Times Interest Earned = EBIT / Total interest payments
```

where EBIT stands for Earnings Before Interest and Taxes. The Times Interest Earned ratio for Orinoco Books is shown in Figure 7.12.

FIGURE 7.12
The Times Interest Earned ratio measures a company's ability to meet the cost of debt.

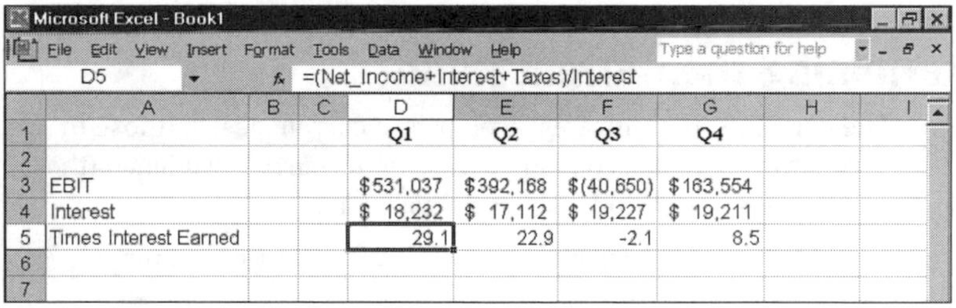

	A	B	C	D	E	F	G	H
1				Q1	Q2	Q3	Q4	
2								
3	EBIT			$531,037	$392,168	$(40,650)	$163,554	
4	Interest			$ 18,232	$ 17,112	$ 19,227	$ 19,211	
5	Times Interest Earned			29.1	22.9	-2.1	8.5	
6								
7								

The formula used in the range D3:G3 of Figure 7.12 is

```
=Net_Income+Interest+Taxes
```

This is a slightly different formulation than is used in Figures 7.8 and 7.9. There, EBIT was calculated for a full year by subtracting operating expenses from gross profit. Here, EBIT is calculated on a quarterly basis by adding interest and taxes back into net income.

The formula used to return the interest amount in the range D4:G4 is

```
=Interest
```

The formula uses the defined name *Interest*, which refers to the range D9:H9 on Orinoco Books' Income Statement (refer to Figure 7.1).

The Times Interest Earned ratio, in reality, seldom exceeds 10. A value of 29.1, such as that calculated in cell D5 in Figure 7.12, is *very* high, although certainly not unheard of during a particularly good quarter. A value of 8.5, such as in cell G5 of Figure 7.12, would usually be considered strong but within the normal range.

Notice that this is a measure of how deeply interest charges cut into a company's income. A ratio of 1, for example, would mean that the company earns enough income (after covering such costs as operating expenses and costs of sales) to cover only its interest charges. There would be no income remaining to pay income taxes (of course, in this case it's likely that there would be no income tax liability), to meet dividend requirements or to retain earnings for future investments.

Analyzing Liquidity Ratios

Creditors, as you might expect, are much concerned by the issue of *liquidity*, or a company's ability to meet its debts as they come due. As earlier chapters in this book have discussed, a company's total assets may be considerable, but if those assets are difficult to convert to cash it is possible that the company might be unable to pay its creditors in a timely fashion. Creditors want their loans to be paid in the medium of cash, not in a medium such as inventory or factory equipment.

Two useful measures of a company's liquidity are the current ratio and the quick ratio.

Determining the Current Ratio

The current ratio compares a company's current assets (those that can be converted to cash during the current accounting period) to its current liabilities (those liabilities coming due during the same period). The usual formula is

```
Current Ratio = Current Assets / Current Liabilities
```

The current ratio during each quarter for Orinoco Books is shown in Figure 7.13.

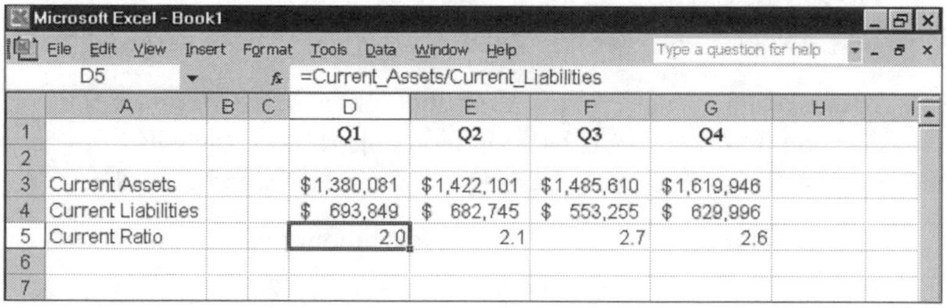

FIGURE 7.13
The current ratio measures the company's ability to repay the principal amounts of its liabilities.

The ranges D3:G3 and D4:G4 in Figure 7.13 simply refer to ranges named Current_Assets (cells D7:G7 on the Balance Sheet, Figure 7.3) and Current_Liabilities (cells D30:G30 on the Balance Sheet, Figure 7.13). The current ratio is simply the current assets divided by the current liabilities. The current ratio values in Figure 7.13, ranging from 1.9 to 2.8, indicate that the company is in a strong position to meet its liabilities as they come due.

The current ratio is closely related to the concept of working capital, discussed in detail in Chapter 5. Working capital is the *difference* between current assets and current liabilities.

Is a high current ratio good or bad? Certainly, from the creditor's standpoint, a high current ratio means that the company is well placed to pay back its loans. Consider, though, the nature of the current assets: they consist mainly of cash and cash equivalents. Funds invested in these types of assets do not contribute strongly and actively to the creation of operating income. Therefore, from the standpoint of stockholders and management, a current ratio that is very high means that the company's assets are not being used to its best advantage.

Determining the Quick Ratio

The quick ratio is a variant of the current ratio. It takes into account the fact that inventory, while it is a current asset, is not as liquid as cash or accounts receivable. Cash is completely liquid; accounts receivable can normally be converted to cash fairly quickly, by pressing for collection from the customer. But inventory cannot be converted to cash except by selling it. The quick ratio determines the relationship between quickly accessible current assets and current liabilities:

```
Quick Ratio = (Current Assets - Inventory) / Current Liabilities
```

Figure 7.14 shows the quarterly quick ratios for Orinoco Books.

FIGURE 7.14
The quick ratio shows whether a company can meet its liabilities from quickly accessible assets.

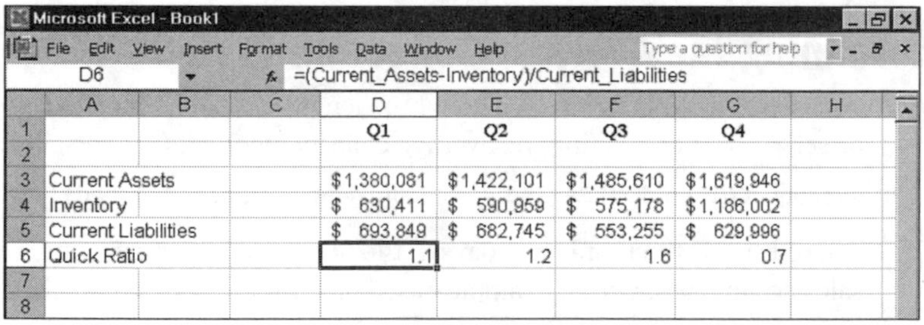

	A	B	C	D	E	F	G	H
				Q1	Q2	Q3	Q4	
1								
2								
3	Current Assets			$1,380,081	$1,422,101	$1,485,610	$1,619,946	
4	Inventory			$ 630,411	$ 590,959	$ 575,178	$1,186,002	
5	Current Liabilities			$ 693,849	$ 682,745	$ 553,255	$ 629,996	
6	Quick Ratio			1.1	1.2	1.6	0.7	
7								
8								

D6 =(Current_Assets-Inventory)/Current_Liabilities

The rather low quick ratio for the fourth quarter is caused by the relatively large portion of current assets that are tied up in inventory. Subtracting that amount from the total current assets results in a smaller numerator and a quick ratio that's less than 1.0.

In practice, a quick ratio of 1.0 is normally considered adequate, with this caveat: the credit periods that the company offers its customers and those granted to the company by its creditor must be roughly equal. If revenues will stay in accounts receivable for as long as 90 days, but accounts payable are due within 30 days, a quick ratio of 1.0 will mean that accounts receivable cannot be converted to cash quickly enough to meet accounts payable.

It is possible for a company to manipulate the values of its current and quick ratios by taking certain actions toward the end of an accounting period such as a fiscal year. It might wait until the start of the next period to make purchases to its inventory, for example. Or, if its business is seasonal, it might choose a fiscal year that ends after its busy season, when inventories are usually low. As a potential creditor, you might want to examine the company's current and quick ratios on, for example, a quarterly basis for at least a full year.

Part
I

Ch
7

Both a current and a quick ratio can also mislead you if the inventory figure does not represent the current replacement cost of the materials in inventory. As you learned from the discussion of inventories in Chapter 3, there are various methods of valuing inventory. The LIFO method, in particular, can result in an inventory valuation that is much different from the inventory's current replacement value; this is because it assumes that the most recently acquired inventory is also the most recently sold.

If your actual costs of materials are falling, for example, the LIFO method could result in an over-valuation of the existing inventory. This would tend to inflate the value of the current ratio, and to underestimate the value of the quick ratio if you calculate it by subtracting inventory from current assets, rather than summing cash and cash equivalents.

Analyzing Activity Ratios

There are various ratios that can give you insight into how well a company manages its operating and sales activities. One primary goal—perhaps, *the* primary goal—of these activities is to produce income through effective use of its resources. Two ways to measure this effectiveness are the average collection period and the inventory turnover rate.

Determining the Average Collection Period

You can obtain a general estimate of the length of time it takes to receive payment for goods or services by calculating the average collection period. One formula for this ratio is

```
Average Collection Period = Accounts Receivable / (Credit Sales / Days)
```

where Days is the number of days in the period for which accounts receivable and credit sales accumulate. For an example based on Orinoco Books financials, see Figure 7.15.

FIGURE 7.15
The average collection period is an indicator of how well a company manages its accounts receivable.

Microsoft Excel - Book1

D7 =Accounts_Receivable/Credit_Sales_Per_Day

	A	B	C	D	E	F	G
1				Q1	Q2	Q3	Q4
2							
3	Accounts Receivable			$ 657,581	$ 493,151	$ 427,397	$ 660,855
4	Credit Sales			$ 2,652,077	$ 1,860,290	$ 1,498,534	$ 3,134,388
5	Days in Period			90	91	92	92
6	Credit Sales per Day			$ 29,468	$ 20,443	$ 16,288	$ 34,069
7	Average Collection Period			22.3	24.1	26.2	19.4
8							
9							

The formula in the range D3:G3 of Figure 7.15, quarterly accounts receivable for 2002, is

```
=Accounts_Receivable
```

The Accounts_Receivable name refers to the range C4:G4 on the Balance Sheet (refer to Figure 7.3).

For the range D4:G4, labeled *Credit Sales*, the formula is

```
=Sales
```

(The assumption here is that all sales are credit sales.) The number of days in each quarter are entered in D5:G5, and are used as the denominator of the formula that returns Credit Sales per Day. For cell D6 that formula is

```
=Sales/D5
```

Thus, D6 contains simply the average day's worth of credit sales during the first quarter. The range D6:G6 is given the name Credit_Sales_Per_Day. Then, the range D7:G7 is the ratio of Accounts_Receivable to Credit_Sales_Per_Day. This ratio measures the average number of days that any given sale remains in accounts receivable.

You should interpret the average collection period in terms of the company's credit policies. If, for example, the company's policy as stated to its customers is that payment is to be received within two weeks, then an average collection period of 30 days indicates that collections are lagging. It may be that collection procedures need to be reviewed, or it is possible that one particularly large account is responsible for most of the collections in arrears. It is also possible that the qualifying procedures used by the sales force are not stringent enough.

N O T E The calculation of the average collection period assumes that credit sales are distributed roughly evenly during any given period. To the degree that the credit sales cluster at the end of the period, the average collection period will return an inflated figure. If you obtain a result that appears too long (or too short), be sure to check whether the sales dates are recorded evenly throughout the period in question. ■

Regardless of the cause, if the average collection period is over-long, it means that the company is losing profit. The company is not converting cash due from customers into new assets that can, in turn, be used to generate new income.

Determining Inventory Turnover

No company wants to have too large an inventory (the sales force excepted: salespeople prefer to be able to tell their customers that they can obtain their purchase this afternoon). Goods that remain in inventory too long tie up the company's assets in idle stock, often incur carrying charges for the storage of the goods, and can become obsolete while awaiting sale.

Just-In-Time inventory procedures attempt to ensure that the company obtains its inventory no sooner than absolutely required in order to support its sales efforts. That is, of course, an unrealistic ideal, but by calculating the inventory turnover rate you can estimate how well a company is approaching the ideal.

The formula for the inventory turnover ratio is

```
Inventory Turnover = Cost of Goods Sold / Average Inventory
```

where the Average Inventory figure refers to the value of the inventory on any given day during the period during which the Cost of Goods Sold is calculated. Figure 7.16 shows the quarterly inventory turnover rate for Orinoco Books.

FIGURE 7.16
The higher an inventory turnover rate, the more closely a company conforms to Just-In-Time procedures.

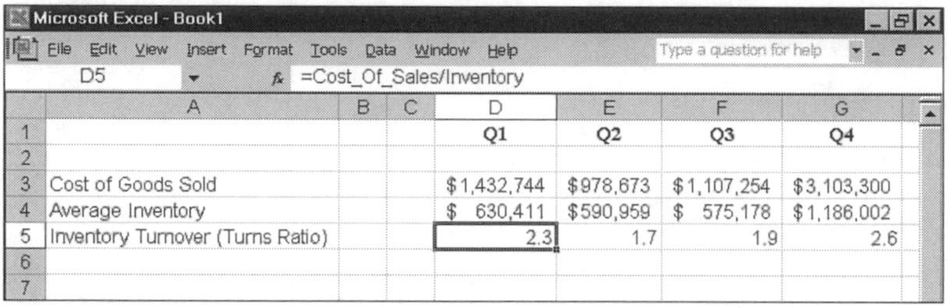

	A	B	C	D	E	F	G
1				Q1	Q2	Q3	Q4
2							
3	Cost of Goods Sold			$1,432,744	$978,673	$1,107,254	$3,103,300
4	Average Inventory			$ 630,411	$590,959	$ 575,178	$1,186,002
5	Inventory Turnover (Turns Ratio)			2.3	1.7	1.9	2.6
6							
7							

Figure 7.16 suggests that this company's inventory is completely replaced around eight or nine times annually.

The figures for Cost of Goods Sold and Average Inventory are taken directly from the Income Statement's cost of sales and the Balance Sheet's inventory levels. In a situation where you know only the beginning and ending inventory—for example, at the beginning and the ending of a period—you would use the average of the two levels: hence the term "Average Inventory."

An acceptable inventory turnover rate can be determined only by knowledge of a company's business sector. If you are in the business of wholesaling fresh produce, for example, you would probably require an annual turnover rate in the 50s. A much lower rate would mean that you were losing too much inventory to spoilage. But if you sell computing equipment, you could probably afford an annual turnover rate of around 3 or 4, because hardware does not spoil, nor does it become technologically obsolete more frequently than every few months.

Summary

This chapter described some of the financial ratios that are important in understanding how, and how well, a company conducts its business. There are variations on virtually every ratio discussed here, and there are ratios that were not covered at all, but their principal forms follow the formulas illustrated.

Only occasionally can you calculate one of these indicators and gain immediate insight into a business operation. More frequently, it is necessary to know the sort of business that a company conducts, because the marketplace imposes different demands on different lines of business. Furthermore, you can usually understand one ratio by considering it in the context of another ratio (the debt ratio and the return on assets is a good example of one ratio providing the context for another).

Keep in mind that it's important to evaluate a financial ratio in terms of its trend over time, of a standard such as an industry average, and in light of other ratios that describe the company's operations and financial structure.

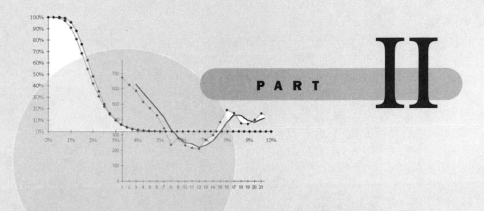

Financial Planning and Control

Budgeting and Planning Cycle

To this point, this book has focused on events that have already occurred. The income, balance sheet, and cash flow statements provide a picture of past performance. But understanding what has already happened is a largely fruitless exercise if you can't use it to plan for the future. This chapter provides an overview of financial planning and budgeting, and discusses how forecasts and projections form one basis for your planning. Chapter 9, "Forecasting and Projections," describes various forecasting techniques along with their Excel applications.

Textbooks prescribe elements for good business planning, such as mission statements, strategies, objectives, and tactics. These elements frequently focus on the customer's requirement for a quality product and for quality service.

After you've read a few mission statements they seem like mere lip service. They can be much more than that, of course, as Johnson & Johnson famously confirmed in 1982, when poison was placed in some Tylenol bottles. That product's market share dropped from 37% to 7% in a few weeks. The company's credo led them to recall every bottle of Tylenol they could, and provide tamper-proof replacements, at a cost of $75 million (which represented serious money in the early 1980s). Within five months Tylenol had rebounded to a 20% share, and was back to 37% within three years.

The point is that no worksheet, financial plan, or budget can prepare you for something as unexpected as that early product-tampering case. To deal effectively with that, you'd need guidance from your company's values.

But once you've decided to take a $75 million hit, you need to know where the money is coming from to cover it. More typically, you need to know where next year's money is coming from and how you're going to spend it.

That knowledge requires an understanding of your profit picture. It's hard to ignore the profit motive in business planning. Very few people can afford to work or to invest without financial rewards. An entrepreneur may start a new business with this goal: "To provide customers with high quality network servers and networking equipment at competitive rates that ultimately maximize profits." Most businesses try to strike a balance between meeting customers' needs and the profit incentive.

The stated goal identifies the business's *raison d'être*: providing high quality network equipment. The business intends to sell, not to manufacture, not to lease. Furthermore, it intends to create profit by selling at competitive prices, rather than by selling specialized equipment to a small market segment of network providers.

The process of business planning involves much more detail than these few concepts suggest. But they underscore that the foundation of good financial planning is good business planning. It's impossible to build meaningful financial plans without knowing what you want to accomplish and how you want to get there.

Creating Pro Forma Financial Statements

The goal of financial planning is to understand and project your financial future. Financial projections are used to evaluate and forecast business plans, to estimate future financing needs, and to establish internal operating budgets. Creating pro forma financial statements is a standard way to forecast a company's financial future. (A *pro forma* is simply a projection. A pro forma balance sheet, for example, projects assets and liabilities at the end of some future period.)

Pro forma statements build on the financial tools and concepts you've already learned about, such as income statements, balance sheets, and cash flow analysis. There are many approaches to developing pro forma statements, ranging from back-of-the-envelope estimates to extensive computerized models that attempt to predict the future. Regardless of the approach, the goal is the same: to develop realistic and useful financial projections.

As you develop a pro forma statement, keep these three drivers in mind:

■ *Known relationships and trends*: Sales commissions might normally have been 8% of revenue.

■ *Information regarding future changes*: A competitor may be preparing to release a new product.

■ *Your business goals*: You intend to reduce expenses by 5% through staff attrition and lay-offs.

There are many approaches to developing pro forma financial statements. The three drivers described previously imply *horizontal* approaches: they focus on changes over time. Another class of *vertical* approaches focuses on industry groups.

For example, you might want to determine whether your cost of goods sold, as a percentage of net sales, is similar to other companies in your industry. Successful companies within an industry group often exhibit similar relationships between key indicators such as these. It can be useful to compare such a relationship, computed for your company, with the industry average. It would be discouraging to find that your cost-to-sales ratio is high, compared with the industry average, and it would probably prompt you to take action to lower costs.

Averages for key ratios within different industry groups are commercially available. The difficulty, of course, is that it might be misleading to compare your company to an industry average. Suppose that you work for a local telephone company. If you choose to compare your company's results to the industry averages for telecommunications firms, you will be comparing your results to those of cable TV firms, cellular communications firms, long-distance providers, firms that offer high-speed dedicated connections, and so on. Their financial structures are likely to be very different from yours, and any comparison could therefore mislead you. A vertical analysis can be enlightening, but it must be prepared with great care.

In contrast, a horizontal approach uses your own historic data as the point of comparison. In effect, your company acts as its own control group. While it requires every bit as much care as a vertical approach, it is relatively straightforward, and the horizontal approach can be a very effective way to project financial results. The next section illustrates a horizontal analysis, based on projections created by means of Percentage of Sales.

Forecasting by Percentage of Sales

The Percentage of Sales forecasting approach is based on the concept that many business activities, such as incurring certain expenses, acquiring assets, and assuming liabilities are directly tied to sales dollars. Without sales, a business would neither incur selling expenses nor generate accounts receivable. An increase in sales should result in additional cash in the bank, greater variable costs, higher income taxes, additional administrative expenses, and so on. Sales is a key driver of most other indicators; therefore, it can be useful to base the projection of other indicators on the projection of sales.

The Percentage of Sales forecasting method entails several steps:

1. Analyze historical trends and financial relationships. It may be, for example, that variable costs have, over several years, averaged 7% of total sales.

2. Forecast the key driver, sales, through the next planning horizon—one year, for example.

3. Estimate future expenses and balances, based on their historical relationships to sales. If you project that sales will increase by 3% during the next year, it would be reasonable to project that sales commissions will also increase by 3%.

4. Prepare the pro forma financial statement using the projected sales and expenses.

Case Study: Cummins Printing

Cummins Printing is a small business that specializes in custom print runs of office stationery and catalogs. It has been in existence for three years, since Jim Cummins incorporated the company and acquired its assets partly through a bank loan and partly through funding that he supplied. Cummins Printing is preparing pro formas for 2005. It does so both to estimate its annual expenses and financial results for the next year, and to guide an operating decision it must make early in the year.

The first step is to review a company's existing financial statements for trends, patterns, and relationships. The statement and ratio analysis tools discussed in Part I of this book make up the platform for the pro forma view. For example, Figures 8.1 and 8.2 display the 2002–2004 income and balance sheet statements for the Cummins Printing Company:

FIGURE 8.1
Cummins Printing income statement for 2002-2004.

	A	B	C	D	E	F
1	Cummins Printing					
2	Income Statement for the year ended:	12/31/02	12/31/03	12/31/04		
3	Sales	$498,541	$367,450	$389,864		
4	Cost of Goods Sold					
5	Inventory, 1/1	$116,081	$85,919	$112,969		
6	Purchases	$115,372	$147,970	$187,540		
7	Available for sale	$231,453	$233,889	$300,509		
8	Inventory, 12/31	$85,919	$112,969	$129,125		
9	Cost of goods sold	$145,534	$120,920	$171,384		
10	Gross profit	$353,007	$246,530	$218,480		
11						
12	Expenses					
13	Advertising	$6,166	$5,915	$6,770		
14	Office lease	$8,750	$9,110	$9,544		
15	Insurance	$3,906	$3,754	$4,010		
16	Office supplies	$2,110	$2,680	$3,862		
17	Salaries	$62,378	$72,924	$94,347		
18	Communications	$3,708	$5,507	$7,014		
19	Travel	$1,070	$8,310	$8,733		
20	Depreciation	$4,192	$4,192	$4,192		
21	Operating expenses	$92,280	$110,392	$138,472		
22	Income before tax	$260,727	$136,138	$80,008		
23	Taxes	$65,182	$34,035	$20,002		
24	Net income	$195,545	$102,104	$60,006		

Cummins now needs to identify the financial trends, patterns, and relationships that flow from these worksheets. While there are many different analytical tools and indicators available, the key for budget planning is to focus on what drives the business. Growth in revenues and an increase in working capital are two examples of these drivers. Cummins Printing focuses on growth in revenue as the key driver, and uses Percentage of Sales as its principal indicator. Figure 8.3 displays the income statements from Figure 8.1, along with a breakdown of components by sales. Each statement component is expressed both in terms of raw dollars and as a Percentage of Sales. The assumption is that as sales dollars vary, other components such as inventory and most operating expenses should vary accordingly.

FIGURE 8.2
Cummins Printing balance sheet for 2002-2004.

	A	B	C	D	E	F
1	Cummins Printing	Balance Sheet for the year ended:	12/31/02	12/31/03	12/31/04	
2	**Current Assets**	Cash	$282,288	$272,787	$281,278	
3		Accounts receivable	$66,567	$158,054	$163,422	
4		Inventory	$85,919	$112,969	$129,125	
5		Total Current Assets	$434,775	$543,810	$573,825	
6	**Fixed Assets**	Equipment	$62,903	$62,903	$62,903	
7		Less-accumulated depreciation	$4,192	$8,384	$12,576	
8		Total Fixed Assets	$58,711	$54,519	$50,327	
9						
10		Total assets	$493,486	$598,329	$624,152	
11						
12	LIABILITIES AND STOCKHOLDERS' EQUITY					
13	**Current Liabilities**	Accounts payable	$169,856	$203,742	$183,592	
14		Notes payable	$62,903	$62,903	$62,903	
15		Income taxes	$65,182	$34,035	$20,002	
16		Total liabilities	$297,941	$300,680	$266,497	
17	**Stockholders' Equity**	Retained earnings	$195,545	$297,649	$357,655	
18						
19		Total liabilities and Stockholders' Equity	$493,486	$598,329	$624,152	
20						
21						
22						
23						
24						

FIGURE 8.3
Cummins expresses statement components as a Percentage of Sales as the first step in creating a pro forma.

	A	B	C	D	E	F	G
1	Cummins Printing					Percentage of Sales	
2	Income Statement for the year ended:	12/31/02	12/31/03	12/31/04		3-year average	2004 Percent
3	Sales	$498,541	$367,450	$389,864		100.00%	100.00%
4	Cost of Goods Sold						
5	Inventory, 1/1	$116,081	$85,919	$112,969		25.21%	28.98%
6	Purchases	$115,372	$147,970	$187,540		37.17%	48.10%
7	Available for sale	$231,453	$233,889	$300,509		62.39%	77.08%
8	Inventory, 12/31	$85,919	$112,969	$129,125		27.03%	33.12%
9	Cost of goods sold	$145,534	$120,920	$171,384		35.35%	43.96%
10	Gross profit	$353,007	$246,530	$218,480		64.65%	56.04%
11							
12	Expenses						
13	Advertising	$6,166	$5,915	$6,770		1.53%	1.74%
14	Office lease	$8,750	$9,110	$9,544		2.23%	2.45%
15	Insurance	$3,906	$3,754	$4,010		0.94%	1.03%
16	Office supplies	$2,110	$2,680	$3,862		0.71%	0.99%
17	Salaries	$62,378	$72,924	$94,347		18.85%	24.20%
18	Communications	$3,708	$5,507	$7,014		1.35%	1.80%
19	Travel	$1,070	$6,310	$8,733		1.39%	2.24%
20	Depreciation	$4,192	$4,192	$4,192		1.02%	1.08%
21	Operating expenses	$92,280	$110,392	$138,472		28.02%	35.52%
22	Income before tax	$260,727	$136,138	$80,008		36.62%	20.52%
23	Taxes	$65,182	$34,035	$20,002		9.16%	5.13%
24	Net income	$195,545	$102,104	$60,006		27.47%	15.39%

With so few data points (only three years worth of information on sales) it is unwise to project sales growth on the basis of prior data alone. For example, if you use an approach based on time snapshots, such as Excel's Moving Average tool, or a regression-based method such as TREND or a chart trendline, you will get an answer but you should give it very little credence.

How can you tell what to believe? The issue is *generalizability*. When you prepare an analysis that seeks to project observed findings to an unobserved situation—such as next year's sales revenues—you make a logical assumption that the future will resemble the past. If you have many data points in the analysis, then you can justify that assumption much more readily than if you have only a few. You can examine the baseline of the data and, perhaps, note that sales revenue in a prior year does a good job of predicting the next year's revenue. But with a very short baseline such as three years, you can obtain an apparently reliable trend that turns out to be utterly misleading.

In a situation such as the one depicted in Figures 8.1 through 8.3, you should attempt to obtain additional evidence. For example:

- Do other indicators, such as local or national economic forecasts, support the notion that your business should continue to produce the results that you've observed?

- Is your competition gearing up or scaling back? Are they taking steps to acquire your customers?

- Are changes occurring in your business's technology? Do they work for you or against you?

- What changes are your existing customers facing? Do these changes suggest that they will continue to buy? And will they continue to buy from you?

- Are you preparing to discontinue or to introduce a new product line?

- What is the market trend for your product? Is demand declining or accelerating?

The answers to questions like these, combined with the actual results from prior years, leads Cummins Printing to the reasonable assumption that the growth in revenues for 2005 will be slightly weaker than that experienced during 2004. In particular, Cummins concludes that this decrease will be due to the combination of a larger customer base, a softer economy, and a new advertising campaign. Cummins projects that its 2005 revenue will be $411,696, a 5.6% increase over 2004.

The next step is to forecast expenses based on their historical Percentage of Sales and applied to your projected 2005 revenue. This forecast is displayed in Figure 8.4.

Those components that are expected to vary with net sales have a percentage in column B. Other components are either calculated from the projections (such as gross profit) or are given best estimates as of the end of the prior period (such as beginning inventory, lease payments, and depreciation).

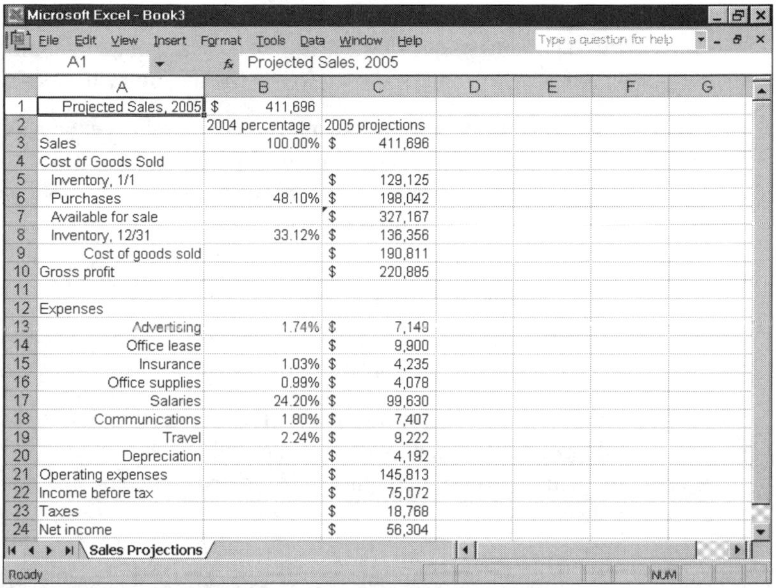

	A	B	C
1	Projected Sales, 2005	$ 411,696	
2		2004 percentage	2005 projections
3	Sales	100.00%	$ 411,696
4	Cost of Goods Sold		
5	Inventory, 1/1		$ 129,125
6	Purchases	48.10%	$ 198,042
7	Available for sale		$ 327,167
8	Inventory, 12/31	33.12%	$ 136,356
9	Cost of goods sold		$ 190,811
10	Gross profit		$ 220,885
11			
12	Expenses		
13	Advertising	1.74%	$ 7,149
14	Office lease		$ 9,900
15	Insurance	1.03%	$ 4,235
16	Office supplies	0.99%	$ 4,078
17	Salaries	24.20%	$ 99,630
18	Communications	1.80%	$ 7,407
19	Travel	2.24%	$ 9,222
20	Depreciation		$ 4,192
21	Operating expenses		$ 145,813
22	Income before tax		$ 75,072
23	Taxes		$ 18,768
24	Net income		$ 56,304

FIGURE 8.4
Applying historical percentages to projected sales results in a pro forma budget for 2005.

The forecast is satisfying as far as it goes, but a disturbing trend emerges from the 2002–2004 income statements. Cummins Printing makes most of its revenues through custom print runs, which often require special paper stock. During the three years of its existence, Cummins has purchased stock for special uses in quantities larger than needed for a particular order. This was done to create lower variable costs, because larger purchases involved lower unit costs. There is also the hope that the customer would make a subsequent order that would require using the remainder of that stock purchase.

Unfortunately, this has not yet happened. Cummins Printing's inventory of paper goods has steadily increased over the three-year period, and has exceeded its growth in sales dollars. Notice in Figure 8.3 that the end-of-year inventory has grown from $85,919 to $129,125 (an increase of over 50%), whereas sales has actually fallen from $498,541 to $389,864 (a decrease of about 28%). Figure 8.4 indicates that unless changes are made, inventory at the end of 2005 will be $136,356.

What impact would a change in purchasing procedures have on Cummins Printing's pro forma income statement and balance sheet for 2005?

Cummins knows that a significant proportion of its sales depends on its ability to provide custom work for its customers. As much as 40% of its business has been due to its willingness to acquire the stock required for special jobs, to purchase stock in bulk, and to apply the unit cost savings to the price it charges its customers.

Cummins has no way of knowing when its existing customers will make further orders (allowing the company to work down the special inventory it has acquired), but must assume that this will happen at some point. In the meantime, one option is to curtail new purchases to its inventory—so doing would slow the rate of increase of its inventory levels—until further orders from existing customers allow it to use the inventory it has already acquired.

Cummins needs to attract new customers. But if Cummins curtails new purchases to its inventory, its ability to perform custom production runs for new customers will suffer. Therefore, the process of working down the existing inventory to a more manageable level will certainly cause the level of new sales to decrease. Is this a sensible business decision?

Cummins explores the effect of reducing its purchase of stock by 50% during 2005, from the pro forma figure of $198,042 to $99,021. Looking at a pessimistic outcome, Cummins assumes that he will lose the 40% of his business that has come from those special jobs. This would bring the sales figure down to $247,018.

Most expenses decrease proportionately with the exceptions of the building lease and the equipment depreciation, which would not normally be expected to vary with net sales. The projected outcome is shown in Figures 8.5 (the pro forma income statement) and 8.6 (the pro forma balance sheet).

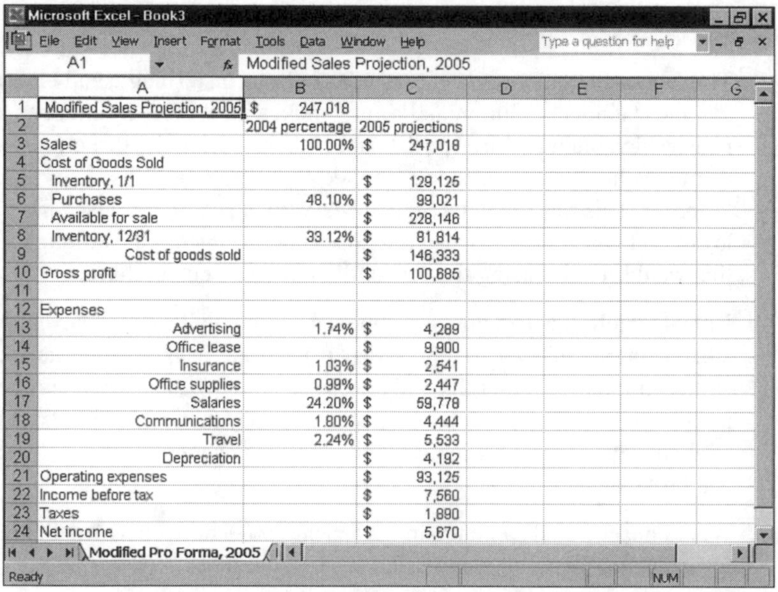

	A	B	C
1	Modified Sales Projection, 2005	$ 247,018	
2		2004 percentage	2005 projections
3	Sales	100.00%	$ 247,018
4	Cost of Goods Sold		
5	Inventory, 1/1		$ 129,125
6	Purchases	48.10%	$ 99,021
7	Available for sale		$ 228,146
8	Inventory, 12/31	33.12%	$ 81,814
9	Cost of goods sold		$ 146,333
10	Gross profit		$ 100,685
11			
12	Expenses		
13	Advertising	1.74%	$ 4,289
14	Office lease		$ 9,900
15	Insurance	1.03%	$ 2,541
16	Office supplies	0.99%	$ 2,447
17	Salaries	24.20%	$ 59,778
18	Communications	1.80%	$ 4,444
19	Travel	2.24%	$ 5,533
20	Depreciation		$ 4,192
21	Operating expenses		$ 93,125
22	Income before tax		$ 7,560
23	Taxes		$ 1,890
24	Net income		$ 5,670

FIGURE 8.5
The 2005 pro forma income statement, based on curtailing inventory purchases, and resulting in lower net sales.

If stock purchases are cut in half, and if net sales consequently falls by 40%, net income will fall by $50,663, or 90%: a huge financial impact for any business. To reduce salaries in accordance with the reduction in net sales by 40%, one employee would have to be laid off: a major human factor for a small business.

FIGURE 8.6

The 2005 pro forma balance sheet in column F reflects the effect of reduced sales on the company's worth.

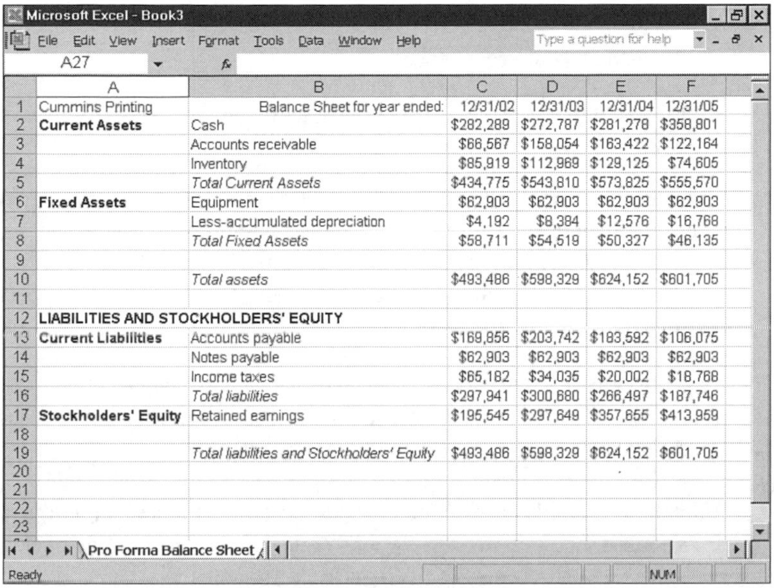

	A	B	C	D	E	F
1	Cummins Printing	Balance Sheet for year ended:	12/31/02	12/31/03	12/31/04	12/31/05
2	**Current Assets**	Cash	$282,289	$272,787	$281,278	$358,801
3		Accounts receivable	$66,567	$158,054	$163,422	$122,164
4		Inventory	$85,919	$112,969	$129,125	$74,605
5		*Total Current Assets*	$434,775	$543,810	$573,825	$555,570
6	**Fixed Assets**	Equipment	$62,903	$62,903	$62,903	$62,903
7		Less-accumulated depreciation	$4,192	$8,384	$12,576	$16,768
8		*Total Fixed Assets*	$58,711	$54,519	$50,327	$46,135
9						
10		Total assets	$493,486	$598,329	$624,152	$601,705
11						
12	**LIABILITIES AND STOCKHOLDERS' EQUITY**					
13	**Current Liabilities**	Accounts payable	$169,856	$203,742	$183,592	$106,075
14		Notes payable	$62,903	$62,903	$62,903	$62,903
15		Income taxes	$65,182	$34,035	$20,002	$18,768
16		*Total liabilities*	$297,941	$300,680	$266,497	$187,746
17	**Stockholders' Equity**	Retained earnings	$195,545	$297,649	$357,655	$413,959
18						
19		*Total liabilities and Stockholders' Equity*	$493,486	$598,329	$624,152	$601,705
20						
21						
22						
23						

All in all, the costs are just too great to justify the (undoubted) benefit to the inventory situation. This is as you might expect when an operational decision exerts such a powerful influence on the way a company does business with its customers.

Excel makes the analysis particularly easy—much easier than the business decision itself might be. The work is in setting up the worksheet that contains the historic data for the income statement and balance sheet. After that is done, the derivation of the percentages is easy and simple. For example, to create the 100% value shown in cell G3 of Figure 8.3, you would enter this formula:

=D3/$D$3

Then, copy that formula and paste it into G5:G10 and into G13:G24. The absolute reference, $D$3, ensures that the denominator in the formula is always the value in cell D3, whereas the numerator in the formula changes according to where the formula is pasted. That is, the formula as pasted into cell G6 changes to D6/$D$3.

TIP

The F4 key gives you a convenient way to convert one reference style to another. If you specify a cell in a formula by using the mouse to point at the cell, Excel uses the relative reference style (such as *D3*) by default. To convert the reference to D3 to the absolute reference style (such as *$D$3*), just highlight that portion of the formula in the Formula Bar and press F4. Pressing F4 repeatedly cycles the reference through mixed reference styles as well: D3, $D$3, D$3, $D3, and then back to D3. This is much more convenient than using the mouse or arrow keys to locate where the $ sign should be placed.

To obtain the values shown in column F of Figure 8.3, enter this formula in cell F3:

```
=(B3+C3+D3)/($B$3+$C$3+$D$3)
```

Then, copy and paste it into F5:F10 and into F13:F24. Another version of this formula is:

```
=AVERAGE(B3/$B$3,C3/$C$3,D3/$D$3)
```

This latter version of the formula, once copied and pasted into other rows, assigns equal weight to each of the three years involved. The former version gives greater weight to a year in which, for example, the advertising expense is high relative to net sales. Your choice of which version to use should be guided by whether you want the average to emphasize or restrain the effect of an unusual value.

TIP Yet another version of the equal-weight formula is =AVERAGE(B5:D5/$B$3:$D$3), array-entered. An array formula uses more memory than its conventional counterpart, but you might find it a more intuitive representation when you see it in the worksheet.

After these formulas are set up, checking the effect of a change in net sales on such variables as expenses, net income, and owner's equity is simply a matter of changing the value of net sales. Because the remaining categories in the income statement and balance sheet depend directly on this value, Excel adjusts them accordingly.

Performing Sensitivity Analysis

After you have created your pro forma statements in Excel, you can use them to analyze different financial scenarios. Evaluating possible changes in your projected financial statements may help identify future risks or opportunities. The Cummins case study illustrated what might happen if sales declined by 40%. It did so by assuming that most costs would follow changes in net sales.

But it is also quite feasible to examine that assumption itself. You might want to understand the effect of lowering your cost of goods sold by 10% on your net income and cash forecast for the year. Or you might ask whether you could stay in business if one of your vendors raised its prices by 20%.

N O T E Excel provides the Scenario Manager to help you keep track of different assumptions in your pro formas. Chapter 13, "Creating a Sensitivity Analysis for a Business Case," discusses the use of the Scenario Manager in some depth. ▪

For a single change to a pro forma, it is usually quicker to simply make a change to the critical cell instead of taking the time to deal with the Scenario Manager.

For example, you could change cell C6 in Figure 8.4 from:

```
=ROUND(B6*$B$1,0)
```

which equals $198,042, to:

```
=ROUND(B6*$B$1*1.2,0)
```

which indicates projected purchases to inventory if the vendor raised its prices by 20%, to $237,650. The effect is to reduce net income from $56,304 to $26,597.

This adjustment can tell you much more than that your net income decreases by about $30,000. Another way of viewing the change in net income is to note that an increase in the cost of purchases to inventory results in a decrease of more than 52% (1–$26,597/$56,304). This means that your net income tracks very closely with your vendor costs: your profit is virtually at the mercy of your vendors' pricing.

Moving from the Pro Forma to the Budget

A pro forma statement can be translated into financial budgets for the upcoming year. The pro forma statement is the forecast. Budgets are used to plan, coordinate, and control a company's operations. The budgeting time period is a matter of judgment. A business may develop annual, quarterly, or monthly budgets depending on such factors as its information needs, its sales patterns (for example, seasonal peaks and valleys versus a steady trend), its operational methods, and its financial structure.

Suppose that Cummins Printing wants to create a quarterly operating budget for 2005, based on its pro forma income statement for that year. The quarterly budget is shown in Figure 8.7.

FIGURE 8.7
The 2005 quarterly operating budget for Cummins Printing created from its pro forma.

	A	B	C	D	E	F	G
1	Cummins Printing	Total		Quarterly projections			
2		for 2005	Q1	Q2	Q3	Q4	
3	Sales	$411,696	$82,339	$164,678	$102,924	$61,754	
4	Cost of Goods Sold						
5	Inventory, 1/1	129,125	129,125	130,571	133,464	135,271	
6	Purchases	198,042	39,608	79,217	49,511	29,706	
7	Available for sale	327,167	168,733	209,788	182,974	164,978	
8	Inventory, 12/31	136,355	130,571	133,464	135,271	136,356	
9	Cost of goods sold	190,811	38,162	76,324	47,703	28,622	
10	Gross profit	220,885	44,177	88,354	55,221	33,133	
11	Expenses						
12	Advertising	7,149	1,430	2,860	1,787	1,072	
13	Office lease	9,900	1,980	3,960	2,475	1,485	
14	Insurance	4,235	847	1,694	1,059	635	
15	Office supplies	4,078	816	1,631	1,020	612	
16	Salaries	99,630	19,926	39,852	24,908	14,945	
17	Communications	7,407	1,481	2,963	1,852	1,111	
18	Travel	9,222	1,844	3,689	2,306	1,383	
19	Depreciation	4,192	1,048	1,048	1,048	1,048	
20	Operating expenses	145,813	29,372	57,696	36,453	22,291	
21	Income before tax	75,072	14,805	30,657	18,768	10,842	
22	Taxes	18,768	3,701	7,664	4,692	2,710	
23	Net income	$56,304	$11,104	$22,993	$14,076	$8,131	
24							

Quarterly Operating Budget

The quarterly budget follows the assumption in the pro forma that the main driver of expenses is the company's net sales. As it happens, revenues for this firm are moderately seasonal: historically, 20% of its sales have occurred during the first quarter, 40% during the second quarter, 25% during the third quarter, and 15% during the fourth quarter. To spread the annual projected net sales of $411,696 across the four quarters, it is necessary to make the following entries:

In cell C3:

`=.2*B3`

In cell D3:

`=.4*B3`

In cell E3:

`=.25*B3`

In cell F3:

`=.15*B3`

These formulas distribute the total projected revenue on a quarterly basis, based on net sales percents for each quarter in prior years.

The inventory level at the start of each quarter is simply the inventory level at the end of the prior quarter.

Inventory purchases during each quarter are a function of both the total projected purchases for the year and the net sales for the quarter. The formula in cell C6 (inventory purchases during the first quarter) is

`=$B6*C$3/$B$3`

The formula represents the amount of anticipated inventory purchases for the year (cell B6), prorated according to the ratio of sales for the quarter (cell C3) to sales for the year (cell B3). Due to the use of mixed references in the formula, copying and pasting from C6 into D6:F6 adjusts the reference to the quarterly net sales from C3 to D3, E3, and F3.

The inventory available for sale during each quarter is the sum of the inventory at the beginning of the quarter plus purchases during that quarter.

The projection for inventory at the end of the quarter is based on the amount that is available for sale, less the cost of goods sold. The cost of goods sold is, again, a function of net sales. For example, the formula in cell C9 is

`=$B9*C$3/$B$3`

Then, the end-of-quarter inventory (cell C8) is projected by means of:

`=C7-C9`

The gross profit is estimated by subtracting the cost of goods sold from the net sales. For example, the gross profit for the first quarter is estimated by:

```
=C3-C9
```

Expenses for each quarter are estimated by prorating the annual expense according to the ratio of the quarter's net sales to the annual net sales. For example, the first quarter's advertising expense is estimated with this formula:

```
=$B12*C$3/$B$3
```

Again, due to the use of the mixed references, this formula can be copied and pasted into the remainder of the range C15:C19, and the cell precedents will adjust accordingly. Rows 13 and 14, which represent the cost of the building lease and depreciation, are assumed *not* to vary with net sales; instead, they are estimated on the basis of the most recent information available at the end of the prior period.

N O T E This book recommends using named ranges in formulas wherever possible. This chapter's discussion of using relative, mixed, and absolute cell addresses in the formula-building process may seem at odds with the use of range names.

But you will find that in situations like the one under discussion here—where you want to fill a large range with related formulas—it's more effective to use relative, mixed, and absolute addresses first, and then build the names. The reason is that addresses respond beautifully to Excel's AutoFill feature, whereas names (even names that use relative addresses) do not.

Total expenses are obtained by summing each quarter's expense categories, and taxes are estimated at 25% of operating income (gross profit less expenses). Net income is the gross profit less the total expenses, less taxes.

Now suppose that Cummins Printing wants to distribute its quarterly operations more evenly. Although the quarterly net sales will continue to be seasonal, it may be possible to obtain, during the first quarter, estimates from customers as to their probable orders during the second through fourth quarters. In that case, it may be possible to balance the quarterly workload more evenly, with consequent savings in overtime salary payments during the busy second quarter.

Cummins estimates that overtime payments during the year are roughly $10,000. Figure 8.8 displays the effect of distributing the workload evenly across quarters.

Notice first that the purchases to inventory shown in Figure 8.8 have been distributed evenly across the four quarters. This is due to the assumption that the workload will be constant, and therefore additional inventory will be needed on a constant basis.

Second, the projection of annual salaries has been reduced from $99,630 to $90,000 (see column G in Figure 8.8). This reflects the anticipated savings in overtime payments. Additionally, the quarterly salary payments are constant across quarters in Figure 8.8. This is done by changing the formula in cell C16 to:

```
=$G16/4
```

FIGURE 8.8
2005 quarterly operating budget for Cummins Printing with workload adjustments to allocate salary costs evenly.

	A	B	C	D	E	F	G
1	Cummins Printing	Total		Quarterly projections			Modified
2		for 2005	Q1	Q2	Q3	Q4	2005 Totals
3	Sales	$411,696	$82,339	$164,678	$102,924	$61,754	$411,696
4	Cost of Goods Sold						
5	Inventory, Start of period	129,125	129,125	140,474	113,660	115,469	129,125
6	Purchases	198,042	49,511	49,511	49,511	49,511	198,042
7	Available for sale	327,167	178,636	189,984	163,171	164,979	327,167
8	Inventory, End of period	136,355	140,474	113,660	115,469	136,358	136,355
9	Cost of goods sold	190,811	38,162	76,324	47,702	28,621	190,811
10	Gross profit	220,885	44,177	88,354	55,222	33,133	220,885
11	Expenses						
12	Advertising	7,149	1,430	2,860	1,787	1,072	7,149
13	Office lease	9,900	1,980	3,960	2,475	1,485	9,900
14	Insurance	4,235	847	1,694	1,059	635	4,235
15	Office supplies	4,078	816	1,631	1,020	612	4,078
16	Salaries	89,630	22,500	22,500	22,500	22,500	90,000
17	Communications	7,407	1,481	2,963	1,852	1,111	7,407
18	Travel	9,222	1,844	3,689	2,306	1,383	9,222
19	Depreciation	4,192	1,048	1,048	1,048	1,048	4,192
20	Operating expenses	145,813	31,946	40,344	34,046	29,847	136,183
21	Income before tax	75,072	12,231	48,010	21,176	3,287	84,702
22	Taxes	18,768	3,058	12,003	5,294	822	21,176
23	Net income	$56,304	$9,173	$36,008	$15,882	$2,465	$63,527

The formula is copied and pasted into cells D16:F16.

Performing these adjustments has two principal effects:

- The annual net income increases by $7,223, as a result of savings in overtime salary payments.

- The net income becomes more variable across quarters. This is because the gross profit for any quarter remains the same, but the quarterly expenses are reduced—and, in the case of the second quarter, the expenses are reduced dramatically, by about 30%.

N O T E Most of the calculations for the modified 2005 totals, shown in column G, are simply the sum of the quarterly amounts. The inventory calculations are different: starting inventory is taken from the first quarter starting inventory, and the ending inventory is taken from the end of the fourth quarter. The cost of goods available for sale is the sum of the beginning inventory and purchases. And the cost of goods sold is the cost of goods available for sale less the ending inventory.

This example illustrates how an operating budget can be used to help you plan and schedule your expenses to increase your profitability. Simply reducing expenses by balancing the workload more evenly has an obvious effect on net income.

Additionally, though, it may be useful to distribute the net income differently than is done by adhering rigidly to percentage of net sales as the only driver. Suppose that Cummins Printing has a large loan payment coming due at the end of the second quarter. By balancing the workload more evenly, net income at the end of the second quarter is increased from 61% of annual net income to 68% of annual net income. Cummins Printing may find it useful to have that additional amount of income earlier in the year to help it meet the loan payment.

This is by no means the only benefit you can realize by re-working a pro forma as an operating budget. For example, if a business projects that its revenue will increase by 10% during the next year, it may want to develop targets for each product line on a quarterly, or even a monthly basis. The entire increase might occur during the month of December. If so, this would very likely have significant implications for the business—December's cash balances, inventory levels, and staffing levels are among the business components that would be impacted. Budgeting, then, is the process of translating the pro forma statements into plans that help you manage your business and optimize your profits.

By comparing your actual results to the budget projections, you can determine whether you are on track to achieve your business goals and financial forecasts. Budget comparisons help you focus on areas of opportunity and concern. If vendor costs increase markedly, you might want to search for a new supplier. An increase in demand for a product may cause you to raise the sales price or alter inventory schedules. Thus, budgets can serve as real time flags for your operational and financial decisions.

Fitting the Budget to the Business Plan

For large companies the planning cycle is extensive. Multi-year business plans are established by top management. Next, managers create operational plans to attain the strategic goals. Pro forma financial statements are then created to quantify and evaluate the plans. Lastly, budgets are developed from the pro forma statements.

Here are three types of budgets that are commonly used:

- *Operating budgets* track projected revenues and expenses to ensure that the projected net income level is achieved.

- *Cash budgets* project cash receipts and disbursements over a period of time. Cash budgets help determine whether it may be necessary to seek outside investment or some other form of external financing.

- *Capital budgets* detail the planned capital (or additions to fixed assets) projects during a designated period.

There are many pitfalls to the budgeting process. One trap is to spend too much time considering the effects of many different scenarios that involve minuscule differences. This can be cumbersome, and tends to add little of value to the analysis. Another trap is to allow budgeting concerns to supersede business goals: budgeting is a means, not an end. It's important to keep budgeting in perspective—used properly, budgets can provide a business a way to plan, coordinate, and monitor its operations. Done improperly, budgeting can waste time and shift your attention away from the bottom line.

Multiple year business plans and pro forma statements are extremely valuable when an endeavor requires more than one year of planning. The company might reasonably ask whether it should continue to invest its resources in a particular division, or it might need to know the anticipated revenue for a product over the next five years. The long-range forecast often impacts operational and financial plans during the current year. Financial plans should extend over the most meaningful planning horizon for your business.

Summary

In this chapter, you have learned how to use historical information to project future revenues and expenses by means of the Percentage of Sales method. This process enables you to create pro forma income statements and balance sheets. Pro formas, in turn, enable you to examine the likely effects on your operations and profits if conditions change or if you modify some aspect of your revenues and expenses.

Operating budgets, which help you plan and manage the way you conduct your business, flow naturally from pro forma statements. You can use budgets to break down your operations and finances into meaningful time periods such as months and quarters. This gives you additional insight into how changes, whether planned or thrust on you, might affect your financial picture.

Key to the entire process is the quality of your projections. Chapter 9 describes how to use Excel to generate the most accurate forecasts possible.

Forecasting and Projections

In business, you often use forecasting to project sales, to estimate what future revenues will be on the basis of past history. This puts you in a position to estimate other quantities, such as cost allocations and staffing, that you need to support the revenue stream.

The term *forecasting*, as used here, is the result of looking back at historic data and figuring out how what came before determined what came after. That process leads to mathematical models that can incorporate your current conditions and forecast what's likely to happen next.

This might sound a bit like reading Tarot cards, but it's not. Consider sunspots. There's a fairly well-known 11-year cycle during which sunspot activity waxes and wanes. Big deal—you could figure that out in just a few decades with a telescope and a calendar. But by using forecasting techniques, astronomers are able to project not just the frequency but the *intensity* of the solar storms that accompany sunspots.

Forecasts that are exactly correct are either very lucky or trivial. Real world systems always have some element of randomness, and no forecasting technique can predict that which is random. If there are components in historic data that vary with some regularity, though, you can use forecasting techniques to make reasonably accurate projections—projections that are better than blind guesses. And that increased accuracy is what reduces your business's operational risk.

Unfortunately, businesses often make an offhand effort at a revenue forecast, and ignore other ways to use forecasts in their planning. Using Excel, you can forecast many other variables, so long as you have a reasonable baseline to create a forecast. For example:

■ If your business depends on high bandwidth telecommunications, you might want to forecast the resources required to keep your users connected to remote computing facilities.

■ If you manage a particular product line, you might want to forecast the number of units that you can expect to sell. This kind of forecast can help you determine the resources necessary to support activities such as installation, warehousing, and maintenance.

■ If you manage customer service, it can be important to forecast the number of new customers you expect. The forecast may lead you to consider changing your staffing levels to meet changing needs.

In this chapter you will learn the fundamentals of creating a useful forecast. You will also learn about different methods of using baseline data to create forecasts, their advantages and drawbacks, and how to choose among them.

Making Sure You Have a Useful Baseline

A *baseline* is a set of numeric observations made over time. Examples of baselines are:

■ Monthly revenue totals for the past four years

■ Daily hospital patient census for the past six months

■ Average annual liquor consumption since 1970

■ Number of calls to customer service per hour for the past week

In short, a baseline consists of a set of quantities measured over time. From the standpoint of forecasting, baselines have four important technical characteristics:

■ A baseline is ordered from the earliest observation to the most recent. This is a fairly simple requirement to meet, but you must meet it. If you have your measurements in a table where rows represent years and columns represent months, it's best to rearrange the numbers into a single column with the earliest at the top.

■ All the time periods in the baseline are equally long. You should not intersperse daily observations with, for example, the average of three days' observations. In practice, you can ignore minor deviations. February and March have different numbers of days, but the two- or three-day difference is usually ignored for baselines that consist of monthly summary observations. The very use of monthly summaries implies that such minor differences are not a matter of concern.

■ The observations come from the same point within each time period. For example, suppose you're monitoring freeway traffic, hoping to forecast when you will have to add new lanes. The conditions that you're measuring are very different on Friday at 5:00 p.m. than on Tuesday at 11:00 a.m. For consistency in the meaning of the baseline, you should stick to a particular time and day.

■ Missing data are not allowed. Even one missing observation can throw off the forecasting equations. If a small fraction of your time series is missing, try replacing that data by estimating it.

> **TIP** A reasonable and quick way to estimate missing data in a baseline is to take the average of the observations immediately before and after one that's missing. For example, if the value for cell A5 is missing, you could enter
>
> =AVERAGE(A4,A6)
>
> in cell A5.

Part
II
Ch
9

If your baseline has these four characteristics, your chances of getting a useful forecast are much better.

Many of Excel's tools, including those that have to do with forecasting, require that you arrange your baseline observations vertically, in columns. For consistency, the examples in this chapter use baselines in columns rather than rows.

In addition to the baseline itself, you also need a method to create a forecast. Excel provides three basic approaches to forecasting: moving averages, regression, and smoothing. This chapter also describes a fourth approach, Box-Jenkins. The *Business Analysis with Microsoft Excel, Second Edition* Web site contains a VBA module that enables you to perform the identification phase of Box-Jenkins forecasting.

Moving Average Forecasts

Moving averages are easy to use, but sometimes they are too simple to provide a useful forecast. Using this approach, the forecast at any period is just the average of several observations in the time series. For example, if you choose a three-month moving average, the forecast for May would be the average of the observations for February, March, and April. If you choose to take a four-month moving average, then the forecast for May would be the average of January, February, March, and April.

This method is easy to compute, and it responds well to recent changes in the time series. Many time series respond more strongly to recent events than they do to long established patterns. Suppose, for example, that you are forecasting the sales volume of a mature product, one that has averages of 1,000 units per month for several years. If your company significantly downsizes its sales force, the units sold per month would probably decline, at least for a few months.

If you were using the average sales volume for the last four months as your forecast for the next month, the forecast would probably overestimate the actual result. But if you used the average of only the last two months, your forecast would respond more quickly to the effect of downsizing the sales force. The two-month moving average forecast would lag behind the actual results for only a month or two. Figure 9.1 gives a visual example of this effect.

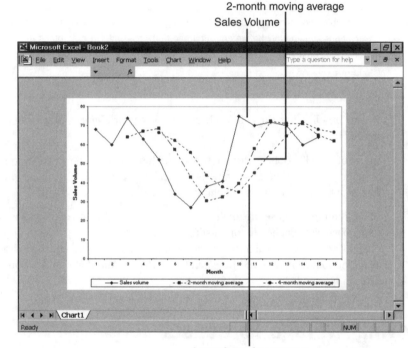

FIGURE 9.1

The two-month moving average for sales volume tracks the actual sales more closely than does the four-month moving average.

The effect depicted in Figure 9.1 occurs because with a two-month moving average, the two most recent months are each responsible for one half of the forecast's value. With a four-month average, the four most recent months are each responsible for only one fourth of the forecast value.

Therefore, the fewer and the more recent the observations involved in a moving average, the more quickly it responds to changes in the level of the baseline.

On the other hand, if you base your moving average forecast on just one or two observations, it can become trivial. In particular, it won't depict an underlying trend in the data any better than the baseline itself does.

Knowing how many observations to include in a moving average is equal parts experience and knowledge of the data series in question. You need to balance the greater responsiveness of a moving average with fewer and more recent observations, against the greater volatility of that average.

One aberrant data point in a three-component average can make a forecast look silly. And the fewer the components, the less the moving average responds to signal and the more to noise. There's no good general rule to use here: you have to use your judgment abetted by your knowledge of the data series you're working with.

Part
II
Ch
9

Case Study: Customer Service

You manage the customer service group for a software development firm. You receive an e-mail from one of your support staff that says she is getting more phone calls from customers who are having a problem with one of your newer applications. You request her to track these calls over a two-week period and report back to you.

The report that you receive has the daily number of calls that she has received concerning this product. You enter the data into an Excel worksheet, laid out as shown in cells A2:A11 of Figure 9.2. To see whether there is any trend in the data, you create a moving average from the number of phone calls, as shown in cells B5:B12 of Figure 9.2.

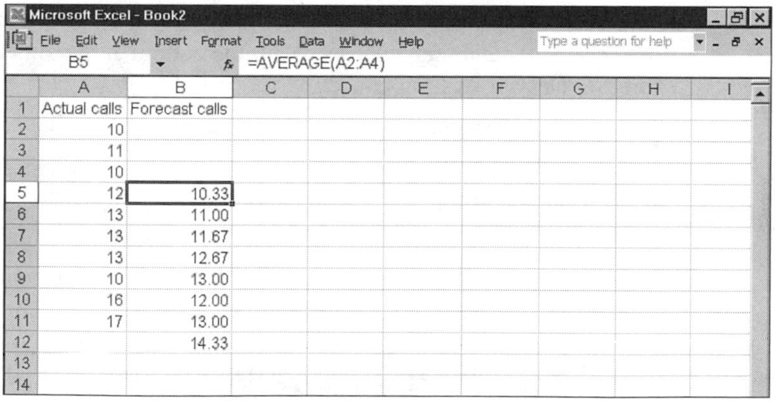

FIGURE 9.2
Moving average forecasts entail the loss of some data at the beginning of the baseline period.

	A	B
1	Actual calls	Forecast calls
2	10	
3	11	
4	10	
5	12	10.33
6	13	11.00
7	13	11.67
8	13	12.67
9	10	13.00
10	16	12.00
11	17	13.00
12		14.33

TIP If you calculate moving averages using formulas like the one shown in Figure 9.2, the Error Checking feature in Excel 2002 might flag them as possibly erroneous. This is because the formulas omit reference to adjacent cells that contain values. You can prevent the error indicator from appearing by choosing Tools, Options and clicking the Error Checking tab. Then, clear the Formula Omits Cells in Region checkbox. Or, if you want to clear the error indicator after the fact, you can select all the cells that contain the indicator, move your mouse pointer over the warning icon to display the menu drop-down, click the drop-down to display the shortcut menu, and click Ignore Error.

You decide to use a three-day moving average: a shorter moving average might not depict the trend well, and a much longer moving average would shorten the trend too much. One way to create a moving average in Excel is to enter the formula directly. To get the three-day moving average for the number of phone calls, as shown in Figure 9.2, you enter

=AVERAGE(A1:A3)

in cell B4, and then AutoFill or copy and paste that formula into B5:B10. The moving average does seem to be trending up, and you might decide to bring the situation to the attention of your company's product testing group.

N O T E To use AutoFill, use your mouse pointer to drag the fill handle of a selected cell or range vertically or horizontally. The fill handle is the small square in the lower-right corner of the selection.

Creating Forecasts with the Moving Average Add-In

Another way to create a moving average is to use the Analysis ToolPak. You invoke this utility from the Tools menu by following these steps:

1. Open an active worksheet.

2. Choose Tools, Add-Ins.

3. Excel displays a dialog box with the available add-ins. Click the box labeled *Analysis ToolPak—VBA*, and then choose OK. At the bottom of the Tools menu, there should now be a Data Analysis option.

4. If necessary, activate a worksheet that contains your baseline data.

5. Choose Tools, Data Analysis.

6. Excel displays a dialog box containing the available data analysis functions. Scroll down the list box until you see Moving Average. Select that tool and then choose OK.

7. Excel displays the Moving Average dialog box that prompts you for the Input Range, Interval, and Output Range, as shown in Figure 9.3.

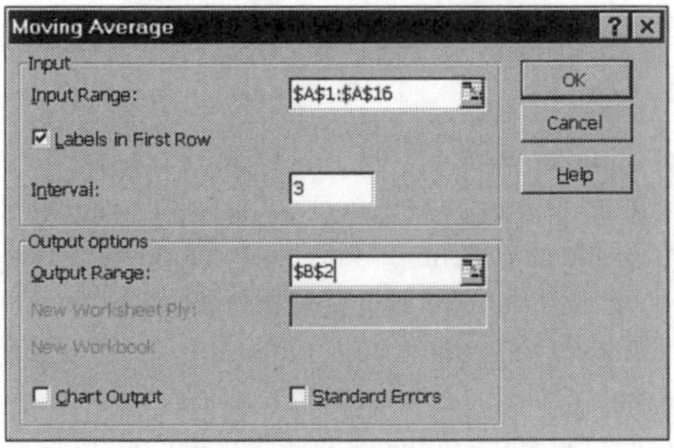

FIGURE 9.3
The Moving Average dialog box enables you to define a period consisting of the observations that go into each average.

8. Click in the Input Range edit box, and either select your baseline data or type its reference.

9. Click in the Interval edit box, and enter the number of intervals that you want to include in each moving average.

10. Click in the Output Range edit box, and enter the address of the cell (or just click the cell) where you want the output to start.

11. Choose OK.

Part

II

Ch

9

Excel fills in the formulas for the moving average on your behalf. The moving averages begin with some #N/A values. There are as many #N/A values as the interval you specified, minus one. This is because there aren't enough data to calculate an average for those first few observations. Figure 9.4 shows the results of using the moving average add-in on the same data as used in Figure 9.1, with a three-period interval.

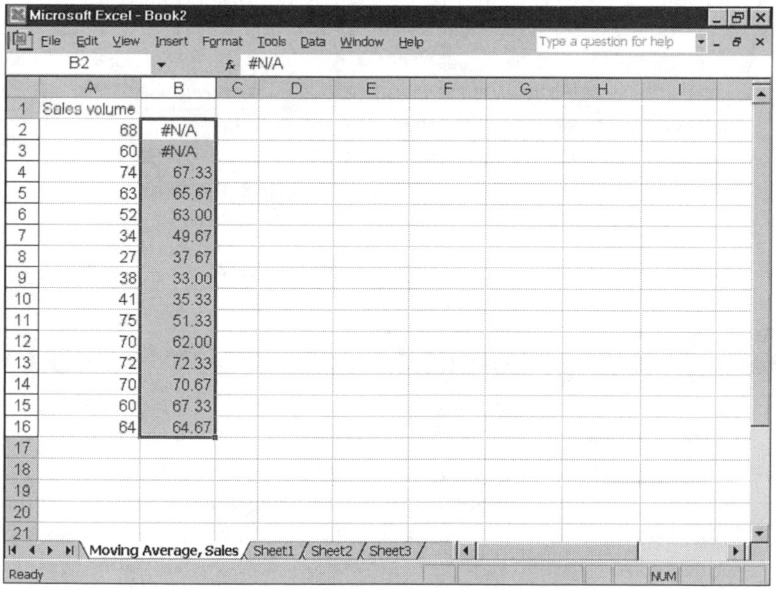

FIGURE 9.4
A three-interval moving average cannot calculate an average for the first two intervals.

Dealing with the Layout of Excel's Moving Averages

It is standard to regard a moving average forecast as a forecast for the first period immediately following the last observation in the average. For example, suppose that you create a three-month moving average of sales revenues, and that the final three observations in your baseline are for January, February, and March. The average of those three observations is usually regarded as the moving average forecast for April: the first period immediately following the last observation.

However, Excel's Moving Average add-in (and, as you will see in the next section, its Moving Average trendline) associate the forecast with the final observation in a given average. Compare, for example, Figure 9.1, where the moving averages were created by entering formulas directly on the worksheet, and Figure 9.4, which was created by the Moving Average add-in. Notice that each moving average in Figure 9.4 is shifted up one position from its position in Figure 9.1. This implies that 550, for example, the first moving average that is computed, is the forecast for the third period.

But it is illogical to regard a number as a forecast for a period that was used to calculate the forecast. The standard interpretation would be that 550 is the forecast for the fourth period, not for the third period.

The best solution is to establish one formula by hand and then use AutoFill to copy and paste it down the column. Here's another solution: after the Moving Average add-in has finished processing, select the values that it outputs and drag them all down by one row. So doing will line up the forecasts with the periods that they are properly associated with.

TIP
If you choose to chart the output by checking the Chart Output checkbox in the Moving Average dialog box, the chart positions the forecasts as it does on the worksheet. After shifting the worksheet values down by one row, edit the chart's forecast series by clicking it and, in the formula bar, change the series' first row to the row that precedes it. For example, change this:

```
=SERIES("Forecast",,'Sales Forecast'!$B$2:$B$25,2)
```

to this:

```
=SERIES("Forecast",,'Sales Forecast'!$B$1:$B$25,2).
```

Creating Moving Average Forecasts with Excel's Charts

You can trade speed for information by creating a chart that uses your baseline data to show a moving average trendline. This method is often faster than using the Moving Average add-in, because it can take several seconds for Excel to load the Add-in Manager, and you can skip this step if you create a trendline on a chart. Furthermore, if you did not install the Analysis ToolPak when you installed Excel, you will need to do so before you can invoke the Moving Average add-in.

The tradeoff is that the chart will not show the actual numeric values of the moving average. Further, it suffers from the defect already noted in the last section of this chapter: the forecast is displayed one time period too early. In this case, there is no workaround, because you cannot shift the location of a chart's trendline.

If you decide that you can live with these tradeoffs, you can create a moving average trendline by following these steps:

1. Select your baseline data.
2. Begin the Chart Wizard, either by clicking the button on the Standard or Chart toolbar, or by choosing Insert, Chart.

3. In step 1 of the Chart Wizard, select the Line Chart. Then select a Line Chart subtype that includes both lines and markers. Click Next.

4. In step 2, verify the data range address and orientation (rows or columns). Click Next.

5. In step 3, set options such as Legend, Chart Title and Axis Titles to the values that you want. Click Next.

6. In step 4, select a location for the chart. Click Finish.

7. Click on the data series in the chart to select it, and choose Chart, Add Trendline.

8. On the Type tab, click the Moving Average box, and either type the periods you want in the edit box or use the Spinner to change the number of periods. The period is the number of observations to include in any given moving average.

9. Choose OK. When you are finished, you see the moving average trendline on the chart (along with the actual observations), as shown in Figure 9.5.

FIGURE 9.5

Excel's Moving Average trendline associates each forecast with the final observation in each moving average.

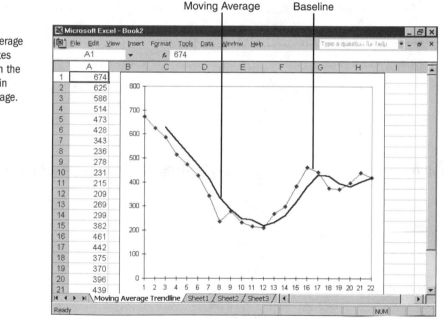

The first few moving averages on the trendline are missing, for the same reason that the Moving Average add-in returns #N/A for the first few moving averages. A moving average consisting of three prior observations cannot be calculated until the third period has been observed.

Forecasting with Excel's Regression Functions

A simple moving average is a quick-and-dirty way to get a feel for the general trend of a time series, but you're likely to want more than that. If you worked through the examples for moving average forecasts, you probably noticed that they don't give you a projection more than one period beyond the final point in your baseline. You can get a projection further into the future by using one of Excel's regression functions.

Each of the regression methods estimates the relationship between the actual observations and some other variable. Applying one of these methods results in an equation whose coefficients you can use to make forecasts. The other variable is often a measure of *when* the observation was made. It could be the numeric position of each observation in the time series, or it could be the date when you made the observation.

Making Linear Forecasts: The *TREND* Function

The TREND worksheet function is the easiest way to create a regression forecast. Suppose that your observations are in A1:A10, and indicators such as day of the month are in B1:B10, as in Figure 9.6. Select cells C1:C10 and array-enter the following formula:

```
=TREND(A1:A10,B1:B10)
```

to get the results in Figure 9.6.

N O T E   Reminder: to array-enter a formula, use Ctrl+Shift+Enter. ■

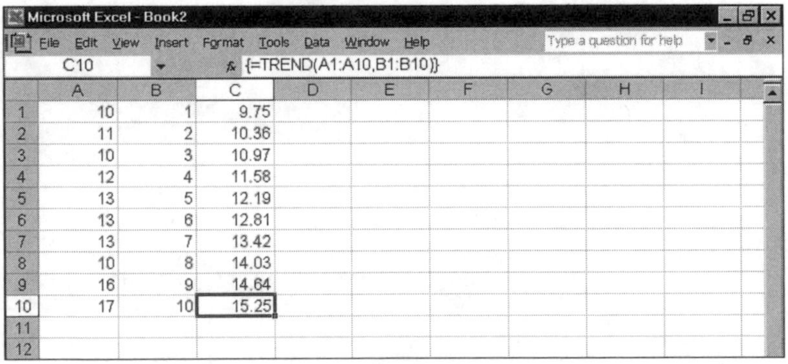

FIGURE 9.6

The TREND function forecasts a baseline of observations on the basis of some other variable.

There are several points to notice about this forecasting method:

■ The same array formula returns each result in C1:C10. Hidden within the array-formula is a more complex expression. Here, the actual, expanded formula is

Cell C1: = 9.13 + .61 * 1

Cell C2: = `9.13 + .61 * 2`

Cell C3: = `9.13 + .61 * 3`

and so on. The value 9.13 is the *intercept* of the forecast line: that is, the value of the forecast at time zero. The value .61 is the *slope* of the forecast line: that is, the change in the value of the forecast for each change in the date of the observations.

■ Because the same intercept and slope values create each forecast value, the forecast doesn't reflect changes in the time series as they occur. For example, the series jumps between the eighth observation (10) and the ninth observation (16). The intercept and slope take account of this jump, but it affects *all* the forecast values. The jump affects the forecast at Time 2, even though Time 2 is six observations before the jump actually occurs.

■ In this example, TREND computes the forecast based on the relationship between the actual observations and the numbers 1 through 10, which could be the first ten days of the month or the first ten months of the year. Excel terms the first argument to the TREND function the *known-y's*, and the second argument the *known-x's*.

TIP If you supply only the first argument, the known-y's, to TREND( ), Excel assumes that the known-x's are a series beginning with 1 and ending with the number of known-y values that you specify. Assuming that the numbers 1 through 20 are in B1:B20, these two formulas are equivalent:
`=TREND(A1:A20)`
`=TREND(A1:A20,B1:B20)`

It was mentioned earlier that the regression approaches to forecasting let you make projections into the future. The regression forecast in Figure 9.6 simply extended through the final actual observation. In practice, you normally want to forecast at least through the value of the next (and, so far, unobserved) point in the time series. Here is how to do that using TREND.

Using the same worksheet data as in Figure 9.6, enter the number 11 in cell B11, and in cell C11 enter

`=TREND(A1:A10,B1:B10,B11)`

N O T E Earlier in this section, examples of the TREND function stated that the formulas should be array-entered. There are several reasons to array-enter formulas, and one is that formulas that return an array of results must be array-entered. The earlier examples returned an array of results. The current example returns one value only and can be entered normally. ■

See the example shown in Figure 9.7 for additional syntax in the TREND function. The first argument, A1:A10, defines the baseline observations (the known y's). The second argument, B1:B10, defines the times when the baseline observations were made (the known x's). The value 11 in cell B11 is a *new x*, and it defines the time to associate with a projection.

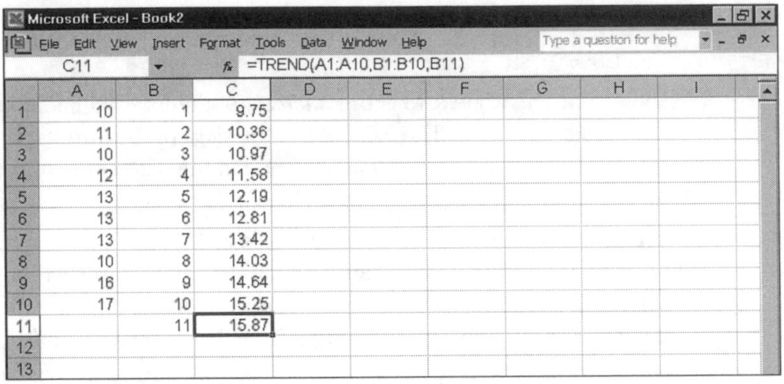

	A	B	C	D	E	F	G	H	I
1	10	1	9.75						
2	11	2	10.36						
3	10	3	10.97						
4	12	4	11.58						
5	13	5	12.19						
6	13	6	12.81						
7	13	7	13.42						
8	10	8	14.03						
9	16	9	14.64						
10	17	10	15.25						
11		11	15.87						
12									
13									

FIGURE 9.7
The TREND function forecasts beyond the end of the baseline by means of its *new-x's* argument.

In effect, the formula says "Given the relationship between the y-values in A1:A10 and the x-values in B1:B10, what y-value would result from a new x-value of 11?" Excel returns the value 15.87, which is a projection of the observed data into the as yet unobserved 11th time point.

TIP You can forecast to dates later than just the next time point by entering a larger value into cell B11. Suppose that the observations in A1:A10 were monthly sales volume for January through October 1995. Then the number 24 in B11 would specify the 24th month: December 1996. The TREND function would return 23.8. This is the projected sales volume for December 1996 on the basis of actual observations from January through October 1995.

You can project to more than one new time point at once. For example, enter the numbers 11 through 24 in cells B11:B24. Then, select cells C11:C24 and array-enter:

```
=TREND(A1:A10,B1:B10,B11:B24)
```

Excel returns, in C11:C24, its forecast for the 11th through 24th time points. It bases the forecast on the relationship between the baseline observations in A1:A10 and the baseline time points 1 through 10 in B1:B10.

Making Nonlinear Forecasts: The *GROWTH* Function

The TREND function creates forecasts based on a *linear* relationship between the observation and the time that the observation was made. Suppose that you chart the data as a line chart with the observations as the vertical axis and time as the horizontal axis. If the relationship is a linear one, the line on the chart is relatively straight, trending up or down, or it may be horizontal. That's your best clue that the relationship is linear, and that TREND is probably the best regression-forecasting tool.

But if the line has a dramatic upward or downward curve to it, then the relationship is probably *nonlinear.* There are many kinds of data that change over time in a nonlinear way. Some examples of this data include new product sales, population growth, payments on debt principal, and per-unit profit margin. In cases where the relationship is nonlinear, Excel's GROWTH function can give you a better picture of the pattern than can the TREND function.

Case Study: Book Sales

The purchasing manager of a large online book retailer has just requested that a new banner be placed on the Web site's home page. The banner advertises a novel that is receiving very favorable reviews. The manager suspects that it will be necessary to order additional copies earlier than normal. To avoid being caught short, the manager starts to track weekly orders for the book, and records the sales shown in Figure 9.8.

FIGURE 9.8

The GROWTH function can be useful in forecasting nonlinear baselines.

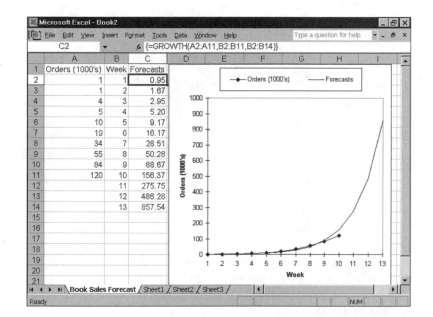

Figure 9.8 shows how both the actual data and the forecasts appear in a standard line chart. Because the line for the actuals curves upward, the decision is to forecast using the GROWTH function. As with TREND, the user can generate forecasts by simply providing new x-values. To forecast into weeks 11 through 13, enter those numbers in B12:B14, and array-enter the following GROWTH function in C2:C14:

```
=GROWTH(A2:A11,B2:B11,B2:B14)
```

Cells C12:C14 forecast the number of orders you can expect for the next three weeks, if the current growth pattern continues. It's necessary to temper such optimistic forecasts with some reality, though. When this sort of forecast projects orders that exceed the weekly total of site hits, it's probably time to back off the forecast.

In cases that display this sort of explosive growth, you might find it more convenient to deal with the logarithms of the observations instead of the observations themselves. For example, you can show the exponential growth as a straight line by using a log scale for the chart's vertical axis. Figure 9.9 shows how the book club data appear in a line chart where the scale of the vertical axis is in log values.

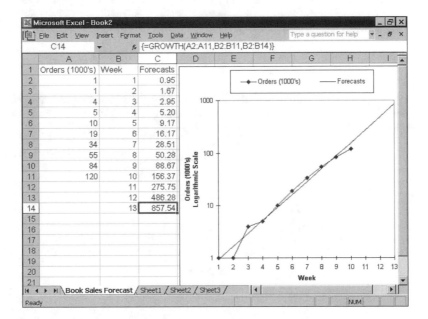

FIGURE 9.9
The logarithmic chart of exponential growth in book sales can be easier to interpret than the standard line chart.

What if TREND instead of GROWTH were used on the book club data? In that case, because the known-x's are linear, TREND would return linear values: values that plot a straight line. In Figure 9.10, note that the TREND series in column C describes that straight line on the chart. Figure 9.10 shows the three series as a standard line chart. The values projected by the GROWTH function are much closer to the ones actually observed, and the GROWTH line is a much better representation of the first ten actual observations than is the TREND line. Therefore, working with this baseline, you are likely to forecast subsequent data more accurately by using GROWTH than with TREND. Using GROWTH acknowledges that the baseline is nonlinear.

N O T E   Figure 9.10 shows the horizontal axis crosses the vertical axis at an Orders value of -20. By default, horizontal axes cross vertical axes at the vertical zero value. You can override this default by clicking the vertical axis to select it, choosing Format, Selected Axis, clicking the Scale tab, and entering the value you want in the Crosses at edit box. ■

FIGURE 9.10

Modeling with GROWTH() can be more convenient than modeling with TREND() when baselines are nonlinear.

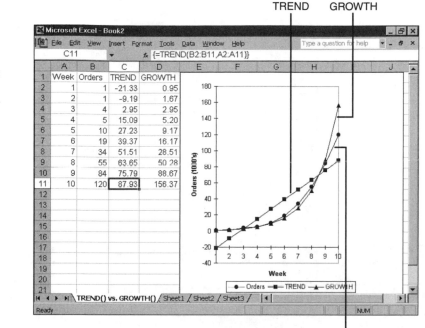

TREND   GROWTH

Baseline

Nevertheless, there's nothing magical about GROWTH: it's simply a convenient way to return specifically logarithmic results. Natural logarithms do not describe all nonlinear series. For example, you might want to project a quadratic trend by squaring its results, like this:

```
=TREND(B2:B11,A2:A11)^2
```

You should often use TREND in these cases, because you can maintain control over your projections by specifying exactly how the model is nonlinear. Although TREND always returns values that describe a straight line, using it together with other worksheet functions (or operators such as the exponentiation operator, as in the previous formula), can bring about the type of result you're after.

Figure 9.11 shows an example of how to use the TREND function to return results identical to the GROWTH function. The array formula used in cells C2:C14 is

```
=EXP(TREND(LN(B2:B11),A2:A11,A2:A14))
```

Note that these values are identical to the ones returned by GROWTH, and would describe the same curve on a line chart. In many cases you will want to use TREND instead of GROWTH, even if the baseline is nonlinear. GROWTH is a useful alternative to TREND when you have data in which natural logarithms fit well.

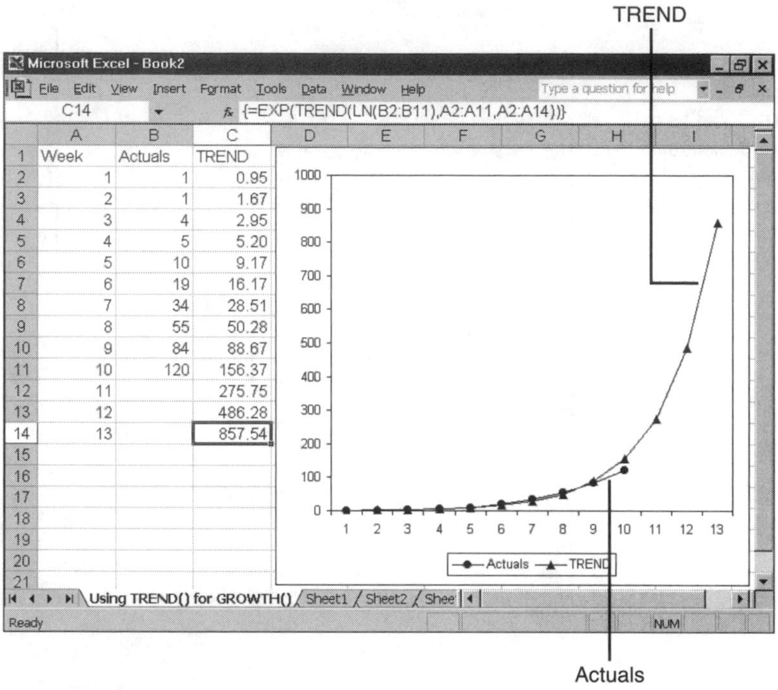

FIGURE 9.11
You can use the TREND function in place of the GROWTH function to handle relationships of any type.

TREND

Actuals

It often helps to keep these points in mind:

- When you chart a variable, the pattern of the data points often suggests a straight line. Then, using the TREND function with no frills is likely the best way to forecast future values.

- If the charted data points suggest a curved line, one possibility is that the GROWTH function will provide your best forecast. Compare the results of using GROWTH on your baseline with the baseline itself. If the fit is good, you should consider using GROWTH to forecast from the baseline.

- If the charted data points suggest a curved line but GROWTH doesn't provide a good approximation, experiment with one of the chart trendlines that Excel provides. These are discussed in the next section.

Creating Regression Forecasts with Excel's Charts

There are plenty of reasons to make extensive use of Excel's charts when you're building a forecast. It always helps to visualize the data. Furthermore, some of the statistical techniques you use in forecasting are sensitive to outliers—that is, data points that are unusually far from the average value. It's much easier to tell if outliers have an effect on your forecasts if you put the data on a chart.

At times, you just want to view a regression forecast on a chart, without calculating the forecast values in worksheet cells. You do so by creating a chart from the baseline values in the worksheet. Then, add a trendline to the chart, in much the same way as you obtain a moving average forecast from a chart. Figure 9.12 displays baseline data and a chart with the baseline, trendline, and forecasts.

FIGURE 9.12
You can create regression-based forecasts directly on a chart by means of trendlines.

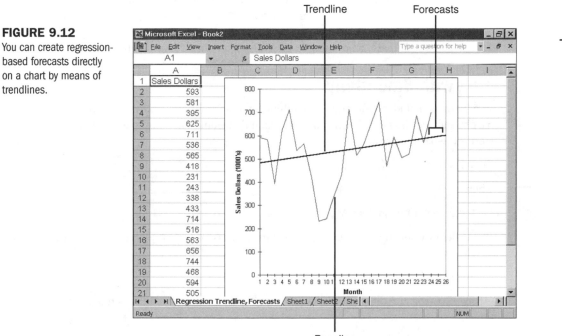

To create the chart in Figure 9.12, use the Chart Wizard to create a line chart of the baseline data in cells A2:A25. Click the chart to open it for editing, and click the data series on the chart to select it. Then:

1. Choose Insert, Trendline.
2. Choose Linear under Trend/Regression Type.
3. Click on the Options tab.
4. In the Forecast group box, either enter the number of Forward forecast periods you want, or use the spinner to specify the number of forecast periods.
5. If you want, click the Display Equation on Chart checkbox. Doing so will place the forecast equation (intercept and slope) as text on the chart. Excel's placement of the equation may obscure the chart's data or trendline, or the equation may not be fully visible. You can select the equation by clicking on it and then dragging it to a new location.
6. Choose OK.

Unlike the Moving Averages trendline, a Linear trendline can return forecast values, and if specified it displays them on the chart.

Forecasting with Excel's Smoothing Functions

Smoothing is a way to get your forecast to respond quickly to events that occur during the baseline period. Regression approaches such as TREND and GROWTH apply the same formula to all the forecast points, and getting a quick response to a shift in the level of the baseline becomes quite complex. Smoothing is a useful way around this problem.

Projecting with Smoothing

The fundamental idea behind the smoothing approach is that each new forecast is obtained in part by moving the *prior* forecast in a direction that would have improved the old forecast. Here's the basic equation:

$$F[t + 1] = F[t] + a \times e[t]$$

where:

t is the time period, such as Month 1, Month 2, and so on.

$F[t]$ is the forecast at time *t*, and $F[t + 1]$ is the forecast at the time period immediately following time *t*.

a is the *smoothing constant*.

e[t] is the error: the difference between the forecast for time *t* and the actual observation at time *t*.

So a smoothing forecast is, in a sense, self-correcting. In words, each new forecast is the sum of the prior forecast, plus a correction factor that moves the new forecast in the direction that would have made the prior forecast more accurate. Later in this chapter you will see how best to select a smoothing constant.

Consider the example shown in Figure 9.13.

Notice that the level of the series increases dramatically at time 8. This is known as a *step function* or *step change*. Smoothing is useful when there are large differences between levels of data in the time series. The linear trendline does not do a good job of reflecting the step increase that occurs between time 7 and time 8. It overestimates the level of the series through time 7, and it underestimates the series thereafter. But the smoothing forecast tracks the actual baseline fairly closely.

FIGURE 9.13
The linear trendline forecast misses the baseline's step change, but the smoothing forecast tracks it.

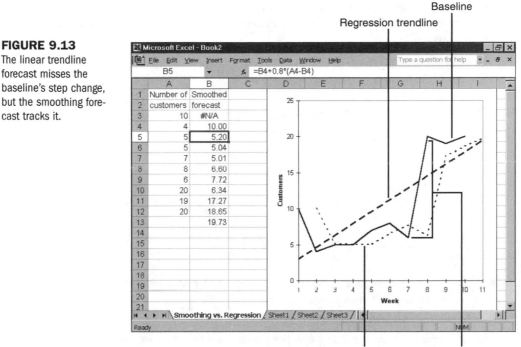

Baseline

Regression trendline

Smoothing forecast   Step change

Using the Exponential Smoothing Add-In

The forecasting methods collectively known as *smoothing* handle the step function effect much better than regression methods do. Excel provides one such method directly with the Exponential Smoothing tool in the Analysis ToolPak.

The Exponential Smoothing tool creates forecasts that are identical to the one shown in Figure 9.13. It uses a different but algebraically equivalent formula to calculate each forecast. Each component—prior observation and prior forecast—in each forecast is multiplied by a factor that represents the component's contribution to the current forecast.

You can invoke the Exponential Smoothing tool by choosing Tools, Data Analysis after you have loaded the Analysis ToolPak.

Case Study: Rental Cars

Suppose that you operate a car rental agency in the Rocky Mountain region. As winter approaches, you start to track customer requests for vehicles that have ski racks. After a few days of monitoring these requests, an early winter storm passes through the area and, as expected, the number of requests per day increases substantially. You would like to know, on the tenth day, how many cars equipped with ski racks you should arrange to make available on the eleventh day.

You enter the data for the first ten days in cells A1:A10 of a worksheet, and start Excel's Exponential Smoothing add-in (see Figure 9.14).

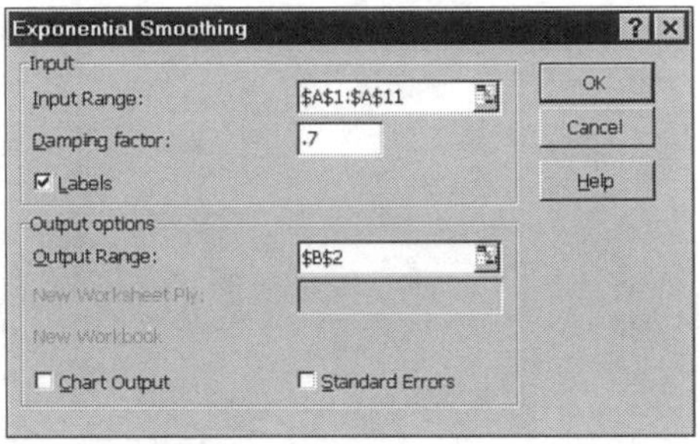

FIGURE 9.14

The Exponential Smoothing dialog box asks you for a damping factor, rather than a smoothing constant.

N O T E The *damping factor* in the Smoothing dialog box and the *smoothing constant* mentioned in the prior section are related as follows:

1 - smoothing constant = damping factor

Therefore, knowing the damping factor means that you also know the smoothing constant, and vice versa. Excel chooses to ask you for the damping factor. ■

You use A1:A11 as the Input Range, fill the Labels checkbox, use B1 as the Output Range, and .7 as the Damping factor. Excel returns the results shown in Figure 9.15.

TIP To forecast one time period beyond the end of the baseline, enter one extra row in the Smoothing dialog box's Input Range edit box.

According to the smoothed forecast, the best estimate of the required number of cars with ski racks on day 11 is 16 or 17. This estimate reflects both the overall level of the baseline data and the increase in requests that occurred on the eighth day. The actual number needed on the eleventh day could drop by several units, as a result of anything from a change in weather conditions to an increase in airline fares. The smoothed forecast strikes a good balance between the recent surge in requests and the average number of requests for the entire 10-day period.

N O T E Even though you might fill the Labels checkbox in the Smoothing dialog box, Excel does not show the label in the resulting chart. ■

FIGURE 9.15
Car rental data with smoothed forecasts; notice the lag in the forecasts.

Baseline

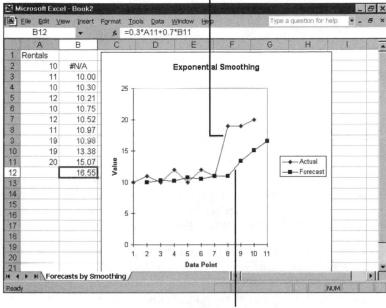

Smoothed forecasts

Notice in Figure 9.15 that the forecast increases on day 9, reflecting the increase in the baseline that occurs on day 8. Generally, simple smoothing approaches lag one step behind occurrences in the time series itself.

The smaller the damping factor, the more responsive the forecast is to recent observations. On the other hand, the larger the damping factor, the longer the forecasts will lag behind recent observations. This is useful if recent observations reflect random occurrences that do not alter the overall level of the time series for long.

Choosing a Smoothing Constant

You should avoid using a damping factor smaller than .7. If exponential smoothing appears to work *significantly* better with a larger smoothing constant, it is likely due to a substantial amount of autocorrelation in the time series. If so, you need to deal with it by means of a forecasting technique other than simple smoothing.

Autocorrelation is an important concept in forecasting. It occurs when there is a dependency between observations that occur at a given time and observations that occur some number of time periods earlier. For example, if you pair up each observation with the observation that immediately precedes it, you can calculate the correlation between the two sets of data that result from the pairing. If the correlation is strong—say, .5 or greater—then there is a substantial amount of autocorrelation in the time series. The autocorrelation—the dependable relationship between earlier observations and later ones—is at the heart of a regression-based forecast. But a baseline time series with much autocorrelation does not lend itself well to the smoothing approach to forecasting.

TIP

You can use Excel's CORREL function to test for autocorrelation. Suppose that your baseline is in A1:A10. You might use

```
=CORREL(A1:A9,A2:A10)
```

to estimate the autocorrelation between each observation and its predecessor. If it is strong, then each observation depends largely on the value of the observation that immediately preceded it.

Another kind of autocorrelation has to do with seasonality in the series. In a time series that consists of months in a year, the observation in each February might be dependent on the prior February. In such cases, you should use seasonal smoothing (see the next section) or a Box-Jenkins model (see the section in this chapter titled "Using the Box-Jenkins ARIMA Approach: When Excel's Built-In Functions Won't Do").

Given that the amount of autocorrelation in your baseline is not too great, you might use Solver to help you arrive at the optimal smoothing constant. The idea is to calculate the amount of error in the forecasts using one smoothing constant, and then to direct Solver to minimize that error value by changing the smoothing constant. To do so, take these steps (based on Figure 9.15):

1. Install Solver from Office Setup if necessary.

2. In cell B15, enter this formula:
   ```
   =SQRT(SUMXMY2(A3:A11,B3:B11)/9)
   ```

3. Give a cell the name SmoothingConstant and enter the value **0.3** in that cell.

4. Give another cell the name DampingFactor and enter the formula
   ```
   =1-SmoothingConstant
   ```

5. Choose Tools, Solver. Set the Target Cell to B15 and click the Min option button. Set the Changing Cells to the SmoothingConstant. Click Solve.

The formula in cell B15 calculates what's sometimes termed the *root mean square error*. It uses the SUMXMY2 worksheet function to return the sum of the squared differences between the actual observations and the smoothed forecasts: these are the squared errors. The formula then divides by the number of forecasts, and takes the square root of the result. The root mean square error is one standard way of measuring the amount of error in forecasts.

When you invoke Solver, it tries other values of the smoothing constant until it finds the one that minimizes the root mean square error—that is, the one that provides the most accurate smoothed forecasts.

Making Smoothed Forecasts Handle Seasonal Data

If you want to forecast sales, you almost certainly need to account for seasonal trends. Sales data and related time series are frequently seasonal. For example, sales may spike at the beginning of the year and then return to a lower level until the next year.

This effect can be due to the nature of the product: the demand for parkas is lower during spring and summer than during fall and winter. It can also be due to fiscal years: buyers might increase their purchases at the point in the fiscal year when dollars are plentiful. In cases like these, the regression and simple smoothing methods may be inadequate to forecast a seasonal trend.

When a time series displays a seasonal trend, it is usually necessary to modify the smoothing formula. Instead of forecasting just on the basis of the prior observation, a seasonal forecast works on the basis of two components:

- A trend component, which represents any upward or downward drift in the baseline.
- A seasonal component, which represents any upward or downward spikes in the baseline that occur at regular intervals.

The seasonal smoothing process takes place in two phases: an initialization phase, which quantifies the magnitude of the trend and seasonal components, and a forecasting phase, which makes the projections based on those components. Consider the time series in Figure 9.16.

FIGURE 9.16
Sales data from baselines greater than one year in length usually display a seasonal component.

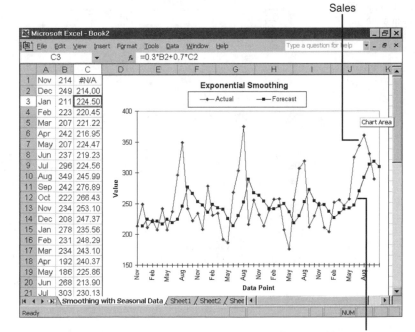

The series in Figure 9.16 has considerable seasonality. It trends up each August and down again each November. A forecast that used simple exponential smoothing would have some undesirable lag, because a current forecast is based only on the prior observation and the prior forecast. Therefore, a forecast of the surge in the series' value that occurs each August would lag by a month each year. Figure 9.16 also shows the forecast based on the time series by means of simple exponential smoothing.

Seasonal smoothing takes account of this regularity in the data by looking back at the pattern in prior years. The current forecasts then reflect the prior pattern. This minimizes the lag from the prior observation to the current forecast. Figure 9.17 shows the same baseline as in Figure 9.16, along with a seasonally smoothed forecast. There is still some lag, but not as much as with simple smoothing. Furthermore, because each forecast depends in part on an observation from a prior *year*, it is possible to extend the forecast further into the future than it is with simple smoothing.

N O T E This kind of analysis can be useful to a business even if it never prepares a formal forecast. Just knowing about seasonality in revenues, costs, or profits helps you make more effective operational decisions. Knowing the degree of change that the seasonality causes makes these decisions more effective yet. ▓

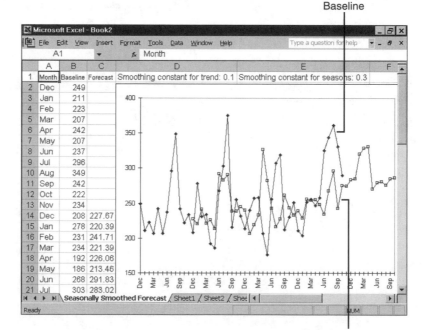

FIGURE 9.17
Seasonality can sometimes let you forecast further into the future than can a one-step-ahead forecast.

Two smoothing constants are necessary for seasonal smoothing: one for any trend there may be in the series, and one for the seasonal component. You can use Solver, much as in the prior section, to help you find the best values for the constants. Just include both as the changing cells.

The *Business Analysis with Microsoft Excel, Second Edition* Web site contains a file named Smooth.xls. The file contains a module, also named Smooth. The module contains a VBA procedure, SeasonalSmooth. SeasonalSmooth performs seasonally smoothed forecasts on a baseline of observations. To run the SeasonalSmooth code, follow these steps:

1. Have a worksheet with your baseline open. The baseline should occupy a single column.

2. Open Smooth.xls, and switch back to the worksheet that contains your baseline observations.

3. From the Tools menu, select Macro.

4. In the Macro Name/Reference list box, select Smooth.xls!SeasonalSmooth.

5. Choose Run.

When you run that macro, a dialog box similar to the Exponential Smoothing dialog box appears on your screen, giving you the opportunity to identify these items:

- An input range—your baseline—found on your worksheet in a single column.

- The number of periods in each season. For example, if your input data consist of one observation for each month in the year, then the number of periods in each season (Spring, Summer, Fall, and Winter) would be 3. If your input data consists of one observation for each week in the month, then the number of periods in each season would be 4, if you consider that a month is a season, or 12, if you consider that a quarter is a season.

- The number of seasons per calendar block. A calendar block is the period of time during which a seasonal cycle becomes complete. For example, if you are concerned with quarterly cycles, then the calendar block would likely be one year. If you are concerned with weekly cycles, then the calendar block might be one month.

- The two smoothing constants: one for the trend, and one for the seasons. Both constants should be set to a fractional value between 0 and 1.

Using the Box-Jenkins ARIMA Approach: When Excel's Built-In Functions Won't Do

Box-Jenkins methods, often called *ARIMA* (for *A*uto*R*egressive *I*ntegrated *M*oving *A*verage) models, have much broader scope than simple moving average, regression or smoothing forecasts, and they can often remove most of the drawbacks of the approaches discussed previously.

However, Box-Jenkins methods are also much more complex, well beyond the scope of this book to cover in detail. This chapter discusses only the preliminary phase of these methods, the identification phase. Completing the identification phase helps you to decide whether to make your forecast using a program written specifically for Box-Jenkins, or whether you can choose a regression or smoothing approach that Excel supports directly.

The Web site includes VBA code that will assist you in determining whether a Box-Jenkins model is necessary to forecast your time series properly.

Understanding ARIMA Basics

Suppose that you have a baseline of observations from which you want to make a forecast. Excel provides little in the way of guidance as to whether you should use a regression approach such as TREND or GROWTH, or a smoothing approach such as the Exponential Smoothing add-in, to create forecasts from your baseline. Many people choose one or the other on an *ad hoc* basis: they might be more familiar with one approach than with another, or they might want to save time by forecasting with a chart trendline, or they might simply flip a coin.

Box-Jenkins models provide you with a quantitative basis for deciding between regression and smoothing—and, carried to their conclusion, can apply both regression and smoothing simultaneously to create the best forecast. The process does this by examining the patterns of correlations in the baseline and returning information to you that suggests whether a regression approach (in ARIMA, AutoRegressive) or a smoothing approach (in ARIMA, Moving Average), or a combination, is optimal.

The Box-Jenkins identification phase, covered in this section, is a formal, rather than *ad hoc*, means of choosing an approach to forecasting. To understand this more fully, consider that a time series can have:

- An autoregressive component. Each observation is dependent on a prior observation (not necessarily the immediately prior observation). An example is revenue from leases, where the amount of revenue each month reflects the amount of revenue the prior month. This is very similar to the concept of autocorrelation, described previously in the section on Choosing a Smoothing Constant.

- A trend component. The series level drifts regularly up or down over time. An example is unit sales of a new product that is gaining market acceptance. Eventually the unit sales figures will become constant and the trend will disappear, but during the early phases there is often a clear, sometimes explosive trend.

- A moving average component. In the Box-Jenkins context this means that the series experiences random shocks over time. The effect of these shocks may linger in the level of the series long after the shock itself has occurred.

These three components may exist separately or in combination in any time series. There are AR (autoregressive) models, MA (moving average) models, and ARMA (autoregressive moving average) models. In some cases it's necessary to work with the differences between one observation and the next; then, before forecasting, the observations have to be un-differenced or integrated. Then, an "I" becomes part of the model: ARI models, IMA models, and ARIMA models. Furthermore, there may be seasonality in the series, leading to (for example) a series that has both a regular and a seasonal AR component, as well as a regular and a seasonal MA component.

With all these models from which to choose, how do you select the one that best fits your time series, and is thus the best one to use for forecasting? ARIMA jargon refers to this as the *identification* phase. Early in the analysis, charts called *correlograms* are created. These correlograms help identify what sort of forecasting model, if any, you should consider.

A Box-Jenkins module can be found in the file named ARIMA.xls on the *Business Analysis with Microsoft Excel, Second Edition* Web site. This module contains a macro named ARIMA, which creates correlograms for your time series. By examining the correlograms, you can determine whether you should use one of the complete Box-Jenkins computer programs to complete the analysis, or whether you can use an Excel regression function or the Exponential Smoothing add-in. There are many programs available that perform complete Box-Jenkins analyses; the more familiar ones include SAS and SPSS.

To run the ARIMA macro, have a worksheet open that contains your baseline in a single column. Then, follow these steps:

1. Open ARIMA.xls, and switch back to the worksheet that contains your baseline observations.
2. From the Tools menu, select Macro.
3. In the Macro Name/Reference list box, select ARIMA.
4. Choose Run.

The ARIMA code displays a dialog box where you enter the address of your baseline data, whether to compute first differences, and how many lags you want to view for the autocorrelations. (The effects of these options are covered later in this section.) The remainder of this section describes the choices you have in the dialog box, and how to interpret the procedure's output.

You should not use Box-Jenkins models with fewer than 50 observations in the time series. It takes at least this many observations to model the data with any accuracy. In practice, it is usual to obtain well over 100 observations prior to starting the forecast process.

TIP This recommendation is not limited to Box-Jenkins forecasts: it could and should be used for most forecasts based on any regression method. Before you place much faith in a regression forecast, use the worksheet function LINEST or LOGEST to determine the standard error of estimate for the regression (this is the value returned in the second column of the array's third row). If the standard error is large relative to the precision that you need so as to have confidence in a forecast, it's probably best to obtain a longer baseline before you proceed with a forecast.

In sum, before you decide to employ these methods with any real baseline data, be sure that you have enough data points for the task to be worthwhile.

Starting with Correlograms to Identify a Model

A *correlogram* displays correlation coefficients in graphic form, one for each lag in a time series. Figure 9.18 shows a correlogram for lags 1 through 20.

FIGURE 9.18

The correlogram for ACFs for lags 1 through 20: this could be either an AR or an ARMA process.

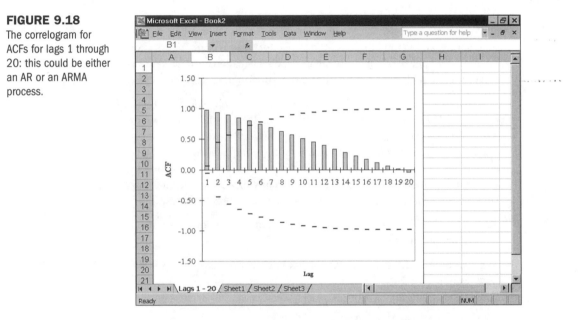

N O T E The time series used in Figures 9.18 through 9.23 are far too long to include here. You can find them in a workbook titled ARIMA Series.xls on the Web site. ■

The ACF is the *autocorrelation function*, and is a type of correlation coefficient, akin to the autocorrelations discussed in Choosing a Smoothing Constant earlier in this chapter. The dashed lines show two standard errors of the ACFs. An ACF that extends above an upper dashed line, or one that extends below a lower dashed line—thus over two standard errors from zero—is usually considered statistically significant. Here, the ACFs gradually tail off. This pattern in the ACFs is typical of an autoregressive (AR) model.

The lags simply identify which data are used in the ACF. For example, consider the ACF at lag 1 in Figure 9.18. It is the autocorrelation between the second through twentieth observations, and the first through nineteenth observations.

The second series, consisting of observations one through nineteen, lags one step behind the second through twentieth observations. Similarly, the ACF at lag 2 is based on the data in the third through twentieth observations and the first through eighteenth observations. The second set lags two steps behind the first set (see Figure 9.19).

FIGURE 9.19
Lags are relationships between different subsets of a time series.

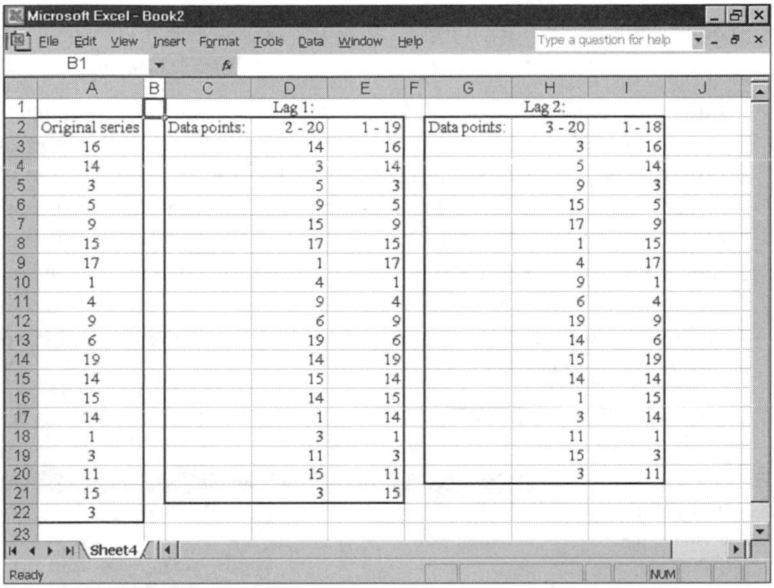

A	B	C	D (Lag 1:)	E	F	G	H (Lag 2:)	I	J
Original series		Data points:	2 - 20	1 - 19		Data points:	3 - 20	1 - 18	
16			14	16			3	16	
14			3	14			5	14	
3			5	3			9	3	
5			9	5			15	5	
9			15	9			17	9	
15			17	15			1	15	
17			1	17			4	17	
1			4	1			9	1	
4			9	4			6	4	
9			6	9			19	9	
6			19	6			14	6	
19			14	19			15	19	
14			15	14			14	14	
15			14	15			1	15	
14			1	14			3	14	
1			3	1			11	1	
3			11	3			15	3	
11			15	11			3	11	
15			3	15					
3									

NOTE When a baseline has trend—that is, when it has a pronounced upward or downward slope—it is often necessary to *difference* the observations. First-differencing usually removes the trend in the baseline, making it stationary—that is, roughly horizontal. (Subsequently undifferencing the differenced observations is termed *integrating*, the "I" in ARIMA.) The ACFs of a stationary baseline can be interpreted; the ACFs of an undifferenced baseline that has a trend are ambiguous: you don't know how to attribute them in identifying a model.

The ARIMA macro's dialog box has a checkbox for first-differencing. If your baseline has a pronounced slope, click the checkbox. ARIMA will then difference your baseline, removing the trend and making the ACFs interpretable.

Identifying Other Box-Jenkins Models

To identify a particular Box-Jenkins model, it is necessary to examine two correlograms: one for the ACF at different lags, and one for the PACF (partial autocorrelation function) at the same lags.

A PACF is conceptually similar to a partial correlation coefficient, which is the relationship between two variables after the effect of another variable or variables has been removed. For example, a partial correlation coefficient might measure the relationship between revenue and profit margin, after the effects of number of salespeople and advertising costs have been removed from the relationship.

Similarly, a PACF at lag 4 would measure the relationship between, say, A5:A20 and A1:A16, after the effects of the intervening series have been removed.

Each Box-Jenkins model (AR, MA, ARMA, and so on) has a distinctive signature in the pattern of the ACFs and PACFs in their correlograms. Figure 9.18 shows the ACF of an autoregressive series. It is characterized by either a gradual decline in the ACFs (as shown) and by a single spike in the PACF. For a baseline that displays this pattern of ACFs and PACFs, you could use an Excel regression technique, and regress the baseline onto itself, according to the location of the PACF's spike. For example, suppose that the spike were at lag 1. In that case, your known-y's would begin at the second observation in the baseline, and end at the end of the baseline. Your known-x's would begin at the start of the baseline, and end at its next-to-last observation.

Figure 9.20 shows the ACFs for a moving average process, and Figure 9.21 shows its PACFs.

FIGURE 9.20

ACFs of a moving average process: notice the single spike at lag 1.

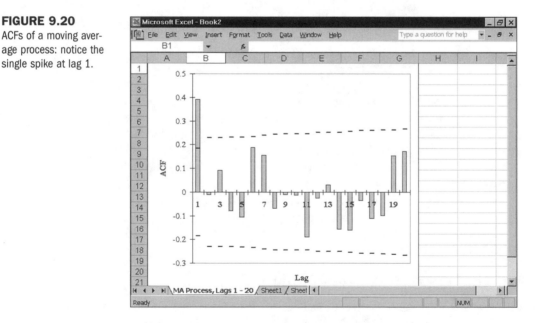

FIGURE 9.21

PACFs of a moving average process: notice the gradual decline in the absolute magnitude of the PACFs.

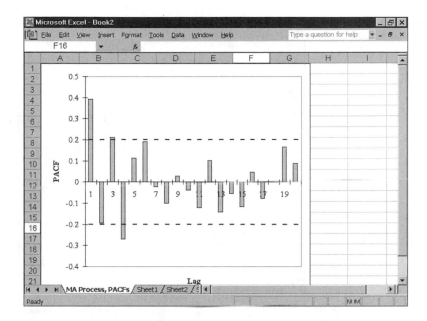

Notice the large, statistically significant ACF value at lag 1 in Figure 9.20. (A value such as this is often termed a "spike" in a correlogram.) It is the only significant ACF in the correlogram.

Also notice that among the first six PACF values in Figure 9.21, three are statistically significant and two just miss significance. This suggests that the PACFs are gradually dying out—in contrast to the single spike in the ACF correlogram in Figure 9.20.

This pattern—single spike in the ACF, gradual decline in the PACF—is characteristic of an MA process. If the ACF's spike is at lag 1, you can use Excel's Exponential Smoothing add-in with some confidence that it is the proper forecasting tool. If the single spike occurs at some other lag, you should resort to an application that provides specifically Box-Jenkins forecasting.

Figures 9.22 and 9.23 show the ACFs and the PACFs in the correlograms for a mixed process, one with both autoregressive and moving average (ARMA) components.

Notice the gradual decline in the ACFs in Figure 9.22, as well as in the PACF in Figure 9.23. This pattern in the correlograms is typical of a mixed, ARMA process. To forecast properly from this baseline, you would need to use an application that performs Box-Jenkins forecasting.

If your time series show any patterns similar to these when you run the Box-Jenkins add-in, you should consult a text that specifically covers Box-Jenkins models, and use one of the standard statistical programs that offer Box-Jenkins options. You are likely to get a much more accurate forecast of your data if you do so than if you use simple moving averages, regression, or exponential smoothing.

FIGURE 9.22
ACFs of an autoregressive, moving average process gradually decline.

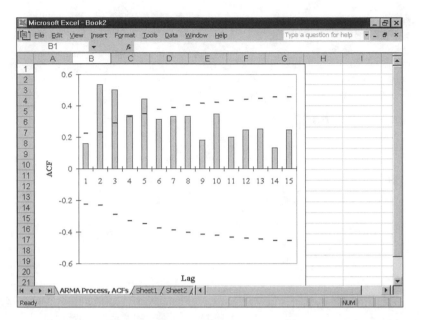

FIGURE 9.23
The PACFs of an autoregressive, moving average process, like its ACFs, gradually decline.

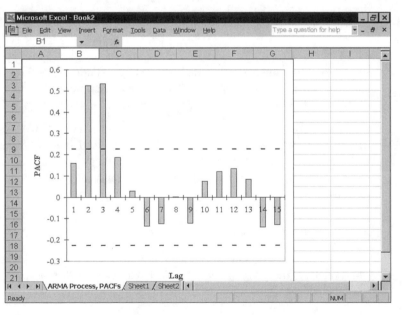

Summary

Forecasting can be trappy. To create a good forecast, you need a well-measured, well-defined baseline of data. You should use the suggestions made in this chapter to choose the most appropriate approach (moving average, regression, smoothing, or Box-Jenkins). At times, your baseline might not suggest an appropriate method, and you might need to wait for a longer baseline before you can be confident of your forecast.

Even if you feel you've done everything right, conditions have a way of changing unexpectedly—making your careful forecast look like a blind guess. Be sure to regard your forecasts with a healthy dose of skepticism. The more variables you have to work with, the more ways there are to view the future. Changes in one forecast can tip you off to the possibility that another forecast is about to change.

The methods described in this chapter are accurate ways to help you build your business plan. They can help you answer questions such as whether to anticipate an increase or a decrease in demand, whether price levels are rising or falling, and (perhaps more importantly) to what degree. Because the discussion has not explored the underlying theory of these approaches in great depth, you should consider studying a text (such as *Time Series Analysis, Forecasting and Control* by Box, G.E.P., and Jenkins, G.M.) devoted to the topic if you make many forecasts in the course of your work.

Part
II

Ch
9

CHAPTER 10

Measuring Quality

Product quality is an important component of profitability. Other things being equal, a product with a reputation for high quality tends to sell more units than a product without that reputation. A product with good quality suffers fewer customer complaints, fewer free service calls, and fewer warranty repairs. Poor product quality goes directly to the bottom line in the form of lost profit.

It is also true that the quality of *operations* drives profit margins. When customer service representatives spend too much time chatting with one customer, that means another customer is on hold, planning to buy someone else's product. When invoices are incorrect or indecipherable, there is usually a delay in receipts. When the purchasing department orders unnecessary parts from a supplier, there is an unnecessary increase in carrying costs. When the quality of goods purchased is *too* high, the cost of the goods is probably also too high: zero-defect manufacturing is very expensive.

You can monitor each of these sorts of processes using Excel. The only other item you need is a source of data. This chapter describes how to use Excel to help you track and control these processes.

In this chapter, you learn to create and interpret statistical process control charts for both variables and attributes, create sampling plans to help you determine whether shipments of goods are acceptable, and decide whether a tested sample's defects are representative of those in its population.

Monitoring Through Statistical Process Control

The idea behind statistical process control (SPC) is that over a period of time you can take measurements on a process and determine whether that process is going out of control. Examples of process measurements include

- Number of defective units in a manufacturing run
- Average number of defects in a unit
- Average diameter of a part that must meet a precise specification
- Average number of errors in an invoice
- Average length of time that customers remain on hold
- Average available capacity of a data communications circuit

or virtually any other process that your company uses.

The key phrases here are "over time," "average," and "out of control." *Over time* means that SPC depends on repeatedly and regularly measuring the process—daily, perhaps, or hourly or weekly. Your choice of how often to measure the process depends on how closely you want to monitor it.

For example, if it is a continuous process, and one that is critical to your company's success, you might decide to monitor it hourly. This could happen if you were in the business of manufacturing ceramic tiles, and the color of the glaze as it leaves the kilns is a standard that is important to your customers.

Average has two implications. First, it means that SPC often depends on sampling several units at any given time. Suppose that you decide to monitor errors in invoices that your accounts receivable department prepares. It would be too costly and time consuming to examine every invoice. On the other hand, if you examine only one invoice per day you probably won't get a good estimate of the overall accuracy of the invoices.

In cases like these, SPC uses a random sample of the process, and it uses the average of that sample as an estimate of the process for that time period. You might decide to sample five invoices daily, and to use the average number of errors in that sample as the process estimate for that day.

On the other hand, you might use a 100% sample, in which case you would monitor every instance of the process. For example, this could occur in a manufacturing environment if you use a procedure that tests every unit as soon as assembly is complete.

The second implication of SPC averaging is the calculation of the typical value of the process. The periodic measurements that you take combine to form an overall value. For example, you might find that over a several-week period the average number of ceramic tiles you produce with defective glazing is 1 in 500. This long-term average forms a central point, the process's average level, and your periodic measurements vary around that level—some higher, some lower.

Out of control means that SPC uses information not only about the average level of a process, but about its variability too. Suppose that you run the customer service department for a financial services company, and that 20 people answer your phones to take orders from your customers. You arrange to monitor the call length of 16 randomly sampled calls per day, and learn that the average call length is two minutes and twenty seconds.

One hundred forty seconds for the average phone call seems satisfactory until you notice that 12 calls took less than a minute, and four calls took over six minutes each. You might decide that you need to learn why some calls take so long. (Are some of them personal calls? Is a representative putting callers on hold to look up something that he should have known?) You would not have known about the variations if you looked only at the average call length.

Using X-and-S Charts for Variables

SPC typically uses charts to depict the data in graphic form, as shown in Figure 10.1.

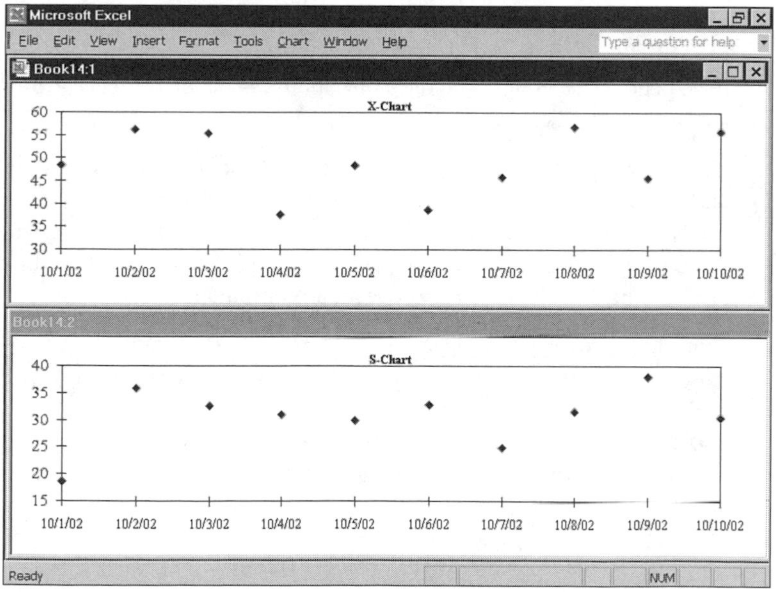

FIGURE 10.1
These SPC X-and-S charts summarize the actual observations, but control limits are needed to interpret them properly.

Figure 10.1 shows two charts: one for the process average (the X-chart) and one for the process standard deviation (the S-chart).

N O T E A *standard deviation* is a measure of how much individual scores vary around an average. Conceptually, it is similar to the range between the highest score and the lowest
score. It is a more useful measure than the range, though. The range tells you only the difference
between the two most extreme observations. The standard deviation takes all the scores into account
in measuring how much variability there is in the group of scores.

If you're not familiar with standard deviations, just keep in mind that a standard deviation, like a
range, is a measure of variability. This book explains standard deviations more fully in Chapter 15,
"Making Investment Decisions Under Uncertain Conditions." ▪

Many SPC charts are laid out in a fashion similar to the ones shown in Figure 10.1. The horizontal axis always shows the time (which hour, which day, which week, and so on) that a
measurement was taken. The X-chart's vertical axis always represents the average measurement of a sample at a particular time. The S-chart's vertical axis always represents the standard deviation of the sample at a particular time. They are known as X-and-S charts because
the statistical symbol for an average is x, and the statistical symbol for the standard deviation
is s.

An alternative to X-and-S charts is the X-and-R chart, which substitutes the range of
measures—the largest measure minus the smallest measure—for the standard deviation as
an estimate of the variability in the process. The principal rationale for using the range
instead of the standard deviation is that in the mid-20th century, when these techniques were
developed, calculating a standard deviation was tedious and error prone, whereas calculating
a range was quick and easy.

Even with tools such as Excel that make it a snap to get a standard deviation, some tradition-
alists prefer the range as a measure of process variability. Its main defect, of course, is that
the size of the range is entirely dependent on two observations. Change every measure but
the maximum and the minimum, and the range remains constant. In contrast, all measures
are used in the calculation of the standard deviation.

This chapter does not cover X-and-R charts. It does discuss the use of X-and-MR (for *moving
range*) charts, required for processes that have one measure only per time period.

N O T E You may have seen charts like those shown in this chapter referred to as Deming or
Shewhart charts, after the people who developed the technique. There are many varia-
tions in the way that these charts are created. But regardless of the name—SPC or Deming or
Shewhart—the basic approaches described here are standard. ▪

Figure 10.2 adds three refinements to the charts in Figure 10.1.

FIGURE 10.2

X-and-S charts with Center Line and Upper and Lower Control Limits: these limits put the observed values into context.

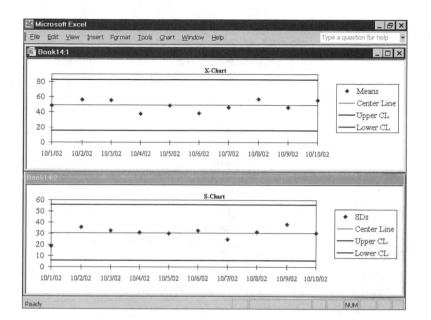

The charts in Figure 10.2 have three horizontal lines that can help you understand the nature of the process being studied. These horizontal lines are called the Upper Control Limit (UCL), the Center Line (CL), and the Lower Control Limit (LCL). For example:

- If too many points are either above the UCL or below the LCL, then something's wrong with the process.

- If a long series of points are between the CL and the UCL, or between the CL and the LCL, something may be wrong with the process.

- If a series of points are trending up toward the UCL, or down toward the LCL, something may be going wrong with the process.

You can see how useful this sort of information can be. It alerts you not only to the possibility that the process is out of control, but also to when it started going out of control. Knowing when might help you to pinpoint the cause of the problem: perhaps it always occurs during a staff change, such as at the end of a shift. Perhaps it occurs during a change from daylight savings time to standard time, which might interfere with people's sleep for a few days. Perhaps it's associated with drops in ambient temperature that cause the heating system to come on, introducing dust into a delicate manufacturing environment.

Whatever the cause, if you know that a problem has occurred as well as when it occurred then you are well on your way to identifying its cause.

The CL is a double-average. In an X-chart that uses each point to represent a particular day, the observations for a given day are averaged to get the point for that day. Then, the averages for all the days are averaged to get the overall average: this is the CL for the X-chart. You create the CL for an S-chart in the same way, except that you start by calculating each day's standard deviation, and then average those standard deviations to get the CL for the S-chart.

The UCL and the LCL are a little more complicated. A UCL is usually three standard deviations above the CL, and an LCL is usually three standard deviations below the CL. (It's actually more complicated than that. The standard deviations are really standard errors, and the gamma distribution gets involved.) Unless you're really interested, don't worry about it. If you are really interested, examine the SPC VBA module, SPC.XLS, on the Web site, as shown in Appendix A, "What's on the Web Site?"

NOTE Although it is obviously impossible in many cases to actually *observe* a value below zero, SPC calculations sometimes result in a negative LCL value. Some texts replace a negative LCL with a zero value. To make it clear that UCLs and LCLs are equidistant from the center line, both SPC.XLS and the figures in this book allow for a negative LCL. ▪

Due to the way that standard deviations behave, it is known that in the long run less than three tenths of one percent (0.3%) of the charted observations occur above the UCL or below the LCL, *unless something unexpected is going on*.

So, in the normal course of events, you would expect to see about one observation in 300 that is outside either control limit. If you do find more than 0.3% of the observations outside the limits, it suggests that something might have happened to the process.

It's easy (and often correct) to conclude that observations occurring outside a control limit are "bad": consistency is usually a desirable trait for a process. More broadly, though, it means that something unusual has occurred. For example, suppose that you found an observation *below* a lower control limit on an S-chart. This means that the variability among the individual observations made at that time is very low. Is that bad?

It's hard to tell: it depends on the nature of the process. It could mean that something changed in the way the observations are measured. Or, it could mean that all the observations were made on one machine, or one person, or any other process component, when the other samples were taken from multiple components. Or it could be one of the 300 cases that we expect, just by chance, to exceed a control limit.

Whatever the cause, the outcome might be "bad" or it might not: the main point is that something unusual has occurred that probably warrants closer attention.

Case Study: Manufacturing

Suppose that your company manufactures floppy disks, and that you are monitoring the disks' storage capacity. There are too many disks manufactured on a given day to test each of them, and you decide to test a random sample of eight disks from each day's production run. You measure the disks' storage capacity in bytes, and over a 10-day period you obtain the results shown in Figure 10.3.

FIGURE 10.3
The X-and-S charts for
floppy disk storage
capacity point to a
process that's in con-
trol.

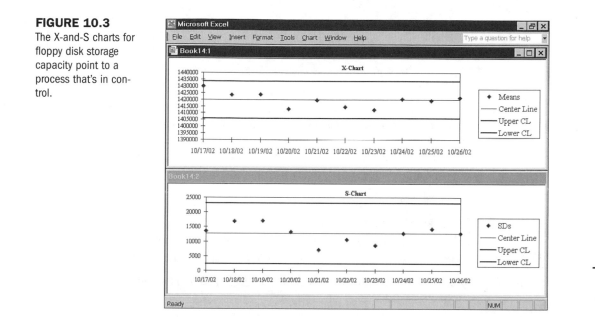

In Figure 10.3, all appears to be fine. All of the points are between the UCL and the LCL on
both the X-chart and the S-chart, there are no long runs above or below the CL, and there
appears to be no trend in the values.

On the other hand, suppose that your SPC charts looked like those in Figure 10.4.

FIGURE 10.4
The X-and-S charts with
outliers suggest a prob-
lem with the process
on 10/26.

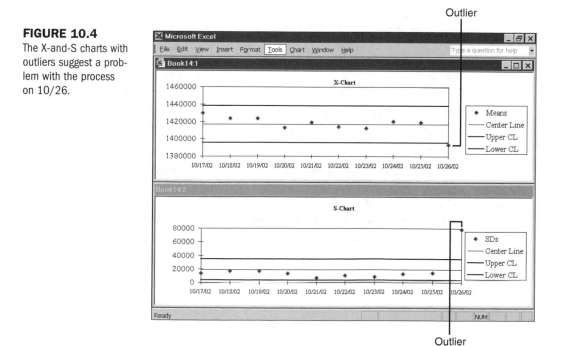

In Figure 10.4, the average capacity for floppy disks manufactured on 10/26 is below the LCL on the X-chart, and the standard deviation for the disks' capacity on 10/26 is well above the UCL on the S-chart. These two points are known as *outliers*, because they lie outside the charts' control limits.

What does this mean to you? Because the 10/26 average capacity dropped, there must be one or more disks on 10/26 that have relatively low storage capacity. The standard deviation for 10/26 is relatively high because the capacity of at least one disk was far from that day's average measured capacity. Thus, the variability in storage capacity among those disks is relatively large.

There are two possibilities:

- There was something unusual going on with the production process on 10/26/01.
- The average of the observations on 10/26/01 was one of the 300 expected, by chance, to diverge so far from the overall process average.

While it may be a chance finding, there is evidence that you should look into the production conditions on 10/26.

The observations used to create the charts in Figure 10.4 are shown in Table 10.1. Notice that the fourth measurement on 10/26 (boldface) is well below the level of all the other measurements, thus lowering the average and raising the standard deviation for that day.

Table 10.1 Data for Figure 10.4: Floppy Disk Storage Capacity

Date	Disk: 1	2	3	4	5	6	7	8
10/17	1421970	1445852	1406897	1436859	1446271	1434959	1420128	1426424
10/18	1444357	1415618	1409933	1429544	1446601	1410771	1400657	1430475
10/19	1449892	1431635	1427423	1436118	1408108	1405997	1400926	1429746
10/20	1400088	1443116	1410786	1409694	1406425	1418465	1405021	1410238
10/21	1423175	1406126	1416449	1420671	1427192	1413840	1421505	1426484
10/22	1401442	1429202	1426506	1424363	1408183	1405559	1410345	1409108
10/23	1402426	1427257	1408280	1403981	1418220	1411746	1419280	1407419
10/24	1413475	1414245	1403137	1426422	1406381	1432664	1437300	1429160
10/25	1407405	1417666	1446294	1428254	1428110	1405154	1406399	1413903
10/26	1408183	1416470	1439869	**1200863**	1404776	1429217	1434428	1412609

Why is it necessary to look at both the X-chart and the S-chart? Consider Figure 10.5.

FIGURE 10.5

The X-and-S charts with an outlier on the S-chart *only* suggest the presence of compensating problems.

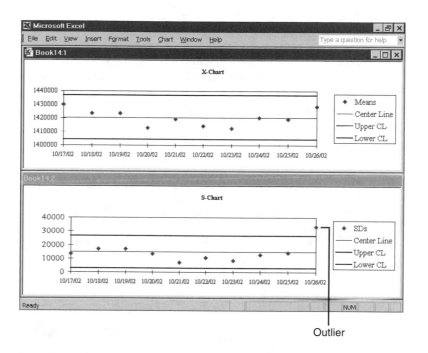

Outlier

Here, there is nothing unusual about the X-chart, but the standard deviation on 10/26 is well above its UCL. The data for Figure 10.5 are shown in Table 10.2.

Table 10.2   Data for Figure 10.5: Floppy Disk Storage Capacity

Date	Disk: 1	2	3	4	5	6	7	8
10/17	1421970	1445852	1406897	1436859	1446271	1434959	1420128	1426424
10/18	1444357	1415618	1409933	1429544	1446601	1410771	1400657	1430475
10/19	1449892	1431635	1427423	1436118	1408108	1405997	1400926	1429746
10/20	1400088	1443116	1410786	1409694	1406425	1418465	1405021	1410238
10/21	1423175	1406126	1416449	1420671	1427192	1413840	1421505	1426484
10/22	1401442	1429202	1426506	1424363	1408183	1405559	1410345	1409108
10/23	1402426	1427257	1408280	1403981	1418220	1411746	1419280	1407419
10/24	1413475	1414245	1403137	1426422	1406381	1432664	1437300	1429160
10/25	1407405	1417666	1446294	1428254	1428110	1405154	1406399	1413903
10/26	**1361867**	1439561	1446806	1432533	1403855	**1473898**	1440723	1430756

Part

II

Ch

10

Notice that the first and sixth measurements on 10/26 (in boldface) are, respectively, well below and well above the average. In the average observation for that day, the two measurements cancel one another out, but they increase the variability around the mean—thus increasing the standard deviation for that day. This is evidence that something unusual went on in the production process, resulting in less consistency in the disks' storage capacity. Again, the process for that day should be examined.

Even if neither the X-chart nor the S-chart contains outliers, you may find a trend that causes you to examine a process. Consider Figure 10.6.

FIGURE 10.6
When X-and-S charts display a trend, it suggests problems in the process, even though there are no outliers.

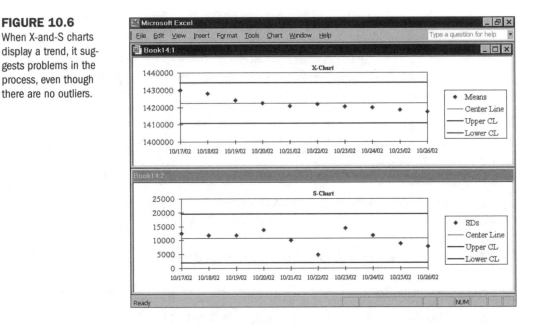

Here, the daily average capacity of the floppy disks is gradually but consistently declining. It is probable that the operating specification of some device or the quality of some raw material is progressively degrading.

Creating P-Charts for Dichotomies

Sometimes it is necessary to make a more general measurement of a unit than a variable such as the storage capacity of a floppy disk. There are, for example, many ways that a floppy disk can be unacceptable: it won't initialize, or there are too many bad clusters when it is formatted, or the write safe tab won't slide back and forth, and so forth.

Or, if you were monitoring the quality of invoices produced by an accounts receivable department, you might not be interested in exactly how an invoice falls short of being acceptable—just that it does. In cases such as this, you might want your measurement to be a dichotomy such as acceptable versus unacceptable (other terms used in quality control are conforming versus nonconforming and defective versus nondefective).

An SPC chart for this kind of analysis is based on the fraction of a sample that is nonconforming. For example, if you find that five invoices in a sample of 50 are unacceptable, then the fraction nonconforming is 0.1. This is the value that is shown on the chart. In quality control, this is usually termed a P-chart (for *proportion*), and it is analogous to an X-chart.

There is no analog for the S-chart when the measurement is a dichotomy. This is because the standard deviation for a dichotomy is completely represented by the fraction itself, and is defined as

$s = SQRT(p * (1-p))$

where p is the fraction, and SQRT stands for the square root. For example, if the fraction is .2, then its standard deviation is

$SQRT(.2 * (1-.2)) = SQRT(.2 * .8) = SQRT(.16) = .4$

Because knowing the fraction means that you automatically know the standard deviation, it is usual to create only the P-chart.

There are, though, a UCL, an LCL, and a CL on a P-chart. The CL is the overall average fraction nonconforming for the process, just as the CL on an X-chart is the overall average of the process. The UCL and LCL are based on the overall fraction nonconforming: they represent three standard deviations above and below the CL. These standard deviations are calculated from the fraction nonconforming for the process, taking the sample size into account. (See Figure 10.7.)

For example, if the overall fraction nonconforming is .2, and the size of each sample is 50, then the UCL is

$.2 + 3 * SQRT((.2 * (1-.2) / 50)) = .37$

and the LCL is

$.2 - 3 * SQRT((.2 * (1-.2) / 50)) = .03$

With P-charts, it is better to maintain a constant size for each sample, if possible, so that the UCL and LCL be constant for all samples. If it is not possible to maintain a constant sample size, there are transformations that you can apply to make the UCL and LCL constants. For information on these transformations, consult an advanced text on statistical process control.

Choosing the Sample Size

The size of the sample you take, for either an X-and-S or a P-chart, is important both to the accuracy of the average or fraction, and to the distance of the control limits from the center line. From that point of view, the larger the sample that you take, the better.

FIGURE 10.7

P-charts for conforming/ nonconforming are not normally accompanied by an S-chart.

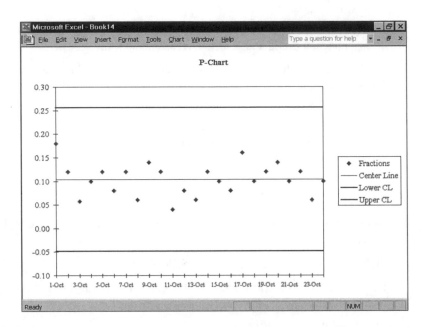

However, it is also true that the larger the sample you take, the greater the cost of quality control. This is particularly true of destructive testing, where the test makes an item unsalable. Suppose that you manufacture automobiles, and one quality test that you run is how well the front bumper stands up to a collision. It will be difficult to sell the cars that you have tested.

Therefore, you would like to take samples that are small enough to be affordable, but large enough to yield accurate estimates. One useful way to define an accurate estimate is that there is a 50% chance of detecting that a process has gone out of control.

A 50% chance may not seem too accurate, but keep in mind that you have multiple opportunities to detect the problem. Suppose that you are monitoring a process hourly. If the process goes out of control at, say, 10:15 a.m., then you have an opportunity to detect it at 11:00, 12:00, 1:00, and so on. The probability that the problem will remain undetected at, say, 2:00 p.m. is .5×.5×.5×.5 = .0625. You have nearly a 94% chance to detect that the process is out of control.

The previous examples used samples of size 8 for X-and-S charts, and of size 50 for a P-chart. In combination with the process standard deviation, these sample sizes defined the location of the UCL and the LCL. You can, instead, turn it around and begin by defining the location of the UCL and the LCL. So doing determines the required sample size. In effect, you ask, "How large a sample do I need if I want the UCL to be at a given criterion?"

Suppose that the overall fraction nonconforming for a process is .1. You decide that a fraction nonconforming of .25 is unacceptable. You also decide that you want to have a 50% chance of detecting that the fraction nonconforming has increased from .1 to .25. If the process average increases to .25, then half the samples would be larger than .25, and half would be smaller. (This assumes that defects are distributed symmetrically around their average, which is the usual assumption in statistical process control.) In that case, you would have your desired 50% chance to detect a shift in the process average: 50% of the observations would exceed .25.

You can set the UCL, three standard deviations above the CL, to equal the fraction nonconforming that you want to detect. The size of the change to detect is .25–.1 = .15, and you can set up this equation:

$$.25 - .1 = .15 = 3 * \text{SQRT}((.1 * (1 - .1) / N))$$

where N is the sample size. Rearranging this equation, you have

$$N = (3/.15)^2 * .1 * (1 - .1)$$

$$N = 36$$

or, more generally

$$N = (s/d)^2 * p * (1 - p)$$

where d is the size of the shift you want to detect, p is the fraction nonconforming, and s is p the number of standard deviations above and below the CL for the UCL and LCL. Given that the UCL and LCL are three standard deviations above and below the CL, that the process average is .1, and that you want a 50% chance of detecting a shift from .1 to .25, you should take samples of 36 observations each. The Excel worksheet formula is

```
= (3 / .15)^2 * .1 * .9
```

N O T E Setting the probability of detecting a shift to 50% simplifies the equation that determines the necessary sample size. If you wanted to increase that probability to, say, 80%, you would need to determine or assume the shape of the distribution of defects, make reference to the resulting theoretical distribution, and add to the equation a term that represented the units of measurement associated with an increase of 30% (that is, 80% – 50%). For detailed information, consult an advanced text on statistical quality control.

Deciding That a Process Is Out of Control

So far, this chapter has waffled and weaseled about whether or not a process is in control. It has used phrases such as "might be going out of control" and "something may be wrong with the process."

The reason for this bobbing and weaving is that the decision that a process is out of control is a completely arbitrary one. Suppose that you observe a measurement that's beyond an upper or lower control limit. You're going to make that observation once for every 300 measures you take, and that has everything to do with the mathematical definition of a standard deviation and may have *nothing* to do with the process.

In that case, what if you observe two measures in 300 beyond the control limits? Is the process then out of control? No? What about three or four outliers? When do you decide the process is out of control?

It's just as well not to ask the question because the usual suspects—logic, mathematics, probability, statistics—won't help here. But don't regard this as a defect of SPC analysis. You've already suffered losses by the time a process has gone out of control, whether or not you decide that's happened. No, the great strength of SPC is to give you an early warning that not all is right. Then, you can look carefully into the situation and *perhaps* decide to take action.

N O T E It's often best to do nothing, even when you have evidence that a process may be failing. A famous exercise used in quality control classes involves dropping balls through a funnel at a target on the floor. Students note where the balls hit. Those who decide to move the funnel to correct its aim typically wind up with less accurate scores: they're adding systematic variation into the process, amplifying its naturally occurring random variation. Those who appreciate the effect of that random variation, and how random errors often sum to zero, leave the funnel where it is and get a much tighter clustering than do the activists.

Tradition offers a guide, though. There are rules, often termed the *Western Electric rules*, that many analysts use to make a decision about a process. (The "rules" are really just recommendations published in a handbook by the Western Electric Company in 1956.) These rules involve the center line, and the upper and lower control limits. They also involve four more control limits, not yet discussed in this chapter:

- The upper 1 sigma control limit. This control limit is one standard deviation, or *sigma*, above the center line.

- The upper 2 sigma control limit. This control limit is two standard deviations above the center line.

- The lower 1 sigma and 2 sigma control limits. Like the upper 1 sigma and 2 sigma limits, these control limits are one and two standard deviations from the center line, but they are below it instead of above it.

- Using this terminology, the 3 standard deviation control limits that have been discussed so far in this chapter are called the upper and lower 3 sigma control limits.

Those additional control limits are used to determine if there's been a violation of the Western Electric rules as follows:

- One or more observations above the upper 3 sigma limit, or one or more observations below the lower 3 sigma limit, constitute a violation.

- At least two of three consecutive observations above the upper 2 sigma limit signal a violation. Similarly, at least two of three consecutive observations below the lower 2 sigma limit constitute a violation.

- At least four of five consecutive observations above the upper 1 sigma limit signal a violation. Similarly, at least four of five consecutive observations below the lower 1 sigma limit constitute a violation.

- Eight or more consecutive observations on either side of the center line constitute a violation.

Under these decision rules, a violation of any one of the four rules defines a process as out of control. A few examples follow. Figure 10.8 shows a 3 sigma violation.

FIGURE 10.8

When the process returns to its original level after a violation, it's possible that violation was caused by an incorrect measurement.

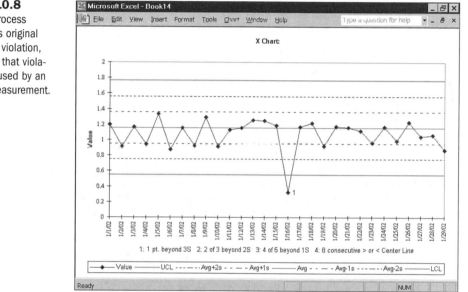

Part

II

Ch

10

If a 3 sigma violation is followed by a shift in the apparent level of the process, it's easier to believe that the violation was meaningful. In contrast, if the process resumes after the violation at roughly its original level, then you should suspect that a one-time event occurred—perhaps someone entered the data wrong.

Violations of the other rules are easier to believe than are 3 sigma violations. These violations have their own confirmation built in. For example, the violation shown in Figure 10.9 requires not just one, but two out of three observations beyond a 2 sigma limit.

Notice in Figure 10.9 the three observations labeled with the number *2*. Two of them lie outside the -2 sigma limit. The third of the three points that cause the violation actually lies above the center line. Had it fallen outside the -2 sigma limit, the three observations would still have resulted in a violation. The rule calls for at least two of three consecutive observations outside a 2 sigma limit.

FIGURE 10.9
One sigma and two sigma violations require that the observations in question occur outside the *same* sigma limit.

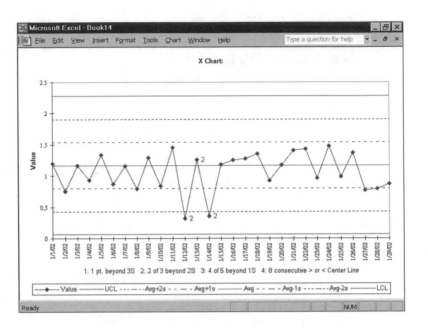

But had either of the two observations that is below the -2 sigma limit fallen above the +2 sigma limit, then these three observations would not constitute a violation. Two of three consecutive observations must lie outside the same 2 sigma limit.

Violations that involve four of five consecutive observations are more convincing yet, as seen in Figure 10.10.

FIGURE 10.10
A 1 sigma violation requires more observations, but the observations can occur closer to the center line.

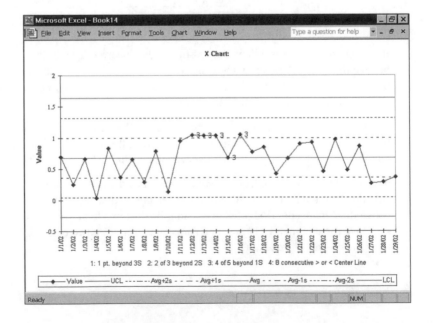

Although a 1 sigma violation requires four of five consecutive observations to lie outside a limit, that limit is only one standard deviation away from the center line. So the observations do not have to be as discrepant, but there needs to be more of them to confirm an out-of-control situation.

Don't be misled by the wording of these rules, by the way: an observation can be more discrepant than a given rule calls for. Suppose that of five consecutive observations, three fall between the +1 sigma and the +2 sigma limits, and a fourth falls outside the +2 sigma limit. Those four discrepant observations create a 1 sigma violation. It doesn't matter how far beyond the limit in question an observation is, so long as it is beyond the limit.

Figure 10.11 shows an example of the fourth type of violation.

FIGURE 10.11

Eight consecutive points on the same side of the center line almost always signal a process shift.

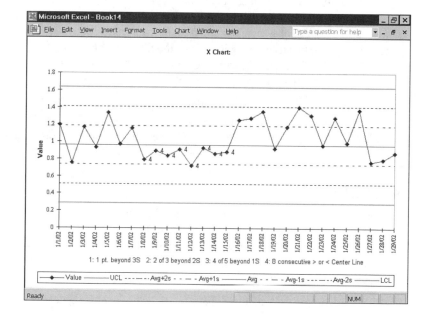

Part
II

Ch
10

Using X-and-MR Charts for Individual Observations

It often happens that you have only one observation available for a given time point. Perhaps the process that you're measuring takes so much time or resources that you can't wait for a reasonably large sample before starting your analysis. Or perhaps the process defines only one measure per time point: one example is budget variance analysis, where there is only one variance per account during a given accounting period.

In this sort of case, X-and-S analysis doesn't help you, because you can't calculate a standard deviation based on one observation only. The range suffers the same defect, so X-and-R charts are useless here. But you can use the *moving range*, or MR, instead. The MR is defined as the absolute value of the difference between one observation and the next. So, if you observe the value 23 on January 5, and the value 31 on January 6, the MR is 8: the absolute value of 23 – 31.

The X-and-MR analysis estimates a standard deviation by these steps:

1. Find the value of each moving range. There are as many moving ranges as there are observations, minus 1.

2. Take the average of the moving ranges.

3. Divide the average of the moving ranges by 1.128. The result is an estimate of the variability in the data set.

Couldn't you just take the standard deviation of all the observations instead? Sure. But that method addresses the wrong kind of variability. Taking the moving range approach stresses the variability due to the difference between sequential observations. Using the standard deviation of all the observations stresses the (squared) difference between each observation and the overall mean. In many instances, the difference between the moving range estimate and the actual standard deviation might be trivial. But when there is an actual process shift, you can expect the difference to be substantial.

Even when you have many observations available at each time point, it can be useful to average them as in X-and-S analysis and use X-and-MR analysis as described here. When the variability you're interested in stems from differences in sequential observations, the moving range can be the right way to estimate that variability.

Creating SPC Charts Using Excel

SPC charts are easy to create by using the VBA module *SPC Chart Maker* in the file named SPC.XLS on the Web site. To create SPC charts, you will need a worksheet that contains data laid out as in Tables 10.1 and 10.2. There should be a range of dates or times of day in a column, and a range of observations for each date or time, also in columns. The two ranges should occupy the same rows.

The observations can be either one or more columns of variable measurements (such as floppy disk storage capacity) or one column of dichotomies (such as the fraction nonconforming). In the case of dichotomies, the module assumes that there is one column for the measurements. This is because it's easier for you to enter the fraction nonconforming than to enter several columns, each with a 1 or a 0 to indicate conforming/nonconforming.

When you have opened SPC.XLS, a new item appears in the Data menu: SPC. With a worksheet active and laid out as described previously, choose that item to begin SPC analysis. When you close SPC.XLS, the SPC item is removed from the Data menu.

When you start the code by choosing Data, SPC, it displays a user form prompting you to enter the range that contains the times or dates, and the range that contains the actual observations. The form is Step 1 of a three-step wizard. Figure 10.12 shows the Step 1: SPC Charts page of the wizard.

FIGURE 10.12
Click the Collapse
Dialog button at the
right of each reference
edit box to collapse the
user form—this can
make it easier to locate
the cells you want.

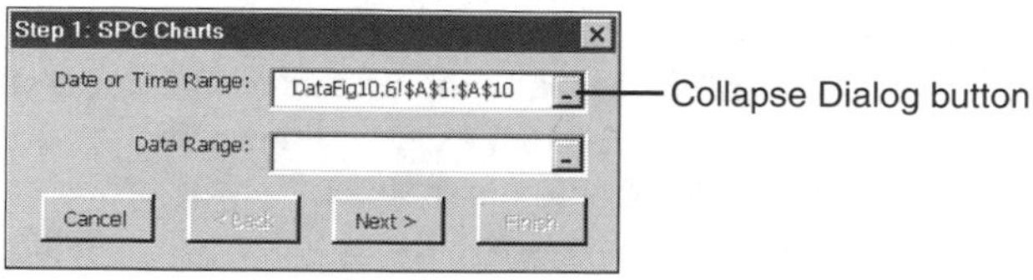

Collapse Dialog button

Click in the Date or Time Range reference edit box, and either type the range of dates or times, or drag through that range on your worksheet. That range does not need to have actual date or time values. You can leave that range blank, but the code requires you to identify a worksheet range.

When you click the Next button in Step 1, the Step 2: SPC Charts page of the wizard appears as shown in Figure 10.13.

FIGURE 10.13
Fill the Retain These
Options checkbox if you
want to use the SPC
wizard several times
(your choices will be
kept on the user
forms).

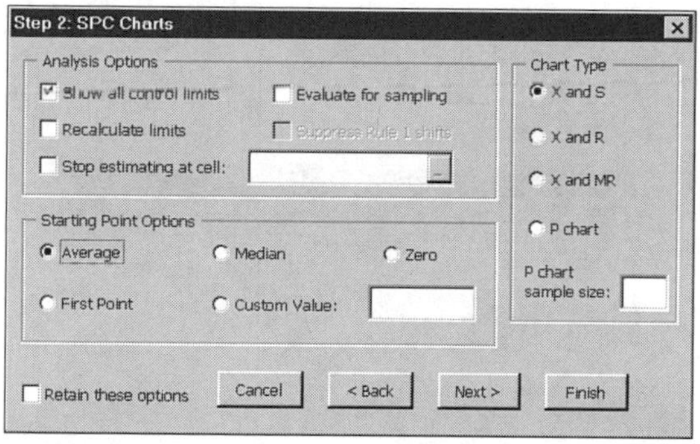

Use Step 2 to define the options you want to use. You can select X-and-S, X-and-R, X-and-MR, or P-charts. If you select a P-chart you must also supply the sample size: the number of observations that comprise each fraction in the input range.

You have several options as to the X chart's starting point: this refers to the first point in its center line. The custom value is often useful in process capability analysis.

The Analysis Options are not available for P-charts, but for other chart types they have the following effects:

- *Show All Control Limits.* If you check this box, the X-chart will show the center line, the UCL, the LCL, and the upper and lower 1 and 2 sigma limits. If you clear this box, the X-chart will show only the center line, the UCL, and the LCL.

- *Evaluate for Sampling.* Checking this box causes an additional worksheet to be included in the output workbook. The worksheet assists you in calculating the minimum sample size needed to detect a shift in the process. You are asked to provide the size of the shift that you would want to detect.

■ *Recalculate Limits.* Some analysts like to recalculate and redraw the center line and the sigma limits in response to a shift in the level of the process. That is, when one of the Western Electric rules is violated, the center line can be recalculated at the point where the shift occurred. So doing has consequences for the probability statements that you can make about the SPC analysis, and these consequences differ according to the nature of the data and the location of the shift. The option is provided if you feel that you need it: to invoke it, fill the checkbox.

■ *Stop Estimating at Cell.* Particularly when you have planned an intervention in a process, you might want SPC to stop estimating the process parameters before the process endpoint. For example, suppose that you intend to change an important piece of equipment after Day 20. You expect that change to have an impact on the process. To measure that impact accurately, you want to stop estimating the process average and variability as of Day 20. You can arrange that by filling the Stop Estimating at Cell checkbox, clicking in the associated edit box, and then clicking the cell on the worksheet that represents Day 20.

As usual with Excel wizards, you can click the Back button in Step 2 to return to Step 1, Cancel to stop processing, Finish to skip setting any other options, or Next to go to the next step. In this case, Step 3: SPC Charts is the final page of the wizard, as shown in Figure 10.14.

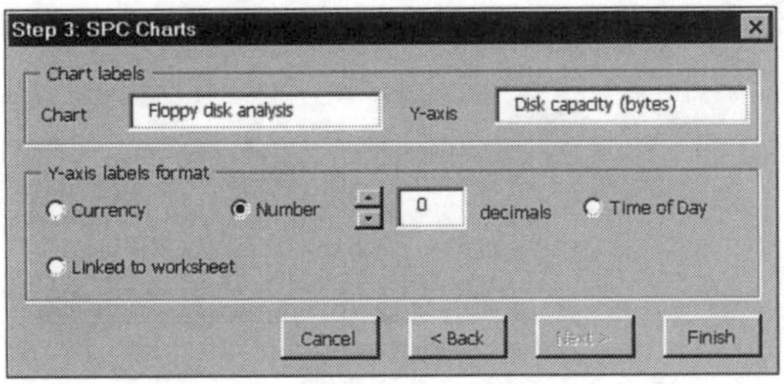

FIGURE 10.14
On the SPC charts shown in this chapter, the Y axis is the vertical axis.

Use this step to set a chart title, a label for the Y axis (which represents the values of your observations), and the format used by the tick labels on the Y axis. When you're through, click Finish to create your charts.

Performing Acceptance Sampling

Acceptance sampling often enables you to reduce the cost of goods that you purchase. It can also enable you to control the costs you incur when a purchaser returns products to you due to defects.

You do not want to purchase materials, whether supplies or equipment, that are faulty. Nor do you want to offer defective goods for sale. However, it is normal for the purchaser and the seller of large amounts of merchandise to negotiate an acceptable fraction of that merchandise that may be defective.

Here's the reasoning. It is extremely expensive to produce any appreciable amount—one lot, say—of goods that has no defective units. To do so, the producer would have to perform 100% testing, because any less would run the risk of having at least one defective product in the lot. And, because testing itself is not perfect, a test result of 0% defective is not a guarantee that no defects exist. Furthermore, the producer would always bear the sunk cost of having manufactured the defective units.

The producer is presumably in business to make a profit. So as to cover the costs of attaining 0% defects, the producer would have to raise the selling price. You, as a purchaser, might then decide to purchase the goods elsewhere. But if you demand 0% defects from another producer, that producer also has to raise the selling price to meet your requirement.

If you, as the purchaser, can tolerate some relatively small percent defective in the lots that you purchase, you might be in a position to negotiate a lower price from your suppliers.

This is the "invisible hand" at work: Adam Smith's principle that optimum values result when participants in an economic activity act in their own self-interest.

Now consider it from the producer's viewpoint. Suppose that the contract that you, the producer, enter into with your customer allows you to make shipments that contain some small percentage of defective product. In that case, you could test a *sample* of the product that you ship, instead of the entire lot. Your testing costs therefore immediately drop. Your costs drop again when you consider that you do not have to bear the cost of returned, defective goods, if you have met the customer's criterion for an acceptable shipment. This puts you in a position to gently reduce your selling price, thus retaining the customer but still making a profit.

However, the moment that you enter the domain of sampling, you enter the domain of probability. Suppose that the contract with your customer calls for you to ship no more than 1% defective units. You test 20 units, and you find one defective. How likely is it that there are only 1% defective in your entire shipment? Put another way, how likely is it that any shipment from your inventory will exceed the 1% limit? How large a sample should you take? And if you start finding defects in the sample, when should you stop testing sample units?

Excel provides several functions that answer these questions, and the next sections explore them.

Charting the Operating Characteristic Curve

An operating characteristic curve shows how an agreement between buyer and vendor works out in practice. The curve in Figure 10.15 is an example.

FIGURE 10.15

The operating characteristic curve helps you visualize the relationships among the different kinds of risk assumed by the buyer and the seller.

Supplier's risk

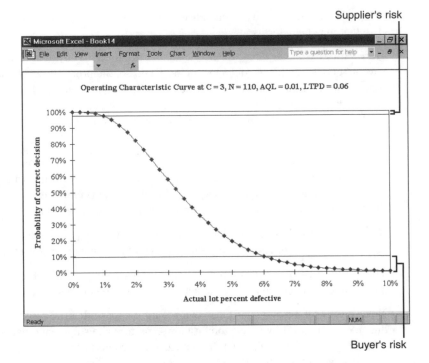

Buyer's risk

The curve shows the probability that a lot will be acceptable (vertical axis) with different percents of defects (horizontal axis). Notice that, as you would expect, the lower the number of actual defects, the higher the probability that a lot will be accepted. Four factors define the curve:

- The acceptable quality level (AQL) of the supplier's goods. This is the worst percent of defects that the buyer is willing to accept *as a process average*.

- The lot tolerance percent defective (LTPD) of a given lot. This is the worst level of quality that the buyer is willing to accept *in a given shipment*.

- The amount of risk to the supplier that a good shipment will be rejected due to sampling error. The *distance between* the upper horizontal line and the 100% point in Figure 10.9 represents this amount of risk.

- The amount of risk to the buyer that a bad shipment will be accepted due to sampling error. The lower horizontal line in Figure 10.9 represents this amount of risk.

Taken together, these four factors can provide a great deal of information to the supplier and buyer:

- The operating characteristic curve itself

- The sample size necessary to keep both the supplier's risk and the buyer's risk acceptably low

■ The maximum number of defects in a sample before a lot is rejected (usually termed *c*)

■ The actual supplier's risk and the actual buyer's risk, at a specific sample size and a specific *c*

Figure 10.16 shows the curve for a an AQL of 1%, an LTPD of 3%, and supplier's risk of 5% and buyer's risk of 10%. The upper horizontal line represents the supplier's risk: the distance between this horizontal line and the top of the vertical axis indicates the probability that a good shipment will be rejected. The lower horizontal line represents the buyer's risk: the distance between this horizontal line and the bottom of the vertical axis indicates the probability that a bad shipment will be accepted.

FIGURE 10.16

The steepness of operating characteristic curves usually depends largely on their sample sizes.

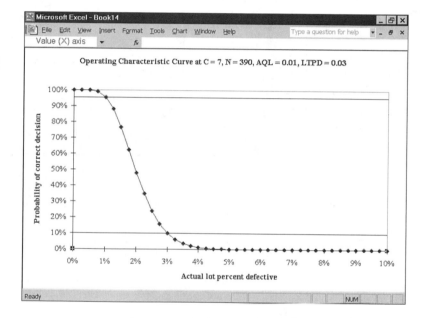

Also shown at the top of Figure 10.16 is N, the sample size needed, and c, the maximum number of defects that you can find in a sample before concluding that the entire lot contains too many defects. Therefore, this operating characteristic curve tells you that you should sample 390 units. As you test those units, when and if you find as many as eight defective units, you can stop testing and conclude that the full lot contains too many defects.

N O T E Excel offers a function, CRITBINOM, that returns a number similar to the *c* that this section discusses. It is normally different from *c*, because it takes into account only the supplier's risk or the buyer's risk. The procedures discussed here, and that are contained on the *Business Analysis with Microsoft Excel, Second Edition* Web site VBA module, take both types of risk into account. Therefore, *c* is usually different from the value you would obtain if you used CRITBINOM. ■

The curve shown in Figure 10.16, while steeper than the curve in Figure 10.15, is not extremely steep. Generally, the larger the sample size, the more capable you are of discriminating between an acceptable and an unacceptable lot. Contrast Figure 10.16 with Figure 10.17, where the sample size is larger and the curve is steeper.

FIGURE 10.17

The required sample size of an operating characteristic curve depends to some degree on the value of the AQL.

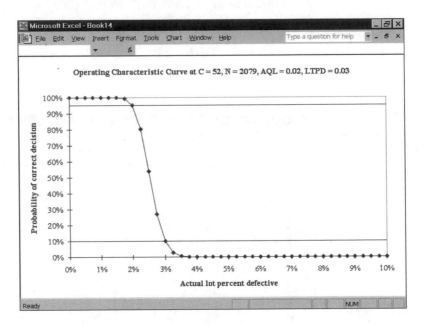

In Figure 10.16, an increase in the actual defect rate from 2% to 3% is accompanied by a drop in the probability of acceptance from about 48% to 10%.

In Figure 10.17, the increase in actual defect rate from 2% to 3% is accompanied by a drop in probability of acceptance from about 95% to 10%.

What causes the sample size to increase? The operating characteristic curve in Figure 10.16 uses an AQL of 1%, whereas the curve in Figure 10.17 uses an AQL of 2%. The Web site's workbook, *Operating Characteristic Curves.xls*, that created these charts seeks the minimum sample size that satisfies all four criteria (AQL, LTPD, supplier's risk, and buyer's risk). The smaller the AQL, the smaller the sample required. This is because the smaller the AQL, the fewer defects there are to find. Further, the smaller the AQL, the smaller the value of c that's required to determine whether the current lot is a bad one.

N O T E The VBA module named *Derive Op Char Curve* can be found in the file named *Operating Characteristic Curves.xls* on the Web site. To run it, open that file and choose Tools, Macros. Select OC_Macro from the Macro list box, and choose Run. ■

So, when you change the AQL from, say, .01 to .02, you also change the necessary sample size from a smaller figure to a larger one. This effect can be quite pronounced: in the case of Figures 10.16 and 10.17, the increase in sample size is from 390 to 2079.

LTPD also exerts an influence on the required sample size. Figure 10.18 shows the operating characteristic curve with the same inputs as 10.16, except that instead of an LTPD of 3%, it uses an LTPD of 4%.

FIGURE 10.18
An operating characteristic curve with a smaller Lot Tolerance Percent Defective reduces the required sample size.

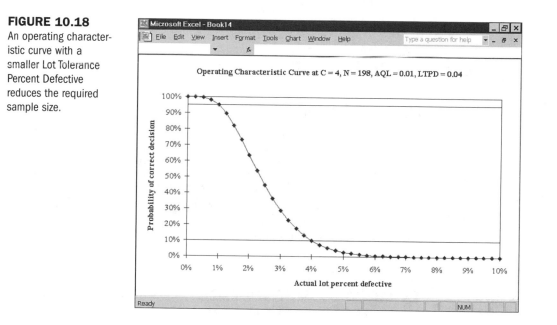

Modifications of supplier's risk and buyer's risk have relatively small effects on sample size. Figure 10.19 shows the effect of reducing the supplier's risk from 10% to 5%, and Figure 10.20 shows the effect of reducing the buyer's risk from 10% to 5%.

Note that in all the cases discussed previously, if you want to lower the degree of risk, you need to increase the power of the testing to discriminate between a good lot and a bad lot. You increase the power of the testing by increasing the size of the sample. So doing causes the curve to steepen: the steepness of the curve is a visual guide to how well the testing will discriminate between lots that meet the criteria and lots that are substandard. And, of course, the better the discrimination, the better the degree of protection for both the buyer and the supplier.

Again, you can generate these curves by running the VBA procedure OC_Curve in the file named *Operating Characteristic Curves.xls*, found on the *Business Analysis with Microsoft Excel, Second Edition* Web site. When you do so, Excel will display a dialog box that prompts you to supply an AQL, an LTPD, a fraction that represents supplier's risk, and a fraction that represents buyer's risk. After you choose OK, Excel searches for the minimum sample size and c that satisfy these four criteria. A set of summary data are placed on a worksheet, and the curve is plotted on a separate chart sheet.

Part
II

Ch
10

FIGURE 10.19
Operating characteristic
curves that vary the
supplier's risk tend to
shift, and gently
steepen, the curve.

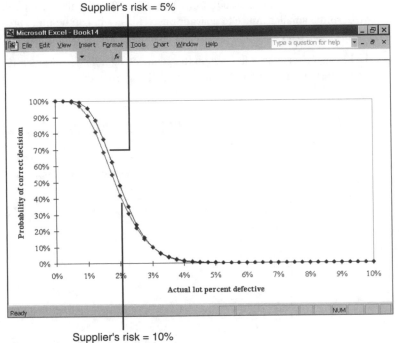

Supplier's risk = 5%

Supplier's risk = 10%

FIGURE 10.20
Varying the buyer's risk
also shifts the curve to
the right or left.

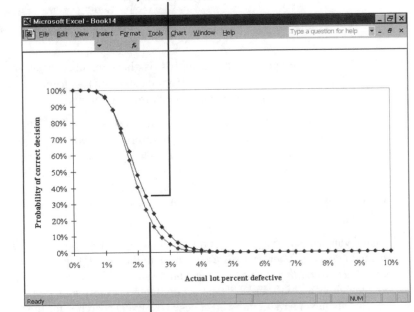

Buyer's risk = 10%

Buyer's risk = 5%

N O T E   Depending on the input values that you choose, it can take the VBA code a long time to execute. Press the Esc key to halt a lengthy search. ■

You can use these curves and the associated summary data in negotiations between suppliers and buyers. As a buyer, you might be willing to increase your LTPD requirement slightly to reduce the required sample size. This would save the supplier some testing costs that could be reflected in the cost of the goods.

As a supplier, you might be willing to accept a slightly increased level of risk that a good shipment will be rejected due to sampling error. Accepting this additional risk would save sampling and testing costs, and you might be able to apply these savings to another negotiating point where you need additional bargaining room.

The operating characteristic curves discussed in this section are based on a single sample from a lot. There are other, more complex sampling plans that include double samples, multiple samples, and sequential samples. For further information, consult an advanced text on quality control.

Using Worksheet Functions for Quality Control

You can use Excel to help answer a variety of questions that occasionally arise in quality control situations. It's important to understand the nature of the tools that are available to you when such questions come up. Because statistical quality control is largely an exercise in probability—and in choosing the right tool in a given case—this chapter concludes with a discussion of some of these questions and how you can use Excel to answer them.

Sampling Units from a Finite Population

To this point we have discussed statistical process control and acceptance sampling in terms of theoretically infinite populations. There has been no limit to the size of the population of products that has been sampled to create X-and-S charts, P-charts or operating characteristic curves.

Things change some when you sample from a finite population. You have a finite population when you are interested only in a specific group, such as the items in a special production run, or your own company's sales staff, or customers' responses to a temporary price reduction.

When you sample from a finite population, it's usual to do so *without replacement*: that is, if you are going to sample two items, you select the first item, and then select the second item without putting the first item back into the pool. Suppose that you have a population of 10 items. The chance of selecting any given item at random is 1/10, or 10%. If, after selecting the item, you put it back into the pool, the chance of selecting any given item is still 10%. If, however, you do not return the item to the pool, the chance of selecting at random any given item as your second choice is 1/9, or 11%.

Case Study: Manufacturing

A customer wants you to manufacture 200 coffee cups with a glazing that differs substantially from the glazing of those that you normally make. This will be a special production run, and therefore the 200 cups constitute a finite population. Your agreement with the customer allows for a 5% defect rate.

You plan to sample 20 cups, without replacement, from your production run, and to reject the run if you find unacceptable imperfections in the glazing on more than 5% of the sample. That is, you will reject the run if the sample contains two or more defectives. What is the probability that your full run has met the 5% criterion if you find zero or one defective cup?

You answer this question with Excel's HYPGEOMDIST function. It takes four arguments:

- The number of "successes" in the sample. Here, that argument is zero or one: the number of imperfect cups in your sample if you are to accept the production run.

- The sample size. Here, that argument is 20, the number of cups you sample.

- The number of "successes" in the population. Here, that argument is 10. If you tested all 200 cups, then the 5% criterion implies that not more than 10 would be imperfect.

- The size of the population. Here, that argument is 200, the number of special cups that you manufactured.

HYPGEOMDIST returns the probability that you would observe an exact number of successes, given the sample size, the successes in the population, and the population size. So, if you entered

=HYPGEOMDIST(0,20,10,200)

then Excel would return .34. Therefore, there's a 34% probability of finding no imperfect cups in a sample of 20, when there are exactly 10 imperfect cups in the population of 200.

You also need to know the probability of finding exactly one defective cup in your sample, so you enter

=HYPGEOMDIST(1,20,10,200)

Excel returns .40. Therefore, there's a 40% probability of finding exactly one imperfect cup in your sample. Together, these two probabilities add up to 74%. So it is more likely (74%) than not (100% − 74% = 26%) that there are 10 imperfect cups in the full production run.

TIP

You can use an array constant in HYPGEOMDIST, and similar functions, to get the sum of the function's results. Instead of entering

=HYPGEOMDIST(0,20,10,200)

and

=HYPGEOMDIST(1,20,10,200)

and summing the results, you can enter

=SUM(HYPGEOMDIST({0,1},20,10,200))

This formula executes HYPGEOMDIST twice: once for the first element in the array {0,1} and once for the second element. It then adds the results together, and in this case it returns .74, or 74%.

Sampling Units from a Nonfinite Population

When you monitor a nonfinite population, you are interested in a larger group than when you monitor a finite population. For example, instead of testing a special, finite production run, you might be testing your normal, ongoing, nonfinite product line. If you were testing a new invoice format, you might try it for a week before deciding to adopt it; then, sampling for invoice accuracy would involve a finite population. On the other hand, if you were monitoring invoice accuracy as a normal procedure, you would probably consider your sample to be from a nonfinite population.

To make probability statements about a sample from a nonfinite population, you use Excel's NORMSINV function.

Case Study: Videotape Rentals

Suppose that you are in the business of renting videotapes to the public. After tapes have been viewed some number of times, their quality deteriorates to the point that you consider them to be defective. Furthermore, some customers own tape players that are defective, and they can ruin your videotapes.

You want to maintain an inventory of tapes that is at least 85% acceptable; you would really prefer 95%, but because you can't keep your customers' machines from damaging the rental tapes, you relax the criterion a little. Although you have a finite number of tapes on any given day, your inventory is constantly changing due to the acquisition of new tapes, and the removal of old ones. You therefore consider your population of tapes to be nonfinite.

Testing video tapes is a time consuming process, and you would like to keep the sample as small as possible. A rule of thumb that works well in quality testing is to make sure both of these equations result in a number that is 5 or greater:

$n * p$

and

$n * (p-1)$

where n is the sample size, and p is the probability of an acceptable unit in the population. If your tapes meet your criterion of 85% acceptable, p is .85. To make sure that both n * p and n * (p–1) are both greater than 5, you will need n, the sample size, to be at least 43. To keep the numbers easy to work with, you decide to take a sample of 50.

NOTE The rule of thumb described previously is due to the relationship between the binomial and the normal distributions. The sampling distribution of a binomial variable such as defective/acceptable is very close to a normal distribution when both n * p and n * (1–p) are greater than 5. ▪

You test the random sample of 50 tapes, finding three that are defective and 47 that are acceptable, so 94% of your sample is acceptable. What is the probability that at least 85% of your population of tapes is acceptable?

You decide that you want to make a correct decision about the defects in your population of tapes 95% of the time that you test samples. The following Excel formula returns the criterion that you need if you are to have that amount of protection (it is known as a *critical value*):

```
=NORMSINV(.95)
```

Excel returns 1.64. This critical value is the number that your test statistic needs to exceed if you are to make a correct decision.

TIP   NORMSINV() is easier and quicker to use than NORMINV(). However, NORMINV() gives you greater control over the characteristics of the underlying distribution.

To get the test statistic itself, enter the Excel formula

```
=(0.94-0.85)/SQRT(0.15*0.85/50)
```

which returns 1.78. The general formula is

= (x–p)/SQRT(p * (p–1)/n)

where x is the percent acceptable in the sample, p is the hypothetical percent acceptable in the population, n is the sample size, and the denominator is the standard error of p.

Because your test statistic of 1.78 exceeds your critical value of 1.64, you conclude that your inventory of tapes is at least 85% acceptable.

Sampling Defects in Units

This chapter has so far discussed one particular attribute: whether a unit is acceptable or defective. A related measure is the number of defects in a particular unit. For example, if you were concerned with the quality of the purchase orders that your company distributes, you might want a more detailed measure than acceptable/defective. It might be important to understand the frequency of occurrence of critical defects in the purchase orders (such as account number or ship-to address) versus minor defects (such as the spelling of the supplier's street address).

To make inferences about numbers of defects, as distinct from numbers of defective units, the Excel POISSON function is often useful.

Case Study: Forms

As the manager of the purchasing department for a large firm, you have noticed an unusual number of complaints that deliveries from suppliers have been late. Following up on some of the complaints, you find that some suppliers report that the deliveries have been delayed because of errors on the purchase orders relating to unit pricing, want-dates, model numbers, and contract references.

Because suppliers sometimes place inappropriate blame on buyers, you decide to examine a sample of purchase orders to see whether the overall rate of defects per form might be high enough to cause these delays.

You decide that an overall defect rate of .5 defects per purchase order is acceptable. If Purchase Order A is perfect and Purchase Order B has only one defect (therefore, the average rate is .5 defects per purchase order), there should be enough good information on B for the supplier to be able either to fill the order or to quickly resolve the incorrect information.

You also decide that you want to limit the likelihood of deciding that the average defect rate is one-half of one defect per order, when in fact it is some other number, to 5%.

You sample 10 purchase orders at random and examine them for inaccuracies. You find 12 instances of misinformation in the sample. Given this data, should you continue to believe that the average number of defects in all your purchase orders is .5?

Use Excel's POISSON function. Enter

```
=1-POISSON(11,5,TRUE)
```

which returns .005. The first argument, 11, is 12–1: that is, the number of inaccuracies that you found, minus 1. The second argument, 5, is the number of inaccuracies that you would expect to find in 10 purchase orders if the average number of inaccuracies were .5. The third argument, TRUE, specifies the cumulative form of the Poisson distribution: that is, the sum of the probability for zero inaccuracies, plus the probability for one inaccuracy, and so on.

You decided beforehand that the level of protection you wanted against an incorrect decision was 5%, or .05. Because .005 is less than .05, you reject your hypothesis that there are .5 errors per form among all your purchase orders. You probably need to make sure that your staff is properly trained on your new system, and that the system itself is operating as it was designed.

Part

II

Ch

10

Summary

This chapter has described how to use Excel to create X-and-S statistical control charts and P-charts, to monitor the ongoing performance of systems. X-and-S charts are used for variables such as the capacity of floppy disks, the length of telephone calls or the profit margin on daily sales. P-charts are used for attributes: for example, the percent of defective units such as manufactured goods, or forms that you can classify as either defective or acceptable. These statistical control charts enable you to judge the performance of a system over time.

Another topic in this chapter is operating characteristic curves. Studying these curves puts you in a position, as a supplier, to limit the risk that an entire shipment of goods will be rejected because the number of defective units in a sample is an overestimate of the entire shipment. As a purchaser, you can use operating characteristic curves to limit your risk of accepting an entire shipment of goods because the number of defective units in a sample is an underestimate of the entire shipment.

This chapter has also discussed three ways to estimate overall process quality on the basis of sampling:

- The overall rate of defective items in a finite population. You can estimate this rate using the HYPGEOMDIST function.

- The overall rate of defective items in a nonfinite population. Use the NORMSINV function to make this estimate.

- The overall rate of defects per unit. Use the POISSON function to determine whether your estimate of this overall rate is accurate.

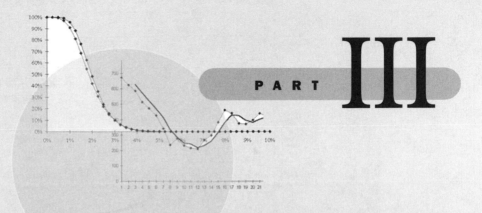

PART **III**

Investment Decisions

CHAPTER 11

Examining a Business Case: Investment

Business case analysis is one of the most important activities a finance department can undertake to support management decision making. A business case can take any of a variety of forms, depending on the question that's been asked and the decision that needs support.

For example, a very basic question on the use of capital is "Should we lease a copy machine or should we buy one?" Although it may seem trivial, the answer to the question depends in part on an analysis of the cost effects of purchasing versus leasing. This is because there are tax implications to a capital expenditure that differ from those of an operating lease.

At the other end of the complexity spectrum, management might ask, "Should we enter a new line of business?" A major decision such as this involves activities that include

- Investing capital to purchase equipment
- Hiring new staff to operate the equipment
- Acquiring market research to quantify the potential costs and revenues
- Assessing cross-elasticities among product lines

Each of these involves costs that must be taken into account when making the decision.

This chapter discusses these activities from two viewpoints: why they are important to making a good business decision, and how they flow into an Excel workbook that supports the eventual decision.

Developing a Business Case

Most business case development is incremental. That is, the business case focuses on changes—increments to revenues and to costs—that would occur only if a company adopts a proposal. The business case emphasizes the relevant benefits of a proposed decision, including

- New revenues
- Larger market share
- Lower expenses
- Product diversification

The business case analysis also emphasizes the relevant costs of the proposal, such as

- Incremental investment
- Additional operating expenses
- Additional taxes
- Losses to existing line of business

A business case does not typically include the costs of doing business as usual, because you generally regard those costs as set. You would incur them whether or not the business case is approved for implementation. For example, the costs of doing general ledger accounting and the cost of rent for corporate headquarters would not change if you decide to lease a new copier. It is possible that these costs would not change even if you decide to expand your line of business.

In the first stage of business case analysis, you should undertake a qualitative review of all potential benefits and costs. The stakeholders within the firm (those on whom the business decision would have substantial impact) should participate in the review. This approach is similar to obtaining agreement from individual operating units on their annual budgets.

In large organizations, it frequently happens that the marketing or product management group offers up an idea for a new product. The proposal often defines an opportunity in terms of a customer need. The marketing group might identify this need by means of focus groups, general awareness of the industry, or an understanding of the life cycle of current product sets—in short, any of a variety of subjective and objective indicators.

No analysis tool such as Excel can create a business case on your behalf. It can help you analyze the business decision, but only after you provide it with some quantitative basis. Therefore, the marketing or product group's proposal should usually frame its product description with several types of numeric analysis. These analyses often include the product's market potential, the competitive environment, and the plans to bring the product to market.

The proposal usually describes the product's market potential in terms of

- Current size: How many product units would the marketplace purchase if the product were available for sale today?
- Growth potential: What is the forecast for additional sales during the life cycle of the product?

These estimates are normally in terms of unit sales, and the unit sales projections form part of the basis for projecting new product revenue. To complete the projection, an analysis of the competitive environment translates unit sales estimates into dollars. In assessing the competitive environment, it's useful to understand these aspects of the competition's offerings:

- Product alternatives: Do they have products or options that compete directly with your new product?
- Pricing: Is it a single price? Is it tiered in some way? Can your product meet that pricing, and does it need to?
- Costs: What level of resources must they commit to the production and sale of their product? Do they have a technological edge that holds down their costs relative to yours?
- Profitability: Faced with price pressure from your product, is their product profitable enough that they would continue production and sales?
- Competitive advantage: What hurdles can they put in your way? These include market presence, name recognition, brand loyalty, long-term contracts with resellers, and so on.

Each of these considerations influences the pricing that you plan for the product. By combining that pricing estimate with unit sales forecasts, you can create a credible projection of revenue for the product.

To complete the initial quantitative picture, you need to give Excel information about the variable costs associated with bringing the new product to market. In particular, it's useful to assess the costs of

- Market research: What leads you to believe that the new product will generate additional revenue? Is there evidence from prior product rollouts? What about external sources of information, such as trade association data? How good is the evidence that's available? How much will it cost to obtain the data?
- Distribution channels: What are the costs, such as reseller discounts and warehousing, of getting the product to your customers?
- Promotion and advertising: How much must you pay different media to run your advertisements? How much will it cost to produce new brochures and other product literature? Should you purchase mailing lists?

Part

III

Ch

11

- Rollout and implementation: Is it necessary to travel to meet with your distributors or salespeople? Should you offer special incentives to those in the distribution channel so that they will focus their efforts on selling this product? Does the distribution channel need any special training to understand the product's price structure, its market niche, and its competitive strengths and weaknesses?

- Product cross-elasticities (any characteristics that compete with your existing products): Is the proposed product likely to cut into the sales of existing product lines? Will this reduce existing revenue? By how much?

- Objectives for market share and penetration: Will the cost of attaining one more percentage point of market share outweigh the additional revenue? Is the cost of filling the last seat in the airplane more than the price of the ticket?

These kinds of questions are not just useful adjuncts to a product concept. You need the answers to quantify the projected costs and revenues that are associated with the new product. The estimated costs and revenues form the quantitative basis for deciding whether to go ahead with the product development, or to pass on the opportunity.

So far, only marketing issues have been considered. You also need to quantify the operational and customer service costs to determine the new product's profit potential. The drivers of these costs include

- **Technology:** Is the technology that is required to produce this product available, or must it be acquired? If it must be acquired, how much will it cost to purchase and maintain it? If existing capacity is available, what is the opportunity cost of exploiting it?

- **Systems:** Are appropriate methods and processes in place, or must they be developed? Such systems usually include sales support, product tracking, billing and collections, inventory management, and the software needed to manage them.

- **Implementation plans:** Are they feasible? Are the timelines reasonable and achievable for existing staff, or are there any incremental staffing requirements?

- **Training:** Will company personnel or customers require additional training in the production or use of the new product? If so, should training be developed in-house or obtained externally? How much will it cost? And how much will it cost to deliver it?

It's useful for a company to develop a formal process for business case development. Once in place, formal procedures make it much easier to repeat the process the next time the company considers bringing new products to market. A formal and repeatable process can help you validate a business case that's currently under consideration against the results of earlier business cases.

All research and analysis should be documented. It can be difficult to take this step, particularly with research. Early on in the planning process, research is often anecdotal, non-replicable, soft. Only later, perhaps not until well after product release, is sufficient hard data available to support decisions with real confidence. Documenting soft research data often seems futile, and this may be one reason that it's so seldom done. But if you do not document it, it's very difficult to assess your business case after the fact, to determine the basis for either a bad decision or a good one.

Analysis is another matter, particularly if you use the tools that Excel provides to document and audit your work. After you've completed your analysis, it's then easier to determine how you came to make a decision. As you develop your analysis worksheets, give names to your constants and your ranges. Fill in the summary information for the workbook. Add notes to cells. Where appropriate, create scenarios and associate them with the names of the groups who defined them.

Once approved, the business case should state how to compare its assumptions with actual results. It is important to establish accountability early, and to track significant milestones. If it addresses these issues, the business case process can become an integral piece of the firm's strategic and tactical operations.

Developing the Excel Model

Part
III

Ch
11

A model for a business case built using Excel synthesizes concepts and methods that you have already learned about in this book: income statement formation (discussed in Chapter 1, "Working with Income Statements"), cash flow analysis (in Chapter 5, "Working Capital and Cash Flow Analysis"), budget planning (in Chapter 8, "Budgeting and Planning Cycle"), and forecasting (in Chapter 9, "Forecasting and Projections").

The first step in developing the model is to create a pro forma income statement. The pro forma income statement takes into account the relevant benefits and costs involved in the proposed course of action.

Case Study: A New Type of Wireless Phone

Your manufacturing company has been a market leader in the wireless telephone business for the last 10 years. Other firms have imitated your product with some degree of success, but you occupy a dominant position in the marketplace because you were there first with a quality product.

Is life too comfortable at the phone factory? What would happen if you offered a new, enhanced wireless phone? This new phone would not replace your current product, but would offer additional features, greater durability, and better performance for a somewhat higher price. As a result, some of your current distributors might migrate from your current product to the new phone.

Offering this enhanced phone would establish a new revenue stream for your company. Using the forecasting tools developed in Chapter 9 along with some market research, you can identify the incremental margin associated with this new product (see Figure 11.1).

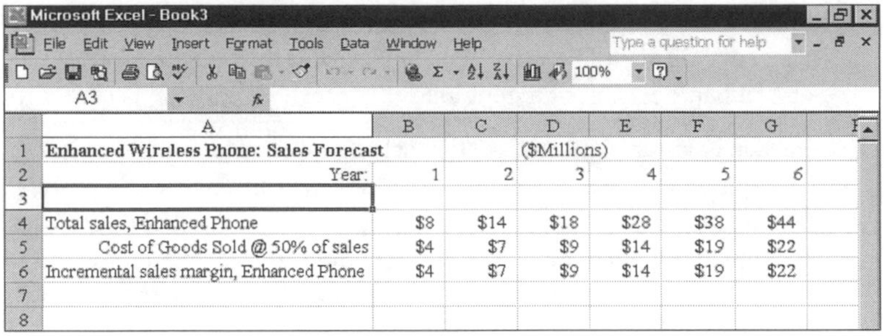

	A	B	C	D	E	F	G
1	Enhanced Wireless Phone: Sales Forecast			($Millions)			
2	Year:	1	2	3	4	5	6
3							
4	Total sales, Enhanced Phone	$8	$14	$18	$28	$38	$44
5	Cost of Goods Sold @ 50% of sales	$4	$7	$9	$14	$19	$22
6	Incremental sales margin, Enhanced Phone	$4	$7	$9	$14	$19	$22
7							
8							

FIGURE 11.1
The added value (the incremental margin) of the new wireless phone takes into account both the new phone's total sales and lost sales of the existing phone.

Your marketing department has provided you with a total sales forecast for the new phone, shown in row 4 of Figure 11.1. The range B4:G4 is named TotalSales. One way to name the range is to select it—here, cells B4:G4—and then click in the Name Box, type the name in the box, and press Enter.

Row 5 shows the cost of goods sold, and assumes that this cost will be 50% of revenue. Select B5:G5, and type `=0.5*TotalSales` into the Formula box. Then press Ctrl+Enter. (This is ***not*** the same as array-entering a formula with Ctrl+Shift+Enter.) Pressing Ctrl+Enter causes the formula to be entered into each of the six highlighted cells. The formula takes advantage of Excel's implicit intersection. Each column in row 5 is matched to its corresponding column in the range that's named TotalSales, and the value in that column is multiplied by 0.5.

TIP A good way to think of an implicit intersection is that it is *implied* by the location of a formula—that is, by the row or column where the formula is located. In this case, the intersection is implied by the column in which each instance of the formula exists and the row in which the range TotalSales exists.

As long as you have B5:G5 selected, you might as well name this range by clicking in the Name box, typing **COGS** (for "cost of goods sold"), and pressing Enter.

The cost of goods sold reflects only the purely variable costs of material and labor to produce the phone: that is, it does not include any cost allocations for overhead. Sometimes these variable costs are referred to as the direct cost of sales. Revenue minus the associated cost of sales is the sales margin—in this case, the incremental sales margin: the additional margin that the company expects to derive from the new product. This line item, shown in row 6 of Figure 11.1, is linked to the main worksheet shown in Figure 11.2.

You can make this linkage easily by taking these steps:

1. In the Sales Forecast worksheet, name the B6:G6 range IncrementalMargin.
2. In the same workbook, activate a worksheet that will become your pro forma income statement.
3. To duplicate the information for the product's incremental value, as shown in Figure 11.2, highlight the B4:G4 range of cells.
4. Type the formula `=IncrementalMargin` and then press Ctrl+Enter.

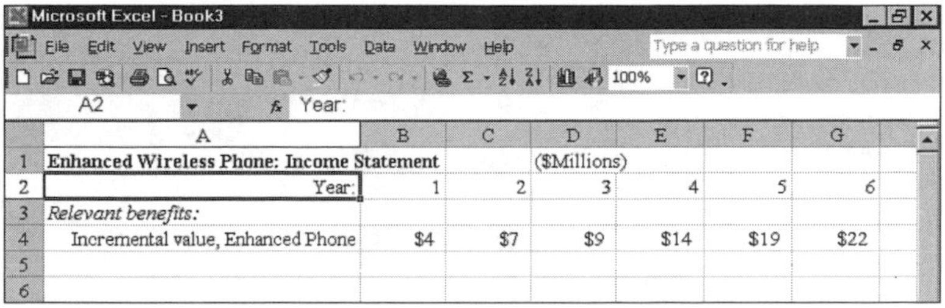

FIGURE 11.2

The pro forma income statement begins by identifying a relevant benefit–the incremental margin–of the new wireless phone.

	A	B	C	D	E	F	G
1	Enhanced Wireless Phone: Income Statement			($Millions)			
2	Year:	1	2	3	4	5	6
3	*Relevant benefits:*						
4	Incremental value, Enhanced Phone	$4	$7	$9	$14	$19	$22
5							
6							

Step 4 used another instance of the implicit intersection. The formula you just entered spans columns B through G, just as the range named IncrementalMargin does. If you entered this formula anywhere outside those six columns, you would get the #VALUE! error value. Column S, for example, is not among IncrementalMargin's columns, so in column S there's nothing for the implicit intersection to intersect.

With B4:G4 on the new pro forma still selected, click the Name box, type **IncrementalValue**, and press Enter.

TIP

Again, the use of range names makes it easier to re-use data that you have already entered, to document your work, and to ensure that any changes you make in the data are reflected in dependent formulas. Suppose, for example, that at some later time you need to adjust the sales forecast. The combination of these formulas and the named ranges lets the adjustment migrate throughout the workbook into formulas that depend, either directly or indirectly, on the sales forecast.

After a qualitative review of this product offering with the stakeholders in your organization, you identify the following relevant costs:

- Some of the current distributors of the existing type of phone will prefer the new features and performance enhancements in the new phone. You can expect that they will stop buying your existing phone and start buying the new one. An estimate of the gross margin of these lost sales is shown in Figure 11.3 in row 7, Lost value, Current Phone.

- Advertising will be necessary to inform the public about your new product. Row 8, Advertising, in Figure 11.3 quantifies the budget for an initial marketing blitz and for ongoing commercials.

- The new phone has characteristics (relating to its design, consumer market, compatibility with existing networks, and so on) that make it necessary to hire a new product management team. This group will oversee the new phone's product introduction, its future development, and its life cycle. Row 9, New product management team, in Figure 11.3 shows the ongoing cost of this group.

- The market research expenses needed to launch the product are directly related to the new phone itself, and are incremental to business as usual. Row 10, Market research expenses, shows this cost.

FIGURE 11.3

The relevant costs in the pro forma statement include only the costs that are directly attributable to the new product.

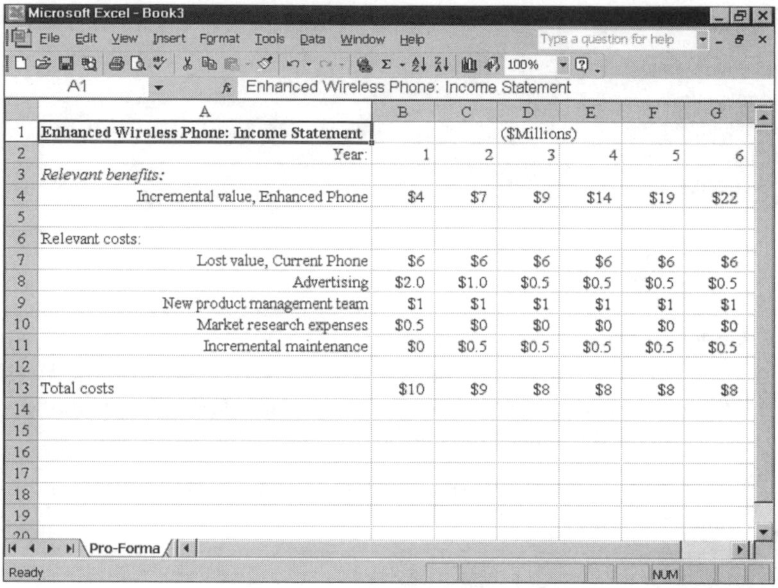

	A	B	C	D	E	F	G
1	**Enhanced Wireless Phone: Income Statement**			($Millions)			
2	Year:	1	2	3	4	5	6
3	*Relevant benefits:*						
4	Incremental value, Enhanced Phone	$4	$7	$9	$14	$19	$22
5							
6	Relevant costs:						
7	Lost value, Current Phone	$6	$6	$6	$6	$6	$6
8	Advertising	$2.0	$1.0	$0.5	$0.5	$0.5	$0.5
9	New product management team	$1	$1	$1	$1	$1	$1
10	Market research expenses	$0.5	$0	$0	$0	$0	$0
11	Incremental maintenance	$0	$0.5	$0.5	$0.5	$0.5	$0.5
12							
13	Total costs	$10	$9	$8	$8	$8	$8

■ New equipment is needed to produce the new phone. The maintenance on the new equipment will increase total maintenance expense for the company by about $5,000 per year. Row 11, Incremental maintenance, contains this cost. Notice that the firm does not begin to incur these maintenance costs until Year 2, after the equipment has been in use for one year.

A pro forma income statement (see Figure 11.4) can now be constructed from the data you have entered so far. The relevant costs are totaled in row 13: enter the formula =SUM(B7:B12) in cell B13, and then copy and paste it into C13:G13. Name range B13:G13 TotalIncrementalCosts. It shows the total relevant costs that are projected for each year.

The total incremental costs are then subtracted from the new product's incremental value. Select the range B15:G15, enter the formula

```
=IncrementalMargin - TotalIncrementalCosts
```

and press Ctrl+Enter.

The result, usually referred to as *EBITDA* and shown in row 15, constitutes the estimated earnings from the product before taking other indirect costs into consideration. As awkward an acronym as EBITDA is, it's easier than what it stands for: "Earnings Before Interest, Taxes, Depreciation, and Amortization." The name EBITDA is given to the worksheet range B15:G15.

Row 16 contains the cost of depreciation on the new production equipment as a line item in order to arrive at a pre-tax income figure (row 17). The cost of the equipment itself, $10 million, is shown in cell B21; name that cell CapitalCost.

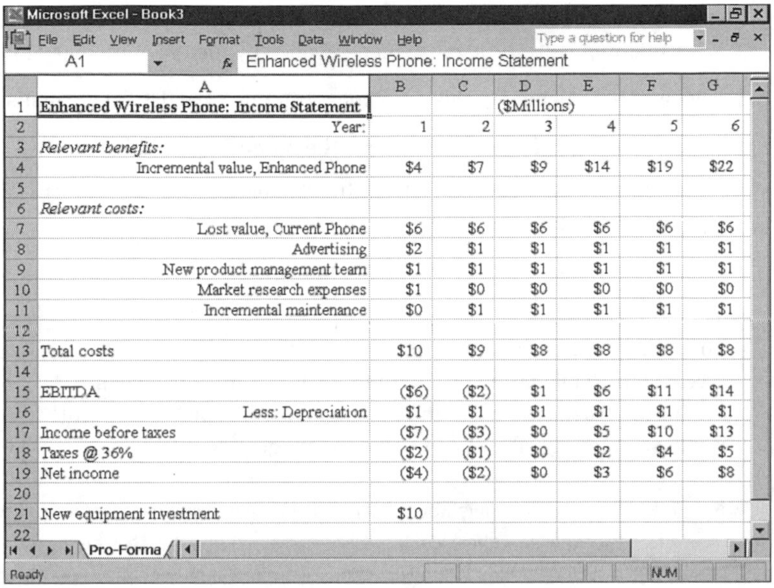

FIGURE 11.4

The pro forma income statement arrives at a figure for net income by taking depreciation and income taxes into account.

Besides the cost of the equipment, two other bits of information are needed to calculate the annual depreciation expense: its salvage value and its useful life. The useful life is taken to be 10 years, and the salvage value will be set to zero. These two constants are given names by taking these steps:

1. Choose Insert, Name, Define.
2. In the Names in Workbook box, type **UsefulLife**.
3. In the Refers to box, type **=10**.
4. Click Add.
5. In the Names in Workbook box, type **SalvageValue**.
6. In the Refers to box, type **=0**.
7. Click OK.

TIP

These steps, which give names to the salvage value and the length of the useful life, cause the names to refer to actual values. You could instead have made the names refer to cells where you enter the values (10 and 0, in this case), as is done with the CapitalCost name. It's mainly a matter of personal preference. Putting the values on the worksheet makes them easier to see. Having the names refer directly to values keeps the worksheet from looking cluttered.

The cost of the equipment, $10 million, will be depreciated over a 10-year period, and its salvage value at the end of that period will be zero. The formula for depreciation cost is therefore =SLN(CapitalCost,SalvageValue,UsefulLife), where the SLN function returns straight-line depreciation. You can enter this formula either in a single cell and copy it across the remaining cells, or in all six cells at once by means of the Ctrl+Enter key combination.

You can now calculate pre-tax income as, in this case, EBITDA minus depreciation:

1. Select cells B16:G16 and name the range Depreciation.
2. Select cells B17:G17. Click in the Formula Box and type =EBITDA-Depreciation.
3. Press Ctrl+Enter.
4. While B17:G17 is still selected, name the range by clicking in the Name box and typing **PreTaxIncome**.

To calculate taxes, create a constant with the value .36 named TaxRate, or give the name TaxRate to a cell and enter **.36** in that cell. Then, select cells B18:G18, type =TaxRate*PreTaxIncome in the Formula box, and press Ctrl+Enter. While the B18:G18 range is still selected, go ahead and name the range Taxes.

N O T E Some accountants would (legitimately) quarrel with the projection of a negative income tax expense. Others would (also legitimately) find it a sensible usage, because early losses from a new operation can offset income from profitable operations, thus reducing the total tax expense. To keep this example simple (by avoiding reference to other, profitable operations), the negative figure is used here.

After figuring in taxes, calculate net income by subtracting taxes from income before taxes. Row 19, Net income, is the end result of the income statement. It denotes the additional, incremental income that the company can anticipate as a result of the combined revenues and costs due to offering a new product.

However, net income is seldom identical to net cash flow. You will want to know the amount of cash that will flow into and out of the business each year if your company decides to proceed with bringing this new product to market.

To quantify the cash flow, it's necessary to extend the pro forma income statement so that it becomes a cash flow statement. In this case, there are two items needed to derive annual cash flow from the income statement: the depreciation on the new equipment (reprising its earlier role) and its purchase price. Figure 11.5 shows these modifications.

N O T E Again, to keep this example simple, factors due to working capital requirements (such as additional inventory and accounts receivable on incremental sales) have been omitted. If you worked through Chapter 5, you will find it a straightforward process to add these considerations to your pro forma income statement.

FIGURE 11.5
Adding the depreciation back in and accounting for the equipment expenditure clarify the actual cash flows for the new product.

Microsoft Excel - Book3

A1 = Enhanced Wireless Phone: Cash Flow Statement

	A	B	C	D	E	F	G
1	**Enhanced Wireless Phone: Cash Flow Statement**			($Millions)			
2	Year:	1	2	3	4	5	6
3	*Relevant benefits:*						
4	Incremental value, Phone	$4	$7	$9	$14	$19	$22
5							
6	*Relevant costs:*						
7	Lost value, Current Phone	$6	$6	$6	$6	$6	$6
8	Advertising	$2	$1	$1	$1	$1	$1
9	New product management team	$1	$1	$1	$1	$1	$1
10	Market research expenses	$1	$0	$0	$0	$0	$0
11	Incremental maintenance	$0	$1	$1	$1	$1	$1
12							
13	Total costs	$10	$9	$8	$8	$8	$8
14							
15	EBITDA	($6)	($2)	$1	$6	$11	$14
16	Less: Depreciation	$1	$1	$1	$1	$1	$1
17	Income before taxes	($7)	($3)	$0	$5	$10	$13
18	Taxes @ 36%	($2)	($1)	$0	$2	$4	$5
19	Net income	($4)	($2)	$0	$3	$6	$8
20	Plus: Depreciation	$1	$1	$1	$1	$1	$1
21	Minus: New Equipment Investment	$10	$0	$0	$0	$0	$0
22	Net Cash Flow	($13)	($1)	$1	$4	$7	$9
23							

Pro-Forma

Ready NUM

Begin by adding the depreciation expense from row 16 back into the statement in row 20, as shown in Figure 11.5. Row 17, which contains income before taxes, subtracts depreciation from EBITDA, and now that process is reversed in row 20.

Why deal with depreciation twice? Because depreciation is not an actual cash outlay but an accrued expense. Depreciation assigns to each time period a portion of the loss in the value of the capital investment. As an *expense*, you can use it to reduce income, for the purpose of calculating tax liabilities. As a *non-cash* expense, it should not count as a cost reducing the net cash flow. Therefore, you subtract it from pre-tax income for the purpose of calculating taxes, and add it back in for the purpose of estimating actual net cash flow.

As mentioned earlier, your company needs new machinery to produce the new product. It will also be necessary to retool some of the assembly lines' production facilities that at present are dedicated to your current product. You require $10 million in capital expenditures to purchase the new equipment and to accomplish the retooling, and this amount is shown in cell B21.

After adding depreciation back in, the $10 million capital investment in the new machinery is subtracted in row 21 to produce the net cash flow figure for the period (row 22).

These steps extend the original pro forma income statement and make it a pro forma cash flow statement.

Summary

The topics covered in this chapter constitute the basic inputs to a full business case. Chapters 12, "Examining Decision Criteria for Business Case Analysis," and 13, "Creating a Sensitivity Analysis for a Business Case," explain how to analyze these inputs to determine whether the business case makes financial sense. So, while the process is by no means complete, by this point you have accomplished the following:

- Identified all the relevant benefits and costs of this business decision.
- Quantified all the relevant benefits and costs of the decision, and entered them in a workbook format.
- Merged the benefits and costs to construct a pro forma income statement.
- Extended the pro forma income statement to depict a pro forma cash flow statement.

The result is a projection of future cash flows that would result if the company embarked on this business venture.

How can management use this information? It should base its decision of whether to proceed with the new product on an analysis of the cash flows' current value to the business.

Put another way, investments must be made at the outset to implement the proposal. The company must provide funds for retooling, anticipate the loss of revenues from the current product, support promotional activities, hire more staff, and so on.

Are the anticipated returns adequate to justify these investments? Chapter 12 discusses the additional financial concepts and indicators that assist in the decision-making process. It also demonstrates how you can use Excel to extend the pro forma cash flow model, and how you can apply valuation tools to help determine whether a decision to implement the proposal is a sound one.

Examining Decision Criteria for Business Case Analysis

Chapter 11, "Examining a Business Case: Investment," looked at the relevant facts surrounding a business case decision. If you worked your way through the case study, you constructed a pro forma income statement and a pro forma cash flow statement. These statements help you to describe the decision quantitatively, but that's far from the end of the process.

An important criterion to use in the evaluation of an income or cash flow statement is the discount factor. The term *discounting* refers to the estimation of the present value of future cash flows. For example, every dollar you own today has a different value in the future. If you deposit $100 in a savings account that yields 5% annually, that $100 will be worth $105 in one year. Its future value one year from now is $105.

The future value depends on several issues, including the length of time that you hold the money and the rate of return you can obtain on the dollar. This chapter shows you how to take discounting into account in your income and cash flow statements. By doing so, you can make these statements more meaningful.

This chapter also covers payback periods, discounted payback periods, and the concepts of future value, present value, and net present value.

Understanding Payback Periods

The *payback period* is the length of time between an initial investment and the recovery of the investment from its annual cash flow. Suppose, for example, that you purchase a store for $500,000. Taking into account the income from the store, your expenses and depreciation, and your taxes, it takes you 48 months to earn back the $500,000. The payback period for your investment is 48 months.

Figures 12.1 and 12.2 show the full cash flow statement from the case study presented in the previous chapter, including the discounting, payback, and other numbers you'll learn about in this chapter.

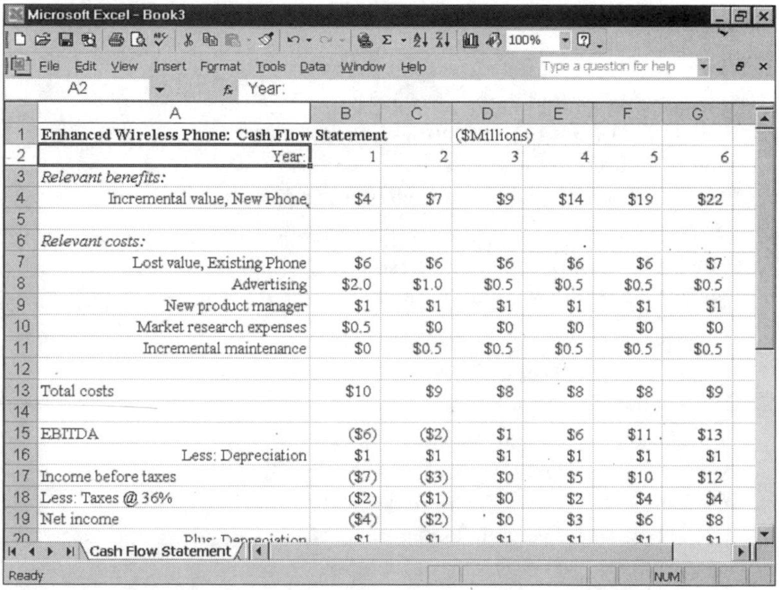

FIGURE 12.1

The cash flow statement's benefits and costs summarize the relevant business case inputs.

	A	B	C	D	E	F	G
1	**Enhanced Wireless Phone: Cash Flow Statement**			($Millions)			
2	Year:	1	2	3	4	5	6
3	*Relevant benefits:*						
4	Incremental value, New Phone	$4	$7	$9	$14	$19	$22
5							
6	*Relevant costs:*						
7	Lost value, Existing Phone	$6	$6	$6	$6	$6	$7
8	Advertising	$2.0	$1.0	$0.5	$0.5	$0.5	$0.5
9	New product manager	$1	$1	$1	$1	$1	$1
10	Market research expenses	$0.5	$0	$0	$0	$0	$0
11	Incremental maintenance	$0	$0.5	$0.5	$0.5	$0.5	$0.5
12							
13	Total costs	$10	$9	$8	$8	$8	$9
14							
15	EBITDA	($6)	($2)	$1	$6	$11	$13
16	Less: Depreciation	$1	$1	$1	$1	$1	$1
17	Income before taxes	($7)	($3)	$0	$5	$10	$12
18	Less: Taxes @ 36%	($2)	($1)	$0	$2	$4	$4
19	Net income	($4)	($2)	$0	$3	$6	$8
20	Plus: Depreciation	$1	$1	$1	$1	$1	$1

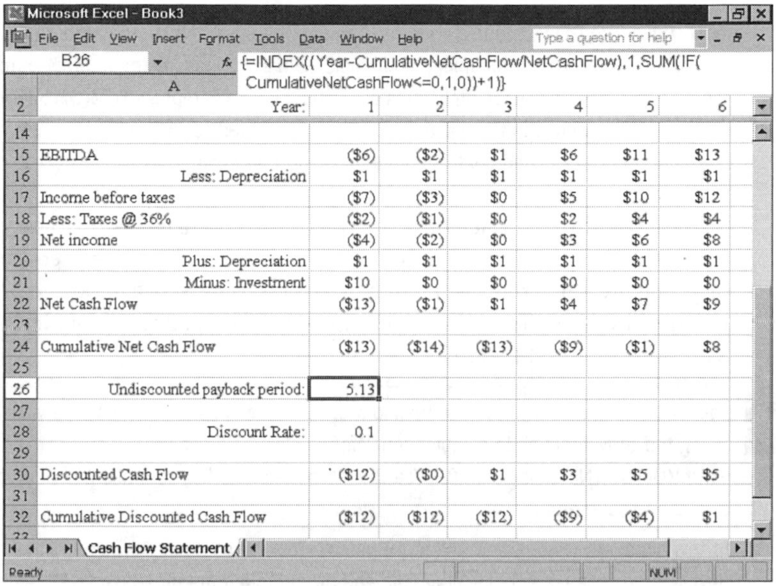

FIGURE 12.2

The cash flow statement's adjustments take account of depreciation, taxes, and capital investment to arrive at net cash flows.

	Year:	1	2	3	4	5	6
14							
15	EBITDA	($6)	($2)	$1	$6	$11	$13
16	Less: Depreciation	$1	$1	$1	$1	$1	$1
17	Income before taxes	($7)	($3)	$0	$5	$10	$12
18	Less: Taxes @ 36%	($2)	($1)	$0	$2	$4	$4
19	Net income	($4)	($2)	$0	$3	$6	$8
20	Plus: Depreciation	$1	$1	$1	$1	$1	$1
21	Minus: Investment	$10	$0	$0	$0	$0	$0
22	Net Cash Flow	($13)	($1)	$1	$4	$7	$9
23							
24	Cumulative Net Cash Flow	($13)	($14)	($13)	($9)	($1)	$8
25							
26	Undiscounted payback period:	5.13					
27							
28	Discount Rate:	0.1					
29							
30	Discounted Cash Flow	($12)	($0)	$1	$3	$5	$5
31							
32	Cumulative Discounted Cash Flow	($12)	($12)	($12)	($9)	($4)	$1

B26 = {=INDEX((Year-CumulativeNetCashFlow/NetCashFlow),1,SUM(IF(CumulativeNetCashFlow<=0,1,0))+1)}

Microsoft Excel - Book3 — Cash Flow Statement

The next general step in developing the business case is to determine the payback period. To make the calculations clearer, add a row labeled Cumulative Net Cash Flow to the cash flow statement that you developed in Chapter 11. To add the row, follow these steps:

1. Select cells B2:G2. Click in the Name box, type **Year**, and press Enter.
2. Select cells B22:G22. Click in the Name box, type **NetCashFlow**, and press Enter.
3. Select cell A24, and enter the label **Cumulative Net Cash Flow**.
4. Select cell B24, and enter the formula =SUM(OFFSET(NetCashFlow,0,0,1,Year)).
5. Copy cell B24 and paste it into C24:G24, either by choosing Edit, Copy and Edit, Paste, or by dragging B24's fill handle into the C24:G24 range.
6. Select the range B24:G24, click the Name box, type **CumNetCashFlow**, and press Enter.

Figure 12.2 shows the result. The formula you entered in step 4 returns the running total of the range NetCashFlow for each consecutive year.

The range named Year occupies cells B2:G2 on the worksheet, and has the values 1 through 6. As you fill row 24 with its formula, the fifth argument of the OFFSET function adjusts for each successive value of Year, so that 1 becomes 2, then 3, and so on. This argument specifies the number of columns in NetCashFlow to return to the SUM function by way of OFFSET.

Part III

Ch 12

N O T E The OFFSET function returns a range that is shifted some number of rows or columns from its first argument. It can also be used to specify the number of rows and columns in the shifted range, but those arguments are optional. For example, =SUM(OFFSET(A1,2,1,3,4)) returns the sum of the values in the range B3:E5, which is shifted (or *offset*) down by two rows and right by one column from A1, and contains three rows and four columns. ■

So, because the first value of Year is 1, OFFSET returns just the first column of NetCashFlow to SUM in B24. In C24, the formula refers to the second value of Year, or 2, and OFFSET returns the first two columns of NetCashFlow to be added together by SUM. The result is a cumulative, summed value for NetCashFlow in row 24, Cumulative Net Cash Flow.

TIP This book encourages you to use named ranges as a means of documenting your work in Excel. Using the SUM function in combination with the OFFSET function—
=SUM(OFFSET(NetCashFlow,0,0,1,Year)) in step 4—is one way to make use of a named range to get the result you're after.

In this case, a quicker way would make use of a mixed reference. You could enter =SUM($B$22:B22) in B24, and then click B24's fill handle and drag through the range C24:G24. As you do so, the absolute reference portion remains fixed, and the relative reference adjusts. So in cell G24, for example, you wind up with the formula =SUM($B$22:G22). The tradeoff is speed and convenience in entering the formulas, in exchange for clarity when you examine them later on.

By visually inspecting the CumNetCashFlow range you can see that sometime after five years this project will have recouped the original investment for the company. It is at this point that CumNetCashFlow changes from negative values to a positive value. This is the payback period for this example. However, you cannot as yet tell exactly when the payback period has ended. All you can tell so far is that the payback period ends sometime during the sixth year.

You can modify the worksheet to calculate the payback period exactly by array-entering the formula

```
=INDEX((Year-CumNetCashFlow/NetCashFlow),1, SUM(IF(CumNetCashFlow<=0,1,0))+1)
```

Cell B26 is selected in Figure 12.2 so you can see the formula, and the result in that cell. This is a lengthy formula. As is the case with most complicated formulas, it is easier to understand if you break it up into segments, and enter those segments on your worksheet. Figure 12.3 shows these segments, and how they combine to return the payback period.

Row 1 in Figure 12.3 shows the number of each year in the calculation of the payback period. Row 3 contains the net cash flow, and row 5 contains the cumulative net cash flow. Each of these rows is a named range—Year, NetCashFlow, and CumNetCashFlow, respectively.

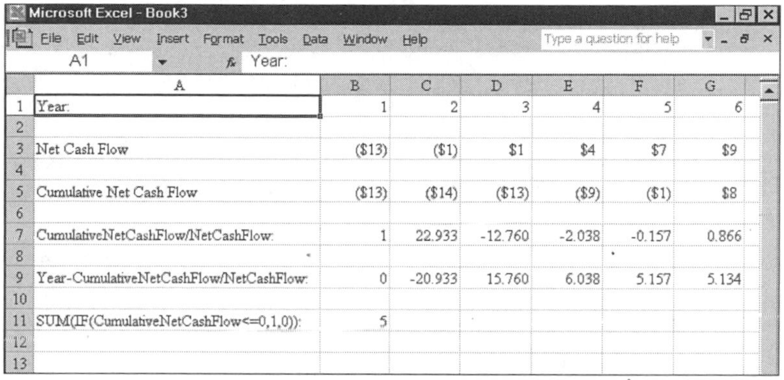

FIGURE 12.3

All of these calculations are summarized in the single array formula in cell B26 of Figure 12.2.

	A	B	C	D	E	F	G
1	Year:	1	2	3	4	5	6
2							
3	Net Cash Flow	($13)	($1)	$1	$4	$7	$9
4							
5	Cumulative Net Cash Flow	($13)	($14)	($13)	($9)	($1)	$8
6							
7	CumulativeNetCashFlow/NetCashFlow:	1	22.933	-12.760	-2.038	-0.157	0.866
8							
9	Year-CumulativeNetCashFlow/NetCashFlow:	0	-20.933	15.760	6.038	5.157	5.134
10							
11	SUM(IF(CumulativeNetCashFlow<=0,1,0)):	5					
12							
13							

Microsoft Excel - Book3 — File Edit View Insert Format Tools Data Window Help — Type a question for help — A1 ▼ *fx* Year:

 TIP The three named ranges in Figure 12.3 are not the same ranges as those with the same names in Figures 12.1 and 12.2. In Figure 12.3, the ranges are *sheet level*, and in the Define Name dialog box their names appear as, for example, Fig12.3!Year. The reference to the sheet where they are found distinguishes them from *book level* names, which are not qualified by a worksheet name. These sheet level names are used in formulas on the same sheet where they are defined, so the formulas do not need to qualify the names with that of their worksheet.

Row 7 in Figure 12.3 shows the ratio of each year's cumulative net cash flow to that year's net cash flow. To enter the formula, select B7:G7 and type
=CumNetCashFlow/NetCashFlow.

TIP If you use named ranges in formulas, you might find it easier to paste the name instead of typing it. After selecting a cell, type = (the equal sign), and then choose Insert, Name, Paste to display any defined names. Clicking a name moves it into the formula bar.

Then press Ctrl+Enter. This key combination enters the formula in each of the selected cells, taking advantage of the implicit intersection (discussed in the Chapter 11 section, "Case Study: A New Type of Wireless Phone").

The ratio in row 7 of Figure 12.3 has a particularly useful meaning for the year during which the payback period is complete. The ratio expresses the proportion of that year during which the cumulative net cash flow has exceeded the payback of the investment.

Notice that it is not until the end of year 6 that cumulative net cash flow becomes a positive number. The ratio of the cumulative net cash flow to the net cash flow for year 6 is $7,520,000/$8,680,000, or .866. (The dollar amounts are formatted with no decimals in Figure 12.3, and represent millions of dollars.) If you assume that cash flows are evenly distributed throughout the year, then the initial investment has been recouped at about 13.4% (1–.866) of the way through year 6. Put another way, when 13.4% of year 6 has elapsed, the cumulative net cash flow reaches zero; therefore, the amount of the initial investment has been paid back.

Subtracting that ratio (.866) from the year number (6) results in 5.134: it will take about 5.134 years to pay back the initial expenses and capital investment. This calculation is shown for each of the six years in row 9 of Figure 12.3. These cells contain the array formula `=Year-CumNetCashFlow/NetCashFlow`. How can you get Excel to determine which of the values in row 9 represents the true payback period? Again, the payback period cannot have elapsed so long as the cumulative net cash flow is negative. Therefore, you want Excel to ignore all years until the cumulative net cash flow turns positive.

The array formula `=SUM(IF(CumNetCashFlow<=0,1,0))` assigns a 1 if the CumNetCashFlow is less than or equal to 0, and assigns a 0 otherwise. It then sums the assigned numbers and returns the result, which is the number of years during which the cumulative net cash flow is less than or equal to zero. In this case, the array formula returns 5 (see cell B11 in Figure 12.3), because the cumulative net cash flow is still negative at the end of year 5. Adding 1 to this result returns the first year during which the cumulative net cash flow is greater than 0: `=SUM(IF(CumNetCashFlow<=0,1,0))+1`.

Finally, you are in a position to express all this with one array formula, `=INDEX((Year-CumNetCashFlow/NetCashFlow),1,SUM(IF(CumNetCashFlow<=0,1,0))+1)`, which you saw in cell B26 of Figure 12.2.

The general syntax of the INDEX function is `=INDEX(ARRAY,ROW,COLUMN)`.

Here, the ARRAY argument is the row of six values expressed by (Year-CumNetCashFlow/NetCashFlow) and shown as row 9 in Figure 12.3. The ROW argument is 1, because there is only one row in the array. The COLUMN argument is the result of `=SUM(IF(CumNetCashFlow<=0,1,0))+1`, which is the first year during which the cumulative net cash flow is positive, or 6.

The result of the full array formula is 5.13—the sixth column in the only row of the array of the ratios—which is in cell G9 of Figure 12.3, and in cell B26 of Figure 12.2.

N O T E The approach outlined here returns the length of time required for the cumulative net cash flow to become a positive number *for the first time.* There are instances where additional investments must occur subsequent to the initial investment, and these subsequent investments can cause the cumulative net cash flow to turn negative again. ■

Thus, the undiscounted payback period for this series of cash flows is 5.13 years.

Understanding Future Value, Present Value, and Net Present Value

This analysis so far has not taken into account the time value of money. One dollar received today is worth more than one dollar received five years from today. But how much more? That would depend on how much the recipient thinks he could earn on that dollar: in other words, what's an adequate rate of return?

Calculating Future Value

A dollar received today and invested in a financial instrument that yields 10% would be worth $1.10 after one year. $1.10 is the future value of your dollar given the time period for investment (one year) and the rate of return (10%). After five years, the future value of your dollar would be $1.61. This value is

$1.00×1.1×1.1×1.1×1.1×1.1 = $1.61

or

$1.00×1.1^5 = $1.61

Calculating Present Value

Conversely, what is today's value of a dollar to be received five years from now? You can calculate the present value of that dollar (again, assuming a rate of return of 10%) by means of

$1.00÷1.1÷1.1÷1.1÷1.1÷1.1 = $0.62

or

$1.00/1.1^5 = $0.62

You can set up a formula in your worksheet to compute present value discount factors, given a selected interest rate. You can then apply the discount factors to the period's cash flow (see Figure 12.4). To do so, follow these steps.

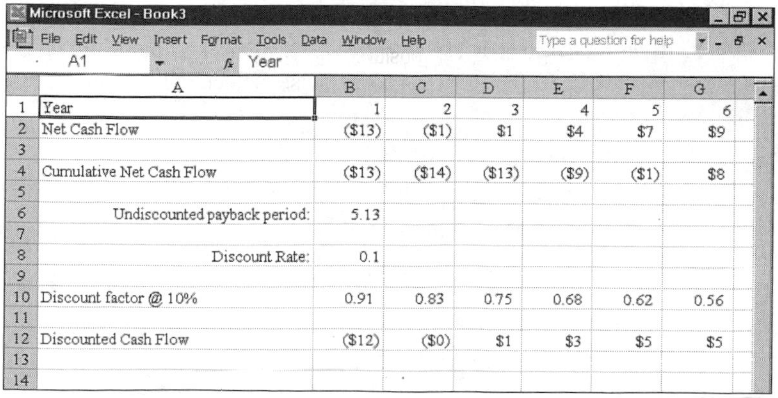

Part III

Ch 12

FIGURE 12.4
The discounted cash flow takes account of the time value of money.

	A	B	C	D	E	F	G
1	Year	1	2	3	4	5	6
2	Net Cash Flow	($13)	($1)	$1	$4	$7	$9
3							
4	Cumulative Net Cash Flow	($13)	($14)	($13)	($9)	($1)	$8
5							
6	Undiscounted payback period:	5.13					
7							
8	Discount Rate:	0.1					
9							
10	Discount factor @ 10%	0.91	0.83	0.75	0.68	0.62	0.56
11							
12	Discounted Cash Flow	($12)	($0)	$1	$3	$5	$5
13							
14							

1. Select cell A8, and enter the label **Discount Rate**.

2. Select cell B8, and enter **0.1**.

3. With B8 selected, click in the Name box, type **DiscountRate**, and press Enter. You have now created a range named DiscountRate, whose value is the number (0.1) that you entered in cell B8.

4. Select cells B10:G10, and type this formula:

   `=1/(1+DiscountRate)^Year`

   Press Ctrl+Enter to place the formula in all six selected cells.

5. With B10:G10 still selected, select Format, Cells and click the Number tab. Choose Number from the Category list box, and set the Decimal places to 2.

The result is as shown in Figure 12.4.

Notice that the discount factor ranges from .91 at the end of the first year, to .83 at the end of the second year, to .56 at the end of the sixth year. This represents the value of a dollar that you have today at the end of one, two,..., six years. For each year, the number 1 is divided by (1 +DiscountRate), or 1.1, raised to the number of years that have elapsed.

Line 12 in Figure 12.4, labeled Discounted Cash Flow, is the result of multiplying line 2 (NetCashFlow) by line 10 (the discount factor). This represents the discounted value of NetCashFlow—that is, the value in today's dollars of future annual cash flows.

For example, the NetCashFlow in year 6 is $8,680,000. The discounted cash flow in year 6 is $4,900,000. This means that, under the assumption of an annual 10% rate, the funds needed to start producing the new product return $4,900,000 six years later—taking into account that you could make 10% per year in an alternative investment.

Calculating Net Present Value

This discussion has described the discounting process in two steps—creating each year's discount factor, and multiplying that discount factor by the annual net cash flow. The discussion used two steps to make what happens in the discounting process a little clearer. Excel provides a function, NPV (Net Present Value), that enables you to perform the discounting process with just one formula:

1. If you have already created the range name DiscountRate on the worksheet shown in Figure 12.2, skip to step 4. Otherwise, select cell A28, and enter the label **Discount Rate**.

2. Select cell B28, and enter **0.1**.

3. With B28 still selected, click in the Name box, type **DiscountRate**, and press Enter.

4. Select cells B30:G30, enter the formula

   `=NetCashFlow/(1+DiscountRate)^Year`

   and press Ctrl+Enter.

5. With B30:G30 still selected, choose Format, Cells and click the Number tab. Select Currency from the Category list box, and set the Decimal places to 0.

The result is the discounted cash flow, which is shown in row 30 of Figure 12.2.

Line 32 in Figure 12.2, Cumulative Discounted Cash Flow, is calculated in much the same way as CumNetCashFlow is calculated. It shows the running total for each year of the *discounted* cash flows rather than the *undiscounted* cash flows. To obtain the cumulative discounted cash flow, select cells B32:G32 and array-enter this formula:

```
=NPV(DiscountRate,OFFSET(NetCashFlow,0,0,1,Year))
```

The outer portion of this formula, initiated by NPV, returns the net present value of its arguments. The OFFSET component of this formula returns as many elements from the NetCashFlow range as are specified by the Year argument. For cell B32, Year is equal to 1, so OFFSET returns the first element of NetCashFlow. For cell C32, Year is equal to 2, so OFFSET returns the second element of NetCashFlow.

The cumulative discounted cash flow amount in the sixth year, $654,920 (shown rounded and in millions in Figure 12.2 as $1), is the net present value of the cash flows for the six-year period of this project. It is simply the sum of the discounted cash flows for the full six-year life of the business case.

At this point, you can also add into your worksheet a payback calculation similar to the one that you developed for the undiscounted cash flows. In cell B34 of the worksheet shown in Figure 12.2, enter the following array formula:

```
=INDEX((Year-CumDiscountedCashFlow/DiscountedCashFlow),
1,SUM(IF(CumNetCashFlow<=0,1,0))+1)
```

Notice that the payback period for the discounted cash flows is 5.87 years, instead of the payback period of 5.13 years for the undiscounted cash flows. This makes sense because actual dollars being paid back are worth less the farther into the future you go; therefore, payback takes longer.

Shortening the Payback Period

It's an unfortunate but immutable fact of business life that, after you have gone through these careful calculations to derive payback periods based on both undiscounted and discounted cash flows, your executive director of finance says, "Smith, your analysis is close, but we have to keep the undiscounted payback to a maximum of five years. Go do it again."

Here's how to meet that five-year requirement.

Part III

Ch 12

Case Study: Optimizing Costs

As you analyze the effects of costs on the payback period for offering a new wireless phone product, you see that there are several cost categories that you must take into account. Some costs, such as taxes, are beyond your company's control. Other costs, such as the initial capital investment of $10,000,000, the advertising budget, salary for the product management group, and the market research, are all controllable.

You need a way to simultaneously modify all the controllable costs so as to meet the newly imposed conditions for the payback periods. Other examples in this book have used Excel's Goal Seek function to adjust one value by changing another. Goal Seek is faster than trial-and-error in finding a particular precedent value, but it limits you to just one changing cell. Furthermore, that changing cell cannot contain a formula: it must contain a value.

You can use Solver instead. Solver is an add-in that comes with Excel, and if you did a complete installation of Excel, it is available to you. With the Solver, you can modify more than one cell at once to get to a desired outcome. The changing cells do not need to contain values, and can contain formulas (although Solver converts the formulas to values if you save the Solver's solution at the end of the process).

To access Solver, follow these steps:

1. Choose Tools, Add-Ins from Excel's main menu.
2. If the checkbox for the Solver Add-in is empty, check it, and then choose OK; if the box is already checked, choose Cancel.
3. Excel works for a few moments loading the Solver add-in. When it has finished, Solver is a new option in the Tools menu.

NOTE If you cannot find the Solver add-in in the Add-ins dialog box, try choosing Browse to find SOLVER.XLA. It is normally in the SOLVER folder, within the LIBRARY folder that is within the folder where you have stored the Excel application file itself. SOLVER.XLA may have inadvertently been moved to another location. If you cannot locate it, you will have to re-install it from your installation CD-ROM. Make sure that you request the installation of the Solver when you set the installation options. ■

You want Solver to change your controllable costs, but you need to give it some criteria to work with. For example, Solver has no way of knowing *a priori* that you must pay the product manager a positive amount of money each year. Unconstrained, the Solver might suggest that you pay the product manager a negative amount of money to shorten the payback periods.

Because this is unacceptable, establish some minimum values. In cell H4, enter the formula =MIN(B4:G4).

Then copy that formula and paste it into cells H5 and H6. These cells will act as *constraints* on the solution that the Solver reaches. The formulas return the minimum values for advertising, the product manager's annual salary, and the market research expenses.

Select cell B22, which contains the undiscounted payback period. Then, choose Tools, Solver.

Complete the entries in the Solver Parameters dialog box as follows:

1. The Set Target Cell box should contain $B$22. If it does not, click in that box and then click on cell B22 on the worksheet.

2. Click the Value option button, and enter **5** in the edit box to its right. This informs Solver that you want it to modify various changing cells until the value in B22 is 5—in this context, until the undiscounted payback period is 5 years.

3. Click in the By Changing Cells box, and then select cells B4:G5 on the worksheet. These cells contain the annual costs for advertising and for product management's salary. Type **,** (a comma) following the G5 reference in the edit box, and click cell B6, which contains the market research cost. Type **,** (a comma) after G6 in the edit box, and click cell B17, which contains the amount of the initial investment.

4. Click the Add button. In the Add Constraint dialog box, click in the Cell Reference box and then select cell H4 on the worksheet. H4 contains the minimum value of the annual advertising cost.

5. Click the down arrow next to the operator symbol, and select the >= operator.

6. Click in the Constraint box, and enter **0**. The Add Constraint dialog box should appear as shown in Figure 12.5.

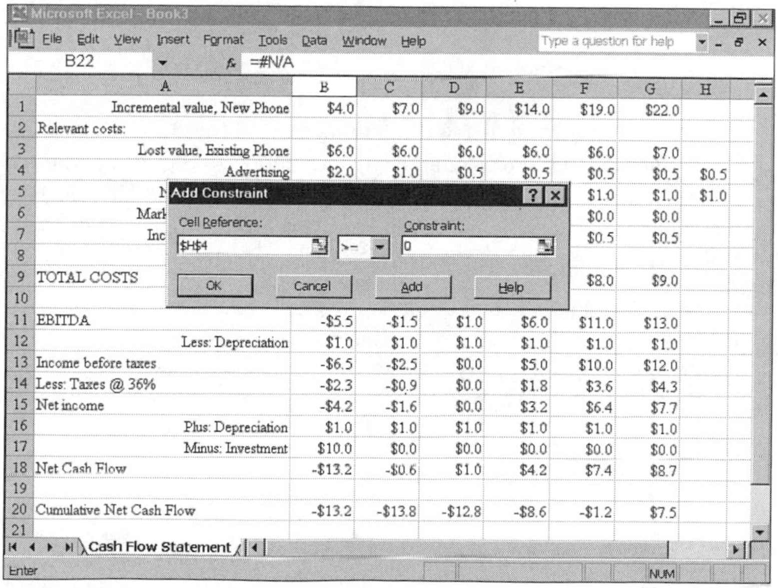

FIGURE 12.5

Setting a constraint on advertising expenses prevents Solver from changing them to negative values.

7. Choose Add.

8. Repeat steps 4 through 7 for cells H5, B6, and B17 to establish constraints for product management's salary, the market research expense, and the initial capital investment. Use a >= value of 8 for the constraint on the initial investment: although you may have to forego advertising, a product manager, and market research by means of zero costs, you cannot forego the initial investment entirely.

9. When you have finished entering cell B17 as a constraint, click OK to return to the Solver Parameters dialog box, which is shown in Figure 12.6.

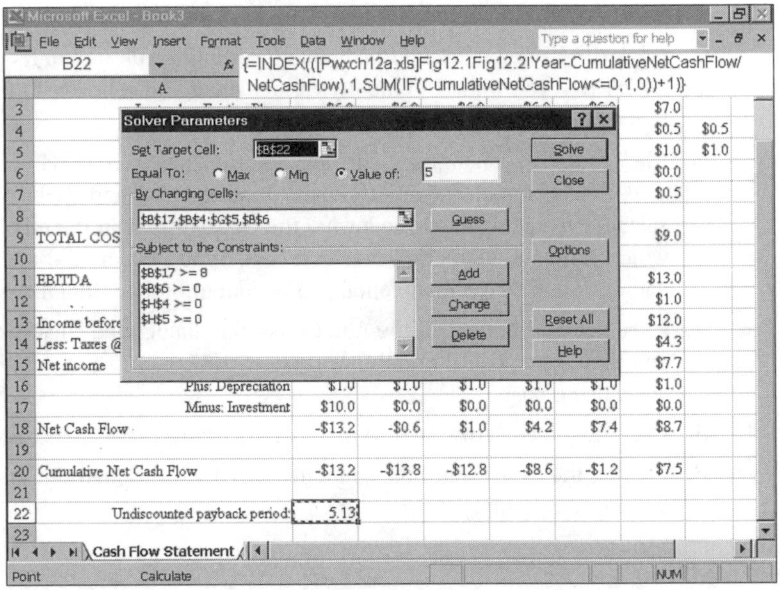

FIGURE 12.6

Using Solver to opti-mize costs involves set-ting the target cell, the changing cells, and any necessary constraints.

10. Click Solve.

Solver now begins adjusting the various costs in the changing cells in order to reach the value 5 for the undiscounted payback period (5 represents the *end* of year 4). Because you specified 0 as the minimum allowable value for cells H4:H5, B6, and B17 via the Add Constraints dialog box, the Solver will not attempt to establish a negative value in B4:G5, B6, or in B17.

When Solver has reached a solution the Solver Results dialog box appears. On occa-sion, the specifications that you supply—the target value, the constraints, or even the way the formulas are set up on the worksheet—may make it impossible for Solver to reach a solution. The Solver Results dialog box lets you know whether a solution was reached or not. With the example data, though, the Solver is able to shorten the undiscounted payback period to 5.

Because Solver is capable of modifying a variety of cells to reach a specified result, there may be many ways to achieve that result. It is useful to save the different solutions as *Scenarios*. One of the scenarios that you should save contains the original values in your worksheet. To save it, click the Save Scenario button in the Solver Results dialog box. The Save Scenario dialog box appears, and you can type a descriptive name such as *Initial Values* or *Five-Year Payback* in the Scenario Name box. Click OK to return to the Solver Results dialog box. Click the Restore Original Values radio button in the Solver Results dialog box, and then click OK.

As a result of this manipulation of values and saving them in a scenario, you have an easy way of going back and forth between your original input values, and the values that Solver found to bring the undiscounted payback period to 5. Just choose Tools, Scenarios; select the name of the scenario that you want to view in the Scenarios list box; and click Show. Solver has saved the proper addresses and values for the changing cells into the scenario.

Figure 12.7 shows one way that Solver can change the advertising, product management, market research, and initial investment costs to shorten the undiscounted payback period.

FIGURE 12.7

Controllable costs are reduced to shorten the payback period.

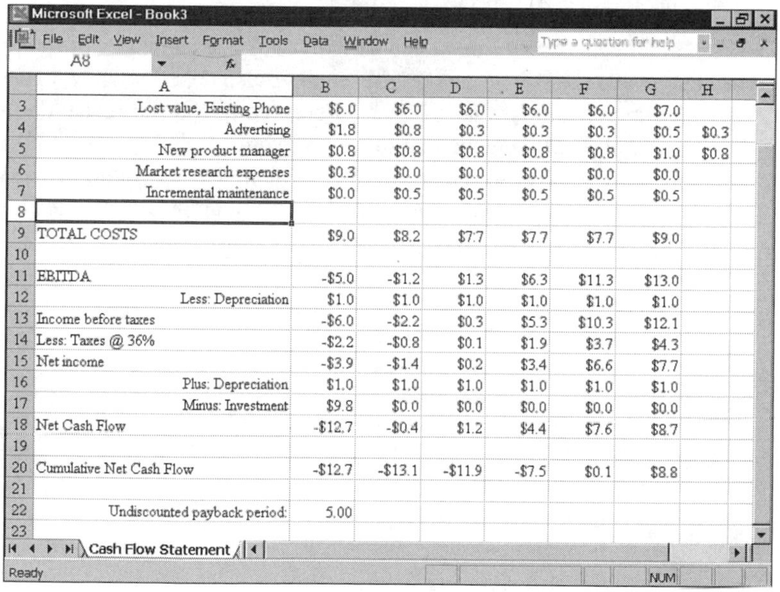

	A	B	C	D	E	F	G	H
3	Lost value, Existing Phone	$6.0	$6.0	$6.0	$6.0	$6.0	$7.0	
4	Advertising	$1.8	$0.8	$0.3	$0.3	$0.3	$0.5	$0.3
5	New product manager	$0.8	$0.8	$0.8	$0.8	$0.8	$1.0	$0.8
6	Market research expenses	$0.3	$0.0	$0.0	$0.0	$0.0	$0.0	
7	Incremental maintenance	$0.0	$0.5	$0.5	$0.5	$0.5	$0.5	
8								
9	TOTAL COSTS	$9.0	$8.2	$7.7	$7.7	$7.7	$9.0	
10								
11	EBITDA	-$5.0	-$1.2	$1.3	$6.3	$11.3	$13.0	
12	Less: Depreciation	$1.0	$1.0	$1.0	$1.0	$1.0	$1.0	
13	Income before taxes	-$6.0	-$2.2	$0.3	$5.3	$10.3	$12.1	
14	Less: Taxes @ 36%	-$2.2	-$0.8	$0.1	$1.9	$3.7	$4.3	
15	Net income	-$3.9	-$1.4	$0.2	$3.4	$6.6	$7.7	
16	Plus: Depreciation	$1.0	$1.0	$1.0	$1.0	$1.0	$1.0	
17	Minus: Investment	$9.8	$0.0	$0.0	$0.0	$0.0	$0.0	
18	Net Cash Flow	-$12.7	-$0.4	$1.2	$4.4	$7.6	$8.7	
19								
20	Cumulative Net Cash Flow	-$12.7	-$13.1	-$11.9	-$7.5	$0.1	$8.8	
21								
22	Undiscounted payback period:	5.00						
23								

Notice that the cumulative net cash flow is now $0 at the end of the fifth year; therefore, the payback period is now exactly five years. The advertising, product management, and market research expenses have all been reduced from a total of $10 million to a little more than $8 million. The initial investment cost has been reduced much more gently, from $10,000,000 to $9,800,000.

You might want to modify the Solver constraints on the ongoing costs, to force more of the savings into the capital cost category. Doing so could cause the capital cost to drop so far that you wouldn't be able to acquire the equipment. Or it may make it impossible for Solver to reach a solution that meets the required criteria. In that event, you might request additional guidance in setting the criteria, or you could report that the business case analysis suggests that the numbers do not support developing the new product.

Summary

In this chapter, you learned about payback periods, which quantify the length of time required to break even on an investment. The concepts of future value, present value, and net present value set the stage for discounted payback periods, which can vary as the value of money changes over time. And you learned how to use a very powerful add-in, the Solver, to optimize a variety of input values in order to achieve an outcome that you specify.

Each of these concepts and tools plays a part in developing a business case that conforms to your decision criteria. This chapter also described how to save different combinations of input values in scenarios, so that you can revisit them and eventually select the best combination to achieve your plan's objectives. The next chapter takes up the topic of sensitivity analysis, which enables you to quantify the magnitude of changes to the case's outcomes as you manipulate changes to its inputs.

Creating a Sensitivity Analysis for a Business Case

A business case is a snapshot of a set of assumptions surrounding a business activity that your firm is considering. Some of these assumptions can be made with relatively high confidence; others are little more than educated guesses. A well-prepared business case recognizes that at least some of its inputs are bound to be inaccurate.

The business case should document the logic behind the numbers, and should also test the sensitivity of its results to variations in its input assumptions. Suppose that a business case assumes, among other things, that a company can obtain a loan at 9%. If it gets that loan, according to the business case, the company can expect profits to increase by 12%. The business case should also report the expected profits for other interest rate assumptions (8% and 10%, for example). By varying the input assumption (interest rate), decision makers can determine how *sensitive* certain measures (profits) are to changes in assumptions.

When you first construct a business case, you undertake a qualitative review of all the potential drivers of costs and benefits. As discussed in Chapters 11, "Examining a Business Case: Investment," and 12, "Examining Decision Criteria for Business Case Analysis," you then attempt to quantify those drivers—to attach credible numbers to them. After constructing the basic framework and reviewing its output, you have an opportunity to review each of those drivers. This review enables you to determine your level of confidence in their accuracy; remember, the drivers are variables that can be anything from hard data to vague estimates.

In some cases, the accuracy of your estimate doesn't make much difference. In other cases, an apparently minor change to an estimate has a profound effect on the outcome. Sensitivity analysis enables you to calculate the importance of a particular assumption. This puts you in a position to focus on the accuracy of the critical drivers, and to avoid being distracted by drivers that have little effect on the outcome. If a crucial driver is very difficult to estimate with enough confidence, it will be equally difficult to place much faith in the results of the business analysis.

Excel provides several ways to manage and manipulate these drivers. One, scenario management, helps you to manage the inputs to your business case. Using scenarios, you can alter different assumptions about decision drivers such as the discount rate or the cost of capital.

Another Excel function that gives you more insight into your business case's outcomes is IRR, or *internal rate of return*. And by using Excel's Goal Seek function, you can enhance the usefulness of a sensitivity analysis.

This chapter covers each of these topics in detail.

Managing Scenarios

Chapters 11 and 12 explained how to construct a base business case. During the initial case development, the tendency is to be neither optimistic nor pessimistic about the initial inputs: these estimates are starting points, and they are usually just best guesses. After constructing the basic business case, it's useful to continue with a sensitivity analysis—an examination of each input variable, and the assignment of base case, worst case, and best case values to each.

Scenario management is the process of examining individual variables, and assigning ranges of values to them. Each combination of values results in a different view, or *scenario*. You can then focus on each scenario, and assess the sensitivity of the most likely outcome (the base case) to changes in the assumptions that underlie the business opportunity. Again, this helps you keep your eye on the variables that matter.

The input variables involved in the decision to produce an enhanced wireless phone, developed in Chapters 11 and 12, include the following:

- Incremental sales
- Lost sales

- Cost of goods sold for incremental sales
- Cost of goods sold for lost sales
- Advertising expense
- New product manager salaries and benefits
- Market research expense
- Capital required for new equipment
- Incremental maintenance expense

A quick scan of this list makes it evident that the two items in which you would have the lowest level of confidence are the incremental sales and the lost sales. (Lost sales represent the purchases that current customers would make in the absence of a new product. You expect that some, but not all, of these lost sales will be recovered through purchases of the new product when you introduce it).

You normally have confidence in your estimates of the other input variables, because they involve controllable costs. For example, you expect to have an accurate estimate of the factors that influence the cost of goods sold. These line items include both labor and material costs. You can often exert considerable control over these by entering into long-term purchasing agreements for material, and long-term wage agreements for labor. Often, these agreements are already in place at the time that you undertake the sensitivity analysis.

You can also estimate capital costs for new equipment and for retooling, and the associated incremental maintenance, with a high degree of certainty. You can obtain quotes from vendors for the required equipment, and ensure that the quotes will remain firm during the process of evaluating the business case.

You can estimate the costs associated with hiring new product managers fairly closely. For instance, you can find out what other employers are offering new hires in product management at different experience levels, and also check the salaries and benefits offered for similar positions within your company.

Market research is also a controllable expense, and it's also your source of information on both the new revenue and the degree of lost sales you can expect. You might decide to spend very little on market research, and just guess at the level of lost sales, or you could spend millions of dollars on focus groups and test marketing. Because the volume of lost sales is a critical input variable, you might use the $2 million initially budgeted for market research as a minimum amount. You could retain the option to consider additional research expenses if, after reviewing preliminary research results, you find you have little confidence in their accuracy.

Advertising expenses are also under your control. Assume that, historically, sales of this product have had a strong positive correlation with the dollar level of advertising. If so, varying the advertising expenditures would have a known impact on sales, and sales have a corresponding impact on profitability. Of course, there is a level of advertising expenditure at which returns begin to diminish.

New sales revenue is the remaining input variable that you can't control directly, and that you can't estimate as accurately as you'd like. To determine how sensitive the business case is to both underestimates and overestimates of new sales revenue, it is useful to create scenarios that specify different conditions, such as:

- Incremental sales are doubled
- Incremental sales are halved
- Advertising expense is doubled, causing incremental sales volumes to increase by 20%
- Advertising expense is halved, causing incremental sales volumes to decline by 30%

N O T E These conditions, such as double the incremental sales and half the advertising expenses, are just examples. In your own situation, you would probably be concerned about other variables in addition to advertising and incremental sales. Further, you would want to identify a *relevant range* for each variable. Depending on the particular business case, other upper and lower limits would apply—for instance, plus and minus 15% of the base case's incremental sales assumption. ■

In the previous list, the first two scenarios give you both an optimistic and pessimistic view of the opportunity, considering large variations in incremental sales only. The second two scenarios enable you to analyze the impact on profitability of changing the advertising plan.

The base case is the starting point for the sensitivity analysis (see Figure 13.1).

FIGURE 13.1

The base case analysis of the decision to produce an enhanced wireless phone depicts only one possible outcome.

	A	B	C	D	E	F	G
1	Enhanced Wireless Phone: Cash Flow Statement			($Millions)			
2	Year:	1	2	3	4	5	6
3	*Relevant benefits:*						
4	Incremental sales	$4	$7	$9	$14	$19	$22
5							
6	*Relevant costs:*						
7	Lost value, Existing Phone	$6	$6	$6	$6	$6	$7
8	Advertising	$2.0	$1.0	$0.5	$0.5	$0.5	$0.5
9	New product manager	$1	$1	$1	$1	$1	$1
10	Market research expenses	$0.5	$0	$0	$0	$0	$0
11	Incremental maintenance	$0	$0.5	$0.5	$0.5	$0.5	$0.5
12							
13	Total costs	$10	$9	$8	$8	$8	$9
14							
15	EBITDA	($6)	($2)	$1	$6	$11	$13
16	Less: Depreciation	$1	$1	$1	$1	$1	$1
17	Income before taxes	($7)	($3)	$0	$5	$10	$12
18	Less: Taxes @ 36%	($2)	($1)	$0	$2	$4	$4
19	Net income	($4)	($2)	$0	$3	$6	$8
20	Plus: Depreciation	$1	$1	$1	$1	$1	$1
21	Minus: Investment	$10	$0	$0	$0	$0	$0
22	Net Cash Flow	($13)	($1)	$1	$4	$7	$9
23							

Use Excel's Scenario Manager to document each scenario. With the Base Case sheet open, take these steps:

1. Choose Tools, Scenarios. The Scenario Manager dialog box appears as shown in Figure 13.2.

FIGURE 13.2
You can manipulate scenarios in several different ways by using the Scenario Manager.

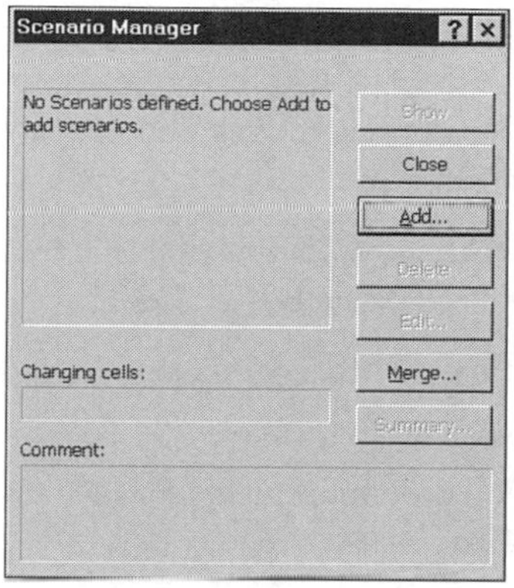

2. Click Add. The Add Scenario dialog box (see Figure 13.3) appears.

FIGURE 13.3
The Add Scenario dialog box enables you to store several different sets of values for the same worksheet.

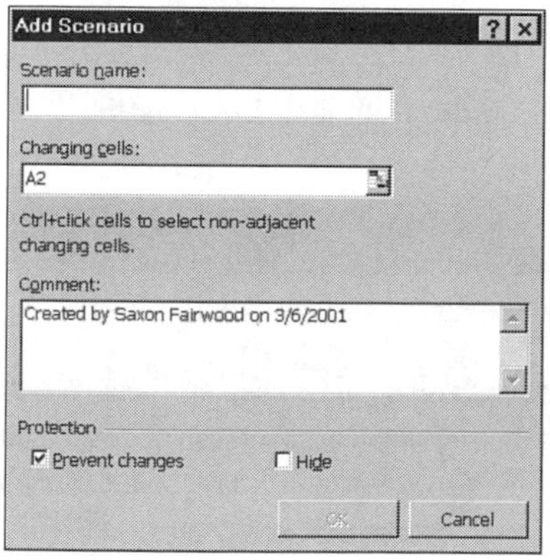

3. In the Scenario Name box, type **Base Case**. It's important to establish the current base case values as a scenario, so that you can quickly get back to them.
4. Click in the Changing Cells box.
5. Enter the address of the changing cells in the Changing Cells box, either by selecting the range on the worksheet or by typing the address in the edit box. In this case, the changing cells are B4:G4, the incremental sales shown in Figure 13.1.
6. Click OK. The Scenario Values dialog box appears, as shown in Figure 13.4. Click OK to accept the current base case values.

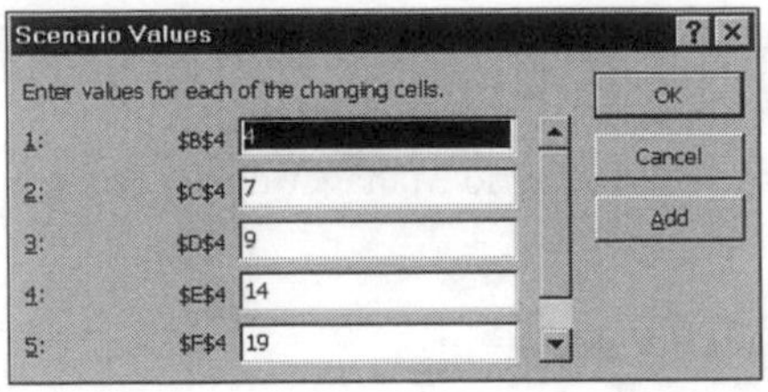

FIGURE 13.4
In the Scenario Values dialog box, values are saved under the scenario's name after you add the scenario to the worksheet.

7. The Scenario Manager dialog box reappears. Click Show to activate the worksheet and show the values for the Base Case scenario.

With the Base Case scenario defined, take the following steps to create the scenario under which the incremental sales are twice those of the Base Case.

1. Choose Tools, Scenarios. The Scenario Manager dialog box appears.

2. Click Add. The Add Scenario dialog box appears.

3. In the Scenario Name box, enter a descriptive name for the new scenario. For this case, type **Incremental Sales Two Times Base Case**.

4. Click in the Changing Cells box.

5. Select the range B4:G4 on the worksheet, or type the address of that range into the box. These are the same changing cells that you used to establish the Base Case scenario.

6. If you want, you can click in the Comment box and enter more information about the scenario. That way you'll have more than just the scenario name documented in your worksheet.

7. Check the Prevent Changes checkbox if you want to protect the scenario from modification (even by you). You can also check the Hide checkbox to prevent the scenario's name from appearing in the Scenario Manager dialog box.

N O T E Neither the Prevent Changes nor the Hide option has an effect unless the worksheet is protected, which you can do by choosing Tools, Protection, Protect Sheet. Scroll down in the list box that's labeled Allow All Users of This Worksheet To, make sure that the Edit Scenarios checkbox is cleared, and click OK. Then, if you checked Prevent Changes, the Edit and the Delete buttons on the Scenario Manager dialog box are dimmed. If you checked Hide only, the scenario name is missing from the Scenarios list box. The Edit and Delete buttons are available only if the worksheet has another scenario that does not have its Prevent Changes or Hide options selected. ■

8. Click OK. The Scenario Values dialog box appears. This scenario doubles the sales assumptions for the Base Case, so you would change the 4 entry in cell $B$4 to =4*2, the 7 entry in $C$4 to =7*2, and so on, doubling the existing value of each cell, as shown in Figure 13.5.

FIGURE 13.5
Excel converts these
formulas to static val-
ues when you click the
Scenario Values dialog
box's OK button.

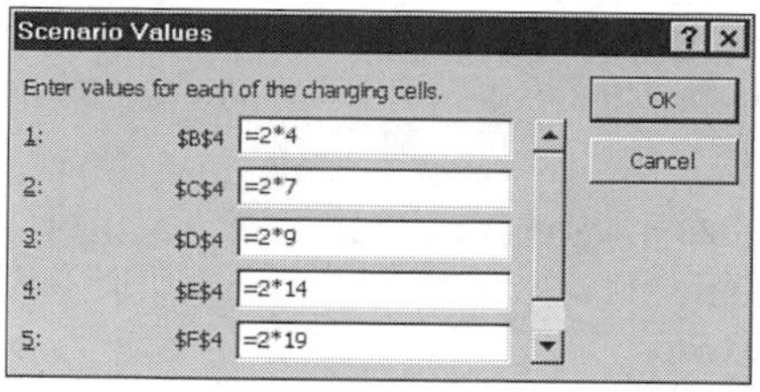

9. Click OK. The Scenario Manager dialog box reappears. Click Show to activate the worksheet and show the values for the scenario highlighted in the Scenarios list box. You can also click Close to activate the worksheet with its current values.

CAUTION

If you happen to be using Excel 97, beware of hiding the only scenario on a worksheet, and then protecting the worksheet. When you next start the Scenario Manager on that worksheet, Excel 97 crashes. One workaround is to create more than one scenario on that worksheet.

In the Scenario Manager dialog box, you can also click the Add, Edit, Merge, and Summary buttons to bring up the appropriate dialog boxes for managing your scenarios. With Merge, you can add scenarios from other worksheets or workbooks into the list of available scenarios for the active worksheet. Clicking the Summary button enables you to create a summary of the available scenarios.

You now have a scenario that represents the optimistic input assumption that incremental sales will be twice as great as those represented in the Base Case. Now create a scenario that represents a pessimistic input assumption: that incremental sales will be half those of the Base Case.

First, ensure that the worksheet shows the Base Case values (select Tools, Scenarios; highlight Base Case in the Scenarios list box; and click Show). Then, repeat the nine steps you followed for the scenario that doubled the incremental sales, except:

- In step 3, enter **Incremental Sales Half of Base Case** as a scenario name.
- In step 8, enter a value for each Changing Cell that is half that of the Base Case. Change the 4 entry for cell $B$4 to =4/2, the 7 entry for $C$4 to =7/2, and so on through cell $G$4.

You now have a Base Case scenario, an optimistic scenario, and a pessimistic scenario associated with the worksheet. The latter scenarios assume that the market research was wrong, and that with no additional effort the sales of the new wireless phone will be either double the Base Case values or, sadly, half the Base Case values.

There are two more scenarios to consider—those in which you change the cost of the advertising expense. While the optimistic and pessimistic scenarios assume that incremental sales will differ from the Base Case even though you use Base Case advertising levels, you should also assume that changing the advertising expenditure will change the level of incremental sales.

First, assume that you will double the Base Case advertising budget, and that this additional expenditure will increase incremental sales by 20%. To create this scenario, repeat steps 1 through 9 shown previously, except:

- In step 3, enter **Incremental Sales 120%, Advertising Twice Base Case** as a scenario name.

- In step 5, select cells $B$4:$G$4, and then hold down the Ctrl key and select cells $B$10:$G$10. This enables you to change both the incremental sales values and the advertising budget values.

- In step 8, enter values for cells $B$4:$G$4 that are 1.2 times the Base Case values. Change the 4 entry for cell $B$4 to =4*1.2, the 7 entry for $C$4 to =7*1.2, and so on through cell $G$4. For cells $B$10:$G$10, double the advertising budget by changing the 2 value in $B$10 to =2*2, the 1 value in $C$10 to =1*2, and so on through cell $G$10.

Then, assume that you will cut the Base Case advertising budget by 50%, and that this additional expenditure will decrease incremental sales by 20%. To create this scenario, repeat the nine steps, except:

- In step 3, enter **Incremental Sales 70%, Advertising 50% of Base Case** as a scenario name.

- In step 5, select cells B4:G4, and then hold down the Ctrl key and select cells B10:G10. This enables you to change both the incremental sales values and the advertising budget values.

- In step 8, enter values for cells $B$4:$G$4 that are 0.7 times the Base Case values. Change the 4 entry for cell $B$4 to =4*.7, the 7 entry for $C$4 to =7*.7, and so on through cell $G$4. For cells $B$10:$G$10, halve the advertising budget by changing the 2 value in $B$10 to =2/2, the 1 value in $C$10 to =1/2, and so on through cell $G$10.

> **N O T E** You can enter static values instead of equations for the changing cell values. The instructions given in this section use equations only to emphasize the purpose of creating the scenarios: to see the effects of doubling the revenues, of halving the revenues, and so on. ▪

This completes the preparation of individual scenarios that reflect different input assumptions. It is useful to summarize the results of these scenarios on one worksheet. You can do this by selecting Tools, Scenarios and clicking the Summary button. The Scenario Summary dialog box appears (see Figure 13.6).

FIGURE 13.6
Use the Scenario Summary dialog box to summarize the results of the worksheet's scenarios.

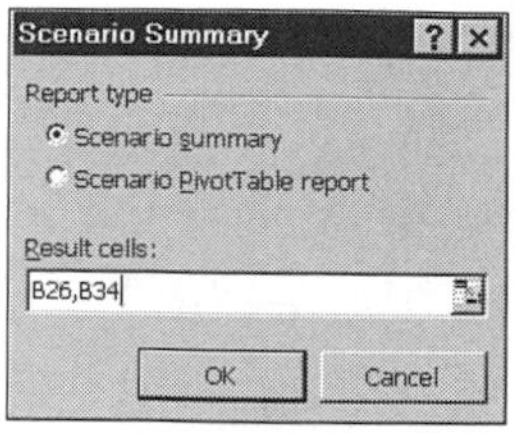

The Scenario Summary dialog box proposes default result cells to show in the summary. You can add to these if you want more results. When you choose OK, Excel creates a new worksheet in the active workbook that contains a summary of the scenarios available to the active worksheet. See Figure 13.7 for an example.

FIGURE 13.7
Summary of the five scenarios for the sensitivity analysis.

	Current Values	Incremental Sales Two Times Base Case	Base Case	Incremental Sales Half of Base Case	Adverti
Changing Cells:					
$B$4	$4	$8	$4	$2	
$C$4	$7	$14	$7	$4	
$D$4	$9	$18	$9	$5	
$E$4	$14	$28	$14	$7	
$F$4	$19	$38	$19	$10	
$G$4	$22	$44	$22	$11	
$B$8	$2.0	$2.0	$2.0	$2.0	
$C$8	$1.0	$1.0	$1.0	$1.0	
$D$8	$0.5	$0.5	$0.5	$0.5	
$E$8	$0.5	$0.5	$0.5	$0.5	
$F$8	$0.5	$0.5	$0.5	$0.5	
$G$8	$0.5	$0.5	$0.5	$0.5	
Result Cells:					
$B$26	5.13	2.99	5.13	#REF!	
$B$34	5.87	3.27	5.87	#REF!	

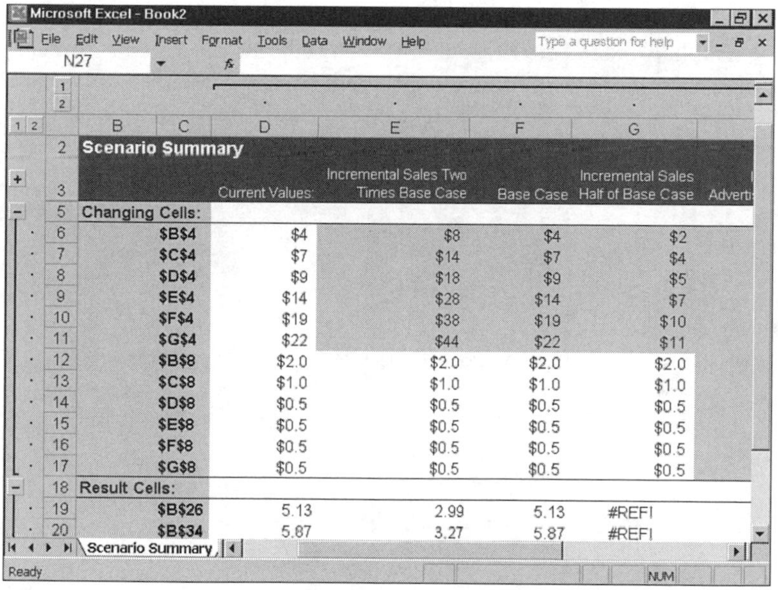

Decision makers can now examine the Summary sheet and make a subjective judgment about the risk of undertaking this product enhancement. If, for example, an undiscounted payback period of 7.5 years is regarded as too long, you might decide either to repeat the sensitivity analysis with a different set of input assumptions. It may be that you cannot settle on a set of assumptions that result in a satisfactory outcome. In that case, you might decide that the risk is too great to undertake the project at all.

N O T E Notice in Figure 13.7 that both the undiscounted and discounted payback periods have the #REF! error value for the scenario whose sales are half the Base Case. In that scenario the cumulative net cash flow does not turn positive during the six years under consideration. There is therefore no index value to present to the OFFSET function that the formulas use to calculate the payback periods. The result is the #REF! error value. ■

Measuring Profit

To this point, the sensitivity analysis has been simplified by considering only one measure of profit: payback period. There are other measures that you can use, and each of these alternatives provides another point of view on your profit. These include the Internal Rate of Return and the Profitability Index.

Calculating Internal Rate of Return

Given the assumptions used in the Base Case, it is apparent that introducing a new product will generate more than a 10% return on the funds that the project requires. This is easy to determine from the net present value of the project. Taking the discount rate (10%) into account, the project returns a positive net present value. The company therefore has positive earnings compared to the 10% alternative.

But how much better than the 10% discount rate does the investment perform? Asked differently, what discount rate would cause the net present value to be zero? Excel's IRR function answers that question, and Figure 13.8 shows the result returned by IRR for the Base Case in cell B38.

FIGURE 13.8
You can use various financial indicators to summarize the results of different scenarios in different ways.

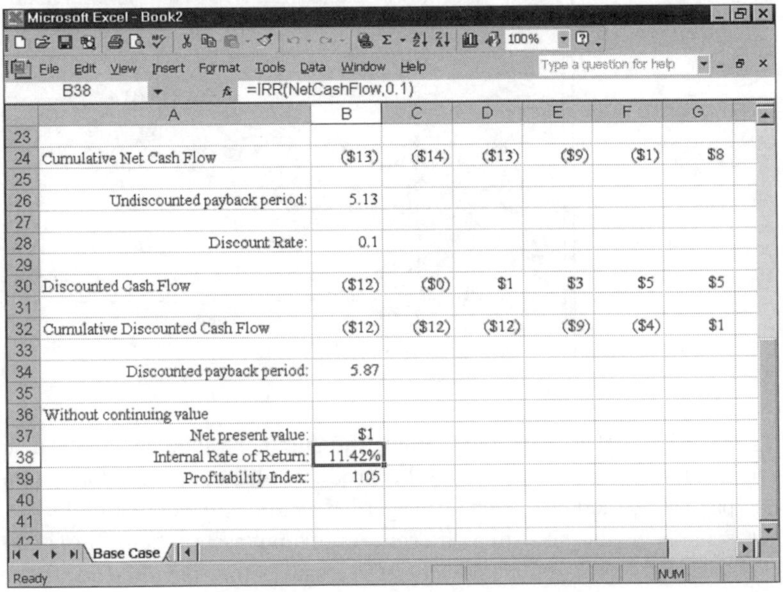

Excel gives 11.42% as the internal rate of return for the project's Base Case. As compared to the discount factor of 10%, this is not a spectacular increase, but it is useful.

Put differently, if the discount factor were 11.42% instead of 10%, the net present value of the funds required for the new product would be zero. IRR returns a value greater than the 10% assumed by the discount rate. Therefore, this business case represents a more attractive use of the funds than a 10% alternative investment.

The formula that returns the 11.42% figure in cell B38 is

```
=IRR(NetCashFlow,.1)
```

The first argument, NetCashFlow, represents the values that IRR uses to determine the rate of return. Notice that the result of 11.42% reflects the return on values *prior* to applying the discount factor of 10%.

> **N O T E** You can infer from this discussion that you would not want to apply IRR to *discounted* cash flows. To do so would be to ask what discount rate would return a net present value of zero on cash flows that have already been discounted. ▪

The second argument, .1, is simply an assist that you can give Excel. Excel calculates the internal rate of return by an iterative method, and it gives up (returning #NUM!) if it cannot reach a meaningful result within 20 iterations. By providing a second argument that is fairly close to what you guess the internal rate of return might be, you give IRR a head start on its iterations. This makes it a little more likely that you will get a usable result. If you do not supply the second argument, Excel uses a default value of .1.

Note that at least one of the values in the first argument must be positive and at least one must be negative. Otherwise, IRR returns the #NUM! error value. In the Base Case, net cash flow conforms to this requirement: there is only one change in sign (negative to positive) in the series of cash flows.

> **N O T E** Use caution if the series of cash flows you use as the first argument to the IRR function changes sign more than once. There is one distinct internal rate of return for each change in sign in the series. In most of the cases where the sign changes more than once, there is only one internal rate of return that makes sense. But if you do not supply a reasonable initial guess as IRR's second argument, it is possible that IRR will iterate to an unacceptable value. ▪

Calculating Profitability Indices

Discounted payback, net present value, and internal rate of return are all indicators of the profitability of a business case. They can be used as tools that help a company decide which projects to undertake. The company may have decision criteria specifying, for example, that a project must have a payback period of no more than five years, or that it must have an internal rate of return greater than 15%, to be considered for implementation.

But in all likelihood there is a limit to the amount of investment that a firm is willing or able to undertake during a given time period. If a company is presented with two projects, both with net present values of $500,000, which project is the right one to select? In a case such as this, it may be useful to calculate a profitability index.

A *profitability index* is simply a comparison of the present value of the inflows that result from an investment to the value of the investment amount itself. The present value of the inflows is the net present value of the project, with the initial investment added back. To calculate a profitability index, two values are required: the project's net present value and its initial investment.

In the worksheet shown in Figure 13.8, two named ranges have been established:

- NetPresentValue represents cell B37, the net present value of the cash flows given the discount rate.
- InitialInvestment represents cell B24, the funds that would initially be committed to the project.

The formula for the profitability index shown in cell B39 of Figure 13.8 is

```
=(NetPresentValue + ABS(InitialInvestment))/ ABS(InitialInvestment)
```

(The ABS function converts a negative value to a positive value.) In other words, the formula adds the project's net present value to the value of the first year's investment, and divides the sum by the value of the first year's investment. It is a way of expressing the project's value as a function of the initial investment amount: expressed in this way, for every dollar invested at inception, the project returns $1.05.

The profitability index is useful for ranking projects that have similar internal rates of return or net present values, but that require very different initial investment amounts.

Estimating the Continuing Value

The impact of a decision made today often has effects that last beyond the period that the business case studies. In evaluating a startup business opportunity, for example, you can review the financials of a forward-looking, ten-year business planning horizon (as done in the case of the new phone, albeit for six years). Such an analysis, however, would be missing a critical element: after ten years, the business would have some sort of value in the market-place. How can that value be incorporated into the discounted cash flow analysis?

The concept of continuing value attempts to quantify this element. It assigns a future value to the startup opportunity. It then discounts that value back to the present (when the decision is to be made) and incorporates that amount into the net present value.

Not all business cases should necessarily incorporate continuing value. For example, suppose that a computer software manufacturer announced that it would make major changes to a popular operating system in three years. And suppose that another company prepares a business case that involves improvements to application software that requires the current operating system. In that event, the business case would look at no more than three years of cash flow, and would not incorporate any continuing value estimates.

Figure 13.9 shows an estimate of continuing value in cell B46, and uses a common method of estimating continuing value: as a multiple of after tax cash flows. The formula used for continuing value is

```
=G27/DiscountRate
```

where cell G27 contains the net cash flow during the final year of the Base Case.

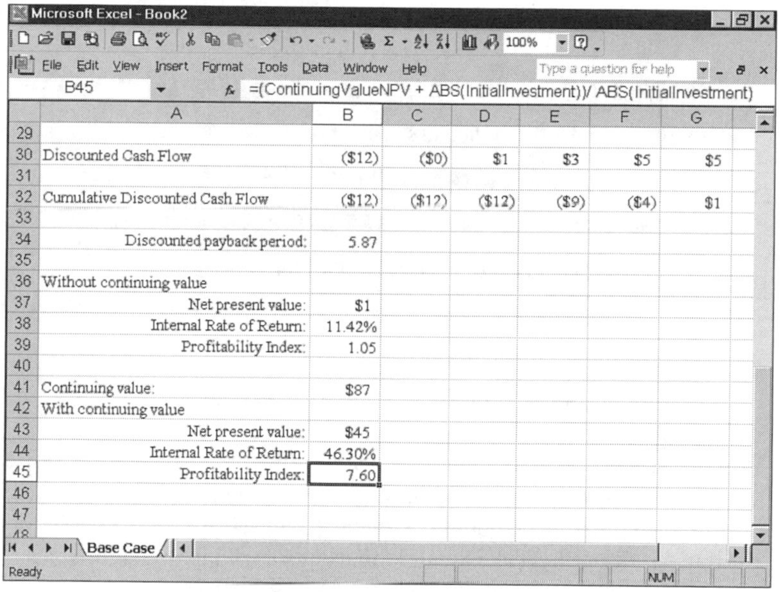

	A	B	C	D	E	F	G
29							
30	Discounted Cash Flow	($12)	($0)	$1	$3	$5	$5
31							
32	Cumulative Discounted Cash Flow	($12)	($12)	($12)	($9)	($4)	$1
33							
34	Discounted payback period:	5.87					
35							
36	Without continuing value						
37	Net present value:	$1					
38	Internal Rate of Return:	11.42%					
39	Profitability Index:	1.05					
40							
41	Continuing value:	$87					
42	With continuing value						
43	Net present value:	$45					
44	Internal Rate of Return:	46.30%					
45	Profitability Index:	7.60					
46							
47							

FIGURE 13.9
Establishing a continuing value extends your business case to the point that the product is well established.

Dividing the basis of $8.7 million (rounded on the worksheet to $9) by the discount rate of 10% results in a continuing value of $87 million, measured as a net cash flow. In effect, this assigns a multiple of 10 to after tax cash flows because of the value chosen for the discount rate. It is one possible answer to this question: What value would you place on a business that generates $8.7 million after taxes, if your target return rate is 10%?

Figure 13.9 also shows several other values that follow from the continuing value. The cumulative net cash flow, discounted cash flow, and cumulative discounted cash flow can be extended to take the continuing value into account. Now you can calculate another set of indicators that include net present value, internal rate of return, and the profitability index (cells B43:B45 in Figure 13.9). The indicators reference the cash flows that incorporate the continuing value of the project.

It's convenient to establish two new names on the worksheet: NetCashFlowContinuingValue, that extends the NetCashFlow name to include the continuing value figure, and ContinuingValueNPV, that represents the net present value of the project under the continuing value assumption. To establish these names do the following:

1. Select the cell that contains the continuing value formula (in Figure 13.9, this is cell B41).
2. Click in the Name Box, type **ContinuingValueNPV**, and press Enter.
3. Click in the Name Box and then select the NetCashFlow name. This selects the NetCashFlow range.
4. Hold down the Ctrl key and then click cell B41, which contains the continuing value figure. This creates a multiple selection, consisting of the existing NetCashFlow range plus the cell that contains the continuing value.
5. Click in the Name Box and type **NetCashFlowContinuingValue**.

The formulas for the indicators are:

For net present value, in cell B43:

```
=NPV(DiscountRate, NetCashFlowContinuingValue)
```

For internal rate of return, in cell B44:

```
=IRR(NetCashFlowContinuingValue,.1)
```

For the profitability index, in cell B45:

```
=(ContinuingValueNPV + ABS(InitialInvestment))/ ABS(InitialInvestment)
```

This puts you in a position to compare profitability indicators during the period covered by the business case with indicators that assess the project beyond the business case's horizon. And, using the techniques for sensitivity analysis discussed earlier in this chapter, you can compare these indicators under different sets of input assumptions.

Varying the Discount Rate Input

One input assumption that can have a major influence on your profitability is the discount rate. Chapter 14, "Planning Profits," discusses the effects of the relationship between fixed costs and variable costs, and the amount of debt financing a company uses. If a company borrows funds to obtain fixed cost assets, then the discount rate—the cost of borrowing funds—has effects on profitability that go well beyond the interest charges.

How sensitive are the financial indicators to changes in the size of the discount factor? Figures 13.10 through 13.12 recapitulate the indicators that result from the base case assumptions.

FIGURE 13.10
Indicators with discount rate of 10%: this is identical to the base case.

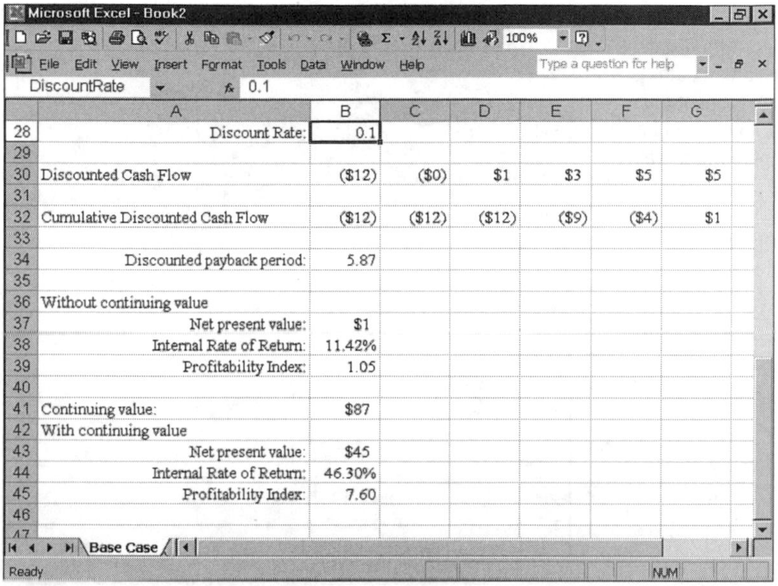

	A	B	C	D	E	F	G
28	Discount Rate:	0.1					
29							
30	Discounted Cash Flow	($12)	($0)	$1	$3	$5	$5
31							
32	Cumulative Discounted Cash Flow	($12)	($12)	($12)	($9)	($4)	$1
33							
34	Discounted payback period:	5.87					
35							
36	Without continuing value						
37	Net present value:	$1					
38	Internal Rate of Return:	11.42%					
39	Profitability Index:	1.05					
40							
41	Continuing value:	$87					
42	With continuing value						
43	Net present value:	$45					
44	Internal Rate of Return:	46.30%					
45	Profitability Index:	7.60					
46							

FIGURE 13.11
Indicators with discount rate of 5%: the business case is much more attractive than with a discount rate of 10%.

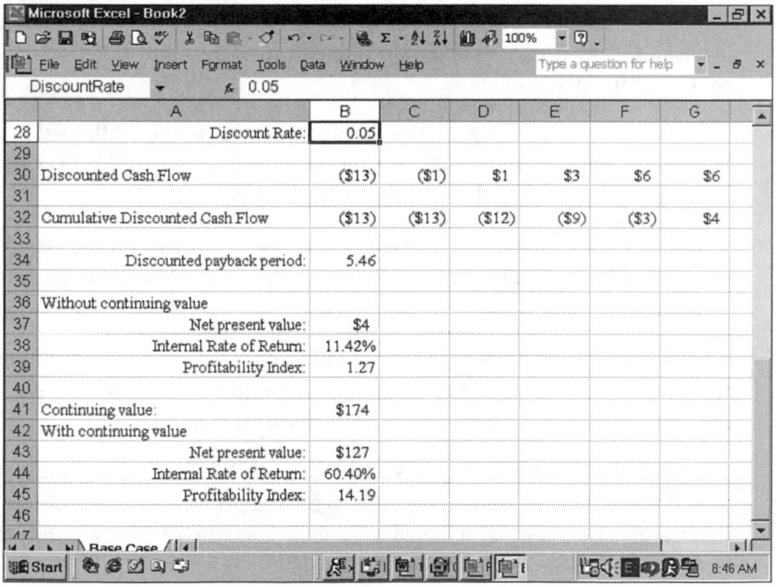

	A	B	C	D	E	F	G
28	Discount Rate:	0.05					
29							
30	Discounted Cash Flow	($13)	($1)	$1	$3	$6	$6
31							
32	Cumulative Discounted Cash Flow	($13)	($13)	($12)	($9)	($3)	$4
33							
34	Discounted payback period:	5.46					
35							
36	Without continuing value						
37	Net present value:	$4					
38	Internal Rate of Return:	11.42%					
39	Profitability Index:	1.27					
40							
41	Continuing value:	$174					
42	With continuing value						
43	Net present value:	$127					
44	Internal Rate of Return:	60.40%					
45	Profitability Index:	14.19					
46							

Part
III

Ch
13

FIGURE 13.12

Indicators with discount rate of 15%: an alternative investment that returns 15% would be much more attractive.

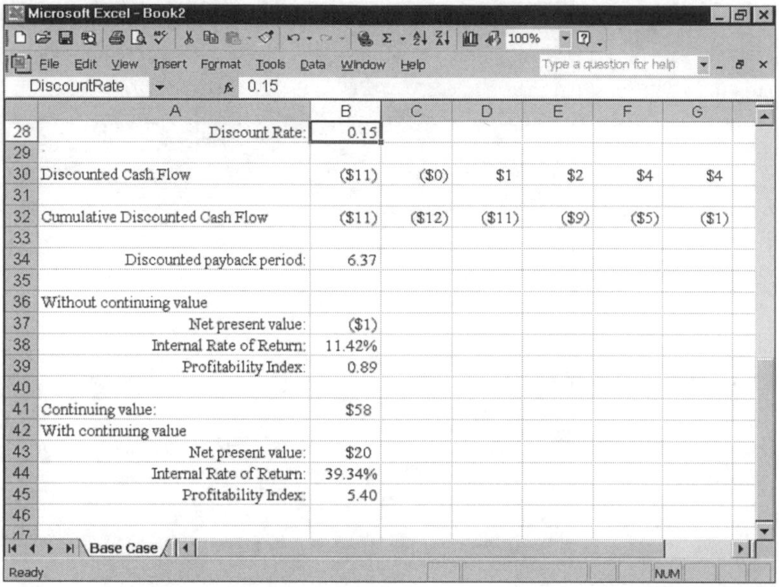

The IRR results are the same in each figure for the Without Continuing Value analysis. This is because they are independent of the choice of discount rate: they measure the rate of return of the investment.

Net present value, however, uses the discount rate to adjust the value of the future cash flows back to the value of money at the present time. This quantifies how many dollars this project would generate over and above the cost of capital.

The profitability index also varies as a function of the discount rate. This is because it is a function of both the net present value of an investment and the actual dollar investment amount.

These same sensitivities hold for the indicators that include continuing value. In addition, the IRR indicator is sensitive to changes in the discount rate, because the formula for computing continuing value uses the discount rate in its calculation.

The analysis depicted in Figures 13.10 through 13.12 tells you that you can be comfortable with the discount rate you have chosen for the project. A discount rate should reflect, at a minimum, a firm's weighted cost of capital. This rate can vary from year to year as a firm undergoes changes in its capital structure.

Using this minimum value as a benchmark enables you to adjust the rate upward so as to consider the relative risk of the project, over and above normal business operations. In the Base Case example, enhancing the current product line does not represent a substantial deviation from the firm's core business: the enhancement is simply a newer version of an existing product.

However, if the business case involved the development of a new product that is substantially different from the firm's current operations (for example, if the product were network hubs instead of phones), it would be wise to employ a higher discount rate than the one used for existing operations. Doing so would reflect the greater risk involved in developing an entirely new product line.

Using the Goal Seek Function

When you perform a sensitivity analysis, you usually try to identify the value of an input variable that is necessary to produce a specific output. For example, it may be useful to quantify the level of incremental sales required for this project to break even, or the level that is required to produce a 15% internal rate of return. Rather than using the trial and error method of changing the sales inputs and visually inspecting the relevant outputs, you can use Excel's Goal Seek function.

Goal Seek is similar to the Solver in that it backtracks to an input value (the Changing Cell) that satisfies a result value that depends on the input value. Goal Seek is easier to use than the Solver, however, and it often finds the optimal input value faster than does the Solver. (This is because the Solver offers more options than does Goal Seek, and the Solver can modify more than one Changing Cell.)

You can use the Goal Seek function when you want to find an input value that generates the answer you want in a formula cell. To find the level of sales required to break even, for example, the formula cell would contain the net present value, and you would want the NPV function to return a zero value (which represents a break-even figure).

Because the Goal Seek function adjusts the value in *one* cell that is a precedent to the formula cell, you need to make an adjustment to the Base Case worksheet. Refer back to Figure 13.1, where the relevant cells appear. Treating year 1 as an anchor point, notice that each subsequent year's sales is a multiple of the year 1 sales. You can then express sales for years 2 through 6 as a function of year 1 sales:

> In cell C4, enter: **=B4*3**
>
> In cell D4, enter: **=B4*4**
>
> In cell E4, enter: **=B4*6**
>
> In cell F4, enter: **=B4*10**
>
> In cell G4, enter: **=B4*20**

These changes make the values of sales in years 2 through 6 dependent on the value in cell B4. Now, even though net present value depends on sales values for all six years, you can use the single Changing Cell B4 in Goal Seek to answer a variety of questions. For example: What level of incremental sales would be required for this project to break even? To answer that question, follow these steps:

1. Select cell B37, which contains the NPV function.

2. Choose Tools, Goal Seek. The Goal Seek dialog box appears as shown in Figure 13.13.

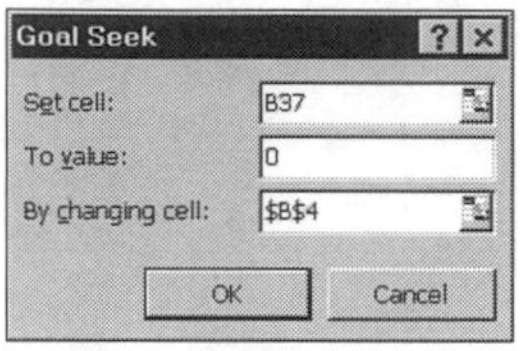

FIGURE 13.13
You can use Goal Seek to modify a business case's inputs and determine their effect on its results.

3. The Set Cell box should already contain the reference B37; if not, select that cell on the worksheet.

4. Click in the To Value box, and enter **0** (zero).

5. Click in the By Changing Cell box, and select worksheet cell B4 (or simply type **B4** in the box).

6. Choose OK.

Goal Seek returns a value for year 1 sales. Because you changed the values for years 2 through 6 to formulas that depend on year 1, their values also change. The result is the incremental sales required for the project to break even—that is, to have a net present value of zero.

What level of incremental sales would be required for this project to return a 15% internal rate of return? Simply repeat steps 1 through 6 shown previously, but begin by selecting the cell that contains the IRR function, and specify in step 4 that the To value is to be .15.

Summary

When sensitivity scenarios are included in a business case package, management obtains a better overall feel for the project under review. The analyst who constructs the business case also has the opportunity to answer pertinent "what if" questions proactively. It provides multiple points of view on a project, and enables the review team to focus on the business drivers that have the most significant impact on potential outcomes.

In this chapter, you have learned how to use Excel's Scenario Manager to establish and examine the effect of variances in the input assumptions of a business case, as well as how to establish upper and lower limits on the sensitivity of the business case's outputs. You have extended your understanding of profitability indicators to different ways of measuring the rate of return, and have learned a quicker (although less powerful) means of optimizing a value by means of Goal Seek. Chapter 14, "Planning Profits," examines the effect that changing the relationship between your fixed and variable costs, as well as the effect of borrowing, has on the profitability of your enterprise.

Planning Profits

The concepts of *operating leverage* and *financial leverage* are key to understanding how a company will fare in fluctuating market conditions. A firm is said to be leveraged whenever it incurs either fixed operating costs (operating leverage) or fixed capital costs (financial leverage). More specifically, a firm's degree of operating leverage is the extent to which its operations involve fixed operating expenses, such as fixed manufacturing costs, fixed selling costs, and fixed administrative costs.

A firm's degree of financial leverage is the extent to which that firm finances its assets by borrowing. More specifically, financial leverage is the extent to which a firm's Return on Assets exceeds the cost of financing those assets by means of debt. The firm expects that the leverage acquired by borrowing will bring it earnings returns that will exceed the fixed costs of the assets and of the sources of funds. The firm expects that these added earnings will increase the amount of returns to shareholders.

In the business environment of recent years, it has been nearly impossible for a firm to succeed financially without using some form of leverage. Firms commonly use leverage as a tool to help bolster their financial position and operating condition (for example, their return to stockholders).

However, with increased leverage comes increased risk. If your company chooses to be highly leveraged, it must be willing to accept the risk that the downside losses will be as great as its upside profits. This can easily occur if a firm's sales volume is not large enough to cover its fixed operating expenses and the required interest payments on its debt.

You can find plenty of examples of this phenomenon in a stack of annual reports from the 1980s. Within that stack you can find several companies that were highly leveraged. Tracking these firms through the 1990s, you would see trends depicting peaks and troughs: the positive and the negative impacts of using leverage to operate a business. Many firms were acquired via *leveraged buyouts*, where the funds needed to make the acquisition were themselves borrowed (hence the qualifier *leveraged*).

The likelihood of experiencing these kinds of swings is one reason that managers, analysts, and stockholders must apply the concepts of operating and financial leverage to accurately analyze a firm's overall value and financial health. These concepts also provide the background required to fully understand how the firm conducts its business operations.

An additional concept that's important in this context is that of *business risk*. Business risk is the inherent uncertainty of doing business. It represents the risk that a company assumes by the nature of the products it manufactures and sells, its position in the marketplace, and its pricing structure—in short, all the fundamental aspects involved in the creation of profitable revenues. Assuming a higher degree of operating or financial leverage is seldom hazardous when the business risk is very low. But if the business risk itself is high, then increasing the degree of either type of leverage compounds the risk.

Analyzing Operating Leverage

Operating leverage is the extent to which a firm's operations involve fixed operating expenses. Managers can define the degree of operating leverage they want the firm to incur, based on the choices they make regarding fixed expenses. They can, for example, acquire new equipment that increases automation and reduces variable labor expenses. Alternatively, they can choose to maintain their variable labor expenses. Other things being equal, the more automated equipment a firm acquires through capital investment, the higher its operating leverage will be.

Case Study: Business Forms

You own a small company that prints business forms such as invoices, letterheads, envelopes, and business cards. At present, your variable operating costs are $0.03 per card to print a box of 500 business cards, which you sell for $35.

One of your employees suggests that, if you purchase some additional electronic and communications equipment, your customers could send their own designs for business cards to you electronically. This would save you the cost of doing the design and layout of the cards for each order.

You review some recent orders and find that you paid an employee an average of $3 per order to do the design and layout. So your costs and profit per order are as follows:

- Variable $0.03 per card for 1 box of 500 cards = $15
- Fixed design and layout per box = $3
- Total cost per box: $18
- Operating income per box: $17

If you can remove the cost of design and layout, your total costs will drop from $18–$15 per order and your operating income per box will increase from $17–$20.

On the other hand, purchasing additional equipment will cost $1,400. This will introduce a new, fixed cost to the production of the cards. You will have to sell 70 boxes of business cards (70 boxes * $20 profit) to cover the cost of the equipment—that is, to break even on the investment.

You should base your decision on how dependable your business card orders are. Suppose that you have a steady stream of around 60 orders per month—because of the stability of the flow of orders, the business risk is low. In that case, you break even on the investment in a little over a month, and after that you show an additional $3 profit for every order. That added profit is the result of *leveraging* your capital investment.

Now supposethat your business card orders are not so dependable—the business risk is a little higher. Most of your business depends on the patronage of one large account. When its business is good, and your customer is hiring and promoting staff, it makes frequent orders for business cards. But when its business is not so good, you can go for several months with only a few orders.

If the timing of your investment coincides with a drop in orders for business cards, the equipment could sit nearly idle for several months. There will be little profit to cover the cost, the break-even point will be pushed well into the future, and you will have lost the opportunity to invest the $1,400 in some other manner, such as advertising. The leverage is actually working against you.

Of course, there are other considerations you must take into account. You would want to consider how many of your customers have the inclination and equipment to send their own designs to you, whether they would demand a price break if they do so, maintenance on the equipment, and so on. Business decisions are seldom clear-cut.

So, operating leverage cuts both ways. A good decision can increase your profitability dramatically, once you have broken even on the fixed cost. Bad timing can cut your profitability dramatically if it takes longer than anticipated to break even on the investment.

Case Study: Comparing the Degree of Operating Leverage

For a more detailed example, consider three different paint stores whose operations are identical in all respects, except for the decisions they have made regarding their variable and fixed expenses:

- Store A has decided to incur the lowest fixed and highest variable costs. It has little in the way of special equipment, and relies heavily on the experience and knowledge of its salespeople. At this store, sales commissions are relatively high.
- Store B has decided to incur higher fixed costs than Store A, but to keep its variable costs lower. This store has invested a moderate amount of money in color-matching equipment that enables a salesperson to match paint samples automatically. It believes that reliance on this equipment allows it to hire salespeople who are less experienced. Its salespeople therefore earn less than do Store A's.
- Store C has decided to incur the highest fixed and lowest variable costs of the three stores. It has invested heavily in equipment that not only matches paint samples exactly, but mixes paints automatically to produce a gallon of matching paint. Its salespeople need no special knowledge, and receive lower commissions than the staff are paid at Stores A and B.

Figures 14.1, 14.2, and 14.3 display an analysis of each store's sales and Earnings Before Interest and Taxes (EBIT) for a given quantity of sales at their existing fixed costs, variable costs, and unit sales rates.

FIGURE 14.1
Store A breaks even quickly, but has relatively low profit growth after break-even.

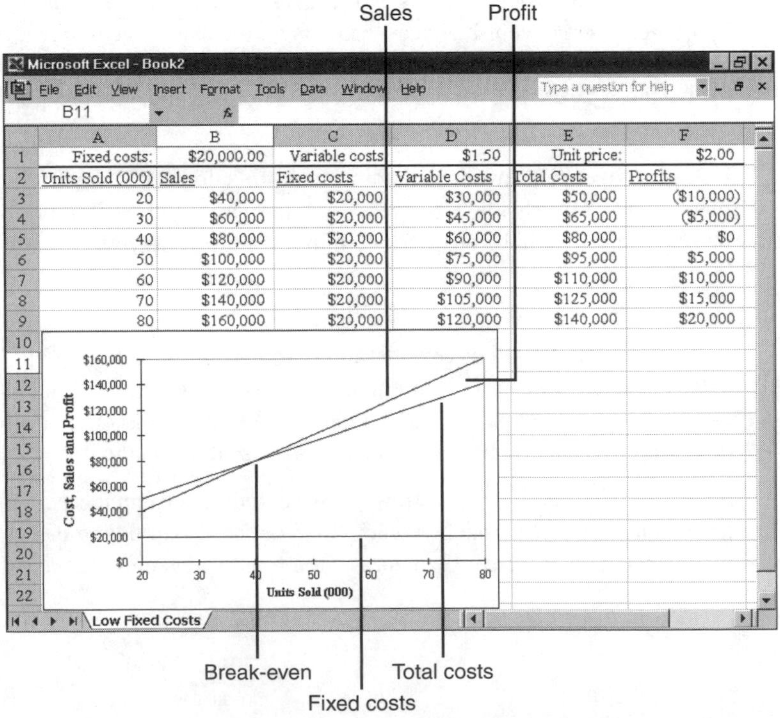

Fixed costs:	$20,000.00	Variable costs	$1.50	Unit price:	$2.00
Units Sold (000)	Sales	Fixed costs	Variable Costs	Total Costs	Profits
20	$40,000	$20,000	$30,000	$50,000	($10,000)
30	$60,000	$20,000	$45,000	$65,000	($5,000)
40	$80,000	$20,000	$60,000	$80,000	$0
50	$100,000	$20,000	$75,000	$95,000	$5,000
60	$120,000	$20,000	$90,000	$110,000	$10,000
70	$140,000	$20,000	$105,000	$125,000	$15,000
80	$160,000	$20,000	$120,000	$140,000	$20,000

FIGURE 14.2
Store B breaks even
more slowly, but its
profitability grows faster
than Store A after
break-even.

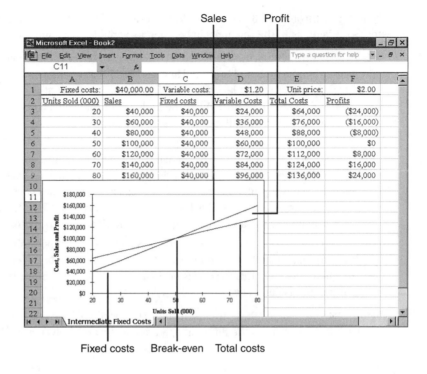

FIGURE 14.3
Store C breaks even
more slowly, but experi-
ences fast profit growth
thereafter.

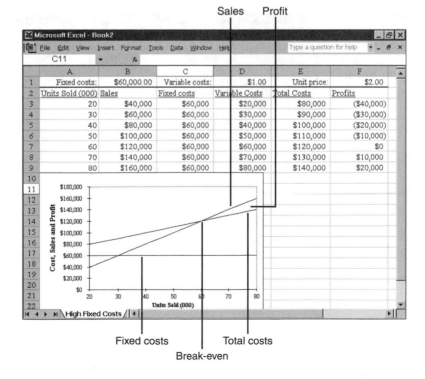

Figures 14.1 through 14.3 make some trends evident. These trends are consequences of each store's decision as to the relationship between its variable costs and its fixed costs:

- Store A, which has the lowest fixed cost and the highest per unit cost, will break even faster than Store B and Store C. However, once the break-even point has been met, Store A's EBIT will be less than both Store A and Store B at any given level of production. This is because Store A has the highest per unit sales cost. No matter how many gallons of paint it sells, it incurs the same, relatively high sales commission on each unit.

- Store B, which has fixed costs that fall between Store A and Store C, reaches the break-even point later than Store A but earlier than Store C. Once it reaches its break-even point, it is more profitable than Store A because its unit sales cost is lower. However, after breaking even, Store B is less profitable, in terms of EBIT, than Store C as sales increase: it pays its sales staff a higher commission than does Store C.

- Store C, which has the highest fixed costs and the lowest per unit sales cost, breaks even more slowly than the other two stores. But after the break-even point has been reached, Store C's EBIT rises faster than either Store A or Store B because of its low sales commission rates.

Figure 14.4 summarizes these trends. It shows the profitability of each store across its range of units sold. This reflects the different operating leverage involved at each store:

FIGURE 14.4
Comparison of profitability of three stores with different degrees of operating leverage.

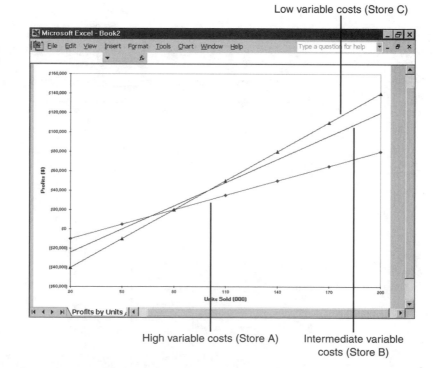

Another way to understand how operating leverage impacts your company's profitability is by calculating the Degree of Operating Leverage (DOL):

```
DOL = Units*(Price-Variable Cost)/(Units*(Price-Variable Cost)-Fixed Cost)
```

or, equivalently:

```
DOL = Contribution Margin/(Contribution Margin - Fixed Cost)
```

(Chapter 19, "Analyzing Contributions and Margins," discusses contribution margins in some detail.) Using the data for the three paint stores, one can calculate the DOL at the point where unit sales are $120,000 (as shown in Figure 14.5).

FIGURE 14.5
The Degree of Operating Leverage accelerates EBIT as unit sales increase.

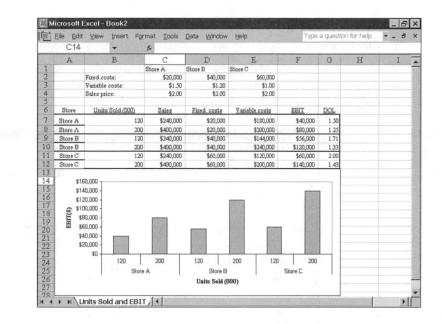

N O T E The charts shown in Figures 14.5 and 14.6 are pivot charts, introduced in Excel for Office 2000. In addition to being much stronger and more flexible than traditional Excel charts, pivot charts make it possible to group levels of one field within another, just as different Units Sold levels are grouped within Stores in Figures 14.5 and 14.6.

This effect is equivalent to the grouping of levels of an inner field within those of an outer field in a pivot table. Traditional Excel charts do not group in quite this way, and they require the user to take extra steps in order to use two columns (or rows) for the axis labels. ■

Store A, for example, has a DOL of 1.5 with unit sales of $120,000:

```
DOL = 120,000*($2.00-$1.50)/(120,000*($2.00-$1.50)-$20,000)
DOL = 1.5
```

These calculations quantify the data shown in Figure 14.5. The numbers indicate that the EBIT of the companies that have the greatest operating leverage are also the most sensitive to changes in sales volume.

Each store sells the same number of units: 120,000 or 200,000. Each store sells them for the same price: $2 per unit. But because the stores differ in their fixed and variable costs, they also differ in their EBIT. For Store A, a 67% increase in unit sales from 120,000–200,000 results in a (67% * 1.5 DOL) or 100% increase in EBIT. For Store B, a 67% increase in unit sales results in a (67% * 1.7 DOL) or 114% increase in EBIT. And Store C experiences a (67% * 2.0 DOL) or 133% increase in EBIT. So, the higher the DOL, the greater the EBIT as unit sales increase.

Expressed in raw dollar amounts, an increase in unit sales from 120,000 to 200,000 means an increase in profits of $40,000 for Store A, $64,000 for Store B, and $80,000 for Store C.

However, the calculated DOL will be the same on the downside. So for every decrease in sales volume, each firm's DOL will cause an unwanted decrease in EBIT corresponding to the desired increase in EBIT (see Figure 14.6).

FIGURE 14.6
The Degree of Operating Leverage accelerates loss of profit as unit sales decline.

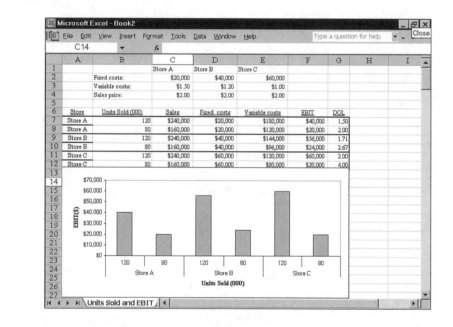

The DOL gives managers a great deal of information for setting operating targets and planning profitability. For example, you would want to make operating leverage decisions based on your knowledge of how your sales volume fluctuates. If your company experiences large swings in sales volume throughout the year, it would be much riskier to maintain a high degree of leverage than it would be if your company has a predictable, steady stream of sales.

Case Study: Coffee Sales

Java Man is a small business that sells specialty coffee drinks at office buildings. Each morning and afternoon, trucks arrive at offices' front entrances, and the office employees purchase various stimulants with names such as Java du Jour. The business is nevertheless profitable.

But Java Man's offices are located to the north of town, where lease rates are less expensive, and the principal sales area is south of town. This means that the trucks must drive cross-town four times each day.

The cost of transportation to and from the sales area, plus the power demands of the trucks' coffee brewing equipment, is a significant portion of the variable costs. Java Man could reduce the amount of driving—and, therefore, the variable costs—if it moves the offices much closer to the sales area.

Java Man presently has fixed costs of $10,000 per month. The lease of a new office, closer to the sales area, would cost an additional $2,200 per month. This would increase the fixed costs to $12,200 per month (see Figure 14.7).

FIGURE 14.7
Profit analysis for the lease of existing offices by Java Man, Inc.

Although the lease of new offices would increase the fixed costs, a careful estimate of the potential savings in gasoline and vehicle maintenance indicates that Java Man could reduce the variable costs from $0.60 per unit to $0.35 per unit. Total sales are unlikely to increase as a result of the move, but the savings in variable costs could increase the annual profit from $82,986–$88,302. This is a 6.4% growth in profit margin: not an insignificant amount in relative terms (see Figure 14.8).

Part
III

Ch
14

FIGURE 14.8

Profit analysis for the lease of new offices by Java Man, Inc.: variable costs fall and Degree of Operating Leverage increases.

	A	B	C	D	E	F
			D4 ▼ ƒ× =Contribution_Margin/(Contribution_Margin-SUM(Fixed_Costs))			
1	Units sold per month:	20,000	Unit variable costs:	$0.35		
2	Average unit sales price:	$2.20	Current fixed costs:	$10,000		
3	Added lease payment, new offices:	$2,200	Contribution margin:	$234,702		
4	Projected fixed costs:	$12,200	DOL:	2.66		
5						
6				Fixed	Variable	
7	2002 sales month	Units	Sales	costs	Costs	EBIT
8	January	6,582	$14,480	$12,200	$2,304	($23.30)
9	February	11,121	$24,466	$12,200	$3,892	$8,374
10	March	14,178	$31,192	$12,200	$4,962	$14,029
11	April	13,692	$30,122	$12,200	$4,792	$13,130
12	May	11,597	$25,513	$12,200	$4,059	$9,254
13	June	9,599	$21,118	$12,200	$3,360	$5,558
14	July	9,913	$21,809	$12,200	$3,470	$6,139
15	August	10,926	$24,037	$12,200	$3,824	$8,013
16	September	14,349	$31,568	$12,200	$5,022	$14,346
17	October	12,965	$28,523	$12,200	$4,538	$11,785
18	November	6,972	$15,338	$12,200	$2,440	$698
19	December	4,972	$10,938	$12,200	$1,740	($3,002)
20						
21					Sum:	$88,302
22					Standard Deviation:	$5,738

Cost Analysis, New Lease

But look at the change in the variability of the profit from month to month. From November through January, when it is much more difficult to lure office workers out into the cold to purchase coffee, Java Man barely breaks even. In fact, in December of 2002, the business loses money.

Figure 14.8 indicates that by moving some of the expenses from the category of variable costs to that of fixed costs, Java Man increases total annual earnings but the variability of the earnings from month to month also increases. Although the company earns more during the spring and fall by reducing the variable costs, it loses more during the winter months because it must continue to meet its higher fixed costs.

This increase in variability is reflected in the month-to-month standard deviation of earnings, which is shown both in Figures 14.7 and 14.8 directly under the annual sum of earnings. The current cost structure results in a standard deviation of $4,963, but the projected cost structure has a month-to-month standard deviation of $5,738. (To learn more about the meaning and use of standard deviations, which measure the amount of variability in a set of numbers, see Chapter 15, "Making Investment Decisions Under Uncertain Conditions.")

The increase in variability is also reflected in the Java Man's DOL. As shown in cell D4 of Figures 14.7 and 14.8, the DOL would increase from 2.45 to 2.66 as a result of increasing fixed costs and decreasing variable costs. Both the DOL and the business risk would increase if Java Man moved its offices.

N O T E The DOLs calculated in Figures 14.7 and 14.8 use the *contribution margin* to shorten the formulas. The contribution margin is defined as revenues less total variable costs. ■

If Java Man has plenty of money in the bank to meet unexpected expenses, such as major repairs to its trucks or the trucks' coffee brewers, then the acceptance of greater fixed costs may make good financial as well as operational sense.

But if Java Man's owners frequently take profits out of the business, so that it has relatively little in the way of resources to cushion the impact of unexpected expenses, it might be unwise to add to its fixed costs. Where will the money come from to repair a truck that breaks down at the end of January?

Managers can use the DOL to plan not only their operations, as was done in the Java Man case study, but also their net income and their pricing. It is useful to perform sensitivity analysis around sales volume levels, and around adjustments to both fixed and variable expenses. (For a detailed example of sensitivity analysis see Chapter 13, "Creating a Sensitivity Analysis for a Business Case.")

N O T E   Variability in profit levels, whether measured as EBIT, operating income, or net income does not *necessarily* increase the level of business risk as the DOL increases. If the variability is predictable—if the timing and size of the swings can be forecast with confidence—then a company can anticipate and allow for them in its budgets.

Planning by Using the DOL

Suppose that each of the three paint stores discussed earlier in this section plans to capture additional market share. In January the managers of Stores A, B, and C might set out their annual operations and profit targets by means of the following assumptions:

- Each store wants to increase its sales volume from 120,000 to 200,000 units.
- Each store's research leads it to believe that to sell an additional 80,000 units it must lower its unit sales price from $2 to $1.70.
- None of the three stores expects that its total fixed costs or its unit variable costs will change during the year.

Based on these assumptions, the change in net operating income for each firm would be as shown in Figure 14.9.

Store A immediately sees that its DOL prevents it from pursuing expansion in this way. Store B has so little to gain that it probably should decide to stand pat. It looks like it makes sense for Store C to expand, because by dropping its price 15%, it increases its net income by 30%.

This comes about because Store C has a higher DOL than either Stores A or B. Although the managers of Store C believe that this leverage works to their advantage, they should also perform the same analysis on the downside.

FIGURE 14.9

Changes to net operating income with higher unit sales and lower sales prices.

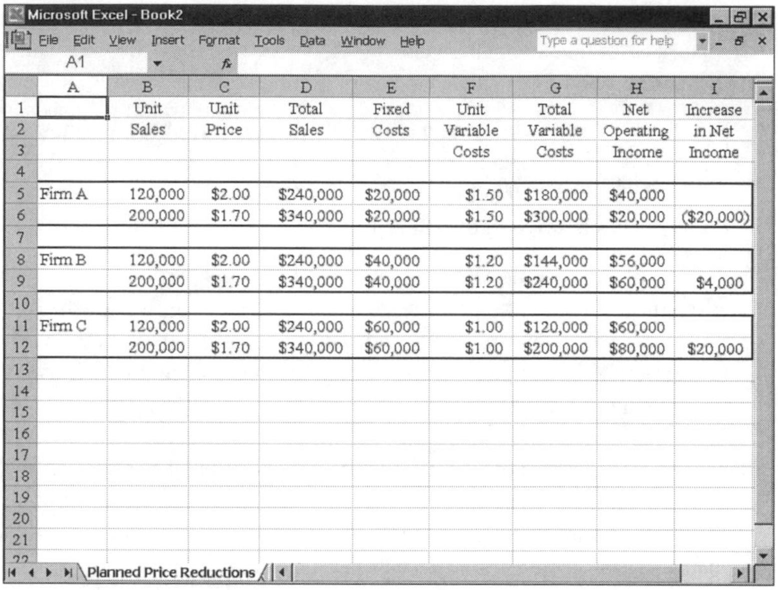

	A	B	C	D	E	F	G	H	I
1		Unit	Unit	Total	Fixed	Unit	Total	Net	Increase
2		Sales	Price	Sales	Costs	Variable	Variable	Operating	in Net
3						Costs	Costs	Income	Income
4									
5	Firm A	120,000	$2.00	$240,000	$20,000	$1.50	$180,000	$40,000	
6		200,000	$1.70	$340,000	$20,000	$1.50	$300,000	$20,000	($20,000)
7									
8	Firm B	120,000	$2.00	$240,000	$40,000	$1.20	$144,000	$56,000	
9		200,000	$1.70	$340,000	$40,000	$1.20	$240,000	$60,000	$4,000
10									
11	Firm C	120,000	$2.00	$240,000	$60,000	$1.00	$120,000	$60,000	
12		200,000	$1.70	$340,000	$60,000	$1.00	$200,000	$80,000	$20,000

Planned Price Reductions

If, despite reducing their unit sales price, their total sales remain at 120,000 instead of increasing to 200,000, the reduction in unit price would lower profits by $36,000 instead of raising them by $20,000. It is for this reason that companies with a high degree of leverage must be confident that their sales volumes will not fall. Otherwise, they run a significant risk of missing their profit objectives.

Performing an analysis of the impacts that leverage can have on a firm's profitability is essential to a clear picture of the risk a company has decided to take on. However, the DOL is only one of the indicators that a manager, shareholder, or creditor uses to measure the value and risk to a firm's financial health. Another important measure is a company's degree of financial leverage.

Analyzing Financial Leverage

Financial leverage is the extent to which a company finances the acquisition of its assets by means of debt: that is, a company that borrows money to acquire assets engages financial leverage. This type of leverage is a critical component in the measurement of the financial health and value of a company. It helps managers, analysts, stockholders, as well as long and short-term creditors distinguish between a firm's level of business risk and the financial risk that the firm has assumed.

In contrast, financial risk is the additional exposure, above and beyond business risk, that a firm incurs by using financial leverage: that is, the debt that the firm assumes by financing the acquisition of its assets.

Suppose, for example, that you decide to start a business that offers training classes in the design of databases and the use of database management systems. Your business risk is defined by factors such as the desirability of the training, the number of people who might want it, the number of other firms that offer similar training classes, the market share of the database management systems that you choose to focus on, and the quality and price of your service relative to that of your competition.

If you obtain a loan to finance the purchase of a server and workstations for your clients to use during training, you have assumed an additional financial risk, beyond your business risk: the possibility that your firm will be unable to repay that loan from its earnings.

It is useful to consider business and financial risk separately when you make decisions pertaining to financial leverage. One way to focus on financial risk is to analyze a firm's financial structure: in particular, the way that the firm has gone about financing its assets. Part of a company's overall financial structure is its capital structure. The company's capital structure is the mix of debt and equity that is used to finance the acquisition of its assets.

A thorough understanding of the debt that your company has assumed significantly enhances your ability to make good decisions about acquiring new debt. As a creditor, it is essential to understand a borrower's capital structure in order to measure the risk of making a loan, and to determine whether the interest rate is in line with that risk.

The acquisition of additional debt changes a company's degree of financial leverage, and can have either a positive or a negative impact on the evaluations made by creditors and stockholders.

Suppose that you can obtain a loan at 9% interest to finance the acquisition of new computer workstations. If the return on the assets represented by the new workstations is 12%, you will have *leveraged* the loan, to your benefit. But if the return on these assets turns out to be only 6%, the leverage works against you: you will pay more in interest than you will earn from the asset.

Clearly, financial leverage is an important indicator to investors (Should I buy this stock?), to managers (Will this decision get me a promotion or a pink slip?), to stockholders (Should I sell or stand pat?) and to creditors (Can they repay this loan?). There are several financial leverage ratios that help you analyze a company's capital structure. These ratios include the Debt Ratio and the Times Interest Earned Ratio.

The ratios provide managers, analysts, investors, and creditors with useful indications of how financial leverage impacts the level of financial risk a company has assumed. The ratio information is critical for determining the stability, and even the solvency, of a company.

Determining the Debt Ratio

The Debt Ratio is the ratio of total debt to total assets. (Another term for the Debt Ratio is the *Leverage Factor*.) Figure 14.10 calculates the Debt Ratio of three firms that are identical in all respects except for the amount of debt that they have assumed.

Part

III

Ch

14

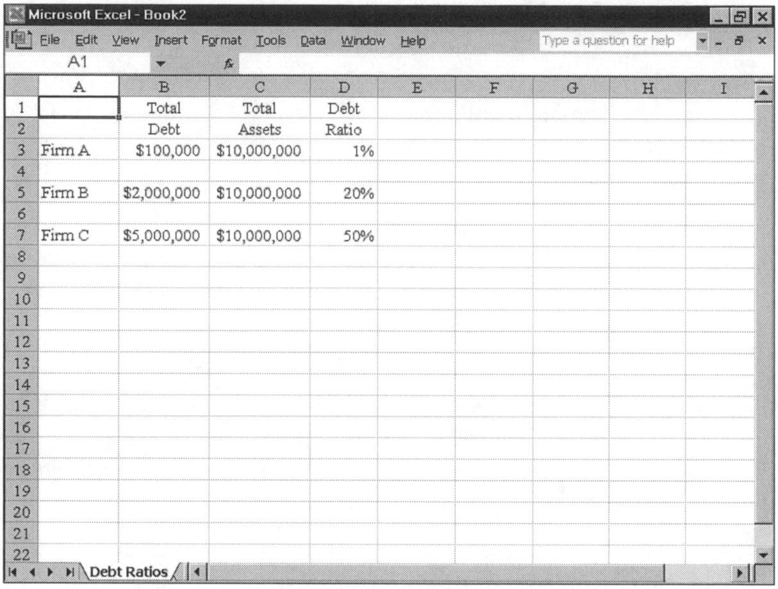

	Total Debt	Total Assets	Debt Ratio
Firm A	$100,000	$10,000,000	1%
Firm B	$2,000,000	$10,000,000	20%
Firm C	$5,000,000	$10,000,000	50%

FIGURE 14.10
The Debt Ratio is one way of measuring financial leverage.

The Debt Ratio measures the proportion of a firm's total assets that are financed, both short-term and long-term, by means of creditors' funds. Managers, analysts, shareholders, and creditors use the Debt Ratio as one indicator of how much risk a firm is carrying.

For example, a company's value is in large measure a function of the value of its assets. If a firm has a high Debt Ratio, then a high proportion of its assets have been financed by means of debt. This implies that the company must spend a greater proportion of its earnings to pay off those debts, instead of reinvesting its earnings in the company.

On the other hand, a company with a low Debt Ratio has used its equity to acquire assets. This implies that it requires a smaller proportion of its earnings to retire debt, and the company can make more dollars available for reinvestment and dividends.

A firm's Debt Ratio is also a useful indicator of how well it will weather difficult financial times. For example, if a company with a high Debt Ratio suffers significant earnings losses, it will be hard pressed to continue operations and simultaneously pay off its debts. But a company with a low Debt Ratio is in a much better position to continue operations if earnings decrease, because it will not need to use a significant amount of its earnings to help retire its debt.

In Figure 14.10, Firm C has the highest Debt Ratio. This implies that if the firm were to experience a business slowdown, the cash flow it generates may not be sufficient to meet principal and interest payments on the debt acquired. In this example, the Debt Ratio indicates that Firm C is at the greatest financial risk.

NOTE The Equity Ratio, discussed in Chapter 7, "Ratio Analysis," is the opposite of the Debt Ratio. It returns the ratio of a firm's equity to its assets. The higher the Equity Ratio, the lower a firm's financial leverage.

Determining the Times Interest Earned Ratio

Times Interest Earned refers to the number of times that interest payments are covered by a firm's earnings. It is calculated by dividing the EBIT by interest charges: that is, the income that is available for the payment of interest, divided by the interest expense. Thus, the Times Interest Earned Ratio indicates the extent to which a firm's current earnings are able to meet current interest payments out of net operating income or EBIT. Figure 14.11 shows possible Times Interest Earned Ratios for three firms.

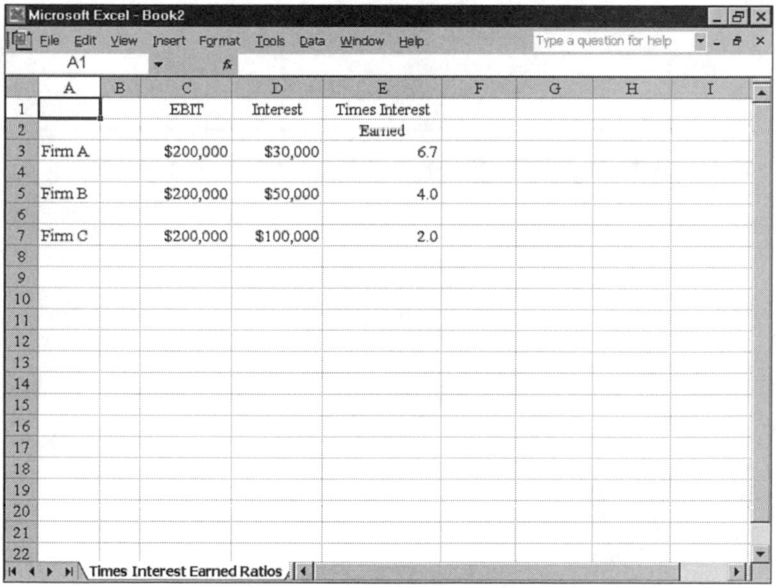

	EBIT	Interest	Times Interest Earned
Firm A	$200,000	$30,000	6.7
Firm B	$200,000	$50,000	4.0
Firm C	$200,000	$100,000	2.0

FIGURE 14.11
The Times Interest Earned Ratio measures a company's ability to meet its interest payments.

The Times Interest Earned Ratios in Figure 14.11 indicate that Firm A, because it has relatively low debt, uses a lower proportion of its earnings to cover interest payments. Firm B covers annual interest payments four times at its current earnings level, and Firm C covers annual interest payments two times at its current earnings level.

Firm C runs a greater risk of financial difficulty than the other two firms. This is because it must cover interest payments before applying earnings to any other purpose, such as reinvestment.

Summary

Operating and financial leverage are important ingredients in determining the success or demise of many companies. Firms acquire leverage to bolster their financial position, thus increasing shareholder value. However, with increased leverage comes increased risk. Managers, analysts, shareholders, and creditors must be very clear about the implications of the risks associated with a firm's operating and financial leverage to make investment decisions. Knowing these implications brings their decisions in line with their desired level of risk.

CHAPTER 15

Making Investment Decisions Under Uncertain Conditions

At times you have access to dependable, objective information as the basis for your business decisions. For example, you might know how much you must pay in interest charges for a loan that will enable you to retool a manufacturing operation. Or, you might know what it will cost to hire an employee who can perform a critical role for your company.

More frequently, though, you must make a decision without access to solid information. In this case, if you are fortunate, you can look to historical data or acquire new empirical information that bears, even if indirectly, on your decision. The appropriate analysis of that data can enable you to make probability statements about different courses of action: for example, "If we pursue Course A, the likelihood that we'll achieve an additional 10% profit is 95%. If we pursue Course B, achieving an additional 10% profit has a probability of only 45%."

Being able to make statements like that with confidence can be useful when you are confronted with a business decision that depends on uncertain, variable conditions. This chapter explores the use of information about variability in data to help you make such statements. There are three concepts, and associated Excel tools, that are fundamental to this sort of decision making: standard deviations, confidence intervals, and regression analysis.

Standard Deviations

A *standard deviation* is a measure that expresses how much a set of numbers varies from one another. It is one important method of determining the spread of different numbers across the range of values that the numbers are able to take. For example, and as a practical matter, the age of individual human beings can range from 0 to 90. But the ages of 500 high school students spread differently across the possible range of values than do the ages of 500 college students.

Because people's ages vary, there is uncertainty about people's ages. Because supplier prices vary, there is uncertainty about supplier prices. A business manager is confronted by uncertainty every day and needs to understand how to deal with it.

Suppose that you are interested in analyzing the commissions that you pay salespeople who work for your firm. You want to know, of course, the total amount of money in commissions that you are paying the sales force. After you have determined the total commission amount, it is natural to inquire about the average, or mean, commission earned by the salespeople. This is easy to obtain by dividing the number of salespeople into the total commissions paid.

The average commission is a measure of the central tendency of the individual observations—an estimate of the amount that each individual earns in commission. It is a point on the scale of commission payments that lies somewhere between the smallest commission and the largest commission.

In contrast, the standard deviation is a distance along that same scale of numbers. Like the range, which is the distance between the smallest and largest commissions, the standard deviation expresses a distance along a scale of numbers, and is a measure of how the individual amounts vary from one another.

For example, suppose that you find the average annual sales commission is $15,000. You also find (by using functions described later in this section) that the standard deviation of these commissions is $6,000. In that case, the individual commissions vary from one another more than if you found that the standard deviation was $1,000.

Why is this kind of information useful? One reason—and there are many—is that it immediately gives you information about the performance of your sales force. It turns out, for example, that about two-thirds of the individual observations lie between one standard deviation above and one standard deviation below the mean.

In the previous example, where the average annual commission is $15,000, you might take a very different view of the performance of the sales force if the standard deviation were $1,000 than if it were $6,000. If about two thirds of the sales force makes between $14,000 (mean − 1 standard deviation, or $15,000 − $1,000) and $16,000 (mean + 1 standard deviation, or $15,000 + $1,000), then most salespeople are performing at roughly the same level, as shown in Figure 15.1.

FIGURE 15.1

A smaller standard deviation means that the observations cluster around their average.

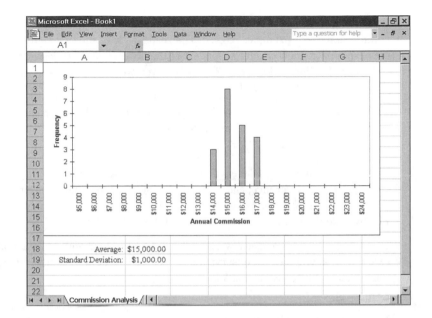

On the other hand, if you found that the standard deviation is $6,000, then about two thirds of the sales force is earning between $9,000 (mean − 1 standard deviation, or $15,000 − $6,000) and $21,000 (mean + 1 standard deviation, or $15,000 + $6,000) in commissions, as seen in Figure 15.2. You might then conclude that most salespeople are performing very differently, and you might want to investigate the reasons for those differences.

FIGURE 15.2

A larger standard deviation means that the observations are more dispersed around their average.

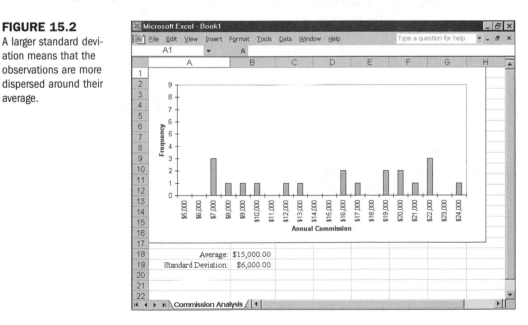

In both Figures 15.1 and 15.2, the horizontal x-axis shows different values of annual commissions—for example, $16,000. The vertical y-axis shows a count of the number of observations in each category. Notice that the observations are less spread out, left to right, in Figure 15.1 than in Figure 15.2. This is as you would expect, given the relative sizes of the standard deviations in each figure.

The formula for a standard deviation is not as intuitively obvious as is the formula for an average. The definitional form of the formula is

```
Standard deviation = √ Σ(X-μ)²/n
```

where $\Sigma(X-\mu)^2$ means to take each number (X), subtract from it the average of the numbers (μ), square that difference, and then take the sum of the squared differences. The rightmost fragment of the formula, $/n$, means to divide that sum by n, or the number of observations. Finally, take the square root of the result of the division.

Fortunately, Excel provides a worksheet function for the standard deviation. Suppose, for example, that you have 20 observations in A1:A20. To get the standard deviation of these observations, the Excel formula is

```
=STDEV(A1:A20)
```

Unfortunately, it's not quite that simple, because there's more than one way to calculate a standard deviation: you use one way when your observations are a sample from a population and another when your observations *are* the population.

The standard deviation as previously defined is properly used on a population of values. It is a *biased* statistic when you apply it to a sample. That is, it underestimates the standard deviation of the population that the sample comes from.

Therefore, Excel provides two functions that return a standard deviation. If you're working with a sample, you should use the STDEV function. If you're working with a population, use the STDEVP function instead,

```
=STDEVP(A1:A20)
```

where the P at the end of the function name is a mnemonic for "Population."

Applied to a sample, the proper formula is

```
Standard deviation = √ Σ(X-μ)²/(n-1)
```

Notice that the denominator of the ratio is now (n–1): the number of observations minus 1. STDEV uses (n–1) in the denominator, whereas STDEVP uses n in the denominator.

CAUTION

Be cautious when you use STDEV or STDEVP on data whose magnitude is either very large (on the order of, say, 10^5 or greater) or very small (say, 10^-5 or smaller). With such data, rounding errors can occur in any PC application, not just Excel, because of the cumulative effect of squaring the differences between the observations and their mean. If you work with data such as this, you might consider re-scaling the numbers before applying STDEV or STDEVP, and interpreting their results in terms of the re-scaling.

Finding the standard deviation of a set of numbers enables you to make precise statements about their variability. This knowledge by itself can be useful. Suppose your company manufactures equipment that must fall within certain physical limits, such as diameters. In that case, you need to know whether the variability of your product line's diameters is comfortably inside those limits or is likely to exceed them.

But there are many other uses for the standard deviation than were discussed in this section. This is particularly true in the area of inferential statistics, which help you make inferences about a population on the basis of a sample. For example, Chapters 9, "Forecasting and Projections," and 10, "Measuring Quality," in this book make extensive use of standard deviations in statistical process control and of standard errors (a type of standard deviation; see "Using Regression Analysis in Decision Making" later in this chapter) in forecasting.

Understanding Confidence Intervals

In many situations, it is either too expensive or completely impossible to acquire all the information that would allow you to make a decision with 100% confidence.

Suppose you manufacture cars, and want to test how well the bumpers perform in a 15 mph crash. To conclude, "Less than $1,000 damage" with complete confidence, you'd have to test all your cars. And then you'd have nothing left to sell.

In this case (and in less drastic ones), the best that you can do is to obtain a sample of the information. With the sample in hand, you can calculate a statistic that you hope is a close approximation of the value you would calculate if you had access to the entire information set. You can measure the "closeness" of the approximation by means of confidence intervals.

A confidence interval is a bracket around a sample statistic such as the mean. It expresses an interval in terms of both an upper and a lower bound, within which you can have some level of confidence that the population value exists. And when you have that objective measure—when you can quantify the degree of risk that you're running—you're much better placed to make the right decision than if you were to take a more subjective approach.

Using Confidence Intervals in a Market Research Situation

Your company is considering the acquisition of a new retail store, and foot traffic past the store's location is, for you, an important measure of its desirability. Each day for two weeks, you have the ex-CEO of a dot-com firm count the number of people who walk past the location. This constitutes a 14-day sample from the population of all possible days that you might own the store.

You calculate the average of each daily observation, which turns out to be 403. How accurate is this average, obtained from a sample, as an estimate of the number of people who would walk past the site on *any* given day? Put differently, how well does the sample mean of 403 represent the unknown population mean: the mean of the population of all possible days, a figure that you can't observe directly?

A confidence interval around the sample mean value of 403 helps answer this question. The raw data and analysis are shown in Figure 15.3.

FIGURE 15.3
A confidence interval around a sample mean helps you locate the mean of the population.

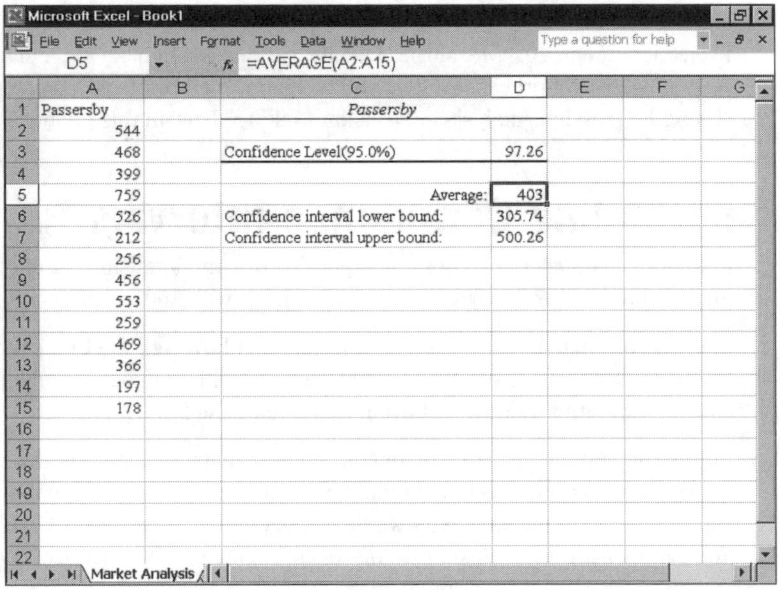

To obtain this analysis, take the following steps:

1. Choose Tools, Add-Ins.
2. Check the Analysis ToolPak check box. If you do not see this option in the Add-Ins dialog box, you need to run Add/Remove Programs in the Windows Control Panel and reinstall Office. Be sure to specify that Setup should install Excel's Analysis ToolPak add-in.

3. Choose OK.
4. After the add-in manager has finished processing, choose Tools, Data Analysis.
5. Choose Descriptive Statistics from the Analysis Tools list box.
6. Choose OK.
7. With the flashing cursor in the Input Range edit box, highlight cells A1:A15.
8. Check the Labels in the First Row check box, and make sure that the Confidence Level for Mean is set to 95%.
9. Click the Output Range radio button. Ensure that the flashing cursor is in the Output Range edit box, and then enter (or select) $C$1.
10. Choose OK.

For this set of data, the Descriptive Statistics tool returns a result of 97.26. You can add this number to the mean, and also subtract it from the mean, to obtain a confidence interval of 305.74 to 500.26. Assume that the result of 97.26 appears in cell D3. Then enter this formula in a blank cell:

`=AVERAGE(A2:A15)+D3`

This returns the confidence interval's upper bound. In another cell, enter this formula
`=AVERAGE(A2:A15)-D3`

to return the confidence interval's lower bound.

What does this interval mean? If you repeated your experiment 100 times, you would have 100 two-week means and associated confidence intervals. Ninety-five of the confidence intervals would capture the population mean: that is, the true population mean would lie between the interval's lower bound and its upper bound. Five of the confidence intervals would *not* span the true population mean.

So, it's 95 to 5, or almost 20 to 1, that the confidence interval you calculated captures the true population mean. You move forward on the sound assumption that the number of people walking past this site on *any* given day is somewhere between 306 and 500.

It's up to you to decide whether this is a precise enough estimate for your purposes, and whether the figure 403, as your best estimate of the population mean, is large enough to make it an attractive retail location.

For example, you might take a formal approach to this experiment and specify *beforehand* that you will consider this site if there is an average of 520 people who walk by it on any given day. After collecting and analyzing the information, you find that the confidence interval's upper limit is 500. Therefore, you can conclude with 95% assurance that this site does not meet your criterion: the confidence interval does not capture the average number of 520 that you require.

Refining Confidence Intervals

Several factors are involved in the calculation of a confidence interval. One is the standard deviation of the observations: you can't do much about this, because it's based on the data that you observe.

Another is the confidence level that you specify in the Descriptive Statistics analysis tool, and here you can exercise some control. The greater the confidence level that you specify, the larger the confidence interval. Of course, there's a tradeoff involved: you can make the interval smaller by specifying, say, 90% instead of 95% as a confidence level. But while this reduces the size of the interval, it also reduces the confidence that you can place in the estimate.

The surest way to narrow the interval and yet retain an acceptable level of confidence is to increase the sample size. By taking three weeks of observations, rather than two weeks, you might be able to narrow the confidence interval to between, say, 353 and 453. You might find this interval to be a precise enough basis for your decision of whether to acquire the location.

Although increasing the sample size is your best bet to reduce the size of a confidence interval, it is not guaranteed to do so. It is possible that an increase in the sample size will cause an increase in the standard deviation. This is virtually certain to happen if the additional observations that you obtain are quite low or quite high relative to the mean of the original sample. (It would also suggest that your original sample was non-random.)

The meaning of a confidence interval is one that many people misinterpret. Suppose that you have created a 95% confidence interval. It is easy to think, "The probability is 95% that this confidence interval captures the true population mean," but this is a false conclusion. Either the interval captures the mean or it does not: so, the probability that it captures the mean is either 1 or 0. However, out of 100 95% confidence intervals, 95 *will* capture the mean, and it would be illogical to believe that yours is one of the 5% that fail to do so.

Using Regression Analysis in Decision Making

Regression analysis is a powerful tool that can help you make sense of much larger amounts of data than was used in the case study on confidence intervals in the prior section. It is a technique that's fundamental for exploring and understanding relationships among variables. When you're faced with uncertain situations, you can use it to guide decisions about everything from operations to finance and from sales commissions to marketing.

Excel provides good support for regression analysis. There are 15 worksheet functions that bear directly on regression analysis, and other capabilities such as the Regression add-in; menu items such as Edit, Fill, Series, and Linear; and trendlines on charts that make certain regression computations more convenient.

Regressing One Variable onto Another

Suppose that you are considering an increase in your advertising budget for a particular product to boost that product's unit sales. You're concerned, though, that you will not sell enough additional units to justify the increased cost of advertising, and this would depress your earnings. In this case, you would be interested in the relationship between your company's advertising budget for each product and the number of unit sales of those products. Can you estimate the effect of an increase in advertising on unit sales?

Yes, if you have the data necessary to do a regression analysis. Many—perhaps most—retail stores have point-of-sale terminals that can capture information about product sold, sales price, date, and location sold, and (if the customer pays by credit card) about the customer. Operations, marketing, and finance groups have learned to mine the resulting databases for insight into how best to distribute, price, and sell their companies' products. (They have learned to *do* it, but not necessarily how to do it to create useful information. Read on.)

Figure 15.4 shows two variables, advertising budget and unit sales, for 18 different models of a product sold by a company. The figure also shows an XY chart that summarizes the relationship between advertising budget and unit sales. Each point on the chart represents one of the 18 models, and shows visually where its advertising budget and unit sales intersect.

FIGURE 15.4
Unit sales increase as advertising dollars increase.

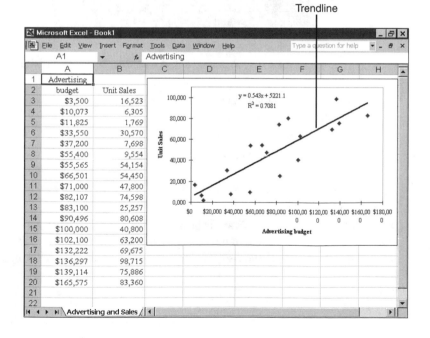

To create the embedded chart shown in Figure 15.4, open the workbook, activate the data worksheet, and follow these steps:

1. Highlight the data in A3:B20.

2. Choose Insert, Chart, or click the Chart Wizard button. Step 1 of the Chart Wizard appears. See Figure 15.5.

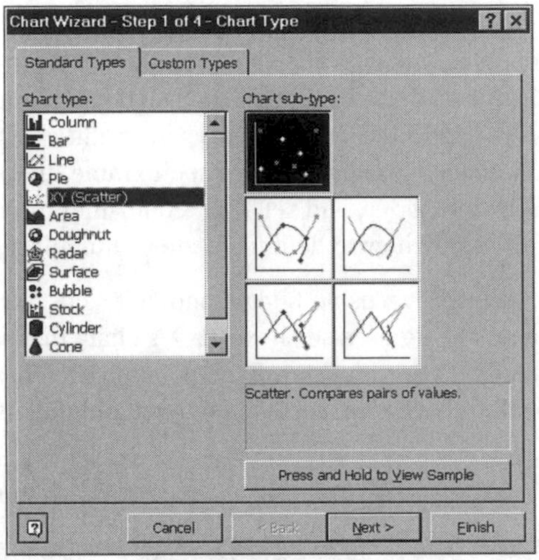

FIGURE 15.5
Other chart types, accessible from the Custom Types tab, are just variations on the standard chart types.

3. In Step 1 of the Chart Wizard, click the XY (Scatter) chart option in the Chart type list box.

4. Still in Step 1 of the Chart Wizard, click the first (that is, the markers only) XY chart format option. Click Next.

5. In Step 2 of the Chart Wizard (see Figure 15.6), make sure that the Data Series in Columns radio button is selected. In this step, you can also verify the worksheet address of the data that you want to chart. Click Next.

6. In Step 3 of the Chart Wizard, shown in Figure 15.7, add axis titles if you want, and click Next.

7. Step 4 of the Chart Wizard appears as shown in Figure 15.8. Click Finish to accept the default chart location in the active worksheet. Or, if you prefer to place the chart on its own sheet, check the As New Sheet radio button and then click Finish.

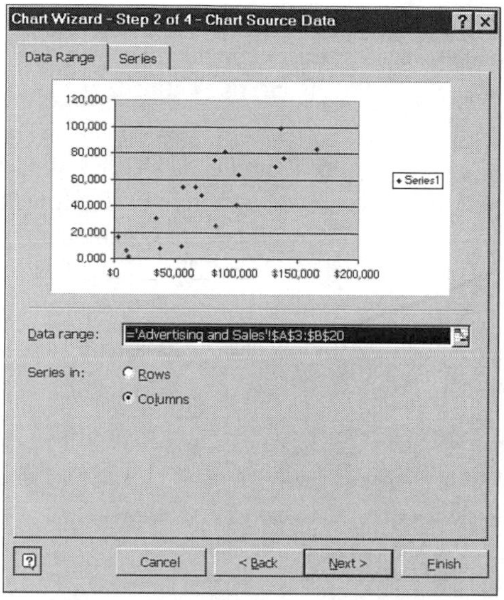

FIGURE 15.6
If you don't see a sample of your chart in Step 2, then you haven't selected a range containing numeric data before starting the Chart Wizard.

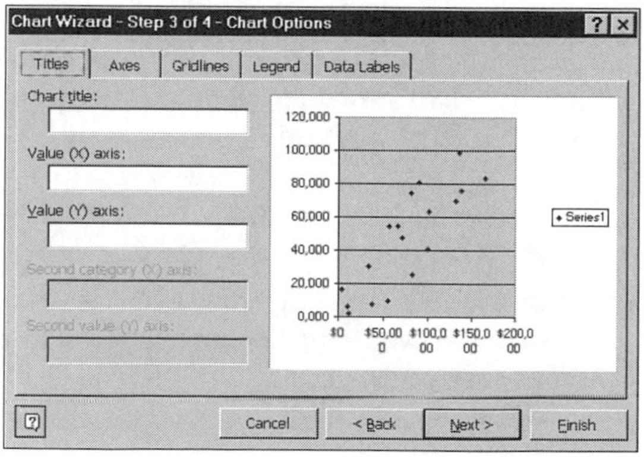

FIGURE 15.7
After you have completed the chart, you can access all these options by choosing Chart, Chart Options.

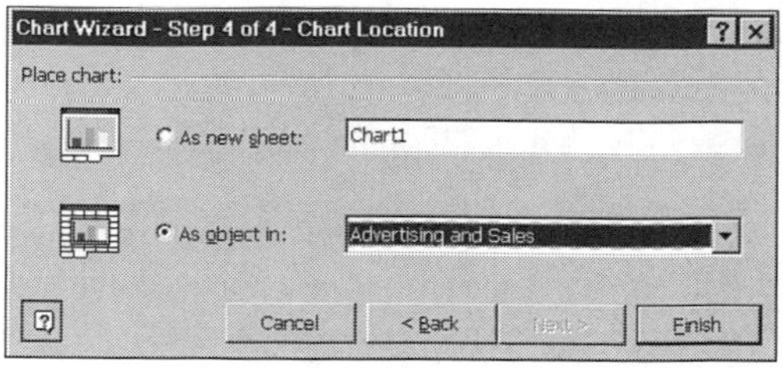

FIGURE 15.8
The combo box list contains the names of all the sheets in the active workbook.

8. Assume that you chose to place the chart in the active worksheet. When the chart appears in the worksheet, sizing handles should appear on its border. If you don't see the sizing handles, single-click the chart. Also notice that a Chart menu appears on the menu bar.

9. If the chart that you create has more than one data series (this example has one only) then you need to select the series that you want to base a trendline on: click on any of that series' markers to select the series. If you have one data series only, just make sure the chart is selected. Choose Chart, Add Trendline, and click the Type tab if necessary. Choose the Linear type.

10. Click the Options tab, and check the Display Equation on Chart and the Display R-squared Value on Chart check boxes. Choose OK.

TIP If your columns of data have header rows that contain labels, you can use the header rows in the chart's legend. Step 2 of the Chart Wizard has a Series tab. Select it and then identify the worksheet address of the headers in its Name box. Refer to Figure 15.6. If you want to do this without invoking the Chart Wizard, then with the chart active you can also choose Chart, Source Data, click the Series tab, and enter the worksheet address. You can also type a label in the Name box.

What can you learn from the information in Figure 15.4? It's clear that as advertising dollars increase, so do unit sales. That's termed a positive or direct relationship. If one variable increases as the other falls, it's termed a negative or inverse relationship. The trendline (the straight line that runs from the chart's lower-left corner to its upper-right corner) emphasizes that the budgets and the unit sales grow jointly.

The chart also contains this equation:

$y = 0.543x + 5221.1$

This is the *regression equation* for the data in the worksheet. It expresses numerically the relationship between dollars spent on advertising these products and their unit sales volume. In the equation, y stands for unit sales and x stands for advertising dollars. It gives you the best estimate of the unit sales volume, y, given any value of advertising dollars, x.

This does not mean that you can estimate unit sales precisely, given knowledge of advertising dollars. For example, plug the value $55,400 advertising dollars into the equation as x, and it returns 35,302 units sold. Notice that $55,400 is one of the actual observations in Figure 15.4, but the units sold for that product is 9,554. To repeat: regression gives you the best estimate (35,302 units) on the basis of the data at hand, not a precise prediction.

N O T E If you use the values in the chart's regression equation to predict a y-value, you are likely to obtain a slightly different value than if you use a worksheet function. This is because the values for the intercept and the slope in a chart's regression equation are rounded to fit inside the chart. ▪

There are two terms in the right side of this regression equation. The number 0.543 is called the *slope*, and the number 5221.1 is called the *intercept*. The slope is simply a measure of the steepness of the trendline: the higher the number that represents the slope, the more steep the trendline. The slope might be a negative number, and in that case the trendline would run from the upper-left corner of the chart to the lower-right corner. If you were to chart unit price against unit sales, for example, you would be likely to get a trendline with a negative slope: the higher the unit price, the lower the number of unit sales.

The intercept indicates where the trendline crosses the y (that is, the vertical) axis. In this case, it is 5221.1. One way to interpret this number is to state, "If we spend zero dollars on advertising a product, we estimate that we will sell about 5220 units." But see the next section, "Avoiding Traps in Interpretation: Association Versus Causation," for more on this.

The chart also shows a statistic called R^2, pronounced "R squared." This statistic is absolutely fundamental to regression analysis (R stands for regression). It expresses the proportion of the variance in y (here, unit sales) associated with the variance in x (here, advertising dollars).

N O T E   The *variance* is the square of the standard deviation. Like the standard deviation, it is a measure of the degree to which individual scores are dispersed about their mean. But while the standard deviation can be thought of as a distance, the variance can be thought of as an area: the square of a distance. It's often useful to keep this in mind when considering the relationship between variables, as in Figure 15.9. ■

The R^2 shown in Figure 15.4 is .7081, which means that about 71% of the variability in unit sales is associated with variability in advertising dollars. Figure 15.9 illustrates this relationship.

FIGURE 15.9
The overlapping areas indicate shared variance: changes in the values of one variable are associated with changes in the values of the other variable.

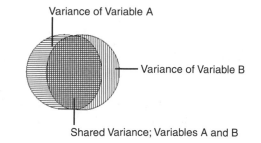

Variance of Variable A

Variance of Variable B

Shared Variance; Variables A and B

Why R *squared*? Because R^2 is the square of the correlation coefficient, which is usually symbolized as *r*. If you entered, on Figure 15.4's worksheet, the formula:

```
=CORREL(A3:A20,B3:B20)^2
```

it would return .7081: the same as the R^2 for this data set.

Using Excel charts and trendline options is the most visually appealing and informative way to examine the relationship between two variables, but there are other worksheet functions that are quicker and sometimes more convenient. Referring again to the data in Figure 15.4:

- This worksheet formula uses the RSQ function to return R^2 just as does the chart trendline option:

  =RSQ(B3:B20,A3:A20)

- You can get the intercept for the equation by means of:

  =INTERCEPT(B3:B20,A3:A20)

- The slope of the regression equation is available from:

  =SLOPE(B3:B20,A3:A20)

- If you want both the slope and intercept from one function, select a two-cell range consisting of one row and two columns, and array-enter:

  =LINEST(B3:B20,A3:A20)

Why bother with these functions when the chart trendline options are so convenient? One reason is that you might want to include the values returned by the functions in a report, or use them with other utilities such as the Scenario Manager or the Solver. And it will become apparent in the section titled "Regressing One Variable onto Several Other Variables" that worksheet functions such as LINEST are much more powerful than anything you can display with a trendline option.

Avoiding Traps in Interpretation: Association Versus Causation

When you interpret the results of a regression analysis, it's important to understand that regression expresses an *association* between or among variables. This is not necessarily the same as *causation*, which means that manipulating one variable necessarily results in a change to another variable.

Many (by no means all) data mining efforts ignore this distinction. Such efforts stumble when management changes the value of some variable—say, types of household to target in a direct mail campaign—that a data mining project says is associated with revenues. The two variables, revenues and mailing targets, may very well be associated. But that doesn't mean that changing the target of a direct mail campaign will necessarily increase revenues, any more than putting more books in a school library will necessarily increase student test scores.

These points don't represent a defect in regression analysis itself. Whether you get your data from a formal, planned experiment or from a grab sample you find in a data mining project, you probably use the same regression technique. The difference is in how the data set is established.

For instance, in this section's example concerning advertising expenditures and unit sales, you could plug the value $200,000 into the regression equation and get 113,818 as the estimated number of units sold. That does not necessarily mean that spending $200,000 to advertise a product would result in the sale of 113,818 units (although it certainly might do so). There are many reasons other than amount of advertising budget for unit sales to vary, and these other reasons (for example, unit sales price) are not represented in the regression equation.

Furthermore, even if the relationship between variables is a causal one, you have no way of knowing for sure the direction of the causation. It is entirely plausible that as unit sales increase, the marketing department has increased that product's advertising budget—thus, unit sales may have driven spending on advertisements, instead of the other way around.

Yet another possibility is the existence of some third variable that exerts a causal influence on both sales and advertising. An upturn in either the national or a local economy is typical of this effect.

The only way to be sure of cause and effect is to conduct a formal experiment, in which you manipulate one or more input variables and measure the outcome on some result variable. You also need to arrange for a comparison that isn't subjected to the manipulation of the input variables. This helps you quantify and thus control for the effect of other, unmanipulated, "nuisance" variables.

Regressing One Variable onto Several Other Variables

Suppose that, besides increasing advertising dollars for a product, you are considering lowering its unit sales price. Again, you might look to the data on all your product lines for guidance. Figure 15.10 shows, in addition to the advertising budget and unit sales, the sales price for 18 different models of a product.

What is the best estimate of the *combined* effect of changing both the advertising budget and the sales price on units sold? Because neither equation addresses both advertising and price simultaneously, neither chart's regression equation can answer this question.

To answer it, it's necessary to resort to the worksheet function LINEST. LINEST is capable of analyzing the relationship between a variable such as units sold (sometimes called a *criterion* variable or *dependent* variable) on the one hand, and multiple variables such as advertising dollars and sales price (sometimes called *predictor* variables or *independent* variables) on the other. Figure 15.11 shows LINEST in this context.

FIGURE 15.10
Unit sales increase as advertising dollars increase and sales price decreases.

	A	B	C
1	Advertising	Sales	
2	budget	Price	Unit Sales
3	$3,500	$88	16,523
4	$10,073	$110	6,305
5	$11,825	$85	1,769
6	$33,550	$28	30,570
7	$37,200	$101	7,698
8	$55,400	$71	9,554
9	$55,565	$7	54,154
10	$66,501	$82	54,450
11	$71,000	$62	47,800
12	$82,107	$24	74,598
13	$83,100	$91	25,257
14	$90,496	$40	80,608
15	$100,000	$45	40,800
16	$102,100	$21	63,200
17	$132,222	$40	69,675
18	$136,297	$8	98,715
19	$139,114	$63	75,886
20	$165,575	$5	83,360

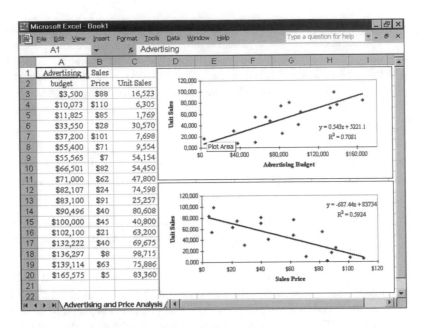

FIGURE 15.11
The `LINEST` worksheet function returns statistics that describe the relationship between one criterion variable and one or more predictor variables.

	A	B	C	D	E	F	G	H	I
1	Advertising	Sales							Derived
2	budget	Price	Unit Sales						variable:
3	$3,500	$88	16,523						6634.401
4	$10,073	$110	6,305						1236.780
5	$11,825	$85	1,769						10888.068
6	$33,550	$28	30,570						39441.960
7	$37,200	$101	7,698						14840.194
8	$55,400	$71	9,554	LINEST(C3:C20,A3:B20,TRUE,TRUE):					32614.096
9	$55,565	$7	54,154		-358.4634	0.3818	36842.9715		55669.921
10	$66,501	$82	54,450		129.5278	0.0936	13164.5770		32837.390
11	$71,000	$62	47,800		0.8068	14339.4362	#N/A		41724.264
12	$82,107	$24	74,598		31.3176	15.0000	#N/A		59729.636
13	$83,100	$91	25,257		1.29E+10	3.08E+09	#N/A		35948.302
14	$90,496	$40	80,608						57053.546
15	$100,000	$45	40,800						58889.619
16	$102,100	$21	63,200						68402.008
17	$132,222	$40	69,675			RSQ(C3:C20,I3:I20):	0.8068		72983.490
18	$136,297	$8	98,715			F9/F10:	4.0799		86096.075
19	$139,114	$63	75,886			TDIST(F9/F10,15,1):	0.0005		67549.256
20	$165,575	$5	83,360			TDIST(ABS(E9/E10),15,1):	0.0072		98382.993

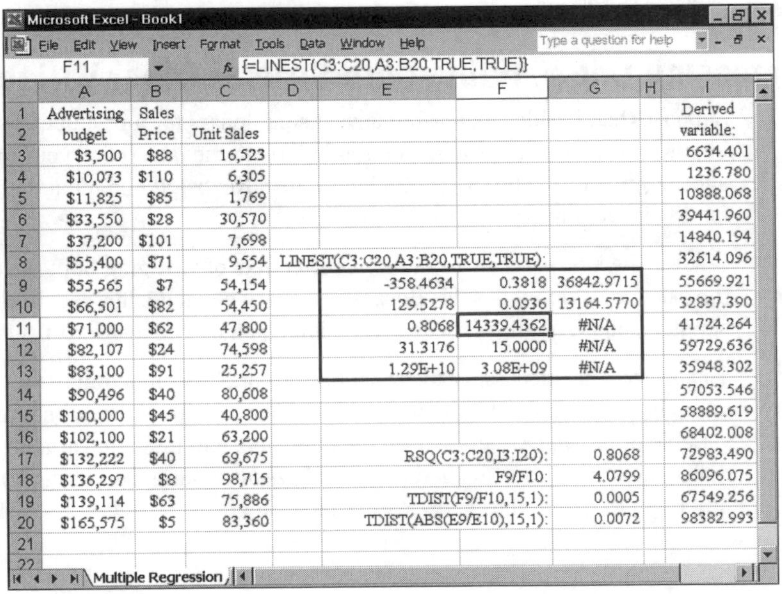

The range E9:G13 contains the `LINEST` function, which in this case is array-entered as

```
=LINEST(C3:C20,A3:B20,TRUE,TRUE)
```

The result of the function is rich in information. First, it provides the best-estimate multiple regression equation to predict units sold from the combination of advertising dollars and sales price. The equation is

```
y = 36842.9715 + (.3818 * x1) + (-358.4634 * x2)
```

where y represents units sold, x1 represents advertising dollars, and x2 represents sales price.

Notice first that there are three terms to the right of the equal sign in the equation. The first, 36842.9715, is the intercept, as it is in two-variable regression. The second and third terms contain .3818 and –358.4634. These are no longer slopes, because there is only one regression line to consider and one straight line can't have two different slopes. They are, instead, termed *regression coefficients*. They are coefficients that you can multiply times a value for advertising dollars and a value for sales price, to estimate units sold.

Also notice that LINEST does not return the regression coefficients in the same order as the predictor variables on the worksheet. That is, the first coefficient (–358.4634) applies to the rightmost predictor variable, Sales Price (found in B3:B20). The second coefficient (.3818) applies to the leftmost predictor variable, Advertising Budget (found in A3:A20). This is an inconvenience in the LINEST function, and there is no way around it: the order that LINEST returns the coefficients is always the reverse of the order of the arguments that refer to the worksheet ranges.

What else does the LINEST function tell you? The value 0.8068, in the third row and first column of the LINEST results, is the R^2 between units sold and the best combination of advertising budget and sales price. When you optimally combine sales price and advertising budget by means of the regression equation, you get a new variable that shares 80.68% of its variance with units sold.

Figure 15.11 shows this new variable in cells I3:I20. The formula in cell I3 is

```
=$G$9+($E$9*B3)+($F$9*A3)
```

This formula is copied and pasted into cells I4:I20. Finally, this formula is entered in cell G17:

```
=RSQ(C3:C20,I3:I20)
```

Recall that the RSQ function returns the R^2 between two variables: the percent of variance that they have in common. In this case, it returns 0.8068, which is identical to the value returned in cell E11 by the LINEST function.

More importantly, 0.8068 is larger than .7081, which is the R^2 between units sold and advertising dollars alone. This means that by combining advertising dollars and sales price as predictor variables, you can explain an additional 10% (80.68% – 70.81%) of the variability in unit sales.

What of the second row in the LINEST results, cells E10:G10 in Figure 15.11? These speak to the statistical significance, or the dependability, of the regression coefficients. They are the standard errors of the regression coefficients and the intercept. A standard error is a kind of standard deviation. If you divide each regression coefficient by its standard error, you get what's known as a *t-statistic*. For example, using the data shown in cells F9 and F10 of Figure 15.11:

```
=.3818/.0936
```

```
=4.0799
```

This means that .3818 is slightly more than four standard errors away from zero. Four standard errors is a considerable distance. (Until and unless you've had a fair amount of experience working with standard deviations and standard errors, it's difficult to know that intuitively, and for now it's okay to take the statement at face value.) You can use Excel's TDIST function to determine whether you think it's statistically significant. For example, you could enter this formula on the worksheet:

```
=TDIST(F9/F10,15,1)
```

which returns .0005. Taking the formula's components one-by-one:

- F9/F10 is the ratio of the regression coefficient for advertising dollars to its standard error. Again, this is the t-statistic, whose value is 4.0799.

- 15 is the number of degrees of freedom for the t-statistic. It is the number of observations, minus the number of terms in the equation. Here, there are 18 observations in the data set (A3:C20). There are three terms in the equation (one intercept and two regression coefficients), so the degrees of freedom is $18 - 3 = 15$. It is the same as the value returned by the LINEST function in the second column of its fourth row (see cell F12 in Figure 15.11). Other things being equal, the larger the number of degrees of freedom, the more powerful and sensitive the analysis—and therefore the more accurate your estimate can be.

- 1 is the number of tails to reference in the t-distribution. This book does not go into sufficient detail about the directionality of statistical hypotheses to fully explain this argument to the TDIST function. However, you can use this as a rule of thumb: if you expect, before you look at the data, a positive (or a negative) relationship between a predictor variable and a criterion variable, use 1 as TDIST's third argument. If you don't know whether to expect a positive or a negative relationship, use 2 as TDIST's third argument. Here, it's reasonable to expect a positive relationship between advertising dollars and unit sales (the more you advertise, the more you sell), so 1 is used.

- The TDIST function itself, given its three arguments, returns the probability of observing a ratio of the regression coefficient to its standard error as large as this one, if the regression coefficient for all such products were really zero. For these data, the probability is .0005 (or 5 chances in 10,000) of getting a t-statistic of 4.08 if the population regression coefficient were really zero.

Why do you care whether the regression coefficient is significantly different from zero? Consider the implication of a regression coefficient whose value is zero. If you multiply zero times all the values of the associated predictor variable, as you would in the regression equation, you add nothing—zero—to the predicted value of the criterion variable. Therefore, the predictor variable would be of no use to you.

But most people would consider 5 chances in 10,000 good evidence of a statistically significant finding. They would conclude that the regression coefficient is in fact non-zero, and would retain the predictor variable in the equation. In the current example, they would choose to predict unit sales as a function of both advertising and sales price, not just one or the other.

N O T E Excel's TDIST function requires a value greater than or equal to zero as its first argument; it returns #NUM! if its first argument is negative. You can get a negative ratio of the coefficient to its standard error if the coefficient itself is negative (neither a standard error nor a standard deviation can ever be negative). A negative regression coefficient can be every bit as informative as a positive one: the coefficient's sign is just a matter of whether the relationship is direct (as with advertising dollars and units sold) or inverse (as with sales price and units sold).

The significance level of a regression coefficient is unrelated to the direction of the relationship between the predictor and the criterion variables. Therefore, to get around TDIST's insistence on a positive value for its first argument, use Excel's ABS function, which returns the absolute value of a number. For example:

```
=TDIST(ABS(E9/E10),15,1)
```

If all this seems like a lot of work to you (array-entering LINEST, accounting for the order of the regression coefficients in LINEST's results, noting the R^2 value, getting the degrees of freedom, getting the ratio of the coefficients to their standard errors, using TDIST correctly), it should. If you want to reduce the degree of uncertainty that surrounds many business decisions, you'll find that this sort of analysis is necessary—but it can be exacting and tedious.

Fortunately, Excel's Regression add-in provides a shortcut: it returns all this information, and more, from the choices you make in just one dialog box. Figure 15.12 shows the results of running the Regression add-in on the data in Figure 15.11.

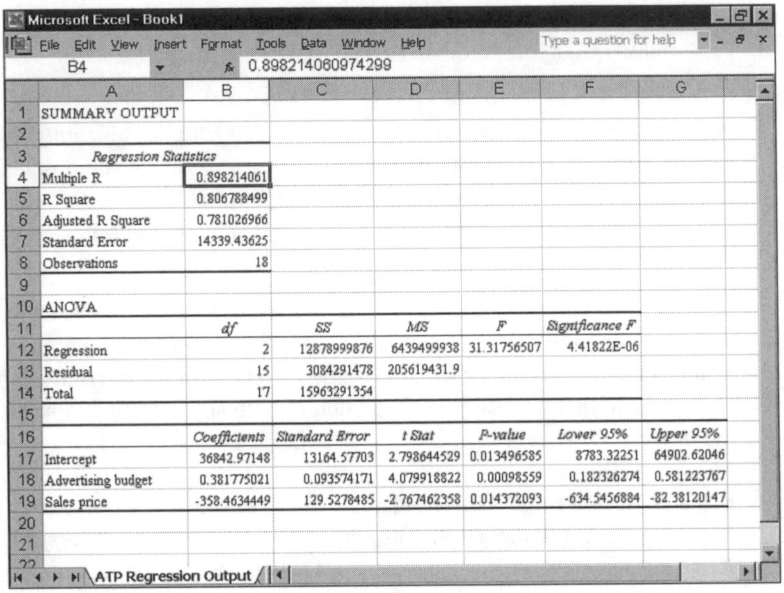

	A	B	C	D	E	F	G
1	SUMMARY OUTPUT						
2							
3	*Regression Statistics*						
4	Multiple R	0.898214061					
5	R Square	0.806788499					
6	Adjusted R Square	0.781026966					
7	Standard Error	14339.43625					
8	Observations	18					
9							
10	ANOVA						
11		*df*	*SS*	*MS*	*F*	*Significance F*	
12	Regression	2	12878999876	6439499938	31.31756507	4.41822E-06	
13	Residual	15	3084291478	205619431.9			
14	Total	17	15963291354				
15							
16		*Coefficients*	*Standard Error*	*t Stat*	*P-value*	*Lower 95%*	*Upper 95%*
17	Intercept	36842.97148	13164.57703	2.798644529	0.013496585	8783.32251	64902.62046
18	Advertising budget	0.381775021	0.093574171	4.079918822	0.00098559	0.182326274	0.581223767
19	Sales price	-358.4634449	129.5278485	-2.767462358	0.014372093	-634.5456884	-82.38120147

FIGURE 15.12
The Regression add-in automates much of the work involved in a multiple regression analysis.

To obtain this analysis, verify that you have loaded the Analysis ToolPak via Tools, Add-Ins. Follow these steps with a worksheet containing the data for Figure 15.11 active:

1. Choose Tools, Data Analysis.
2. Choose Regression from the Analysis Tools list box.
3. Choose OK. The dialog box shown in Figure 15.13 appears.
4. With the flashing cursor in the Input Y Range edit box, select cells C3:C20 or type the address directly in the edit box.
5. Click in the Input X Range edit box, and select cells A3:B20 or type the address.
6. Make sure that the Confidence Level edit box contains 95, and that the New Worksheet Ply option button is selected. (There's nothing magic about these settings: they are simply the ones use to create Figure 15.12.)
7. Choose OK.

CAUTION

If you use the Regression tool in the Analysis ToolPak, be careful when you change the Output Options shown in Figure 15.13. Output Range is the default. Whenever you change the selected output option button, the Input Y Range edit box (unaccountably) gets the focus. An unwary user finds himself replacing the input Y range address that he wants to use with the address of the location where he wants the output to go; or, he finds himself typing a new sheet name (a ply is a worksheet) in place of the input Y range address. Other tools in the Analysis ToolPak share this defect.

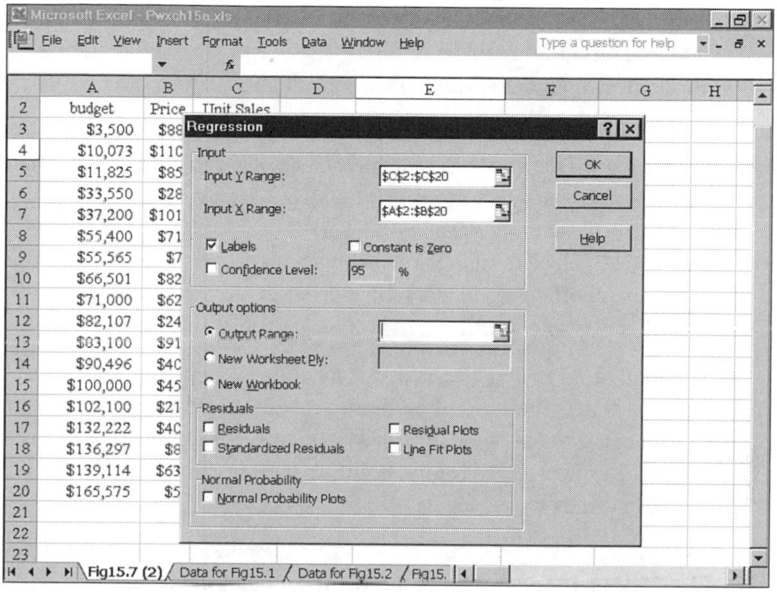

FIGURE 15.13
With the Regression add-in dialog box you can specify just a few options to obtain a complete multiple regression analysis.

There's plenty of useful information in the Regression output, even though no special options such as residual analysis were used. For example, Figure 15.12's cell B5 shows the R^2 between the units sold and the combination of advertising dollars and sales price. In cell B4 it also shows the multiple R, which is, as mentioned earlier, the square root of R^2. The multiple R is a correlation coefficient, and expresses the correlation between units sold and the derived combination of the predictor variables.

The adjusted R^2, shown in cell B6, takes into account the number of observations and the number of predictor variables. In multiple regression analysis, when the number of observations is small, relative to the number of predictor variables, the R^2 tends to be biased upward. The adjusted R^2 informs you what value you would expect to obtain in another sample of data, one that would have many more observations than does the current one. Compare the actual R^2 with the adjusted R^2. By doing so, you can tell that if this example had been based on, say, 100 observations instead of just 18, then the adjusted R^2 would have been only trivially different from the observed R^2.

N O T E The formula for the adjusted R^2 is

$$1-(1-R^2) \times ((N-1)/(N-k-1))$$

where N is the number of observations and k is the number of predictor variables. ▨

A discussion of the ANOVA (Analysis Of Variance) table is beyond the scope of this book, and would add little to the object of this analysis, the regression coefficients. If you are interested in more information about ANOVA, consult an intermediate text on statistical analysis.

The third section of Figure 15.12 provides detailed information about the terms in the regression equation. The intercept and coefficients are reported, as are their standard errors, and are identical to those returned by LINEST. The Regression add-in, however, returns them in the same order as they exist on the worksheet. (LINEST's reversal of the order of the coefficients is the source of much confusion among users. The fact that the Regression add-in returns the coefficients in worksheet order is often reason enough to prefer the add-in over the worksheet function.)

The add-in also returns the t-statistic for the intercept and for each regression coefficient: recall that this is the ratio of each term to its standard error. For example, cell D18 in Figure 15.12 reports the t-statistic for sales price as 4.079918822. This is the same value as is shown in Figure 15.11, cell G18, which is 4.0799 (the apparent difference between the two values is due to the different cell formats).

The P-values reported by the add-in are different than those shown in Figure 15.11. There, cell G19 reports the results of the TDIST function for advertising dollars as 0.0005, whereas the add-in reports it as 0.00098559. The reason for the difference is in the third argument to TDIST, which specifies using a one- or two-tailed test (see the discussion earlier in this section). The analysis in Figure 15.11 used a one-tailed test, because the direction of the relationship between the predictor and the criterion was known (or, at least, strongly suspected) before the data were examined.

However, the Regression add-in has no way of knowing or suspecting the direction of the relationship prior to performing the analysis. Therefore, it is programmed to supply a two-tailed test. If you were to enter this formula

```
=TDIST(F9/F10,15,2)
```

on the worksheet shown in Figure 15.11, it would return 0.00098559, just as does the Regression add-in.

Finally, the add-in reports the upper and lower limits of a 95% confidence interval around the intercept and around each coefficient (see the section on confidence intervals earlier in this chapter for a fuller explanation of their interpretation). Notice that none of the three confidence intervals spans zero: this is as you would expect, because the P-values are each significant beyond the 5% level. If a P-value were .05 or greater, the 95% confidence interval for that term would span zero.

So, you can conclude with 95% confidence that the intercept and regression coefficients are non-zero: that the predictor variables add information meaningfully to the regression equation, and that you can predict unit sales from advertising dollars and sales price with reasonable accuracy.

Estimating with Multiple Regression

After you have verified that a meaningful relationship exists between a criterion variable and a set of predictor variables, how do you go about estimating the outcome of modifying the value of one or more of the predictors? More concretely, what unit sales might you hope for, in a product whose advertising budget is $200,000 and whose unit sales price is $10?

NOTE Bear in mind that data mining efforts such as the one discussed in this example almost never enable you to infer causation. They are not the result of formal experiments, but represent convenience samples. They can point the way to possible cause-and-effect relationships, though, and that's their real value. This is the reason that the prior paragraph used the phrase "might you hope for" instead of "should you expect." ■

The most intuitive method is simply to apply the multiple regression equation, with the values for the predictor variables inserted. In this case, you would use

```
=36842.97+(.3818*200000)+(-358.4634*10)
```

```
=109613.34
```

If you sold 109,613 units at $10 each, your revenues would be over $1 million, and this might be a good investment. (However, there are plenty of other tests for the quality of an investment discussed in Chapters 11, 12, and 13 on business case development; this is only one preliminary test you might make when you are uncertain of the investment's outcome.)

A slightly easier method of applying the multiple regression equation is to use Excel's TREND function. It is *much* easier to use TREND when there are many predictor values that you want to manipulate. TREND calculates the regression equation as does LINEST, and optionally applies that equation to new predictor values, returning the values you would obtain if you entered the multiple regression formula itself.

For example, suppose that you enter the value 200000 in cell A21 and the value 10 in cell B21 in the worksheet shown in Figure 15.10. If you then entered this formula:

```
=TREND(C3:C20,A3:B20,A21:B21)
```

it would return 109613.34, just as does the explicit entry of the multiple regression equation. In the TREND equation, C3:C20 is the address of the range containing the criterion variable, A3:B20 is the address of the range containing the predictor variables, and A21:B21 is the address of the range containing the new predictor variable values that you want to apply.

This may not seem much easier than entering the regression equation explicitly, but what if you had 20 pairs of new values to test? If these new values were in A21:B40, you could array-enter this formula in a one-column by 20-row range:

```
=TREND(C3:C20,A3:B20,A21:B40)
```

and in that way obtain all 20 predicted values with one array formula.

Case Study: Improving Profit Margin

As product manager for a manufacturer of frames for eyeglasses, you manage a product line comprised of 47 different frames. One of your primary responsibilities is to maximize the profit margin returned by your individual products.

You have just completed a survey of the retail outlets that market your frames. The survey collected a variety of information about the products, and included variables such as retail price, perceived quality of the frames, and satisfaction with the warranty terms that you extend to the resellers.

Your product line includes everything from conservatively designed frames that do little other than hold lenses in place to so-called "designer" frames that are inexpensive to manufacture but are perceived as stylish by the customer. You also have at hand information on your profit margin for each product, the total of your fixed and variable manufacturing costs, and the share of your total product line achieved by each frame.

Each of these variables could be related in some way to your profit margin. For example:

- A higher average retail price charged by the outlets might mean that you could increase the wholesale price.
- It may be that the greater the perceived quality of the frames, the more you can charge for them.
- It may be that the greater the frames' actual quality, the more it costs to manufacture them.
- The more that each type of frame contributes to your overall sales, the more popular it is likely to be—and, perhaps, the more you could charge the retail outlets.
- The better the warranty terms, the more it costs you in product replacements, thus reducing your margin.
- And, of course, the more it costs you to manufacture the frames, the lower your profit margin.

How, if at all, can you manipulate any or all of these variables to boost profit margins? The price that you charge the retail outlets is under your control, but if you raise some prices you run the risk that the outlets will promote the less expensive frames; or, worse, will promote frames made by your competitors. You could modify your manufacturing operations in a way that would reduce the quality of the product, and therefore make it less expensive to produce. But then the retail outlets might demand a price reduction. There is little you can do about the popularity of a given frame, but if it is a powerful driver of profit margin you might decide to do nothing about the other variables: any action you take is likely to entail some cost, to no benefit. You might modify the warranty terms or retool your manufacturing operation to reduce costs, but would doing so materially increase your profit margin?

The data that you have collected are shown in part in Figure 15.14.

FIGURE 15.14
A partial listing of the product data for the multiple regression analysis shown in Figure 15.15.

Profit Margin	Product Quality	Warranty Terms	Retail Price	Unit Cost	Component Share
0.99%	1.22	1.24	$130	$35.19	2.08%
1.21%	1.45	1.54	$104	$80.00	1.09%
2.07%	1.90	1.31	$100	$23.31	2.28%
2.14%	2.53	1.36	$164	$80.00	1.44%
3.05%	3.41	2.65	$119	$80.00	1.75%
3.87%	1.96	1.63	$126	$68.84	1.54%
4.78%	2.71	1.66	$128	$80.00	0.47%
5.45%	1.76	1.40	$142	$30.32	2.51%
5.55%	2.09	2.61	$165	$80.00	2.81%
6.12%	1.10	2.42	$124	$32.94	0.59%
6.51%	3.62	3.50	$109	$28.56	0.64%
6.95%	3.53	1.29	$129	$78.75	1.73%
7.24%	2.09	2.44	$165	$38.63	1.83%
7.45%	1.54	2.60	$119	$48.67	0.76%
8.88%	2.41	2.11	$164	$40.83	0.14%
10.08%	3.64	2.06	$146	$80.00	3.53%
10.25%	2.61	1.85	$159	$80.00	2.13%
10.81%	2.62	2.28	$157	$80.00	3.86%
11.09%	3.29	4.07	$178	$80.00	1.28%
11.64%	1.24	1.84	$138	$31.20	4.25%

Eyeglasses Analysis

You run the Regression add-in on the data, using product margin as the y-range and the remaining variables as the x-range. You obtain the results shown in Figure 15.15.

FIGURE 15.15
The multiple regression analysis of product data for eyeglass frames forms the basis for avoiding a useless change in pricing and operations.

SUMMARY OUTPUT

Regression Statistics	
Multiple R	0.71684266
R Square	0.51386340
Adjusted R Square	0.45457845
Standard Error	0.04694102
Observations	47

ANOVA

	df	*SS*	*MS*	*F*	*Significance F*
Regression	5	0.09549447	0.01909889	8.66768713	0.00001137
Residual	41	0.09034183	0.00220346		
Total	46	0.18583630			

	Coefficients	*Standard Error*	*t Stat*	*P-value*	*Lower 95%*	*Upper 95%*
Intercept	-0.11895439	0.04970656	-2.39313270	0.02136750	-0.21933887	-0.01856990
Product Quality	0.02980053	0.00767474	3.88293909	0.00036802	0.01430108	0.04529998
Warranty Terms	0.00693261	0.00889049	0.77977789	0.44000000	-0.01102212	0.02488734
Retail Price	0.00119016	0.00039374	3.02269683	0.00430578	0.00039498	0.00198534
Unit Cost	-0.00083227	0.00033930	-2.45288035	0.01851416	-0.00151751	-0.00014703
Component Share	0.63455512	0.59762352	1.06179743	0.29454224	-0.57237072	1.84148096

Eyeglasses Analysis Results

You notice, first, that there is variation in profit margin that is associated with variation in the predictor variables. The amount of variation is around 50%: the multiple R^2 (labeled *R Square* by the Regression add-in) is .51 and the adjusted R^2 is .4546. The difference between the observed R^2 value and the adjusted value is not so great that you would conclude that you have either too many predictors or too few observations. 50% is a useful amount of shared variance. It's not perfect, but at least there's a substantial amount of variation in profit margin that is associated with variation in the predictor variables.

Turning your attention to the analysis of the regression coefficients, you see that product quality, retail price, and unit cost are all significantly related to profit margin at the 95% confidence level. The P-values for the t-tests of these three variables are lower than .05, and the 95% confidence intervals do not span zero. (See cells E18:G21 in Figure 15.15.)

The coefficients for product quality and retail price are positive, so the relationships are direct: for example, the higher the retail price, the higher the profit margin. The coefficient for unit cost is, as expected, negative: the higher the unit cost, the lower the profit margin.

This suggests, then, that there might be room to raise the price that you charge your retailers, given the average retail prices that they charge. There might also be an opportunity to modify your manufacturing operations, simultaneously reducing the product quality a bit and lowering your unit production costs.

Keep in mind, though, that these data come from a snapshot sample, not from a true experimental design in which you purposely manipulate the independent variables and note the effect of doing so on the dependent variable. The results are suggestive, and it's reasonable to hypothesize that changes in the predictors will influence the criterion variable. But without evidence from a true experiment, it's very dangerous to adopt a firm conclusion that changing a predictor will *necessarily* cause a change in the criterion.

Before you undertake such possibly drastic measures as raising prices or modifying your manufacturing operations, you should estimate the effect of doing so on your present results. At present, for example, you have one product that has a profit margin of 10.25%. Its unit cost is $80 and its perceived quality is 2.61. What would happen if you were to find a way to reduce its unit cost to, say, $20 and if the perceived quality of the eyeglass frame therefore fell from 2.61 to 1.30?

Begin by copying its predictor values (cells B19:F19 of Figure 15.14) to a blank range such as G19:K19. Change the unit cost in that range from $80 to $20, and the value of perceived quality from 2.61 to 1.30. Selecting another blank cell, enter this formula:

```
=TREND(A3:A49,B3:F49,G19:K19)
```

The result is 11.84%, about 1.6% greater than 10.25%, your current profit margin for that product. This is not a dramatic increase, certainly not one that should convince you to invest money in drastic changes to your manufacturing operations or the price you charge your retailers.

This analysis might well persuade you to let well enough alone. But if the analysis had suggested that you could bring about a 5% or 10% increase in profit margin, that might warrant a pilot test. You'd want to make sure to design that pilot test to deliberately manipulate the wholesale price and the changes to your manufacturing operations. By doing so you could later infer real causation. You would also make sure that you had a comparison group: products that are manufactured using existing procedures and that are wholesaled at existing prices.

Summary

In this chapter you have learned how to use information about the variability in an indicator to make decisions about investment options when you do not have perfect information at your disposal. In particular, confidence intervals can help you to bracket the likely outcome by means of worst- and best-case scenarios, which gives you a range within which you can make your decision.

You have also learned how to use the powerful multiple regression technique to analyze data and to estimate the potential effect of a change in such variables as pricing, quality, and component share on an important outcome like profit margin. Excel provides convenient and powerful tools to assist you in these analyses, but it's necessary to understand the meaning of the results so you can apply them sensibly.

CHAPTER 16

Fixed Assets

Your company probably owns various tangible assets that it uses to produce revenue. These assets might include buildings, land, manufacturing equipment such as dies, office equipment such as computers, and transportation equipment such as trucks.

Together, these assets are known as *fixed assets*. Your financial statements and reports may also refer to them as *plant and equipment* or *property, plant and equipment*. In contrast to supplies, these assets are regarded as long-lasting. In contrast to intangible assets such as trademarks, fixed assets have an objective value. And in contrast to goods, such as an inventory of products that your company manufactures, fixed assets are not intended for resale.

Of course, categorizing an asset depends not only on the asset itself but on your line of business. If your company resells computers, you would usually regard a computer component as a unit of inventory. But if your company uses computers to help sell real estate, you would regard the same computer component as a fixed asset.

There are two principal ways that your treatment of fixed assets contributes to your company's profitability and worth: the determination of its original cost and the determination of its current value. This chapter explores these two processes in detail.

Determining Original Cost

If you acquire a new fixed asset—a telephone system, for example, or a new building—you need to account for that asset in your books. The asset's value contributes to your company's worth on its balance sheet. Furthermore, it's likely that you obtain the fixed asset to help you produce revenue over time, and you need to be able to match the asset's cost to the revenue it helps to produce. Therefore, it can be critically important to value the asset accurately if you are to understand your company's worth and profitability.

Among the issues involved in determining an asset's original cost are the choice of which costs to include, which assets to treat as capital expenses, and whether to use the actual expenditure or its replacement value as the cost of the asset.

Choosing Costs

Suppose that you purchase a new computer to help you run your business, expecting that this computer will contribute to the creation of revenue over a period of several years. Figure 16.1 shows the costs involved in acquiring the computer.

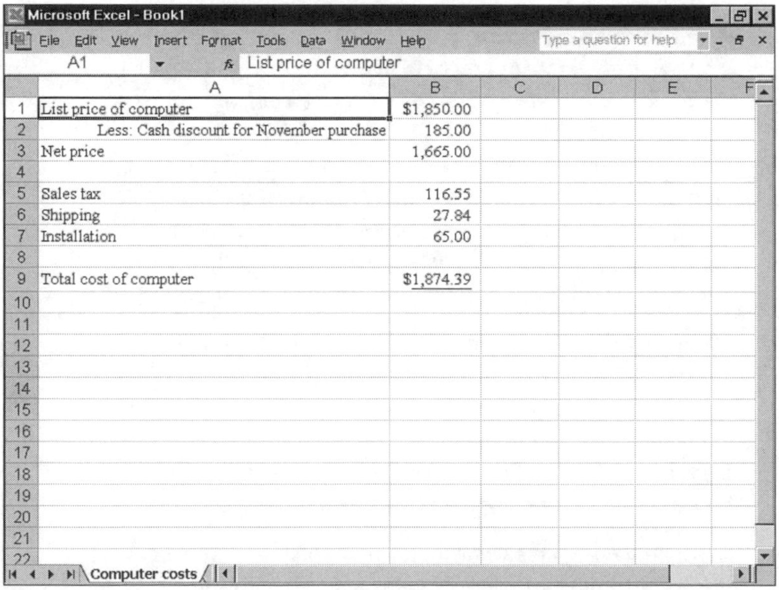

	A	B
1	List price of computer	$1,850.00
2	Less: Cash discount for November purchase	185.00
3	Net price	1,665.00
4		
5	Sales tax	116.55
6	Shipping	27.84
7	Installation	65.00
8		
9	Total cost of computer	$1,874.39

FIGURE 16.1
Fixed asset acquisition costs involve more than just the list price of the asset.

The main portion of the expenditure is, of course, the computer's list price. But the list price does not represent the actual cost of the equipment. Suppose that the supplier is trying to clear its inventory of this particular model, and offers a cash discount of 10% if a purchase is made before the end of November. You take advantage of this offer, reducing the basic price from $1,850 to $1,665. A sales tax of 7% applies, increasing the cost by $116.55. Shipping adds an additional $27.84, and you pay a local firm $65 to install the computer and its connection to your company's local area network.

> **N O T E** The rules that govern how you capitalize and depreciate assets are complex and protean. It's unlikely that rules used by this chapter's examples are the same as the ones that pertain to your firm. You should discuss these issues with your accountant; then, when you are sure you understand how the rules work in your case, you can use the techniques described in this chapter to apply them. ■

These additional costs are not really part of the computer itself. Shouldn't you treat them as expenses for the month of November? No—you should normally treat them as part of the cost of the fixed asset. The reason is once again due to the basic principle of matching costs to revenues.

The computer will presumably remain in service for several years, and will contribute to the generation of your revenue during that time. The ancillary costs are necessary aspects of putting the equipment into service: you could not use the computer to generate revenue unless you pay the sales tax on it, have it shipped to your place of business, and arrange for its installation. Therefore, these costs should be matched to revenue generated not only this month, not only this year, but generated during the entire useful life of the equipment.

If you allocated the costs to expenses for the current period, you would understate your income for that period and overstate it for subsequent periods. All the costs associated with the acquisition of the equipment should be included in its valuation and, via the depreciation process, allocated against revenue during all the periods that the equipment retains a value.

Are there any other costs that you should apply to the computer's valuation? Possibly: it depends on whether the costs are reasonable and necessary for its use. Suppose that you erroneously told the firm that installs the computer that it already has a network interface card installed, when in fact it doesn't. The technician must make a special trip to obtain additional equipment, and charges you extra for this trip. Your accountant might tell you that the extra charge is not a reasonable and necessary cost, and you should not include it as part of the depreciable cost of the asset.

Choosing Assets

Companies frequently acquire equipment that has a useful life that extends over several accounting periods, but that they hesitate to treat as fixed assets. Items such as staplers, postage scales, beverage carafes, and inexpensive office decor all tend to be long-lasting (*particularly* the decor) and have an objective value. But the effort the company will make to account for their depreciation usually costs more than the benefit derived from the additional accuracy of accounting for the assets.

Therefore, it is useful to have a company policy that establishes a minimum cost (for example, $500) for an item before it is treated as a capital expense. Items that cost less are treated as current expenses, even if they are tangible, continue in use over more than one accounting period, and in theory represent fixed assets.

Choosing Between Actual Cost and Replacement Cost

Depending on the nature of the fixed asset, as well as the way that you put it into service, you might need to use the replacement or market value of the asset to determine its cost. If you contribute an asset to the business as capital, this choice can become important. (Generally Accepted Accounting Principles state that other assets are to be valued at their historical cost.)

Suppose that you own a house that cost you $150,000 to purchase, and that after living in it for some time you convert it to a rental property. For your own business purposes, it might be necessary to value the house at its current market value, which could be $175,000, $325,000, or virtually any other figure.

In some cases such as this, the Lower of Cost or Market principle can come into play. This principle, which can apply to inventory valuation as well as to the valuation of fixed assets, states that an item should be valued at either the price you paid for it, or the current market value of an identical item: whichever is lower.

However, this principle does not apply in all cases. You should consult an accountant to determine whether to use an asset's actual cost, its replacement cost, or the lower of its actual cost or its market value.

The choice of the appropriate valuation method affects both your company's worth on the balance sheet and its earnings on the income statement. Clearly, the greater the asset's valuation, the greater the company's worth. But as you depreciate the asset over its useful life, you will be showing some portion of its cost as an expense attributable to each accounting period.

The greater the cost of the asset, then, the greater the depreciation expense for any given period of time. Other things being equal, the greater the depreciation expense, the lower your reported income and the lower your income tax liability.

This is fine in theory, but in practice it can be difficult to determine either a replacement cost or a market cost—and the two are not necessarily the same. Suppose that you want to determine the replacement cost of a personal computer, two years into its useful life. Because two years have passed since you acquired the asset, the technology has changed: a computer is not a chair. It could (and probably would) be extremely difficult to obtain a price on a computer that is both new and directly comparable to the one you own.

Even if you were able to find several replacement sources for an asset, it could be difficult to determine the market price. When many sources exist for a product, it is likely that their prices vary. Deciding when to stop searching for additional pricing information, which price to adopt as an estimate of market value, whether to average several values as your estimate, and so on can take an amount of effort that is not commensurate with the benefits that you might derive.

Your choices as to valuing an asset are of course restricted by the tax laws and regulations, and for this reason it's recommended that you consult an accountant or tax lawyer for advice on how to value any significant asset. You should be aware, though, of how establishing a cost for an asset has implications both for the valuation of a company and for its reported income.

Depreciating Assets

Depreciation, in accordance with the accrual principle, influences the timing of your company's earnings by matching revenues and costs. It is the means by which a company can spread the cost of an asset over its expected useful life. In other words, *depreciation* is the allocation of prior expenditures to future time periods, so as to match revenues and expenses.

Typically, you make the cash outlay to purchase an asset during the first year of the asset's useful life. The cash outlay itself is not reflected in the depreciation line of an income statement. Depreciation does not represent a cash outlay: it is a non-cash charge that you use to match the first year's expenditure with the subsequent flow of revenue.

Suppose that you match the entire cost of an asset to the earnings shown in the income statement for the year you make the purchase. Your operating income for that year would then be lower than if you spread the cost over the asset's useful life. Furthermore, the following years of the asset's useful life would get a free ride. The asset will contribute to revenue generation, but the income statements in subsequent years would not reflect the associated expense.

Depreciation enables you to properly match the first year's expenditure to subsequent revenue (see Figure 16.2).

Suppose that your company purchases a vehicle to pick up materials from your suppliers and to deliver products to your customers. Figure 16.2 shows how the vehicle depreciates over a four-year period, which here is considered to be the asset's useful life. At the end of that period, the vehicle still has a *salvage* value of, say, $3,000. The salvage value is subtracted from the purchase cost to obtain the amount that is depreciated: $8,000. The expense in each of the four years is therefore $2,000. By spreading the expense equally over the asset's useful life (instead of taking the entire expense during the first year) you can more accurately match the expense to the revenue the vehicle will help to produce.

If this company sold $20,000 annually in goods and services, the impact to operating profit would be substantial. During year 1, without depreciation, earnings would be $20,000 – $8,000, or $12,000. During year 1, with depreciation, earnings would be $20,000 – $2,000, or $18,000. The difference between the two calculations is $6,000, or 30% of the company's annual revenue.

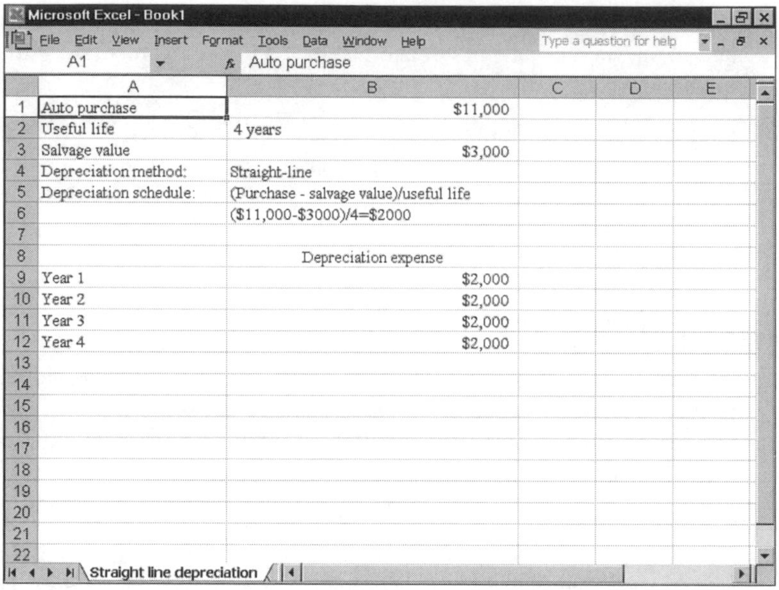

FIGURE 16.2
The straight-line method results in an equal amount of depreciation during each period.

	A	B	C	D	E
1	Auto purchase	$11,000			
2	Useful life	4 years			
3	Salvage value	$3,000			
4	Depreciation method:	Straight-line			
5	Depreciation schedule:	(Purchase - salvage value)/useful life			
6		($11,000-$3000)/4=$2000			
7					
8		Depreciation expense			
9	Year 1	$2,000			
10	Year 2	$2,000			
11	Year 3	$2,000			
12	Year 4	$2,000			

Four items are needed to determine the annual amount of depreciation:

■ The asset's useful life

■ The asset's original cost

■ The asset's salvage value (its value at the end of its useful life)

■ The depreciation method employed

There are two general methods of allocating an asset's cost over its useful life: *straight-line depreciation* and *accelerated depreciation*. Under the straight-line method, you depreciate the asset by a constant amount each year, as shown in Figure 16.2.

The second general method of depreciation is actually a family of techniques, together known as accelerated depreciation. Each accelerated technique charges more depreciation in the early years of an asset's life and less in later years. Accelerated depreciation does not enable a company to take more depreciation in total, but simply alters the timing of the depreciation.

The basic rationale for accelerated depreciation is the recognition that when an asset is new, it tends to operate more efficiently than after it has been in service for several accounting periods. The assumption is that when the asset operates at a high level of efficiency, its contribution to the creation of revenue is greater than after its efficiency has declined. The timing of the acquisition expense—the depreciation—should reflect the asset's contribution to revenue creation. Therefore, more depreciation should be recognized earlier, and less later, during the asset's useful life.

This rationale is, of course, rather disingenuous. One effect of accelerated depreciation is to increase reported expenses, and thus to decrease reported income, during the early periods of an asset's useful life. In turn, this has the effect of reducing income taxes early on. If you suspect a political rationale for the laws and regulations that enable accelerated depreciation schedules, in addition to a rationale based on the matching principle, then your suspicion is probably correct.

N O T E It is not required that a company use the same method of depreciation for tax purposes as it does for purposes such as internal planning or external reporting. Many businesses use an accelerated method in figuring their taxes, and straight-line depreciation when presenting financial information to, say, a bank. Again, check with your accountant. ■

Excel offers several different methods to calculate depreciation. These are shown in Figures 16.3 through 16.9.

Using Straight-Line Depreciation

Straight-line is the simplest method to calculate an asset's depreciation. It is the cost of the asset, less its salvage value, divided by its number of years of useful life.

Excel's SLN function returns the amount of depreciation taken each year using the straight-line method. It requires three arguments: the asset's cost, its salvage value, and its useful life. Figure 16.3 shows these values (in named ranges on the worksheet), and the formula used in cells B6:B10 is

=SLN(Cost,Salvage,Life)

FIGURE 16.3

The cumulative depreciation taken over time, using straight-line depreciation, describes a straight line.

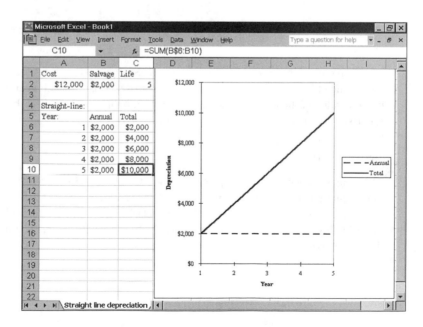

The SLN function is the simplest of Excel's depreciation methods. It takes only three arguments, but gives you very little control over the amount of depreciation that occurs during any given accounting period.

Using Declining Balance Depreciation

Figure 16.4 shows depreciation calculated by the *declining balance* method, one of the accelerated depreciation techniques.

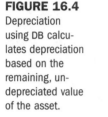

FIGURE 16.4
Depreciation using DB calculates depreciation based on the remaining, undepreciated value of the asset.

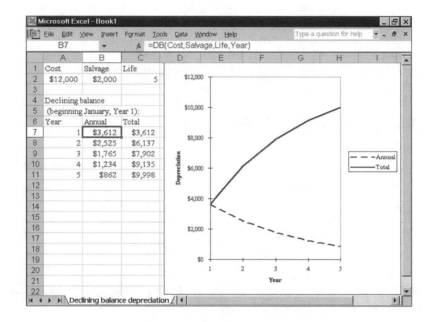

Excel's DB function returns the amount of depreciation taken each year using the declining balance method. This method calculates the depreciation each year according to the current value of the asset. (In contrast, the straight-line method uses the original value of the asset to return each year's depreciation.) The range B6:B10 in Figure 16.4 contains this array-formula:

```
=DB(Cost,Salvage,Life,Year)
```

The ranges named Cost, Salvage, and Life are the same as in Figure 16.3. The DB function requires one more argument than SLN. DB's fourth argument is the period for which it calculates the amount of depreciation. For clarity here, that argument has been named "Year," although Excel refers to it as "Period." In Figure 16.4, "Year" actually refers to the named range A7:A11.

Notice that there is a different amount of depreciation that is taken during each year. In this example, the amount of depreciation taken in each period is almost exactly 70% of the amount taken during the prior period.

There is nothing special about 70%: the ratio of the current period's depreciation to that of the prior period depends on the asset's original cost and the number of periods in its useful life. However, this ratio is always a constant figure with the DB function.

Also notice the slight inaccuracy induced by the DB function: the sum of the depreciation is $9,998 instead of $10,000. This is due to the fact that DB calculates a constant rate that it uses to obtain the depreciation in all periods following the first period. This constant factor is limited to three significant digits, which results in small rounding errors. See "Correcting Rounding Errors" later in this chapter for a method to correct these inaccuracies.

Declining Balance Depreciation, Incomplete Year

Figure 16.5 introduces a wrinkle to the DB function. DB can take a fifth argument, an optional one termed "Month." By specifying this argument, you can take account of the fact that a purchase may have been made, not in the first month of the year, but well into the year. Figure 16.5 assumes that the purchase has been made at the end of June, and that depreciation begins in July.

FIGURE 16.5
When an asset is put into use part-way through a period, the matching principle states that depreciation should begin at that time.

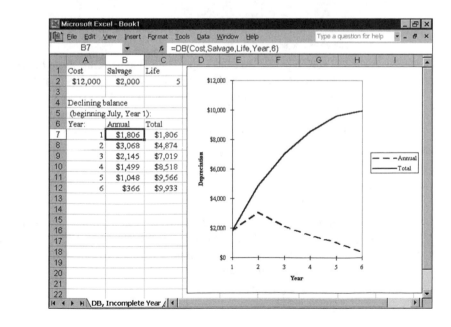

Notice that the amount of depreciation during the first year is less than that in the second year. This reflects the fact that revenues have been matched to the cost of the asset during the second six months of the first year. It was during the second six months, not the full twelve months, that the asset was available to help produce revenue.

The formula used in cells B7:B12 of Figure 16.5 is

```
=DB(Cost,Salvage,Life,Year,6)
```

where 6 represents the number of months during which depreciation will be taken in year 1 (July through December).

Also notice that Figure 16.5 shows six years, not five as in Figure 16.4. This is because the five years during which depreciation is taken begin halfway through year 1 and end halfway into year 6.

Correcting Rounding Errors

The inaccuracy induced by rounding error in the DB function is somewhat more severe in Figure 16.5 than in Figure 16.4. Here is a method to eliminate the rounding error in both cases. It assumes that you have set up your worksheet as shown in Figures 16.4 and 16.5 (or that you use the worksheets containing these figures, found in Appendix A, "What's on the Web Site?"), with the appropriate named cells and ranges (Cost, Salvage, and Life):

1. In an empty cell such as A15, enter this formula:
   ```
   =1-((Salvage/Cost)^(1/Life))
   ```

2. With A15 selected, choose Edit, Copy. Then, choose Edit, Paste Special and check the Values radio button in the Paste Special dialog box. This converts the formula to a value. (It is necessary to have a value in this cell because you will be using it as the changing cell for the Goal Seek command in step 8, and Goal Seek requires that the changing cell contain a value, not a formula.) Choose OK.

3. Name cell A15 as Rate. With A15 still selected, click in the Name Box, type **Rate**, and press Enter.

4. In another empty cell such as A17, enter this formula:
   ```
   =Cost*Rate*12/12
   ```
   where you would use 12/12 for 12 months of depreciation in the first year (thus, depreciation begins in the first month, as in Figure 16.4). Or, you could use 6/12 for 6 months of depreciation in the first year (thus, depreciation begins in the seventh month, as in Figure 16.5).

5. In A18, enter this formula:
   ```
   =(Cost-SUM($A$17:A17))*Rate
   ```

N O T E The formula shown in step 5 uses a combination of an absolute reference ($A$17) and a relative reference (A17). This is a standard and useful technique to create a running total. As the formula is copied or dragged into other cells, the absolute reference does not change, but the relative reference does. ■

Copy this formula, and paste it into cells A19:A21. The formula in A21 should now be:

`=(Cost-SUM($A$17:A20))*Rate`

6. In cell A22, enter this formula:

`=((Cost-SUM(A17:A21))*Rate*(12))/12`

for depreciation starting in January, or

`=((Cost-SUM(A17:A21))*Rate*(6))/12`

for depreciation starting in July.

7. In cell A23, enter this formula:

`=SUM(A17:A22)`

8. With cell A23 selected, choose Tools, Goal Seek. The Set cell will be A23.

9. In the To Value box, enter **10000** (or whatever the difference is between the asset's cost and its salvage value).

10. In the By Changing Cell box, enter **A15**, or highlight cell A15 after clicking in the By Changing Cell box.

11. Choose OK.

The Goal Seek tool now adjusts the value of Rate, in cell A15, so that the sum of the depreciation taken equals the difference between the cost of the asset and its salvage value. This procedure duplicates the DB function but without its errors of rounding.

Using Double Declining Balance Depreciation

Figure 16.6 showshow you can accelerate depreciation even faster than with the declining balance method. It shows the results of using Excel's DDB (double declining balance) function:

The DDB function used for the data in Figure 16.6 is:

`=DDB(Cost,Salvage,Life,Year,2)`

Double declining balance doubles the rate that you would depreciate an asset under the straight-line method, and applies that rate to the original cost minus the sum of prior depreciation amounts.

Excel's DDB function allows you to use a value other than 2 as its fifth argument. If, for example, you did not want to double the straight-line rate per period, but instead use 1.5 times that rate, you could enter:

`=DDB(Cost,Salvage,Life,Year,1.5)`

Excel terms the final argument to the DDB function the *Factor*.

FIGURE 16.6

Depreciation using DDB (double declining balance) causes faster depreciation: compare with Figure 16.4 and 16.5.

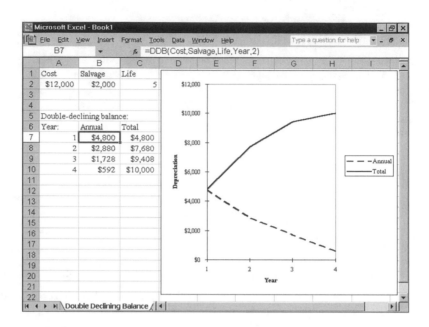

Using Variable Declining Balance Depreciation

The variable declining balance function (VDB) is the most flexible (and the most complex) of Excel's depreciation functions. VDB's general syntax is

```
=VDB(Cost,Salvage,Life,StartPeriod,EndPeriod,Factor,NoSwitch)
```

The Cost, Salvage, and Life arguments operate in exactly the same way as with the other depreciation functions. The Factor argument operates as it does in the DDB function: the larger the Factor argument, the faster that depreciation accumulates.

The StartPeriod and EndPeriod arguments enable you to focus on a particular time period during the asset's useful life. For example, to obtain the depreciation on an asset during the first year of a five-year Life, you could use this formula:

```
=VDB(Cost,Salvage,5,0,1,Factor,NoSwitch)
```

where using a StartPeriod of 0 and an EndPeriod of 1 specifies a span of time from when the asset is first placed in service until the end of the first period. Similarly,

```
=VDB(Cost,Salvage,5,0,.5,Factor,NoSwitch)
```

returns the depreciation on the asset during the first half of the first period. And this formula

```
=VDB(Cost,Salvage,5,1,3,Factor,NoSwitch)
```

returns the *total* depreciation on the asset that occurs during the second and third periods of its five-period life.

The NoSwitch argument is a little convoluted. Suppose that you specify a depreciation factor low enough that the asset does not fully depreciate to its salvage value during its useful life. Figure 16.7 illustrates this situation.

FIGURE 16.7
Depreciation using VDB (variable declining balance): NoSwitch is FALSE, so Excel switches to straight-line depreciation.

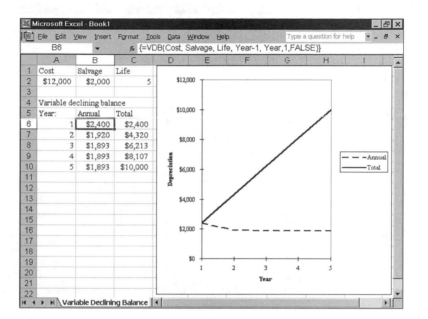

The array-formula used to return the annual depreciation amounts shown in Figure 16.7 is

=VDB(Cost, Salvage, Life, Year-1, Year,1,FALSE)

The depreciation factor is 1, and the NoSwitch argument is FALSE. Setting the NoSwitch argument to FALSE means that VDB switches to straight-line depreciation in the event that, and when, the straight-line depreciation for that period would be greater than the depreciation under declining balance. In Figure 16.7, the total accumulated depreciation over the five years of the asset's useful life is $8,068. This situation arises because the depreciation factor, 1, is so low that depreciation does not accumulate fast enough to fully depreciate the asset to its salvage value during five periods.

TIP Recall that accelerated depreciation methods depreciate faster early on than does the straight-line method. This means that they depreciate more slowly toward the *end* of the asset's useful life. Setting NoSwitch to FALSE causes VDB to use straight-line depreciation at the point that straight-line begins to depreciate faster than VDB.

This can occur when tax accounting regulations for a particular type of asset limit your accelerated depreciation factor to a relatively low value, given your estimate of the asset's useful life.

If you set the NoSwitch argument to TRUE, the VDB function *does not* switch to straight-line depreciation (see Figure 16.8).

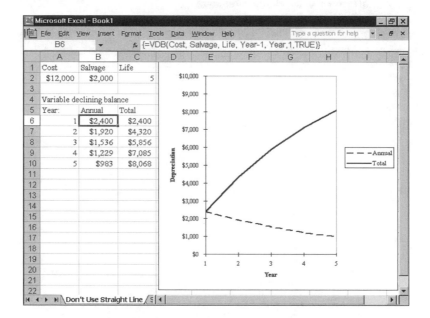

FIGURE 16.8

Depreciation using VDB (variable declining balance): NoSwitch is TRUE, so VDB does not switch to the straight-line method.

The array-formula used to return the depreciation in Figure 16.8 is

```
=VDB(Cost, Salvage, Life, Year-1, Year,1,TRUE)
```

Notice that, with NoSwitch set to TRUE, VDB continues to return smaller depreciation amounts in each period. The result is that the asset is not depreciated to its salvage value at the end of the final period. VDB would, however, fully depreciate the asset if the depreciation factor were, say, 2 instead of 1—in fact, it would depreciate the asset by the end of the fourth period.

Setting the NoSwitch argument to FALSE, as in Figure 16.7, causes the VDB function to return constant, straight-line depreciation values for periods 3 through 5 ($1,893). As has been discussed, one effect of this is to fully depreciate the asset to its salvage value by the end of the fifth period. Notice that the total depreciation by the end of the fifth period is $10,000, which is the difference between the asset's cost ($12,000) and its salvage value ($2,000).

Another effect of setting NoSwitch to FALSE is to increase the amount of depreciation taken in period 3: $1,893 in Figure 16.7 versus $1,596 in Figure 16.8.

TIP   You can replicate VDB explicitly with simple worksheet formulas. For any period, VDB is =MIN(Cost-Salvage-TotalSoFar),BookValue*Factor/Life) where TotalSoFar is the total depreciation taken in prior periods and BookValue is Cost-TotalSoFar.

Using Sum-of-Years-Digits Depreciation

Yet another method of accelerated depreciation, sum-of-years-digits, is shown in Figure 16.9:

FIGURE 16.9

The SYD (sum-of-years-digits) method is easy to understand, but gives you little control in situations such as mid-year asset purchases.

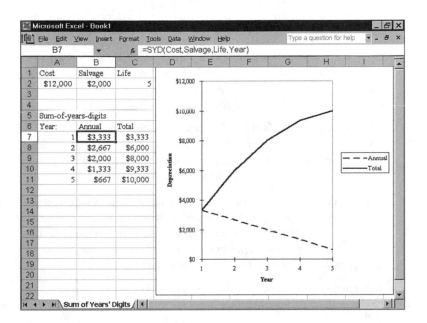

This method, which is used in Excel's SYD function, sums the number of years of the asset's useful life. For example, if the useful life is five years, the sum would be 1 + 2 + 3 + 4 + 5 = 15. Each year, this sum is divided into the *remaining* years of useful life. For example, during the first year, the fraction would be 4/15; during the second year, the fraction would be 3/15, and so on. The appropriate fraction for each year is multiplied by the difference between the asset's cost and its salvage value, to compute each year's depreciation expense.

Thus, in Figure 16.9, $2,000 will be taken in depreciation during the third period. At the beginning of period 3, there are three periods remaining in the asset's useful life (period 3, period 4 and period 5). Three remaining periods divided by the sum of the years digits is 3/15, or 20%. The difference between the cost and the salvage value is $12,000 – $2,000, or $10,000. Twenty percent of $10,000 is $2,000.

Summary

This chapter discussed the process of valuing fixed assets—usually defined as a company's property, plant, and equipment—for the purposes of determining the company's worth as well as its income for an accounting period.

An asset contributes to the creation of a company's revenue during the time that it is in service. The principle of matching expenses to revenue over time suggests that some portion of the expense involved in acquiring the asset be attributed to the revenue created during an accounting period. This is done by means of depreciation: even though the entire cash outlay for the asset usually occurs during the first accounting period, this expense is distributed across the useful life of the asset.

Excel offers five methods of calculating depreciation: straight-line, declining balance, double declining balance, variable declining balance, and sum-of-years-digits. The latter four methods adopt an accelerated approach, under which more depreciation is allocated early during an asset's useful life, and less is allocated later.

With all these methods at hand to determine depreciation, how do you select the appropriate method? The tax laws allow you to use different methods depending on the type of asset that you are depreciating. It's wise to check with your accountant to determine which method you should use for a particular kind of asset.

The depreciation method that you choose has an impact on the earnings that you show for a given period. If you depreciate quickly, early profits tend to be understated: you expense more depreciation early on and therefore reduce the earnings for those periods. If you depreciate slowly, early profits tend to be overstated because you do not expense as much in earlier time periods as you would if you accelerated the depreciation.

This chapter concludes Part III, "Investment Decisions." Part IV, "Sales and Marketing," begins with a discussion of the issues surrounding the recognition of revenue.

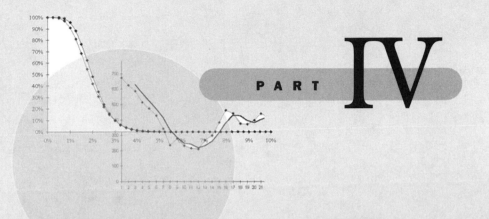

Sales and Marketing

Revenue Recognition and Income Determination

This book has had much to say about the matching principle: timing the occurrence of costs so as to match them with the occurrence of revenues. Depreciation, for example, is one way of doing so, by recording a portion of an asset's cost during the period that it helps to generate revenue. The entire basis for calculating profit, and determining how and why you make it, is accrual accounting and its corollary, the matching principle.

The other side of the coin hasn't yet been discussed: timing the occurrence of revenues to match them with the occurrence of costs. *Recognition* and *realization* are two closely related concepts that help you match revenues to costs. To recognize revenue is to record it in your company's books. To realize revenue is to determine that it has in fact been earned.

Revenue Recognition in Theory

Many—perhaps even most—companies use accrual as the basis of their accounting systems. Again, *accrual* means that when a company transacts business involving the receipt of revenue for a service or a product, they record the transaction when the transaction occurs. This can be, and often is, at a different time than when the revenue is actually in hand in the form of, say, a check.

The use of accrual accounting can make it more difficult to manage information about revenues and costs, because normally there are differences between the date of the transaction and the date that payment is received. It's important, then, to have standard procedures and rules in place that maintain the accuracy of the reporting, even if it is more difficult to do so.

The Financial Accounting Standards Board (FASB) is a private board, an advisory authority that is generally recognized by both the private sector (for example, the American Institute of Certified Public Accountants)and the public sector (for example, the Securities and Exchange Commission). It promulgates accounting guidelines as Generally Accepted Accounting Principles, or GAAP. One rationale for these rules is to help companies better understand how to use the theory of accrual accounting, as it applies to realization, revenue recognition, and income determination.

It's common to assume that the processes of realizing and recognizing revenue are one and the same. For accounting purposes, this is not always the case:

- *Recognition* is the act of recording revenue in the accounting records and reporting it in the financial statements.

- *Realization* is a more abstract process, used to determine when revenue should be recognized. Realization, applied to recognition, brings the issue of timing into the picture.

More formally, FASB has defined realization as the occurrence of an event that reduces uncertainty about future cash flows. Such an event makes the decision to objectively recognize revenue justifiable. When applied to GAAP, the following criteria are used to determine when you should treat revenue as realized:

- When you can determine the amount of the revenue, and when you know its timing, on an objective basis

- When the process of earning the revenue has been completed, or is virtually complete

Put differently, you should realize revenue—that is, decide that it is time to recognize it—and recognize it in the income statement when an event that is critical to the earning of revenue has occurred. Furthermore, you should do so when you can objectively measure the amount and timing of the revenue that you will receive.

For example, suppose that a bicycle shop sells a bicycle, but the buyer has not yet taken possession of it. The recognition of the sale takes place when the bicycle is sold, not when the buyer picks it up. The critical event is the sale of the bicycle, not the act of riding it away.

The Earning Process

The process of earning revenue has a great deal to do with when revenue recognition occurs. Consider two major industries: manufacturing and merchandising. These two industries have very different earning processes, but from the standpoint of recognizing revenue they are quite similar.

A manufacturing firm acquires materials for production, makes the finished product from the materials, sells it to a wholesaler, a retailer, or end user, and finally collects payment for the product. The sale and the collection of the payment might occur simultaneously. They might also occur over a long period of time, if the manufacturer and the customer have negotiated conditions for a long-term receivable.

The earning process for a merchandiser differs from that of a manufacturer in that the merchandiser acquires inventory, holds it for an indeterminate period, perhaps rotates it back to the manufacturer under an exchange agreement, advertises it, and so on. Although their operating activities are very different, their earning processes are identical.

Both a manufacturer and a merchandiser produce something: a manufacturer produces goods, and a merchandiser produces sales. Both assume that as their level of production grows, their level of income will also grow (see Figure 17.1).

Part

IV

Ch

17

FIGURE 17.1
Revenue recognition over time: it's normal to recognize revenue when the product is sold. It's coincidental if that's when payment is received.

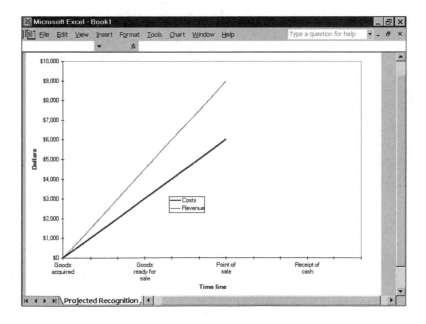

Figure 17.1 suggests a parallel assumption: that over time, costs grow along with revenues. It's easy to see how either a manufacturer or a merchandiser can incur costs during its production cycle. It's not quite so easy to see how they can be generating revenue—how they can

be realizing and recognizing it—before a sale is actually completed. And yet the matching principle requires that they associate revenues with costs as they occur.

To understand how this can happen, consider that there are four different times in the process of moving from production to sales when a company might recognize revenue:

- During production
- At the completion of production
- At the point of sale
- During the cash collection process

In practice, revenue is almost always recognized at the point of sale. However, there are a few exceptional cases when it might be necessary to recognize revenue either before the sale or subsequent to it. The remainder of this chapter describes each of the points in time that revenue can be recognized, along with the reasons for recognizing revenue at that point.

N O T E Although the discussion proceeds from the earliest time (during production) to the latest time (subsequent to sale), keep in mind that recognizing revenue before or after the point of sale is the exceptional case. ▩

Recognizing Revenue During Production

Some companies engage in long-term projects, in which the production of goods extends over several accounting periods. It's usually a straightforward process to assign those costs to the period in which they are incurred. But should any revenue be recognized during the course of production? And if so, how?

For example, suppose that it takes a prime contractor several years to complete construction of a major highway. Should the contractor recognize any portion of the expected revenue while the highway is under construction? So doing would help investors to better understand the revenue, cost, and profit implications of the contractor's current activities.

Therefore, the contractor should recognize some revenue during the construction period. If the contractor can make a reasonable determination of the amount and the timing of revenue, or if the earning process is virtually complete, then some portion of the revenue can and should be recognized during the construction process.

So, at least some revenue should be recognized prior to the completion of the project. How should the contractor determine the timing and the amount of revenue to recognize?

There are two ways to account for revenue recognition when long-term projects are in progress. These are the *percentage of completion* method and the *completed contract* method.

Using the Percentage of Completion Method

To determine how much revenue the contractor should recognize during any given period in a long-term contract, the contractor needs to know or estimate four quantities:

- The total price of the contract—that is, the price that the buyer will pay
- The total cost that the contractor will incur during the life of the construction project
- The cost that the contractor incurred during the current accounting period
- The percentage of the project that has been completed

Using the percentage of completion method, the contractor would estimate the total cost, the total price, and the current cost for the production that is in progress.

There are various convenient ways to determine the portion of the project that has been completed to date, but each is based on costs expended. For example, before the project begins, the contractor estimates the number of labor hours that will be needed to complete the project. This estimate is used as a base to determine the percentage of completion at a given point in time (see Figure 17.2).

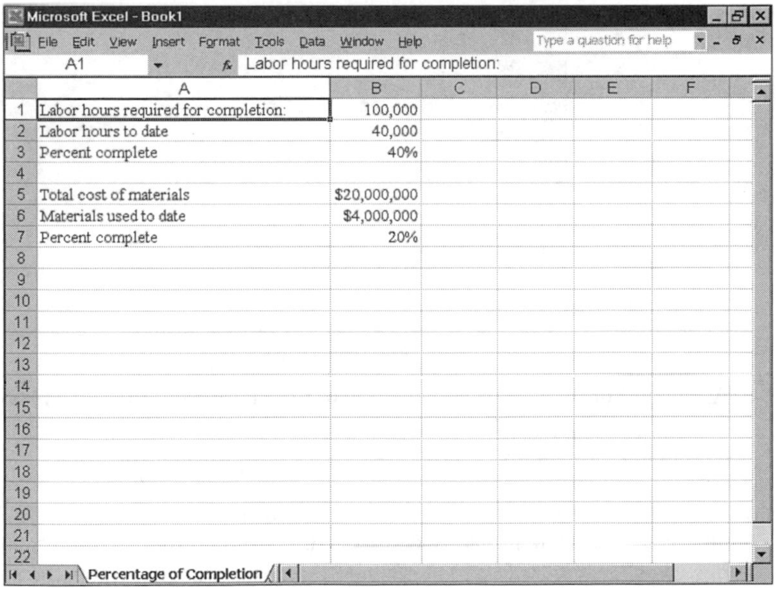

FIGURE 17.2
Determining percentage of project completion is one way to estimate costs and revenues while work is in progress.

Suppose that the contractor estimates that a total of 100,000 labor hours will be needed to complete the project. After the first year, 40,000 labor hours have actually been used, so it's reasonable to estimate that 40% of the project is complete.

Or, another contractor could compare the costs that have been incurred through the current date to the total estimated construction costs. For example, given an estimate of $20,000,000 in materials needed to complete the project and a first year cost of $4,000,000, the percentage of completion would be 20%.

For the purpose of recognition, the contractor applies the percentage of completion method at the end of each accounting period. The total contract price is compared to the estimated total contract cost to determine the estimated total income.

For example, suppose that a contractor wins a bid for a four-year building construction project, with a total price of $20,000,000 and with estimated total costs of $16,000,000. The estimated income from project completion is therefore $4,000,000 (see Figure 17.3).

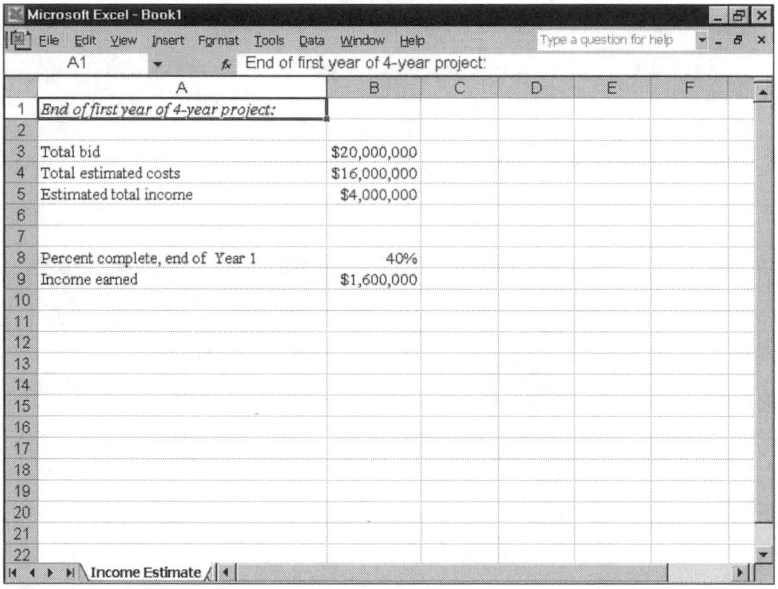

FIGURE 17.3

The percentage of project completion can be different than the percentage of time elapsed.

At the end of the first year, using one of the methods to measure percentage of completion, the contractor determines that the project is 40% complete; $8,000,000 should be recognized as revenue. Further, $1,600,000 should be recognized as income.

Now suppose that due to bad weather during the final year of the contract, progress slows, and only 90% of the project is complete after 48 months. The contractor estimates revenue *through* year 4 at 90% * $20,000,000 = $18,000,000, and subtracts the revenue that has already been recognized. So in this example, at the end of year 4 the total revenue to be recognized would be calculated as $18,000,000. Prior revenues of, say, $14,000,000 are subtracted, so revenues for year 4 are $18,000,000 – $14,000,000, or $4,000,000 (see Figure 17.4).

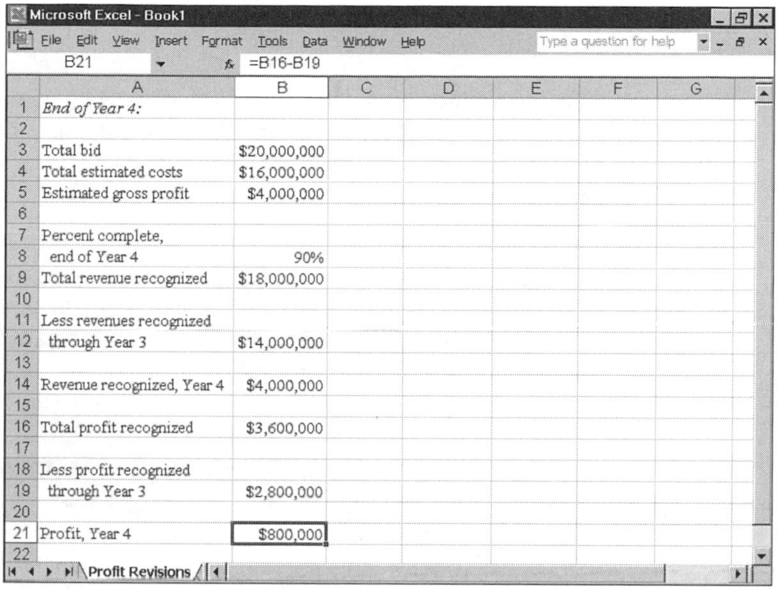

	A	B
1	*End of Year 4:*	
2		
3	Total bid	$20,000,000
4	Total estimated costs	$16,000,000
5	Estimated gross profit	$4,000,000
6		
7	Percent complete,	
8	end of Year 4	90%
9	Total revenue recognized	$18,000,000
10		
11	Less revenues recognized	
12	through Year 3	$14,000,000
13		
14	Revenue recognized, Year 4	$4,000,000
15		
16	Total profit recognized	$3,600,000
17		
18	Less profit recognized	
19	through Year 3	$2,800,000
20		
21	Profit, Year 4	$800,000
22		

FIGURE 17.4
It's important to re-estimate profit as a project nears completion: both revenues and income may have been over-recognized.

The Completed-Contract Method

The completed-contract method should be used when you cannot make reasonable estimates concerning the percentage of project completion. Using this method, revenue recognition occurs when deliverable products are transferred from seller to buyer once the project has been completed. Until this time, however, no revenue should be recognized.

In the highway construction example, if the contractor cannot make a reasonable estimate of either the total cost or total revenue, it might be appropriate to use the completed-contract method. Then, the contractor would recognize the entire $30,000,000 revenue, $20,000,000 in costs, and $10,000,000 in gross profit in the final year of the project. By that point, it should be possible to determine these amounts with reasonable accuracy.

Recognizing Revenue at Completion of Production

For certain types of commodities, such as agricultural products and some precious metals, it is best to recognize revenue when production is complete. To recognize revenue when production has been completed, it is necessary to meet the following criteria:

- The product is sold in a market with a reasonably assured selling price.
- The costs of selling and distributing the product are not significant and can be reasonably estimated.

■ Production is considered the most critical event in the earning process, not the sale itself.

For example, the most critical event in a wheat farmer's earning process is the harvesting of the grain, not the act of selling the grain. This is because the grain price has already been determined by the marketplace. In fact, in the commodities markets, options to buy or sell at a certain price are often negotiated well in advance of the actual production of the commodity.

Once again, the recognition of revenue using the completion of production method, as distinct from its recognition using some other method, is purely a timing issue. For example, suppose that a farmer harvests grain in late 1995, sells 75% of the harvest in 1995, and sells the remainder in 1996. According to the completion of production method, the total value of the farmer's harvest would be recognized in 1995. Using the point of sale method (see the next section), 75% would be recognized in 1995 and 25% in 1996 (see Figure 17.5).

FIGURE 17.5

Assigning revenue to accounting periods at completion of production can cause full recognition prior to the point of sale.

	A	B	C	D
1	*Completion of production*			
2		Percent of harvest complete	Sales made	Amount recognized
3	Activities, 2001	100%	$56,250	$75,000
4	Activities, 2002	0%	$18,750	$0
5				
6	*Point of sale*			
7		Percent of harvest complete	Sales made	Amount recognized
8	Activities, 2001	100%	$56,250	$56,250
9	Activities, 2002	0%	$18,750	$18,750

Of course, the total revenue recognized is the same using both the completion of production and the point of sale methods. Using completion of production, the producer might recognize $75,000 in 1995. Using the point of sale method, the producer might recognize $56,250 in 1995 and $18,750 in 1996. The difference lies in *when* the revenue is recognized.

Recognizing Revenue with the Point of Sale Method

Without a sale a company would not generate revenue, and for many businesses the sale itself is the most important part of the entire earning process. It is for this reason that most companies use the point of sale as the point of revenue recognition. As a rule of thumb, a sale takes place when one or more of the following events takes place:

- Ownership of goods is transferred to a buyer
- Services are performed
- Asset services (such as apartment rentals) have been provided

Revenue recognition at the point of sale is the most intuitive method, and can be the least complicated of the possible methods of recognizing revenue. A sale has been made and cash is received; the revenue is recognized immediately because there is no uncertainty about the timing of cash flows. Point of sale also represents the completion of the earning process because the merchandise has been physically transferred to the buyer.

While apparently simple, recognizing revenue at the point of sale can be complicated by factors such as these:

Part
IV
Ch
17

- Sales made on credit
- Trade and cash discounts
- Uncollectible accounts
- Costs related to the sale that are incurred after the date of sale
- Return privileges on merchandise sold

Each of these factors can snap the direct connection between the point of sale and the recognition of revenue, making it necessary to accrue costs or revenues into some later period. Their effects, and how to resolve them, are discussed in the next section.

Making Sales on Credit

When you make a sale on credit, you record the revenue from the sale net of any discounts, and at the value of the merchandise at the time of the sale.

For example, assume that your store sells a sweater in April, to a customer who uses a credit card to make the purchase. The price of the sweater at the time of the purchase is $56. Your store is offering a discount of 10% from list during April (see Figure 17.6).

The buyer puts the purchase on a credit card and does not pay it off until three months from the time of purchase. Based on the criteria described previously, the sale would be recorded for $50.40 in revenue: the present value at the time of sale of $56 less the 10% purchase discount.

When a business deals with credit sales, it is normal to establish a special kind of account called a *contra-revenue* account. There are different kinds of contra accounts, such as contra-liability and contra-asset (for example, depreciation is one kind of contra-asset account, because it continually reduces the value of depreciable assets). You use a contra-revenue account to allow for uncollectible sales.

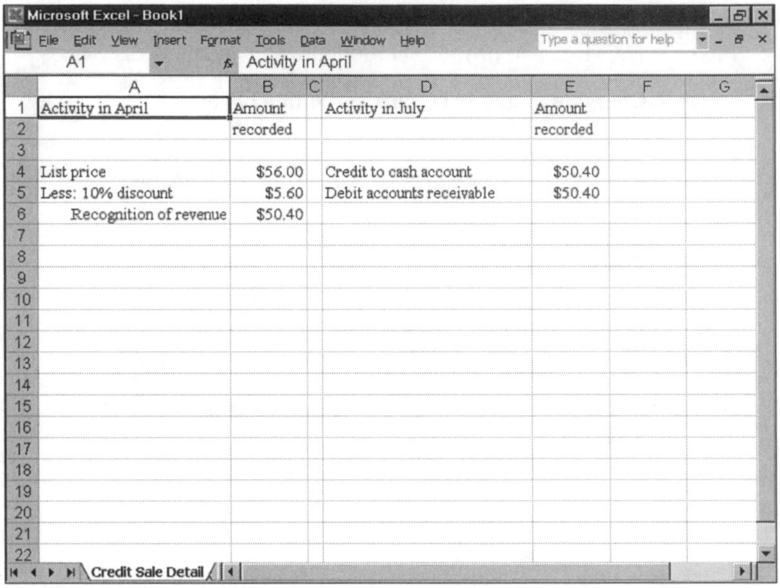

	A	B	C	D	E
1	Activity in April	Amount		Activity in July	Amount
2		recorded			recorded
3					
4	List price	$56.00		Credit to cash account	$50.40
5	Less: 10% discount	$5.60		Debit accounts receivable	$50.40
6	Recognition of revenue	$50.40			

FIGURE 17.6
Recognizing net income from a credit sale occurs when the sale is made; additional postings occur when payment is made.

Not all consumers pay off their credit debts, so the seller must make estimates for those credit sales that will never be collected to present a true picture of actual cash flows. Usually, this is done by using historical data: for example, you might find that over the past five years, it has proved impossible or impractical to collect 3% of the apparent revenue from your credit sales. Figure 17.7 depicts this situation.

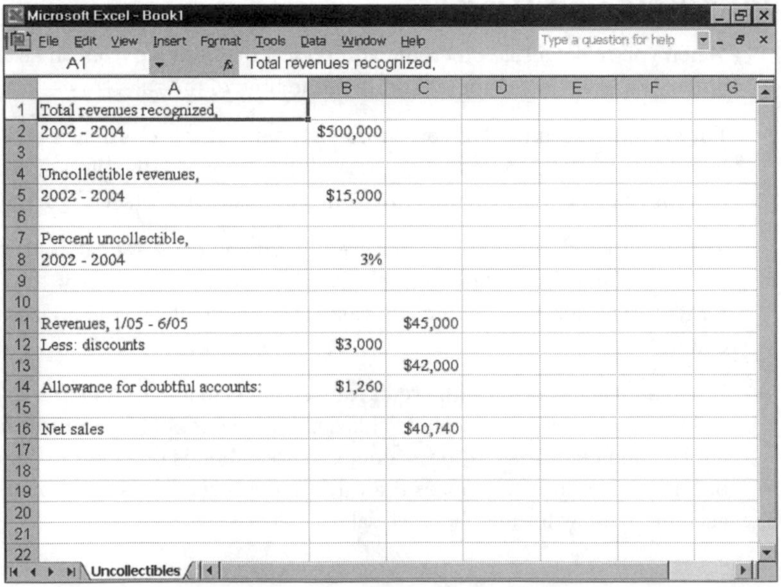

	A	B	C
1	Total revenues recognized,		
2	2002 - 2004	$500,000	
3			
4	Uncollectible revenues,		
5	2002 - 2004	$15,000	
6			
7	Percent uncollectible,		
8	2002 - 2004	3%	
9			
10			
11	Revenues, 1/05 - 6/05		$45,000
12	Less: discounts	$3,000	
13			$42,000
14	Allowance for doubtful accounts:	$1,260	
15			
16	Net sales		$40,740

FIGURE 17.7
Accounting for doubtful collectibles by means of a contra account helps to prevent the over-estimation of revenue.

Therefore, you might use a contra-revenue account to allow for the sales during the current period that turn out to be uncollectible. You would record 3% of the current period's sales in the contra account, and use it as an offset to Sales (along with other offsets such as Sales Discounts) to arrive at a Net Sales figure for the period.

Incurring Costs After the Point of Sale

Using the point of sale method, even though revenue is recognized at the time of the sale, it does not necessarily follow that the earning process is complete. In some cases, you incur costs associated with selling a product after the sale itself has been made. However, you need to estimate and accrue these costs as of the time of the sale.

For example, if you sell cameras, you will very likely include a warranty as a part of the sale. According to accrual accounting, the cost of servicing that warranty must be estimated and recognized and accrued at the time of sale. In this way, revenues and associated expenses are recorded at the same time.

Allowing for Returns Privileges

In some types of sales, the buyer can return the item for various reasons. In fact, in many states, the buyer can even cancel a sale made somewhere other than the seller's normal place of business, without citing a reason of any sort.

For revenue recognition purposes, the seller needs to make some assumptions about how much revenue might be returned to the customer, and include this assumption in the amount of revenue that is recognized. Just as with uncollectible credit sales, an allowance for expected returns should be used, at the date of sale, as a contra-revenue account in order to properly measure the expected cash flows resulting from the sale.

Recognizing Revenue During the Cash Collection Process

As mentioned before, there are certain criteria that must be met before revenue can be recognized at the point of sale. It was also mentioned that complications occur when you recognize revenue at the point of sale, and when those sales are made on credit. In some cases the complications due to credit sales are so great that the collection of the amounts due for those sales become highly uncertain. In that case, revenues should not be recognized at the point of sale.

This is the sort of situation that might call for the application of the concepts and methods for recognizing revenue during the cash collection process. There are two ways to do so: the installment method and the cost recovery method.

Part
IV

Ch
17

Using the Installment Method

If the criteria for point of sale revenue recognition have been met, you would simply recognize the revenue for installment sales at the point of sale.

However, if the criteria are not met (for example, the collection period on credit sales extends well beyond the normal time in which a credit sale should be paid, and there is no reasonable basis for estimating uncollectibles), then you might use the installment method to recognize the revenues associated with these sales. The basis for the installment method is that gross profit on the sale of the goods in question is deferred. Recognition occurs over time, as the cash is collected.

For example, suppose that a company sells stereos on a deferred payment plan. The total sale price for a stereo is $500, and the plan requires a $100 down payment, with the remaining payments to be made over the next 10 months. Each of the stereos sold costs $400 to produce. You can calculate the amount of revenue to be recognized under the installment method as follows:

```
Gross Profit Percentage = (Sales - Cost of Goods Sold)/Sales
```

```
=($500 - $400) / $500 = 20%
```

So, in this example, each time that additional cash is collected over the 10-month period, 20% of the cash would represent profit and the remaining 80% of cash would be used to recover costs. If the remaining $400 in sales is collected over the 10-month period, the company receives $40 each month.

Twenty percent of the $40, or $8, is recognized as gross profit and $32 would be used to recover costs of producing the stereo. These calculations are shown in Figure 17.8.

FIGURE 17.8

Recognizing revenues using the installment method pushes recognition past the point of sale.

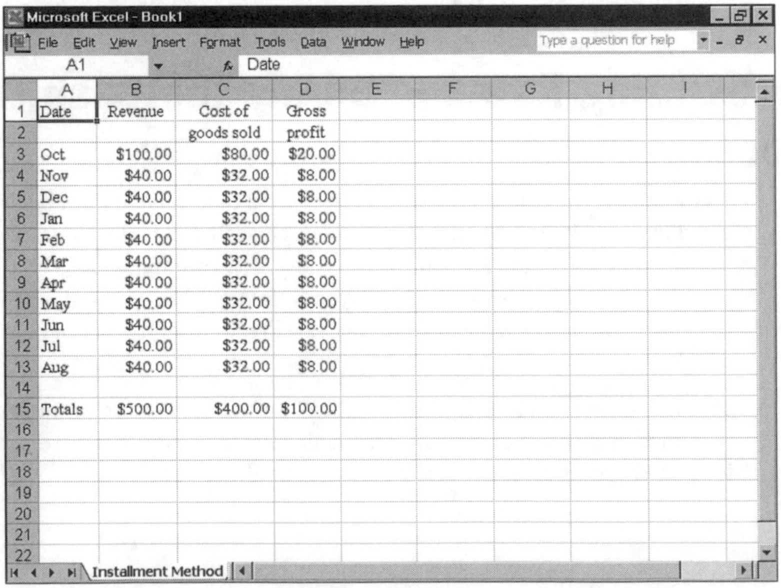

	A	B	C	D
1	Date	Revenue	Cost of	Gross
2			goods sold	profit
3	Oct	$100.00	$80.00	$20.00
4	Nov	$40.00	$32.00	$8.00
5	Dec	$40.00	$32.00	$8.00
6	Jan	$40.00	$32.00	$8.00
7	Feb	$40.00	$32.00	$8.00
8	Mar	$40.00	$32.00	$8.00
9	Apr	$40.00	$32.00	$8.00
10	May	$40.00	$32.00	$8.00
11	Jun	$40.00	$32.00	$8.00
12	Jul	$40.00	$32.00	$8.00
13	Aug	$40.00	$32.00	$8.00
14				
15	Totals	$500.00	$400.00	$100.00

N O T E   Although the installment method is not used frequently in the preparation of financial statements, it is sometimes used in the preparation of income tax records. By deferring the recognition of income until it is actually in hand, a company might be able to adjust its tax liability to its benefit. ▪

Using the Cost Recovery Method

Under the cost recovery method, no revenue is recognized on credit sales until the cost of the product sold has been fully recovered by cash collections. When enough cash has been collected to recover the costs, any remaining cash collections are reported as income in the period in which they are collected.

To continue the example given previously, if a stereo was sold in October of 1995 with a $100 down payment and $300 additional was received by April of 1996, the $400 cost of the stereo would then have been recovered. Using the cost recovery method, therefore, all cash collected from May to June 1996 would be recognized as income during the remaining two months (see Figure 17.9).

FIGURE 17.9
Distributing recognition by means of the cost recovery method.

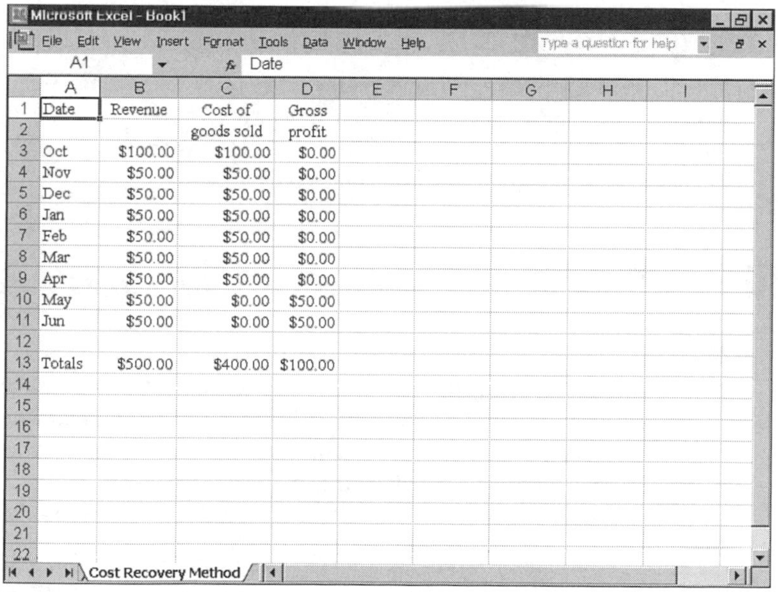

	Date	Revenue	Cost of goods sold	Gross profit
3	Oct	$100.00	$100.00	$0.00
4	Nov	$50.00	$50.00	$0.00
5	Dec	$50.00	$50.00	$0.00
6	Jan	$50.00	$50.00	$0.00
7	Feb	$50.00	$50.00	$0.00
8	Mar	$50.00	$50.00	$0.00
9	Apr	$50.00	$50.00	$0.00
10	May	$50.00	$0.00	$50.00
11	Jun	$50.00	$0.00	$50.00
13	Totals	$500.00	$400.00	$100.00

This method is occasionally used when there is a great deal of uncertainty surrounding the profitability associated with a new venture or contract.

Recognizing Revenue in Different Industries

Although the methods of revenue recognition are standard across all industries, industries differ as to the methods they use to implement recognition.

Recognizing Revenue in Service Industries

Revenue recognition in service industries is composed of four different methods. These four methods are described here:

- The *specific performance method* occurs when performance of a service consists of a single act. Under this method, revenue is recognized when the service has been completed.

- The *proportional performance method* occurs when several similar acts are performed. Under this method, revenue is recognized as it is under the percentage of completion method.

- The *completed performance method* occurs when more than one act is required and the final act is considered the critical event in the earning process. Under this method, the revenue recognition process is similar to the completed production method.

- The *collection method* is used when there is a great deal of uncertainty surrounding the collectibility of revenue. Under this method, revenue is recognized only when cash collection has been made.

Recognizing Revenue in Manufacturing Industries

Manufacturing industries operate on the same basis for revenue recognition as do service industries. The primary difference is that a large portion of manufacturing operate on long-term contracts. As described previously, the methods specific to long-term projects include the percentage of completion and completed contract methods.

Understanding the Impact of Revenue Recognition Methods

No matter which method of revenue recognition you use, the eventual, total amount of recorded revenue should be the same. What differs is the time at which the revenue is recognized. The timing of revenue recognition carries significant implications for different aspects of your business. For example, if your firm's primary activity is sales, then the timing of revenue recognition can become critical both to you and to your employees.

Suppose that you compensate your employees by means of commissions, and that commissions are paid when revenue is recognized. If, as is very likely, you recognize revenue on a point of sale basis, then your employees have an advantage. This is because you must pay them their commissions no matter when you actually receive the cash payment from the customer.

On the other hand, if you recognize revenue only at the completion of a contract, you will have the advantage because you will not have to pay commissions on earnings not yet recognized. You might have received payment, but you can defer the commission expense until the contract is complete.

There are various ways to structure sales commission plans, and many companies structure their plans to benefit both the company and the employee. One deceptively straightforward plan is to pay 40% of the commission at the point of sale, and to pay the remaining 60% at the time payment is actually made. Notice that, depending on the recognition method you use, you could record the cost of the full commission amount as of the point of sale, and defer the actual cash payment of 60% of the commission until you receive the full amount due from the customer.

Summary

Part
IV

Ch

17

Under accrual-based accounting, the realization and the recognition of revenue are critical to determining a company's financial position at any given time. In this chapter, you have seen how different circumstances can alter this timing.

Normally, you will find it both necessary and expedient to recognize revenue at the point of sale, along with its associated costs and the profit that results. However, the critical event that produces the revenue is not always the sale itself, or a project that generates revenue extends over a very long period of time, or certain subsequent events make it difficult to determine the revenue amount as the sale occurs. In such cases, it can be necessary to alter the timing of the recognition.

CHAPTER 18

Importing Business Data into Excel

Chapter 3, "Valuing Inventories for the Balance Sheet," discussed how a small retail establishment named Evans Electronics manages its inventory, both with regard to counts of different products and valuation. That case study mentioned that the company keeps its sales information in a true database file. Evans Electronics imports the information into Excel when it is time to close the books on an accounting period.

In choosing to bring data into Excel from a database, isn't Evans Electronics needlessly complicating things? After all, you can store data in Excel worksheets by means of structures that Excel terms *lists*. And Excel provides many approaches to extracting data from lists, from AutoFilter to the various Lookup functions to pivot tables.

All true. And for a very small application it probably *would* be overkill to involve a true database, one managed by Microsoft Access or Oracle or some other system. But managing data isn't what Excel does best. Excel is designed and optimized to synthesize, analyze, and display data. It has some rudimentary database capabilities, and you should use them when your judgment tells you that the tradeoff favors simplicity over power.

In the same way, Access has some rudimentary analysis tools, built-in functions such as Sum and Avg (average). But if your application requires as straightforward a statistic as the median, you'll want to get Excel involved. While Access doesn't calculate the median for you, Access is a *lot* better than Excel at data storage.

The point is that Excel's strengths are in calculating results with functions and displaying data with charts and formatted worksheets. The strengths of a database manager such as Access have to do with storing, indexing, and retrieving data very efficiently.

Perhaps most telling is that database managers are designed to be multi-user applications. When you have more than one user who wants to modify the same record, and when they want to do so simultaneously, then you have the potential for conflicts. Good database management systems have the tools to handle these issues, and those tools were built into them when they were first designed.

Applications such as Excel also have tools for resolving multi-user conflicts. But those tools were included late in the day, tacked on as afterthoughts. They *can't* work as well as tools that are integral to the design of the application. They weren't intended to and they don't.

But Excel does have methods that let you integrate it tightly with true database management systems. If you use these methods, you can create systems that leverage the strengths of the database management system as well as those of the worksheet. This chapter covers several of the available methods, including Microsoft Query, Data Access Objects, and Web queries.

Creating and Using ODBC Queries

The acronym ODBC stands for Open Database Connectivity. It's a standard that many database programs and database management systems subscribe to. If you have a data source, such as an Access database, that is what's called ODBC-compliant, then you can import data from it into Excel.

But just because the standard exists and software manufacturers use it doesn't mean that all databases have the same structures. To make sure that these databases can be used in conjunction with other applications the manufacturers provide *drivers*—in this context, a driver is software that applications such as Excel can use to establish a connection to the database.

When you install Microsoft Office, the setup routine automatically installs several drivers, including ones for Access, Paradox, dBASE, and SQL Server. Early in the process of importing data from a database into Excel, you need to identify which kind of database you intend to use. This informs Excel which driver Excel should use to connect with the database.

After you have identified the type of data source you want to use, you also must provide a *query*. A query is a sequence of instructions written in a standard language called Structured Query Language, often abbreviated as SQL and pronounced "sequel." Those instructions provide information such as what tables in the database are to be used, which fields in a table are needed, and whether to apply any criteria in selecting records to retrieve.

Microsoft Office comes with a program named Microsoft Query. Shortly after you start the process of importing data from a database, Microsoft Query starts to run. It helps you design the query that will retrieve the records you want from the database. Depending on whether or not you arranged for the Office setup routine to install Microsoft Query you may need to have the Office installation CD handy.

Once the data source is identified and the query created, the data is automatically imported into Excel. As you will see, you need to go through this process only once for any given query. Your specifications are saved and Excel will subsequently update the data so that you can be sure you are using the most current information in the database.

Bear in mind that importing data from a database into Excel is a two-step process: you need to identify a data source and you need to construct a query. The next two sections provide the details on how that's done.

Specifying Data Sources

When, back in Chapter 3, Evans Electronics closed its books on its first accounting period, it needed to import sales data from its Access database into Excel. Were you the owner, you would have taken the following steps to specify the data source:

1. With an Excel workbook open (and preferably a blank worksheet active) choose Data, Import External Data, New Database Query. The Choose Data Source dialog box appears, as shown in Figure 18.1.

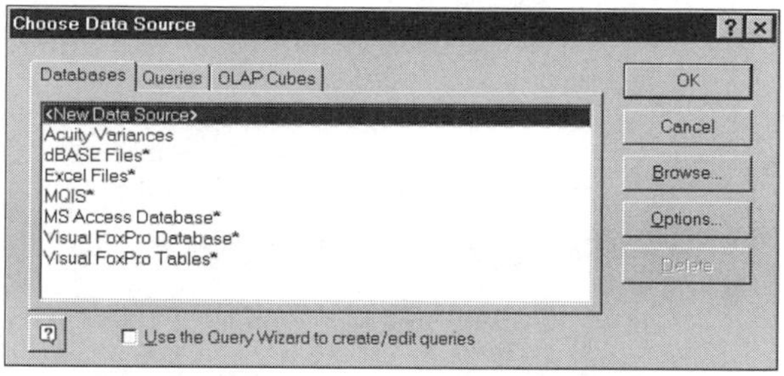

FIGURE 18.1
The Databases list box contains the names of installed drivers and data sources you have already specified.

2. Select New Data Source from the list box and click OK. The Create New Data Source dialog box appears (see Figure 18.2).

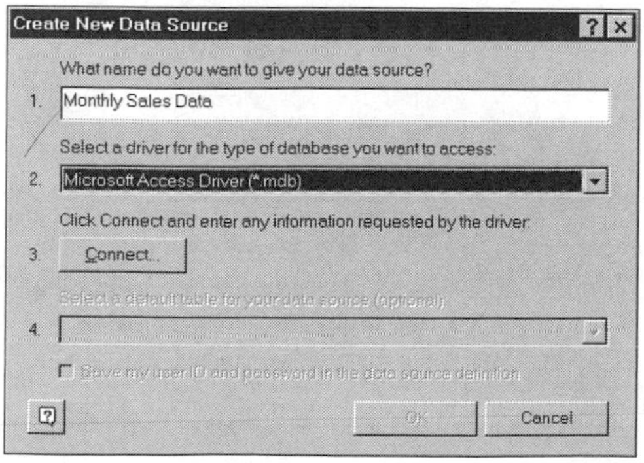

FIGURE 18.2
The combo boxes and buttons in items 2, 3, and 4 become enabled only after you make your selection for the preceding item.

Part
IV

Ch
18

3. Type a descriptive name such as **Monthly Sales Data** in the text box found in item 1. This name will appear in the Choose Data Source dialog box the next time it opens.

4. Click the down arrow in the combo box found in item 2. The drop-down list displays the available drivers. For this example, choose Microsoft Access Driver (*.mdb). (Microsoft Access databases all have the .mdb filename extension.)

5. Click Connect. The ODBC Microsoft Access Setup dialog box appears, as shown in Figure 18.3.

FIGURE 18.3

In the case of Access, a System Database contains information about database permissions for specific users and groups.

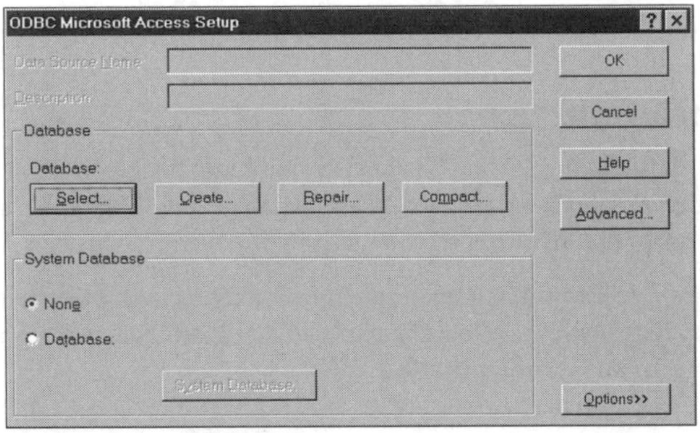

6. Click Select to open the Select Database dialog box, shown in Figure 18.4, and then browse to the database you want to use. In this example, you would browse to Evans Electronics.mdb.

FIGURE 18.4

In a networked environment, it helps to put the Excel workbook in the same folder as the source database, in case a drive letter gets remapped.

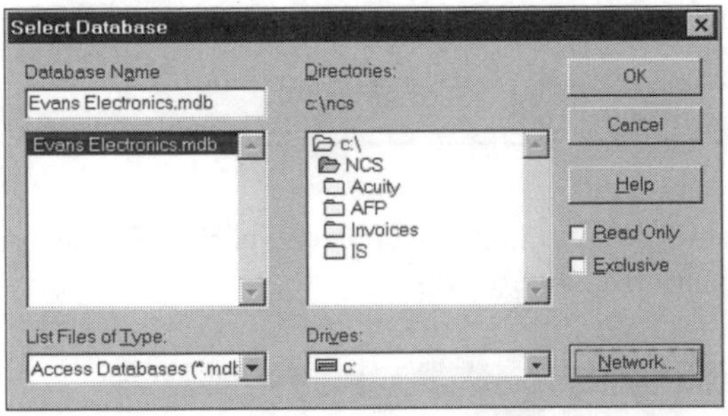

TIP

Suppose that the database is located on a network server, and it's not convenient to store the database and Excel workbook in the same folder. In that case it's best to use a Universal Naming Convention (UNC) address instead of a drive letter such as H:\. From time to time, drive letters are remapped and no longer point to the location they did when you specified your data source. Your network administrator can give you the UNC address for the server. It will usually have a pattern such as \\EvansServer\UserData\Sales\. Type that sequence followed by the database name and extension into the Database Name box shown in Figure 18.4.

7. Click OK to close the Select Database dialog box, and OK to close the ODBC Microsoft Access Setup dialog box. You are returned to the Create New Data Source dialog box. Click OK to close it, too.

N O T E Notice the combo box in item 4 of the Create New Data Source dialog box (refer to Figure 18.2). When clicked, it displays a list of the available tables and queries. You can usually skip this, because you will usually be selecting a table (or tables, or an existing query) next anyway. ■

These seven steps are all that's needed to specify a data source. A couple of items were skipped over that occasionally will be important:

■ In the Choose Data Source dialog box (see Figure 18.1) there is a checkbox labeled Use the Query Wizard to create/edit queries. If you fill that checkbox you will create the query itself by using the Query Wizard—not unlike the guided sequence of steps that constitute Excel's Chart Wizard or PivotTable Wizard. If you leave the checkbox cleared, you will use Microsoft Query directly and you won't be guided through the process. The tradeoff is one of convenience for power: the Query Wizard is easier to use, but offers less functionality. To use Microsoft Query directly requires some experience, but gives you more control over the process.

■ The Create New Data Source dialog box (see Figure 18.2) also has a checkbox, one that enables you to save your user ID and password with the data source definition. If your database requires you to supply a user ID and password you can avoid having to do so every time you execute a query against this data source. Just fill the checkbox. But bear in mind that the data source definition is just an ASCII file. Anyone who knew where to look could open the data source definition with something as simple as Notepad, and learn your user ID and password. As you will see in a subsequent section in this chapter, "Working with External Data Ranges," you can save your ID and password in an encrypted format when you work with the query itself. So it's usually best to leave this checkbox cleared.

Creating Queries with the Query Wizard

The first major step in importing the external data into Excel is now complete: you have specified your data source. The second major step is to create the query to extract records from that data source.

Suppose that you filled the checkbox on the Choose Data Source dialog box (refer to Figure 18.1) so that the query will be created with the Query Wizard. In that case the Query Wizard – Choose Columns dialog box shown in Figure 18.5 appears as soon as you've finished specifying the data source.

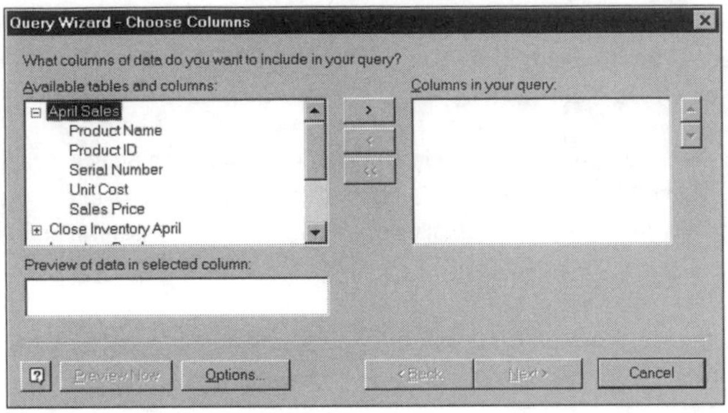

FIGURE 18.5
Use the Options button to specify that you want to see tables only, views (another term for queries) only, or both.

Continue by following these steps:

1. Examine the Available Tables and Columns list box. If the box to the left of April Sales contains a plus sign, click it to display the columns in April Sales.

2. Select Product Name and then click the > button to move your selection into the Columns In Your Query list box. Because the standard multiple selection shortcut keys (Shift and Ctrl) do not work here, each item needs to be moved individually. Continue as previously and move Product ID, Serial Number, Unit Cost, and Sales Price. Click Next.

N O T E   You can preview the values in the currently selected field by clicking the Preview Now button. If you do so, keep in mind that not all values in the table appear in the Preview of Data in Selected Column box. Only unique values appear there.

3. The Query Wizard – Filter Data dialog box appears, as shown in Figure 18.6. The Query Wizard is not as powerful as is Microsoft Query itself, and allows you to filter on one column only; however, you can specify multiple conditions for that single column. In contrast, Microsoft Query does not limit the number of columns you can use as filters.

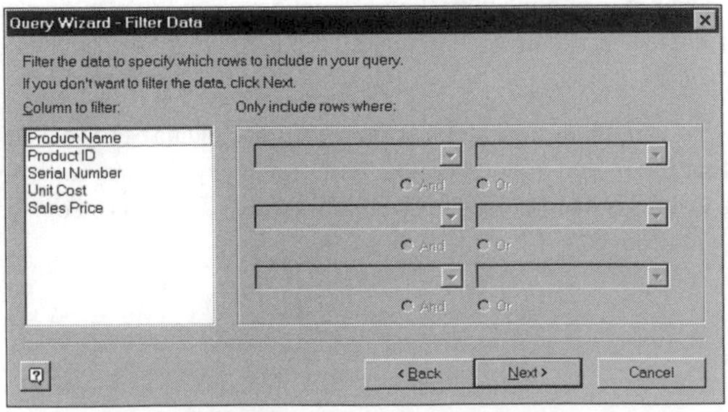

FIGURE 18.6
To filter data is to exclude records that do not meet your selection criterion.

4. April Sales, selected in Step 1 previously, contains only sales made during April. No other filtering is needed, so click Next. The next step in the wizard, the Query Wizard – Sort Order dialog box, appears as shown in Figure 18.7.

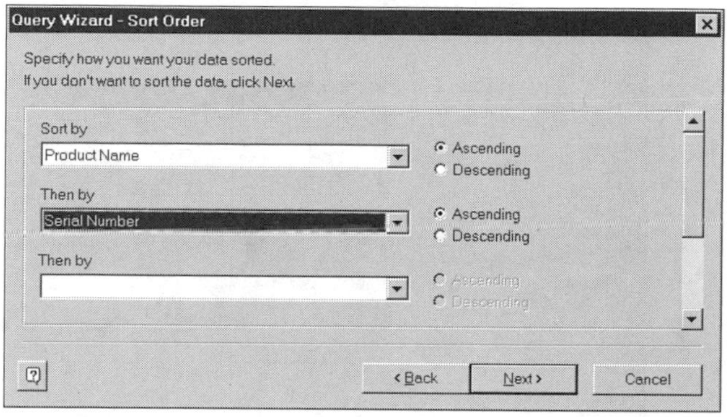

FIGURE 18.7
Use the vertical scroll bar at the right of the dialog box to display more sorting combo boxes.

5. It's useful to return the data to Excel sorted first by Product Name and then by Serial Number. It's generally more helpful to see data in some kind of order rather than in a random sequence. Use the Sort By drop-down list to select Product Name, and the first Then By drop-down list to select Serial Number. This creates a nested sort: records are sorted by Serial Number within each level of Product Name. Click Next.

6. The Query Wizard – Finish dialog box appears (see Figure 18.8) where you can choose to return the data to Excel, view the data in Microsoft Query, or create an OLAP cube. Click Finish.

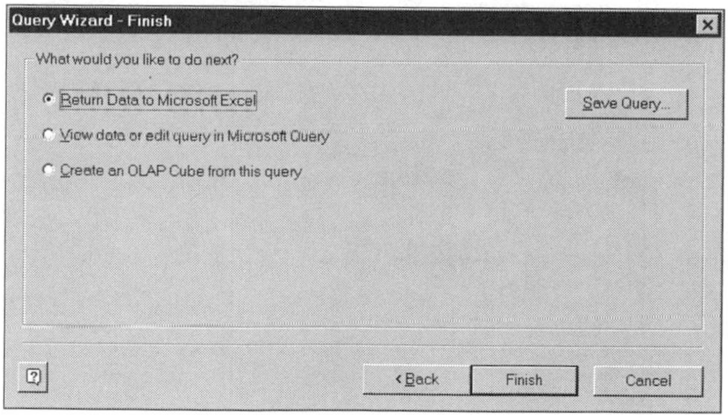

FIGURE 18.8
Choose Create an OLAP Cube from this query only if you're dealing with a huge number of records.

7. The Import Data dialog box appears, as shown in Figure 18.9. Use it to identify where on the active worksheet, on another existing worksheet, or on a new worksheet, you want to locate the data. Click OK.

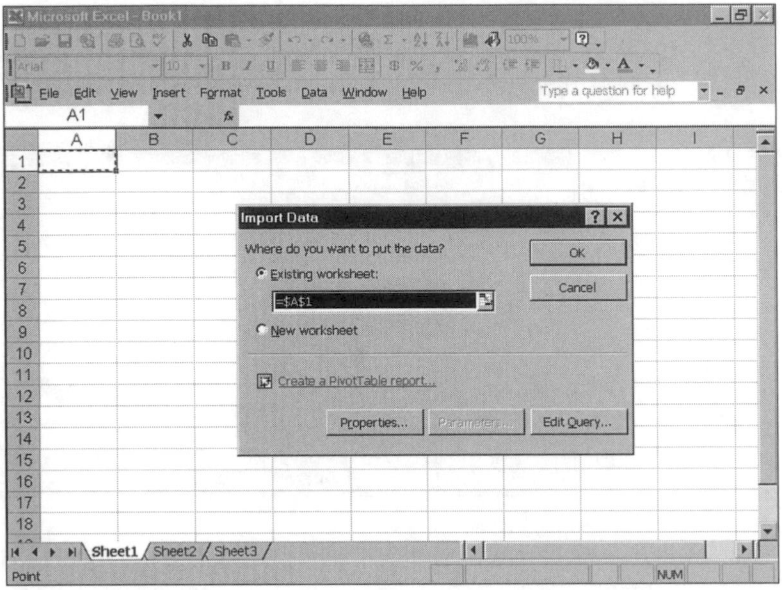

FIGURE 18.9
Because you began with the Query Wizard, clicking Edit Query here takes you to the Choose Columns step of the Wizard.

The data appears on the worksheet as shown in Figure 18.10.

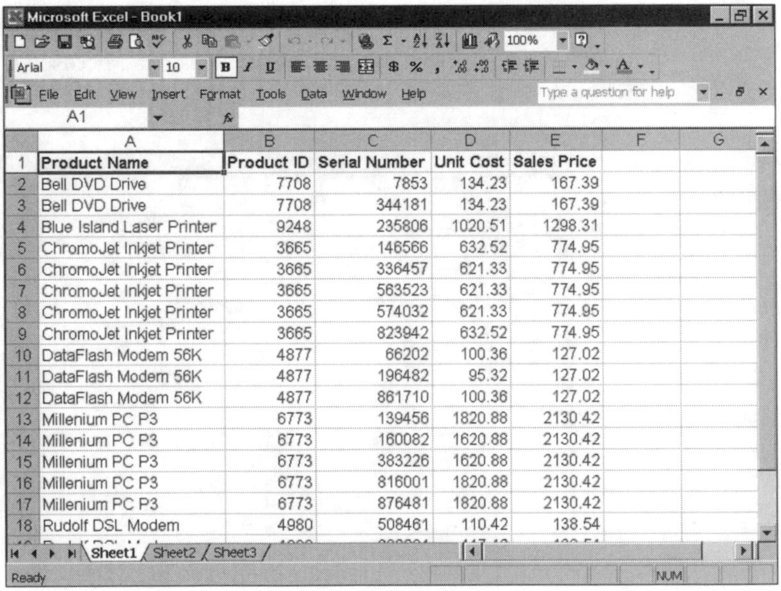

FIGURE 18.10
The data appears as an Excel list: fields in columns, records in rows, and a header row with the field names.

	A	B	C	D	E	F	G
1	**Product Name**	Product ID	Serial Number	Unit Cost	Sales Price		
2	Bell DVD Drive	7708	7853	134.23	167.39		
3	Bell DVD Drive	7708	344181	134.23	167.39		
4	Blue Island Laser Printer	9248	235806	1020.51	1298.31		
5	ChromoJet Inkjet Printer	3665	146566	632.52	774.95		
6	ChromoJet Inkjet Printer	3665	336457	621.33	774.95		
7	ChromoJet Inkjet Printer	3665	563523	621.33	774.95		
8	ChromoJet Inkjet Printer	3665	574032	621.33	774.95		
9	ChromoJet Inkjet Printer	3665	823942	632.52	774.95		
10	DataFlash Modem 56K	4877	66202	100.36	127.02		
11	DataFlash Modem 56K	4877	196482	95.32	127.02		
12	DataFlash Modem 56K	4877	861710	100.36	127.02		
13	Millenium PC P3	6773	139456	1820.88	2130.42		
14	Millenium PC P3	6773	160082	1620.88	2130.42		
15	Millenium PC P3	6773	383226	1620.88	2130.42		
16	Millenium PC P3	6773	816001	1820.88	2130.42		
17	Millenium PC P3	6773	876481	1820.88	2130.42		
18	Rudolf DSL Modem	4980	508461	110.42	138.54		

Creating Queries with Microsoft Query

As you become more comfortable with the process of querying a database, you might become impatient with the Query Wizard. You may want to exercise more control over the structure of the query: after all, that's what defines which records are returned, in what order, with which fields, and so on. This section shows you how Evans Electronics returns its April sales data, bypassing the Query Wizard.

You can invoke Microsoft Query in several ways. One is to start from scratch: Choose Data, Import External Data, New Database Query. In the Choose Data Source dialog box (refer to Figure 18.1) clear the checkbox labeled Use the Query Wizard to create/edit queries. Continue with the data source definition until you click OK on the Create New Data Source dialog box. Now instead of the Query Wizard, Microsoft Query appears.

If you're not starting from scratch you can use Microsoft Query to edit an existing query. The existing query will have returned data to an Excel worksheet, as shown in Figure 18.10. The worksheet range that the data occupies is termed the *external data range*. Right-click in the external data range and choose Edit Query. Microsoft Query appears as shown in Figure 18.11.

Part
IV

Ch
18

FIGURE 18.11
If you're creating a new query, the Add Tables dialog box appears automatically when Microsoft Query starts.

Table pane

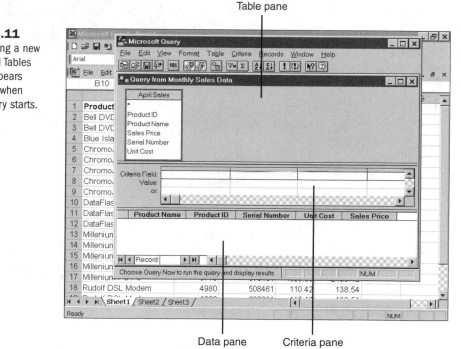

Data pane   Criteria pane

There are three panes in the Microsoft Query window:

- Put tables and existing queries from the active database into the Table pane. In Figure 18.11, for example, you see April Sales in the Table pane.

- Specify the criteria you want to apply to the records in the Criteria pane. This pane does not appear automatically when Microsoft Query starts, unless you are editing an existing query that contains criteria. To establish the Criteria pane, choose View, Criteria.

- Put the fields that you want the query to return into the Data pane. You can drag field names from a table into a Data pane column, or double-click a field name in a table, or choose a field name from the drop-down box at the top of the Data pane.

Suppose that it's now the end of May and you want to return the May sales data to Excel. Follow these steps:

1. If a table is visible in the Table pane, remove it by clicking on it and then choosing Table, Remove Table.

2. Choose Table, Add Tables to open the Add Tables dialog box as shown in Figure 18.12.

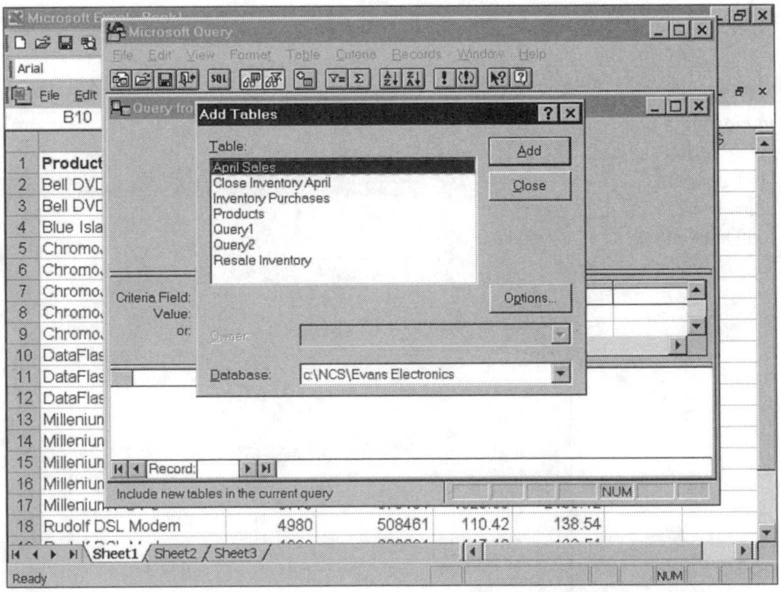

FIGURE 18.12

If the active database is in a folder with other databases, you can add a table from one of them by using the Database drop-down list.

3. Click Resale Inventory in the Table list box, and click Add. Click Products in the Table list box, and click Add. Click Close.

4. In the Products table, double-click the Product Name field.

5. In the Resale Inventory table, double-click Product ID, Serial Number, Unit Cost, and Sales Price.

6. If you do not see the Criteria pane, choose View, Criteria. Click in the first column of the Criteria row. The cell becomes a drop-down box. Click its arrow to view a list of available fields. Click *Resale Inventory.Date Sold*. It appears in the Criteria row as *Date Sold*, no longer qualified by its table name.

7. In the Value row below the criterion *Date Sold*, type **Between 5/1/2001 And 5/31/2001** and then press Enter. Notice that Microsoft Query surrounds the date values with pound signs as separators.

8. If you want, you can choose Records, Query Now to see the records that Microsoft Query will return to Excel. The Microsoft Query window should now appear as shown in Figure 18.13.

FIGURE 18.13

If the active database is in a folder with other databases, you can add a table from one of them by using the Database drop-down list.

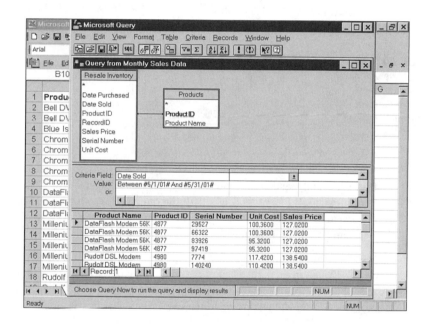

9. Choose File, Return Data to Microsoft Excel. The Microsoft Query window disappears and the Import Data dialog box appears (refer to Figure 18.9).

Consider some of the other actions you might have taken while Microsoft Query was active. You could have added another criterion, or even several, by putting more field names into the Criteria Field row and appropriate expressions into the Value row. Using the Query Wizard you're limited to one field as a criterion.

You can specify a sort order on one or multiple fields. Click on a field name in the Data pane and then click the Sort Ascending (or the Sort Descending) button. To sort on multiple fields, arrange the field names contiguously in the Data pane. Click the leftmost field name for the sort, press Shift, and click the rightmost field name; this selects the fields simultaneously. Then click one of the Sort buttons. (The Query Wizard does allow you to sort on multiple fields.)

Creating Parameterized Queries in Microsoft Query

Had the owner of Evans Electronics read this book, he would not have found it necessary to create a query to return April sales records and a separate one to return records from May. He would have known that he can create a *parameterized query*, which would prompt him for the range of sales dates he wants to import from the database.

Step 7 in the previous section specified that the criterion for the Date Sold field should be entered as Between 5/1/2001 And 5/31/2001. Evans can arrange to be prompted for a new range of dates if instead he enters something similar to Between [Enter the Starting Date] And [Enter the Ending Date] as the criterion value.

If he does so, Evans can refresh the data whenever he wants and he will be prompted to enter a starting date. See Figure 18.14.

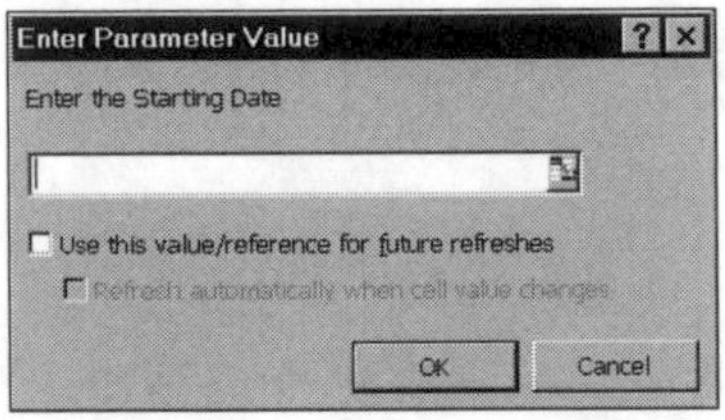

FIGURE 18.14

A parameterized query can be used repeatedly to return records that meet the user's changing requirements.

After entering a starting date such as 5/1/2001 and clicking OK, Evans is prompted to enter an ending date. If he enters 5/31/2001, the query returns from the database all records whose Date Sold field is between 5/1/2001 and 5/31/2001, inclusive. This is much more efficient than creating a new query for each accounting period.

This is another example of how Microsoft Query gives you more control than does the Query Wizard. You cannot create a query that prompts you for criteria using the Query Wizard. You can enter something such as [Enter a Start Date] in the Filter Data step of the Query Wizard, but if you do you will get an error message when you click Finish.

Using Joins in Microsoft Query

Notice the dark line that connects the Resale Inventory and the Products tables in the Table pane in Figure 18.13. It is termed a *join line*, because it shows how two tables are joined. It's not the purpose here to discuss relational database design in great detail, but you will find it useful to understand a few aspects of joins.

In the Evans Electronics database, the full names of the products are stored in the Products table, along with a product ID, a unique numeric value for each product name. The product ID is also stored in the Resale Inventory table. Each time a sale is recorded, it is the product ID rather than the product name that is recorded. There are many good reasons for taking this approach: data integrity, ease of data entry, and conserving disk space are three.

When it comes time to view the data, you want to see the product name, not just its ID. So you join the table with the ID of the product that was sold, Resale Inventory, to the table that contains the product name, Products. You join the tables by means of the field they have in common, Product ID. When the query runs, it notes the value of Product ID in Resale Inventory, finds the corresponding Product Name in the Products table, and returns it to the screen where you can see it or to Excel where you can save it.

Microsoft Query creates the join line in the Table pane on your behalf if the tables meet two conditions:

- The common field (in this instance, Product ID) has the same name in both tables. If the fields have incompatible data types (for example, in one table it's text and in the other table it's numeric), Microsoft Query will draw the join line but it won't function as intended and you'll get an error message.

- The common field is the key field (in Microsoft Access jargon, a *primary key*) in one table. A primary key is a field that contains no duplicate values and serves to uniquely identify a particular record.

If the designer of the database did not fulfill these two conditions, Microsoft Query will not create the join line for you. You can do it yourself by clicking the common field in one table, holding down the mouse button, and dragging to the common field in the other table. When you release the mouse button Microsoft Query draws the join line between the two fields.

Joins can have powerful effects and they have a variety of uses beyond the rather simple one described here. Joins are in fact the foundation of relational database design. If you find that you frequently have reason to import from a database into Excel you will want to become familiar with the different types of joins and their uses. A book on Microsoft Access, one published by Que for choice, would be a good next step.

Part

IV

Ch

18

Working with External Data Ranges

When you have imported data into a worksheet as the previous section described, you have more than just the data set itself. A new range name is automatically defined, and refers to the range of cells defined by the fields and records that were returned. That data range has properties that you can manipulate. You can access the properties by clicking the Properties button on the Import Data dialog box (see Figure 18.9).

But it's usually best to have a look at the data before you start changing the ranges properties. You can modify the properties after the data has been written to the worksheet. Just right-click any cell in the external data range and choose Data Range Properties from the shortcut menu. When you do so, the External Data Range Properties dialog box appears, as shown in Figure 18.15.

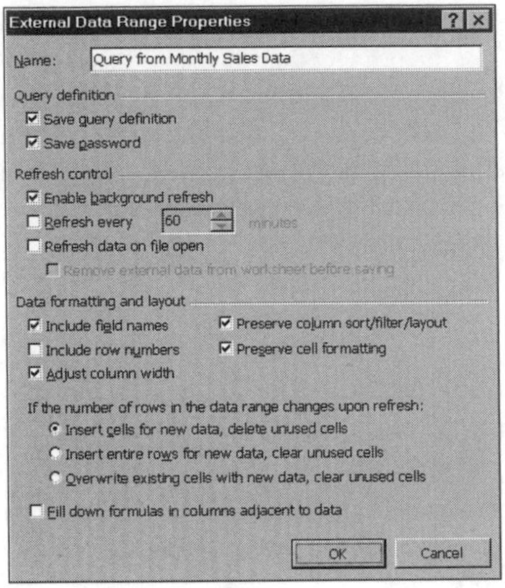

FIGURE 18.15
Give some thought to how you set these properties: they can make your analyses much easier to carry out.

Setting Security Information

Refer to Figure 18.8 and notice that the Finish step of the Query Wizard contains a checkbox that you can use to save the query. Filling that checkbox has much the same effect as filling the checkbox labeled Save My User ID and Password in the Data Source Definition in Figure 18.2.

Saving the user ID and password *with the data source definition* can compromise the security of a database. When you save a query by using the checkbox in the Query Wizard, you save not only the information that defines the query but also save the data source definition.

It's a little circuitous, but the chain of events is logical. Suppose that the database requires you to supply a password. You choose to save the ID and password with the data source definition. Subsequently you choose to save the query, in the Finish step of the Query Wizard. So doing saves yet another ASCII file, with the SQL of the query and the data source definition, which contains the ID and password.

Of course it's convenient to save that information. If it's saved, you don't need to supply it each time you want to run the query and get more data. But it's the rule, not the exception, that information in business databases is sensitive—the information ranges from employee social security numbers and salaries to confidential medical information concerning hospital patients. If you've taken care to guard the database by means of passwords, you're endangering its security by leaving the passwords strewn around in unprotected disk files.

That's where the external data range properties come in handy. Figure 18.15 shows that two of the properties you can set are Save Query Definition and Save Password. If you fill either or both checkboxes, that information is saved on the Excel worksheet *in hidden names*. If a snoop can open the workbook, he can see the data that's been returned from the database, but at least he can't tell what the password is. And saving the query definition in this way means that it doesn't need to sit out there unprotected.

Both checkboxes are filled by default, so both a password and the query definition are saved unless you specify otherwise.

If it's a serious outcome for someone who's unauthorized to see the data, you should password protect the workbook as well as the database. To protect the workbook, use Tools, Protection, Protect Workbook to supply and confirm a password.

Arranging Automatic Refreshes

It's possible to waste a lot of time working with a set of data that's not current. One way to prevent this from happening is to update the data automatically. Excel refers to the process of updating the data as *refreshing* it.

You can refresh the data yourself whenever you want. Right-click on any cell within the external data range and choose Refresh Data from the shortcut menu; or, left-click any cell in that range and choose Refresh Data from the Data menu. If you clear the Save Query Definition checkbox, Excel loses information about the query and you cannot subsequently refresh the data, either manually or automatically: you have to re-establish the query.

Using the external data range properties you can arrange for the data to be refreshed automatically. One good way is to fill the Refresh Data on File Open checkbox, on the External Data Range Properties dialog box. Then, save the workbook. With that checkbox filled, each time you open the workbook the query will run again. That ensures that you are working with all the records in the database that meet your query's criteria.

If you fill the Refresh Data on File Open checkbox, you automatically enable the checkbox labeled Remove External Data from Worksheet before saving. This option is helpful only if the query has returned a large number of fields and records. Then, if disk storage space is a concern, you might want to use this option to clear the data prior to a save.

There might be times that you work with a database that contains an extremely large number of records. In that case the query can take quite some time to return the records to Excel—the wait can easily be several minutes. The problem is that you won't have control of Excel until the query has completed running.

If you encounter this situation, make sure that the Enable Background Refresh checkbox is filled. That way you'll be able to continue using Excel while the query executes. The tradeoff is that a background refresh often causes more time to elapse between starting the query and its completion.

Particularly if you're querying from an active database, one that constantly acquires new data, you might want to refresh Excel's data automatically while you have the workbook open. If so, fill the Refresh Every X minutes checkbox and use its spinner to set the refresh frequency.

Setting Other Data Range Options

With the records laid out as a row of field names followed immediately by rows of records, with each field occupying a different column, they are arranged properly for input to a pivot table or a chart. That's why it's usually helpful to see the names of the fields on the worksheet. If you find it so, fill the Include Field Names checkbox.

Sometimes database administrators use field names that are more arcane than useful. In that case, consider supplying your own labels on the worksheet and start the external data range below them. Of course it's your responsibility to make sure that, for example, the field that contains revenue information is the one lined up below your Revenue label.

Filling the Include Row Numbers checkbox is seldom useful and can be misleading. Because records can be returned by a query in many different orders, a particular record is not uniquely and consistently identified by its row number. If someone noted that, say, Mr. Smith was in row number 5 in your data range, that person might expect to find information about Mr. Smith in database record number 5. (Believe it: this happens and causes no end of confusion when it does.) If you do decide to include row numbers, be aware that many databases start counting at Row 0.

Importing Data into Pivot Tables and Charts

If the eventual destination you have in mind for imported data is a pivot table or pivot chart, there's no particular reason to import the data into an external data range. You can bring the data directly into the pivot table.

Begin by choosing Data, PivotTable and PivotChart Report. The PivotTable Wizard's first step appears, as shown in Figure 18.16.

FIGURE 18.16
The pivot chart report must initially be accompanied by a pivot table but if you want you can delete the table later.

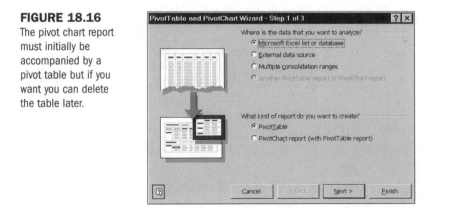

Choose the External data source option. When you click Next, the wizard's second step appears as in Figure 18.17.

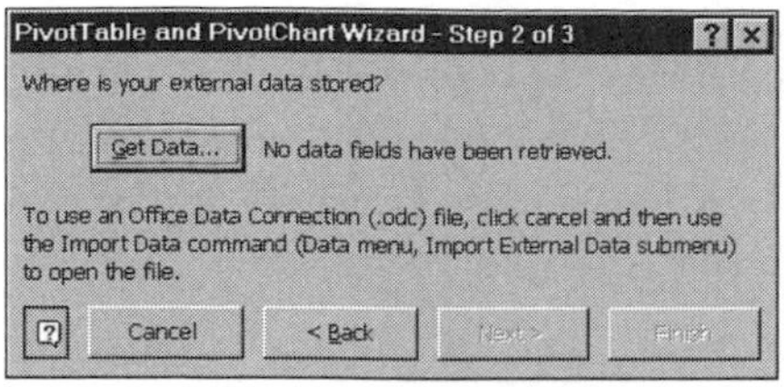

FIGURE 18.17
Follow the instructions on this dialog box to put an odc file into a pivot table.

When you click Get Data, the Choose Data Source dialog box appears. You have seen this dialog box before, in Figure 18.1. And in fact the entire process from this point is identical to that illustrated in Figures 18.1 through 18.13, from defining a new data source (or using an existing source) to defining the query (or, again, using an existing query).

At the end of the process you dismiss Microsoft Query by choosing File, Return Data to Microsoft Excel (or you dismiss the Query Wizard by clicking Finish). Instead of seeing the Import Data dialog box you see the PivotTable Wizard's second step. At this point you can click Next to get to the third step, if you want to set options, or just click Finish. The pivot chart appears, ready for you to locate the fields, as shown in Figure 18.18.

FIGURE 18.18
Drag the Product Name field into the Category Fields area and the Sales Price field into the Data Items area.

Data Items area

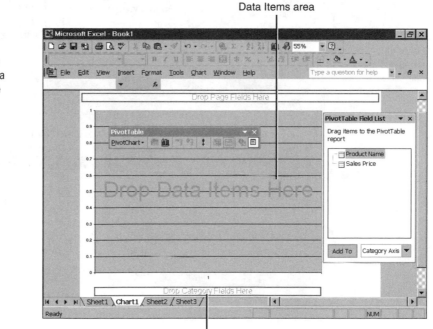

Category Fields area

Creating and Using Web Queries

Chapter 7, "Ratio Analysis," discussed a variety of indicators of a company's financial status. It did not go into detail about where to find those indicators or how best to get them into an Excel worksheet. This section shows you one good way.

A Web query is a special kind of query: it obtains data not from a database but from Web pages, which are usually constructed using Hypertext Markup Language (HTML) or one of its variants such as Extended Markup Language (XML). Web queries return data from the Web page directly to your Excel worksheet.

Required is Excel 2000 or 2002 and a Web connection. If you have those, you're ready to go.

1. Choose Data, Import External Data, New Web Query. The New Web Query dialog box opens to the Home page you've specified for your browser (see Figure 18.19).

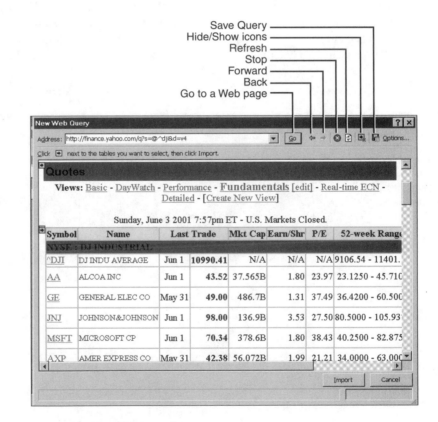

FIGURE 18.19
Web queries do not retrieve graphics to your workbook.

2. Type your destination's URL in the Address box and click Go, or select it from the Address drop-down list. The Web page shown in Figure 18.19 contains a table with EPS and P/E ratios.

Notice the squares with the arrows inside them pointing right. These are termed *icons*, somewhat unhelpfully. Their purpose is to indicate the location of a table that you can import, and they are located at the upper-left corner of those tables. When you click one its arrow turns into a checkmark.

3. After you have finished selecting tables by clicking their icons, click the Import button at the bottom of the dialog box. Excel imports the data into your worksheet (see Figure 18.20).

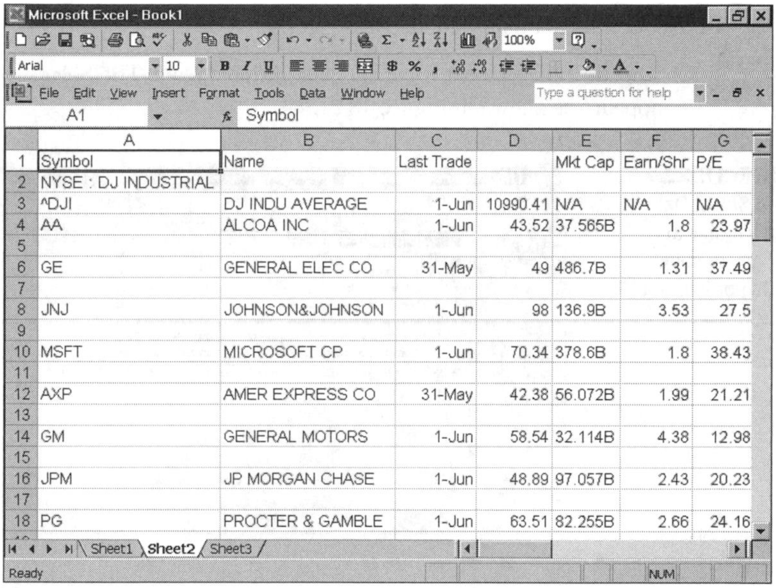

FIGURE 18.20
Just like an external data range, this information updates when you right-click in it and choose Refresh Data.

	A	B	C	D	E	F	G
1	Symbol	Name	Last Trade		Mkt Cap	Earn/Shr	P/E
2	NYSE : DJ INDUSTRIAL						
3	^DJI	DJ INDU AVERAGE	1-Jun	10990.41	N/A	N/A	N/A
4	AA	ALCOA INC	1-Jun	43.52	37.565B	1.8	23.97
5							
6	GE	GENERAL ELEC CO	31-May	49	486.7B	1.31	37.49
7							
8	JNJ	JOHNSON&JOHNSON	1-Jun	98	136.9B	3.53	27.5
9							
10	MSFT	MICROSOFT CP	1-Jun	70.34	378.6B	1.8	38.43
11							
12	AXP	AMER EXPRESS CO	31-May	42.38	56.072B	1.99	21.21
13							
14	GM	GENERAL MOTORS	1-Jun	58.54	32.114B	4.38	12.98
15							
16	JPM	JP MORGAN CHASE	1-Jun	48.89	97.057B	2.43	20.23
17							
18	PG	PROCTER & GAMBLE	1-Jun	63.51	82.255B	2.66	24.16

Part
IV

Ch
18

The toolbar buttons shown in Figure 18.19 are used as follows:

- Go: Takes you to a Web page. Use this button if you've typed a URL into the Address box.
- Back, Forward, Stop, and Refresh: These work just as in a standard browser, taking you to a prior or subsequent page, stopping the refresh of a page, and initiating the refresh of a page.
- Hide/Show icons: Suppresses the icons that indicate the location of tables, or displays them. If you suppress them, all tables on the page are returned when you click Import.
- Save query: Saves your query definition in a separate file. This makes it convenient to re-use in a different workbook.

The Options button displays some choices that enable you to preserve the Web page's formatting, such as colors and fonts.

Using Parameterized Web Queries

"Creating Parameterized Queries in Microsoft Query" earlier in this chapter showed how you can create queries that have one or more parameters. A parameter prompts you for a selection criterion that must be met by any records it returns to Excel.

Microsoft Office comes with some Internet query files, which have the filename extension .iqy. These queries also have parameters, which make them handy for returning from the Web information about companies you specify.

To use an Internet query, follow these steps:

1. Choose Data, Import External Data, Import Data. The Select Data Source dialog box appears as shown in Figure 18.21.

FIGURE 18.21
Use the Select Data Source window to invoke any existing database or Internet queries.

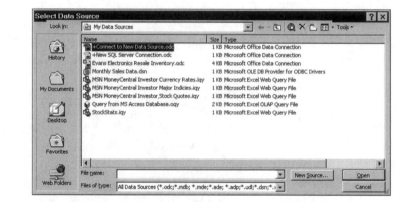

2. Select either MSN MoneyCentral Investor Currency Rates or MSN MoneyCentral Investor Major Indicies (sic), depending on whether you're interested in currency exhanges or stock index figures. Click Open.

3. The Import Data window appears (refer to Figure 18. 9). Correct the cell reference if necessary and click OK. The Internet query returns the data to Excel. An example of the stock index query results appears in Figure 18.22.

N O T E   If the Import Data command is disabled when you choose Data, Import External Data, it is likely that the active cell is part of an existing external data range. The data may have been cleared away but the range name and the underlying query are still in place. Click the down arrow in the Name box to display any range names. If you see one that could represent an external data range, click it to select it; then, choose Edit, Clear, All. You will see a warning message that asks you if you want to remove the query along with the data range. Assuming that you want to do so, click Yes. The Import Data command should now be enabled. ▪

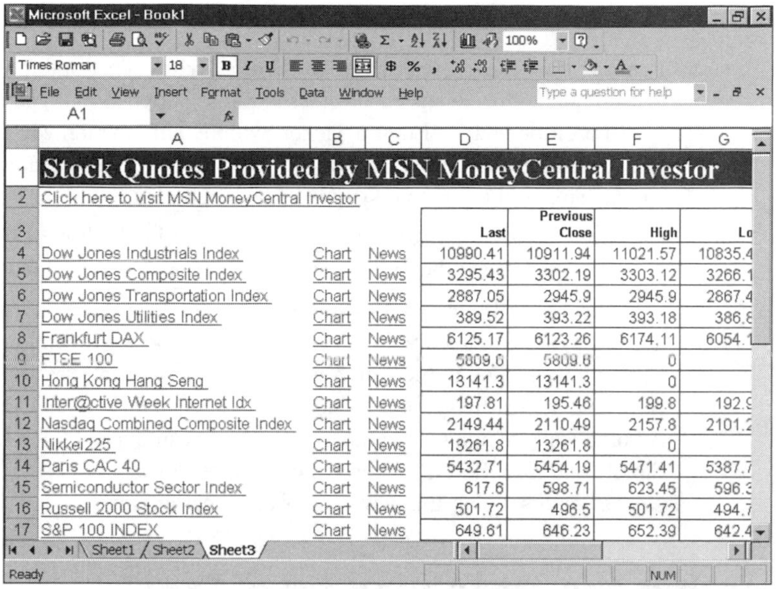

FIGURE 18.22
Click one of the CHART hyperlinks to see, in your browser, a 52-week chart of that index's performance.

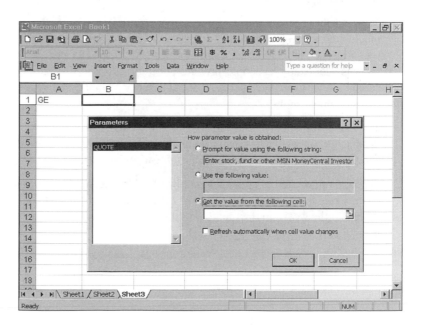

There is something different about the MSN MoneyCentral Investor Stock Quotes Internet query. Begin by entering a stock ticker symbol in a worksheet cell. Then, choose Data, Import External Data, Import Data. Select MSN MoneyCentral Investor Stock Quotes in the Select Data Source window and click Open. You see the Import Data window, but with the Parameters button enabled. If you click the Parameters button, the window shown in Figure 18.23 appears.

FIGURE 18.23
This window also appears when you right-click a cell in the external data range and click Parameters in the shortcut menu.

You have three options. Your choice controls how the data is subsequently refreshed.

- **Prompt for Value Using the Following String.** This option is similar to the parameterized query that Evans Electronics created. Suppose that you select this option, and type a prompt such as Enter a Ticker Symbol. Later, when you refresh the data, you will see that prompt and a box where you can enter a new ticker symbol. The query will be executed using that symbol as its parameter.

- **Use the Following Value.** If you select this option its box becomes enabled and you can type a ticker symbol into it. The query automatically returns data for that symbol.

- **Get the Value from the Following Cell.** It was suggested that you begin by entering a ticker symbol in a worksheet cell. Now you choose this option, click in the associated box, and then click in the worksheet cell where you entered the symbol. The query returns data for the symbol in the cell. If you also fill the checkbox labeled Refresh Automatically When Cell Value Changes, you can bypass the Refresh Data command. Simply enter a different ticker symbol in that worksheet cell and the query automatically executes, using the new symbol as its parameter.

Updating the Database from Excel

Throughout this chapter, you have learned various ways to get data from Web sites and databases into Excel workbooks. There are times when you want to reverse the process: to move data that you have in an Excel workbook to a database.

The reasons to do so have to do with both user convenience and technical issues. There are many people who find an Excel worksheet a familiar, even intuitive work environment, but feel at a complete loss when working directly with a database program.

Many database programs, of course, can present information to the user in a grid that looks much like an Excel worksheet, with rows and columns. But in a technical sense the tables are very different. In a database program such as Microsoft Access, the rows always represent records—for example, people, products, or transactions—and columns always represent variables—for example, a person's Social Security Number, or a product's name, or a transaction's account number.

The Excel worksheet is much less rigid. While Excel lists require the same structure as a database, you may have many other uses for rows and columns, and this flexibility is one reason that some people are more comfortable with the worksheet.

Suppose you wanted to create a monthly calendar in Excel. It's easy enough to let the first column represent Sundays, the second Mondays, and so on. And you can let four or five rows represent the weeks in the month. Put the number of the day in each cell's upper-left corner by setting the cell's alignment format.

You can't do these things in a database because it's not primarily intended to be a display mechanism. But the attractive and functional display of information is one of Excel's great strengths. There are ways that you can provide a user, whether yourself or someone else, with the comfortable and flexible Excel interface, and yet use that interface to put data directly into a database. To do so requires some ability to program in VBA, a BASIC dialect. The remainder of this chapter demonstrates how Evans Electronics can use VBA and Data Access Objects (DAO) to move data the other direction, from its Excel workbook to its Access sales database.

Structuring the Worksheet

Evans begins by creating the worksheet shown in Figure 18.24.

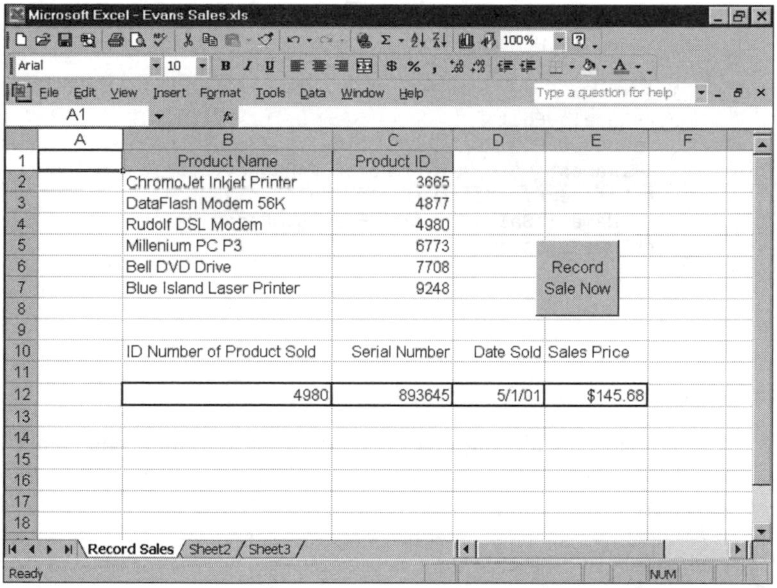

FIGURE 18.24
The worksheet provides a convenient place for Evans to record data that describes a sale.

Evans uses cells B12:E12 to enter the sales information. Each cell in that range has been named: Product_ID, Serial_Number, Date_Sold, and Sales_Price. Evans uses the table at the top of the sheet as a reminder of the numeric product ID that's associated with the product name.

Because Evans wants to uniquely identify a particular item sold, it's necessary to supply both the product's ID number and serial number. Suppose that by coincidence both a Rudolf DSL modem and a Bell DVD drive had the same serial number. In that case, supplying only the serial number would not enable the database to locate the specific item that was sold.

Part IV
Ch 18

Editing the Record's Values

After entering the information, Evans clicks the Record Sale Now button. That button, created by using the Forms toolbar, is associated with the following VBA code; clicking the button causes the code to run.

```
Sub RecordASale()
Dim dbSales As Database
Dim rsResale As Recordset
Set dbSales = OpenDatabase(ThisWorkbook.Path & "\Evans Electronics.mdb")
Set rsResale = dbSales.OpenRecordset("Resale Inventory", dbOpenDynaset)

With ThisWorkbook
    rsResale.FindFirst "[Serial Number] = " _
        & .Names("Serial_Number").RefersToRange.Value _
        & " And [Product ID] = " _
        & .Names("Product_ID").RefersToRange.Value
    If rsResale.NoMatch Then
        MsgBox "Couldn't find that item in the database."
    Else
        rsResale.Edit
        rsResale.Fields("[Date Sold]") = _
          .Names("Date_Sold").RefersToRange.Value
        rsResale.Fields("[Sales Price]") = _
          .Names("Sales_Price").RefersToRange.Value
        rsResale.Update
    End If
End With

End Sub
```

Here's a walkthrough of the code:

The first line just identifies the procedure as a subroutine and names it. Then, two variables are declared with Dim statements. The variable named dbSales is declared as a Database, and rsResale is declared as a recordset.

TIP

Many people who write code find it useful to begin the names of variables with short tags that help identify what the variable represents. Using these mnemonic devices helps the coder remember that dbSales represents a *database* and that rsResale represents a *recordset*.

Before the VBA code can assign these variables properly, it's necessary to make an object library available to the code. The following steps show you how.

1. Open the Visual Basic Editor from Excel by choosing Tools, Macros, Visual Basic Editor.

2. Begin a code module by choosing Insert, Module.

3. Choose Tools, References. The References - VBAProject dialog box opens, as shown in Figure 18.25.

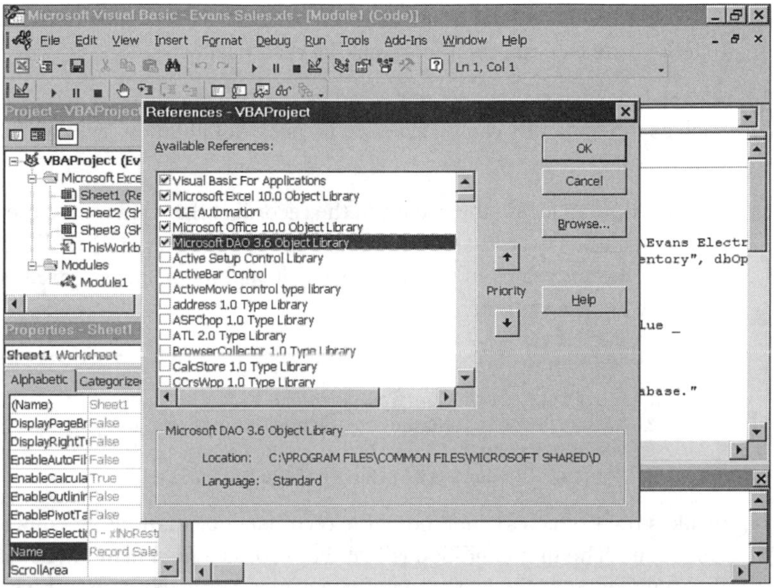

FIGURE 18.25

The list of references contains a variety of libraries and controls, such as the Calendar Control, that you can make available to VBA.

4. Scroll down the Available References list box until you find the item named Microsoft DAO 3.6 Object Library. Make sure the checkbox is checked, and click OK.

The entire DAO object library is now available to your module. In VBA for Excel, you often refer to Excel objects such as workbooks, worksheets, charts, cells, and so on. But because it's VBA for Excel, it doesn't come with objects that are contained in databases, such as databases themselves, tables, queries, and so on. By making a reference to DAO, you make these database objects available to your Excel VBA code.

With those objects available, you can set the two variables that you declared equal to the objects they represent:

```
Set dbSales = OpenDatabase(ThisWorkbook.Path & "\Evans Electronics.mdb")
Set rsResale = dbSales.OpenRecordset("Resale Inventory", dbOpenDynaset)
```

The variable `dbSales` is set equal to the database named Evans Electronics.mdb, which is found in the same path as the workbook that contains the VBA code.

A *recordset* is a group of records that have fields. A recordset could be a table—which by definition has records and fields—in a database, or it could be the results of a query that extracts particular records and particular fields from one or more tables.

The code sets the variable `rsResale` to the table named Resale Inventory. VBA is instructed that it can find that recordset in the database that's represented by the variable `dbSales`. The `OpenRecordset` method is used; that method actually opens the table and assigns its records and fields to the `rsResale` recordset.

The recordset is defined as a Dynaset type of recordset. This means, among other things, that the code can edit the records in the recordset.

A With block is established, governed by the ThisWorkbook object. That means that objects such as range names can be referred to using dot notation, without having to repeatedly mention ThisWorkbook.

Now it's time to locate the record in the recordset that represents the item that Evans just sold. Once that record has been located, by means of its product ID and its serial number, the code will assign values to its Date Sold field and to its Sales Price field. The record is located with this statement:

This command:

```
rsResale.FindFirst "[Serial Number] = " _
    & .Names("Serial_Number").RefersToRange.Value _
    & " And [Product ID] = " _
    & .Names("Product_ID").RefersToRange.Value
```

invokes the FindFirst method of the recordset object. It takes as its argument two search conditions. The first condition is that the recordset field named [Serial Number] must equal the value found in the worksheet range named Serial_Number. The second condition is that the recordset field named [Product ID] must equal the value found in the worksheet range named Product_ID.

In words, VBA tries to find a record in the Resale Inventory recordset that has a product ID the same as the one found in worksheet cell B12, and a serial number equal to the one in cell C12.

N O T E The reason that the recordset field names, such as [Serial Number], are enclosed in square brackets is because an Access database field name that contains a space must be so enclosed. By contrast, workbook- and worksheet-level names in Excel are not allowed to contain spaces, and underscores (as in Serial_Number) are convenient standins for spaces. ▪

The next statement is

```
If rsResale.NoMatch Then
    MsgBox "Couldn't find that item in the database."
```

The NoMatch property applies to recordset objects such as rsResale. You use it after sending VBA on a hunt for a record in the recordset. If VBA found a record that matches your specifications, the recordset's NoMatch property has the value False. If VBA failed to find such a record, the NoMatch property is set to True.

In this instance, the code has looked in the rsResale recordset for a record with a particular product ID and serial number. If Evans mis-typed either value on the worksheet, VBA probably would be unable to find the record (unless Evans happened to type in error a pair of values that do exist in the recordset). Then, NoMatch would be true and a message that the item wasn't found is displayed on the screen. This informs the user that an error has been made somewhere, either in the Product_ID or Serial_Number range on the worksheet, or when the records were entered in the database. In either event, the user would not continue trying to record the sale until the error was found and corrected.

But if the record was found, then NoMatch is set to False, and the code continues with the next line following the MsgBox statement.

```
Else
    rsResale.Edit
```

The Else statement just says that should the prior If condition not have been met—here, if the record that VBA looked for was found—then the following statements are to be executed. The first of those invokes the recordset's Edit method. Using DAO, when your code attempts to change the value of a field you must preface that attempt with an Edit statement.

The next two statements are then able to modify the values of the [Date Sold] and [Sales Price] fields:

```
rsResale.Fields("[Date Sold]") = _
  .Names("Date_Sold").RefersToRange.Value
rsResale.Fields("[Sales Price]") = _
  .Names("Sales_Price").RefersToRange.Value
```

In words, locate the value in the range that's referred to by the name Date_Sold. Put that value in the recordset's field named [Date Sold]. Then, locate the value in the Sales_Price field and put it in the field named [Sales Price]. These values will be associated with the record that has the product ID and serial number from the worksheet: when VBA found that record it became active.

```
    rsResale.Update
```

The changes to the fields' values do not fully take effect until the recordset's Update method is executed. It's helpful to remember that when you are modifying a record's fields using DAO, you begin the process with the Edit method and complete the process with the Update method.

The subroutine finishes with these commands:

```
    End If
End With

End Sub
```

The End If terminates the If that checks to see if the specified record was found in the recordset. The End With terminates the With block governed by the ThisWorkbook object. And the End Sub terminates the subroutine.

This is a rather simple procedure. It consists of only 17 statements, and only seven of them actually *do* anything. But it's powerful: it enables the user to locate a record in a database and

Part

IV

Ch

18

to change the values of its fields without knowing what table the record is located in, what database contains that table, where the database is located, or even that the database exists.

If you were to employ an approach such as this in your business—arranging to use Excel as the user interface, an Access database, or another database to store the data, writing VBA code to manage the data transfer, making a DAO object library available to the code—then you would surely add other checks and protections in the code.

For example, you would want to provide a sequence of commands to execute if the code for some reason couldn't find the database where you expected it would be stored. Or, after updating the values in the fields, you might find the record again, read the values in its fields, and show the user those values in a message box as confirmation that the update occurred properly.

Adding New Records to the Recordset

Suppose now that Evans wanted to adopt a similar approach for the purpose of adding records to the database. Records would be added when the store acquires new stock for sale and it must be recorded in the Resale Inventory table. The Excel worksheet might be structured much like the one shown in Figure 18.26.

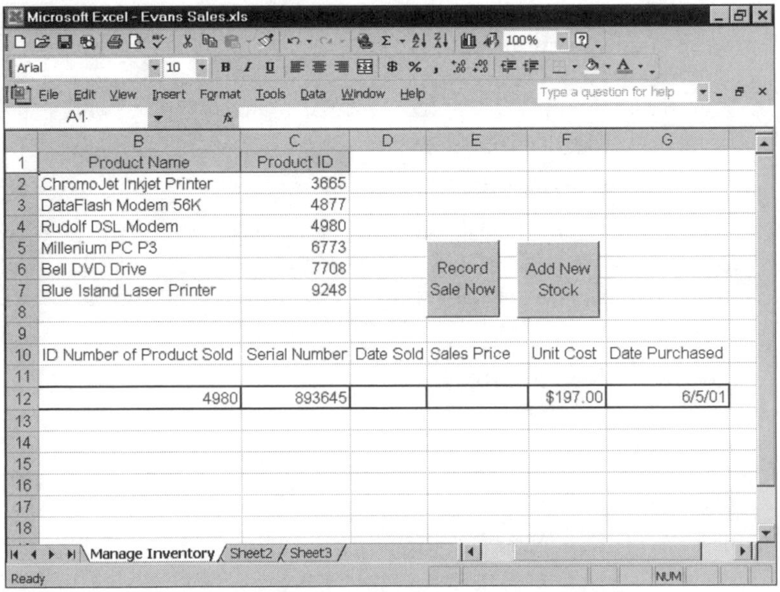

FIGURE 18.26
This worksheet just adds two named ranges and a command button to the worksheet shown in Figure 18.24.

The worksheet in Figure 18.26 has a command button that records a sale in the database and one that adds an item to the resale inventory. The act of recording a sale does not involve changing either the unit cost or the date acquired; when Evans adds an item to inventory, the sales price and date sold are not yet known. In practice it might be wise to put those two capabilities on separate worksheets, if only to keep named ranges that are not involved in the data transaction off the active worksheet.

The code that's associated with the Add New Stock button is as follows:

```
Sub AddAnItem()
Dim dbSales As Database
Dim rsResale As Recordset
Set dbSales = OpenDatabase(ThisWorkbook.Path & "\Evans Electronics.mdb")
Set rsResale = dbSales.OpenRecordset("Resale Inventory", dbOpenDynaset)

With ThisWorkbook
    rsResale.FindFirst "[Serial Number] = " _
        & .Names("Serial_Number").RefersToRange.Value _
        & " And [Product ID] = " _
        & .Names("Product_ID").RefersToRange.Value
    If Not rsResale.NoMatch Then
        MsgBox "Already have that item in the database."
    Else
        rsResale.AddNew
        rsResale.Fields("[Serial Number]") = _
          .Names("Serial_Number").RefersToRange.Value
        rsResale.Fields("[Product ID]") = _
          .Names("Product_ID").RefersToRange.Value
        rsResale.Fields("[Unit Cost]") = _
          .Names("Unit_Cost").RefersToRange.Value
        rsResale.Fields("[Date Purchased]") = _
          .Names("Date_Purchased").RefersToRange.Value
        rsResale.Update
    End If
End With

End Sub
```

Part

IV

Ch

18

> **TIP**
> If you put this subroutine in the same workbook as the RecordASale subroutine, you do not need to establish a new reference to the DAO object library. Once that reference is established, it is available to all subroutines and modules in the workbook.

This subroutine is similar to the RecordASale subroutine in several ways. The same database and recordset variables are declared and set in the same way, and the With block has the same functionality. The code searches for a record with a particular product ID and serial number.

The first difference between the two subroutines comes in the If test:

```
If Not rsResale.NoMatch Then
    MsgBox "Already have that item in the database."
```

This time, Evans expects that the record is *not* in the database: it is just now being added to the resale inventory. So the `If` test gets the `Not` keyword added to it. If it is *not* the case that a match is not found—skirting the double negative, you could say "If a match is found"—that means that an item with that product ID and serial number is already in the database. In that case, warn the user with a message box. Something's wrong and should be corrected before the item is added to the database.

On the other hand, if `NoMatch` is `True`, the record wasn't found and the code can go ahead and add it to the recordset:

```
Else
    rsResale.AddNew
```

This time, instead of using `rsResale.Edit` to modify an existing record, the code uses `rsResale.AddNew` to put a new record in the recordset. Then the appropriate fields of that new record are given values. Those values are obtained from the named ranges in the Excel workbook: Serial_Number, Product_ID, Unit_Cost, and Date_Purchased.

```
rsResale.Fields("[Serial Number]") = _
        .Names("Serial_Number").RefersToRange.Value
    rsResale.Fields("[Product ID]") =
        .Names("Product_ID").RefersToRange.Value
    rsResale.Fields("[Unit Cost]") =
        .Names("Unit_Cost").RefersToRange.Value
    rsResale.Fields("[Date Purchased]") =
        .Names("Date_Purchased").RefersToRange.Value
```

With the values in the fields, the `Update` method is invoked to fully establish the record in the recordset:

```
    rsResale.Update
```

The final three statements that end the `If`, the `With`, and the subroutine itself are as in `RecordASale`.

Choosing to Use DAO

Couldn't Evans Electronics have handled all this with Access as the user interface? Sure. Someone could have created a couple of forms in Access, linked directly to the Resale Inventory table, that Evans could use to edit records and add new ones. VBA wouldn't be involved. DAO wouldn't be needed. Perhaps the author just wasn't sufficiently creative to come up with examples that were spare enough to serve as introductions, and yet complicated enough to require the use of DAO.

The DAO object model contains many more objects, properties, and methods than the few illustrated in the preceding sections. Using DAO you can:

- Create a new database
- Build new tables in databases

■ Create new queries, store them in databases, and use them to return data to the worksheet

■ Delete records from tables

■ Use indexes to find *very rapidly* particular records in huge tables

■ Perform just about any action that you might perform using the database program itself

There are many business situations that you would choose to use Excel as the user interface and (say) an Access database to store the information. As just one example, consider the user who wants to review quality control data that pertains to a manufacturing operation.

From time to time that user must correct what he judges to be erroneous information in the database. When the factory turns out thousands of units per day, even fairly small quality control samples can quickly become too large to manage conveniently—or at all—in an Excel worksheet.

So why not examine that data in the database itself? Because then the user does not have easy access to supporting documents such as charts, reference distributions such as the normal curve and the Poisson, and tools such as Solver and Goal Seek. These are the items in Excel that enable the user to make inferences and judgments about the data: perhaps to determine that a measure in the database is so egregious an outlier that it simply has to be wrong. That judgment suggests that information in the database should be corrected, and what better place to do that from than the active application? To do so directly requires the use of DAO.

Summary

This chapter has focused on Microsoft Access as the database program used in examples of database queries and of DAO. That is because Excel and Access work very well together. For example, you can take VBA code that you have developed and written in an Excel workbook, copy it into a module in an Access database, and execute the code in that context with very few changes—quite possibly none at all.

But don't let that kind of smooth interaction cause you to forget that you can use the techniques developed in this chapter with databases other than Access. The examples of queries and of using DAO apply equally to any ODBC-compliant database, and there are many such in use in business, scientific, educational, and other institutions.

Part
IV
Ch
18

CHAPTER 19

Analyzing Contributions and Margins

Management accounting concerns itself with the internal operations and drivers of business performance. Among its primary tools are contribution analysis and break-even analysis, which use financial indicators such as these:

- *Contribution margin.* This is usually defined as the sales revenue less the variable costs of production.

- *Unit contribution.* This is the margin contributed by each unit sold.

- *Break-even point.* This is the point in the sales process at which the revenues equal the costs of production.

These indicators enable you to make decisions about how you can:

- Increase product profitability

- Manage your product sales mix

- Optimize your resources to hold your costs down and raise your profits

These decisions often involve making assumptions about the profitability, resources, and product mix. You can test the assumptions by considering what effect they have on variables such as unit contribution.

For example, suppose that you manage a product whose contribution margin is $1 million per year. If your company is to meet its targeted profit for next year, you must assume that you can raise your product's contribution margin by 10% to $1.1 million. What options could you exercise that would cause your product to return an additional $100,000 profit?

To guide you in a search for your options, you could refer back to a contribution margin analysis and perhaps a unit contribution analysis. These analyses spell out the factors that tend to hold your revenues down or keep your costs up. Examining those factors can help you determine which costs, sales prices, and volume levels you can modify to achieve your assumed $1.1 million target.

This chapter explores the relationships among these variables. It shows you how to use Excel to identify which inputs you can modify to meet your goals.

Calculating the Contribution Margin

All firms have costs that are directly associated with their product or service. One of the most powerful means of understanding and controlling those costs is *contribution margin* analysis. The contribution margin itself is calculated by subtracting the variable costs required to manufacture the product from the revenue achieved by selling that product.

Variable costs are those that change as production levels rise and fall. For example, the cost of raw materials is a variable cost because the more goods you manufacture the more raw materials you need. In contrast, fixed costs are those that do not change along with differences in production levels. For example, the cost of salaried workers is a fixed cost.

In practice, the definition of the contribution margin is often expanded to "revenue minus directly traceable costs." This is because it can be extremely difficult to distinguish between some fixed and variable costs. But the directly traceable costs should include all those that are variable.

Case Study: Producing Digital Video Disks

Discography, Inc. produces DVDs. To make the DVDs, it costs Discography:

- $5 per DVD for the materials used in the DVD itself
- $1 per DVD for the packaging materials (the jewel box, the paper insert, the shrink wrap, and the enormous clear plastic container that's supposed to prevent you from stealing the DVD and that requires that you use the Jaws of Life to get it open)
- $0.50 per DVD for the factory employees

for a total production cost of $6.50 per DVD. You would calculate the contribution margin for this product line as shown in Figure 19.1:

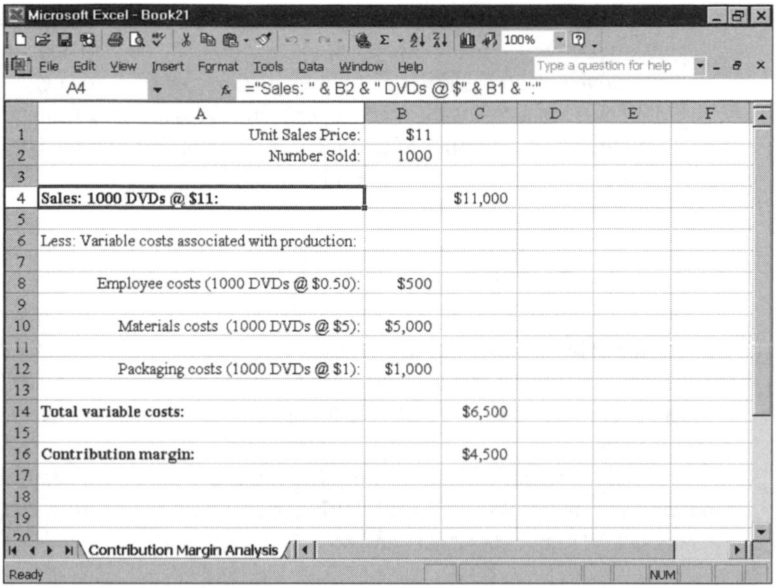

FIGURE 19.1

The contribution margin is defined as revenues less variable costs.

The $6,500 required to make the production run shown in Figure 19.1 is called the *variable cost*, the cost that varies with the number of units produced. When production goes down variable costs decrease, and when production goes up variable costs increase.

Besides variable costs, Discography also has *fixed costs*. Fixed costs do not vary with the level of production. For example, rent paid for a building, legal fees, and business insurance are usually the same regardless of how many DVDs Discography produces. In contrast, when Discography makes more DVDs, the total amount that it pays for materials such as blank disks increases: that is a variable cost of production.

In practice, and even when you can separate variable from fixed costs, the distinction is not quite as crisp as it is in theory. Consider, for example, the $0.50 per DVD that Discography pays its factory employees. There are several ways that Discography can incur that cost:

- The employee is paid for each DVD that's produced and, as long as the current labor contract is in force, the nature and amount of the payment cannot be changed. If that is the arrangement, the payment is a variable cost: the more DVDs produced, the greater the total payments to the employees.

- The employee receives a fixed wage, regardless of the number of DVDs produced, and the $0.50 per DVD is just a long-term average. In this case, the employee's wage represents a fixed cost. Unless you negotiate payment terms that are based directly on production, you should not include this sort of cost in the contribution margin analysis.

Part

IV

Ch

19

■ The employee is paid by the DVD, but the rate of payment changes according to how many DVDs are made. For example, for up to 1,000 DVDs made per day, you pay the employee $0.50 per DVD, but you pay $0.60 per DVD for between 1,000 and 2,000 DVDs. This is termed a *semi-variable* cost. A semi-variable cost changes along with changes in the number of units, but the size of that change is not precisely *proportional* to that of the change in the number of units.

NOTE Semi-variable costs are often *step functions*. A step function is one whose value changes suddenly when a variable reaches a certain threshold. In this example, when the production level reaches the threshold of 1,000 DVDs, the employee cost jumps from $0.50 per unit to $0.60 per unit.

Up to 1,000 DVDs, the ratio of total employee cost to units made is exactly $0.50. After 1,000 DVDs, the ratio is exactly $0.60. But across the full range of production (say, from 0–5,000 DVDs produced) the ratio is inexact: it depends on the number of DVDs that are produced above the threshold. ■

Figure 19.2 shows an example of how you might account for a semi-variable cost: in this case, an employee makes $0.50 for each DVD produced up to and including 1,000 DVDs per day, $0.60 per DVD for 1,000–2,000, and so on.

FIGURE 19.2

Calculating semi-variable costs in a contribution margin analysis: employee costs are purely and proportionately variable within a quantity range, but describe a step function across ranges.

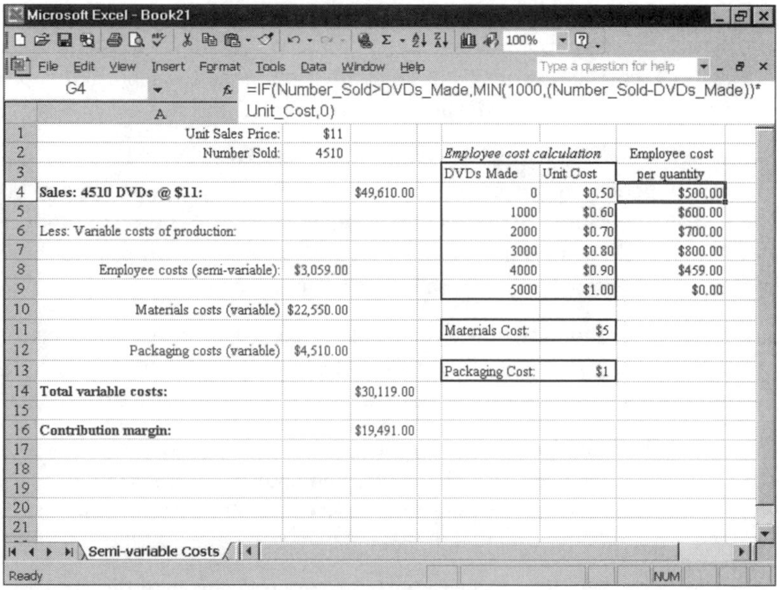

Three named ranges are used in Figure 19.2:

■ Number_Sold refers to cell B1.

■ DVDs_Made refers to cells D3:D8.

■ Labor_Cost refers to cells E3:E8.

The implicit intersection with the ranges named DVDs_Made and Labor_Cost causes the following IF statement to return different values to the cells in the range F3:F8.

```
=IF(Number_Sold>DVDs_Made,MIN(1000,(Number_Sold-DVDs_Made))*Labor_Cost,0)
```

The MIN function appears in the formula because no more than 1,000 units should be counted for any level of DVDs_Made. In the figure example, Number_Sold is 4,510. For the 4,000 level of DVDs_Made, Number_Sold–DVDs_Made = 510, and this amount is multiplied by the corresponding Labor_Cost of $0.90 to return $459.

In contrast, at the 3,000 level of DVDs_Made, Number_Sold–DVDs_Made = 1,510. But this is too many units to count: 1,000 is the maximum number of units to count for any given level. Therefore, the formula makes use of the MIN function to return the smaller of 1,000, or the difference between Number_Sold and DVDs_Made.

The smaller of those two values is multiplied by the corresponding Labor_Cost to return the cost of the DVDs made at that level of production.

Finally, Number_Sold can be less than any given level of DVDs_Made. In the figure example, 4,510 is less than 5,000, so no units should be counted for that level. The IF function returns 0 in that case.

Using Unit Contribution

The analysis of contribution margin in the case study of DVD production involved total variable costs and total revenues. You can also break the information down to a per unit and percent of sales basis. Doing so often gives you a different view of the relationship between your costs and revenues.

Calculating the Unit Contribution Margin

To continue the Discography case study, consider the information summarized in Figure 19.2 from the perspective that's provided in Figure 19.3.

The detailed per unit and percent of margin information gives you a better idea of:

- The product's individual contribution to total revenue
- The source of the greatest percentage of variable costs
- The relationships among the magnitudes of the variable costs

The detail that you obtain from this type of analysis gives you the tools you need to make decisions that maximize your profits. For example, Figure 19.3 makes it clear that if Discography pays its employees an extra $0.10 per DVD for every additional 1000 DVDs produced, the contribution margin goes down (39.29% at the 4,510 level, 38.84% at the 5,510 level). The company's total gross margin for the product line increases with more production, from $19,491 to $23,540. But the unit contribution decreases.

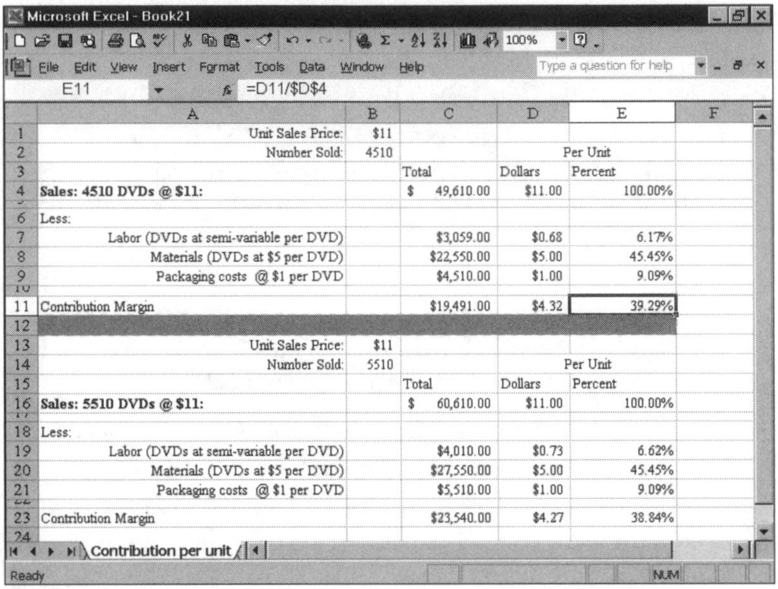

	A	B	C	D	E
1	Unit Sales Price:	$11			
2	Number Sold:	4510		Per Unit	
3			Total	Dollars	Percent
4	Sales: 4510 DVDs @ $11:		$ 49,610.00	$11.00	100.00%
6	Less:				
7	Labor (DVDs at semi-variable per DVD)		$3,059.00	$0.68	6.17%
8	Materials (DVDs at $5 per DVD)		$22,550.00	$5.00	45.45%
9	Packaging costs @ $1 per DVD		$4,510.00	$1.00	9.09%
11	Contribution Margin		$19,491.00	$4.32	39.29%
12					
13	Unit Sales Price:	$11			
14	Number Sold:	5510		Per Unit	
15			Total	Dollars	Percent
16	Sales: 5510 DVDs @ $11:		$ 60,610.00	$11.00	100.00%
18	Less:				
19	Labor (DVDs at semi-variable per DVD)		$4,010.00	$0.73	6.62%
20	Materials (DVDs at $5 per DVD)		$27,550.00	$5.00	45.45%
21	Packaging costs @ $1 per DVD		$5,510.00	$1.00	9.09%
23	Contribution Margin		$23,540.00	$4.27	38.84%

FIGURE 19.3
You can derive a greater level of detail by breaking down the total cost information to a per unit and percent of sales basis.

Increasing the Contribution Margin

Suppose that Discography wants to increase the contribution margin, expressed as a percentage of sales, from 39.29% to 45% at the 4,510 unit sales level. By analyzing the information in Figure 19.3, Discography notices that if it can lower the cost of its materials from $5 per DVD to $4.37 per DVD, it can increase the contribution margin to 45%. One way of doing so might be by using a different supplier. Lowering the cost of materials will decrease the direct material cost to 39.73% of total costs. This enables Discography to achieve its desired contribution margin of 45%.

The fastest way to perform that analysis is to use Goal Seek. Follow these steps:

1. Select the cell with the contribution margin that you want to change. In Figure 19.3 that's cell E11. Make sure that it contains the necessary formula, `=D11/$D$4`.
2. Choose Tools, Goal Seek. In the To Value box, enter **0.45**. In the By Changing Cell box enter **D8**, which contains the unit materials cost.
3. Click OK.

The required material cost appears in D8 and the desired unit contribution margin appears in E11.

In summary, when you're in the process of making operational decisions, a contribution margin analysis can help you in several ways:

- It helps you decide what price to charge for your product. For example, if you want an additional $10 contribution margin on every unit you sell, you will either have to increase your selling price by $10, reduce your unit variable costs by $10, or arrange some combination of price increase and cost reduction that sums to $10. The contribution margin analysis makes it easy to quantify those changes.

- It helps you focus on controlling those costs that are directly related to making the product. For example, if you are currently using a vendor who charges $50 per 10 units of materials, you may be able to find a vendor that charges $45 at no loss in quality. But suppose that you focused on reducing fixed costs. Although this is frequently a useful activity, it does not usually increase your profit as a function of increased production.

- It helps you understand the relationships among the volume of products produced and sold, their costs, and your profits. This is especially useful in the case of semi-variable costs, which are usually difficult to account for and to fully understand without doing the formal analysis.

Creating an Operating Income Statement

Once created, an Excel worksheet can make it very easy to analyze contribution margin. You should first structure an operating income statement on a worksheet. The statement contains your sales, variable cost, and volume information on a total, per unit, and percent of margin basis. This portion of the worksheet contains the values that depend on unit pricing (see Figure 19.4).

FIGURE 19.4
An operating income statement should detail the product's sales price, variable costs, and quantities.

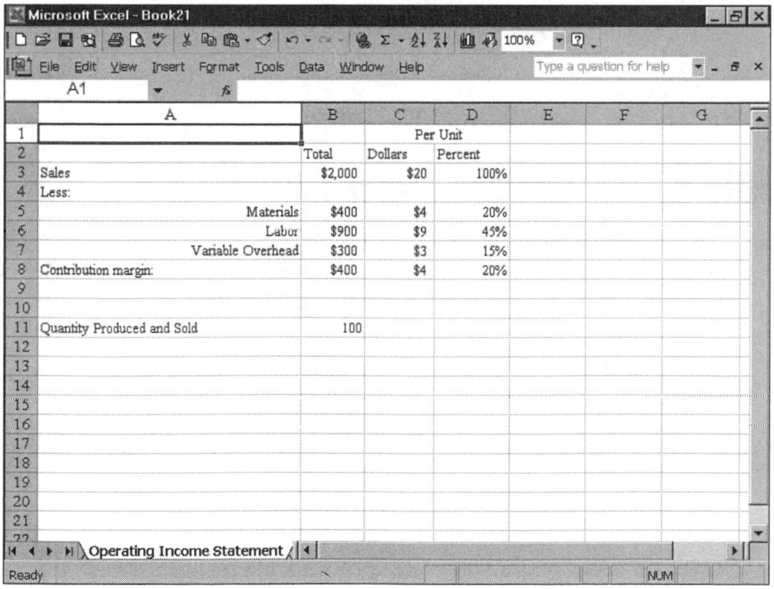

	A	B	C	D
			Per Unit	
2		Total	Dollars	Percent
3	Sales	$2,000	$20	100%
4	Less:			
5	Materials	$400	$4	20%
6	Labor	$900	$9	45%
7	Variable Overhead	$300	$3	15%
8	Contribution margin:	$400	$4	20%
11	Quantity Produced and Sold	100		

Operating Income Statement

Part
IV

Ch
19

The formulas used to create the information in Figure 19.4 are shown in Figure 19.5.

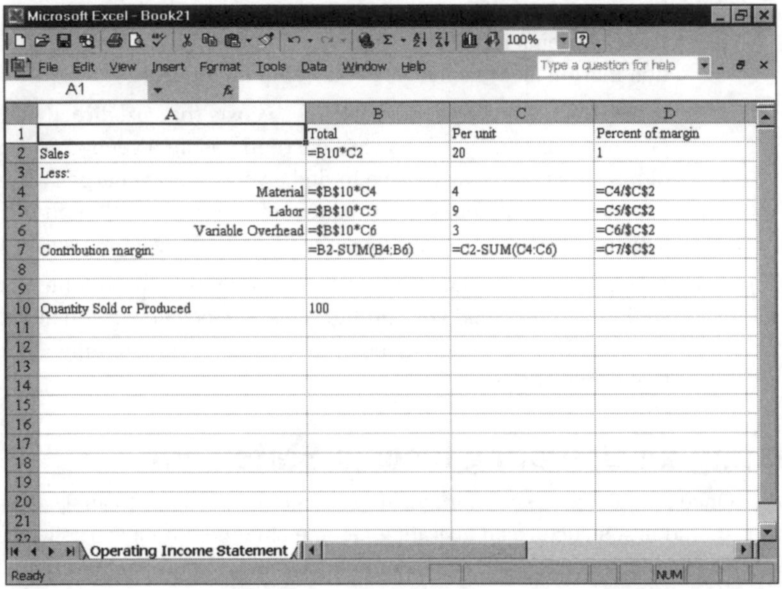

FIGURE 19.5
Excel formulas for the operating income statement.

	A	B	C	D
1		Total	Per unit	Percent of margin
2	Sales	=B10*C2	20	1
3	Less:			
4	Material	=$B$10*C4	4	=C4/$C$2
5	Labor	=$B$10*C5	9	=C5/$C$2
6	Variable Overhead	=$B$10*C6	3	=C6/$C$2
7	Contribution margin:	=B2-SUM(B4:B6)	=C2-SUM(C4:C6)	=C7/$C$2
8				
9				
10	Quantity Sold or Produced	100		

By detailing your price, cost, and quantity information separately in your operating income statement, you can easily modify selling prices, costs, and quantities to represent different assumptions. (It helps to save the values as scenarios.) The modified values will flow through the formulas in the operating income statement, and will raise or lower your calculated contribution margin.

Finding the Break-Even Point

Another way that you benefit from studying a product's contribution margin is the ability to perform a cost/volume/profit analysis. Creating this analysis is often little more than the manipulation of the information derived from your contribution analysis. By doing so, you can determine the combination of production volume and sales price that will enable you to maximize your gross profits and minimize your production costs.

One way to turn your contribution margin analysis into a cost/volume/profit analysis is to calculate the break-even point. This is the point where total revenues equal the total of fixed and variable costs.

```
Total Revenues          =       Total Costs
(Unit Price * Quantity) =          (Fixed Costs + (Variable Costs * Quantity)
```

Break-even analysis allows you to plan for the level of sales that you need to cover your total costs. It also provides you with information on the level of sales that will be necessary to achieve your desired level of profitability.

There are several ways to calculate the break-even point. Each calculation method provides you with a different slant, and your choice should depend on your information requirements. The break-even calculations include break-even in units, break-even in dollars, and break-even with an expected level of profit.

Calculating Break-Even in Units

Break-even in units is the number of units that must be sold at current price levels to cover fixed and variable costs. The break-even point measured in units is:

```
Break-even [units] = Total Fixed Costs/( Unit Sales Price - Unit Variable Costs)
```

Calculating the break-even point in units is most useful when managers need to analyze current or projected volume levels. You might know, for example, that with your current sales force you can expect to sell 10 units per month. By calculating break-even in units, you can determine whether your company can be profitable at 10 units sold per month. If your company cannot be profitable at that level, you might decide that you need to add sales staff.

Suppose that total fixed costs are $50, unit sales price is $20, and unit variable costs are $15. You can calculate the break-even point in units by means of this formula:

```
Break-even [units] = $50 / ($20 - $15)
```

The result is 10. Therefore, the company needs to sell 10 units during the period when the fixed costs are incurred to break even.

Or, you might find it useful to turn this relationship around. Suppose that you know that your total fixed costs will increase by $10 per month, from $50 to $60. You do not want to change your unit sales price, and your unit variable costs will not change. How many units must you sell to break even?

Begin by rearranging the formula for break-even point in units, as follows:

```
Total Fixed Costs = Break-even [units] * (Unit Sales Price - Unit Variable Costs)
```

You can use Goal Seek to quickly determine your new break-even point in units. See Figure 19.6 for a sample worksheet layout.

Cell A2 contains this formula:

```
=D2*(B2-C2)
```

Part

IV

Ch

19

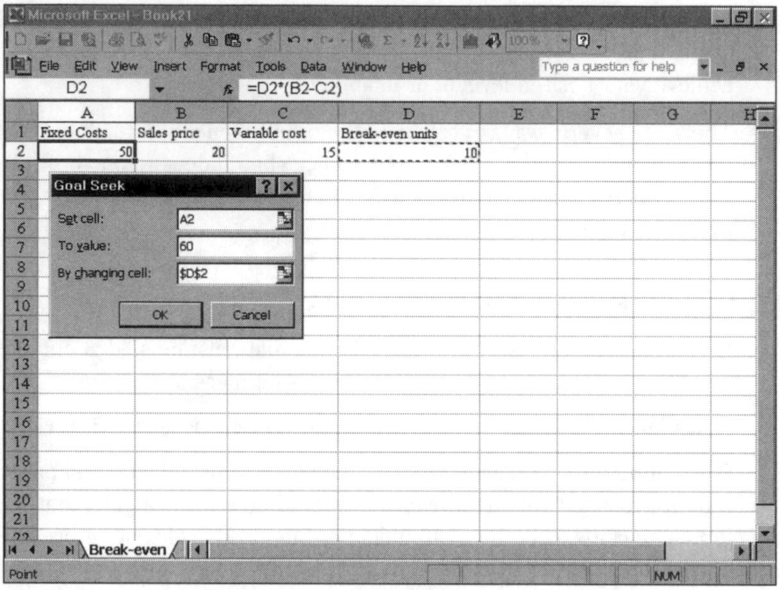

FIGURE 19.6
Using Goal Seek to
find a new break-even
point.

Cells B1 through D1 contain the values shown (not formulas). Follow these steps:

1. Select cell A2, and choose Goal Seek from the Tools menu. The reference to cell A2 appears in the Set Cell box.
2. Click in the To Value box, and enter the number **60**. This is the new total fixed costs.
3. Click in the By Changing Cell box and then click cell D2.
4. Choose OK.

Goal Seek now changes the value in cell D2 until the value in cell A2 equals 60. The result is 12: the number of units you must sell to cover the new total fixed costs.

Calculating Break-Even in Sales

Break-even in sales is the number of dollars of sales revenue that are needed to cover fixed and variable costs. There are several ways to calculate break-even in sales. Each provides the same result, but each method uses slightly different inputs. One method is:

```
Break-even [sales] = (Break-even [units] * Unit Sales Price)
```

Suppose that the break-even units is 10 and the unit sales price is $20. These data result in a break-even in sales dollars of $200:

```
$200 = (10 * $20)
```

Here, you already know how many units you need to sell to break even, and you simply multiply that by the price of each unit.

Another formula that you can use if you haven't yet calculated break-even units is

```
Break-even [sales] = Total Fixed Costs / ((Unit Sales Price - Unit Variable
Costs) / Unit Sales Price)
```

Here, the total of the fixed costs is $50, unit sales price is $20, and unit variable cost is $10. The data result in

```
$50 / (($20 - $15)/ $20)
$50 / ($5 / $20 )
$50 / .25 = $200
```

It's easier to understand if you restate the formula in words. Find your profit per unit ($20 – $15 = $5) and divide by the unit sales price: $5 / $20, or .25. This is the proportion of unit sales price that is profit over and above your variable costs. Dividing the additional costs that you need to cover, your total fixed costs, by that profit proportion results in the sales dollars needed to meet total costs.

A third approach is

```
Break-even [sales] = (Break-even [units] * Unit Variable Cost) + Total Fixed
Costs
```

or, where break-even units is 10, unit variable cost is 15, and total fixed costs is $50:

```
(10 * $15) + $50
$150 + 50 = $200
```

This formula simply determines the total variable cost for break-even units, and adds to that the total fixed cost.

In each case, you find that you need $200 in sales to break even.

Break-even as measured in sales dollars will provide you with valuable information regarding how much sales revenue is required to cover your operating costs. It can give you an understanding of how aggressively you must market your product to meet your operating costs. It also gives you some indication of how efficiently you are using the resources that are available to you.

Part
IV

Ch
19

TIP   In practice, it is easiest to set up one formula that involves each component as a named cell reference. The formula might be

```
= Units * (Unit_Price – Unit_Cost) – Fixed_Costs
```

Then, you can use Goal Seek to set the value of the formula to zero (the break-even point) by varying any one of the formula's precedent cells.

Calculating Break-Even in Sales Dollars with an Expected Level of Profit

Break-even in sales dollars represents the sales revenue needed to cover fixed and variable costs, and still return a profit at the level you require. Conceptually, this is similar to treating profit as a cost. You need to meet your fixed costs, and you need to meet your variable costs; you simply consider that profit is another cost category that you need to meet.

You can calculate break-even in sales dollars by using this formula:

```
Break-even [sales] = Variable Costs + Fixed Costs + Expected Profit
```

Suppose that a company wants to make a $5 profit on every unit it sells. The variable cost is $15 per unit, 10 units are sold, the fixed costs total to $50, and the expected profit is $5 per unit. Then, the formula that provides the break-even point in terms of sales dollars is:

```
Break-even [sales] = (Unit Variable Cost * Units) + Fixed Costs + (Expected
Profit * Units)

= ($15 * 10) + $50 + ($5 * 10)
= $250
```

and the company's break-even point, measured in sales dollars, is $250 for 10 units with a profit of $5 per unit.

Charting the Break-Even Point

Using equations to perform a break-even analysis is one valuable way to analyze the cost/volume/profit relationship. Another is to depict the break-even point graphically. Figure 19.7 displays a chart that depict the elements of a cost/volume/profit analysis.

Figure 19.7 represents the relationship between total costs and total sales at different levels of production. The chart illustrates the quantity at which loss, break-even, and profit are achieved. Below 10 units on the X-axis, the company loses money because the unit profit has yet to make up for the fixed costs. At 10 units, there is exactly enough unit profit to cover fixed costs, and the total sales equals total costs. Above 10 units, the company is making a profit at the rate of $5 per unit over 10.

The graphic representation of a company's current cost/volume/profit relationship gives you an effective tool for determining what adjustments you need to make to volume, cost, or both to increase your profit level. Relationships among these variables can become extremely complex, especially when several different products are involved. When you are dealing with a complicated situation, it is usually easier to make sense of the relationships by viewing them on a chart, rather than by gazing at a table of raw numbers.

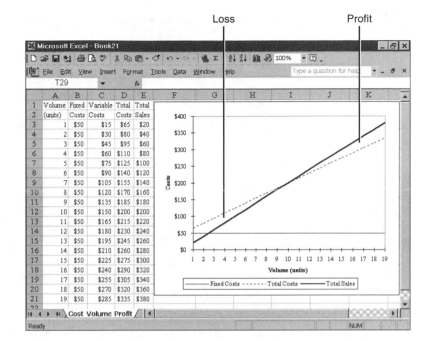

FIGURE 19.7
Relationships between costs, volume, and profit: profit begins at the break-even point.

To create the chart shown in Figure 19.7, follow these steps:

1. Select cells A1:B21. Press the Ctrl key and select cells D1:E21. You now have a multiple selection that consists of two ranges and that skips column C.

2. Click the Chart Wizard button on the main toolbar, or choose Insert, Chart to display the Chart Wizard's first step.

3. In the Chart Wizard's first step, choose Line as both the Chart type and the Chart sub-type. To avoid visual clutter, choose a Chart sub-type without markers. Because the break-even chart's three data series are not additive, do not choose a Stacked line sub-type. After choosing a sub-type click Next.

4. In the Chart Wizard's second step, click the Series tab, as shown in Figure 19.8. The Chart Wizard assumes that each of the columns you selected in the first step is a different data series. You need to arrange for the Chart Wizard to treat the data in Column A as category labels. With Volume (units) selected in the Series list box, click Remove. The Volume (units) series is removed from the chart.

5. Click the Collapse Dialog button at the right end of the Category (X) axis labels box. Doing so gets the dialog box out of the way so you can select worksheet ranges unencumbered, but leaves the Category labels box itself visible. Select A1:A21, and click the button again to restore the full dialog box. Notice that the Category labels box now contains the reference to cells $A$1:$A$21. Click Next.

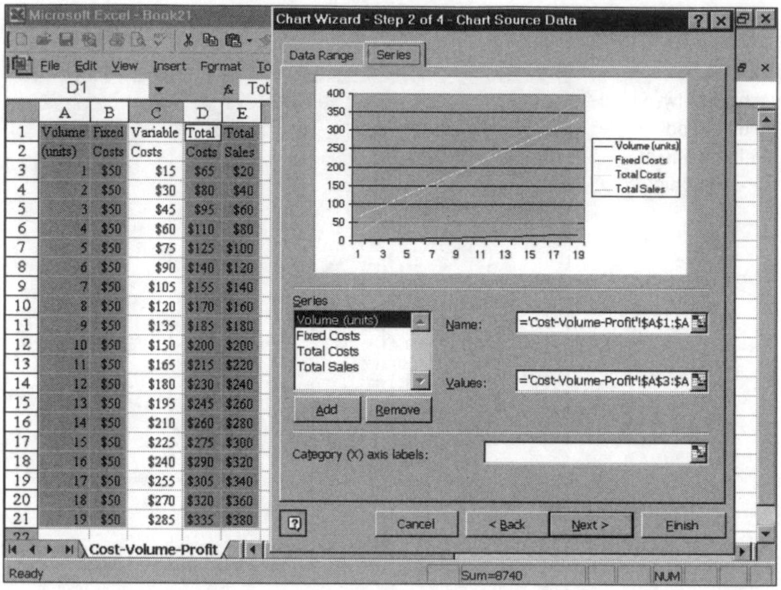

FIGURE 19.8

Treat the data in column A as axis labels, not as a data series.

6. In the Chart Wizard's third step, click the Titles tab if necessary and enter **Volume (units)** in the Category (X) axis box. Enter **Costs** in the Value (Y) axis box. Click the Legend tab and choose the Bottom placement option. If you want to suppress gridlines, click the Gridlines tab and clear its checkboxes. Click Next.

7. In the Chart Wizard's fourth step (see Figure 19.9), select As New Sheet if you want the chart to occupy its own sheet. If you want the chart to exist as an object on the active worksheet, select As Object In and click Finish. You can use the combo box to the right of the As Object In button to locate the chart in a different worksheet.

8. Right-click the chart's Plot Area, the rectangle that's defined by the two axes. Choose Format Plot Area from the shortcut menu and then choose None Under Area. Click OK.

N O T E In Step 1 of the preceding instructions, you could begin by selecting B1:B21 and D1:E21. That way, you would not have to remove A1:A21 as a series prior to establishing it as a set of axis labels. ■

FIGURE 19.9

It's a good idea to locate the chart on the worksheet if you still have it under development.

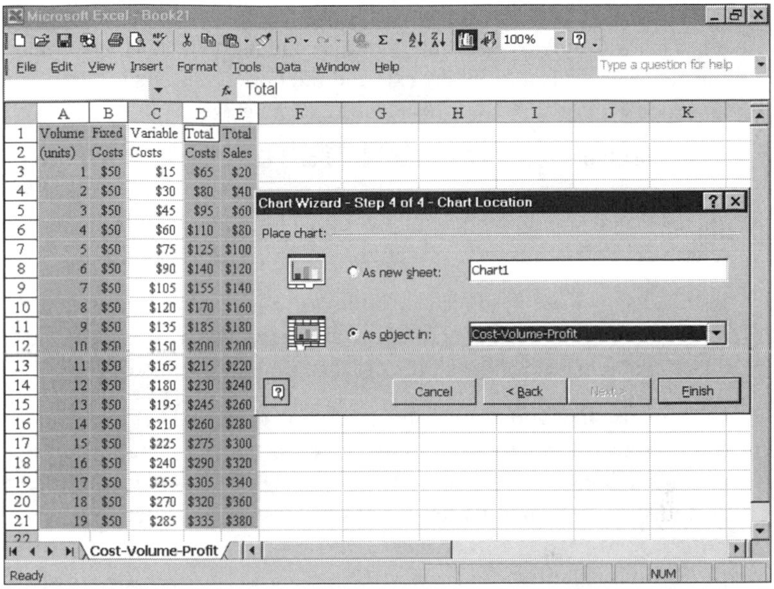

Choosing the Chart Type

The preceding section advised you to create the break-even chart using the Line chart type. It did so because it can be more straightforward to create a Line chart that contains several data series than to use the usual alternative, the XY(Scatter) chart.

The most apparent difference between Excel chart types is their appearance: lines, dots, columns, bars, bubbles, pies, and so on. Beyond the appearance, and sometimes obscure, is the issue of axis type. Excel charts have two types of axis: category and value.

A category or X axis (Excel uses the terms interchangeably) is appropriate for qualitative variables, such as the names of products. A value or Y axis (again, the terms are interchangeable) is appropriate for quantitative variables, such as number of units produced.

These two types of axis have different effects. Items on a category axis are always spaced evenly. Suppose you create a Line chart showing units sold for Ford, General Motors, and Toyota. The horizontal, category axis would put each data marker equidistant from its immediate neighbors. If the middle data marker represented General Motors, it would be as far from the Ford marker as it was from the Toyota marker. On a category axis, distance between points conveys no special meaning.

In contrast, distance between points has meaning on a value axis. The value 4 is half as far from 2 as it is from 0: the distance between the points denotes their relative magnitude.

Part
IV

Ch
19

Most chart types in Excel have one category axis and one value axis. For example, a Column chart's horizontal axis is a category axis and its vertical axis is a value axis. On a Bar chart, the vertical axis is a category axis and the horizontal axis is a value axis. The Line chart shown in Figure 19.7 has a horizontal category axis.

Two chart types, the XY(Scatter) chart and the Bubble chart, have two value axes (no 2-D chart type has two category axes). This aspect makes them valuable for analyzing relationships between numeric, quantitative variables. For example, if you wanted to analyze how job tenure is related to salary, you might use an XY(Scatter) chart.

In the chart shown in Figure 19.7, the horizontal axis represents production level. The axis displays levels of production that are all one unit apart. Because they're equidistant, the Line chart's category axis doesn't distort the numeric relationships.

But suppose that you wanted to run a break-even analysis over different ranges of production. For reasons of equipment capacity and allocation, you might want to view the break-even analysis at levels of 20 to 40, 60 to 80, and 100 to 120—skipping the irrelevant ranges of 40 to 60 and 80 to 100. Your worksheet has the relevant production levels sorted in ascending order.

In that event, if you use a Line chart, its horizontal axis will place the production levels in the same order on the axis as they are on the worksheet, and it will put 39 just left of 40 and 40 just left of 60. It's a category axis and ignores differences in magnitude. This distorts the relationship between level of production, costs, and profits. An XY(Scatter) chart would preserve the numeric relationship.

N O T E   There is another reason to use an XY(Scatter) chart instead of a Line chart when you have two numeric variables. Adding any trendline other than a Moving Average trendline to a Line chart will almost certainly return erroneous results. The trendline will be based not on the numeric values shown on the horizontal axis, but on the order in which they appear on the axis (1, 2, 3, 4, and so on). Only when the numeric values happen to match their sequential order will the trendline be correct. ■

Making Assumptions in Contribution Analysis

The analysis of contribution margin, break-even points, and the relationships among costs, volume, and profit makes some assumptions that must be met before you can put much trust in the results of the analysis. The assumptions discussed in the next few sections are particularly important.

Linear Relationships

Contribution margin analysis assumes that revenues and expenses are linear across the relevant range of volume. Suppose that you offer volume discounts to your customers. In that case, when you sell more goods, each additional, incremental sale generates less revenue per unit than when you sell fewer units. The revenue line would be similar to that in Figure 19.10. Notice that it is no longer straight (*linear*), but that it increases more slowly as volume increases (*non-linear*).

FIGURE 19.10

Volume discounts can cause non-linear revenue growth.

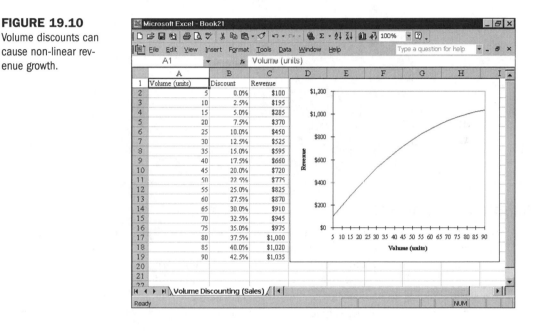

Or suppose that you take advantage of volume discounts from your suppliers—in that case, the more supplies you buy, the less you pay in unit costs. The contribution margin line might be similar to that in Figure 19.11.

FIGURE 19.11
Purchase discounts can cause non-linear increases in the contribution margin.

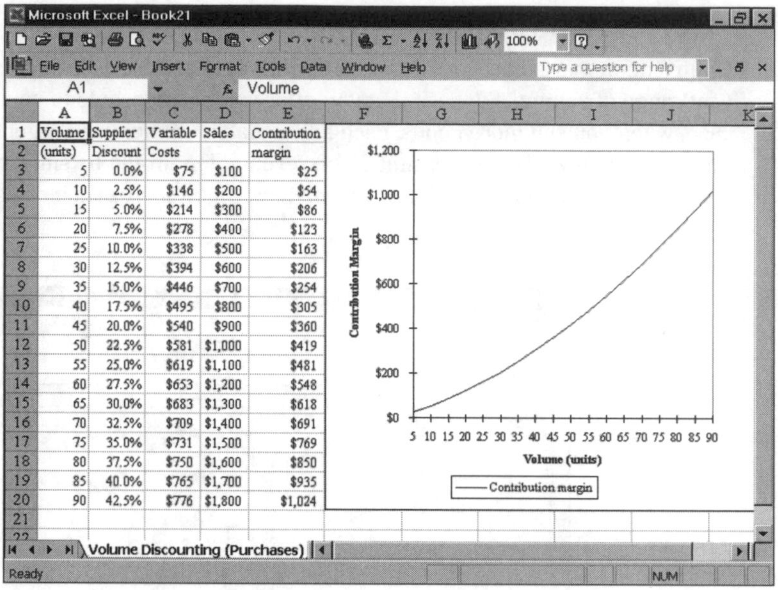

Volume (units)	Supplier Discount	Variable Costs	Sales	Contribution margin
5	0.0%	$75	$100	$25
10	2.5%	$146	$200	$54
15	5.0%	$214	$300	$86
20	7.5%	$278	$400	$123
25	10.0%	$338	$500	$163
30	12.5%	$394	$600	$206
35	15.0%	$446	$700	$254
40	17.5%	$495	$800	$305
45	20.0%	$540	$900	$360
50	22.5%	$581	$1,000	$419
55	25.0%	$619	$1,100	$481
60	27.5%	$653	$1,200	$548
65	30.0%	$683	$1,300	$618
70	32.5%	$709	$1,400	$691
75	35.0%	$731	$1,500	$769
80	37.5%	$750	$1,600	$850
85	40.0%	$765	$1,700	$935
90	42.5%	$776	$1,800	$1,024

Assignment of Costs

Contribution margin analysis assumes that you can accurately allocate expenses to fixed and variable cost categories, and in most cases you will be able to do so. For example, up to the point that you need to acquire additional space, your monthly office lease is fixed regardless of how many units you sell. In some cases, however, it can be difficult to decide whether to treat a particular expense as fixed or variable. In particular, it can be difficult to assign an expense that bears a relationship to volume but not necessarily a direct, one-to-one relationship.

An example is your monthly long-distance phone bill. Unless your sales are restricted to your local calling area, it is likely that the more you sell, the higher your bill will be. But some of those long distance calls probably have nothing to do with incremental sales volume, and everything to do with discussing an upcoming audit with your company's chief financial officer. The accuracy of your analysis of contribution margin and break-even will depend on how accurately you can assign the long distance charges to fixed costs versus variable costs.

Constant Sales Mix

The analysis assumes that the sales mix is constant: that, from one period to the next, your total sales are based on the same percent of each product line. Sales mix is discussed in greater detail in the section "Determining Sales Mix," later in this chapter, but for now note that different products usually have different cost and profit structures. If the sales mix changes so that, overall, either costs or contribution margins also change, then the break-even points will vary.

Worker Productivity

The analysis assumes that worker productivity does not change. If, at a constant rate of pay, your workers begin to produce more product per period of time, then the structure of your variable costs will change: the break-even points will come earlier, and the product's contribution margin will rise. Conversely, if your workers begin to produce less per period of time, due perhaps to illness or procedural changes, variable costs will increase, and you will reach your break-even points later.

Determining Sales Mix

More often than not, a company manufactures or offers for sale several product lines. In these cases, you should consider the sales and costs value of *each* of those product lines as you analyze the company's sales as a whole.

For example, suppose that a company sells three product lines. A side-by-side view of each of these products' price and cost information is a valuable way to analyze each product's impact on the bottom line. For a sample analysis, see Figure 19.12.

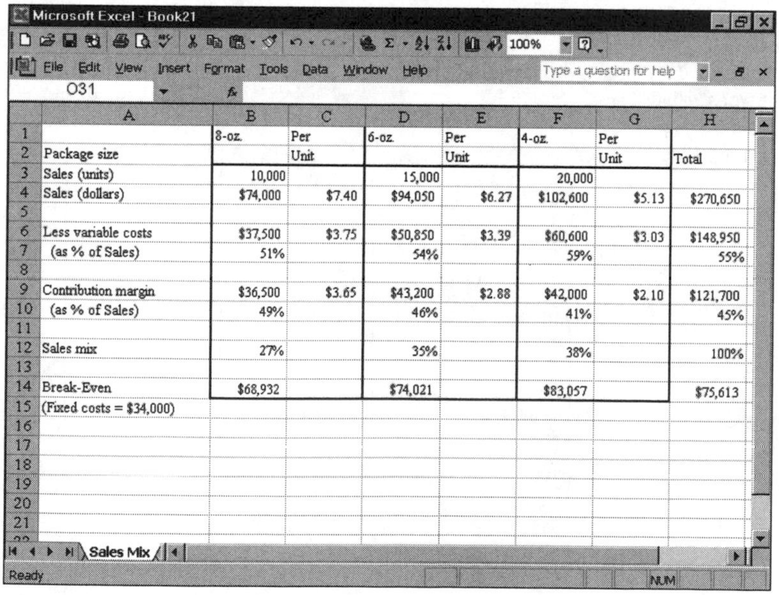

FIGURE 19.12
The sales mix analysis focuses on contribution margins for each type of product sold.

	A	B	C	D	E	F	G	H
1		8-oz.	Per	6-oz.	Per	4-oz.	Per	
2	Package size		Unit		Unit		Unit	Total
3	Sales (units)	10,000		15,000		20,000		
4	Sales (dollars)	$74,000	$7.40	$94,050	$6.27	$102,600	$5.13	$270,650
5								
6	Less variable costs	$37,500	$3.75	$50,850	$3.39	$60,600	$3.03	$148,950
7	(as % of Sales)	51%		54%		59%		55%
8								
9	Contribution margin	$36,500	$3.65	$43,200	$2.88	$42,000	$2.10	$121,700
10	(as % of Sales)	49%		46%		41%		45%
11								
12	Sales mix	27%		35%		38%		100%
13								
14	Break-Even	$68,932		$74,021		$83,057		$75,613
15	(Fixed costs = $34,000)							

Part
IV

Ch

19

A sales mix analysis helps you understand the relative value of the products in your current sales mix. You can determine which of your products provides the greatest contribution to your company's total sales. Suppose that your company produces an over-the-counter medicine in three different package sizes: an 8-ounce, a 6-ounce, and a 4-ounce package.

Figure 19.12 shows that the variable costs to make the 8-ounce package are 1.10 times greater than to make the 6-ounce package ($3.75 per unit versus $3.39 per unit), and 1.24 times greater than the 4-ounce package ($3.75 per unit versus $3.03 per unit). However, the contribution margin from selling the 8-ounce package is 1.27 times greater than from selling the 6-ounce package ($3.65 versus $2.88), and 1.74 times greater than from selling the 4-ounce package ($3.65 versus $2.10).

The difference in contribution margin is due to the fact that variable costs are only 51% of the selling price for the 8-ounce package, whereas they are 54% of the selling price for the 6-ounce package, and 59% of the selling price for the 4-ounce package. So even though it costs more to make the larger package, the sales price of the 8-ounce package is high enough to recover more of its variable costs than do the prices of the other sizes.

This type of analysis is valuable in helping you determine which products you want to market most actively, which products (if any) you should discontinue, and which products you wish to keep but at a reduced level of production. For example, if you focused sales and production efforts on the larger sizes, and de-emphasized the 4-ounce product, your total profit might appear as in Figure 19.13.

FIGURE 19.13
A redistribution of product types within the sales mix can increase profitability.

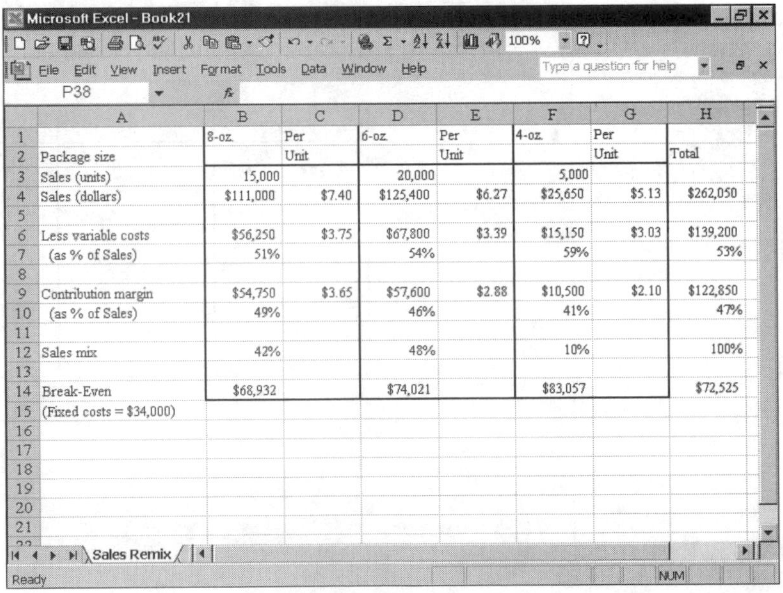

	8-oz.	Per Unit	6-oz.	Per Unit	4-oz.	Per Unit	Total
Package size							
Sales (units)	15,000		20,000		5,000		
Sales (dollars)	$111,000	$7.40	$125,400	$6.27	$25,650	$5.13	$262,050
Less variable costs	$56,250	$3.75	$67,800	$3.39	$15,150	$3.03	$139,200
(as % of Sales)	51%		54%		59%		53%
Contribution margin	$54,750	$3.65	$57,600	$2.88	$10,500	$2.10	$122,850
(as % of Sales)	49%		46%		41%		47%
Sales mix	42%		48%		10%		100%
Break-Even	$68,932		$74,021		$83,057		$72,525
(Fixed costs = $34,000)							

In Figure 19.13, sales and production efforts have been shifted from the 4-ounce package to the 8- and 6-ounce packages. The effect has been to decrease sales of the 4-ounce package by 15,000 units, and to increase sales of the 8-ounce package and 6-ounce package by 5,000 each. The total sales revenue has dropped by $8,600, but the total contribution margin has increased by $1,150.

This result, of course, is achieved by selling more of the higher-profit products and fewer of the lower-profit products. And while it is obvious that doing so will increase profit, it is useful to carry out this sort of analysis: both to quantify the potential results and to focus attention not just on the revenues but on the contribution margins as well.

The previous analysis is a very basic snapshot of the impacts that are associated with de-emphasizing or discontinuing a product line. In addition, you should also consider such issues as:

- The incremental costs of discontinuing a product line—for example, the value of an existing contract to purchase the materials used.

- The difficulty of shifting resources to a different product line—for example, can those employees who produce one product also produce another product with no additional training?

There can be a variety of reasons that you might want to change the sales mix. An obvious one is that discontinuing a low-margin product can create additional profit. Another is that discontinuing a product that is out of line with the company's long-range strategic goals might outweigh the associated incremental costs. In either case, the best decision is probably to change your sales mix to achieve your profit target and strategic goals.

Achieving the optimum sales mix is a more difficult task in reality than it is in a book. Nevertheless, it is wise to monitor your sales mix closely. The wrong mix can prevent your company from being profitable. Using the tools that have been presented in this chapter, and extending them to your actual line of business, will help you achieve the optimum sales mix for your company's expectations, both short- and long-term.

Part
IV

Ch
19

Analyzing Segment Margin

Suppose that a ceramics company has three divisions: household ceramics, ceramic tiles, and ceramic conductors. It may be that each division uses a different physical plant, employs different operating and sales staff, has a different overhead structure, and so on.

If so, the divisions' fixed costs are likely to differ. An analysis of segment margin—so called because each division is termed a segment—is primarily an extension of contribution margin analysis for products to segments. You can determine the segment margin by deducting the direct fixed costs from the segment's contribution margin, as shown in Figure 19.14:

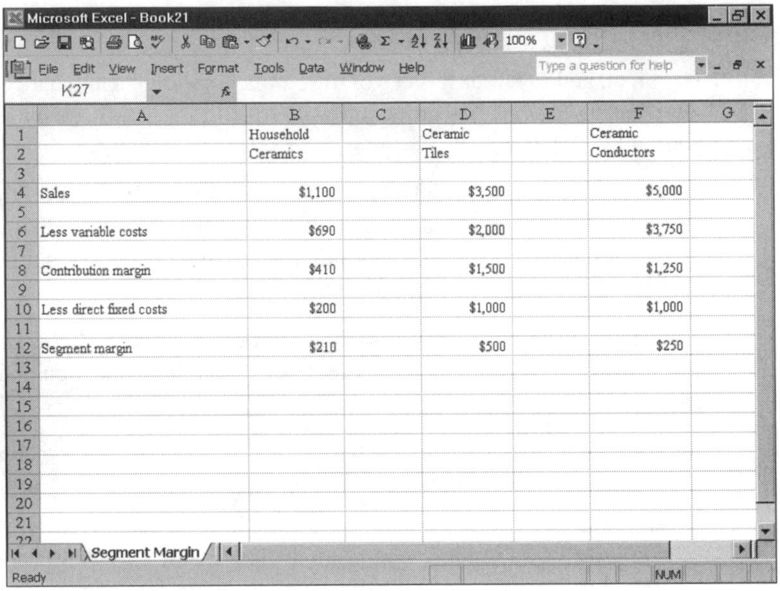

FIGURE 19.14
A segment margin analysis can shed light on the profitability of product lines that incur different fixed costs.

Unlike a contribution margin analysis, which focuses on short-term impacts, the segment margin can help you understand a segment's long-term profitability. It gives you information on how much revenue is available after a segment has covered all its direct costs. The remaining revenue can be used to cover the common costs incurred by the total company, and any extra represents the segment's contribution to the company's total net income.

By deducting direct fixed costs from the segment's contribution margin, you have a better picture of each segment's contribution to the cost/volume/profit relationship for the company as a whole.

Summary

This chapter has discussed several important tools that can help you understand how your company's profit picture is structured:

- The contribution margin analysis gives you a snapshot of how a particular product is performing, in terms of both its variable costs (which increase with each additional unit produced) and its contribution margin (sales revenue less variable costs).

- The unit contribution analysis puts you in a position to consider the profitability of a given product in greater detail.

- The break-even point in sales tells you how much revenue you must generate to cover both your products' variable costs as well as your fixed costs. This may imply that you need to lower your costs, increase your sales price, or increase the number of units sold.

- The break-even point in units tells you how many units you need to sell to cover your fixed and variable costs. You may find that you need to increase sales staff to reach the break-even point in units. This can be a complex decision when increasing staff leads to a concomitant increase in fixed costs.

- The sales mix analysis helps you understand how your product lines combine to result in a profit or loss. It can help pinpoint which products are performing best, and where you may need to make adjustments to costs to lift the performance of a given product.

- The segment analysis gives you a broader perspective on a company with several divisions, each with its own set of products. You would typically use this sort of analysis to gain a longer-term understanding of the source of a company's profits.

Part
IV

Ch
19

CHAPTER 20

Pricing and Costing

Whether a business operates at a loss or makes a profit depends almost exclusively on how much it costs to produce a product and how much the business can sell it for. Costs and prices are closely related, and this chapter goes into some detail concerning ways to analyze that relationship.

Although neither costs nor prices are under your complete control, you can exercise some influence on both. There are many methods of cost control: from reducing the company's payroll to lowering inventory levels to exerting greater control over travel and entertainment expenses.

Regarding prices, another truly wicked variable enters the equation: competition. Competitors are often intent on capturing some of your market share, or on forcing you into a precarious position in the marketplace. They can usually do so by cutting their prices for products that are comparable to yours. Yes, selling on the basis of features and quality, and engaging in so-called "relationship selling," can mitigate the impact of a head-on assault on price structures. In the long run, though, even the most skilled sales force cannot make up for a dramatic price disadvantage.

But there are some techniques that put you in a position to better understand the relationship between the costs of production and the prices you charge for your products. By understanding these relationships, you are sometimes able to make adjustments in the cost components without having to resort to measures that disrupt your business's operations. In turn, these adjustments sometimes have an effect on how you price your products.

"Buy low and sell high" is one of those deceptively simple epigrams that is both true and utterly useless. How low is low? As the next section shows, that depends on the costs that are fixed and the costs that are variable.

Using Absorption and Contribution Costing

Two important methods of determining costs are absorption and contribution costing. Although they can yield very different results, there is only one major difference between the two approaches: absorption costing allocates certain production costs between the total cost of goods sold and the ending inventory, while contribution costing allocates those production costs entirely to the cost of goods sold.

The result is that the income for a period can differ depending on which method is used. The specific reasons are discussed in the two sections that follow.

Understanding Absorption Costing

A problem in determining profitability arises when, at the end of a period, you have some quantity of goods that remain in your ending inventory. Because you normally have some goods on hand at all times, including at the end of a period, this is the usual situation. The difficulty stems from the fact that your valuation of inventories includes both variable and fixed costs.

Case Study: QuickData Modems

QuickData Modems is a subsidiary of a large electronics manufacturer. QuickData purchases modems from DataPump, another of its owner's subsidiaries. QuickData then puts its own logo on the modems, and sells them at a lower price than does DataPump. QuickData keeps its total costs lower than DataPump's by offering a much more restricted product warranty.

QuickData's production process therefore consists of placing its logo on each product and preparing the product for sale—among other things, QuickData packages software along with the modem itself. QuickData's production costs involve those of purchasing the modem from DataPump, stamping its logo on the modem, and boxing the product.

Figure 20.1 shows some basic operating data and an (incomplete) income statement for QuickData for the first quarter of 2002:

QuickData prepares 10,000 modems for sale during the first quarter, and sells 8,000 of them for $110 each. The *variable* production cost of each modem is $38. Additionally, QuickData has *fixed* production costs of $90,000 per quarter that it must meet, regardless of how many modems it produces—whether 1 or 100,000.

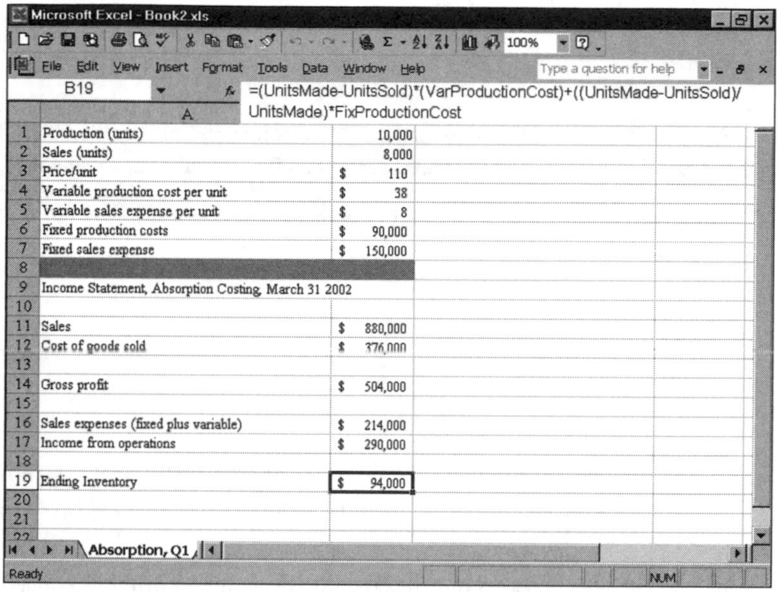

	A	B
1	Production (units)	10,000
2	Sales (units)	8,000
3	Price/unit	$ 110
4	Variable production cost per unit	$ 38
5	Variable sales expense per unit	$ 8
6	Fixed production costs	$ 90,000
7	Fixed sales expense	$ 150,000
8		
9	Income Statement, Absorption Costing, March 31 2002	
10		
11	Sales	$ 880,000
12	Cost of goods sold	$ 376,000
13		
14	Gross profit	$ 504,000
15		
16	Sales expenses (fixed plus variable)	$ 214,000
17	Income from operations	$ 290,000
18		
19	Ending Inventory	$ 94,000
20		
21		

FIGURE 20.1
Under absorption costing, some production costs are allocated to the value of the ending inventory.

NOTE The purpose of this case study is to focus on the different effects of fixed and variable costs on the valuation of finished goods. To keep the example clear, it is assumed that QuickData has no beginning inventory at the start of the period. By the end of the case study, you will see how two different approaches to costing lead to two different valuations of the ending inventory—which is, of course, the beginning inventory for the next period.

When you understand how the approaches lead to two different valuations of the ending inventory, you will be better placed to understand how they affect the value of the beginning inventory for the next period. ■

In addition to production costs, QuickData also has sales expenses, both variable and fixed. The variable sales expense is $8 per modem, and this amount includes the sales force's commission as well as a reserve for fulfilling the restricted product warranty. The fixed sales costs include such items as the printing of product brochures and the salaries paid to the sales force.

By selling 8,000 modems at $110 each during the first quarter, QuickData realizes revenue in the amount of $880,000. To arrive at its gross profit, QuickData computes its cost of goods sold as

```
=Units_Sold*(Variable_Cost+(Fixed_Cost/Units_Made))
```

or, using actual values

```
=8000*(38+(90000/10000))
```

which is $376,000. Notice that this is the sum of the number of units sold (8,000) times the sum of the variable production cost ($38) and the average fixed production costs of each unit that was made.

8,000×($90,000/10,000) equals $72,000, which is 80% of the $90,000 in fixed production costs: the portion that can be allocated to the 8,000 modems that were sold.

The gross profit, sales less cost of goods sold, is $504,000. The fixed sales costs and the variable sales costs are calculated by

```
=Units_Sold*Variable_Sales_Expense+Fixed_Sales_Expense
```

or, again using actual values

```
=8000*8+150000
```

which returns $214,000.

The income from operations is therefore $290,000 ($504,00–$214,000). This is simply the difference between the gross profit on the modems and the expenses associated with the sales process.

QuickData sells 8,000 of the 10,000 units it produces during the quarter. The remaining 2,000 units constitute its ending inventory, which is calculated as

```
=(Units_Made-Units_Sold)*(Variable_Cost+(Fixed_Cost/Units_Made))
```

Again, this formula multiplies the units remaining in inventory (10,000 – 8,000 = 2,000) times the sum of their variable production costs and the average fixed production costs for all units made.

2,000×($90,000/10,000) equals $18,000, which is 20% of the fixed production costs: the portion that can be allocated to the 2,000 modems that went unsold. This is the remaining 20% of the fixed production costs that were not allocated to the 8,000 modems that were sold. The result of the full formula is $94,000, which is the total value of QuickData's inventory at the end of the first quarter.

Notice that neither the fixed nor the variable sales expense is involved in the valuation of the ending inventory: because these 2,000 modems have not yet been sold, the expenses of selling them have not yet been incurred.

At the end of the second quarter, QuickData prepares another income statement (see Figure 20.2).

Comparing the two income statements in Figures 20.1 and 20.2, notice that

- The number of units sold has not changed.
- The sales price has not changed.
- Neither the fixed production cost nor the fixed sales expenses have changed.

■ Neither the per unit variable production cost nor the per unit variable sales expense has changed.

■ The number of modems produced has increased from 10,000 during the first quarter to 11,000 during the second quarter.

■ The net income from operations has increased from $290,000 in the first quarter to $294,909 in the second quarter.

FIGURE 20.2
Absorption costing causes operating income to vary with production levels.

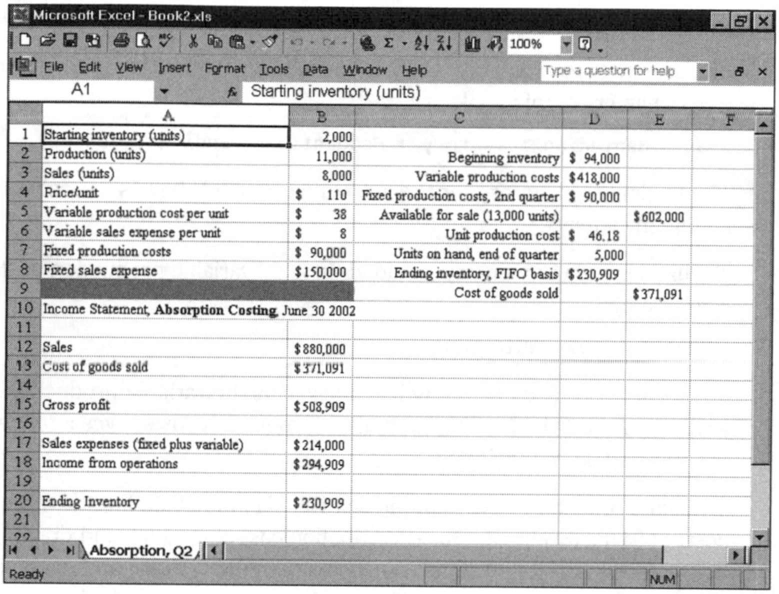

	A	B	C	D	E	F
1	Starting inventory (units)	2,000				
2	Production (units)	11,000	Beginning inventory	$ 94,000		
3	Sales (units)	8,000	Variable production costs	$418,000		
4	Price/unit	$ 110	Fixed production costs, 2nd quarter	$ 90,000		
5	Variable production cost per unit	$ 38	Available for sale (13,000 units)		$602,000	
6	Variable sales expense per unit	$ 8	Unit production cost	$ 46.18		
7	Fixed production costs	$ 90,000	Units on hand, end of quarter	5,000		
8	Fixed sales expense	$150,000	Ending inventory, FIFO basis	$230,909		
9			Cost of goods sold		$371,091	
10	Income Statement, **Absorption Costing** June 30 2002					
11						
12	Sales	$880,000				
13	Cost of goods sold	$371,091				
14						
15	Gross profit	$508,909				
16						
17	Sales expenses (fixed plus variable)	$214,000				
18	Income from operations	$294,909				
19						
20	Ending Inventory	$230,909				
21						

You might not have expected this. When the number of units sold, the selling price, and the costs and expenses are constant, as they are here, you would intuitively expect that the net income would also be constant.

Instead, the only change in the basic inputs is that the number of units produced has increased. Therefore, *a different proportion of the fixed production costs is allocated to the cost of goods sold.* A larger proportion of the $90,000 in fixed production costs—which do not vary as the number of units produced rises or falls—has been allocated to the ending inventory, and a smaller proportion has been allocated to the cost of goods sold. When the cost of goods sold falls, the gross profit increases, as does the net income from operations.

From management's perspective, this can be an unwelcome development. A manager for QuickData would want the gross profit from operations to vary as a function of sales quantities and prices, less costs and expenses. Instead, using the approach displayed in Figures 20.1 and 20.2, net income has varied as a function of production.

Part
IV

Ch
20

For that reason, QuickData might not want to use this approach to support its decision-making process. (It is termed the *absorption* approach to costing. This term is used because the fixed production costs are absorbed partly by the goods sold and partly by the goods that remain in inventory at the end of the period.) A more informative approach would be one that allows QuickData to estimate income independent of changes in the volume of products that it produces.

To get a better feel for what happens with absorption costing, consider some of the additional information shown in Figure 20.2, focusing on the range of cells C2:E9.

The cost of goods sold, or COGS, is calculated using a formula that has appeared in several other chapters of this book:

```
COGS = Beginning Inventory + Production - Ending Inventory
```

The beginning inventory for the second quarter, $94,000, is the value of the first quarter's ending inventory.

To that beginning inventory is added the total variable production costs of $418,000, which is returned by

```
=Units_Made*Variable_Cost
```

or 11,000 * $38. The beginning inventory, plus the variable production costs, totals to $512,000. Adding in the $90,000 in fixed production costs gives a total value of goods available for sale of $602,000 (cell D5).

The unit production cost, found in cell D6, is found by adding the total variable production costs of $418,000 plus the fixed production cost of $90,000, and dividing by the number of units produced (11,000). This distributes both the variable and fixed production costs across the 11,000 units, and returns $46.18 as the total cost of producing a single unit.

By multiplying the unit production cost by the ending inventory of 5,000 units, QuickData can establish a total value for its ending inventory: 5,000 units times $46.18 is $230,909. The first-in, first-out (FIFO) method is used in this method of inventory valuation (see Chapter 4, "Summarizing Transactions: From the Journals to the Balance Sheet," for a discussion of the various methods of inventory valuation, including FIFO).

Finally, QuickData can arrive at a figure for cost of goods sold during the second quarter. The figure of $371,091 in cell D9 represents the cost of goods available for sale, $602,000, less the ending inventory of $230,909.

Notice that part of the fixed production costs of $90,000 appears in the valuation of the ending inventory. The unit production cost includes a per-unit fixed production cost, and is used to value the 5,000 units that remain in inventory at the end of the quarter. And because the cost of goods sold depends partly on the valuation of the ending inventory, it includes the remaining portion of the fixed production costs.

Another way to look at it is to start with the beginning inventory, instead of starting with the ending inventory (see Figure 20.3).

FIGURE 20.3
With absorption costing, fixed costs are allocated according to the ratio of units sold to units produced.

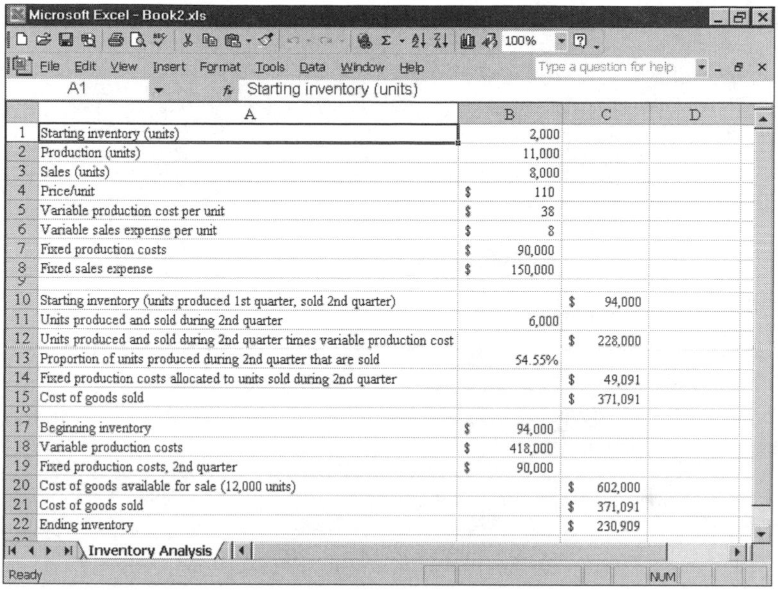

Because FIFO is the valuation method used, the assumption is that the first 2,000 of the 8,000 modems sold come from the beginning inventory; its cost is $94,000.

To that $94,000, add the total variable cost of the other 6,000 modems sold: 6,000 times $38 is $228,000. The third component in the cost of goods sold is the proportion of fixed production costs that are allocated to the 6,000 newly produced modems: 6,000 divided by 11,000 (54.55%) times $90,000 is $49,091. The total of the ending inventory, plus the variable costs of production of 6,000 modems, plus the sold goods' share of $90,000, is $371,091.

And because the cost of the goods available for sale is $602,000, the ending inventory is 230,909: $602,000 − $371,091 = $230,909. However you go about calculating the cost of goods sold and the cost of the ending inventory, a portion of the fixed costs of production appears in—is absorbed by—each quantity. *The portion of the fixed production costs that is attributable to either quantity depends on the ratio of number of units sold to the number of units remaining in inventory at the end of the period.* This is the reason that a change in units produced causes a change in net income, even though the number of units sold remains constant.

Understanding Contribution Costing

Contribution costing (also known as *variable costing*) adopts a different point of view toward the allocation of fixed production costs. Instead of allocating these costs in part to goods that are sold and in part to goods that remain in inventory, this approach allocates the entire amount of fixed production costs to the cost of goods sold. Figure 20.4 shows how this works.

Part
IV

Ch
20

FIGURE 20.4
Contribution costing allocates all fixed costs to the products that are sold.

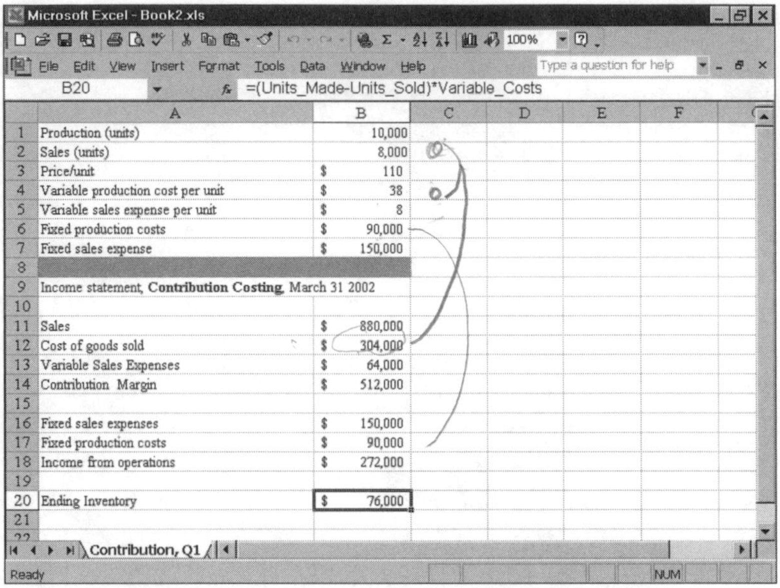

	A	B	C	D	E	F
1	Production (units)	10,000				
2	Sales (units)	8,000				
3	Price/unit	$ 110				
4	Variable production cost per unit	$ 38				
5	Variable sales expense per unit	$ 8				
6	Fixed production costs	$ 90,000				
7	Fixed sales expense	$ 150,000				
8						
9	Income statement, **Contribution Costing**, March 31 2002					
10						
11	Sales	$ 880,000				
12	Cost of goods sold	$ 304,000				
13	Variable Sales Expenses	$ 64,000				
14	Contribution Margin	$ 512,000				
15						
16	Fixed sales expenses	$ 150,000				
17	Fixed production costs	$ 90,000				
18	Income from operations	$ 272,000				
19						
20	Ending Inventory	$ 76,000				
21						

Compare Figure 20.4 with Figure 20.1, which shows QuickData's first quarter income statement under the absorption approach. The first major difference is in the calculation of the cost of goods sold. Using contribution costing, the cost of goods sold is

=Units_Sold*Variable_Costs

which is 8,000 times $38, or $304,000. The absorption approach included in this figure a portion of the fixed production costs.

The variable sales expense is entered in cell B13 as

=Units_Sold* Variable_Sales_Expense

which returns $64,000. As is discussed in Chapter 19, "Analyzing Contributions and Margins," when the cost of goods sold and the variable sales expense are subtracted from the sales figure of $880,000, the result is the product's contribution margin (hence the term "contribution costing").

Then, just as is done when using the absorption approach, the fixed sales expenses are entered. But in contrast to the absorption approach, the total fixed production costs are entered into the computation: they are subtracted from the contribution margin to return the income from operations, in cell B18, of $272,000.

Notice that this is $18,000 less than the $290,000 income from operations reported in Figure 20.1. The reason is that in Figure 20.1, 20% (2,000 modems in ending inventory divided by 10,000 modems produced) of the fixed production costs were allocated to the ending inventory. Twenty percent of the $90,000 fixed production costs is $18,000. Using the contribution approach, that 20% is charged to income instead of to the value of the ending inventory.

Compare the income statement in Figure 20.4 with the one shown in Figure 20.5, for the second quarter of 2002.

FIGURE 20.5
Contribution costing makes income independent of production quantities.

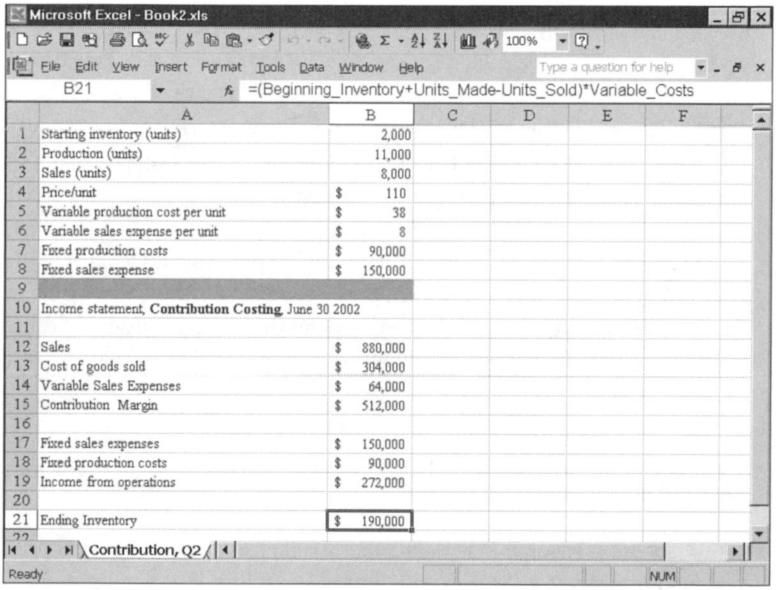

The input information shown in Figure 20.5 is the same as in Figure 20.4. The income statements in both Figures use contribution costing. However, and in contrast to absorption costing, Figures 20.4 and 20.5 show that the income from operations is the same in the second quarter as in the first quarter. This is because sales, cost, and expense data have remained constant despite the fact that production has increased from the first to the second quarter.

This is the desirable effect of contribution costing: changes in income are a function of changes in revenue and costs, and are not due to changes in levels of production. From a management perspective, it is more efficient to analyze the effect of changes in pricing, expenses, and quantities sold on a variable that responds directly to those inputs. It is less efficient to perform that analysis on a variable that also responds to production levels.

Of course, contribution costing has a consequence for the value of the ending inventory. Figure 20.4 shows that, under contribution costing, income from production is $272,000 for the first quarter. That's $18,000 less than income from production for the first quarter under absorption costing. Furthermore, the value of the first quarter's ending inventory under the contribution approach is $76,000, versus $94,000 at the end of the first quarter under the absorption approach: again, the difference is $18,000.

Part
IV

Ch
20

The $18,000 in costs that appeared in ending inventory under the absorption approach is shifted to a current period expense under the contribution approach. This has the simultaneous effects of reducing the valuation of ending inventory and of reducing the income from operations, both by $18,000.

NOTE Because of the way that it values inventories, the contribution approach is *not* normally used to prepare income statements and balance sheets that are used outside the company—for example, by potential creditors and investors. The contribution approach tends to undervalue inventories because it omits a portion of fixed production costs from their valuation, and it tends to understate income because it charges the full amount of fixed production costs for a period against the contribution margin.

Therefore, although it's a useful tool for internal planning and analysis purposes, the contribution approach is not normally used for external reporting.

It should not surprise you that the matching principle appears in a discussion of the relative merits of absorption costing versus contribution costing. According to this principle, costs should be matched with the revenues that they help to produce, during the period that the costs were incurred and the revenue occurred.

Absorption costing causes the costs associated with the production of products to remain with those products until they are sold. It is proper to show those costs after they have been recovered: when a product that remains in one period's ending inventory is sold during a subsequent period.

Equally, it is reasonable to argue that fixed costs of production represent the cost of being able to produce a product in the first place. Without incurring those costs, a company would be unable to produce *any* product. Therefore, these costs should not be regarded as attributable to one collection of goods or another—not some to goods sold and some to ending inventory—but as a cost of the period in which they were incurred. In that case, these costs should be fully charged to the period, not distributed among the products that were manufactured and subsequently were either sold or held in inventory.

These are philosophical positions, though, and are moot. What matters is the dictum that absorption costing should normally be used for external reporting purposes. For internal planning purposes, in which you want to investigate the relationships among costs, volume of sales, and profitability, you are of course free to use any method of analysis that you and your company approve.

Applying the Contribution Approach to a Pricing Decision

How can a contribution analysis of a product line help you decide how best to set its sales price? Suppose that QuickData's income statement for the first quarter is as shown in Figure 20.6.

FIGURE 20.6
Absorption costing
makes it difficult to
arrive at cost-volume-
profit decisions.

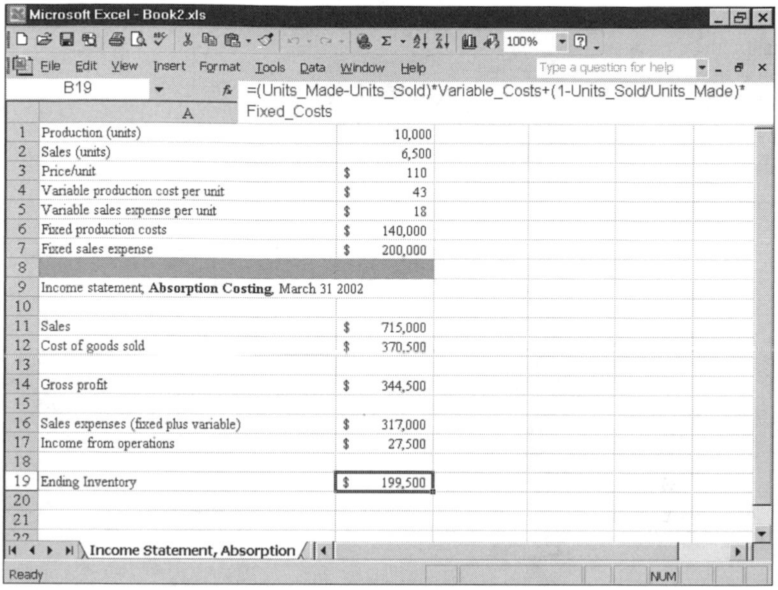

	A			
	B19	f_x =(Units_Made-Units_Sold)*Variable_Costs+(1-Units_Sold/Units_Made)* Fixed_Costs		
1	Production (units)		10,000	
2	Sales (units)		6,500	
3	Price/unit	$	110	
4	Variable production cost per unit	$	43	
5	Variable sales expense per unit	$	18	
6	Fixed production costs	$	140,000	
7	Fixed sales expense	$	200,000	
8				
9	Income statement, **Absorption Costing**, March 31 2002			
10				
11	Sales	$	715,000	
12	Cost of goods sold	$	370,500	
13				
14	Gross profit	$	344,500	
15				
16	Sales expenses (fixed plus variable)	$	317,000	
17	Income from operations	$	27,500	
18				
19	Ending Inventory	$	199,500	
20				
21				
22				

This income statement, which uses absorption costing, depicts QuickData as not doing quite so well as suggested in earlier figures in this chapter. All of QuickData's costs and expenses have been increased, and the quarter's unit sales have been decreased to 6,500. As a result, the income from operations has fallen to $27,500.

QuickData's management wants to know how changes in the sales price of its modems, or changes in the quantities that it sells, might affect its net income from operations. As a first step, QuickData prepares an income statement in a contribution costing format (see Figure 20.7).

The first item to notice in this contribution analysis is that QuickData's operating income from this product is actually negative. When QuickData deducts the entire amount of the fixed production costs, $140,000, from the contribution margin—instead of allocating the fixed production costs in part to the ending inventory—the net income becomes a loss of $21,500.

Using the contribution approach, QuickData's management can isolate the effect of changes in sales quantities and pricing on income from operations. Recall that under the absorption approach, income is in part a function of production levels and costs. But when you use the contribution approach instead, the act of varying production volume has no effect on the net income attributable to the product. Therefore, if management can find the proper mix of sales price and quantity sold, it can be confident that the product will remain profitable regardless of changes that might occur in the production volumes.

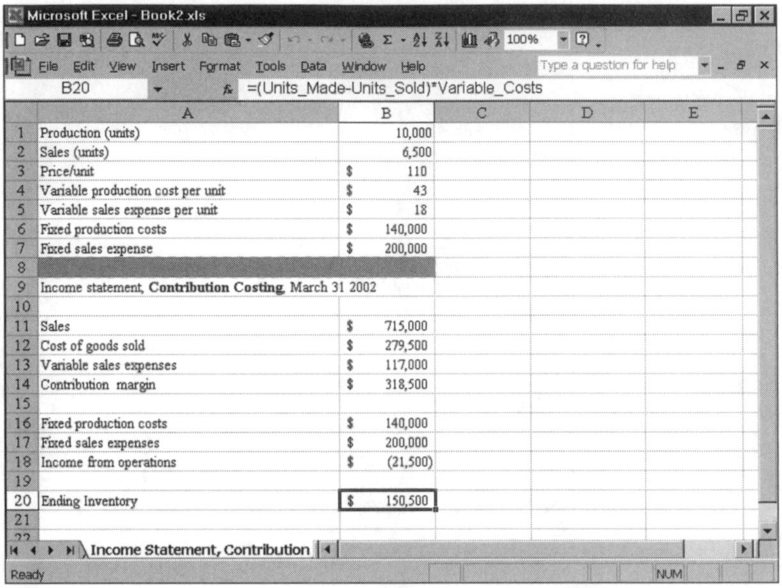

FIGURE 20.7
With contribution costing, the relationships between pricing, costing, and sales volumes become more clear.

The image shows a Microsoft Excel screenshot with the following spreadsheet content:

Cell reference: B20, formula: =(Units_Made-Units_Sold)*Variable_Costs

	A	B
1	Production (units)	10,000
2	Sales (units)	6,500
3	Price/unit	$ 110
4	Variable production cost per unit	$ 43
5	Variable sales expense per unit	$ 18
6	Fixed production costs	$ 140,000
7	Fixed sales expense	$ 200,000
8		
9	Income statement, **Contribution Costing**, March 31 2002	
10		
11	Sales	$ 715,000
12	Cost of goods sold	$ 279,500
13	Variable sales expenses	$ 117,000
14	Contribution margin	$ 318,500
15		
16	Fixed production costs	$ 140,000
17	Fixed sales expenses	$ 200,000
18	Income from operations	$ (21,500)
19		
20	Ending Inventory	$ 150,500

Sheet tabs: Income Statement, Contribution

If QuickData's management wants to focus solely on sales price, it can use Excel's Goal Seek function to determine its break-even point for income. To do so using the worksheet in Figure 20.7, follow these steps:

1. Select cell B18.
2. Choose Tools, Goal Seek to open the Goal Seek dialog box. The Set Cell edit box is selected by default, and contains B18.
3. Click in the To value edit box, and enter **0** (zero).
4. Click in the By changing cell edit box, and click in cell B3 on the worksheet.
5. Choose OK.

Cell B18, income from operations, will now equal $0 and cell B3 will now equal $113.31. This is the price that QuickData must charge to arrive at a break-even point (see Figure 20.8).

TIP

If QuickData's management wants to increase its income from operations beyond the break-even point, and yet to allow both price and sales quantities to fluctuate, it could use the Solver rather than the Goal Seek function. The Solver is able to modify several inputs simultaneously, whereas Goal Seek is restricted to one input variable (in this example, sales price).

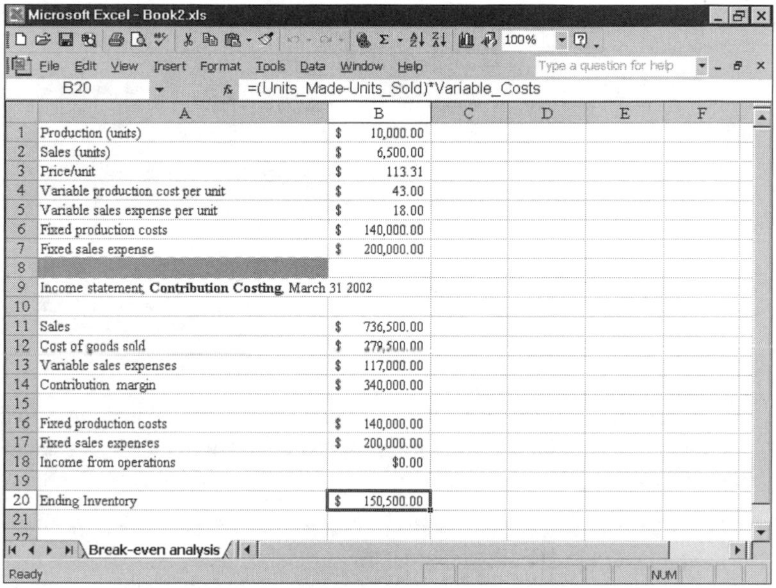

FIGURE 20.8
Break-even points are
easier to find using
contribution costing.

	A	B	C	D	E	F
1	Production (units)	$ 10,000.00				
2	Sales (units)	$ 6,500.00				
3	Price/unit	$ 113.31				
4	Variable production cost per unit	$ 43.00				
5	Variable sales expense per unit	$ 18.00				
6	Fixed production costs	$ 140,000.00				
7	Fixed sales expense	$ 200,000.00				
8						
9	Income statement, **Contribution Costing**, March 31 2002					
10						
11	Sales	$ 736,500.00				
12	Cost of goods sold	$ 279,500.00				
13	Variable sales expenses	$ 117,000.00				
14	Contribution margin	$ 340,000.00				
15						
16	Fixed production costs	$ 140,000.00				
17	Fixed sales expenses	$ 200,000.00				
18	Income from operations	$0.00				
19						
20	Ending Inventory	$ 150,500.00				
21						

Using Contribution Analysis for New Products

Several figures used in the previous section show that the contribution margin is calculated by subtracting a product's variable costs from its revenue. For example, in Figure 20.8, the contribution margin is $340,000. This is the result of subtracting the cost of goods sold ($279,500) and variable sales expenses ($117,000) from the sales figure of $736,500. The cost of goods sold is returned by this formula:

```
=Units_Sold*Variable_Cost
```

So the contribution margin is obtained by the combination of sales revenue, variable sales expenses, and the variable production cost. This in fact defines the contribution margin: it is the difference between sales revenue and variable costs and expenses. No fixed costs enter into the equation.

This method of segregating variable costs from fixed costs to determine contribution margin can be very useful in other situations, such as deciding whether to bring a new offering into your product sct. Suppose, for example, that DataPump, Inc. currently manufactures two kinds of data communications devices: a conventional analog modem for telephone lines and a cable modem. DataPump needs to decide whether to begin the manufacture of DSL modems. The company makes the preliminary calculations shown in Figure 20.9, using the contribution approach.

Part
IV

Ch
20

FIGURE 20.9

This initial view of a new product line suggests that it would lose money.

	A	B	C	D	E	F
1	Annual income projection for all models					
2						
3	Model:	56 Kbps	Cable modem	DSL	Total	
4	Projected unit sales	50,000	40,000	10,000	100,000	
5	Sales price	$ 90	$ 110	$ 160		
6	Revenue	$ 4,500,000	$ 4,400,000	$ 1,600,000	$ 10,500,000	
7	Costs of production	$ 1,762,500	$ 1,960,000	$ 1,585,000	$ 5,307,500	
8	Gross profit	$ 2,737,500	$ 2,440,000	$ 15,000	$ 5,192,500	
9	Operating expenses	$ 1,537,500	$ 1,560,000	$ 1,180,000	$ 4,277,500	
10	Income	$ 1,200,000	$ 880,000	$ (1,165,000)	$ 915,000	
11						
12						

This analysis suggests that the outlook for a new model is poor. The actual revenue, cost, and expense results for the existing models are shown in columns B and C. These figures indicate that the existing models have been doing reasonably well in the marketplace.

DataPump's management believes that certain of the costs of producing the proposed DSL modem can be shared among all three models. They also believe that some operating expenses can be kept to a minimum because a portion of the marketplace will seek out the new model due to its much greater speed over existing telephone lines. Management's hope is that this feature will help to reduce the amount of time and money required for the sales force to market the product effectively.

Even so, the projections for the proposed new model are not good. The projected revenue of $1,600,000 is just enough to cover the costs of production, with $15,000 to spare. And when the operating expenses associated with the new model are figured in, the DSL modem is projected to lose over a million dollars per year.

What if the projected sales quantity of 10,000 units is too conservative—that is, what if the new model proves popular enough that DataPump can sell 20,000 or 30,000 units?

The analysis in Figure 20.9 cannot answer that question. Some of the cost of production is fixed, as are some of the operating expenses. These fixed dollar amounts would not change if more units were produced and sold. On the other hand, some of the costs and expenses are variable, and would increase as production and sales increase. To estimate the effect of greater sales, it's necessary to break the costs and expenses into fixed and variable categories.

The first step in extending the analysis is shown in Figure 20.10.

For each model, the analysis estimates four dollar amounts: fixed production and sales amounts, and variable production and sales amounts.

The key word in the prior sentence is "estimates." In practice, it is often very difficult to determine which actual costs and expenses are fixed and which ones are variable. It can be even more difficult to allocate these dollar amounts to different products.

FIGURE 20.10
Accurate cost and expense breakdowns can be very difficult to achieve, but are necessary components of pricing analysis.

	A	B	C	D
1	Model:	56 Kbps	Cable modem	DSL
2				
3	Fixed sales expenses	$ 750,000	$ 800,000	$ 1,000,000
4	Fixed production costs	$ 1,200,000	$ 1,300,000	$ 1,400,000
5	Variable production costs	$ 11.25	$ 16.50	$ 18.50
6	Variable sales expenses	$ 15.75	$ 19.00	$ 18.00

Suppose, for example, that DataPump's customers purchase both the conventional and the cable modems. The cost of sales calls made by DataPump's sales force must somehow be allocated between the two models to arrive at a variable sales expense for the conventional model and one for the wireless model. To do so with a reasonable degree of accuracy, DataPump management must undertake a careful analysis of customer purchasing records and compare it to sales expense reports. Even so, the analyst will have to exercise judgment in allocating expenses to different products.

The process is not easy, but it is feasible and this discussion assumes that the costs and expenses shown in Figure 20.10 are reasonably accurate. The next step is to use the cost analysis to create a contribution analysis. See Figure 20.11.

FIGURE 20.11
A product contribution analysis puts the new product in a different light.

	A	B	C	D
1	*Contribution analysis, unit basis*			
2				
3	Model:	56 Kbps	Cable modem	DSL
4	Price	$ 90.00	$ 110.00	$ 160.00
5	Variable costs of production	$ 11.25	$ 16.50	$ 18.50
6	Variable sales expenses	$ 15.75	$ 19.00	$ 18.00
7	Total	$ 27.00	$ 35.50	$ 36.50
8				
9	Per unit contribution margin ($)	$ 63.00	$ 74.50	$ 123.50
10	Per unit contribution margin (% of revenue)	70%	68%	77%

The amounts shown in Figure 20.11 are based on unit revenue—the sales price for one unit of each model—and on unit variable costs and expenses. Keep in mind that the definition of a contribution margin is the product's revenue, less its associated variable costs and expenses.

The situation starts to become a little clearer. Because DataPump can share some variable production costs among the three models, the incremental cost of producing each DSL modem can be kept in check. Furthermore, the estimate of the variable sales expense of each DSL modem is actually lower than that of the cable modem. However, these amounts are no more than educated guesses provided by the manufacturing department and by sales management. The decision maker must bear that in mind while interpreting the analysis.

Nevertheless, if the estimates are even reasonably accurate, the contribution margin for the proposed model is impressive. The proposed model is expected, before taking fixed costs into account, to contribute over three quarters of its sales price to gross profit. Again, only variable costs are used in conjunction with sales revenue to arrive at the contribution margin. DataPump's management can therefore estimate which costs will rise—and by how much—as production and sales volumes increase. The remaining, fixed costs should remain stable, and DataPump can get a better picture of how adding the new model to its product set will affect its net income from operations.

Now that the unit contribution margins have been estimated, it remains to determine the net income under different volume assumptions (see Figure 20.12).

FIGURE 20.12
An aggregate contribution analysis clarifies the relationship of sales volume to operating income.

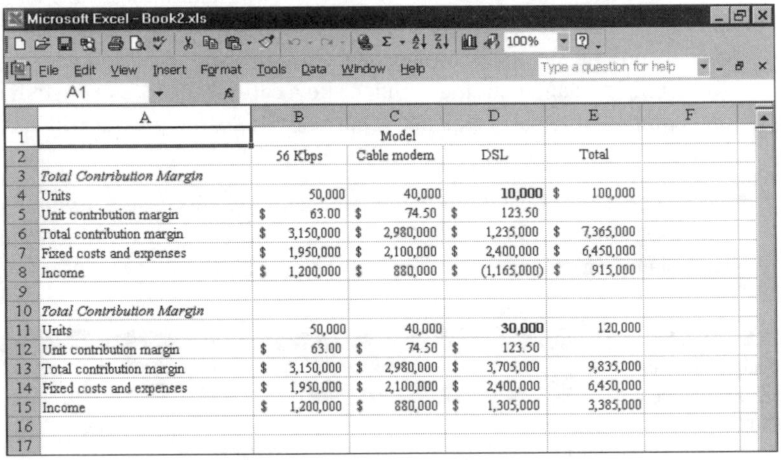

	A	B	C	D	E
1			Model		
2		56 Kbps	Cable modem	DSL	Total
3	*Total Contribution Margin*				
4	Units	50,000	40,000	**10,000**	$ 100,000
5	Unit contribution margin	$ 63.00	$ 74.50	$ 123.50	
6	Total contribution margin	$ 3,150,000	$ 2,980,000	$ 1,235,000	$ 7,365,000
7	Fixed costs and expenses	$ 1,950,000	$ 2,100,000	$ 2,400,000	$ 6,450,000
8	Income	$ 1,200,000	$ 880,000	$ (1,165,000)	$ 915,000
9					
10	*Total Contribution Margin*				
11	Units	50,000	40,000	**30,000**	120,000
12	Unit contribution margin	$ 63.00	$ 74.50	$ 123.50	
13	Total contribution margin	$ 3,150,000	$ 2,980,000	$ 3,705,000	9,835,000
14	Fixed costs and expenses	$ 1,950,000	$ 2,100,000	$ 2,400,000	6,450,000
15	Income	$ 1,200,000	$ 880,000	$ 1,305,000	3,385,000
16					
17					

Figure 20.12 shows the effect of two different assumptions about sales volume: the range D4:D8 contains the estimated outcomes if 10,000 units (cell D4) of the proposed model are sold, and D11:D15 contains the estimates given a sales volume of 30,000 units (cell D11).

As was the case in Figure 20.9, the new model shows a net loss of $1,165,000 (cell D8) if DataPump sells 10,000 units. This is due largely to the fixed costs and expenses that are associated with producing and selling any number of units, from 1 to 100,000.

However, if DataPump sells 30,000 units, it stands to increase its income by $1,305,000 (cell D15). As DataPump sells more and more units, the contribution margin grows, concomitant with the sales volume. But the fixed category remains fixed, and detracts—on a relative basis—less and less from the product's contribution margin.

Thus, this analysis suggests that should DataPump be able to sell more than the 10,000 units initially assumed, it will begin to make money on the product (19,433 units is the break-even point).

You have probably noticed several qualifications and caveats in this discussion. Predicting the future is a risky undertaking, fraught with uncertainties and unknowns. Not only does the model itself involve many assumptions, but the realities of the marketplace can change during the period for which the company has made its projections. Following is a summary of the assumptions, both explicit and implicit, that the analysis makes:

- It is possible to distinguish fixed production costs from variable production costs.
- It is possible to distinguish fixed sales expenses from variable sales expenses.
- It is possible to allocate these costs and expenses accurately to the product lines in question.
- It is possible to estimate with reasonable accuracy the number of units that the company will actually produce and sell.
- The fixed costs and expenses remain fixed across the probable range of units produced and sold.

Although for clarity we have assumed that the fixed costs and expenses are constant across a very broad range of quantities, in practice there are usually breakpoints: for example, when a company must acquire new equipment to keep pace with increased production levels.

Even though it might seem difficult to justify this set of assumptions, you will find that you generally have a good sense of their validity, and therefore of the projections.

There is one more major assumption remaining: the introduction of the new product will have no effect on the sales of the existing products. It is necessary to test this assumption, and the next section describes how to do so.

Estimating the Effect of Cross-Elasticity

When a company introduces a new product, it is likely that the product will compete to some degree with products that it already produces and sells. This is termed *cross-elasticity*: the tendency of similar products to draw sales from one another, instead of expanding market penetration, due to the fact that the products function in similar ways.

There are many reasons that a company might want or need to introduce a new product. It might be necessary to do so because its customers demand it, because technological advances make the new product feasible, to maintain the marketplace's perception of the company, or—most typically—because the competition has introduced its own version.

If the new product is so clearly superior to existing products that very few customers would continue to purchase from the current product lines, it is often best to simply discontinue the existing products. However, if there are real differences in function, appearance, or cost, it is often sensible to introduce a new product and continue to offer the existing lines.

What effect might the introduction of DataPump's DSL modem have, both on the company's overall profitability and on the individual products? See Figure 20.13.

FIGURE 20.13
It's necessary to account for cross-elasticity when a new model is similar to existing models.

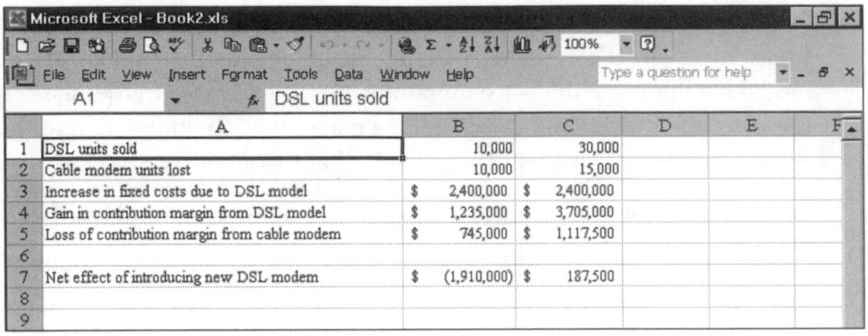

	A	B	C	D	E	F
1	DSL units sold	10,000	30,000			
2	Cable modem units lost	10,000	15,000			
3	Increase in fixed costs due to DSL model	$ 2,400,000	$ 2,400,000			
4	Gain in contribution margin from DSL model	$ 1,235,000	$ 3,705,000			
5	Loss of contribution margin from cable modem	$ 745,000	$ 1,117,500			
6						
7	Net effect of introducing new DSL modem	$ (1,910,000)	$ 187,500			
8						
9						

The analysis in Figure 20.13 depends on DataPump's capability to estimate the quantity of sales of an existing product that will be lost to the new product. Ideally, DataPump is in a position to test market the new product in a restricted market. DataPump would want to restrict the market to hold down the cost of actually performing the test.

If it can undertake a market test, DataPump will be able to observe the effect of the product introduction in one area on the sales of its existing modems. The company can then compare the outcomes in the test market to the outcomes in a control market. It should not focus solely on the test market, because other influences might be at work.

Suppose, for example, that a cable service happened to drop its monthly rates at the same time that DataPump's market test is occurring. This might encourage some users to purchase new cable modems, but there might be no similar motivation for them to purchase DSL modems.

In that case, the market for the cable modem might remain strong, and the effect of introducing the DSL model could be masked. But by comparing the test market results with a control market, where DataPump does not introduce the DSL model, it is possible to isolate the effect of the DSL product on sales of the cable modem: in other words, to quantify the cross-elasticity of the two products.

For one reason or another, it might not be feasible to conduct a market test (for example, DataPump might not market on a geographic basis and thus could not control where its new product is sold). In that case, a typical alternative is to ask the sales force to estimate the degree of loss in the existing product that would come about as a result of the introduction of a new product. This approach is not, of course, as satisfying as conducting an empirical trial, but a carefully conducted survey of the sales force can be reasonably informative.

Assume, then, that DataPump has by one means or another been able to estimate how many sales in its existing cable modem it will lose to its new DSL product. Figure 20.13 projects the financial outcomes under two scenarios: column B describes what will happen should each of 10,000 customers purchase DataPump's DSL model instead of its cable modem. Column C describes what will happen if 30,000 customers purchase the DSL modem: 15,000 customers purchase the DSL instead of the cable modem, and 15,000 new customers purchase the DSL. The latter 15,000 customers represent new sales, not losses to the existing product.

If DataPump's customers purchase the DSL model rather than the cable modem (column B), DataPump will lose nearly $2,000,000 in income. This is due to assuming $2,400,000 in fixed costs, at a level of sales that fails to generate sufficient contribution margin ($1,235,000) to cover those costs, and at a level that reduces the contribution margin for the cable modem ($745,000). The latter amount is returned by this formula:

=C5*B2

where the amount represented by the reference to cell C5 is the cable modem's unit contribution margin. Multiplied by the amount in cell B2, the cable modem units that are lost to the DSL model, this is the contribution margin that DataPump loses to its new model.

The loss of $1,910,000 shown in cell B7 is returned by

=B4-B3-B5

which is simply the margin gained from the DSL model, less the fixed costs due to the DSL model, less the contribution margin lost from the cable modem.

In contrast, if DataPump sells 30,000 units of the DSL model, suffering a loss of 15,000 units of the cable modem, it can expect to increase its net income by $187,500. However, in the context of the fixed costs it must assume to produce any appreciable number of the DSL modem, this increase in margin appears negligible. On the basis of this financial analysis alone, it would be unlikely that DataPump's management would opt to introduce the new product.

Suppose that DataPump decides that it needs to increase its net income by at least $1,000,000 to justify the risk to its existing product line and the additional fixed costs that it would have to undertake. DataPump can try the effect of raising the sales price of the DSL model, to increase its contribution margin (see Figure 20.14).

By raising the proposed sales price of the DSL model from $160 to about $187, the net effect of introducing the model is a $1,000,000 increase in income. Separating the DSL from the cable modem by an additional $27 in sales price would certainly reduce its cross-elasticity with the existing product lines, and it might be that the number of cable modem sales lost would be less than the estimated 15,000.

However, raising the sales price would also tend to reduce the number of sales of the DSL model. DataPump must be convinced that the features in the DSL model are superior to its existing products by a similar margin: one that is wide enough to justify in the new customer's mind the additional cost.

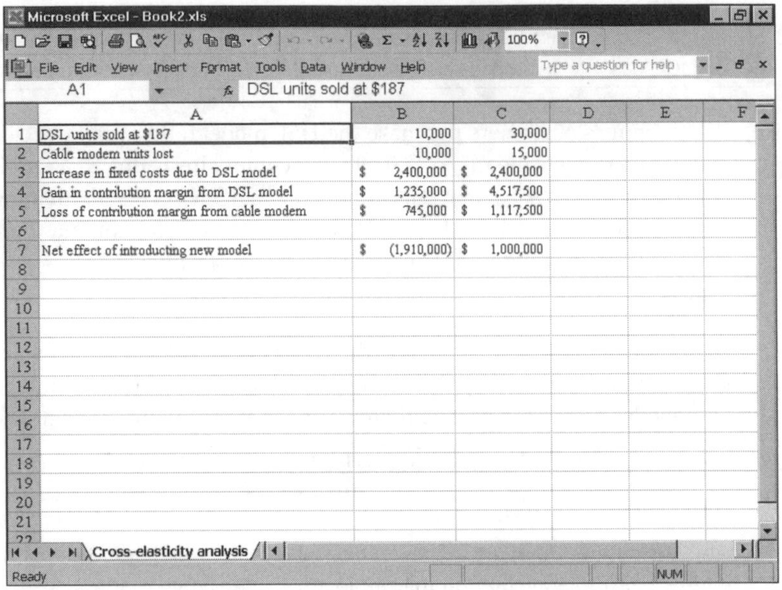

FIGURE 20.14

It's often necessary to revisit pricing decisions when two products or models share common characteristics.

	A	B	C	D	E	F
1	DSL units sold at $187	10,000	30,000			
2	Cable modem units lost	10,000	15,000			
3	Increase in fixed costs due to DSL model	$ 2,400,000	$ 2,400,000			
4	Gain in contribution margin from DSL model	$ 1,235,000	$ 4,517,500			
5	Loss of contribution margin from cable modem	$ 745,000	$ 1,117,500			
6						
7	Net effect of introducting new model	$ (1,910,000)	$ 1,000,000			

Summary

This chapter has discussed the effect of the relationship between fixed costs and variable costs on your income from operations. There is a complex interplay among these costs, the price that you charge for your products and the product quantities that you produce.

The absorption approach to costing allocates the fixed costs of production between goods that are sold and goods that remain in inventory at the end of an accounting period. This approach is used for external reporting purposes, because it more accurately estimates the value of the inventory asset as well as the income earned during the period.

The contribution approach to costing assigns the total fixed costs of production to the goods that are sold. While this assignment understates the value of the company's inventory asset as well as its income, it makes the income for a period insensitive to variations in levels of production (a useful effect for cost-volume-profit planning). The contribution approach is also useful for determining the potential profitability of a new product under alternative pricing structures, and for assessing the impact on profitability of a product's cross-elasticity with other product lines.

What's on the Web Site?

Owners of this book will have access to all of the worksheets that are depicted in the book's figures by going to Que's Web site at www.quehelp.com. This makes it easy for you to re-create the business analyses that are described in the text. The Web site will also contain several special VBA modules that you can use to automate some business analyses such as forecasting and quality control. These author example files can be found at www.quehelp.com and then by searching for the book title. Once the book has been accessed and loaded on to the screen, you can download the example files by clicking the executable file.

The only figures that do not have associated worksheets on the Web site are those figures that display nothing other than an Excel dialog box.

VBA Modules and Subroutines

The Web site also contains several VBA files that automate the creation of forecasts, quality control charts, and sales and marketing analyses.

Forecasting Modules

Chapter 9, "Forecasting and Projections," describes how to use Excel to make forecasts of variables such as revenues and product demand. It also describes how to extend Excel's built-in functions to make your forecasts more accurate. These extensions depend on VBA modules that you can find on the Web site in the folder named *Chap09*:

- Smooth.xls contains code that you can use to extend Excel's Exponential Smoothing add-in to take account of seasonality in a baseline, to make annual forecasts more accurate.

- ARIMA.xls contains code that you can use to determine whether a Box-Jenkins analysis would provide a better forecast than Excel's functions and tools will make. This module displays ARIMA correlograms that help to identify the proper Box-Jenkins model.

Quality Control Modules

Chapter 10, "Measuring Quality," describes various ways that you can perform quality control analyses using Excel, including statistical process control (SPC) charts. On the Web site in the folder named *Chap10*, there is a VBA module that creates SPC charts for you, named *SPC.xls*. The folder also contains an extensive Help file, named *SPC.hlp*. The VBA module creates SPC charts for both variables (X- and S-charts) and attributes (P-charts).

Instructions for installing and running each of these VBA modules are located in the appropriate chapters of *Business Analysis with Microsoft Excel, Second Edition*.

Glossary

3-D reference A reference to a range that spans more than one worksheet in a workbook. A reference to the range A1:D4 is *not* a 3-D reference. A reference to the range Sheet1:Sheet5!A1:D4 is a 3-D reference. Only certain Excel functions can make use of 3-D references: for example, `=SUM(Sheet1:Sheet5!A1:D4)` is legal, but `=MMULT(Sheet1:Sheet5!A1:D4,F1:I4)` is not.

Absolute reference Compare with relative reference and mixed reference. An absolute reference contains a dollar sign ($) before its row component and before its column component. $A$1 is an example of an absolute reference. If you enter **=$A$1** in cell C1, and then copy the formula in C1 to cell D1, the formula in both C1 and D1 will be =$A$1. The reference is *absolute*, and will not change, regardless of where you might copy it.

Absorption costing Also called full costing. A method of assigning both the variable and fixed costs of production to the goods produced on a pro-rata basis, and regardless of whether the goods are sold during the current period. Compare with *contribution costing*.

Accelerated depreciation   Any of a variety of methods of calculating depreciation that do not necessarily assign an equal amount of depreciation to an asset during each period of its useful life. Declining balance and variable declining balance are two examples of accelerated depreciation.

Acceptable Quality Level   Used in acceptance sampling. The lowest proportion of non-defective goods that a buyer considers an acceptable *average for the supplier's production process*. Compare with *Lot Tolerance Percent Defective*.

Accounts payable   Amounts that a business has agreed to pay its suppliers for items purchased on credit.

Accounts receivable   Amounts owed to a business for products and services purchased on credit.

Accrual accounting   Recording revenue when it is earned and expenses when they are incurred. It is coincidental if this is the same period that cash is collected from customers or paid to suppliers.

Actual cost   The price paid to a supplier for an asset. Compare with *replacement cost*.

Adjusted Trial Balance   A balance of accounts, struck at the end of an accounting period, that includes adjusting entries.

Adjusting entry   An entry to an account, made at the end of an accounting period, that records any account activity that is not driven by an actual business transaction. Examples include depreciation, accrued salaries, and interest due for the period.

Aging approach   A method of estimating the amount in Accounts Receivable that might never be collected. Under this approach, open accounts are classified according to the length of time that they are past due, and a different percentage of each category is treated as doubtful. Compare with percentage of sales approach.

Argument   A value or a variable that is used by a function (or, in VBA, by a procedure). For example, in the formula =SUM(1,2,3), the numbers 1, 2, and 3 are all arguments to the SUM function. Excel worksheet functions can take up to 30 arguments. But note that a reference such as A1:A1000 counts as one argument, so worksheet functions are not limited to 30 *numbers*.

Array formula   A special kind of formula in Excel. To enter a formula as an array formula, type it as usual but instead of pressing Enter, press Ctrl+Shift+Enter. You will be able to tell that Excel has accepted it as an array formula if you see a pair of curly braces {} surrounding the formula in the Formula Bar. Do not try to enter the braces from the keyboard: this would indicate a text entry to Excel. Array formulas are required in certain worksheet functions such as LINEST() and MMULT(), and in these cases you must highlight a range of cells that corresponds to the function's requirements before you array-enter the formula. They are also required when one or more of their arguments consist of arrays that do not already exist on the worksheet, but instead are calculated by the formula. Array formulas that occupy one cell only are legal and occur frequently.

Asset Anything of value that a business owns and that contributes to its capability to make a profit.

Autocorrelation function (ACF) A measure, used in ARIMA analysis, of the degree to which the current observation is dependent on a prior observation. Given that observations are recorded in the worksheet range A1:A20, a close approximation to a lag-1 ACF can be found by =CORREL(A2:A20,A1:A19), and lag-2 ACF by =CORREL(A3:A20,A1:A18).

Autoregressive Integrated Moving Average (ARIMA) Also known as Box-Jenkins analysis. A method used in forecasting that combines the advantages of regression approaches with moving-average and smoothing approaches to forecasting.

Average collection period The average length of time it takes to recover costs and earn profit on credit sales. The usual formula is Accounts Receivable divided by the ratio of sales made on credit to the number of days in the period. The longer the average collection period, the longer the company does not have access to its assets for reinvestment.

Average cost A method of inventory valuation that assigns a value to each unit in the inventory that is the average of the cost of all units in inventory, regardless of when or what specific cost they were acquired.

Balance sheet A financial statement that summarizes a business's assets in one section, and its liabilities and owner's equity in the other. The totals of the two sections should equal one another: that is, they should be in balance.

Block A group of VBA statements that is initiated and terminated by certain keywords. For example, statements between an If condition and an End If statement are a block. Similarly, statements between a With statement and an End With statement are a block.

Break-even point The date that the costs of an investment are fully recovered by the income it produces.

Collection In VBA, a group of objects. For example, the Worksheets collection consists of a group of Worksheet objects.

Common sizing The conversion of the numbers in a financial statement from dollar amounts to another metric. This is often done by dividing each dollar amount by total sales for the period: in this way, each entry in the statement represents a percentage of sales. Different divisors, such as headcount and total assets, can be used for different analysis purposes.

Confidence interval   The size of the range between an upper and a lower value, such that some proportion of the averages of repeated samples from a population are expected to fall within the range. That proportion is the probability, or confidence, level associated with the interval. Therefore, a 95% confidence interval around a sample average is expected to capture 95 of 100 averages from other, usually hypothetical samples.

Continuing value   An estimate of the total value of an investment after some specified period of time. This estimate is often based on the value of an alternative investment that would return the same cash flow as the existing investment.

Contra account   A type of ledger account established to accumulate amounts that work against other accounts. For example, a contra-revenue account, such as Sales Returns or Uncollectible Accounts, is used as an offset to Sales to calculate Net Sales.

Contribution costing   Also called variable costing. A method of assigning all the fixed costs of production to the goods sold during the current period. Compare with *absorption costing*.

Contribution margin   The revenue created by the sale of a single product unit, less the variable costs associated with its production.

Control limits   Values used in Statistical Process Control that help define whether a process is in control. Usually, it is three standard deviations above and below the average value of the process.

Control variable   A variable that defines the number of times a loop executes. For example, this For statement: *For Counter = 1 to 10* causes the subsequent statements to execute 10 times. The control variable is *Counter*.

Correlogram   A graph, used in ARIMA analysis, of the correlations of observations with observations that occurred earlier in the baseline. Correlograms are used in the identification phase of an ARIMA analysis to help specify a model (AR, MA, IMA, and so on) for the data.

Cost of Goods Available for Sale   The sum of the value of a period's beginning inventory, plus the value of goods produced (or acquired for resale) during the period.

Cost of Goods Sold   Compare with Cost of Goods Available for Sale. The cost to a company of the acquisition and manufacture of the products that it sells. The components of Cost of Goods Sold include the cost of raw materials, any labor costs involved in manufacture or other preparation for sale, and any overhead associated with production. It is usually most convenient to determine the Cost of Goods Sold by subtracting the value of the Ending Inventory from the Cost of Goods Available for Sale. On the Income Statement, the Cost of Goods Sold is subtracted from Sales (or from Net Sales, if goods have been returned by the customer) to find Gross Profit.

Cost/Volume/Profit analysis   Analyses of the relationships among the costs paid to produce or acquire goods, the number of such goods, and the profit obtained from their sale. Particularly important in these analyses is the understanding of the relative effects of Fixed and Variable Costs, and the products' contribution margin.

Credits   The right side of a T-account.

Cross-elasticity   The functional similarity of different products offered by a business. Products that are cross-elastic tend to cut into one another's sales.

Current assets   Cash, plus assets that a business can convert into cash, usually within one year, in the course of conducting its normal operations.

Current liabilities   Debts or obligations to creditors and suppliers that must be satisfied within the current period.

Current ratio   A measure of a company's capability to meet its current liabilities from its current assets. Current assets include inventory; compare with the Quick Ratio, which subtracts inventory from current assets.

Data Access Objects (DAO)   A library of objects (and their associated methods and properties) that can be used to represent objects in databases. By making DAO available to VBA, the user can write VBA code that enables Excel to interact directly with databases.

Date serial number   In Excel, each possible day is assigned a different serial number. In Excel for Windows, the default system assigns serial number 1 to January 1, 1900; the serial number 2 to January 2, 1900; and so on. Optionally, you can use the 1904 date system (use Tools, Options and select the Calculation tab), under which serial number 1 is assigned to January 2, 1904.

Debits   The left side of a T-account.

Debt ratio   The ratio of a company's total debt to its total assets. From a creditor's standpoint, the lower the debt ratio the better.

Declining balance   A method of depreciation that bases the amount of depreciation of an asset for the current period on the value of the asset at the end of the prior period.

Depreciation   The loss in the value of an asset (typically, buildings and equipment) that occurs through its use in the production of revenue. This loss in value is recognized periodically, as the asset ages. Excel supports several methods of calculating depreciation, including straight-line, declining balance and sum-of-years'-digits.

Dim statement   The typical method of declaring a VBA variable. You can use the Dim statement to name the variable, to declare it as a specific type such as String or Integer, to declare it as an array of values, and (if an array) to specify the bounds of its dimensions.

Discount factor   The factor used to determine the future value of a given present value, or the present value of a given future value.

Discounted payback period   The length of time required to recover the cost of an investment, taking into account losses in the investment's value due to discounting.

Double Precision   A variable type. Compare with Single Precision. A VBA variable declared as Double occupies 64 bits of memory, and is therefore more precise than a Single Precision variable, which occupies only 32 bits of memory.

Double-entry accounting   The method of accounting under which every business transaction appears as a debit to one account and as a credit to another account.

Earnings Before Interest, Taxes, Depreciation, and Amortization (EBITDA)   This figure is frequently used in financial analysis because it represents a company's earnings due to its normal business operations, undiluted by ancillary obligations.

Earnings per share (EPS) ratio   A company's earnings (usually defined as its net income less an allowance for preferred dividends), divided by the number of shares of common stock outstanding. EPS is a measure of the attractiveness of an investment to a common stockholder.

Equity ratio   The complement of debt ratio. The ratio of a company's total equity to its total assets, and thus the portion of the company's asset base that has been acquired through investment rather than through borrowing.

Event   In the Excel object model, something that happens to an object. Events and methods are closely related. VBA code might apply the Open method to a workbook. When that happens, the Open event has occurred, and other code might execute in response to and as a result of the event.

First-in, First-out (FIFO)   A method of inventory valuation that assumes that the value of the goods that were sold from inventory during the period is the value of the goods acquired earliest. Compare with LIFO and average cost.

Fixed Assets   Assets that, in contrast to consumable supplies, are long-lasting, and that have an objective value.

Fixed Costs   Compare with Variable Costs. Costs of conducting operations that are the same regardless of how many product units are produced or services rendered.

Future value   The value at some future time of an investment made today: its original value plus whatever amount the investment earns between today and some date in the future.

General Journal   Compare with Special Journal. A journal that contains, usually in chronological order, records of business transactions that do not belong in any of the Special Journals that a company has established. It is usually reserved for exceptional transactions, such as a one-time bonus to an employee, whereas a Special Journal is reserved for frequently occurring transactions such as weekly salary payments or cash sales.

General ledger   A grouping of all the accounts that pertain the to operation of a business, showing the debits and credits that apply to each account. Detailed information about very active accounts, such as Cash Receipts, Accounts Payable, and Accounts Receivable, are maintained in subsidiary ledgers, and their total debits and total credits are transferred to the associated account in the general ledger.

Generally Accepted Accounting Principles (GAAP)   Methods used in accounting that help ensure accurate financial reporting, and that help make possible accurate comparisons of the results reported by one business entity with those reported by another.

Gross profit margin   A measure of a company's profitability before operating expenses are taken into account. It is usually calculated by subtracting the Cost of Goods Sold from Sales, and dividing the result by Sales. This returns Gross Profit as a Percentage of Sales.

Horizontal analysis   The comparison of a company's financial results with its own, prior results. Compare with *vertical analysis*.

Implicit intersection   The intersection of a row and a column that is implied by a formula, rather than explicitly defined in the formula. If cells A1:E1 constitute a range named "Prices", you could enter, using the key combination Ctrl+Enter, into cells A2:E2 the formula **=Prices*.06** to return the sales tax. This formula implies that cell A2 should use the value in cell A1, cell B2 should use the value in cell B1, and so on. It implies an intersection between the first row and the column that contains a particular value in the range named Prices.

Income statement   A report of the changes in the financial position of a business during an accounting period, usually composed of a summary of its revenues, less the Cost of Goods Sold, less operating expenses, less other expenses such as taxes, resulting in an estimate of earnings. Income statements used for external reporting must follow GAAP guidelines and rules, but income statements used for internal planning may take any of a variety of forms that help the user focus on a particular product, operation, or business strategy.

Intercept   The y-axis value of a line at the point that its value on the x-axis is zero. Combined with knowledge of the line's slope, the intercept helps to forecast an unknown y-value given its known x-value.

Internal Rate of Return (IRR)   A measure of the profitability of an investment based on a series of cash flows generated by the investment. IRR assumes that the cash generated can be reinvested at the same rate.

Inventory profit   The profit that can be created simply by holding goods in inventory as their replacement price increases due to changes in market conditions.

Just In Time (JIT)   An approach to inventory management that calls for goods required for production or resale to be obtained no earlier than absolutely necessary.

Last-in, First-out (LIFO)   A method of inventory valuation that assumes that the value of the goods which were sold from inventory during the period is the value of the goods acquired most recently. Compare with *FIFO* and *average cost*.

Liability   A debt incurred by a business: thus, a claim by a creditor against the business's assets.

Long-term note payable   An obligation to a creditor that must be satisfied at some point following the end of the current accounting period.

Loop   A series of VBA statements that execute repetitively. The loop can be under the control of a For statement, in which case the statements usually execute a fixed number of times. It can also be under the control of a Do statement; if so, the statements usually execute until some Boolean condition changes. Or, it can be under the control of a For Each statement; then, the statements execute once for each member of a collection, such as for each worksheet in a workbook.

Lot Tolerance Percent Defective   The lowest level of non-defective products that a buyer is willing to accept *in an individual lot*. Compare with *Acceptable Quality Level*.

Matching principle   A basic principle of accrual accounting: revenues should be matched with the expenses that helped to produce them.

Method   In VBA, an action that can be performed on or applied to an object. For example, the Range object has the Delete method: you would use that method to delete a worksheet range. Compare with *event*.

Mixed reference   Compare with absolute reference and relative reference. A mixed reference is a combination of an absolute and a relative reference. It has a dollar sign before either its row component or its column component but not both. $A1 and A$1 are examples of mixed references. If you enter **=$A1** in cell C1, and copy it to cell D1, the reference will not change, but if you copy it from C1 to C2, the formula will change to =$A2. On the other hand, if you enter **=A$1** in cell C1, and copy it to cell D1, the reference will change to =B$1, but if you copy it from C1 to C2, the formula will not change.

Modified Internal Rate of Return (MIRR)   The Internal Rate of Return, modified by eliminating IRR's assumption that cash flows can be reinvested at the same rate.

Moving average   A method used in forecasting under which the variation of individual observations from a long-term trend is suppressed by converting each observation into an average of several prior observations.

Named range   A range of cells that is assigned a name, usually by means of the Name Box, or by means of Insert, Name, Define or Insert, Name, Create. After you have assigned a name to a range, you can use the name in place of the range's address in formulas. This makes the structure and function of a worksheet much easier to understand. For example, suppose that cells A1:A12 are given the name MonthlySales. It is easier to understand the intent of the formula =SUM(MonthlySales) than it is to understand the intent of =SUM(A1:A12).

Net Present Value   The value of an investment as of today, less its loss in value due to discounting.

Net Profit Margin   A measure of a company's profitability after taxes and operating expenses are taken into account. After subtracting Cost of Goods Sold, Operating Expenses, and Taxes from Sales, the result is divided by Sales. This expresses Net Profit—the amount available for distribution or reinvestment—as a percentage of the company's sales.

Object   In VBA, a structure in a workbook, such as a worksheet, a menu bar, or a range (Excel itself, the application, is also an object). Objects belong to collections: for example, the Worksheet collection is the collection of all the worksheets in a specific workbook. Objects have methods, properties, and events.

Object variable   In VBA, a variable that stands in for an object such as a worksheet range. Object variables are assigned to the objects that they represent by means of the Set statement.

Operating Characteristic Curve   A curve used in acceptance sampling that provides a visual representation of the effects of requirements regarding quality that are imposed by the buyer and by the nature of the production process.

Option Explicit   An option that can be set at the beginning of a VBA module. Using this option means that you cannot use a variable name before you have declared it, usually with a Dim statement. If you omit this option from your VBA module, you can declare variables implicitly, simply by using their names. Because variables that are declared implicitly are, by default, Variant variables (and which therefore occupy a relatively large amount of memory) and because it's easy to misspell a variable's name (which would simply create a new variable), it's recommended that you use Option Explicit routinely.

Owner's equity   The difference between a company's total assets and its total liabilities. The sum of the amounts that the owner(s) invested in the business, plus any profits that the business has retained.

Passing a variable   In VBA, the process of making a variable that is available to a calling procedure (a Sub or a Function) accessible to a called procedure. The called procedure might change the value of that variable, and subsequently pass the changed value back to the calling procedure.

Payback period   The time required to recover the cost of an investment from the value (usually, the cash) generated by the investment.

Percentage of completion   A method of determining how much revenue to recognize during any given period of a multi-period contract, usually based on the portion of total costs that have been expended.

Percentage of sales   A method of estimating many items in an Income Statement. Most such items are driven by the dollar amount of sales in a given period, and it's often possible to establish that, for example, Salaries have historically been 35% of Sales. Then, it is possible to estimate Salaries for the upcoming period by first estimating Sales and calculating 35% of that estimate. The percentage of sales approach is also sometimes used to estimate the amount of past due Accounts Receivable that will never be collected.

Periodic inventory system   A method of inventory valuation under which inventory is counted and valued at the end of an accounting period. This method is normally used by businesses that deal in a high unit volume of products whose unit value is relatively low.

Perpetual inventory system   A method of inventory valuation under which the value, and the quantity on hand, of each inventory unit is known and can be recorded as frequently as desired. This method is normally used by businesses that deal with a relatively small number of units, each with a relatively high value.

Post   To move transaction information, initially recorded chronologically in a journal, to the appropriate account in a ledger.

Prepaid expenses   Amounts paid for goods and services prior to the time that the expense is actually incurred. An example is an insurance policy that is purchased at the beginning of the year, and that provides protection throughout the year. The expense is incurred as protection expires; the prepaid expense is the amount originally paid for the policy.

Present value   The value today of an amount you will receive at some future time. For example, present value is the amount you would have to invest in a financial instrument in order that the instrument be worth $1,000 one year from today.

Price-earnings (P/E) ratio   The ratio of the market price of one share of a company's stock to its per-share earnings. Generally, the lower the P/E ratio, the better the stock is as an investment. A company's earnings are usually a good measure of its value, and the smaller the price you must pay for that value, the better the investment.

Pro Forma   A projection or forecast based on a financial statement. A pro forma income statement, for example, might project next year's revenues, costs, and expenses.

Profitability Index   A measure that compares the profitability of investments that have equivalent rates of return, but that require different initial investment amounts.

Property   An aspect of an object. For example, a worksheet Range object has the Address property, which returns the range's reference, such as A1:C3.

Query   A series of statements written in Structured Query Language that add, modify, remove, or return data from a database.

Quick Ratio   A company's current assets less its inventory, divided by its current liabilities. This ratio tests a company's ability to meet its current obligations without having to liquidate its inventory.

R-squared A measure of how well a regression equation predicts one variable on the basis of another variable or variables. R-squared can vary from 0.0 to 1.0; the closer it is to 1.0, the better the prediction.

Range A group of cells on a worksheet, such as A1:D4. Technically, a single cell is itself a range, but in normal usage the term Range means more than one contiguous cell.

Realization The conversion of revenue that has been recognized to actual revenue at the point that you objectively know its amount, when you objectively know when it will occur, and when the earning process is virtually complete. Compare with Recognition.

Recognition The recording of revenue in accounting records and financial statements. Compare with Realization.

RefersTo property Whatever an Excel name represents. Most often this is the address of a worksheet range, as entered in the Refers To edit box in the Define Name dialog box. It can also be a constant value if the name represents a constant.

Regression equation An equation that can be used to predict an unknown value from known values. Excel uses the LINEST function to analyze the relationships among two or more variables and to return a set of coefficients that define the equation. For example, you could use LINEST to analyze the relationship between annual advertising expenses ($20,000, $15,000, . . ., $41,000) and revenues for each year. By applying the equation to a proposed advertising budget figure, you can predict the revenues you would expect to generate with that amount of advertising.

Relative reference Compare with absolute reference and mixed reference. A relative reference contains no dollar signs ($). A1:D4 is an example of a relative reference. Suppose that you enter =SUM(A1:D4) in cell F1. If you then copy the formula in cell F1 to cell G1, the reference adjusts to =SUM(B1:E4). The reference remains *relative* to the location where the formula has been entered.

Replacement cost The cost of replacing an existing asset. This is often used in place of actual cost as a means of valuing the asset.

Return on Assets (ROA) A measure of how well a company uses its resources to create earnings. The usual formula adds net income to interest expense, and divides the result by total assets. Interest expense is added back in to net income because it is normally a cost of acquiring additional assets, and therefore should not be counted against the company's ROA. Compare with *Return on Equity*.

Return on Equity (ROE) A measure of a company's ability to create earnings, as a function of its equity. The usual formula is net income divided by stockholder equity. By comparing ROA with ROE, you can infer how a company tends to raise money: through debt financing (usually used to acquire assets) or through new investment (which contributes to equity).

Revenue   The price paid by customers for a business's goods and services.

Sales mix   The manner in which different products are combined to create a product line.

Salvage value   The value of an asset at the end of its depreciable life.

Seasonality   The tendency of variables such as sales to rise during certain seasons and to fall at other times of the year. The sale of heavy winter apparel tends to be seasonal. Certain forecasting methods can account for and project seasonal variations in sales levels.

Semivariable Costs   Compare with Variable Costs and Fixed Costs. Costs of operations that do not increase on a one-to-one basis with each additional unit that is produced, but that increase markedly as certain production thresholds are reached.

Sensitivity Analysis   An analysis that examines the effects on selected results, such as revenue or earnings, of changing different inputs, such as advertising expenses or depreciation method.

Set statement   A VBA statement that causes an object, such as a range of cells on a worksheet, to be assigned to a VBA variable. For example: Set CurrentRange = ActiveSheet.Range(Cells(1,1),Cells(5,5)).

Sheet-level names   A sheet-level name belongs only to the sheet where it is defined, and contains the name of the sheet as a qualifier of the name. On the sheet where the sheet-level name is defined, you can use the name unqualified by its sheet name. For example, Sheet1!Expenses is a sheet-level name name: it might be defined as =Sheet1!A1:D4. On Sheet1, you can use formulas that refer to Expenses, such as =SUM(Expenses). But unless Sheet2 also contains the name Sheet2!Expenses, you could not use =SUM(Expenses) on Sheet2, because an unqualified sheet-level name is not accessible from another sheet. Instead, on Sheet2 you would have to use =SUM(Sheet1!Expenses). Sheet-level name names enable you to define the same name, qualified by the name of its sheet, in more than one sheet in a workbook.

Short-term note payable   A debt that must be satisfied during the current accounting period.

Single Precision   A variable type. Compare with Double Precision. A VBA variable declared as Single occupies 32 bits of memory. It is less precise than a Double Precision variable for very large or very small numbers. However, it also occupies more memory than a Double Precision variable. If you need to declare a variable that takes on fractional values, or if its possible values are outside the permitted range for Long Integer, and if the variable could be an array, consider using Single Precision instead of Double Precision. However, if the variable would not be an array, the extra memory used by Double Precision is insignificant.

Slope   The change in the level of a line on its y-axis value as a function of a change in the level of the line on its x-axis. Combined with information about the line's Intercept, the slope can be used in regression approaches to forecasting to predict an unknown y-value, given knowledge of the associated x-value.

Smoothing   A type of forecasting technique that uses, for the current forecast, a combination of the prior observation and the error involved in the prior forecast.

Special Journal   Analogous to a subsidiary ledger, a special journal provides a place to record frequently occurring business transactions. This allows the General Journal to function as a place to record infrequently occurring transactions. In this way, similar transactions can be segregated into one location for easy reference.

Standard deviation   A measure of how much different values in a set of numbers vary from their average. In a normal distribution of values, you expect to find about 68% of the values within one standard deviation on each side of the average, about 95% within two standard deviations on each side of the average, and about 99.7% of the values within three standard deviations on each side of the average.

Starting inventory   The value of the goods on hand at the beginning of an accounting period, equal to the value of inventory at the end of the prior accounting period.

Statistical Process Control (SPC)   A method of determining if the results of a process, such as a production line, are in conformance with their specifications. If the process is not in control, SPC can also point to the time when it began to go out of control.

Straight-line depreciation   A method of calculating depreciation that divides the difference between an asset's original and final values by the number of periods that the asset is in service.

Structured Query Language (SQL)   A language that can be used to manipulate databases, structures in databases, and the information stored there. SQL is a standard and most database programs interpret SQL instructions in the same way. A user can embed SQL in VBA code to control a database from the Excel application.

Subsidiary ledger   A representation of all the transactions that occur in a given account during an accounting period. A subsidiary ledger maintains the detail information about the account; its debit and credit totals are transferred to the associated account in the general ledger.

Sum of years' digits   A method of accelerated depreciation that assigns an amount of depreciation based on the number of periods (years) that an asset has been in service, and factored against the asset's original value.

T-account   A format for displaying the debits and credits to an account, so called because the horizontal line under the column headings and the vertical line between the columns form a "T".

Times Interest Earned The ratio of a company's earnings before interest and taxes to its total interest payments. A measure of the company's ability to meet its periodic interest payments from its earnings.

Trend In forecasting and time series analysis, the tendency of data values to increase or decrease over time. A trend might be linear, in which case it describes a straight line. Other frequently occurring, nonlinear trends include quadratic trends (one change of direction over the course of the time series) and cubic trends (two changes in direction over the course of the time series).

Turns ratio The number of times during a period that there is complete turnover in a company's inventory. The usual formula is Cost of Goods Sold divided by Average Inventory. Generally, the higher the Turns ratio, the better: goods that remain in inventory too long tie up the company's resources and often incur storage expenses as well as loss of value.

Unearned revenue Revenue that must be recognized during a period because it has been received from a customer, but that has not as yet been earned (and therefore has no associated expense during the current period).

Union The combination of two different worksheet ranges such that they are treated as one.

User-defined function A function created by the user in VBA code. You can enter a user-defined function in a worksheet cell, just as you enter a built-in worksheet function such as SUM(). In VBA, a user-defined function is identified with the keyword Function, rather than with the keyword Sub. Within the body of the function's code, a value must be assigned to the function's name. When entered on the worksheet a user-defined function can only return a value: it cannot perform other actions such as inserting a row or formatting a range.

Variable Costs Compare with Fixed Costs. Costs that increase as the number of goods produced or services rendered increase.

Variable Declining Balance An accelerated depreciation method that increases the speed with which an asset is depreciated, beyond that provided by Declining Balance depreciation.

Variable type The type of a variable defines what sorts of values it may take on. A variable's type is usually declared with VBA's Dim statement. If a variable is declared as, for example, Integer, it cannot take on either the value "Fred" (which is a string) or 3.1416 (which has a decimal component). See *Variant*.

Variance analysis The comparison of an actual financial result with an expected result. A company might have a negotiated contract with a suppler to purchase materials at a standard cost. If the actual amount of payment for the materials differs from the standard cost, the difference represents a variance. Other, similar comparisons include analyzing the differences between budgeted amounts and actual expenditures.

Variant   A type of variable in VBA. A Variant variable, in contrast to other variable types, can take on any value, such as an integer, a decimal value, text, or a logical value. Declaring a variable as Variant is also a useful way to assign the values in a worksheet range to a VBA array.

Vertical analysis   The comparison of a company's financial information with that of other companies in the same industry grouping. Compare with horizontal analysis.

Visual Basic for Applications (VBA)   The language developed by Microsoft used to write procedures that are executed by Excel.

Weighted average   An average of a set of numbers such that certain numbers receive a greater weight than do other numbers. The formula `=SUM(12*{1,2,3},4,5,6)/6` is a weighted average, because the numbers 1, 2, and 3 are weighted by a factor of 12, and the numbers 4, 5, and 6 are not weighted.

With statement and With block   The With statement initiates a With block; the End With statement terminates the With block. Inside the block, you can refer to methods or properties of the object named in the With statement, and yet not have to qualify the method or property by referring again to the object.

Workbook-level names   Compare with sheet-level names. A workbook-level name belongs to the workbook, and can be used in functions or formulas in any workbook sheet. *Costs* is an example of a workbook-level name; to be a sheet-level name, it would have to be qualified by the name of a specific sheet, as in *Sheet1!Costs*. When you define a name using the Name Box, instead of with Insert, Name, Define, you create a workbook-level name.

Working capital   The difference between current assets and current liabilities: the amount of resources a business has on hand to support its operations.

Index

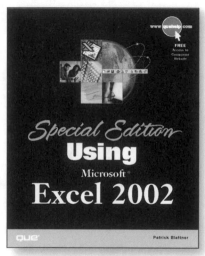